Global Climate Constitutionalism "from below"

Manuela Niehaus

Global Climate Constitutionalism "from below"

The Role of Climate Change Litigation for International Climate Lawmaking

Springer

Manuela Niehaus
Hamburg, Germany

ISBN 978-3-658-43190-7 ISBN 978-3-658-43191-4 (eBook)
https://doi.org/10.1007/978-3-658-43191-4

This Springer imprint is published by the registered company Springer Fachmedien Wiesbaden GmbH, part of Springer Nature.
The registered company address is: Abraham-Lincoln-Str. 46, 65189 Wiesbaden, Germany

Paper in this product is recyclable.

For Leni

Acknowledgements

This thesis was written as part of a Joint PhD Programme between Macquarie University and the University of Hamburg. The study is current as of 31 August 2023.

Every PhD journey is unique—yet what unites all of us who choose to pursue a PhD is that we could not have made it through the dark phases and celebrate the light ones without the support of our supervisors, colleagues, friends and family.

I would like to express my deepest gratitude to my supervisors at both the Universität Hamburg (University of Hamburg) and Macquarie University Sydney—Prof Dr Markus Kotzur, LL. M (Duke), Prof Dr Sarah Sorial and Prof Dr Carlos Bernal Pulido. I am indebted to all of you for the extraordinary supervision, the many helpful comments you have made on my drafts, and the sincere curiosity and openness with which you have approached this topic. A very special thank you is extended to Dr Dr Kirsty Davies who was my main supervisor at Macquarie Law School for most of the project, constantly encouraging me and making me believe in the success of this project.

My gratitude also goes to the members of my transnational examination committee for their helpful remarks and comments—Associate Prof Dr Peter Burdon, Associate Prof Dr Bridgit Lewis, Prof Dr Lothar Michael, Prof Dr Stefan Oeter and Prof Dr Alexander Proelß.

I am very grateful to Macquarie University for awarding me a Commonwealth-Funded scholarship to fund my Joint PhD candidature and an additional stipend to finance my one-year research stay at Macquarie University. This time at Macquarie University gave me the opportunity to learn more conducting research in an international environment and to discuss relevant points of my work.

Furthermore, I am indebted to Prof Dr Henk Botha for his generous invitation to a research visit to Stellenbosch University, which gave me a better insight into South African literature and jurisprudence.

Not to be left unmentioned are the important people in my life who have stood by my side with advice and encouragement, who listened patiently to me endlessly talking either excitedly about my topic or complaining about the idea to pursue a PhD at all: Julia Beckmann, Merret Buurman, Dr Annika Günther, Dr Berenice Möller, Anja Renner and Vanessa Teckenburg as well as my (former) colleagues and friends Verena Kahl and Dr Christina Simmig—and of course, my parents Antina and Günther and my sisters Mareike and Marlen. A huge thank you to all of you!

About the Book

Global climate change poses significant challenges to the law, which international environmental law has so far not been able to adequately address. The unwillingness of many states to tackle the problem decisively and the lack of enforcement possibilities of international law are increasingly becoming a problem for global society. In view of these weaknesses of the Westphalian model of international law, the constitutionalisation of the climate law regime has been discussed for some time now. The constitutionalisation of international climate law is supposed to ensure greater participation of non-state actors such as non-governmental organisations or individuals and a rollback of state sovereignty where states do not care about meeting their climate commitments.

In view of the inability of the international community of states to effectively combat climate change, young people in particular have discovered so-called 'climate change litigation' as a means of forcing states to do more to protect the climate, even against the state's will.

This book takes these lawsuits as an opportunity to reflect on the role of non-state actors in international climate law. Even if they cannot negotiate in 'formal' international climate treaty regimes (such as the United Nations Framework Convention on Climate), the work shows that non-state actors are certainly involved in the creation of climate law outside these formal regimes through the means of strategic litigation. Instead of formal legislative change by parliaments, litigants strive for legal change through the courts, which, thereby, also become important actors in global climate governance.

Against the background of Peter Häberle's theory of the open society of constitutional interpreters, four cases (*Urgenda v Netherlands*, *Leghari v Pakistan*, *Juliana v United States* and *Future Generations v Colombia*) are used to examine how non-state actors can fill the 'space between the text and the law' (Venzke) with new meaning and thus, force states to do more against climate change. In this context, climate lawsuits also offer the possibility of bringing hitherto less-considered problems to the fore, such as questions of intra- and intergenerational justice in the face of the unequally distributed risks and burdens of global climate change. By doing so, climate change litigation can make them a central element of the new transnational climate law.

Based on considerations of democratic theory and the rule of law, it is shown that the international open society can contribute to the constitutionalisation and legitimation of the international climate law regime 'from below' through climate change litigation.

Contents

About the Author

Dr Manuela Niehaus is a fully qualified lawyer and a postdoctoral researcher in law at the German University of Administrative Sciences Speyer. After studying law at the University of Münster and the FGV Direito Rio in Rio de Janeiro, she worked as a research associate at the Institute for International Affairs at the University of Hamburg. She completed her doctorate in a Joint PhD programme of the University of Hamburg and Macquarie University in international environmental law on global climate constitutionalism.

Introduction

1

1.1 Setting the Scene: Climate Change

> The eyes of all future generations are upon you. And if you choose to fail us, I say: We will never forgive you. We will not let you get away with this. Right here, right now is where we draw the line. The world is waking up. And change is coming, whether you like it or not.
>
> Greta Thunberg, United Nations Climate Summit, 23 September 2019

The early 2020s were the years of the COVID-19 pandemic, and they were also years of insight. They demonstrated that most political leaders are capable and willing to sacrifice 'the economy' to keep a catastrophe under control. Many people wish to witness the same determination when it comes to confronting an even bigger crisis: climate change. The COVID-19 pandemic and the climate crisis have both presented devastating global challenges. What is common to both is that they require(d) a public policy response based on scientific expertise and international cooperation. Moreover, both require(d) quick, decisive governmental action on a partly uncertain scientific basis.[1] While the COVID-19 pandemic seems to be under control at the time of writing (three years after the first worldwide lockdown measures were imposed), the same cannot be said for the climate catastrophe that continues to make increasingly urgent headlines. Experts warn that most countries are not meeting their climate targets and that important planetary thresholds have already been or may soon be exceeded.[2]

[1] David Klenert and others, 'Five Lessons from COVID-19 for Advancing Climate Change Mitigation' (2020) 76 Environmental and Resource Economics 751, 752.

[2] Cf. Johan Rockström and others, 'Planetary Boundaries: Exploring the Safe Operating Space for Humanity' (2009) 461 Nature 472.

M. Niehaus, *Global Climate Constitutionalism "from below"*,
https://doi.org/10.1007/978-3-658-43191-4_1

Faced with this existential threat, many (young) people have taken to the streets and the internet demanding that states comply with their climate obligations and provide meaningful participatory opportunities to make better and stronger climate policies. But they do not stop there. Climate activists and concerned citizens have discovered so-called climate change litigation (CCL) as a tool to make states comply with their international and national climate obligations and enforce them, even against the states' will.

This book examines the phenomenon of CCL as an opportunity for non-state actors to engage in international constitutional lawmaking. It argues that plaintiffs of CCL cases can 'force the court to engage in (a legal dialogue)'[3] in which they can present their interpretations regarding states' obligations in the face of the climate crisis. Many of these arguments are based on climate science and international agreements. The courts have shown some sympathy for climate-related concerns under human rights law and ruled in spectacular cases in favour of the plaintiffs and the environment. Cases such as *Urgenda v the Netherlands* (2015–2019), *Leghari v Pakistan* (2015), *Juliana v United States* (2015) and *Future Generations v Colombia* (2018) have attracted attention worldwide, and climate activists and concerned citizens have started to perceive the courts as important allies in their struggle for more ambitious climate action.

This 'wave' of climate lawsuits presents new challenges and opportunities for international law (IL). It fosters dialogue on the constitutionalisation of the international climate regime to constrain state sovereignty on climate matters. The traditional Westphalian model of IL that focuses almost exclusively on states as the main subjects, based on their internal and external sovereignty, seems less and less capable of addressing the climate crisis as 'the defining challenge of our time'.[4] In particular, this model cannot fully display the increasingly important role of non-state actors. This book argues that the participation of non-state actors is of crucial importance for developing and shaping global climate constitutionalism as the law's possible answer to the climate crisis. CCL, then, can be perceived as a form of (international) lawmaking that consistently shapes global climate constitutionalism 'from below'.

---

[3] Peter Häberle, '"The Open Society of Constitutional Interpreters"—A Contribution to a Pluralistic and "Procedural" Constitutional Interpretation (1975)' in Markus Kotzur (ed), *Peter Häberle on Constitutional Theory* (Nomos/Hart 2018) 136.

[4] 'Climate Change Poses "Defining Challenge" of Our Time, Ban Says' *UN News* (7 October 2008) <https://news.un.org/en/story/2008/10/276912-climate-change-poses-defining-challenge-our-time-ban-says> accessed 31 August 2023.

1.2 Exploring the Background: The Challenges of Globalisation and the Westphalian System

Today, there are more than 1300 multilateral agreements that protect the environment or parts of it,[5] including the United Nations Framework Convention on Climate Change (UNFCCC) and its Kyoto Protocol/Paris Agreement, which enjoy quasi-universal membership. However, an 'emissions gap' has been identified between what states promise to do to combat climate change (how much greenhouse gas [GHG] emissions they want to curtail) and what is actually needed to efficiently address the problem.[6] Recent notifications of the Intergovernmental Panel on Climate Change (IPCC) are alarming: the world's leading climate scientists are warning that time is running out to limit global warming to 1.5°C above pre-industrial levels.[7] Beyond that point, the probability of floods, droughts, extreme heatwaves and poverty will increase dramatically and will put millions of lives at risk.[8] Currently, the world is on course to warm by more than 2.8°C.[9]

Climate change is a 'super wicked' problem.[10] The longer it takes the responsible actors to address it efficiently, the more expensive it becomes.[11] Additionally, no state can solve the problem alone. However, the states of the Global North that caused global warming in the first place, and are best suited to address the problem, are not necessarily those willing to act on it.[12] The need for rapid action has been stressed by IPCC reports and climate scientists over the

---

[5] See Ronald B Mitchell, 'International Environmental Agreements (IEA) Database Project' <https://iea.uoregon.edu> accessed 31 August 2023.

[6] UNEP, 'Emissions Gap Emissions Gap Report 2022' (2022) 26ff.

[7] The 2015 Paris Agreement's goal is to limit global warming to well below 2°C, preferably to 1.5° C, see Article 2 para. 1 (a), Paris Agreement to the United Nations Framework Convention on Climate Change, Dec. 12, 2015, T.I.A.S. No. 16–1104. IGOs. A 2018 report of the IPCC stressed the importance to limit global warming to 1.5°C, see IPCC, 'Special Report on Global Warming of 1.5°C' (2018).

[8] 'We Have 12 Years to Limit Climate Change Catastrophe, Warns UN' *The Guardian* (8 October 2018) <https://www.theguardian.com/environment/2018/oct/08/global-warming-must-not-exceed-15c-warns-landmark-un-report> accessed 31 August 2023.

[9] UNEP (n 6) XXI.

[10] Richard J Lazarus, 'Super Wicked Problems and Climate Change: Liberate the Future' (2009) 1234 Cornell Law Review 1153.

[11] Klenert and others (n 1) 753–5.

[12] Lazarus (n 10) 1160.

past two decades,[13] but there seems to be no general sense among state leaders of being bound by the global rule of environmental law to comply with the obligations that international environmental treaties impose on them.[14] The absence of central enforcement mechanisms means that states comply with their climate obligations voluntarily.[15] But when economic interests clash with climate targets, political leaders are often unwilling to prioritise the latter. Sovereignty, therefore, is 'the biggest impediment to dealing with climate change'.[16]

The image of a Westphalian international legal order with strong and sovereign states dating back to the Peace of Westphalia in 1648 seems less suitable for addressing globalisation and its accompanying de-territorialised challenges such as terrorism, cybercrime and climate change.[17] The nation-state is simply no longer capable of comprehensively regulating such problems. Climate change, for example, is a 'glocal' problem, which means that it needs to be addressed by various levels of government (local, subnational, national and international) and by a multitude of stakeholders, including non-state actors and the courts.[18] While non-state actors such as individuals, non-governmental organisations (NGOs), subnational, local governments and businesses are not formally recognised as active subjects of IL, they play important roles, albeit often informally. Many tasks that formerly belonged exclusively to the *domaine réservé* of states, such as military and police activities, are now often carried out by private actors.[19] Some scholars believe that traditional international environmental law (IEL)—in the sense of inter-states law—is unsuitable for solving global problems such as

---

[13] For example, IPCC, 'Summary for Policymakers of IPCC Special Report on Global Warming of 1.5°C'; IPCC, 'Special Report: The Ocean and Cryosphere in a Changing Climate—Summary for Policymakers'.

[14] Louis J Kotzé, 'A Global Environmental Constitution for the Anthropocene's Climate Crisis' in Jordi Jaria-Manzano and Susana Borràs (eds), *Research Handbook on Global Climate Constitutionalism* (Edward Elgar Publishing 2019) 55.

[15] Lazarus (n 10) 1159–61.

[16] Sam Adelman, 'Rethinking Human Rights: The Impact of Climate Change on the Dominant Discourse' in Stephen Humphreys (ed), *Human Rights and Climate Change* (CUP 2009) 166–7.

[17] Eric Allen Engle, 'The Transformation of the International Legal System: The Post-Westphalian Legal Order' (2004) 23 Quinnipiac Law Review 25, 27ff.

[18] Thijs Etty and others, 'Transnational Climate Law' (2018) 7 Transnational Environmental Law 191, 199; Veerle Heyvaert and Thijs Etty, 'Introducing Transnational Environmental Law' (2012) 1 Transnational Environmental Law 1.

[19] Anne Peters, 'Global Constitutionalism Revisited' (2005) 11 Legal Theory 39, 41.

climate change.[20] A shift from government to governance involving other actors, including transnational corporations, environmental NGOs, citizens, grassroots movements such as Fridays for Future and Extinction Rebellion, local and indigenous communities, sub-states and also networks such as the Global Covenant of Mayors for Climate and Energy or the C40 Cities Climate Leadership Group, is not only deemed necessary but is already happening. The growing number of actors and global problems such as climate change confronts IL with its weaknesses. Thus, scholars started looking for new approaches to address these new challenges in the international legal order.

1.2.1 Global Constitutionalism as an Answer to Global Challenges?

One answer to these new challenges is global constitutionalism.[21] In a nutshell, '[g]lobal constitutionalism is a scholarly discourse which diagnoses and/or reclaims that the norms and institutions of global governance follow and respect principles of constitutionalism'.[22]

Legal scholars seek to transfer some features of national constitutional law to the global legal order. These include constitutional principles such as the protection of fundamental rights, the rule of law, the separation of powers, due process, the protection of human rights, democracy, the protection of minorities and solidarity.[23] Moreover, constitutionalism offers the advantage of balancing different interests, such as economic growth and environmental integrity, against

---

[20] See, for example, Rakhyun E Kim and Klaus Bosselmann, 'International Environmental Law in the Anthropocene: Towards a Purposive System of Multilateral Environmental Agreements' (2013) 2 Transnational Environmental Law 285, 286; UNEP, '21 Issues for the 21st Century—Results of the UNEP Foresight Process on Emerging Environmental Issues' (2012) V.

[21] See Jan Klabbers, 'Setting the Scene' in Jan Klabbers, Anne Peters and Geir Ulfstein (eds), *The Constitutionalization of International Law* (OUP 2009); Thomas Kleinlein, 'Non-State Actors from an International Constitutionalist Perspective' in Jean D'Aspremont (ed), *Participants in the International Legal System: Multiple Perspectives on Non-State Actors in International Law* (Routledge 2011).

[22] Max-Planck-Institut für ausländisches öffentliches Recht und Völkerrecht, 'Tätigkeitsbericht für die Jahre 2012, 2013 und 2014' (2015) 25.

[23] Andreas L Paulus, 'The International Legal System as a Constitution' in Jeffrey L Dunoff and Joel P Trachtman (eds), *Ruling the World? Constitutionalism, International Law, and Global Governance* (CUP 2009); Max-Planck-Institut für ausländisches öffentliches Recht und Völkerrecht (n 22) 25.

each other, just as they must be considered and balanced at the national level in accordance with the principle of proportionality.[24] Environmental interests—often defeated by economic interests—could benefit from such an approach.[25]

Constitutionalism is also seen as an answer to the challenge of the ongoing fragmentation of IL. Paradoxically, while the world grows closer in the fields of economy, culture and politics, IL has become more fragmented. This also includes the emergence of 'self-contained regimes' that are relatively isolated from each other. Many scholars fear that fragmentation endangers the unity and coherence of IL.[26] Thus, constitutionalists often argue that a constitutional framework could address fragmentation in the same way a national constitution can unify different specified areas of national law.[27] A fully-fledged constitutional order may never truly come into being, but constitutionalism offers a way of rethinking IL so that it becomes a denser and stronger web of international norms.[28]

Consequently, some scholars argue for establishing a hierarchy among the norms of the international legal order by identifying fundamental norms (e.g., *jus cogens* and *erga omnes* norms) in the same way a national constitution forms the tip of the national norm pyramid.[29] However, the establishment of such a global hierarchy is rejected here. Instead, it will be argued that a multitude of constitutions and institutions in the form of multi-level constitutionalism coexist which are in constant dialogue with each other.[30] Based on theories of societal constitutionalism, these constitutions are not only the result of states making laws but also of non-state actors' setting standards. Societal constitutionalism is based on

---

[24] Anne van Aaken, 'Defragmentation of Public International Law Through Interpretation: A Methodological Proposal' (2009) 16 Indiana Journal of Global Legal Studies 483.

[25] Kim and Bosselmann (n 20).

[26] ILC, 'Report of the Study Group of the International Law Commission (Finalized by Martti Koskenniemi) on "Fragmentation of International Law: Difficulties Arising from the Diversification and Expansion of International Law" (A/CN.4/L.682)' (2006).

[27] Cf. Klabbers (n 21) 18.

[28] Paulus (n 23) 88.

[29] Eva Kassoti, 'The Constitutionalization of International Law and the Challenge of Non-State Actors' (2017) 11 ICL Journal 177, 180–81; JHH Weiler and AL Paulus, 'The Structure of Change in International Law or Is There a Hierarchy of Norms in International Law?' (1997) 8 European Journal of International Law 545.

[30] Ingolf Pernice, 'The Treaty of Lisbon: Multilevel Constitutionalism in Action' (2009) 15 The Columbia Journal of European Law 47; Ernst Ulrich Petersmann, *Multilevel Constitutionalism for Multilevel Governance of Public Goods* (Hart Publishing 2017); Felix Ekardt and Verena Lessmann, 'EuGH, EGMR und BVerfG: Die dritte Gewalt im transnationalen Mehrebenensystem' [2006] Kritische Justiz 381.

the ideas of legal and constitutional pluralism embracing the diversity and plurality of the many different stakeholders, including states but also private actors, in transnational regimes. Such theories argue that several issue-based regimes exist (e.g., the economy, sports, the internet, the environment) and that each regime can develop its own constitution.[31] These constitutions coexist without one being superior to the others, which is similar to the relationship between the European Union (EU) treaties and the constitutions of its member-states.[32] Such a model is better suited to addressing the problem of climate change: a complex polycentric and 'glocal' problem requiring the involvement of many stakeholders at different levels of government, from the local to the supranational.[33]

1.2.2 Climate Justice

Global constitutionalism has been perceived as a strong legal answer to global governance.[34] However, it poses great challenges to traditional understandings of democracy and representation. The principle of democracy is 'the most basic and most important constitutional principle' for domestic constitutional orders and the founding principle for government.[35] It is because of the 'We the people', the demos as the *pouvoir constituent*, that a constitution can establish the supreme legal norms of a nation-state.[36] The people have to agree to constitute a political entity and to subject themselves to majority decisions in the first place. The establishment of a basic consensus, defined as 'the uniformity of opinions on the foundational principles of society', is perceived as a prerequisite for a

[31] Seminal: Gunter Teubner, '"Global Bukowina": Legal Pluralism in the World Society' in Gunther Teubner (ed), *Global Law without a State* (Dartmouth Publishing 1997).

[32] Neil MacCormick, *Questioning Sovereignty. Law, State, and Nation in the European Commonwealth* (OUP 1999) 104.

[33] Samantha Besson, 'Whose Constitution(s)? International Law, Constitutionalism, and Democracy' in Jeffrey L Dunoff and Joel P Trachtman (eds), *Ruling the World? Constitutionalism, International Law and Global Government* (CUP 2009) 396.

[34] Anne Peters, 'Are We Moving towards Constitutionalization of the World Community?' in Antonio Cassese (ed), *Realizing Utopia: The Future of International Law* (OUP 2012) 119f.

[35] Paulus (n 23) 94.

[36] Matthias Kumm, 'The Cosmopolitan Turn in Constitutionalism: On the Relationship between Constitutionalism in and beyond the State' in Jeffrey L Dunoff and Joel P Trachtman (eds), *Ruling the World? Constitutionalism, International Law and Global Government* (CUP 2009) 265.

viable democracy.[37] Generally, this basic consensus stems from shared historical, cultural or ethnic backgrounds, thus, creating a sort of 'we-feeling' and solidarity.[38] It seems difficult, if not impossible, to establish such a basic consensus in a pluralistic global legal community. Thus, scholars such as Peters and Habermas argue that a global basic consensus can only be perceived as a negative consensus on what is not acceptable, for example, the worst human rights violations, such as genocide or crimes against humanity, to which everybody is likely to agree.[39] From such a perspective, 'world domestic politics', including matters of redistribution, need to be addressed by the states, which are or should be themselves democratically legitimised by their citizens.

While convincing in principle, such a minimum approach might not be able to address the complex problem of climate change. Global warming and climate change are a result of the (historical) high-emission activities of the countries of the Global North, especially due to the high consumption of fossil energy. The Global South's contribution to global warming is relatively small, yet its countries have to bear the brunt of the resulting climate change, including an increase in the frequency and severity of extreme weather events such as storms, floods and droughts. This leads to loss and damage of lands, biodiversity, basic needs such as water, food, shelter and culture. Moreover, it is expected that the effects of climate change will worsen in the future. Hazardous climate change affects and continues to affect future generations (young people or generations yet to come) more strongly than adults today, who have benefited from relatively stable environmental and climate conditions for most of their lives. That makes climate change essentially a 'children's rights crisis'.[40] Short-sighted politics today may endanger the course of their lives. Climate change, therefore, is fundamentally a problem of global justice. As such, it requires the redistribution of burdens (especially the costs of climate change), recognition and participation of the affected. These fundamental issues cannot be addressed by a merely negative consensus.

This book seeks to contribute to the discourse on global constitutionalism. It provides a framework that is more suitable for the climate context. It argues that meaningful visions of global climate constitutionalism will need to include

---

[37] Anne Peters, 'Dual Democracy' in Jan Klabbers, Anne Peters and Geir Ulfstein (eds), *The Constitutionalization of International Law* (OUP 2009) 309.

[38] Besson (n 33) 397.

[39] Peters, 'Dual Democracy' (n 37) 309–10; Jürgen Habermas, 'A Political Constitution for the Pluralist World Society?' in Jürgen Habermas (ed), *Between Naturalism and Religion: Philosophical Essays* (Polity Press 2008) 344.

[40] See Chiara Sacchi and others, 'Communication to the Committee on the Rights of the Child' (2019) para 13.

climate justice as a vital element. Climate justice frames the problem of climate change not only in its environmental or physical dimension but also as an ethical and political problem. From this point of view, many questions arise that have aspects of global justice at their core, including who has to reduce GHG emissions, whether richer states are allowed to choose adaptation over mitigation, who has to pay for loss and damage, and how much the present generations have to save for future generations. IL must find answers to the question of who has to give what to whom.

Leaving these questions to national decision-makers, however, excludes those most affected by climate change. Foreigners, especially those from the Global South, and future generations are 'voiceless'[41] in the decision-making process of a nation's climate policies. Although they are affected by national climate policy decisions, such as the licensing of a new coal-fired power plant or a government's decision to reduce fewer GHG emissions than originally planned, the 'voiceless' cannot vote because of their nationality or age. Traditional models of IL are indifferent to this problem. A nation-state has no positive obligations towards non-citizens.[42] Justice is perceived as an exclusive matter of internal democracy. In contrast, this work argues that approaches to global climate constitutionalism need to make global climate justice the main focus. In my argument, global climate constitutionalism should deal with questions of redistributing the benefits and burdens among all countries and citizens equally.

A basic consensus, a demos, a common identity, and particularly global solidarity 'might be a prerequisite of a viable global democracy, especially when it comes to re-distributive policies'.[43] However, given the extreme diversity and plurality of people worldwide, many have doubted that something similar to a nation, a 'We the people', may ever exist at the international level. This book, therefore, analyses on what grounds a 'global climate community' could emerge. By drawing a line to national constitutionalism, this book will explore whether the global community can be socially integrated through a 'sense of common attachment or a common predicament within the putative *demos*'[44]; in the same way, a national constitution integrates the diverse groups and individuals into 'one nation'. Some sense of common attachment and predicament already exists

[41] For this term, see Randall S Abate, *Climate Change and the Voiceless* (CUP 2019).

[42] Thomas Nagel, 'The Problem of Global Justice' (2005) 33 Philosophy and Public Affairs 113.

[43] Peters, 'Dual Democracy' (n 37) 306.

[44] Neil Walker, 'Taking Constitutionalism beyond the State' (2008) 56 Political Studies 519, 531.

at the global level: the care for one's children is a common value, and the risk of hazardous climate change is a shared risk. So far, global solidarity may not exist, but it will be argued here that global solidarity in climate matters may gradually be developed.

1.2.3 Democracy and Deliberation

For climate justice to be realised in frameworks of global climate constitutionalism, not only is global distributive justice important but also recognition and participation.[45] The possibility of participation in decision-making is stressed by several international environmental agreements,[46] but there are no 'formal' participation opportunities at the global level.[47]

The democratic deficit of traditional IL and global governance is nothing new and has been discussed extensively.[48] Within a constitutionalist framework, with its denser quality of norms and structures that aim to reduce state sovereignty, democratic legitimacy becomes even more important. However, many approaches to global constitutionalism do not comprehensively address the issue of transnational democratic legitimacy, if at all.[49] One of the main reasons why scholars do not sufficiently address the democratisation of transnational law or argue that

---

[45] David Schlosberg, 'Reconceiving Environmental Justice: Global Movements and Political Theories' (2004) 13 Environmental Politics 517, 518.

[46] For example, the UNECE Convention on Access to Information, Public Participation in Decision-Making and Access to Justice in Environmental Matters ("Aarhus Convention") 2161 UNTS 447' (25AD).

[47] The Cardoso report, therefore, identifies ways of how the engagement of civil society at the UN could be strengthened, see Fernando Henrique Cardoso, 'We the Peoples: Civil Society, the United Nations and Global Governance—Report of the Panel of Eminent Persons on United Nations–Civil Society Relations (Cardoso Report)' (2004).

[48] See, for example, Gunther Teubner, 'Quod Omnes Tangit: Transnational Constitutions without Democracy?' (2018) 45 Journal of Law and Society S5; Lea Heyne, 'Globalisierung und Demokratie—Führt Denationalisierung zu einem Verlust an Demokratiequalität?' in Wolfgang Merkel (ed), *Demokratie und Krise—Zum schwierigen Verhältnis von Theorie und Empirie* (Springer VS 2015); Michael Zürn, 'Global Governance and Legitimacy Problems' (2004) 39 Government and Opposition 260; Joseph S Nye, 'Globalization's Democratic Deficit: How to Make International Institutions More Accountable' (2001) 80 Foreign Affairs 2; Roland Rich, 'Bringing Democracy into International Law' (2001) 12 Journal of Democracy 20.

[49] Petra Dobner, 'More Law, Less Democracy? Democracy and Transnational Constitutionalism' in Petra Dobner and Martin Loughlin (eds), *The Twilight of Constitutionalism?* (OUP 2010).

such democratisation is impossible is that they try to transfer elements of national constitutional law and democracy to the international sphere without adapting them to the specificities of the transnational legal order.[50] Notably, transnational democracy cannot become a doubleganger of national democracy. Ways in which citizens generally express their will in a nation-state—elections, voting—are not an option at the transnational level. There is no such thing as a world state, and it seems neither likely nor desirable that it would ever come into being. Thus, this book explores alternative ways of conferring democratic legitimacy to a transnational climate order. To do so, this book will draw on theories of deliberative democracy.

Deliberative democracy requires that all people affected by the outcome of a decision should be able to participate in rational discourses about this decision. Deliberative democracy is based on talking rather than voting; therefore, it is better suited to include the interests of the 'voiceless' and to address concerns of global democracy in general. Deliberation occurs in many different forums, including the public sphere and the courts. In the context of climate change, this phenomenon has been coined 'climate change litigation' (CCL). This refers to a series of lawsuits against governmental actors and private entities whose actions are deemed insufficient to address the climate crisis. Such lawsuits have mostly been filed by individuals and NGOs, but also subnational and local governments, and they seek to push policymakers to implement stronger climate policies and enforce them. While each lawsuit is different, plaintiffs commonly rely on climate science and IEL to buttress their claims.

By presenting climate change as a threat to their rights to life, health, private and family life or to a healthy environment, plaintiffs interpret human rights law as containing an ecological dimension. This book argues that where courts follow their interpretations, non-state actors can be perceived as lawmakers in their own right. While non-state actors are not formally equipped with law-making competencies, their interpretations may (gradually) change the black letter law. Litigation, thus, can be understood as a form of participation in self-government.[51]

Formally, only subjects of IL can create law. However, it will be argued in this book that non-state actors participate as lawmakers in the international climate law regime by means of interpretation. Non-state actors—and especially members of civil society—can develop and shape the developing climate constitution of

---

[50] Teubner, 'Quod Omnes Tangit: Transnational Constitutions without Democracy?' (n 48) S 26–7.

[51] Alexandra Lahav, *In Praise of Litigation* (OUP 2017) 84 ff.

the international community by providing their own interpretational concepts of climate law, including inter-temporal approaches that take the interests of future generations into account, the creation of new rights such as the right to a stable climate or whole new legal concepts, such as rights for nature.

For this purpose, however, it is necessary to broaden the circle of interpreters. Often, when we speak about interpreters, we refer automatically to the bodies that are formally authorised to interpret a certain legal text, for example, a constitutional court that is granted the competence of judicial review in the constitution. However, this book argues that interpretation is a task that is not only up to the courts; non-state actors interpret as well. The framework for such an understanding is presented by a German constitutional law theory on interpretation in and by an 'open society of constitutional interpreters' according to which everybody is potentially an interpreter of the constitution.

1.2.4 Häberle on the Open Society of Constitutional Interpreters

In 1975, Peter Häberle developed a theory called 'the open society of constitutional interpreters'.[52] For Häberle, the constitution is 'open': it is an evaluative instrument that can adapt to constitutional reality and, therefore, can take social, political, technological and ecological changes into account. He argues that there is no such thing as a ready and decisive norm. A constitutional norm, once coming into being through the constitutive act, is not simply predetermined but has to be given meaning. A norm, in this sense, is comparable with an empty shell that only interpretation can fill with content:[53]

> There are no legal norms, there are only interpreted legal norms. And: Whether an interpretation remains or should remain the same in time is the problem and result of interpretation.[54]

---

[52] Peter Häberle, 'Die offene Gesellschaft der Verfassungsinterpreten: Ein Beitrag zur pluralistischen und „prozessualen“ Verfassungsinterpretation' (1975) 30 Juristenzeitung 297; see for the English translation Häberle, '"The Open Society of Constitutional Interpreters"—A Contribution to a Pluralistic and "Procedural" Constitutional Interpretation (1975)' (n 3).

[53] Peter Häberle, 'Zeit und Verfassung: Prolegomena zu einem "zeit-gerechten" Verfassungsverständnis' (1974) 21 ZfP 111, 127.

[54] Ibid (tr the author, citations omitted).

A legal norm's meaning may change over time. Its indeterminacy opens it up to time and its public. An interpretation, according to Häberle, can only make sense in the time context in which the norm is interpreted.

The task of interpretation, however, is not assigned exclusively to the judicial branch, in particular, the constitutional court—a concept that Häberle calls the 'closed society of constitutional interpreters'. Instead, he employs a broader understanding of who is interpreting constitutional norms. Informed by Karl Popper's 'open society',[55] in Häberle's 'open society of constitutional interpreters', 'potentially all state entities, all public entities, all citizens and groups are engaged in the process of constitutional interpretation. There is no *numerus clausus* of constitutional interpreters!'[56]

Constitutional interpretation is open to everybody who comes in touch with a constitutional norm. The interpreters do not even need to know that they are interpreting a constitutional provision. Whoever 'fills a norm with "life"' is an interpreter in Häberle's sense.[57] This can happen by simply living in the fundamental right. In this sense, everyone interprets the constitution all the time, independent of their awareness.[58] Additionally, an interpretation does not need to be articulated. Most interpretations never reach a constitutional judge, but 'the substantive constitution "lives" precisely here', where people interpret the constitution on their own and, thus, 'develop an autonomous substantive constitutional law'.[59] However, to convince others of one's interpretation, it does need to be articulated. The courts are an important forum for such deliberation; a citizen can 'force the court to engage in a (legal) dialogue', for example, by filing a constitutional complaint.[60]

Although individuals and groups are not officially authorised to interpret the constitution, they are interpreters in a substantive sense and operate at least as 'pre-interpreters'.[61] This is particularly true for 'open' norms such as freedom of art, freedom of science or religious freedom because all these rights depend on the individual's self-understanding of, for example, the exercise of their religion. Vice versa, it means that constitutional provisions regulating the organisation of

---

55 Karl Popper, *The Open Society and Its Enemies* (Routledge & Kegan 2002).

56 Häberle, '"The Open Society of Constitutional Interpreters"—A Contribution to a Pluralistic and "Procedural" Constitutional Interpretation (1975)' (n 3) 130 (emphasis in original).

57 Ibid 131.

58 Ibid 130.

59 Ibid 150.

60 Ibid 135.

61 Ibid 131.

the state are less open to 'constitutional change' by interpretation but have to be modified through formal amendment.

Häberle's theory of the open society of constitutional interpreters had and continues to have a strong influence on constitutional law all over the world, especially in Latin America. In Brazil, the importance of Häberle's work is openly acknowledged not only by Brazilian legal scholarship[62] but also by the Supreme Court (STF).[63] Some, including former President of the STF (2008–2010) Mendes, argue that the 'open society of constitutional interpreters' had a major influence on the development of the Brazilian system of constitutional review,[64] including the adoption of the amicus curiae (friend of the court) figure in Brazilian law; some lawyers attribute its introduction directly to Häberle.[65] Brazil was the first country of the civil-law circle to establish the amicus curiae to make constitutional processes more pluralistic and open and, thereby, realise

[62] Marcos Augusto Maliska, 'Rezeption von Häberle in Brasilien. Die brasilianische Verfassung im Kontext der internationalen Öffnung, Kooperation und Integration' in Martin Möllers and Robert van Ooyen (eds), *Verfassungs-Kultur. Staat, Europa und pluralistische Gesellschaft bei Peter Häberle* (Nomos 2016) 176; Matheus Souza Galdino, 'Jurisdição constitucional e teoria da decisão: As contribuições de Ronald Dworkin, Peter Häberle e Jürgen Habermas na democratização do debate constitucional' (2016) 21 Revista Jus Navigandi 27; Mônia Clarissa Hennig Leal and Caroline Müller Bittencourt, 'Jurisdição constitucional aberta: Democratizando interpretação constitucional para a sociedade pluralista com a proposta hermenêutica de Peter Häberle' in Clovis Gorczevski and Jorge Renato dos Reis (eds), *Constitucionalismo Contemporâneo* (Norton 2008).

[63] See, for example, 'Notícias STF—Ministros destacam interação do STF com a sociedade na abertura de audiência pública' (2012) <https://stf.jusbrasil.com.br/noticias/3109764/ministros-destacam-interacao-do-stf-com-a-sociedade-na-abertura-de-audiencia-publica> accessed 31 August 2023; Gilmar Ferreira Mendes and André Rufino do Vale, 'O pensamento de Peter Häberle na jurisprudência do Supremo Tribunal Federal' (2008) 2 Observatório da Jurisdição Constitucional; Celso de Mello, 'Discurso de saudação do ministro Gilmar Ferreira Mendes na posse na presidência do Supremo Tribunal Federal (Solemn Ministerial Address on the Occasion of the Official Inauguration of Gilmar Ferreira Mendes as President of the Supreme Federal Court)' 14.

[64] Coelho highlights, among other things, the recognition of non-judicial interpreters, especially indigenous communities, in constitutional processes, the expansion of the number of empowered constitutional translators and the involvement of third parties, see Inocêncio Mártires Coelho, 'As idéias de Peter Häberle e a abertura da interpretação constitucional no direito brasileiro' (1998) 35 Revista de Informação Legislativa 157, 158.

[65] Gilmar Mendes, 'A influência de Peter Häberle no constitucionalismo brasileiro' (2016) 2 Journal of Institutional Studies 30, 33; Gilmar Mendes, 'Homenagem à doutrina de Peter Häberle e sua influência no Brasil (Speech on the Occasion of the Award of an Honorary Doctorate to Prof. Häberle by the University of Brasilía)'.

constitutional guarantees.[66] One of the reasons for the success of Häberle's theory may lie in the fact that Brazilian society is an extremely pluralist one.[67] Pluralism is one of the underlying principles of the Brazilian constitution and is prominent in both the preamble and Article 1 of the 1988 Constitution ('political pluralism').[68] Häberle's 'open society of constitutional interpreters' has also been well-received, inter alia, in South Africa[69] and India.[70] The recognition of the Indian rivers Ganga and Yamuna as living beings/juristic persons can even be understood as the High Court of Uttarakhand resembling 'the people' as 'open interpreters of the constitution'.[71] Kumar understands Häberle's open society of constitutional interpreters as a concept able to include the underrepresented rural, Hindi-speaking masses of India to advance environmental protection.[72]

The theory has not been received everywhere with enthusiasm, in particular, not in Germany. Indeed, Häberle himself foresaw the criticism that an 'open society of constitutional interpreters' could mean the dissolution of constitutional unity in a multitude of interpretations and interpreters. Forsthoff, for example, remarked in disbelief that such a 'quaint' democratisation of constitutional jurisdiction would give theologians, philosophers, sociologists, political scientists and even journalists access to constitutional interpretation.[73] However, Häberle did

---

[66] Mendes and do Vale (n 63).

[67] Ibid; Brazil has one of the most heterogeneous societies in terms of origin, ethics, race, religion, culture and minorities such as the indigenous population, see IBGE, 'Censo demográfico 2010' (2011); Simon Schwartzmann, 'Foro de foco: Diversidade e identidades étnicas no Brasil' (1999) 55 Novos Estudos CEBRAP 83; for some, this is the reason why positivist approaches did not have a great success in Brazil, cf. Mônia Clarissa Hennig Leal, 'As audiências públicas no âmbito do Supremo Tribunal Federal brasileiro: Uma nova forma de participação?' (2014) 19 Novos Estudos Jurídicos 327, 332.

[68] Mendes and do Vale (n 63).

[69] See for example, Lourens du Plessis, 'Legal Academics and the Open Community of Constitutional Interpreters' (1996) 12 South African Journal on Human Rights 214; Dawid van Wyk, 'Values, Values, Values or Mere Words, Words, Words? Values in the 1996 Constitution', *Constitution and Law IV: Developments in the Contemporary Constitutional State* (2000) 26 (fn. 44).

[70] Pratyush Kumar, 'Review Essay: M. Kotzur (Ed.), Peter Häberle on Constitutional Theory: Constitution as Culture and the Open Society of Constitutional Interpreters. Baden- Baden, Germany: Nomos, 2018, 323 Pp., €84' (2019) 65 Indian Journal of Public Administration 769.

[71] Ibid 782–83.

[72] Ibid 783, "The 'atman' of the people became the 'atman' of the court. It would only be about time how this 'spiritual environmentalism' could be used to protect the fragile ecosystems of the Indian sub-continent."

[73] Ernst Forsthoff, *Der Staat der Industriegesellschaft* (CH Beck 1971) 69.

not draw such radical conclusions from his theory but merely aimed to 'determine the democratic-theoretical place and time when law is created in a free society (civil society). The answer was right: "Every day and everywhere!"',[74] but the ultimate responsibility lies with the constitutional judiciary.[75] Häberle's theory is mostly descriptive; thus, he merely offers an alternative to how to understand the role of citizens (and other actors) in constitutional processes as public processes.[76] However, the examples of Brazilian jurisprudence and Kumar's understanding demonstrate how the theory can be made fertile to think about the role of non-state actors in a constitutionalist framework beyond the state.

Recognising this could offer new ways of conferring democratic legitimacy. It would mean a shift from a formal approach that focuses only on 'voting' and 'representation' to interpretation by everybody, thus, considering the democratic side of fundamental rights. It means offering meaningful participation opportunities to non-state actors and giving them a voice. Häberle's theory is opening more venues for public participation, thereby strengthening democracy. The inclusion of the pluralistic public in the processes of interpretation means to include the public and reality of the constitution itself, thereby legitimising the whole process:[77]

> A constitution that not only incorporates the state in a narrow sense, but also structures the public and constitutes society, while directly including the private realm, may not only act passively upon them, treating the societal and private powers as objects. It must actively include them: as subjects.[78]

These ideas form the background against which this book will analyse the role of CCL cases as a form of participation for non-state actors in transnational climate governance. CCL cases allow plaintiffs, often ordinary citizens and NGOs, to

---

[74] Michael Stolleis, Staatsrechtslehre und Politik (Speech Delivered on 7 May 1996) (Müller 1996) 22–3 cited in Roland Lhotta, 'Die kinetische Verfassung: Verfassungstheorie und Verfassungsbegriff bei Peter Häberle und Rudolf Smend' in Martin Möllers and Robert van Ooyen (eds), *Verfassungs-Kultur. Staat, Europa und pluralistische Gesellschaft bei Peter Häberle* (Nomos 2016) 94 (tr the author).

[75] Häberle, '"The Open Society of Constitutional Interpreters"—A Contribution to a Pluralistic and "Procedural" Constitutional Interpretation (1975)' (n 3) 131, 146.

[76] Michaela Hailbronner, 'Hierarchical Authority in German Constitutional Law: The Constitutional Court between Law and Politics', *Traditions and Transformations. The Rise of German Constitutionalism* (2015) 162.

[77] Häberle, '"The Open Society of Constitutional Interpreters"—A Contribution to a Pluralistic and "Procedural" Constitutional Interpretation (1975)' (n 3) 143.

[78] Ibid 144.

present their own interpretations of climate matters. These arguments in court proceedings are not only meant to convince the judge but also the broader public. Where plaintiffs succeed with their arguments against the defending state, they contribute to making and reinforcing international climate law.

The crucial role of the courts for global environmental and climate constitutionalism has been stressed by many scholars, mostly by highlighting the innovativeness and mix of instruments the courts use to subsume climate change under human rights law and other non-climate law.[79] By doing so, judges participate in a worldwide dialogue. Litigation can shape and foster the transnational constitutionalist discourse between many different actors, including non-state actors and courts. From this point of view, global constitutional climate law is not only the product of states' making law but also of non-state actors' actions.

1.3 Objective of the Book: CCL and Non-state Actors as International Lawmakers?

The objective of this book is to analyse whether and how non-state actors can engage in international climate lawmaking by means of CCL.[80] While not allowed to participate formally as subjects in treaty negotiations, non-state actors can at least seek to influence or enforce existing climate policies via the courts.

Global environmental/climate constitutionalism has become a topic of increasing interest in academia. Most contributions in this field are descriptive; they are limited to identifying and comparing provisions in national constitutions related

[79] Cf. Mehrdad Payandeh, 'The Role of Courts in Climate Protection and the Separation of Powers' in Wolfgang Kahl and Marc-Philippe Weller (eds), *Climate Change Litigation—A Handbook* (Beck/Hart/Nomos 2020); James R May and Erin Daly, 'Global Climate Constitutionalism and Justice in the Courts' in Jordi Jaria-Manzano and Susana Borràs (eds), *Research Handbook on Global Climate Constitutionalism* (Edward Elgar Publishing 2019); Louis J Kotzé, 'Global Environmental Constitutionalism in the Anthropocene' in Louis J Kotzé (ed), *Environmental Law and Governance for the Anthropocene* (Hart/Bloomsbury Publishing 2017) 207ff; Jolene Lin, 'Climate Change and the Courts' (2012) 32 Legal Studies 35.

[80] See, for example, James R May and Erin Daly, *Judicial Handbook on Environmental Constitutionalism* (Law Division, UNEP Programme 2017); Erin Daly and James R May, 'Global Environmental Constitutionalism: A Rights-Based Primer for Effective Strategies', *Elgar Encyclopedia of Environmental Law: Decision Making in Environmental Law (Vol. II)* (2017); James R May and Erin Daly, *Global Environmental Constitutionalism* (CUP 2014); Douglas A Kysar, 'Global Environmental Constitutionalism: Getting There from Here' (2012) 1 Transnational Environmental Law 83; Martin Scheyli, 'Der Schutz des Klimas als Prüfstein völkerrechtlicher Konstitutionalisierung?' (2002) 40 Archiv des Völkerrechts 273.

to the protection of the environment.[81] This also means that they employ a strong state-fixed focus. Only recently have scholars started to cover transnational climate constitutionalism independently of national constitutional law from a normative perspective.[82] These approaches seek to identify rules or IEL principles that could or should belong to a transnational environmental constitution. Many of them also discuss strategic litigation as a tool to enforce stronger climate policies.[83]

However, while there is consensus that non-state actors participate in global (climate) governance and, therefore, should play a stronger role in global (climate) constitutionalism than under 'traditional' frameworks of IL, there have been few contributions so far to how they could meaningfully participate and engage in international lawmaking. Some scholars have proposed ideas on how to democratise global climate governance, including the establishment of citizen assemblies at the United Nations (UN) and beyond or forums for treaty drafting.[84] However,

---

[81] May and Daly, *Judicial Handbook on Environmental Constitutionalism* (n 80) 79, for example, describe how three quarters of all constitutions worldwide include a right to a clean and healthy environment or other environment-related rights, see also Roderic O'Gorman, 'Environmental Constitutionalism: A Comparative Study' (2017) 6 Transnational Environmental Law 435; David R Boyd, 'The Constitutional Right to a Healthy Environment' (2012) 54 Environment: Science and Policy for Sustainable Development 3; David Boyd, *The Environmental Rights Revolution: A Global Study of Constitutions, Human Rights, and the Environment* (UBC Press 2011).

[82] See, in particular, the works of Louis J Kotzé, *Global Environmental Constitutionalism in the Anthropocene* (Bloomsbury Publishing 2016); Louis Kotzé, 'A Global Environmental Constitution for the Anthropocene?' (2019) 8 Transnational Environmental Law 11; Louis J Kotzé and Wendy Muzangaza, 'Constitutional International Environmental Law for the Anthropocene?' (2018) 27 Review of European, Comparative and International Environmental Law 278; see also the essay collections in Jordi Jaria-Manzano and Susana Borràs, *Research Handbook on Global Climate Constitutionalism* (Jordi Jaria-Manzano and Susana Borràs eds, Edward Elgar Publishing 2019) and Veerle Heyvaert and Leslie-Anne Duvic-Paoli, *Research Handbook on Transnational Environmental Law* (Veerle Heyvaert and Leslie-Anne Duvic-Paoli eds, Edward Elgar Publishing 2020).

[83] See, for example, May and Daly, 'Global Climate Constitutionalism and Justice in the Courts' (n 79); Jerzy Jendrośka and Moritz Reese, 'The Courts as Guardians of the Environment—New Developments in Access to Justice and Environmental Litigation' in Jonathan Isted (ed), *Environment & Climate Change 2019 (International Comparative Legal Guides)* (Global Legal Group 2019).

[84] Examples of discursive representation such as the ALBA (Bolivarian Alliance for the Peoples of Our America) movement and climate activism on platforms such as TckTckTck, Avaaz, and 350.org, are discussed by Hayley Stevenson and John S Dryzek, *Democratizing Global Climate Change* (CUP 2014) 130–48; for the participation of civil society in UN institutions, see Cardoso (n 47).

these contributions focus on 'formal' channels of international lawmaking and its democratisation. These scholars seek to open avenues for NGOs and citizen groups to formally have a voice in treaty negotiations to influence the outcome of international treaties.[85]

This book seeks to add a perspective to these ideas by focusing on the concept of non-state actors changing the law through interpretation rather than through formal creation or amendment. In many states, 'constitutional change' is an important way of incorporating social, ecological and technological changes and developments into the constitution without the need for formal amendment.[86] This book seeks to transfer this phenomenon to the international level, and in doing so, it argues that CCL can be understood as one (not *the*) tool of self-government through which non-state actors increasingly participate in shaping climate law.

This point is also relevant with respect to climate justice. May and Daly, for example, argue that CCL can advance climate justice by incorporating climate concerns into already existing human rights law, such as the right to life, to health, and to water and food.[87] However, this approach has been limited to national constitutional texts and does not consider climate justice in the larger framework of constitutionalism beyond the state. But it is precisely here where questions of redistribution and socio-economic justice are arising and becoming difficult to solve. In a nation-state, citizenship holds people in a solidarity embrace that compels them to make sacrifices for one another (e.g., redistributive taxation).[88] This book will explore whether there could be such a basis for a transnational global climate society through which global solidarity could emerge. Moreover, it analyses whether global climate constitutionalism with a strong notion of climate justice is bound to a world state or how else democratic legitimacy can be conferred beyond the nation-state without a global democratic system.

---

[85] Barbara B Woodward, 'International Lawmaking and Civil Society' in Catherine Brölmann and Yannick Radi (eds), *Research Handbook on the Theory and Practice of International Lawmaking* (Edward Elgar Publishing 2016) 289–301.

[86] Markus Kotzur, 'Constitutional Amendments and Constitutional Changes in Germany' in Xenophon Contiades (ed), *Engineering Constitutional Change* (Routledge 2013) 134; Ingo Venzke, *How Interpretation Makes International Law: On Semantic Change and Normative Twists* (OUP 2012) 4.

[87] May and Daly, 'Global Climate Constitutionalism and Justice in the Courts' (n 79) 240ff.

[88] Jürgen Habermas, 'The Postnational Constellation and the Future of Democracy' in Jürgen Habermas and Max Pensky (eds), *The Postnational Constellation: Political Essays* (Polity Press 2001) 64–5.

The background for this book will be Häberle's theory of the 'open society of constitutional interpreters'.[89] Against this theoretical background, this work will argue that it is the inclusion of the pluralistic public through interpretation that can legitimise processes of constitutionalisation. Häberle himself recognised the possibility of transferring his theory to the European and international realms. While he subsequently developed a comprehensive version of a European 'open society of constitutional interpreters',[90] he limited himself to a short overview and keywords rather than diving into discussing his points in relation to IL.[91] The emergence of the global climate constitutionalism discourse is a good opportunity to test his theory and identify its value on the international level.

The specific aims of this book, therefore, are to:

1. comprehensively analyse the concepts of 'constitution' and 'constitutionalism' to determine whether global climate constitutionalism could provide a useful framework for addressing climate change
2. shed light on the development of a transnational climate discourse besides the state-fixed regimes established by international treaties, such as the UNFCCC
3. discuss the problem of the absence of democracy in the scholarly discourse of global constitutionalism, in particular, through the lens of climate justice, and offer ways of rethinking democratic legitimacy
4. identify CCL as one possible way of self-governing that allows the members of an open society to develop and shape the content of international (constitutional) norms through the introduction of new interpretations
5. analyse the role of domestic courts in transnational climate dialogues and the limitations on 'judicial lawmaking' under the doctrine of the separation of powers
6. transfer Häberle's theory of the 'open society of constitutional interpreters' to IL and thus, contributing to a more democratic and participatory understanding of global climate constitutionalism, thereby fostering 'bottom-up' approaches.

The importance of this book also lies in addressing an aspect of global climate constitutionalism, which, so far, has received little attention. Dobner has noted that, in discourses of global constitutionalism, the promotion of democracy tends

---

[89] See Section 1.2.4 above.

[90] Häberle, 'The Open Society of Constitutional Interpreters' (n 3) 158–63; Peter Häberle and Markus Kotzur, *Europäische Verfassungslehre* (8th edn, Nomos 2016) 471–510.

[91] Häberle, 'The Open Society of Constitutional Interpreters' (n 3) 164–5.

to be substituted with the promotion of the global rule of law. Visions of normative global constitutionalism are often based on the promotion of universal human rights only.[92] The rule of law is a vital element of global constitutionalism, but it cannot replace the need for the democratisation of global governance. Rather, the global rule of law itself needs to be democratised. 'There is a growing drift between law and democracy' which endangers one of the most important achievements of modernity: the exercise of power based upon the consent of those governed.[93] This book offers an additional perspective on how the problem of the 'dissolution of law and democracy' could be addressed by strengthening the concept of democratic participation and incorporating aspects of deliberative democracy.

1.4 Terminology

Some clarifications concerning the terminology used in this book are necessary. Throughout the next chapters, the text refers to 'transnational', 'global' and 'international' constitutionalism. All of them refer to constitutionalism beyond the nation-state based on several criteria identified by Kotzé, including

> the limitation of a single locus of power; increased participation and greater representation in global governance; the creation of one or more global constitutions and corresponding institutions; legitimization of global governance; effective governance through the institutionalization of power; the existence of one or more higher laws or constitutional norms which place restrictions on states and which create accountability; the existence of a common universal value system based on fundamental rights, among others; the acceptance of the existence of, and the pursuit of, the common interests of mankind; and constitutional standard setting.[94]

This book, therefore, uses 'global', 'transnational' and 'international' to describe constitutionalism beyond the state, as opposed to national or domestic constitutionalism within the nation-state, interchangeably.[95] Where these terms are used by scholars in a particular way relevant to this book, the difference will be

[92] Dobner (n 49) 142.

[93] Ibid.

[94] Louis J Kotzé, 'Arguing Global Environmental Constitutionalism' (2012) 1 Transnational Environmental Law 199, 215.

[95] Cf. Larry Catá Backer, 'Theocratic Constitutionalism: An Introduction to a New Global Legal Ordering' (2009) 16 Indiana Journal of Global Legal Studies 85, 102, 122; Kotzé, 'Arguing Global Environmental Constitutionalism' (n 94) 211.

stressed by using clarifying terms such as 'societal constitutionalism' or 'sectorial constitutionalism'. Moreover, this book employs terms such as 'traditional international law', inter-states law or *jus gentium* to describe IL according to the Westphalian model.

Generally, the term 'climate change litigation' embraces an array of different types and scopes of litigation.[96] Cases can be filed with both judicial and quasi-judicial international bodies, such as the regional human rights courts, and domestic courts. Many cases pursue a pro-regulatory approach, which seeks to improve climate protection. Some CCL cases claim compensation for loss and damage suffered.[97] The term also encompasses the growing body of anti-regulatory litigation filed by business actors and the fossil fuel industry in the aftermath of the landmark *Massachusetts v EPA* decision.[98] So-called 'SLAPP' suits (Strategic Litigation Against Public Participation) that aim to silence criticism, suppress public activism and stop potential plaintiffs from filing suits also fall into this category.[99]

Some cases are related to climate change in some way or another but do not have climate-related arguments at their core; it is not entirely clear whether climate protection is the aspired goal or merely a side effect.[100] The argument that such cases should be excluded for reasons of uninformed judgement about the litigant's motivation[101] is rejected by Peel and Osofsky, who argue that litigants generally rely on the strongest legal argument in court, and this may not be climate protection.[102] The multitude of 'holy grail' cases that have received tremendous attention, such as the *Urgenda* case, are based on human rights

---

[96] An overview is provided by Sandrine Maljean-Dubois, 'Climate Change Litigation', *Max Planck Encyclopedia of International Procedural Law* (OUP 2018) para 5.

[97] See Payandeh (n 79) 15.

[98] Jacqueline Peel and Hari M Osofsky, *Climate Change Litigation: Regulatory Pathways to Cleaner Energy* (CUP 2015) 3.

[99] George (Rock) Pring and Catherine (Kitty) Pring, 'Greening Justice—Creating and Improving Environmental Courts and Tribunals' (The Access Initiative 2009) 53.

[100] Peel and Osofsky (n 98) 5–6 mention the pro/anti hydraulic fracturing ("fracking") cases in the U.S.

[101] David Markell and JB Ruhl, 'An Empirical Assessment of Climate Change in the Courts: A New Jurisprudence or Business as Usual' (2012) 64 Florida Law Review 15, 26.

[102] Peel and Osofsky (n 98) 7.

law or constitutional fundamental rights. However, 'unsexy'[103] cases based on administrative[104] or financial law[105] can be just as successful.

Often, CCL describes litigation against governmental action (or inaction). But plaintiffs also file complaints against major private GHG emitters. The cases of Peruvian micro farmer and mountain guide Lliuya, who sued German energy giant RWE in Germany, of the Dutch NGO Milieudefensie against Shell Oil and

103 Kim Bouwer, 'The Unsexy Future of Climate Change Litigation' (2018) 30 Journal of Environmental Law 483.

104 In the United Kingdom, a court of appeal blocked the construction of a third runway at Heathrow airport after the legal charity "Plan B" had filed a claim based on administrative laws (the UK Planning Act 2008) and the target of the Paris Agreement (R (on the application of Plan B Earth) v Secretary of State for Transport [2020] EWCA Civ 214, [2020] 2WLUK 372). However, the UK Supreme Court overturned the decision in December 2020, inter alia, by finding that the Paris Agreement did not constitute government policy, "Top UK court overturns block on Heathrow's third runway", The Guardian, 16 December 2020, <https://www.theguardian.com/environment/2020/dec/16/top-uk-court-overturns-block-on-heathrows-third-runway> accessed 31 August 2023

105 A class-action suit was filed by 23-year-old Australian student O'Donnell who argued that Australia's economy, and international reputation, will be significantly affected by the Government's inadequate response to climate change. She claims that countless pension funds, central banks, retail investors, insurers and hedge funds have loaned the Australian Government over AUD$700 billion and that the government breaches its duty by not disclosing the risks of global warming and their material impact on investors (Equity Generation Lawyers, 'O'Donnell v Commonwealth and Ors' <https://equitygenerationlawyers.com/cases/odonnell-v-commonwealth> accessed 31 August 2023). In August 2023, the Australian Government agreed to settle the case in exchange for acknowledging that climate change is a risk to government bonds. It is the first country with a AAA credit rating to do so, "Australia to acknowledge climate risk to government bonds after world-first court settlement", The Guardian, 30 August 2023 <https://www.theguardian.com/law/2023/aug/30/australia-to-acknowledge-climate-risk-to-government-bonds-after-world-first-court-settlement> accessed 31 August 2023.

of Greenpeace Southeast Asia suing 50 major carbon companies in the Philippines are exemplary.[106] When governments prosecute civil disobedience, activists may use climate arguments to defend their activities.[107]

In this book, the term 'climate change litigation' is used for lawsuits that strive for stronger regulation or enforcement of (international) norms (pro-regulatory litigation) and either seek to mitigate the problem by addressing the emission of GHGs (mitigation-related litigation) or to adapt to the predicted impacts for ecosystems and communities (adaptation-related litigation).[108] These cases are directed against governmental actors in charge of adopting climate policies or responsible for their enforcement; they employ constitutional fundamental rights and human rights law, and they have climate arguments at their core.

1.5 Methodology

This research objectives in this book will be investigated through an approach that combines the transfer of Häberle's theory of the 'open society of constitutional interpreters' to the international level and an analysis of recent CCL cases. Against these cases, how the interaction of the interpretations of climate activists and the courts can make climate law will be analysed.

Häberle's theory was originally designed to describe the role of those interpreters of the constitution who are not formally authorised by the German Basic Law—in contrast to the Federal Constitutional Court—to interpret the constitution. Transferring Häberle's theory to IL means modifying it in such a way that it can address the particularities of IL without losing its substance. This

[106] The Andean town of Huaraz, where Lliuya lives with his family, is threatened by flooding due to the accelerating melting of the glaciers, which is leading to rising water levels in the glacial lakes near the city, see Brooke Jarvis, 'Climate Change Could Destroy His Home in Peru. So He Sued an Energy Company in Germany.' [2019] *The New York Times Magazine* <https://www.nytimes.com/interactive/2019/04/09/magazine/climate-change-peru-law.html> accessed 31 August 2023; for the case of Greenpeace South East Asia v Philippines, see Alan Boyd, 'Climate Change Litigation in Philippines a Game-Changer?' *Asia Times* (13 April 2018) <https://asiatimes.com/2018/04/climate-change-litigation-philippines-game-changer/> accessed 31 August 2023; The Hague District Court, Milieudefensie et al. v. Royal Dutch Shell plc., Judgement of 26 May 2021, ECLI:NL:RBDHA:2021:5337.

[107] Joseph Rausch, 'The Necessity Defense and Climate Change: A Climate Change Litigant's Guide' (2019) 44 Columbia Journal of Environmental Law 553; Saskia Stucki, 'In Defence of Green Civil Disobedience' *Verfassungsblog* (30 October 2020) <https://verfassungsblog.de/in-defence-of-green-civil-disobedience/> accessed 31 August 2023.

[108] Peel and Osofsky (n 98) 5.

book applies an approach of generalisation and re-specification inspired by Teubner.[109] As opposed to analogy, which, for Teubner, 'either uses vague relations of similarity or generalizes only and fails to respecify',[110] the generalisation and re-specification approach seeks to identify, in a first step, what makes a constitution a constitution. These characteristics will be defined in a more general way, thus, not on the basis of the constitutional understanding of particular nation-states or scholarship to avoid 'methodological nationalism' or a 'self-centered Eurocentric' view.[111] In a second step, these findings are applied to the context of global climate constitutionalism. This establishes the base from which Häberle's theory can be scrutinised against the particularities of transnational climate law. Throughout the chapters, possibilities and criticism of the 'open society of constitutional interpreters' that have been identified by both Häberle and other scholars, including democratic legitimacy and fragmentation/constitutional unity, will be analysed in the context of global climate law, taking into account academic literature and case law.

By doing so, on the one hand, the book adopts a theoretical research approach. Theoretical research (also described as 'jurisprudence research') is defined by the Australian Pearce Committee as 'research which fosters a more complete understanding of the conceptual bases of legal principles and of the combined effects of a range of rules and procedures that touch on a particular area of activity'.[112] Its aim is to provide academic knowledge of the operation of law and, in this respect, is also called 'pure research'. According to the 1983 Canadian Arthurs' report, theoretical research (or, how Arthurs puts it, 'legal theory research') is 'research *in* law' instead of 'research *about* law'.[113] It asks, 'What is the law?' This question is crucial for this book, which seeks to understand how non-state actors can make a meaningful contribution to the creation of international constitutional climate law.

Häberle did not draw any radical conclusions from his 'open society of constitutional interpreters'. Rather, he offered an additional perspective on constitutional theory. This book, however, seeks to make Häberle's theory fertile for notions of normative global constitutionalism by arguing that interpretation can

---

[109] Gunther Teubner, *Constitutional Fragments: Societal Constitutionalism and Globalization* (OUP 2012) 10.

[110] Ibid.

[111] Ibid; Kotzur (n 86) 138.

[112] Dennis Pearce, Enid Campbell and Don Harding, 'Australian Law Schools: A Discipline Assessment for the Commonwealth Tertiary Education Commission' (1987) 17.

[113] Paul Chynoweth, 'Legal Research' in Andrew Knight and Les Ruddock (eds), *Advanced Research Methods in the Built Environment* (Wiley-Blackwell 2008) 30.

fill 'the space between the norm texts and the law'.[114] Such interpretations, however, are presented by many actors, including non-state actors. In doing so, this book relies on cases belonging to the category of CCL. The term encompasses, as seen above, the multitude of lawsuits filed by different actors with different objectives. Based on the aforementioned criteria for CCL relevant to this work (see Section 1.4), four cases (*Urgenda v The Netherlands, Asghar Leghari v Pakistan, Juliana v United States* and *Future Generations v Colombia*) were chosen that will be analysed in detail in Chapter 9. While it is impossible to present the diversity of climate cases worldwide in this book, these four cases attempt to highlight the differences and similarities of global climate litigation. What they all have in common is that they are directed against governments (rather than private entities such as corporations), they are based on fundamental or human rights, and they have climate justice arguments at their core. Moreover, they represent the two legal systems—the common-laws system and the civil-law system—and four different continents with different climate realities. Two of them—*Leghari* and *Future Generations*—belong to the growing wave of climate litigation in the Global South, while *Urgenda* and *Juliana* took place in the Global North.

1.6 Structure of the Book

This book adopts the following structure: Chapters 2 and 3 analyse the concepts that underpin this book. Chapter 2 offers a theoretical understanding of what makes interpretation important for the development of IL. Chapter 3 examines the concepts of constitution, constitutionalism and constitutionalisation and discusses what makes global climate constitutionalism a suitable answer to the global climate crisis.

An important element of global constitutionalism is democracy. Given the plurality and diversity of actors, this element is likely the most difficult to establish on the international plane. Chapter 4 first draws the contours of global climate constitutionalism. It argues that global climate constitutionalism needs to operate under the maxim of climate justice, which includes redistribution, recognition and participation.

Chapter 5 then identifies the basis on which a global climate society, despite its diversity and plurality, can eventually develop global solidarity. Such a base can be found in common attachment and/or common predicament, such as intergenerational equity or the shared risk of survival.

---

[114] Venzke (n 86) 197.

Chapter 6 analyses bottom-up approaches to constitutionalism, in particular through the participation of non-state actors in CCL. It employs theories of deliberative democracy and the possibility of litigation as a form of self-government that confers at least small amounts of democratic legitimacy to an emerging transnational climate regime.

The role of non-state actors as constitution-makers, then, will be discussed in Chapter 7. Contrary to the classical Westphalian model of IL, which focuses almost exclusively on states, theories of societal constitutionalism are examined, according to which non-state actors can develop (civil) constitutional law and help to create new human rights. While theories of societal constitutionalism enhance the circle of participants, under most frameworks, constitutionalism is still established from the top down. The next chapter, Chapter 8, therefore, takes a closer look at the actors involved in litigation.

Chapter 9 analyses four recent CCL cases: *Urgenda v the Netherlands* (2015, 2019, 2020), *Asghar Leghari v Pakistan* (2015), *Juliana v the United States* (2015 ongoing) and *Future Generations v Colombia* (2018). These cases represent litigation in four different countries, continents and the two legal systems. A comparative case analysis reveals similarities and differences between the rulings, including how the courts responded to the different demands put forward by the plaintiffs and applied new legal concepts to grasp the problem of global climate change under the existing legal framework. In doing so, this chapter identifies how and to what extent domestic courts are key actors in the development of international climate law.

Chapter 10 discusses the role of the courts. As a first step, it critically analyses whether the courts are overstepping their competencies under the separation of powers doctrine. By drawing on the theories of Habermas and Möllers, the chapter gives an explanation of the role of the court in the field of tension between popular sovereignty and human rights and the limitations of judicial lawmaking.

The concluding Chapter 11 revisits the complex relationship between the problem of global climate change and state sovereignty. It recaptures that approaches to global constitutionalism meaning to constrain state sovereignty must embrace aspects of climate justice, including offering meaningful participation opportunities to affected populations. CCL can be understood as an informal, indirect participation tool for non-state actors in an emerging transnational climate regime. This section also discusses the limits of CCL in relation to both lawmaking and enforcement. Finally, it demonstrates that Häberle's theory of the 'open society of constitutional interpreters' can offer a fresh theoretical background against which the phenomenon of CCL can be understood as a way of democratising global governance.

Interpretation in International Law 2

'I don't know what you mean by "glory",' Alice said.

Humpty Dumpty smiled contemptuously. 'Of course you don't—till I tell you. I meant "there's a nice knock-down argument for you!"'

'But "glory" doesn't mean "a nice knock-down argument",' Alice objected.

'When I use a word,' Humpty Dumpty said, in a rather a scornful tone, 'it means just what I choose it to mean—neither more nor less.'

'The question is,' said Alice, 'whether you can make words mean so many different things.'

'The question is,' said Humpty Dumpty, 'which is to be master—that's all.'

Lewis Carroll, *Through the Looking-Glass* (1871)

2.1 Introduction

What might seem like a rather curious passage from a children's book demonstrates the dilemma of legal interpretation. Not without reason, this passage from *Through the Looking-Glass* has been used to illustrate the problem of finding meaning through interpretation by both scholars[1] and courts.[2]

[1] Cf. Philip Allott, 'Interpretation—An Exact Art' in Andrea Bianchi, Daniel Peat and Matthew Windsor (eds), *Interpretation in International Law* (OUP 2015) 373; Ingo Venzke, *How Interpretation Makes International Law: On Semantic Change and Normative Twists* (OUP 2012) 55.

[2] See, e.g. United Kingdom House of Lords Decision, UKHL 1, Liversidge v Anderson (1942), AC 206. In the US alone, over 250 judicial decisions quoted Humpty Dumpty, including two rulings of the Supreme Court. Allott (n 1) 374.

M. Niehaus, *Global Climate Constitutionalism "from below"*,
https://doi.org/10.1007/978-3-658-43191-4_2

The dialogue between Alice and Humpty Dumpty highlights the problematic question of the meaning of words and texts in general and—in this present chapter—in international legal texts such as international treaties in particular. The dilemma could be described as whether a legal text contains an existing meaning that needs to be unveiled by the interpreter or whether a text does not possess any meaning at all until it is interpreted in the context of a concrete case. This would mean that meaning needs to be created by the interpreter. If the latter is true, who then is authorised to establish the meaning of the law?

This problem becomes relevant in lawsuits that are concerned with environmental degradation and, especially, climate change. Although climate scientists warn that there is only a limited amount of time to prevent the harshest consequences of global warming and climate change, many countries remain indifferent to their international climate obligations.[3] The Emission Gap reports demonstrate that states are not doing enough to fight climate change; some countries are far in excess of their climate targets.[4] This is where the courts become important. CCL, as a form of public interest litigation, attempts to vest existing laws, especially 'traditional' human rights law, into new interpretational concepts, including the right to a healthy environment, the right to a stable climate or environmental rights for future generations. Some progressive courts have followed these arguments by interpreting 'non-climate' law, for example, the right to life, to include positive obligations to protect humans from the adverse effects of climate change.[5] Courts have found the basis for such claims through a combined reading of human rights law, international and national climate obligations and

[3] See, inter alia, Hans-Otto Pörtner and others, 'Climate Change 2022: Impacts, Adaptation and Vulnerability Working Group II Contribution to the Sixth Assessment Report of the Intergovernmental Panel on Climate Change' (2022); IPCC, 'Special Report: The Ocean and Cryosphere in a Changing Climate—Summary for Policymakers'; IPCC, 'Special Report on Global Warming of 1.5°C' (2018); Special Rapporteur on Extreme Poverty and Human Rights Philipp Alston, 'Climate Change and Poverty (A/HRC/41/39)' (2019); UN Special Rapporteur on Human Rights and the Environment David Boyd, 'Special Report on Human Rights Obligations Relating to the Enjoyment of a Safe, Clean, Healthy and Sustainable Environment (A/74/161)' (2019); UN Special Rapporteur on Human Rights and the Environment John H. Knox, 'Special Report on Climate Change and Human Rights' (2015); Small Island Developing States, 'Male' Declaration on the Human Dimension of Global Climate Change' (2007).

[4] Cf. UNEP, 'Emissions Gap Emissions Gap Report 2022' (2022) XXI. Although there has been a brief decline in GHG emissions due to the COVID-19 pandemic, the report demonstrates that the world is heading towards a 2.8°C scenario instead of the targeted 1.5–2°C.

[5] See, for example, the cases in Chapter 9.

climate reports issued by national and international expert committees such as the IPCC.

This legal development, however, raises important questions that are strongly intertwined. Firstly, the problem of climate change was not known to the member-states of international (human rights) treaty regimes when drafting and concluding these treaties. Can courts introduce new phenomena, such as climate change, to 'old' IL, or are they bound to the original will of the member-states? States, for a very long time, have been seen as the only actors in IL. As 'masters of the treaties', they have decided which rules they want to be bound by. In this context, it has often been assumed that courts merely have to unveil the correct meaning of the international legal text at hand through interpretation and, thus, the will of the states that drafted them. Courts should do nothing else other than apply the so-found correct meaning. However, despite the lack of a (justiciable) human right to a healthy environment, courts have shown themselves open to considering ecological impacts under human rights law. This, secondly, raises the question of whether courts may interpret 'non-climate' law to include climate obligations. The consequences of such activities could eventually mean that courts, and those who bring cases before them, could become important actors in the development and shaping of global climate law. In this sense, it is important to understand what function interpretation fulfils in IL.

This chapter commences with an introduction of the relevance and role of interpretation for IL (Section 2.1.1 and Section 2.1.2). It examines how interpretation shapes the law and how law shapes society (Section 2.2). It then analyses which source of interpretation is decisive from the perspective of the rules of interpretation of the Vienna Convention on the Law of Treaties (VCLT)—whether it is the states' consent (originalism), the text (textualism) or the object and purpose (evolutionary interpretation) (Section 2.3). In Section 2.3.4, human rights law and environmental concerns are more closely examined as the relevant matters of this work, which demonstrates and concludes that interpretation is capable of introducing new subject matters such as climate change to 'old' law.

2.1.1 What is the Relevance of Interpretation?

What does the word 'glory' mean? Most people would agree with Alice: it definitely does not mean 'a nice knock-down argument'. Without going too deep into the matter, 'glory' is associated with terms such as praise and honour.[6] At first glance, however, it does not seem so easy to define, so this section starts with a simpler word: 'sandwich'.

The matter of the word 'sandwich' became important in *White City Shopping Center, LP v. PR Restaurants, LLC.* In this case, a company (PR) had leased a space in a shopping mall to operate a sandwich shop. The lease between PR and the shopping centre forbade the latter to lease space to another bakery or shop if that shop's sales of sandwiches would be greater than 10% of its total sales. When the shopping mall leased space to a Mexican-style restaurant that was planning to sell burritos, tacos and quesadillas, PR claimed that the shopping mall had violated the contract. Thus, the court had to define what 'sandwich' means and decide whether burritos, tacos and quesadillas would fall under such a definition. The court applied the 'ordinary meaning' of the word sandwich and referred to the Merriam-Webster dictionary that defines 'sandwich' as 'two thin pieces of bread, usually buttered, with a thin layer (as of meat, cheese or savory mixture) spread between them'. In an essay, Posner, however, argues that this definition is not complete as there are more types of sandwiches: club sandwiches (with more than two slices of bread) or open-faced sandwiches (with only one slice of bread).[7] Also, the pieces of bread could be thick, and so could be the layer of spread. Hotdogs and hamburgers are considered sandwiches, but their slices are not bread.[8]

What this example illustrates is that even the definition of a 'simple' word such as 'sandwich' can be complicated. The interpretation of international and constitutional law, which often uses vague language that could be understood in different ways and mean different things in different contexts and to different persons, is even more difficult. For example, it has to be asked what the word 'healthy' in the 'right to a healthy environment' means. Would a state that fails to regulate its emissions violate its duty to protect someone's right to a 'healthy' environment? Can the Fifth Amendment, which states that United States (US) citizens cannot be 'deprived of life, liberty, or property, without due process of law', include a right to a stable climate? The answers to these questions depend on what interpretation's role means in relation to the written text.

---

[6] - "glory (noun)", Merriam Webster Dictionary, citing more examples of how to use the word glory.

[7] Richard A Posner, 'The Incoherence of Antonin Scalia' [2012] *The New Republic* <https://newrepublic.com/article/106441/scalia-garner-reading-the-law-textual-originalism> accessed 31 August 2023.

[8] Ibid.

2.1.2 What is Interpretation?

> Interpretation is an act of violence against a text.[9] [...] We disrespect the text for not saying what it means, not meaning what it says, concealing obscurity in delusive clarity.[10]

Interpretation in everyday language means 'to expound the meaning of something',[11] for example, of a play or an expression. The interpretation of legal texts, however, is different. While most people agree that varying interpretations of, say, a piece of music are equally valid, legal interpretation is supposed to disclose *the* one correct intention of a legal text.[12] The reason for this is that the so-found meaning claims normativity and obedience, and from a classical liberal position, only those norms (and therefore, their respective interpretations) to which one has previously consented can restrain one's activities or demand a certain behaviour.[13]

Law serves a special role in and for society. For Allott, the law 'gives to society a range of possible futures which society has chosen as being futures which would serve the common interest'.[14] This means that if a person acts in conformity with the law, even if this is a self-interested choice and/or happens unconsciously, this action actualises the society's determination of its common interest. Such actions can include the exercise of a power, using a freedom, claiming a right, carrying out a duty and so on.[15] For Häberle, all of these actions are interpretations—one interprets the law by simply living in the fundamental

---

[9] Cover argues that interpretation is also an act of violence against the person who is affected by an interpretation, see Cover, 'Violence and the Word', 95 *The Yale Law Journal* (1986) 1601.

[10] Allott (n 1) 373.

[11] – interpret, *v.*, Oxford English Dictionary, <https://www.oed.com> accessed 31 August 2023.

[12] A concept highly doubted by some scholars. Compare, for example, William Baude and Stephen E Sachs, 'The Law of Interpretation' (2017) 130 Harvard Law Review 1079 and Charles P Curtis, 'A Better Theory of Legal Interpretation' (1950) 3 Vanderbilt Law Review 407, 422.

[13] Venzke (n 1) 52.

[14] Philip Allott, 'The Concept of International Law' in Michael Byers (ed), *The Role of Law in International Politics: Essays in International Relations and International Law* (OUP 2001) 74.

[15] Ibid.

right.[16] Extended to all members of a (national) society, this means that law-confirming action is the self-constitution of a (national) society through law.[17] In IL, then, it is 'all humanity' that constitutes itself through law.[18]

A society generates social consciousness, which has to be differentiated from individual consciousness. The former flows from and to the latter and forms and influences the self-consciousness of every society member.[19] A society can only exist if its legal system seeks to safeguard the survival and prosperity of the society as a whole and of the human beings of which it is formed. The international society, therefore, has to have a legal system that strives for the survival and prosperity of *all* human beings.[20] De Vattel applied a theory of natural law to international relations and claimed that a society is established by nature. Each individual has to seek the happiness of the other members of their society, and society would be wretched if individuals were directing their thought only to their own interests. By the very nature of humanity, a 'universal society of the human race' exists, and all persons are bound to cultivate this society and discharge its duties.[21]

Thus, each society, and as such, the international society, has a common interest. The common interest is the self-interest of the members of a particular society, even where it conflicts with their self-interest as individual human beings. The common interest is not only the aggregation of particular interests; it is formed where the real and the ideal meet—where society responds to current and potential situations in the light of its continuing theories, values and purposes.[22] For example, the level of environmental risks that a society is willing to accept as the side effect of certain activities might change over time as knowledge and technology improve.[23] Law's function, then, is to ensure that the

---

[16] Peter Häberle, '"The Open Society of Constitutional Interpreters"—A Contribution to a Pluralistic and "Procedural" Constitutional Interpretation (1975)' in Markus Kotzur (ed), *Peter Häberle on Constitutional Theory* (Nomos/Hart 2018) 131; also Wolfram Höfling, *Offene Grundrechtsinterpretation* (Duncker & Humblot 1987).

[17] Allott (n 14) 74.

[18] Ibid.

[19] Ibid 70.

[20] Ibid 71.

[21] Emer de Vattel, *The Law of Nations: Or, Principles of the Law of Nature, Applied to the Conduct and Affairs of Nations and Sovereigns* (T & JW Johnson 1854) 57.

[22] Allott (n 14) 73.

[23] Yoshifumi Tanaka, 'Reflections on Time Elements in the International Law of the Environment' (2013) 73 Zeitschrift für ausländisches öffentliches Recht und Völkerrecht 139, 142.

actions of society members serve the common interest.[24] Thus, if a society's beliefs about environmental risks change, so does the scope of the precautionary principle.[25] This common interest is an integral part of the international's legal self-constitution, its self-ordering through law.[26]

The law not only responds to social change, but it can also transform social relations. Thus, Bourdieu argues that what the law means is ultimately determined by the predominant group's ethnocentrism: their set of values and moralities. Those professionally engaged in juridical exercise (particularly the judges) are usually part of these dominant groups.[27] However, juridical decisions are given a seal of universality through the process of systematisation and rationalisation, which is both the result and side effect of the juridical formal procedure. From there, jurists are capable of starting a process of 'practical universalisation': what has first been practised just in one or several judgements can expand in terms of geographical or social space to the whole society in a generalising way. It informs the behaviour of all social actors independently of their social class.[28]

Society as a whole, including the non-dominant classes, accepts the emerging legal principles and rules as the result of a supposedly general (moral, ethical) process, which by its very nature is considered neutral and universal, while the true motives for indicating the process—the interests and constraints of the dominant group—remain hidden. Society not only creates law through specific interests and constraints in their respective fields,[29] but it is also shaped and altered through the law to a point where a norm ceases to exist as coercion because it has become part of society's moral and ethical consciousness.[30]

Summarising, three characteristics can be attributed to law:

> (1) Law carries the structures and systems of societies through time. (2) Law inserts the common interest of society into the behaviour of society-members. (3) Law establishes possible futures for society, in accordance with society's theories, values, and purposes.[31]

---

[24] Allott (n 14) 73.

[25] On the inter-temporality of the precautionary principle, see Tanaka (n 23) 165–173.

[26] Allott (n 14) 81–2.

[27] Pierre Bourdieu, 'The Force of Law: Toward a Sociology of the Juridical Field' (1987) 7 Hastings Law Journal 805, 847.

[28] Ibid 845ff.

[29] Ibid 847 also mentions the political and religious fields in addition to the legal field.

[30] Ibid 848 decribes this concept as 'doxa'.

[31] Allott (n 14) 69.

Interpretation, thus, is meant to reinforce and fill out the black letters of the law by providing it with meaning-in-use, with specific instructions and guidelines for action.[32] For Allott, however, it is more than that. He argues that interpretation is a three-fold act of power.[33]

The first aspect is the *re-wording* of a text after *dis-integrating* its linguistic structure and substance. Interpretation is an intra-lingual translation into the same language. This kind of translation adds imagination to the text, which claims relevance over the content of the wording. But this imagination is merely provisional, since it competes with other imaginations created by other interpreters. Against these, it has to prove itself over space and time.[34] Secondly, interpretation imposes one's will on a text. An interpreter might wish to claim that they have found the (only) meaning of a text, but, of course, there can be others. An interpreter, according to the Italian saying *traduttore, traditore*, can easily become a traitor when abandoning the literalness of their exercise and introducing their preferences.[35] The third aspect is what Allot calls the *re-forming* of the semantic *substance* of the text to what is commonly referred to as the science or art[36] of hermeneutics. Interpretation tells the interpreter what the text says that it does not say.[37] In doing so, the interpreter chooses how to reconcile the past with the present, or as Allott puts it, 'interpretation is an act of power across time and space. We interpret in the present, here and now, something created elsewhere in the past.'[38]

Law, thus, shapes both national and international societies' beliefs. But it is interpretation that makes law 'accessible' and changeable, so it can accommodate society's 'updated' social changes and technological developments. Consequently, interpretation is also a game of power, and ultimately, the question arises as to whose interpretation matters (see Section 2.3 ff).

[32] Cf. Venzke (n 1) 18.

[33] Allott (n 1) 373.

[34] Ibid 373–4.

[35] Ibid 374, referring to Humpty Dumpty's speech.

[36] ILC, 'Draft Articles on the Law of Treaties with Commentaries' (1966) 2 Yearbook of the International Law Commission 187, 218.

[37] Allott (n 1) 374.

[38] Ibid; see also Peter Häberle, 'Zeit und Verfassung: Prolegomena zu einem "zeit-gerechten" Verfassungsverständnis' (1974) 21 ZfP 111.

2.2 The Practice of Interpretation

Interpretation serves several purposes. It has an expository, relational, existential and inventive function[39] and potentially a unifying function (see Section 7.4).[40] The expository function of interpretation describes the assignment of meaning to a treaty's norms. The relational function asks whether the subject of international legal interpretation comports, competes or conflicts with other international law(s). In its existential function, interpretative exercise confirms or rejects—explicitly or implicitly—the existence of particular legal concepts (e.g., the figure of the Responsibility to Protect).[41] Without interpretation, there exists no IL.[42] Interpretation rests on a (mostly hidden) iceberg of earlier choices about whether the rule exists in the first place. By the very act of invoking a certain interpretation, the interpreter validates the existence of what is being interpreted.[43] The inventive function of interpretation describes the capability of interpretation to create new law.[44]

Interpretation is not only meant to unveil hidden meanings (at least, according to positivists), but it also always invokes the interpreter to make a decision. The concept of *in claris non fit interpretatio* (clear rules do not require interpretation) is increasingly seen as naïve.[45] As Hart puts it:

> fact situations do not await us neatly labelled, creased, and folded, nor is their legal classification written on them to be simply read off by the judge. Instead, in applying legal rules, someone must take the responsibility of deciding that words do or do not cover some case in hand with all the practical consequences involved in this decision.[46]

---

[39] Duncan B Hollis, 'The Existential Function of Interpretation in International Law' in Andrea Bianchi, Daniel Peat and Matthew Windsor (eds), *Interpretation in International Law* (OUP 2015) 84.

[40] Anne van Aaken, 'Defragmentation of Public International Law Through Interpretation: A Methodological Proposal' (2009) 16 Indiana Journal of Global Legal Studies 483.

[41] Duncan B Hollis, 'Interpretation and International Law' [2015] Legal Studies Research Paper Series, No. 42 14–5.

[42] Hollis (n 39) 78.

[43] Ibid 79.

[44] Ibid 85.

[45] Aharon Barak, *Purposive Interpretation in Law* (Princeton University Press 2005) 13, referring to G. Tedeschi, Masot B'mishpat [Essays in Law] 1 (1978).

[46] HLA Hart, 'Positivism and the Separation of Law and Morals' (1958) 71 Harvard Law Review 593, 607.

Legal interpretation involves decisions: the choice between at least two alternatives. It requires active volition and judgement of the interpreter. Meaning cannot be simply found or recognised; it is the decision that creates the meaning.[47] It has been argued that if the meaning was clear, a treaty is 'applied' and not 'interpreted'.[48] However, although there is a difference between interpretation and application,[49] it is also clear that interpretation always comes before applying a rule. The consequent application of 'the clear meaning of a treaty' is the result of 'making out' that meaning.[50] Only interpretation can fill the 'empty shell' or the 'frame' of the norm. Thus, interpretation is *always* 'giving' meaning to a treaty. 'Giving meaning' assigns an active role to the interpreter, requiring their creativity and subjectivity.[51] This can also mean the incorporation of new concepts that were not known at the moment of drafting the treaty, such as *due diligence* obligations to mitigate hazardous climate change[52] or a right to a stable climate.[53] This raises the question of how interpretation can change the meaning of a particular norm to incorporate such new ideas.

For Bourdieu, the application of a rule means the choice between confronting different agnostic rights. No two cases are completely identical, and, therefore, a rule drawn from a precedent case cannot simply be applied to a new case.[54] What is more, interpretation leads to what Bourdieu calls 'historicization' of the norm: adapting sources to different circumstances, finding new possibilities of how to use them and eliminating what has become obsolete or outdated. Jurists

---

[47] Venzke (n 1) 29.

[48] Arnold Duncan McNair, *The Law of Treaties* (Clarendon Press 1961) 365 n 1.

[49] The question whether there is a difference between 'interpretation' and 'application' of legal rules is fiercely debated among scholars. While Judge Shahabuddeen did not ascribe relevance to the differentiation neither in practical nor theoretical terms (see Separate Opinion of Judge Shahabuddeen in Applicability of the Obligation to Arbitrate under Section 21 of the United Nations Headquarter Agreement of 26 June 1947 [Advisory Opinion], 1988, ICJ Reports 57, at 59), Gourgourinis believed that 'the distinction between the normative processes of interpretation and application rather denotes another normative perspective in existence that can be of practical (normative) importance in international adjudication in times of fragmentation.' Anastasios Gourgourinis, 'The Distinction between Interpretation and Application of Norms in International Adjudication' (2011) 2 Journal of International Dispute Settlement 31, 57.

[50] Richard Gardiner, *Treaty Interpretation* (2nd edn, OUP 2015) 29.

[51] Richard Gardiner, 'The Vienna Convention Rules on Treaty Interpretation' in Duncan B Hollis (ed), *The Oxford Guide to Treaties* (OUP 2012) 478.

[52] See Urgenda v the Netherlands, Section 9.1.

[53] See Juliana v the United States, Section 9.3.1.

[54] Bourdieu (n 27) 826.

have a well-equipped toolbox at hand to ensure the maximum elasticity of the law, for they can broaden or narrow the scope of a rule and use an analogy or the distinction between 'letter and spirit'.[55]

These approaches to understanding interpretation have in common the assumption that meaning is not fixed in the law. Only by using the norms can meaning be attributed.[56] The meaning of a word is its use in the language,[57] and as such, meaning is the product of legal practice.[58] Obeying the law, for example, is a matter of practice.[59] Practice is to be understood as a custom or habit and is acquired through a process of socialisation by internalising the content of a specific rule.[60] This holds true not only for individuals but also for states. In the same way that a person stops at 2 am at a stoplight without a police car in sight, states obey the rules of IL most of the time.[61] They obey the rules not because they are forced to but because rules are learned patterns of obedience as a result of the internalisation of a norm. Thus, internalisation, not coercion, is the main driver of compliance with the rules of IL.[62] Norm change could be thought of as a process of evolution that could lead to new internalisation.[63] A single interpretation cannot bring change over legal norms, but continuous novel action can change the meaning of existing law or lead to the creation of new law.[64] Venzke explains how powerful interpretation in IL is:

> The practice of interpretation then also accounts for the semantic change and legal developments. Interpretations may further provide new reference points for legal discourse and they structure the space for legal argument. The practice of interpretation

---

[55] Ibid 826–7.

[56] Venzke (n 1) 30.

[57] Ludwig Wittgenstein, *Philosophical Investigations* (1953) para 43.

[58] Venzke (n 1) 4.

[59] Wittgenstein (n 57) para 203.

[60] Venzke (n 1) 38.

[61] Harold Hongju Koh, 'Transnational Legal Process' (1996) 75 Nebraska Law Review 181, 183; Harold Hongju Koh, *The Trump Administration and International Law* (OUP 2018) 7.

[62] Koh, 'Transnational Legal Process' (n 61) 203–5.

[63] Venzke (n 1) 38.

[64] Max Weber, *Wirtschaft und Gesellschaft* (JCB Mohr (Paul Siebeck) 1922) para 398 (German: 'Woher stammt dies Neue? Man wird antworten: es entstand durch Änderung der äußeren Existenzbedingungen, welche Änderungen der bisher empirisch geltenden Einverständnisse nach sich ziehen. Die bloße Änderung der äußeren Bedingungen ist dafür aber weder ausreichend noch unentbehrlich. Entscheidend ist vielmehr stets ein neuartiges Handeln, welches zu einem Bedeutungswandel von geltendem Recht oder zur Neuschaffung von Recht führt').

> shifts and generates legal normativity. If nothing else, this position fundamentally challenges the common narrative according to which international law owes its existence and normativity to the consent of its subjects.[65]

Normativity is the sense of legal obligation located at the intersection between validity and effectiveness, between what *should* be a norm and what *is* a norm.[66] As such, it makes rules binding. From a classical positivist position, IL is binding because the states have created it according to procedures (the sources as mentioned in Article 38 of the Statute of the International Court of Justice) and have given their consent to be bound by such law. However, the exact semantic content is only negotiated in the legal practice of interpretation when it comes to applying the norm.[67] Thus, it is not only the legal-political process but also interpretation that creates a common (European) constitutional law.[68]

It becomes apparent how litigation strikes this chord. By filing case after case all over the world, litigants seek to establish a robust body of climate law without the need to amend the 'black letter' law. Instead, they seek to change a norm's meaning-in-use by introducing new interpretational concepts to the courts that may eventually follow their arguments. Each successful case can further promote a climate-friendly environment in which judges are more receptive to climate issues and, thus, gradually add a layer of 'ecological concerns' to non-climate law. It also becomes apparent that states may be keen to avoid such climate-friendly outcomes altogether.[69] While states celebrate themselves for ratifying environmental and climate treaties such as the Paris Agreement, no directly enforceable obligations follow from such membership. An international (human rights) tribunal or national court, however, can 'give teeth' to the treaty objective by incorporating its obligations into existing enforceable law and, thereby, forcing the state to do more than just joining a treaty as a symbolic gesture.

This brings us to the next question: if it is the practice of applying the law in a context that makes the law,[70] whose interpretation counts? Whoever controls interpretation controls the meaning and, therefore, the existence and/or scope of obligations and rights under IL:

---

[65] Venzke (n 1) 4.

[66] Ibid 5.

[67] Ibid 6.

[68] Peter Häberle and Markus Kotzur, *Europäische Verfassungslehre* (8th edn, Nomos 2016) 204.

[69] See, for example the actions of the US government to prevent the case of *Juliana v The United States* (2015) from going to trial. For greater detail, see Section 9.3.1.

[70] Venzke (n 1) 6.

> The meaning of a treaty is not carved in stone at the moment of its conclusion: instead, debates continue, albeit no longer on what words to use in the treaty, but on how to give meaning to the words that are used. Whoever controls this process controls the meaning of the treaty, and therewith controls whether or not the obligations resting upon him are bearable or onerous, and controls whether the acts of States are faithful implementations of a text, or amount to breaches of that same text. And control over the process often presupposes control over the methods to be used: the rules of interpretation.[71]

This is the starting point for a discussion among legal scholars on how to interpret the norms of an international treaty. It concerns this question: to what extent must the past—the original will of the treaty's drafters—be taken into account when interpreting a particular text and whether the text can be 'updated' if technological and social developments occur that the treaty drafters did not predict at the time of concluding the treaty. In other words, who controls the interpretation of norms of the international legal order?

This question has important consequences for legal climate protection. Many industrialised states seem reluctant to have their international environmental and international human rights obligations mixed together. This became clear during the drafting of the 2018 General Comment No. 36 on the right to life (Article 6 ICCPR) and the 2021 General Comment No. 26 to the Convention on the Rights of the Child (CRC) on children's rights and the environment with a special focus on climate change. These General Comments are important tools for the respective UN bodies when it comes to interpreting the norms of the conventions on a case-to-case basis. Although they are not legally binding, they are understood as norm-generating instruments that can increase the density of the interpretation of the conventions and contribute to the process of emerging customary international legal norms.[72]

General Comment No. 36 on the right to life (Article 6 ICCPR) was adopted by the Human Rights Committee in 2018 and now recognises that 'environmental degradation, climate change and unsustainable development constitute some

---

[71] Jan Klabbers, 'On Rationalism in Politics: Interpretation of Treaties and the World Trade Organization' (2005) 74 Nordic Journal of International Law 405, 406–7.

[72] Helen Keller and Lena Grover, 'General Comments of the Human Rights Committee and Their Legitimacy' in Helen Keller and Geir Ulfstein (eds), *UN Human Rights Treaty Bodies: Law and Legitimacy* (CUP 2012) 129.

of the most pressing and serious threats to the ability of present and future generations to enjoy the right to life.'[73]

Moreover, the General Comment explicitly states that:

> The obligations of States parties under international environmental law should thus inform the content of article 6 of the Covenant, and the obligation of States parties to respect and ensure the right to life should also inform their relevant obligations under international environmental law[74]

and points to the preamble of the Paris Agreement. Australia, Canada, the United Kingdom (UK) and the US protested unsuccessfully against this intertwinement of international human rights law with international environmental obligations.[75] In 2019, a group of Australian Torres Strait Islanders claimed that Australia's climate policy was insufficient to protect their low-lying lands from disappearing into the seas over the next decades and would, therefore, inter alia, violate their right to life, including a right to a life in dignity.[76] Australia had claimed that Article 6 ICCPR does not obligate it to prevent foreseeable loss of life from climate change. Moreover, the state argued that it had not agreed to an extension of the right to life as to include a right to life in dignity through GC No. 36, and that this interpretation would, therefore, be unsupported by the rules of treaty interpretation of the VCLT.[77] Australia argued that climate change treaties could 'not provide evidence of the object and purpose of the Covenant, nor the meaning of its terms'.[78] Although the Committee ultimately did not find a violation of Article 6 ICCPR, it rejected Australia's view that foreseeable threats would not fall under the scope of Article 6 ICCPR. Rather, following its line in *Teitiota*

[73] Human Rights Committee, 'General Comment No. 36 (2018) on Article 6 of the International Covenant on Civil and Political Rights, on the Right to Life—(CCPR/C/GC/36)' (2018) para 62 (citations omitted).

[74] Ibid (citations omitted).

[75] Submissions by several countries, NGOs, and individuals can be found at Human Rights Committee, 'Call for Comments on Article 6 of the International Covenant on Civil and Political Rights' <https://www.ohchr.org/en/calls-for-input/general-comment-no-36-article-6-right-life> accessed 31 August 2023.

[76] Katherine Murphy, 'Torres Strait Islanders Take Climate Change Complaint to the United Nations' *The Guardian* (12 May 2019) <https://www.theguardian.com/australia-news/2019/may/13/torres-strait-islanders-take-climate-change-complaint-to-the-united-nations> accessed 31 August 2023.

[77] UN Human Rights Committee, *Daniel Billy et al v Australia*, Views adopted on 21 July 2022, Communication 3624/2019, para 8.4.

[78] Ibid para 6.5.

v New Zealand (2019),[79] it recalled 'that the right to life cannot be properly understood if it is interpreted in a restrictive manner, and that the protection of that right requires States parties to adopt positive measures to protect the right to life',[80] and that such threats may include adverse climate change effects, even where they have not (yet) resulted in the loss of life. The Committee also found that, despite Australia's protest, the right to life includes a right to a life in dignity, stating that the VCLT:

> requires that a treaty be interpreted in good faith in accordance with the ordinary meaning to be given to the terms of the treaty in their context and in the light of its object and purpose. In this regard, the Committee notes that under article 31 of the Convention, the context for interpretation of a treaty includes in the first place the text of the treaty, including its preamble and annexes. The preamble of the Covenant initially recognizes that the inherent dignity and of the equal and inalienable rights of all members of the human family is the foundation of freedom, justice and peace in the world, and further recognizes that those rights derive from the inherent dignity of the human person. While the State party notes that socioeconomic entitlements are protected under a separate Covenant, the Committee observes that the preamble of the present Covenant recognizes that the ideal of free human beings enjoying freedom from fear and want can only be achieved if conditions are created whereby everyone may enjoy their civil and political rights, as well as their economic, social and cultural rights.[81]

In a similar fashion, the draft of the General Comment No. 26 to the CRC, which stresses the importance of a healthy environment and a stable climate for the enjoyment of children's rights, could become an important argumentative tool for children and young people's climate change complaints. To strengthen the rights of children, the GC draft includes some recommendations, including, inter alia, a broadening of legal standing for children before national courts in cases of climate matters, including the consideration of a potential introduction of public interest litigation or class action, the access to free complaint mechanisms for children,[82] and the recognition of a right to a clean, healthy and sustainable environment, which encompasses a safe climate as a substantive element.[83] Several states (e.g., Canada, China, France, Germany and Israel) and the Holy See

---

[79] Human Rights Committee, *Teitiota v New Zealand,* Views adopted on 24 October 2019, Communication, No. 2728/2016, para 9.4.

[80] UN Human Rights Committee, *Daniel Billy et al v Australia*, para 8.3.

[81] Ibid para 8.4.

[82] UN Committee on the Rights of the Child, Draft General comment No. 26—Children's rights and the environment with a special focus on climate change, 2021, para 64.

[83] Ibid paras. 72, 103.

have stressed that this GC cannot create new rights (such as a right to a stable climate) or binding legal obligations, since the states had not accepted such an interpretation of the CRC upon becoming members to it.[84] Some of them argued that climate matters should be dealt with by the more specific UNFCCC regime and that the language of the GC should be harmonised in accordance with the (lesser requirements of) the Paris Agreement. The harshest rejection by the states and the Holy See was made in relation to the GC's claim that 'States have obligations [under the Convention], including *extraterritorial obligations*, to respect, protect and fulfil children's rights'.[85] Some states feared that extraterritorial positive climate obligations were introduced into the CRC through the back door of interpretation.[86] The Committee, however, followed its own interpretation in *Sacchi et. al. vs. Argentina et. al.*,[87] where it found, with reference to the Advisory Opinion OC-23/17 of the Inter-American Court of Human Rights (IACtHR) on the Environment and Human Rights, that extraterritorial obligations can arise in contexts of transboundary harm.[88] Despite the protest, GC No. 27 was adopted by the Committee in May 2023.

Given these recent introductions of climate change obligations into the general comments of some of the conventions,[89] it is necessary to analyse whether states can refuse such new interpretations because they had not agreed to them when they became members to the treaties. Whose interpretation prevails in cases of

---

84 The inputs of States and the Holy See on the first draft of GC No. 27 can be found at OHCHR, 'General Comment No. 26 on Children's Rights and the Environment with a Special Focus on Climate Change' (2021).

85 UN Committee on the Rights of the Child, Draft General comment No. 26—Children's rights and the environment with a special focus on climate change, 2021, para 103 (emphasis added).

86 See the inputs received by Austria, Canada, China, Denmark, France, Germany, and Poland (n. 73).

87 CRC, *Sacchi et. al. vs. Argentina et. al*, Communication No. 104/2019 (Argentina), Communication No. 105/2019 (Brazil), Communication No. 106/2019 (France), Communication No. 107/2019 (Germany), Communication No. 108/2019 (Turkey) (2021).

88 UN Committee on the Rights of the Child, Decision adopted by the Committee on the Rights of the Child under the Optional Protocol to the Convention on the Rights of the Child on a communications procedure in respect of Communication No. 105/2019 (2021), paras. 10.5ff.

89 Another climate-related General Comment recently adopted is the General recommendation No. 37 (2018) on gender-related dimensions of disaster risk reduction in a change climate to the Convention on the Elimination of All Forms of Discrimination Against Women (CEDAW) which highlights the specific risks faced by women and girls due to the intensifying impacts of climate change on gender equality.

conflict between reluctant states and citizens wanting to be protected from the adverse effects of climate change? Can states claim to keep their human rights obligations separate from their climate law obligations?[90] This depends primarily on which method of interpretation the interpreter uses or should use when interpreting international treaties.

2.3 Interpretation Methods

The yardstick and starting point for international treaty interpretation is the 1969 VCLT,[91] in particular Article 31 para. 1 which reads:

> A treaty shall be interpreted in good faith in accordance with *the ordinary meaning* to be given to the terms of the treaty in *their context and in the light of its object and purpose*.[92]

The VCLT is the result of a procedure undertaken by the International Law Commission (ILC) to codify customary law and to clarify the rules according to which a treaty has to be interpreted.[93] However, despite good intentions, the VCLT itself became the subject of many controversies among lawyers. The disunity among legal scholars emerges from different understandings of the very nature of interpretation—between justice and state consent; 'normativity' and 'concreteness'.[94]

Roughly, it is the differentiation of the positions between originalists and proponents of evolutionary approaches. Originalists, who focus on the treaty drafters' (usually the nation-states') will or the treaty text, limit the role of legal interpretation to the momentum of 'unveiling' the meaning that generally stays hidden behind the black letters of a text. By no means is the interpreter legitimised to modify the will or content of the text by taking other considerations into account,

---

[90] Ian Johnstone, 'Treaty Interpretation: The Authority of Interpretive Communities' (1990) 12 Michigan Journal of International Law 371, 372.

[91] Vienna Convention on the Law of Treaties, 23 May 1969, United Nations Treaty Series, vol. 1155, 331.

[92] Emphasis added.

[93] For a critical analysis, see Fuad Zarbiyev, 'A Genealogy of Treaty Interpretation' in Andrea Bianchi, Daniel Peat and Matthew Windsor (eds), *Interpretation in International Law* (OUP 2015) 252ff.

[94] Martti Koskenniemi, *From Apology to Utopia: The Structure of International Legal Argument* (CUP 2005) 513ff.

for example, changing social circumstances. Any changes in meaning are subject to formal treaty amendment or modification. It is this source-fixed view that relies on the traditional sources appointed in Article 38 ICJ Statute[95] and what is called here the originalist's position.

Proponents of an evolutionary approach, conversely, seek to interpret a treaty in the context of a particular time and place. They use different factors, such as time, context and (changing) authority, and focus on the purpose and object of a treaty rather than its wording or the intention of its drafters (a dynamic or teleological approach). They deny the idea that the law is hidden behind the black letters of a text. Instead, meaning is created through interpretation. This view moves away from traditional source-fixation towards an approach that considers a multitude of factors, among them indirect or auxiliary sources of law, and social, political and technological changes occurring after the conclusion of a treaty as well as new actors.[96]

Notably, the VCLT does not mention the intention of the states in Article 31. However, it has been argued that the historical creation of the VCLT and the *travaux préparatoires* should be considered when interpreting a treaty. One of the proponents of such an approach was the first special rapporteur for the VCLT project, Lauterpacht.[97] But the creation-process and the *travaux préparatoires* of the VCLT are subject to as many debates as Article 31 itself.[98] Scholars tend to stress the statements of the ILC, and especially those of Special Rapporteur Sir Waldock, that fit their respective convictions on the best methods.[99] The ILC itself has clarified that there is no hierarchy between the text, the will of the parties, the context, the object and the purpose of a treaty, and that the adopted order followed logic instead of pre-eminence of one of the methods.[100]

---

[95] Venzke (n 1) 16.

[96] See, for example, Häberle, '"The Open Society of Constitutional Interpreters"—A Contribution to a Pluralistic and "Procedural" Constitutional Interpretation (1975)' (n 16) 150.

[97] Hersch Lauterpacht, 'De l'interprétation Des Traités' (1950) 43/1 Annuaire de l'Institut de Droit International 366, 433: 'Le recours aux travaux préparatoires, lorsqu'ils sont accessibles, est notamment un moyen légitime et désirable aux fins d'établir l'intention des parties dans tous les cas où, malgré sa clarté apparente, le sens d'un traité prête à controverse'.

[98] A historical overview of the difficult drafting process of the Vienna Convention is provided by Julian Davis Mortenson, 'The Travaux of Travaux: Is the Vienna Convention Hostile To Drafting History?' (2013) 107 American Journal of International Law 780.

[99] For originalism, see Katharina Berner, 'Authentic Interpretation in Public International Law' (2016) 76 Zeitschrift für ausländisches öffentliches Recht und Völkerrecht 845, 861; for textualism, see Zarbiyev (n 93) 256; for evolutionary interpretation, see Gardiner (n 50) 453ff.

[100] ILC (n 36) 220.

2.3.1 Static Approaches: Originalism and Textualism

Static approaches can be broken down into two main hermeneutic concepts to determine the meaning of a legal text: originalism and textualism. Both seek to serve the aim of discretion-free reasoning, which means that a judge should not be able to interpret the law as to cover new social, technological or ecological developments. Thus, if courts had to interpret in accordance with static approaches, they would not be allowed to derive climate obligations from human rights law or, for that matter, from any other 'non-climate' law.

2.3.1.1 Authentic Interpretation

Proponents of originalism (or intentionalism or authentic interpretation) believe that the intention of the states that concluded the treaty,[101] and, to a lesser extent, international organisations,[102] should be the main reference point for legal reasoning. This view refers to authority: *who* has the power to make and interpret a treaty? It is a subjective approach based on a classical liberal position: one cannot be bound by law against one's will.[103] IL is binding its subjects—the unitary states—only because they have consented to be bound by that law.[104] The doctrine of sources assumes that states as sovereigns—as equal partners—enter a treaty voluntarily. A treaty is no 'accident' but the consequence of states willing to create binding law.[105] Therefore, they own the treaty; they are the 'masters of the treaty'.[106]

State consent as the origin of IL was widely accepted in legal scholarship, especially during the prime time of legal positivism (late nineteenth century until

---

[101] Berner (n 99) 848; Eirik Bjorge, 'The Vienna Rules, Evolutionary Interpretation, and the Intentions of the Parties' in Andrea Bianchi, Daniel Peat and Matthew Windsor (eds), *Interpretation in International Law* (OUP 2015).

[102] Michael N Barnett and Martha Finnemore, 'The Politics, Power, and Pathologies of International Organizations' (1999) 53 International Organization 699, 711–2.

[103] Eirik Bjorge, *The Evolutionary Interpretation of Treaties* (OUP 2014) 56; Alexandru Bolintineanu, 'Expression of Consent to Be Bound by a Treaty in the Light of the 1969 Vienna Convention' (1974) 68 American Journal of International Law 672.

[104] Venzke (n 1) 20.

[105] Berner (n 99) 848.

[106] James Crawford, 'A Consensualist Interpretation of Article 31(3) of the Vienna Convention on the Law of Treaties' in Georg Nolte (ed), *Treaties and Subsequent Practice* (OUP 2013) 31.

the early twentieth century). Accordingly, Article 38 of the ICJ Statute reflects the supreme principle of sovereignty: all of the listed sources are manifestations of state consent, palpably treaties but also customary law, which consists of state practice and *opinio juris*.[107] Both elements are manifestations of state will, as is well demonstrated by the fact that a persistent objector state is not bound by a rule if it rejects being bound by it, with the expectation of *jus cogens* and *erga omnes* obligations.[108] The same applies to general principles. Either they are assumed to derive from municipal legal systems and transplanted into IL, or they emanate from the international context themselves in a way reminiscent of natural law; however, this depends on the established consent of the states.[109]

The purpose of juridical interpretation is to shed light on the will of the parties.[110] Meaning should be attributed to a text in terms of Article 31(1) VCLT without the judge using the criteria of object and purpose or context too much. Proponents of authentic interpretation believe that other methods would give too much power to a judge to disregard the will of the parties as expressed in the treaty.[111] It is what Dupuy calls the 'concept of memory':

> The treaty's object and purpose is at risk of being changed by the judge. Memory must remain loyal and not serve to rewrite history; a treaty belongs to its authors and not to the judge.[112]

Interpretation that clarifies obligations and rights arising under a specific treaty regime is allotted the same value as the interpreted norm itself.[113] For Oppenheim, interpretation, and the creation of the norm in the first place, is a matter of consent between the contracting parties, which does not leave any room for any

---

[107] Venzke (n 1) 22 ff.

[108] Jonathan Charney, 'Universal International Law' (1993) 87 The American Journal of International Law 529, 541–2.

[109] Venzke (n 1) 25.

[110] Francis G Jacobs, 'Varieties of Approach to Treaty Interpretation: With Special Reference to the Draft Convention on the Law of Treaties before the Vienna Diplomatic Conference' (1969) 18 International and Comparative Law Quarterly 318, 320–2.

[111] Pierre-Marie Dupuy, 'Evolutionary Interpretation of Treaties: Between Memory and Prophecy' in Enzo Cannizzaro (ed), *The Law of Treaties Beyond the Vienna Convention* (OUP 2011) 127ff.

[112] Ibid 128.

[113] Berner (n 99) 877.

other interpretation, unless disagreement may require an interpretation based on scientific reasons.[114]

However, in case of disagreement, who has the authority to decide on a final interpretation and meaning of a rule? The lack of a judicial authority on the global level would mean that each state would have the right to interpret and define its rights and obligations: a so-called 'right of auto-interpretation'.[115] The potential for conflicts, if all states' interpretations of their rights and duties were equally valid, is evident.[116] Such a right to auto-interpretation could lead to uncontrolled state activity that is determined entirely by short-term national interests and power politics.[117] Furthermore, it seems impossible that interpreters today can identity a uniform will of the parties, even when the drafting process was documented, as these documents would be subject to interpretation again.[118]

2.3.1.2 Textualism

Contrary to the subjective method of authentic interpretation, textualists take an objective approach, referring to the 'ordinary meaning' as postulated in Article 31 para. 1 VCLT. The main indicator is the text itself.[119] Textualists believe that the words themselves would give away the true meaning of the treaty.[120] It is hidden in the black letters, but interpretation will unveil it. The rules of interpretation

---

[114] Lassa Oppenheim, *International Law, a Treatise, Vol. 1* (2nd edn, Robarts 1912) 582.

[115] Gross, 'States as Organs of International Law and the Problem of Autointerpretation', (1953) reprinted in *Essays on International Law and Organization (1984)*, 386.

[116] Air Service Agreement of 27 March 1946 between the United States of America and France (1978), 18 RIAA 417, at 443 (81): 'Under the rules of present-day international law, and unless the contrary results from special obligations arising under particular treaties, notably from mechanisms created within the framework of international organisations, each State establishes for itself its legal situation vis-à-vis other States. If a situation arises which, in one State's view, results in the violation of an international obligation by another State, the first State is entitled, within the limits set by the general rules of international law pertaining to the use of armed force, to affirm its rights through "counter-measures"'.

[117] Johnstone (n 90) 372.

[118] Venzke (n 1) 3–4.

[119] WTO Appellate Body Report, *United States—Import Prohibition of Certain Shrimp and Shrimp Products*, WT/DS58/AB/R, 12 October 1998, para 114.

[120] Venzke (n 1) 50.

resemble the rules of physics[121] and, accordingly, operate independently of social factors or historical circumstances.[122] Rather:

> norms, verdicts and decrees derive their binding force and validity from the occurrence of certain law-generating events: These decisions must only be processed in the right way and authorized by the right institutions.[123]

Proponents of textualism, such as US Justices Scalia and Garner, argue that, since this approach is objective—contrary to the subjective authentic approach—interpretation remains free from (the judges') ideology.[124] What is more, 'good judges' in Scalia and Garner's sense do not make law, they 'merely apply the content that has been there all along, awaiting application to myriad factual scenarios'.[125] What processes lead to the correct interpretation, who is allowed to claim authority, the establishment of the institutions and so on is also defined by the law and by law only.[126] Thus, for Scalia, a constitution is not a living instrument but a dead one.[127] While the states' intentions should be considered, in the case of remaining uncertainty after considering the words, a 'right to auto-interpretation' is not guaranteed. Literalism, inherent to the positivist legal theory, was meant to keep interpretation within manageable borders and refuses to assign states the right to determine the scope of their rights and duties.[128]

However, the focus on words faces its own problems. Words can and do have many meanings.[129] Posner demonstrates in a thorough study that even judges such as Scalia do not work with words alone but lead their judgements to be

---

121 '[…] facts and theories are different things, not rungs in a hierarchy of increasing certainty. Facts are the world's data. Theories are structures of ideas that explain and interpret facts. Facts do not go away while scientists debate rival theories for explaining them. Einstein's theory of gravitation replaced Newton's, but apples did not suspend themselves in mid-air pending the outcome', Stephen Jay Gould, *Hen's Teeth and Horse's Toes: Further Reflections in Natural History* (WW Norton & Company 1984) 254.

122 Zarbiyev (n 93) 254.

123 Jürgen Habermas, 'On Law and Disagreement. Some Comments on "Interpretative Pluralism"' (2003) 16 Ratio Juris 187, 189.

124 Antonin Scalia and Bryan A Garner, *Reading Law. The Interpretation of Legal Texts* (Thomson/West 2012) 3ff, 56ff, 88–89.

125 Ibid 5.

126 Habermas (n 123) 189.

127 'Scalia Vigorously Defends a "Dead" Constitution' *NPR* (28 April 2008) <https://www.npr.org/templates/story/story.php?storyId=90011526> accessed 31 August 2023.

128 Zarbiyev (n 93) 259.

129 Curtis (n 12) 419–20.

influenced by other factors either because relying on words is impossible or the result undesirable. For example, the sandwich case discussed above was ultimately decided not only based on the dictionary article, but also on other factors such as the location of the shopping centre and the explicit will of the sandwich shop owner.[130] Moreover, textualism, at least in the US, has provoked strong criticism from scholars who argue that it is mainly used by conservative judges who try to impose and disguise their views on issues such as homosexuality, abortion, state rights, illegal immigration and guns under textualism's alleged cloak of neutrality.[131]

Both originalism and textualism do not assign any important role to an open society of interpreters. They rely either on the will of the states or the text itself, which leaves no space for changed moralities or social, ecological and technological developments that have great influences on the daily lives of citizens to be included in an already existing legal text through interpretation.

2.3.2 Evolutionary, Dynamic and Teleological Interpretation

Proponents of an evolutionary (or dynamic or evolutive)[132] approach, conversely, seek to move away from merely textual or consent-based concepts of interpretation. Meaning is not understood as a natural phenomenon that can be discovered by correctly applying hermeneutic tools but the outcome of interpretative exercise that is both time and context sensitive.[133] Interpretation does not discover but creates meaning.[134] The element of time is particularly important, since no rule remains unaffected by time.[135] No interpretation may forever remain 'the

[130] Posner (n 7).

[131] Ibid; Joseph Kimble, 'The Ideology of Textualism' *American Constitution Society Expert Forum* (17 July 2017) <https://www.acslaw.org/expertforum/the-ideology-of-textualism/> accessed 31 August 2023.

[132] Helgesen points out that "evolutive" interpretation refers to a court's answer to new facts while "dynamic" interpretation is a court's new answer to old facts, Jan E Helgesen, 'What Are the Limits to the Evolutive Interpretation of the Convention?', *Dialogue between Judges at the European Court of Human Rights Strasbourg, 28 January 2011* 2 <http://www.echr.coe.int/Documents/Dialogue_2011_ENG.pdf> accessed 31 August 2023.

[133] See, for example, Häberle, 'Zeit und Verfassung: Prolegomena zu einem "zeit-gerechten" Verfassungsverständnis' (n 38); Tanaka (n 23); Zarbiyev (n 93).

[134] Koskenniemi (n 94) 531.

[135] Tanaka (n 23) 139.

right one'; rather, it is justifiable at the respective time. Whether it should 'survive' over time depends on whether it is still 'correct'.[136] Interpretation means to place a legal rule in time and, therefore, public reality. The process of interpretation can only be possible when considering the time element.[137] There are cases where a legal expression or phrase is deliberately informed by an evolutionary concept, to which the parties have agreed upon concluding the treaty. This is often the case when the text is vaguely formulated due to factors that the present lawgiver cannot predict or when the text itself demands that those affected by a certain situation weigh the facts at hand on a case-by-case basis and balance different interests.[138] However, most treaties—of special importance for this work, the human rights conventions—do not choose between interpretative concepts, thus, leaving this problem for the legal practicioner to resolve.

The International Court of Justice (ICJ) generally follows an evolutionary approach to interpretation.[139] In the *Aegean Sea Continental Shelf* case, the Court argued, concerning the expression 'territorial status', that:

> the presumption necessarily arises that its meaning was intended to follow the evolution of the law and to correspond with the meaning attached to the expression by the law in force at any given time.[140]

Moreover, the ICJ made it clear that it tends to interpret treaty provisions in an evolutionary way when the circumstances are changing drastically, particularly

---

[136] Häberle, 'Zeit und Verfassung: Prolegomena zu einem "zeit-gerechten" Verfassungsverständnis' (n 38) 127 (tr the author).

[137] Ibid 123–4.

[138] Martti Koskenniemi, *The Politics of International Law* (Hart Publishing 2011) 339–40; an example in this sense is Article 5(2) of the ILC, 'Draft Articles on the Law of Transboundary Aquifers (Report of the International Law Commission on the Work of Its Sixtieth Session, UN Doc. A/CN.4/L.724)' (2008): 'The weight to be given to each factor is to be determined by its importance with regard to a specific transboundary aquifer or aquifer system in comparison with that of other relevant factors. In determining what is equitable and reasonable utilization, all relevant factors are to be considered together and a conclusion reached on the basis of all the factors. However, in weighing different kinds of utilization of a transboundary aquifer or aquifer system, special regard shall be given to vital human needs.'

[139] For an analysis of ICJ jurisprudence, see Nina Mileva and Marina Fortuna, 'Environmental Protection as an Object of and Tool for Evolutionary Interpretation' in Georges Abi-Saab and others (eds), *Evolutionary Interpretation and International Law* (Hart/Bloomsbury Publishing 2019) 126–9.

[140] ICJ, *Aegean Sea Continental Shelf (Greece v Turkey)*, Judgment, I.C.J Rep 3, 32 (1978), 77.

when it comes to assessing environmental risks or protecting human rights. In *Gabčikovo-Nagymaros*, the Court concluded that:

> newly developed norms of environmental law are relevant for the implementation of the Treaty, and that the parties could, by agreement, incorporate them through the application of [relevant articles] of the Treaty.[141]

Norms addressing environmental protection have to be read in a dynamic sense, and new environmental risks emerging since the conclusion of the treaty in 1977 have to be considered. Through the insertion of evolving provisions, the parties recognised the potential need to adapt the treaty, and, consequently, the treaty was not static.[142] The court continued with this line of jurisprudence in the *Case Concerning Pulp Mills in the River Uruguay (Pulp Mills).* Here, the Court referred to several earlier decisions to find that a customary obligation to undertake an environmental impact assessment exists, inter alia, in the *Dispute Regarding Navigational and Related Rights* case, holding that

> there are situations in which the parties' intent upon conclusion of the treaty was, or may be presumed to have been, to give the terms used—or some of them—a meaning or content capable of evolving, not one fixed once and for all, so as to make allowance for, among other things, developments in international law.[143]

It follows that meaning is dependent on the context in which a norm is applied, as 'principles do not possess a stable meaning beyond, and independent of, their application to concrete cases'.[144] A legal norm cannot be examined in isolation; instead, interpreters must consider historical, social and cultural factors. A treaty is a 'living instrument', and as such, its meaning can change over time.[145] This includes 'thinking in alternatives' or 'thinking of possibilities' of what a norm

---

[141] ICJ, *Gabčikovo-Nagymaros Project (Hungary v Slovakia)*, ICJ GL No 92, (1997) ICJ Rep 7, (1997) ICJ Rep 88, (1998) 37 ILM 162, ICGJ 66, (Judgement) (1997), para 112.

[142] Ibid 112.

[143] ICJ, *Pulp Mills on the River Uruguay (Argentina v. Uruguay)*, Judgment, I.C.J. Reports 2010, p 14, para 204, quoting ICJ, *Dispute regarding Navigational and Related Rights (Costa Rica v. Nicaragua)*, Judgment, I.C.J. Reports 2009, p 242, para 64.

[144] Habermas (n 123) 188.

[145] D Moeckli and ND White, 'Treaties as "Living Instruments"' in Michael J Bowman and Dino Kritsiotis (eds), *Conceptual and Contextual Perspectives on the Modern Law of Treaties* (CUP 2018).

can mean once it is confronted with reality.[146] Therefore, the purpose of a treaty or norm as stated in Article 31 (1) VCLT is the yardstick against which interpretation should be exercised, with the several sub-paragraphs listed in Article 31 (2) and (3) VCLT and Article 32 VCLT that place the purpose into context.[147] Interpretation can also change as a result of subsequent practice—Article 31 (3)(b)—or as a result of systematic interpretation—Article 31 (3)(c) VCLT.[148]

Such an understanding provides the basis for interpreting older treaties in the light of present environmental concerns such as climate change.[149] Unlike originalists, who see a risk in such an understanding, proponents of evolutionary approaches argue that only by accepting that the meanings of treaties might change over time that people would be freed from an 'inter-generational tyranny of constitutional permanence'[150] or a 'government by the dead'.[151] Interpretation needs to be able to 'update' the law according to changing circumstances and thus, respond to the desires and needs of an evolving society.[152]

While the member-states may have different ideas about what has been fixed in a treaty or a legislative act, social circumstances are beyond their control, especially those that are driven by the common interest of the national or international society. The creation of a treaty is similar to legislation in domestic law, which is not the end of the rule-making process but the beginning of new ones.[153] Treaties and law are creating micro-legal systems that derive their legal effect from the general system within which they were constituted and their social effects from

[146] Peter Häberle, 'Demokratische Verfassungstheorie im Lichte des Möglichkeitsdenkens' (1977) 102 Archiv des öffentlichen Rechts 27, 37.

[147] Donald McRae, 'Evolutionary Interpretation: The Relevance of Context' in Georges Abi-Saab and others (eds), *Evolutionary Interpretation and International Law* (Bloomsbury Publishing 2019); Bjorge, 'The Vienna Rules, Evolutionary Interpretation, and the Intentions of the Parties' (n 101).

[148] Geir Ulfstein, 'Evolutive Interpretation in the Light of Other International Instruments: Law and Legitimacy' in Anne van Aaken and Iulia Motoc (eds), *The European Convention on Human Rights and General International Law* (OUP 2018) 83; see also Panos Merkouris, *Article 31(3)(c) VCLT and the Principle of Systemic Integration. Normative Shadows in Plato's Cave* (Brill/Martinus Nijhoff Publishers 2015).

[149] Mileva and Fortuna (n 139) 140.

[150] Frank Michelman, 'Law's Republic' (1988) 97 The Yale Law Journal 1493, 1516.

[151] Christopher L Eisgruber, *Constitutional Self-Government* (Harvard University Press 2001) 40; Dieter Grimm, *Constitutionalism. Past, Present, and Future* (OUP 2016) 11: 'The fundamental question then becomes: how is the acting generation able to acquire the legitimacy to bind future generations? The answer lies in the possibility of changing the law.'

[152] Mileva and Fortuna (n 139) 124.

[153] Allott (n 14) 81.

the society within which they are constituted.[154] It is not only the states' interests but also the common self-interest of the international society as a whole that informs the treaty-making process. It is the open society that updates its own common interests, which is an integral part of the international society's legal self-constituting.[155] Thus, the self-interest of the international society in keeping the planet habitable for the continuation of humanity can inform the subject matter of a treaty, even if it was not considered by the member-states that brought it into being.

If common interests are defined by the international society at large—and not merely states—then interpretative power might be ascribed to non-state actors as well. This would mark a break with the Westphalian model,[156] and it is here where dynamic and evolutionary concepts of interpretation part most clearly from textualism and authentic interpretation. The latter do not close themselves to the idea of change over time and context,[157] but the difference is that the originalist approaches require a formal amendment or modification of the treaty to change its meaning. It is this a quest for the stability of the legal order.[158] Under such a view, newer developments and scientific findings can only be considered if the text was officially modified. Until then, a text is frozen in time and has to be interpreted accordingly.[159] Interpretation must, therefore, not be confused or conflated with lawmaking, which as a task belongs only to the legitimised legislator. Non-state actors may be able to engage in lawmaking, but they cannot change the meaning of norms with any legal value.[160]

---

154 Ibid.

155 Ibid 81–2.

156 See e.g. Venzke (n 1) 64–71.

157 Zarbiyev (n 203) 254, 'the interpretive paradigm of the VCLT is a time- and context-sensitive phenomenon'.

158 Dupuy (n 111) 123, citing Michel Virally: 'Every legal order is a challenge in time, an effort to conserve the social order that it establishes.' (La formation de la pensée juridique moderne, 2nd ed LGDJ 1998).

159 Tanaka (n 23) 141.

160 Berner (n 99) 851.

This idea has been contested by many scholars. In Germany, Häberle was the first leading proponent of a theory that recognises the capacity of 'everyone' to interpret constitutional law.[161] In the US, scholars of the New Haven School and other pluralist strands of legal thought supported a 'jurisgenerative' approach that includes non-state actors, such as transnational corporations, NGOs and individuals.[162] The concept of transnational legal processes (TLP), for example, acknowledges that non-state actors play a role alongside nation-states in making and re-making law through interaction, which generates new interpretations of those rules that become internalised into domestic law, which guides those actors' conduct in the future.[163] Koh identifies the *non-statist* nature as one of the four features of transnational legal processes;[164] both states and non-state actors interact 'in a variety of public and private, domestic and international fora to make, interpret, enforce, and ultimately, internalize rules of transnational law'.[165] These ideas have influenced theories of societal constitutionalism as a domain where constitutional law can be created by non-actors (see Chapter 7).[166]

While intention and the text should be considered, it is the object and the purpose that should inform the interpretative result (the teleological approach). Proponents of the teleological approach see the text merely as 'the formal embodiment' of the parties' shared intentions, but it is for the interpreter to consider

[161] Häberle, '"The Open Society of Constitutional Interpreters"—A Contribution to a Pluralistic and "Procedural" Constitutional Interpretation (1975)' (n 16); the original text was published in 1975 in German, see Peter Häberle, 'Die offene Gesellschaft der Verfassungsinterpreten: Ein Beitrag zur pluralistischen und „prozessualen" Verfassungsinterpretation' (1975) 30 Juristenzeitung 297.

[162] Robert M Cover, 'The Supreme Court, 1982 Term—Foreword: Nomos and Narrative' (1983) 97 Harvard Law Review 4, 11–9.

[163] Koh, 'Transnational Legal Process' (n 61) 186; Koh, *The Trump Administration and International Law* (n 61) 7.

[164] Koh believes that the reason for states obeying international law, even without the coercive force with which domestic law is backed, is TLP. TLP, besides its non-statist nature is non-traditional and thus overcomes the classifications into domestic/international law and private/public law. Furthermore, it is dynamic which means that transnational law is in constant movement: it transforms, changes and percolates on the different levels. And it is normative. The process of interaction produces new legal rules that are again interpreted, internalized and enforced, and thus, the whole process starts all over again. See Koh, 'Transnational Legal Process' (n 61).

[165] Ibid 183–4.

[166] See the contributions in *Global Law without a State* (Gunther Teubner ed, Dartmouth Publishing 1997).

non-textual matters to give effect to its objects and purposes.[167] The question the interpreter should ask themselves is: 'What is intended? What is the purpose?'

This method of interpretation devalues both the framers' historical will and the text. Instead, the point of reference is the interpreter's notion of what constitutes the correct result, according to the 'independent function' of interpretation.[168] What constitutes the correct meaning naturally depends on the interpreter's perspective, which can be influenced by a range of different interests and their corresponding schools of jurisprudence, such as, inter alia, politics (critical legal studies), inclusion and non-subordination (feminist legal theory, race theory) or wealth maximisation (economic theory of the law).[169] It can also aim to find values or a higher moral or political goal beyond the actual law.[170] This method is informed by the social and legal values a society holds. Accordingly, the text is overestimated.[171] It is asked how a particular interpretation fits into the ideas that society has of its political and social life and how to give effect to these understandings. Overarching purposes and values of law and society merge.[172] New values can inform the content of (old) law, and this holds especially for environmental values or the well-being of future generations.

2.3.3 Limits of Evolutionary Interpretation

Critics of evolutionary interpretation express their concerns that interpreters could neglect the most important reference: the text. Articles 31–33 of the VCLT are still the yardstick for the interpretation of all international treaties, not only a certain class.[173] It is this a concern of free-hand interpretations: the fear of judges seeing the legal rules merely as a cloak for their own decision.[174] Textualists

---

[167] Rosalie P Schaffer, 'Current Trends in Treaty Interpretation and the South African Approach' (1976) 7 Australian Year Book of International Law 129, 133.

[168] Winfried Brugger, 'Legal Interpretation, Schools of Jurisprudence, and Anthropology: Some Remarks from a German Point of View' (1994) 2 The American Journal of Comparative Law 395, 397 quoting Justice Frankfurter's concurring opinion in *Adamson v. California*, 332 U.S. 46, 67 (1947).

[169] Compare Table 1 in ibid 403.

[170] Hollis (n 39) 81.

[171] Häberle, 'The Open Society of Constitutional Interpreters' (n 16) 150.

[172] Brugger (n 168) 413.

[173] James Crawford, 'Foreword' in Eirik Bjorge (ed), *The Evolutionary Interpretation of Treaties* (OUP 2014).

[174] Scalia and Garner (n 124) 88–9.

and authentic interpretation supporters are concerned that law and politics will become blurry if the judge is allowed to consider factors that lay outside the law.[175] It is the fear of (hidden) judicial activism, of judges becoming alternative legislators: a fear that is more prominent in domestic settings given the central place of the juridical branch.

Nonetheless, even evolutionary interpretation cannot lead to whatever result the interpreter likes best. Interpretation is limited by at least three factors. First, evolutionary interpretation still must observe the rules of interpretation laid down in Article 31 VCLT.[176] This includes that an interpretative process can never result in a breach of *jus cogens*. Moreover, it must not result in a 'distorted revision' of a treaty—'a completely different text which has neither been negotiated nor agreed'.[177] Additionally, evolutionary interpretation has to be limited by the principle of non-retroactivity.[178]

Second, each interpretation needs to be recognised as a legal claim.[179] It has to be accepted among the members of the relevant interpretative community.[180] It must be consistent with the system of IL and be sensitive to the particular idiosyncrasies of the socio-political context within individual states, but also in the international legal order as a whole, to be successful in its respective community.[181] The interpreter has to respect an explicit code to convince the members of the universe of juridical formalism;[182] it has to fit with what Koskenniemi calls the 'structural bias'.[183]

---

[175] Dupuy (n 111) 127–8.

[176] Mileva and Fortuna (n 139) 135, 138–9; see also Panos Merkouris, '(Inter)Temporal Considerations in the Interpretative Process of the VCLT: Do Treaties Endure, Perdure or Exdure ?' (2014) 45 Netherlands Yearbook of International Law 121.

[177] *Separate Opinion of Judge Bedjaoui, Gabčíkovo–Nagymaros Project (Hungary v Slovakia)* (Judgment) (1997), 123, para 12.

[178] Merkouris (n 176) 150.

[179] Ingo Venzke, 'The Role of International Courts as Interpreters and Developers of the Law: Working Out the Jurisgenerative Practice of Interpretation' (2011) 34 Loyola of Los Angeles International and Comparative Law Review 99, 120.

[180] Venzke (n 1) 40.

[181] Johnstone (n 90) 372ff; on epistemic communities, see Peter M Haas, 'Introduction: Epistemic Communities and International Policy Coordination' (1992) 46 International Organization 1, 3.

[182] Bourdieu (n 27) 849 calls this the 'homologation effect'.

[183] Koskenniemi (n 94) 570: 'Whether a particular justification then seems plausible and the position defended is accepted depends on how it fits with the structural bias in the relevant institutional context. Two patterns emerge: one is the formal style in which arguments must be made in order to seem professionally plausible; the other is the substantive outcome that

In one way or another, all of the above-discussed methods (intention, text, object and purpose) share the common goal of restraining interpretation to keep the amount of possible interpretation from which the interpreter can choose maintainable. They aim to reduce complexity. The need for coherence, certainty and stability in the interpretative communities must not be underestimated.[184]

It follows that interpretation, on the one hand, enables interpreters to choose between at least two alternatives. On the other, and this is the third limitation, interpretation is constrained by past practices.[185] Weber argues that a judge that once consciously and recognisably had chosen a certain maxim as the norm for a decision would face the accusation of bias if they would not apply the same maxim in a similar case. The same then applies to the judges thereafter; all the more when 'tradition' generally dominates life. Because then, every decision made, no matter how they come about, naturally appears as an outflow either as an expression or as part of the only permanently right tradition. It becomes a scheme that at least pretends to have permanent validity.[186] The reference to precedents legitimises the decision by placing it in the light of a neutral and objective process that is safeguarded through the application of specified juridical procedures, even when the result might be motivated by different considerations.[187] It is thus a process of 'natural selection' that decides in which way a norm can be changed, and which of the competing ideas will flourish and which are meant to vanish.[188] Thus, '[t]he current judge is held accountable to the tradition she inherits by the judges yet to come'.[189] A judge's interpretation can only survive if future judges recognise or acknowledge its precedential authority.[190]

---

appears to satisfy the structural bias. The legal justifiability of a decision is not the same as a causal account of why it was taken. The latter has to do with things legal realists have always referred to: ambition, inertia, tradition, ideology, and contingency'.

[184] John Tobin, 'Seeking to Persuade: A Constructive Approach to Human Rights Treaty Interpretation' (2010) 23 Harvard Human Rights Journal 1, 7.

[185] Venzke (n 1) 48.

[186] Weber (n 64) 400.

[187] Bourdieu (n 27) 832.

[188] Oliver Wendell Holmes, 'Law in Science and Science in Law' (1899) 13 Harvard Law Review 443, 449–50.

[189] Robert B Brandom, 'Some Pragmatist Themes in Hegel's Idealism: Negotiation and Administration in Hegel's Account of the Structure and Content of Conceptual Norms' (1999) 7 European Journal of Philosophy 164, 181.

[190] Ibid; Ronald Dworkin, *Law's Empire* (Belknap Press 1986) 229.

However, interpretation should not cling too hard to the past.[191] The European Court of Human Rights (ECtHR) has made this point particularly clear:

> While the Court is not formally bound to follow its previous judgments, it is in the interests of legal certainty, foreseeability and equality before the law that it should not depart, without good reason, from precedents laid down in previous cases [...]. However, since the Convention is first and foremost a system for the protection of human rights, the Court must have regard to the changing conditions within the respondent State and within Contracting States generally and respond, for example, to any evolving convergence as to the standards to be achieved [...]. It is of crucial importance that the Convention is interpreted and applied in a manner which renders its rights practical and effective, not theoretical and illusory. A failure by the Court to maintain a dynamic and evolutive approach would indeed risk rendering it a bar to reform or improvement.[192]

While the text is still the authoritative reference point, rules of interpretation guarantee the possibility of critique.[193] From this perspective, teleological interpretation could be understood as the merging and continuation of the authentic and textualist approaches. It relies on the objects and purposes as they have been expressed in the treaty text. It also aims to go beyond the text and ascertain the history of the treaty, the intention of the parties and the role of the negotiations, in this respect following the authentic approach. The difference is that it determines the object and purpose of the treaty at the time of interpretation, not at the time of the treaty conclusion. This aspect is neither textual, as this 'new' purpose cannot be gathered from the text, nor is it authentic, as it shifts from the original intent of the parties.[194] Instead of theoretically focusing on single elements such as the intention of the states, text, object and purpose, the interpreter should examine interpretation in practice where it resembles an 'eclectic mix' rather than a precise mathematical formula.[195] This 'crucible interpretation' approach has been developed by the ECtHR in *Golder v UK*.[196]

It is also not necessary to employ special rules of interpretation for the human rights regime, which is, due to its non-reciprocal nature, different from general

[191] Curtis (n 12) 415.

[192] ECtHR, *Goodwin v. United Kingdom*, Judgment of 11 July 2002, App. No. 28957/95 (2002), para 74.

[193] Venzke (n 1) 31 n 183.

[194] Schaffer (n 167) 133.

[195] Tobin (n 184) 6.

[196] ECtHR, *Golder v United Kingdom*, Judgment of 21 February 1975, App. No. 4451/70 (1975), para 30: 'In the way in which it is presented in the "general rule" in Article 31 of

IL.[197] Kolb, for example, differentiated between treaties that protect a '*utilitas singulorum*' (then the text should be interpreted in a rather strict manner) or if it protects an international '*utilitas publica*'.[198] If it was the latter, the courts would be more willing to interpret in an evolutionary and teleological manner.[199] While human rights law may be a special system, it is not isolated from general IL and the general rules of interpretation apply without the need for a special hermeneutic system.[200] The interpreter has to use the whole array of hermeneutic methods that Article 31 VCLT offers (wording, context, object, purpose and context) to make human rights law effective.[201] However, one must also not cling to Article 31 VCLT as an 'interpretational straightjacket'.[202] Rather, given their very nature, changing political, social and economic factors need to be considered and human rights provisions interpreted accordingly.[203]

Thus, interpretation should not be seen as a 'one fits it all' concept. In cases that display the classical horizontal relationship between equal states, such as the UN Charter, courts usually base their decisions on state consent.[204] Evolutive approaches and the idea of treaties as living instruments, conversely, are an effective way to broadly interpret states' obligations in human rights law or where a

---

the Vienna Convention, the process of interpretation of a treaty is a unity, a single combined operation; this rule, closely integrated, places on the same footing the various elements enumerated in the four paragraphs of the Article.'

197 Tobin (n 184) 20; Eirik Bjorge, 'The Convergence Methods of Treaty Interpretation: Different Regimes, Different Methods of Interpretation?' in Mads Adenas and Eirik Bjorge (eds), *A Farewell to Fragmentation* (CUP 2015) 498–535.

198 Robert Kolb, *Interprétation et création du droit international* (Bruylant (Editions de l'Université de Bruxelles) 2006) 202–3.

199 Ibid 203.

200 Robert Kolb, 'Is There a Subject-Matter Ontology in Interpretation of International Legal Norms?' in Mads Andenas and Eirik Bjorge (eds), *A Farewell to Fragmentation* (CUP 2015) 484.

201 Cf. Başak Çalı, 'Specialized Rules of Treaty Interpretation: Human Rights' in Duncan B Hollis (ed), *The Oxford Guide to Treaties* (OUP 2012) 527.

202 This expression was coined by Joseph Weiler, 'Prolegomena to a Meso-Theory of Treaty Interpretation at the Turn of the Century', *International Legal Theory Colloquium: Interpretation in International Law,IILJ, NYU School of Law, 14 February 2008* 5–6; Çalı (n 201) 532–3.

203 Çalı (n 201) 531.

204 Dupuy (n 111) 125–6.

court acts as the guardian of a common institution and, therefore, is less bound to the individual will of states.[205]

These thoughts have guided both national courts and international human rights tribunals. The next section demonstrates that national courts and international human rights tribunals do see environmental degradation as a threat to the enjoyment of human rights. This was apparent in a small number of cases concerning pollution from one single source; however, it has given activists hope and encouraged them to file claims that may motivate courts to move to the even larger problem of climate change.

2.3.4 Human Rights and Environmental Law

Many apex courts use an evolutionary approach to interpret constitutional rights. The Canadian Supreme Court, for instance, stated that:

> The 'frozen concepts' reasoning runs contrary to one of the most fundamental principles of Canadian constitutional interpretation: that our Constitution is a living tree which, by way of progressive interpretation, accommodates and addresses the realities of modern life.[206]

Thinking of their conventions as 'living trees' has also been adopted by regional human rights courts and international bodies.

The ECtHR is one of the first courts that has made extensive use of evolutionary interpretation in environmental cases[207] despite the rejection of proposals for an additional protocol including a right to a healthy environment in 1970.[208] It used several rights enshrined in the European Convention on Human Rights (ECHR), in particular the right to life (Article 2) and the right to a private and

---

[205] Andrea Bianchi, 'The Game of Interpretation in International Law' in Andrea Bianchi, Daniel Peat and Matthew Windsor (eds), *Interpretation in International Law* (OUP 2015) 50.

[206] Supreme Court of Canada, Reference re Same-Sex Marriage, [2004] 3 S.C. R. 698, 2004 SCC 79, para. 22. On the debate of originalism and living constitutionalism in national constitutional law, see Lawrence B Solum, 'Originalism versus Living Constitutionalism: The Coceptual Structure of the Great Debate' (2019) 113 Northwestern University Law Review 1432.

[207] For a list of environment-related cases, see ECtHR, 'Environment and the European Convention on Human Rights (Factsheet)' (2021) <http://www.echr.coe.int/Documents/FS_Environment_ENG.pdf> accessed 31 August 2023.

[208] Mileva and Fortuna (n 139) 131.

family life (Article 8), to examine environment-related concerns and determine states' obligations to protect citizens from environmentally harmful activities.[209]

The ECtHR refers to other international instruments even against the member-states' explicit will when determining their obligations under the ECHR.[210] In *Demir and Baykara vs Turkey*, for example, the Turkish government argued that the Court was not authorised to rely on other international instruments (in this case, the Aarhus Convention) than the Convention, since this would risk creating, by way of interpretation, obligations that were not part of the ECHR. Turkey is not a member of the Aarhus Convention. However, the Court stated that it can rely on international instruments, whether a state had ratified them or not, as long as they:

> denote a continuous evolution in the norms and principles applied in international law or in the domestic law of the majority of member States of the Council of Europe and show, in a precise area, that there is common ground in modern societies.[211]

The Court referred to its 'living instrument' jurisprudence and argued that the Convention has to be interpreted 'in the light of present-day conditions', therefore, taking into account the evolution of national and IL.[212] Thus, the Court concluded that in addition to considering the object and purpose of the Convention, it would also consider the IL background to assess the legal question before it:

> Being made up of a set of rules and principles that are accepted by the vast majority of States, the common international or domestic law standards of European States reflect a reality that the Court cannot disregard when it is called upon to clarify the scope

---

[209] For a violation of Article 2, see inter alia: *Öneryildiz v. Turkey*, Judgement of 30 November 2014, App. No. 48939/99; *Budayeva and Others v. Russia*, Judgement of 20 March 2008, App. Nos. 15339/02, 21166/02, 20058/02, 11673/02 and 15343/02; for a violation of Article 8, see: *López Ostra v. Spain*, Judgement of 9 December 1994, App. No. 16798/90; *Guerra and Others v. Italy*, Judgement of 19 February 1998, App. No. 14967/89; *Fadeyeva v. Russia*, Judgement of 9 June 2005, App. No. 55723/00; *Tătar v. Romania*, Judgement of 27 January 2009, App. No. 67021/01; *Cordella and Others v. Italy*, Judgement of 24 January 2019, App. Nos. 54414/13 and 54264/15.

[210] For an analysis of the method of interpretation by referance to other treaties and its missing codification in the Vienna Convention, see Merkouris (n 148) 51ff.

[211] ECtHR, *Demir and Baykara v. Turkey*, Judgement of 12 November 2008, App. No. 34503/97, para 86.

[212] Ibid para 68.

> of a Convention provision that more conventional means of interpretation have not enabled it to establish with a sufficient degree of certainty.[213]

The ECtHR has made it clear in former decisions that:

> Unlike international treaties of the classic kind, the Convention comprises more than merely reciprocal engagements between Contracting States. It creates, over and above a network of mutual, bilateral relationships, objective obligations [...].[214]

Whether the ECtHR understands climate change as a threat to life (Article 2 ECHR) and private and family life (Article 8 ECHR) remains to be seen. Several climate cases are currently, at the time of writing, pending before the ECtHR, including *KlimaSeniorinnen v Switzerland*, *Carême v France* and *Duarte Agostinho and Others v Portugal and 32 other States* before the Grand Chamber.[215]

In the Americas, Article 11 of the San Salvador Protocol explicitly recognises the right to a healthy environment, although this right is not justiciable (Article 19 para. 6). This, however, does not stop the IACtHR from ruling on environmental matters. The Court follows an evolutionary approach and has repeatedly referred to other regional and international human rights instruments.[216]

In *Yakye Axa Indigenous Community v Paraguay*, a positive obligation to protect the right to life has explicitly been recognised by the Court, which interprets Article 4 as including 'not only the right of every human being not to be arbitrarily deprived of his life but also the right that conditions that impede or obstruct access to a decent existence should not be generated.'[217] This includes the state's obligation to generate a minimum of living conditions compatible with the dignity of the human person.[218] It furthermore implies the positive duty to protect the environmental conditions that are necessary for a decent and dignified life.[219]

---

213 Ibid para 76.

214 ECtHR, *Ireland v. the United Kingdom*, Judgment of 18 January 1978, App. No. 5310/71, para 239.

215 See ECtHR, 'Climate Change (Factsheet)' (2023) <https://www.echr.coe.int/documents/d/echr/FS_Climate_change_ENG> accessed 31 August 2023.

216 Dinah Shelton, 'Developing Substantive Environmental Rights' (2010) 1 Journal of Human Rights and the Environment 89, 93ff.

217 IACtHR, *Yakye Axa Indigenous Community v Paraguay*, Judgment of 17 June 2005, para 161.

218 Ibid para 62.

219 Sophie Thériault, 'Environmental Justice and the Inter-American Court of Human Rights' in Anna Grear and Louis J Kotzé (eds), *Research Handbook on Human Rights and the Environment* (Edward Elgar Publishing 2015) 315–6.

In its Advisory Opinion on the Environment and Human Rights (2017), the Court elaborated on the question of how to interpret the human rights provisions enshrined in the Convention in light of both treaty and customary environmental law norms.[220] Colombia raised this question against the background of a planned major infrastructure project that may have affected the marine environment, thereby, risking the coastal states' populations to enjoy their human rights as guaranteed in the Convention. The Court stated explicitly that it was using an evolutionary approach due to the nature of human rights treaties as living instruments.[221] Given the interdependence and indivisibility between human rights and the environment, the Court expressed that it 'can make use of the principles, rights and obligations of international environmental law, which as part of the international *corpus iuris* contribute decisively to set the scope of the obligations derived from the American Convention in this area'[222] when determining the scope of the state's obligations.

Moreover, the Court started to shift the basis for the right to a healthy environment from the non-justiciable Article 11 of the San Salvador Protocol to Article 26 of the American Convention on Human Rights (ACHR).[223] In the recent *Lhaka Honat v Argentina* case, the Court recognised for the first time a direct application of economic, social and cultural rights, including a right to a healthy environment.[224]

However, not all judges supported this decision. Here, the relevance of the different methods becomes visible. Dissenting Judge Vio Grossi argued that such an interpretation was not in accordance with what the member-states had agreed upon. The Court had ignored the differentiation the Convention's text makes between civil and political rights on the one hand, and economic, social and

---

[220] The Environment and Human Rights (State obligations in relation to the environment in the context of the protection and guarantee of the rights to life and to personal integrity—interpretation and scope of Articles 4(1) and 5(1) of the American Convention on Human Rights), Advisory Opinion OC-23/17, IACHR Series A No 23 (15 November 2017), thereafter IACtHR, AO OC-23/17.

[221] IACtHR, AO OC-23/17, para 43.

[222] Ibid para 55.

[223] Mileva and Fortuna (n 139) 135.

[224] IACtHR, *Caso Comunidades Indígenas Miembros de la Asociación Lhaka Honhat (Nuestra Tierra) vs. Argentina*, Judgment of 6 February 2020 (Merits, reparations and costs), see also Paola Patarroyo, 'Justiciability of "Implicit" Rights: Developments on the Right to a Healthy Environment at the Inter-American Court of Human Rights' *EJIL Talk* (2020) <https://www.ejiltalk.org/justiciability-of-implicit-rights-developments-on-the-right-to-a-healthy-environment-at-the-inter-american-court-of-human-rights/> accessed 31 August 2023.

cultural rights on the other.[225] While he recognised the importance of the latter, he claimed that the Court's jurisdiction is limited to finding violations of civil and political rights.[226] Grossi interpreted the Convention from the state's perspective. However, the majority of the judges decided to interpret the Convention in light of international, national and local obligations and the changed circumstances under which indigenous people struggle to live today. It recognised their extremely vulnerable position and drew a concept for the comprehensive protection of their ways of life, which are based on the rights to a healthy environment, adequate food, water and participation in cultural life. Remarkably, the court included a 'right to water', which the Lhaka community had not raised in its communication.[227] Moreover, the court employed a notion of the right to a healthy environment that lends itself strongly to the ideas of rights for nature.[228]

The liberal 'Western' constitutionalism of the eighteenth and nineteenth centuries has strongly influenced constitutionalism in Latin America.[229] However, these conceptions do not fit the reality well in Latin American countries that experienced colonialisation and its long-lasting effects, such as the distribution of wealth and power or the marginalised position of indigenous peoples.[230] These factors are 'ignored' by liberal theories of constitutionalism that focus on state-building and individual rights rather than establishing fair conditions for all citizens. Recently, the IACtHR has started to adjust the law to social realities and incorporated indigenous values in its case law. For example, the IACtHR has recognised that property can belong to a collective entity (and not

225 Partially Dissenting Opinion of Eduardo Vio Grossi, Inter-American Court of Human Rights, Case of the Indigenous Communities of The Lhaka Honhat Association v. Argentina (Judgment of 6 February 2020), para 14.

226 Ibid paras 31, 49.

227 IACtHR, *Caso Comunidades Indígenas Miembros De La Asociación Lhaka Honhat (Nuestra Tierra) vs. Argentina*, Judgment of 6 February 2020 (Merits, reparations and costs, para 200.

228 '[I]t stated that the right to a healthy environment "constitutes a universal value"; it "is a fundamental right for the existence of humankind," and that "as an autonomous right [...] it protects the components of the environment, such as forests, rivers and seas, as legal interests in themselves, even in the absence of the certainty or evidence of a risk to individuals. This means that nature must be protected, not only because of its benefits or effects for humanity, "but because of its importance for the other living organisms with which we share the planet', IACtHR, 'Caso Comunidades Indígenas Miembros De La Asociación Lhaka Honhat (Nuestra Tierra) Vs. Argentina (2020)' para 203.

229 Angela Iacovino, 'Constitucionalismo ecológico en América Latina: De los derechos ambientales a los derechos de la naturaleza' (2020) 31 Cultura Latinoamericana 266, 269.

230 Ibid 270.

only one individual person) since the concept of 'individual property' is unknown to some indigenous peoples.[231] The same holds now for the creation of a right to a healthy environment via Article 26 ACHR and the inclusion of elements of the rights for nature. In Latin America, the concept of '*buen vivir*'—living in harmony with nature—has endured in indigenous cultures despite the colonialisation of the continent and has been passed down from generation to generation.[232] Nature is not seen as a 'provider' of goods that humans need to live. Rather, humans are understood to be a part of nature and not superior to it. National and constitutional courts in South America have experimented with such ecocentric approaches that assign nature its own value for some time now.[233]

Many of the cases that led to landmark rulings were filed by indigenous communities that see their human rights endangered by profit-driven companies and states alike.[234] The fact that the IACtHR has taken up this approach demonstrates that it reacts to developments in the national legal orders and courts and thus, the changing perceptions of (the importance of) nature in their populations. In many member-states to the ACHR, the human right to a healthy environment is already recognised. However, such a human rights–based approach to environmental protection only focuses on the human being, not nature itself.

Here, it becomes quite apparent how the courts react to the ideas of self of their respective open societies. The ECtHR has clarified that it would not protect the environment per se but only where environmental deteriorations are affecting someone's human rights.[235] Its American counterpart, through its definition of the right to a healthy environment, including elements of rights for nature, mirrored a part of cultural identity that is important for large parts of the population but has not found its way into the written Convention yet. This notable shift from a human right to a healthy environment to rights of nature indicates a new form of Latin American ecological constitutionalism with a strong focus on environmental protection and cultural pluralism.[236] Thus, the *Lhaka* ruling can be

---

[231] IACtHR, *Case of the Kichwa Indigenous People of Sarayaku v Ecuador*, Judgement of 27 June 2012 (Merits and Reparations), para145.

[232] Toledo López, 'Sociedad y naturaleza. Contribuciones de la América profunda a la superación de la crisis' [2013] Herramienta Web 1, 3.

[233] For a comprehensive list, see UN Harmony with Nature, 'Rights of Nature Law, Policy and Education' <http://www.harmonywithnatureun.org/rightsOfNature/> accessed 31 August 2023.

[234] See, for example, Constitutional Court of Colombia, 'Tierra Digna v Presidencia de la República (T-622), 2016'.

[235] ECtHR, *Kyrtatos v. Greece*, Judgement of 22 May 2003, App. No. 41666/98, para 52.

[236] Iacovino (n 229) 272.

understood in two ways. First, the Court takes the protection of indigenous peoples seriously, as it has already demonstrated through a series of judgements.[237] Second, indigenous peoples are not only seen as victims but as part of the open society of interpreters who can contribute to a more sustainable legal order by providing their ancient knowledge of the lands and their (legal) understanding of the world—something that the Latin American courts, including the IACtHR, have begun to embrace.

The UN treaty bodies also make use of evolutionary interpretation. In *Billy v Australia*, while the Human Rights Committee could not find a violation of Article 6 ICCPR, but stated that Australia had violated Articles 17 (right to private, family and home life) and 27 ICCPR (right to culture) by failing to take adequate adaptation measures to climate change to protect the complainants' traditional way of life.[238]

2.4 Concluding Remarks

This chapter was concerned with the role of different interpretation methods as postulated in Article 31 VCLT. It explained that originalist positions, such as authentic interpretation based on the intention of the parties and textualism, seek to keep interpretation relatively discretion-free. Originalist interpretation would exclude environmental concerns from international or regional human rights law because these treaties have been concluded before international environmental obligations existed.[239]

Evolutionary approaches, conversely, are based on purpose and context. Treaties are to be interpreted in present daylight conditions that take into account today's time and space. Many international legal bodies apply an evolutionary approach, including the ICJ, the UN human rights treaty bodies and regional human rights tribunals. These are also more likely to consider other IL when interpreting their respective treaties. Such approaches also benefit environmental rights, as an analysis of the jurisprudence of the ECtHR and the IACtHR has

[237] See Thériault (n 219).

[238] UN Human Rights Committee, *Daniel Billy et al v Australia*, Views adopted on 21 July 2022, CCPR/C/135/D/3624/2019, paras. 8.9ff, esp. 8.10, 8.12, 8.14.

[239] Shelton (n 216) 94.

demonstrated. The courts, instead of 'fossilising' the law, consider their respective treaties as a living tissue that should serve the needs of an evolving society.[240]

The role of interpretation, then, can be defined in a completely different fashion. Instead of understanding interpretation as being merely a toolkit that helps the judge (or, for that matter, any other legal practicioner) to find the correct meaning of a text and apply it accordingly, interpretation is a method of law-making. The interpretative process involves creativity and some invention rather than merely applying the rules.[241] It is this interpretative practice that occupies the space between the text and the law and contributes to new understandings of the (same) law. It is the space where practice 'negotiates the contents of commitment' and where all great changes to IL in recent decades have taken place, given the relatively small number of new treaty texts during this time.[242] Therefore, 'interpretation is law-making in all but name'[243] or as Dworkin concisely puts it: 'Law is an interpretive concept.'[244]

[240] Parvez Hassan and Azim Azfar, 'Securing Environmental Rights Through Public Interest Litigation in South Asia' (2004) 22 Virginia Environmental Law Journal 215, 216.

[241] HLA Hart, *The Concept of Law* (Clarendon Press 1961) 204, '[...] the open texture of law leaves a vast field for a creative activity which some call legislative.'

[242] Venzke (n 1) 197.

[243] Berner (n 99) 845.

[244] Dworkin (n 190) 410.

3 Constitution, Constitutionalisation and Constitutionalism

The last chapter demonstrated that interpretation can develop and shape IL. In the following chapters, it will be argued that interpretation can help to constitutionalise the international legal order and, in particular, global climate law.

The basis for this claim is the ongoing academic discourse about the constitutionalisation of IL and global constitutionalism. Both the positive and negative effects of globalisation (trade, increase of wealth, but also global terrorism, international drug wars and cybercrime, to name a few) have led to the erosion of the 'traditional' international legal order: the Westphalian system, which goes back to the *Peace Treaty of Westphalia* of 1648. Accordingly, the international legal order was created and developed by the subjects of IL, primarily the states, which enjoy state sovereignty. However, today, new players participate in the international legal system and take over functions that formerly belonged exclusively to states. Moreover, the *domaine resérvé* of states has decreased over the last decades, in particular, through the rise of international human rights law. A shift from government to (polyarchic and multi-level) governance is notable. Nevertheless, the Westphalian system is officially still in place, and it does not provide any meaningful participation possibilities for non-state actors. Thus, the impression arises that the 'old' IL no longer fits the 'new' global reality.

Constitutionalism addresses this gap between 'de-constitutionalised' states and an ever denser and stronger web of international norms. Constitutionalist approaches aim to constitutionalise global governance. Thus, constitutionalism is a shift from the horizontal legal structure between states—similar to the legal

M. Niehaus, *Global Climate Constitutionalism "from below"*,
https://doi.org/10.1007/978-3-658-43191-4_3

construction of private law—to a 'constitution of the international community'.[1] A constitutionalist reading of IL would still see state sovereignty as an important factor, but it would no longer serve as the only legitimacy point of IL. Instead, it is complemented by other guiding principles, including the common interest, and as such, the protection of the climate. States have to respect these guiding principles and norms.

This makes constitutionalism an interesting approach for environmental law scholars who seek to reduce state sovereignty and hold states accountable for climate and environmental damages. Sovereignty, as constructed in the Westphalian system, is seen as an obstacle to a more sustainable international legal order, since it allows states to emit as many GHGs as they wish without any legal consequences despite having ratified legally binding international climate treaties such as the UNFCCC or the Paris Agreement. The consequence of reconstructing international climate law (or parts of it) as constitutional would mean that these norms cannot simply be 'pushed aside' in the case of a conflict with domestic constitutional law. States would no longer be able (or, at least, would find it more difficult) to sacrifice long-term interests, such as the protection of the climate or the interests of future generations, on the altar of short-term economic benefits. In this respect, global climate constitutionalism holds great advantages for stronger climate protection. It is argued here that global climate constitutionalism can restrict state sovereignty on climate matters and provide more participation opportunities for non-state actors.

This chapter seeks to identify the basis on which Häberle's theory of the open society of constitutional interpreters[2] could be transferred to IL, and in particular, international climate law. His claim that there is no *numerus clausus* of constitutional interpreters, and that everybody interprets the constitution, could serve as the backbone of a theory that assigns non-state actors an active and important role in developing and shaping international climate constitutional law. However, Häberle originally developed his theory for German constitutional law. A 'total' constitution, as we know it from domestic constitutional law, obviously does not exist in IL, and even less so in international climate law. Years after his theory was published, Häberle transferred the open society of constitutional interpreters to the European realm and, subsequently, to the international realm by arguing that constitutional elements can also be found in these international

[1] Anne Peters, 'Compensatory Constitutionalism: The Function and Potential of Fundamental International Norms and Structures' (2006) 19 Leiden Journal of International Law 579, 580.

[2] See Section 1.2.4 above.

legal orders. They are not 'total constitutions' that encompass all subject matters but 'partial constitutions' for their relevant realm, such as the UN Convention on the Law of the Sea.[3]

This chapter first examines the very basics of constitutionalism—the question of what makes a constitution a constitution, as opposed to ordinary law—and what makes it desirable to reproduce it at the international level. To do so, the concepts of constitution, constitutionalisation and constitutionalism are examined, followed by an analysis of whether something like a national constitution could be 'upscaled' to the international level, in particular, to develop environmental constitutionalism. By highlighting the advantages and disadvantages of constitutionalism, it is demonstrated how the climate could profit from a constitutionalist reading of international environmental and climate law.

3.1 From Government to (Environmental and Climate) Governance

Westphalian sovereignty, defined as 'political organization based on the exclusion of external actors from authority structures within a given territory',[4] lasted for almost four centuries.[5] But the *domaine réservé* of states has been continuously reduced throughout the last century, most notably through the development of humanitarian law and international human rights law, which has led to a growing number of treaties, customary law and the emergence of *erga omnes* and *jus cogens* norms that demand state compliance. Moreover, the enforcement of IL (especially in regional human rights courts such as the ECtHR) and international integration, both at the global and regional levels (e.g., the EU), have downsized

[3] Peter Häberle, '"The Open Society of Constitutional Interpreters" – A Contribution to a Pluralistic and "Procedural" Constitutional Interpretation (1975)' in Markus Kotzur (ed), *Peter Häberle on Constitutional Theory* (Nomos/Hart 2018) 165.

[4] Stephen D Krasner, *Sovereignty: Organized Hypocrisy* (Princeton University Press 1999) 3–4.

[5] Eric Allen Engle, 'The Transformation of the International Legal System: The Post-Westphalian Legal Order' (2004) 23 Quinnipiac Law Review 25.

the scope of areas exclusively reserved for states.[6] However, even with the recognition of individuals' rights (in the form of human rights) and duties (international criminal law) to some extent, IL is still focused on states.[7]

Today, IL is shaped both by unifying globalisation and increasing fragmentation.[8] Traditional concepts of nation-states as the sole dominators of IL seem outdated and no longer capable of addressing global challenges such as climate change, terrorism, cybercrime or corruption, which threaten not one nation but many or all of them.[9] Some factors limiting state sovereignty include the universalistic human rights doctrines and globalisation, including global catastrophes, that permeate domestic systems. Climate change is identified as the strongest indicator that certain problems can no longer be solved by single states.[10] Today, the protection of the environment and effective mitigation and adaptation policies are the concern of all states and citizens worldwide on the basis that climate change's adverse effects do not stop at the physical borders of sovereign states. Climate change has become a 'global affair' that threatens not only the lives and health of those living today but also of future generations.[11]

Therefore, a shift from government to governance seems necessary.[12] The UN Commission on Global Governance defined governance as 'the sum of the many ways individuals and institutions, public and private, manage their common affairs. It is a continuing process through which conflicting or diverse interests may be accommodated and co-operative action may be taken. It includes formal institutions and regimes empowered to enforce compliance, as well as informal

---

[6] Katja S Ziegler, 'Domaine Réservé', *MPEPIL* (2013).

[7] Stephen Gardbaum, 'Human Rights and International Constitutionalism' in Jeffrey L Dunoff and Joel P Trachtman (eds), *Ruling the World? Constitutionalism, International Law and Global Government* (CUP 2009) 249.

[8] Cf. ILC, 'Report of the Study Group of the International Law Commission (Finalized by Martti Koskenniemi) on "Fragmentation of International Law: Difficulties Arising from the Diversification and Expansion of International Law" (A/CN.4/L.682)' (2006) 11. This paradoxical phenomenon will be analysed in greater detail in Chapter 7.

[9] Andreas L Paulus, 'The International Legal System as a Constitution' in Jeffrey L Dunoff and Joel P Trachtman (eds), *Ruling the World? Constitutionalism, International Law, and Global Governance* (CUP 2009) 95.

[10] Antonio Cassese, 'Gathering Up the Main Threads' in Antonio Cassese (ed), *Realizing Utopia: The Future of International Law* (OUP 2012) 653–4.

[11] Charlotte Streck, 'Innovativeness and Paralysis in International Climate Policy' (2012) 1 Transnational Environmental Law 137, 138.

[12] Sol Picciotto, 'Constitutionalizing Multilevel Governance?' (2008) 6 International Journal of Constitutional Law 457, 457.

arrangements that people and institutions either have agreed to or perceive to be in their interest.'[13]

Global governance embraces the whole array of governance *by*, *with* and *without* government.[14] Governance *by* governments describes the hierarchic implementation and enforcement of national rules. Due to the absence of a world state, global governance by government is not an option. Instead, governance *with* governments depicts how national governments coordinate and harmonise their policies to cope with transnational problems.[15] The emergence of international treaties and organisations such as the UN, World Trade Organisation (WTO) or International Labour Organisation (ILO) is an expression in this sense.[16] Governance *without* governments describes transnational governing of certain areas by social groupings, such as the domain name allocation system overseen by the Internet Corporation for Assigned Names and Numbers (ICANN).[17] Private–public partnerships are a mixed form that can fall under this category when states do not enjoy a privileged status in such a regime (e.g., the World Commission on Dams).[18] Rules, structures and processes in global governance seeking to regulate certain areas of activity or achieve a particular objective can be either formal or informal.[19] 'Global governance embodies both a pluralism of systems, sources, and norms, as well as a pluralism of interpretive institutions'[20] and has moved

[13] Commission on Global Governance, 'Our Global Neighbourhood' (OUP 1995) 2.

[14] Bernhard Zangl and Michael Zürn, 'Make Law, Not War: Internationale und transnationale Verrechtlichung als Baustein für Global Governance' in Michael Zürn and Bernhard Zangl (eds), *Verrechtlichung—Baustein für Global Governance?* (Stiftung Entwicklung und Frieden 2004) 14–15. Zangl and Zürn define 'Global governance = Governance by + Governance with + Governance without Government' (at 15).

[15] Ibid 14.

[16] Ibid 15.

[17] Ibid.

[18] Ibid. On the other side, Karen Johnston, 'Public Governance: The Government of Non-State Actors in "Partnerships"' (2015) 35 Public Money and Management 15, points out that the state's authoritative role creates asymmetries in governance networks, making the concept of equal partnerships at least questionable.

[19] David Armstrong and Julie Gilson, 'Introduction: Civil Society and International Governance' in David Armstrong and others (eds), *Civil Society and International Governance. The Role of Non-State Actors in Global and Regional Regulatory Frameworks* (Routledge 2011) 1.

[20] Daniel Halberstam, 'Constitutional Heterarchy: The Centrality of Conflict in the European Union and the United States' in Jeffrey L Dunoff and Joel P Trachtman (eds), *Ruling the World? Constitutionalism, International Law, and Global Governance* (CUP 2011) 355.

beyond the nation-state.[21] According to Brown Weiss, the international community is becoming 'a kaleidoscopic world' that has to face increased integration and fragmentation, the involvement of millions of new actors, fast communication and quick changes.[22] While states and international organisations (IOs) remain important players, the international system itself is likely to become less hierarchical, and it faces an explosion of bottom-up initiatives and empowerment by non-state actors.[23] Global governance involves not only intergovernmental relationships but also non-state actors and members of civil society, for example, NGOs, transnational corporations, local and indigenous communities, and individuals.[24] Through new technologies, especially the internet and social media, individuals and NGOs all over the globe are brought together. The result are emerging global ad hoc networks of activists focusing on quickly and effectively changing policies.[25] New 'bottom-up empowerment' leads to 'voluntary commitments' to pursue shared objectives or goals. Soft law serves as a blueprint for civil society to take action and perform functions that, before, belonged exclusively to states.[26]

The importance of the inclusion of non-state actors into global governance becomes particularly clear in relation to the climate change regime. For some scholars, the gap between what countries promise to do and the reduction needed to stay under the 2°C target can only be 'wedged' by the proliferation of initiatives outside the UNFCCC regime.[27]

In this sense, four central elements of climate change governance outside the UNFCCC regime can be identified: 1) it is multi-level and 2) multi-actor, which means that horizontal, vertical and diagonal relationships between both public and private institutions in different countries and across borders including multilateral institutions, states, subnational actors and non-governmental actors, exist, 3) it

---

21 Anne Peters, 'Are We Moving towards Constitutionalization of the World Community?' in Antonio Cassese (ed), *Realizing Utopia: The Future of International Law* (OUP 2012) 119.

22 Edith Brown Weiss, 'Nature and the Law: The Global Commons and the Common Concern of Humankind' [2014] Sustainable Humanity, Sustainable Nature: Our Responsibility. Pontifical Academy of Sciences, Extra Series 41 1, 8.

23 Ibid.

24 Commission on Global Governance (n 13) 3.

25 Edith Brown Weiss, 'International Law in a Kaleidoscopic World' (2011) 1 Asian Journal of International Law 21, 23.

26 Brown Weiss, 'Nature and the Law: The Global Commons and the Common Concern of Humankind' (n 22) 14.

27 Daniel Bodansky, Jutta Brunnée and Lavanya Rajamani, *International Climate Change Law* (OUP 2017) 259.

involves different degrees of legalisation—from 'hard law' (e.g., the norms in the Montreal Protocol on Substances that Deplete the Ozone Layer) to 'soft law' (e.g., the 'Gold standard' for carbon credits and the 'Carbon Neutral protocol') and 4) it is polycentric, in that there is no central, organising authority.[28]

Indeed, today, it is observable that climate change governance is not only exercised by nation-states, supranational and subnational institutions but also by businesses (e.g., mechanisms such as the Verified Carbon Standard developed by the World Business Council for Sustainable Development, the International Emissions Trading Association and others) and environmental groups or other organisations of civil society (e.g., the Gold Standard). A multitude of partnerships and collaborations are thinkable: businesses can collaborate with governmental actors (through the International Organisation for Standardization GHG accounting standard), and so can civil society organisations. Through initiatives such as the Carbon Disclosure Project, civil society organisations cooperate with businesses. And all of them can act together in larger projects such as protecting forests through the voluntary climate change mitigation framework Reduction in Emissions from Deforestation and Forest Degradation (REDD +).[29]

These developments point towards an (emerging) multi-level system of climate governance.[30] In this context, questions arise not only on the matter of how to regulate global governance but also on the quantity and quality of actors. Kennedy argued that little is known about how global civil society works (if there is one) or how public power is exercised in a global legal order.[31] There is no equivalent to the domestic constitution on the international plane. However, legal scholars seek to provide answers to these pressing issues by resorting to a concept they are familiar with: constitutionalism.[32]

---

[28] Ibid 259–60; on polycentrism as a strategy for coping with climate change, see Elinor Ostrom, 'A Polycentric Approach for Coping with Climate Change' [2009] The World Bank—Policy Research Working Paper 5095.

[29] Bodansky, Brunnée and Rajamani (n 27) 264–5.

[30] See, for example, Jacqueline Peel, Lee Godden and Rodney J Keenan, 'Climate Change Law in an Era of Multi-Level Governance' (2012) 1 Transnational Environmental Law 245; Joanne Scott, 'The Multi-Level Governance of Climate Change' (2011) 5 Carbon & Climate Law Review 25.

[31] David Kennedy, 'The Mystery of Global Governance' in Jeffrey L Dunoff and Joel P Trachtman (eds), *Ruling the World? Constitutionalism, International Law, and Global Governance* (CUP 2009) 38.

[32] Ibid 38. Not only lawyers, but also scholars of other fields, including social sciences, economics, political science, and anthropology are looking for visions of how to shape and govern global governance.

3.2 A Global Constitutional Order: Constitution, Constitutionalisation and Constitutionalism

Constitutionalism has become one of the most important ways of rethinking IL. Before analysing the role constitutionalism will play in environmental protection, its general features will be outlined. This is important because constitutionalist approaches are not only meant to reduce state sovereignty but also offer a different place and a more active role for non-state actors within the international legal system. However, 'constitution', 'constitutionalisation' and 'constitutionalism' are often used interchangeably, and although the terms overlap, they mean different things. Therefore, it is important to clarify each of these concepts before turning to global environmental/climate constitutionalism.

3.2.1 Constitution

A constitution is traditionally associated with nation-states.[33] Its basic aim is to keep politics in check[34]:

> What is a constitution all about? It is all about legitimacy. All public powers being exercised have to be *legitimized*, *limited*, and *controlled*. Legitimization, limitation and control of public powers are, since the very beginnings of modern constitutionalism, the *essential functions* of a constitution.[35]

However, this does not answer the question of what distinguishes a constitution as a system of norms from other ordinary law. Why does the constitution sit at the top of the norm hierarchy? What makes it such a powerful tool that international lawyers seek to 'copy' it to the international level? A 'plus'—a criterion that distinguishes it from ordinary law—is needed. This 'plus' could be either a

[33] Peters, 'Compensatory Constitutionalism: The Function and Potential of Fundamental International Norms and Structures' (n 1) 581.

[34] Antje Wiener and others, 'Global Constitutionalism: Human Rights, Democracy and the Rule of Law' (2012) 1 Global Constitutionalism 1, 4.

[35] Markus Kotzur, 'Overcoming Dichotomies: A Functional Approach to the Constitutional Paradigm in Public International Law' (2012) 4 Goettingen Journal of International Law 585, 587 (citations omitted, emphasis in original).

formalistic (in terms of certain formal characteristics) or a substantive element, that is, the characteristics of its content.[36]

In a purely formalistic sense, the reason for its position at the top of the norm hierarchy is its supremacy over all other laws and the difficulty of altering its norms.[37] These characteristics make it the 'fundamental and paramount law of the nation'.[38] A constitution may be a single written document, but this is by no means a requirement, as the constitutions of the UK and New Zealand demonstrate. It is nothing other than 'the greater formal force of law' that distinguishes a constitution from ordinary law.[39] More substantively, the content has to be of a certain quality. In earlier times, a constitution was understood to include regulations on the power relationship between the state and its citizens; modern understandings emphasise the push-back of state power and a commitment to certain democratic and rule-of-law regulations. These find their expression in principles and, particularly, in (human) rights.[40] Importantly, modern (Western) constitutions are unthinkable without the linkage to democracy: the demos as the *pouvoir constituent* that authorises state power.[41]

However, neither a purely formalistic nor a purely substantive concept could explain the constitution's supremacy. Gerber noted in 1880 that its position on top of the legal hierarchy was only to be justified because of the constitution's contents (to limit state power).[42] The substantive approach does not define the constitution's scope; central regulations that organise the state may be found outside the constitutional document, but only those norms established in the document would fall under the supremacy of the constitution.[43] This would miss the

[36] Uwe Volkmann, *Grundzüge einer Verfassungslehre für die Bundesrepublik Deutschland* (Mohr Siebeck 2013) 11–5.

[37] Ibid 12. In Germany, for example, Article 79 para. 3 of the German Basic Law (the so-called eternity clause) prohibits the modification of Article 1 (human dignity) and Article 20 (inter alia, Rechtsstaat [rule of law], separation of powers, democracy).

[38] U.S. Supreme Court, *Marbury v. Madison, 5 U.S.*, (1803) 137, at 176.

[39] Walter Jellinek, *Allgemeine Staatslehre* (O Härig 1914) 534: 'Das wesentliche rechtliche Merkmal von Verfassungstexten liegt ausschließlich in ihrer erhöhten formellen Gesetzeskraft'.

[40] Volkmann (n 36) 13.

[41] Matthias Kumm, 'The Cosmopolitan Turn in Constitutionalism: On the Relationship between Constitutionalism in and beyond the State' in Jeffrey L Dunoff and Joel P Trachtman (eds), *Ruling the World? Constitutionalism, International Law and Global Government* (CUP 2009) 265.

[42] Carl Friederich von Gerber, *Grundzüge Des Deutschen Staatsrechts* (B Tauchnitz 1880) 7–8.

[43] Volkmann (n 36) 14.

point that a 'constitution outside the constitution' exists that (in the case of the US) includes not only the canonical document but also several statutes, regulatory materials, federal common-law rules and established practices.[44] Only a synopsis of both formal and substantive characteristics can grasp the modern concept of a constitution.[45]

Besides formal and material constitutions, different stages of the 'rise of the constitution' can be identified. It has become the normative basic layer of the legal system. Moreover, in today's conception, the constitution not only constitutes the state but has also become the citizen's and society's constitution by reflecting and embodying a nation's identity.[46] This also includes its claim to be a 'just' order embodying the 'good' and 'right'. A constitution is the sum of the basic legal norms that regulate the social and political life of a polity comprehensively.[47] It is legitimised because it is attributable to the people who govern themselves through the constitution, as 'We the people'.[48] As such, the people are not only the addressees of the laws but also its authors, whose wishes have to be respected[49]:

> Constitutions relate to a set of cultural and social conditions within specific contexts, and they represent an agreement (written or not) among representatives of the governed within a community to make sure that the governors proceed according to the wishes of the former.[50]

It is not a ready-made tool but a living instrument. A constitution is an unfinished project, or as Häberle describes it: 'constitution as a public process'.[51] As such,

---

[44] Ernest A Young, 'The Constitution Outside the Constitution' (2007) 117 Yale Law Journal 408.

[45] Volkmann (n 36) 14–5.

[46] On this, see Section 4.4.

[47] Peters, 'Compensatory Constitutionalism: The Function and Potential of Fundamental International Norms and Structures' (n 1) 581.

[48] Kumm (n 41) 260.

[49] Jürgen Habermas, *Between Facts and Norms: Contributions to a Discourse Theory of Law and Democracy* (Polity Press 1996) 120.

[50] Antje Wiener, *The Invisible Constitution of Politics: Contested Norms and International Encounters* (CUP 2008) 21.

[51] Uwe Volkmann, 'Der Aufstieg der Verfassung: Beobachtungen zum grundlegenden Wandel des Verfassungsbegriffs' in Thomas Vesting and Stefan Korioth (eds), *Der Eigenwert des Verfassungsrechts* (Mohr Siebeck 2011) 29–37; see Häberle's essay collection published under the same name: Peter Häberle, *Verfassung als öffentlicher Prozess. Materialien zu einer Verfassungsheorie der offenen Gesellschaft* (3rd edn, Duncker & Humblot 1998).

it depends on the impulses of the open constitutional community to flourish and remain important. This is because a constitution serves as the mirror of a society that shapes its identity and perceptions of self by laying down its basic values in the most important legal text in a nation-state.[52]

A constitution without the nation-state is hardly imaginable for many German scholars.[53] For Kirchhof, for example, 'where there is no state, there is no constitution, and where there is no state's people (*Staatsvolk*), there is no state'.[54] A constitution will usually identify what it is constitutive of—its political community. It lays down provisions about who is included, who is not and on what basis.[55] A state, understood in this sense, is something else or something more than the product of the constitution; it is its premise. A constitution cannot exist without the state and the people that created it.[56] However, state and constitution can also be seen as concepts that are separate from each other. As such, the concept of constitution is not limited to the state. Kant laid the cornerstone for this concept through his idea of a cosmopolitan world order. For Kant, the ideal world order is a cosmopolitical one, where everyone is a fellow world citizen. He believed that 'all men, who have a mutual influence over one another, ought to have a civil constitution',[57] and that there are three constitutions that address different objects:

> Now every legitimate constitution, considered in respect of the persons who are object of it, is I. either conformable to the civil right, and is limited to the people (*jus civitatis*). II. Or to the rights of the nations, and regulates the relations of nations among each other (*jus gentium*). III. Or to the cosmopolitical right, as far as men, or states, are considered as influencing one another, in quality of constituent parts of

---

[52] This point will be analysed in more detail in Section 4.4.

[53] Anne van Aaken, 'Defragmentation of Public International Law Through Interpretation: A Methodological Proposal' (2009) 16 Indiana Journal of Global Legal Studies 483, 487. This becomes clear when taking a closer look at German terms such as Verfassungsstaat, Rechtsstaat, or Staatsvolk.

[54] Paul Kirchhof, 'Kompetenzaufteilung zwischen den Mitgliedstaaten der EU' in Vertretung der Europäischen Kommission in der Bundesrepublik Deutschland (ed), *Europäische Gespräche 2/94. Europäisches Forum: Die künftige Verfassungsordnung der Europäischen Union* (1994) 59.

[55] Jan Klabbers, 'Setting the Scene' in Jan Klabbers, Anne Peters and Geir Ulfstein (eds), *The Constitutionalization of International Law* (OUP 2009) 9.

[56] Thomas Kleinlein, *Konstitutionalisierung im Völkerrecht* (Springer 2012) 123.

[57] Immanuel Kant, *Project for a Perpetual Peace: A Philosophical Essay. Translated from the German* (Vernor & Hood 1796) 13.

> the great state of the human race (*jus cosmopoliticum*). This division is not arbitrary; but necessary in respect of the idea of a perpetual peace.[58]

The idea of a '*peaceable*, though not yet friendly, thorough intercourse of all nations upon earth'[59] is not only a philanthropic but a juridical principle. The *jus cosmopoliticum* is the logical consequence of a community that shares the same ground, not in a legal sense (as in owning the ground) but in 'a thorough relation of the one to all the others, *to offer to traffic or trade*, with one another, and have a right to make a trial of it, without the foreigner's being entitled on that account to treat him as an enemy.'[60]

However, since states assumingly will not be willing to subordinate themselves to such a legal order, a surrogate in the form of a league of nations (*Völkerbund*) would mark a necessary intermediate step on the way to achieving the *jus cosmpoliticum.*[61] Moreover, Kant feared that a sole monopolist of power in a world republic could level the differences between peoples and that religions and languages could 'melt together' and create a 'universal monarchy'. A league of nations should prevent such 'soulless despotism'.[62] Thus, he already saw the potential for constitutionalism beyond the state but, due to the time of writing, could not yet imagine how to safeguard the plurality of cultures. However, Kant's fear of levelling out cultural differences in highly complex societies is unfounded, as the existence of federal states such as the USA or Germany demonstrates.[63]

Accordingly, the state is not the prerequisite, but the opposite: there can be only as much state as the constitution itself creates.[64] The constitution is 'the basic legal order of state *and* society; it is not only a restriction of state power, and it is an authorization to *state* power. It encompasses both the state *and* the society'.[65] Neither the political claim to authority nor the sense of identity (the

---

[58] Ibid 13–4.

[59] Immanuel Kant, *The Metaphysic of Morals, Vol. I* (1799) 128 (emphasis in original).

[60] Ibid (emphasis in original).

[61] Kant (n 57) 21ff, 24ff; Jürgen Habermas, 'A Political Constitution for the Pluralist World Society?' in Jürgen Habermas (ed), *Between Naturalism and Religion: Philosophical Essays* (Polity Press 2008) 314.

[62] Jürgen Habermas, 'Hat die Konstitutionalisierung des Völkerrechts noch eine Chance?' in Jürgen Habermas (ed), *Der gespaltene Westen* (Suhrkamp 2004) 127.

[63] Ibid.

[64] Peter Häberle, *Verfassungslehre als Kulturwissenschaft* (2nd edn, Duncker & Humblot 1998) 620.

[65] Peter Häberle, 'Verfassungsgerichtsbarkeit in der offenen Gesellschaft' in Robert Chr van Ooyen and Martin HW Möllers (eds), *Handbuch Bundesverfassungsgericht im politischen*

community dimension of a constitution)—both characteristic of a constitution—are exclusively bound to the idea of modern nation-states.[66] Thus, a constitution is not dependent on the existence of a state:

> The term 'constitution' has never been exclusively reserved for state constitutions. Today, the notional link between constitution and state has further been loosened in everyday language and in the legal discourse (and thereby the meaning of 'constitution' may have been broadened). It is therefore not *per definitionem* impossible to conceptualize constitutional law beyond the nation or the state. Global constitutionalism advocates non-state constitutional law, and tends to demystify the state and the state constitution.[67]

This is the basic idea that underlies the phenomenon of global constitutionalism. An international constitution, at least in a formalistic way, does not exist (yet). However, legal scholarship seeks to identify constitutional norms and structures at the global level. The methods employed to transfer key elements and/or legal theories about the nature and scope of (domestic) constitutions are comparative constitutional law[68] and a constitutionalist reading of IL.[69] Such attempts generally fall under the categories of constitutionalism and constitutionalisation.

3.2.2 Global Constitutionalism and Constitutionalisation

The definition and scope of the concepts of 'constitutionalism' and 'constitutionalisation' are vaguer than 'constitution'. Complicating the matter is that the terms are not used uniformly.[70] Some concepts or definitions are descriptive and claim that a global constitution already exists (by relying on a set of norms and principles that resemble a global constitution), and others are normative and suggest that some norms, principles or documents (e.g., the UN Charter) could or should

---

System (2nd edn, Springer VS 2015) 39. German: 'Verfassung " ist rechtliche Grundordnung von Staat und Gesellschaft; sie ist nicht nur Beschränkung staatlicher Macht und sie ist Ermächtigung zu staatlicher Macht. Sie umgreift Staat *und* Gesellschaft' (emphasis in the German original).

66 Neil Walker, 'The Idea of Constitutional Pluralism' (2002) 65 Modern Law Review 317, 341.

67 Anne Peters, 'The Constitutionalist Reconstruction of International Law: Pro and Cons' (2006) 1 NCCR Trade working papers 1, 5.

68 Kennedy (n 31) 38.

69 Paulus (n 9) 71.

70 Aoife O'Donoghue, *Constitutionalism in Global Constitutionalisation* (CUP 2014) 136.

become a global constitution in the future.[71] Accordingly, the latter also describes constitutionalisation as the process that may lead to a global constitution.[72]

Here, constitutionalisation means the 'mapping' of various processes of global constitutionalism beyond the state. It seeks to identify and explain the process of the changing nature of IL without making a normative claim towards stronger constitutionalist activism. Constitutionalism, conversely, is the 'shaping' and/or improving of the actual process of constitutionalism through normative encouragement, for example, in the form of concrete proposals for political and legal innovation.[73] Thus, constitutionalism takes on a more active role. It is 'a process of the incorporation of constitutional norms, values, processes or principles, which leads to a deepening of international law, if not to a constitutional structure on a global level'.[74]

3.2.2.1 Constitutionalisation

In its most basic form, global constitutionalisation means the empirical growth of the number of international laws, global legal regimes and the growing impact of international organisations. Between 1848 and 1945, there was a total of 12 000 international treaties, whereas, in the 50 years between 1945 and 1995, the number grew to 55 000.[75] The reference to the growing number of agreements may indicate constitutionalisation. However, Klabbers correctly points out that this growth would better be labelled 'legalisation', as this process is perfectly compatible with a Westphalian, non-constitutional order of IL.[76] Thus, more often, constitutionalisation describes the emergence of a *constitutional* order in an already existing legal order.[77] One or several legal texts can become constitutional to a stronger or lesser degree. Such texts can be called 'constitution-in-the-making'.[78] Different from legalisation, which describes the creation of legal

---

[71] Christine EJ Schwöbel, *Global Constitutionalism in International Legal Perspective* (Martinus Nijhoff Publishers 2011) 12.

[72] Ibid.

[73] Garett Wallace Brown, 'The Constitutionalization of What?' (2012) 1 Global Constitutionalism 201, 227.

[74] Clemens Mattheis, *Die Konstitutionalisierung des Völkerrechts aus systemtheoretischer Sichtweise* (Springer 2018) 147 (tr the author). Note that Mattheis uses the terms constitutionalisation and constitutionalism in the opposite way to Brown.

[75] Brown (n 73) 203.

[76] Klabbers (n 55) 8.

[77] Peters, 'Compensatory Constitutionalism: The Function and Potential of Fundamental International Norms and Structures' (n 1) 582.

[78] Ibid.

regimes with binding force, constitutionalisation also involves social (as well as legal) practices that establish (law-like) rules, institutions and understandings for a particular community.[79] At the global level, it seeks to identify constitution-like elements and explain their emergence and creation and how they influence the development of IL.[80] It enables global law to become a 'good' legal order in the form of a recognised structure of legitimacy, as in the EU, since democracy is one of the principles that is constantly evolving and becoming ever more important.[81]

Furthermore, 'constitutionalisation' is used to describe the increased interconnectedness at the global level. Constitutionalisation is seen as a possible response to the negative effects of globalisation, such as climate change, increased nuclear proliferation, global economic crises and pandemics.[82] The incapability of governments to regulate these problems both at the domestic and global levels results from a lack of unified authority and institutional accountability.[83] Constitutionalisation could be the response that creates a compliance pull and 'generate[s] a more appropriate response to collective concerns of global crisis'.[84] Loughlin, therefore, describes constitutionalisation as 'the attempt to subject all governmental action within a designated field to the structures, processes, principles and values of a "constitution"'.[85]

The decreasing *domaine resérvé* of the state, for example, through the emergence of *jus cogens* and *erga omnes* norms, is interpreted by some scholars as an emancipation of IL from the all-dominating will of the states and another sign that constitutionalisation is already occurring. The increased emphasis on common (environmental) values and interests fosters this development.[86]

---

[79] Antje Wiener, 'Editorial: Evolving Norms of Constitutionalism' (2003) 9 European Law Journal 1, 5.

[80] Peters, 'Compensatory Constitutionalism: The Function and Potential of Fundamental International Norms and Structures' (n 1) 582.

[81] O'Donoghue (n 70) 136; Erika De Wet, 'The International Constitutional Order' (2006) 55 International and Comparative Law Quaterly 51, 63.

[82] Brown (n 73) 204; specifically on COVID-19, see Ezel Buse Sönmezocak, 'The Case for Global Constitutionalism in Pandemic Times' (*Völkerrechtsblog*, 6 June 2020) < https://voelkerrechtsblog.org/the-case-for-global-constitutionalism-in-pandemic-times/ > accessed 31 August 2023.

[83] Brown (n 73) 204.

[84] Ibid.

[85] Martin Loughlin, 'What Is Constitutionalisation?' in Petra Dobner and Martin Loughlin (eds), *The Twilight of Constitutionalism?* (OUP 2010) 47.

[86] Martin Scheyli, 'Der Schutz des Klimas als Prüfstein völkerrechtlicher Konstitutionalisierung?' (2002) 40 Archiv des Völkerrechts 273, 277–8.

3.2.2.2 Global Constitutionalism

Global constitutionalism is an umbrella term encompassing different theories that deal with constitutionalisation beyond the nation-state.[87] These different understandings all hold that constitutionalism is the 'basic understanding of the common good, some sense of a law as a shared project for a reasonably clearly defined [...] objective'.[88]

Global constitutionalism as a scholarly discourse is concerned with diagnosing and/or claiming that the norms and institutions of global governance follow and respect principles of constitutionalism, such as the rule of law, the separation of powers, fundamental rights protection, democracy and solidarity.[89] Modern constitutionalism requires imposing limits on the powers of government.[90] From this perspective, even where states do not consent, they should be bound by global constitutional law and especially comply with their human rights obligations.[91]

Many scholars have come forward with their own ideas of constitutionalism beyond the nation-state. Habermas, for example, proposes a concept of global governance without a world government. Global governance would contain three arenas and three kinds of collective actors. This is different to the Westphalian system of IL, which is composed of one single actor—the nation-states—and two fields—domestic internal affairs and foreign policy or international relations.[92]

The first arena is supranational and dominated by one single world organisation, which would take on the form of a reformed and stronger UN and focus on its two core responsibilities: securing peace and the protection of human rights. Opinion and will formation of this world organisation would have to be backed up not only by the opinions of NGOs and representatives of the global public but also of states, who remain core actors.[93] Political questions such as the balancing

---

[87] Aydin Atilgan, *Global Constitutionalism* (Springer 2018) 71.

[88] Martti Koskenniemi, *The Politics of International Law* (Hart Publishing 2011) 346.

[89] Anne Peters, 'Global Constitutionalism' in Michael Gibbons (ed), *The Encyclopedia of Political Thought* (John Wiley & Sons 2015) 1; Anne Peters, 'Research Concept: Global Constitutionalism and Global Governance' (*Max Planck Institut für ausländisches Öffentliches Recht und Völkerrecht*) < https://www.mpil.de/de/pub/forschung/nach-rechtsgebieten/voelkerrecht/global-constitutionalism.cfm > accessed 31 August 2023.

[90] Michel Rosenfeld, 'Modern Constitutionalism as Interplay Between Identity and Diversity' in Michel Rosenfeld (ed), *Constitutionalism, Identity, Difference, and Legitimacy: Theoretical Perspectives* (Duke University Press 1994) 3.

[91] Koji Teraya, 'Emerging Hierarchy in International Human Rights and Beyond: From the Perspective of Non-Derogable Rights' (2001) 12 European Journal of International Law 917.

[92] Habermas, 'A Political Constitution for the Pluralist World Society?' (n 61) 322.

[93] Ibid 322–3.

of economic against environmental interests will call for regulation and positive integration, which would then—in the second, intermediate arena—be addressed by regional or continental regimes that are equipped with a representative mandate to negotiate and implement binding regulations for whole continents.[94] These intermediate players would need to form shifting coalitions to produce a flexible system of checks and balances.[95] The third level is composed of nation-states that would need to cooperate in regional alliances, such as the EU, to become (or stay) important actors for global domestic politics at the transnational level.[96] Due to expected cultural differences, for example, through the political instrumentalisation of major religions, states would need to learn how to change their behaviour by overcoming stubborn 'nationalism' mindsets and their self-image. Instead, they would not only need to see themselves as peaceful members of a constitutionalised world society but also as strong players in international organisations to avoid a 'clash of civilizations'.[97] Here, one aspect becomes visible that has already been mentioned and will constantly influence this work: global constitutionalism is not bound to the existence of a world state. Rather, it is multi-levelled and polyarchic.

It is not until recently that constitutionalism has been used exclusively in national settings to identify the quality of a nation-state's constitution. With a shifting focus from states to the global realm, constitutionalism has regained importance.[98] As in the eighteenth century, constitutionalism today refers to society and not to the state (which is separated from society).[99] This is mostly the consequence of realising that international instruments such as the UN Charter were not capable of regulating the 'untamed side' of sovereignty in a way that would overcome the dependence on unpredictable states.[100]

Global constitutionalism is essentially perceived as one response to the shift from government to governance on the international plane that goes along with

---

[94] Ibid 324.

[95] Ibid 325.

[96] Ibid 325–6.

[97] Ibid 326–7; The term 'clash of civilizations' was coined by Samuel P Huntington, 'The Clash of Civilizations?' (1993) 72 Foreign Affairs 22, passim.

[98] Cf. Loughlin (n 85).

[99] Hauke Brunkhorst, 'Die Legitimationskrise der Weltgesellschaft. Global Rule of Law, Global Constitutionalism und Weltstaatlichkeit' in Mathias Albert and Rudolf Stichweh (eds), *Weltstaat und Weltstaatlichkeit* (VS Verlag für Sozialwissenschaften 2007) 64.

[100] Bardo Fassbender, 'Sovereignty and Constitutionalism in International Law' in Neil Walker (ed), *Sovereignty in Transition* (Hart 2003) 142.

legitimacy and efficiency concerns.[101] It aspires to regulate social life on all levels of governance in a comprehensive way.[102] Moreover, Peters ascribes a compensatory function to it. Constitutionalism compensates for hollowed-out constitutions, given that many tasks that belonged to the tasks of the state, such as guaranteeing security, freedom and equality, have been transferred to 'higher' levels of governance and became dysfunctional or empty at the national level.[103] Beyond the nation-state, constitutionalism, thus, seeks to restrain the free will of states at the international level in the conduct of their relations and at the national level in designing their domestic constitutional orders. Constitutionalism strengthens the autonomy of IL and limits the traditional *domaine réservé* of states.[104]

With the shift of IL from the 'law of nations' to 'transnational law',[105] the common good of the world community and the well-being of the individual are becoming ever more important; additionally, the ideas of interdependency, shared responsibility and solidarity are expressed in many international provisions, both in rules and international environmental principles.[106] Thus, the 'international legal order is in the process of shifting from an order based on 'Westphalian sovereignty' (conceived as carte blanche for national governments to organize their domestic legal and political structures without any authoritative external interference) to a 'hybrid' or 'dualistic' world order, based on (modified) state sovereignty *and* the autonomy or self-determination of the individual.'[107]

Where IL is undergoing a process of constitutionalisation, global constitutionalism seeks 'to improve the effectiveness and the fairness of the international legal

[101] Eva Kassoti, 'The Constitutionalization of International Law and the Challenge of Non-State Actors' (2017) 11 ICL Journal 177, 177–8.

[102] Fassbender (n 100) 142–3.

[103] Peters, 'Global Constitutionalism' (n 89) 2; also Peters, 'Compensatory Constitutionalism: The Function and Potential of Fundamental International Norms and Structures' (n 1).

[104] Thomas Kleinlein, 'Non-State Actors from an International Constitutionalist Perspective' in Jean D'Aspremont (ed), *Participants in the International Legal System: Multiple Perspectives on Non-State Actors in International Law* (Routledge 2011) 41–2.

[105] Markus Kotzur, 'Weltrechtliche Bezüge in nationalen Verfassungstexten' (2008) 39 Rechtstheorie 191, 195 (tr the author).

[106] Kleinlein, *Konstitutionalisierung im Völkerrecht* (n 56) 8–12.

[107] Peters, 'Compensatory Constitutionalism: The Function and Potential of Fundamental International Norms and Structures' (n 1) paras 586–7 (emphasis in original).

order'[108] by giving fundamental values, including democracy and legitimacy, priority over state consent as the ultimate rule of recognition.[109] To do this, global constitutionalism puts individuals at the top. Similar to modern national constitutional law, individuals are seen as 'subjects' that have to be protected against the exercise of public power. The state is the 'object' that finds the justification for its existence in protecting the individual's rights and, therefore, is legitimised and limited by the constitution.[110] States gain sovereignty in exchange for protecting individuals from threats to their health, well-being and wealth, and for respecting and protecting their human dignity,[111] but only to the extent that they are upholding and enacting democratic law.[112] Whether an action is legitimate will not be assessed against a state's sovereignty (or power), but whether it serves to protect an individual or community interest.[113] This is the logical consequence of a conception of IL that finds its justification and objective in protecting the well-being of natural persons, along with the emergence of human rights law that elevates natural persons to subjects in IL.[114] 'Humanity is the A and Ω of sovereignty.'[115] Not only must national constitutions flow from human dignity, but, seen as a cultural-anthropological premise, even IL could find its ultimate

[108] Anne Peters, 'The Merits of Global Constitutionalism' (2009) 16 Indiana Journal of Global Legal Studies 397, 397.

[109] Kassoti (n 101) 178.

[110] Kleinlein, 'Non-State Actors from an International Constitutionalist Perspective' (n 104) 43.

[111] Cf. Christian Tomuschat, 'International Law: Ensuring the Survival of Mankind on the Eve of a New Century' in Académie de Droit International (The Hague Academy of International Law) (ed), *Recueil des Cours*, vol 281 (Martinus Nijhoff Publishers 2001) 162, who speaks of states being nothing 'more than instruments whose inherent function it is to serve the rights of their citizens as legally expressed in human rights'.

[112] David Held, *Democracy and the Global Order: From the Modern State to Cosmopolitan Governance* (Polity Press 1995) 233.

[113] Anne Peters, 'Membership in the Global Constitutional Community' in Jan Klabbers, Anne Peters and Geir Ulfstein (eds), *The Constitutionalization of International Law* (OUP 2009) 187.

[114] Anne Peters, '*Der Mensch im Mittelpunkt des Völkerrechts*', Lecture given on 27 November 2013 in the context of the farewell of Prof. Dr. Dr. h.c. Rüdiger Wolfrum as Director of the Max Planck Institute for Comparative Public Law and International Law and introduction of Prof. Dr. Anne Peters as new Director (2013) 1 < http://www.mpil.de/files/pdf3/Peters_Der_Mensch_im_Mittelpunkt_des_Voelkerrechts._Vortrag_zur_Amtseinfuehrung_als_neue_Direktorin_am_Max_Planck_Institut_fuer_Voelkerrecht_27.11.20131.pdf > accessed 31 August 2023.

[115] Anne Peters, 'Humanity as the A and Ω of Sovereignty' (2009) 20 European Journal of International Law 513.

point of accountability in human dignity.[116] In this sense, the preamble to the Universal Declaration of Human Rights (UDHR) recognises the inherent dignity and the equal and inalienable rights of all humans as the foundation of freedom, justice and peace in the world. Such an understanding could extend to future generations. The notion of 'all members of the human family' has a temporal dimension that encompasses all human beings, even those unborn, and declares equality between the generations.[117] This point is especially relevant when it comes to issues such as climate change that affect those not yet born. Thus, global constitutionalism has to focus on human beings, both born and unborn, and balance their interests against each other to strike a fair balance.

Importantly, constitutionalism does not mean that developments in IL necessarily amalgamate or result in a perfect global constitution one day.[118] Global constitutionalism should not be understood as a final destination but rather as a continuing (and nonlinear) process that is bolstered by a strong academic discourse and during which elements in the international legal order are identified or emerge, which are induced by the actions of both academic and juridical actors.[119] A 'check list approach to constitutionalization', where boxes are ticked off to describe the status of constitutionalisation, 'mistakenly suggest[s] that international constitutionalism is a binary, "all or nothing" affair', and that 'constitutionalism consists of a type – rather than a quantum – of rules'.[120] It is equally unlikely that there will ever be a single 'constitutional moment' or a single foundational document for the whole of the international community.[121] Instead, scattered legal texts and jurisprudence together can form a body of

---

[116] Peter Häberle, 'The Rationale of Constitutions from a Cultural Science Viewpoint' in Markus Kotzur (ed), *Peter Häberle on Constitutional Theory* (Nomos/Hart 2018) 255.

[117] Edith Brown Weiss, 'In Fairness To Future Generations and Sustainable Development' (1992) 8 American University International Law Review 19, 20–1.

[118] Christine EJ Schwöbel, 'Organic Global Constitutionalism' (2010) 23 Leiden Journal of International Law 529, 530. She describes the concept of Organic Global Constitutionalism as 'based on four themes: (a) constitutionalism should be regarded as an ongoing process, (b) the debate on global constitutionalism should be political and discursive, (c) a vision of global constitutionalism should be predicated on the idea of the universal as a negative or, in other words, constitutionalism as an "empty space", and (d) global constitutionalism should be viewed as a promise for the future – a future devoid of predetermined content' (539).

[119] Peters, 'The Merits of Global Constitutionalism' (n 108) 397–8.

[120] Jeffrey L Dunoff and Joel P Trachtman, 'A Functional Approach to International Constitutionalization' in Jeffrey L Dunoff and Joel P Trachtman (eds), *Ruling the World? Constitutionalism, International Law, and Global Governance* (CUP 2009) 9.

[121] Kotzur (n 35) 589.

international constitutional law within the international legal order that enjoys a particular normative status.[122]

3.2.3 Criticism

Constitutionalism is criticised from both cultural and legal points of view. Constitutionalism, it has been argued, would be to too Western- or European-oriented, which would make it even more difficult for developing states to have a serious say in the development of IL.[123] Constitutionalism would impose Western conceptions of what a constitution is on all other societies.[124] Constitutionalism that attempts to create an 'empire of uniformity' is incapable of dealing with social and cultural diversities.[125] Tully claims that, instead of accommodating diversity, modern schools of constitutionalism share a language designed to exclude or assimilate cultural diversity and justify uniformity[126]—the 'soulless despotism' that Kant feared.[127] Diversity, then, is eliminated in favour of the assertion that there is only 'the people' as the single locus of authority.[128] In this sense, 'traditional' and non-European societies are seen as being 'less developed' or at a less progressive stage than the European societies ('the primitive and "child-like" Aboriginal' compared to the 'universal European'[129]). Such a position is based on an entirely European and masculine point of view, yet it pretends to be universal.[130] The constitutional language was seen as too masculine, too European and too imperialist by radical feminists in the 1960s and 1970s and was, therefore, rejected by women's movements and replaced by mechanisms of rotating responsibilities and validating personal experience as political expressions. However, the absence of formal structures was not only found to be too demanding but also, paradoxically, made many women feel excluded and silenced. The lack

---

[122] Peters, 'Global Constitutionalism' (n 89) 2.

[123] Carol Harlow, 'Global Administrative Law: The Quest for Principles and Values' (2006) 17 The European Journal of International Law 187, 189.

[124] James Tully, *Strange Multiplicity. Constitutionalism in an Age of Diversity* (CUP 1995) 63ff.

[125] See Chapter 2 and 3 in Tully (n 124).

[126] Ibid 58.

[127] Kant (n 57) 40, here 'a despotism, which destroying the minds [...]'. The wording 'soulless despotism' was only introduced by a translation of W. Hastie in 1891.

[128] Tully (n 124) 67.

[129] Ibid 65.

[130] Ibid 65–6.

of accountability was another issue and made feminists return from the 'tyranny of the structurelessness' to constitutional frameworks.[131]

In visions of normative constitutionalism, human rights are often understood as the authoritative expression of the values of humankind. In addition to the criticism that the interpretation of human rights law is too closely oriented towards the ideals of the West and, therefore, not necessarily universal, the invisible hierarchy and preference for civil and political rights over economic, social, cultural and environmental rights also contributes to the critique of the vision that global constitutionalism is truly universal instead of being merely a Western concept.[132] The gap between the values promoted by (normative) constitutionalism and reality is another point of critique. Marx argued that the law of the state not only blurred but also consolidated the indifferences between formal legal equality—people are equal and have the same rights under the constitution as citizens—and their unequal positions in daily, material life as members of the civil society.[133] Human rights would not help to overcome this gap between the proposed equality in the law and the inequality of conditions in real life, as they precisely seek to guarantee the basis for this gap by protecting private property and, thus, consolidating inequality.[134] Marx explains:

> But liberty as a right of man is not founded upon the relations between man and man, but rather upon the separation of man from man. It is the right of such separation. The right of the *circumscribed* individual, withdrawn into himself. The practical application of the right of liberty is the right of private property.[135]

Consequently, constitutionalism would not be able to deliver on its promises, and while it would perhaps strengthen the rule of law or the separation of powers at the international level, it could not change the lives of people positively. Moreover, the people would not necessarily have a say in these developments. The strengthening of juridical review in visions of global constitutionalism has been seen as an attempt to replace democratic processes with a rigid 'legalist' constitutionalist reading that relies too heavily on overly powerful international

131 Judith Squires, 'Liberal Constitutionalism, Identity and Difference' in Richard Bellamy and Dario Castiglione (eds), *Constitutionalism in Transformation: European and Theoretical Perspectives* (Blackwell Publishers 1996) 212f.

132 Schwöbel (n 71) 118.

133 Karl Marx, 'On the Jewish Question (1843)' in Robert Tucker (ed), *The Marx-Engels Reader* (Norton & Company 1978) 33f (emphasis in original).

134 Ibid 42.

135 Ibid.

courts composed of non-representative judges instead of a democratic process that alone can legitimise constitutionalism.[136] This phenomenon has been labelled the 'judicialization of politics'[137] Some critics argue that of the two sides of constitutionalism—legalism and democracy—the latter has often been neglected.[138] Furthermore, the underlying historical focus on the state as the main actor in frameworks of constitutionalism would continue to neglect the role of non-state actors in the development of global constitutionalism and their influence on formerly exclusively public affairs.[139] Even where theories of global constitutionalism strive towards post-state frameworks, the Eurocentric core of constitutionalism, including its seventeenth-century assertions of sovereignty, remains prescient; its imperialist roots are still in place.[140]

Despite these criticisms, many scholars agree that instead of abolishing the idea of global constitutionalism, it should be adjusted to modern realities. Tully, for example, finds that 'the composite, contemporary language of constitutional thought and practice need not be either blindly defended against any claim to cultural recognition or blindly rejected for its male, imperial and Eurocentric bias. Rather, it can be amended and reconceived to do justice to demands for cultural recognition.'[141]

The constitutionalist language has not only been used by imperialists but also by anti-imperial movements and minorities to have their interests included in current and prevailing versions of constitutionalism. Thus, constitutionalist language has not only proven to be stable but also flexible and adjustable and, therefore, can accommodate diversity under constitutionalist frameworks. Cultural recognition allows for 'negotiation and mediation of claims to recognition in a dialogue governed by the conventions of mutual recognition, continuity and consent'.[142]

---

[136] Richard Bellamy, *Political Constitutionalism: A Republican Defence of the Constitutionality of Democracy* (CUP 2007) 4.

[137] David Boyd, *The Environmental Rights Revolution: A Global Study of Constitutions, Human Rights, and the Environment* (UBC Press 2011) 5.

[138] See, for example, Petra Dobner, 'More Law, Less Democracy? Democracy and Transnational Constitutionalism' in Petra Dobner and Martin Loughlin (eds), *The Twilight of Constitutionalism?* (OUP 2010); Anne Peters, 'Dual Democracy' in Jan Klabbers, Anne Peters and Geir Ulfstein (eds), *The Constitutionalization of International Law* (OUP 2009); 408–09 Peters, 'The Merits of Global Constitutionalism' (n 108); Schwöbel (n 71) 150.

[139] See Boyd (n 137) 6.

[140] O'Donoghue (n 70) 220, 241.

[141] Tully (n 124) 31.

[142] Ibid 209.

Given this adjustability—and the experiences from the radical feminist movement—Schwöbel argues that the language of constitutionalism has the advantage that it 'is a language that all may be comfortable with as a language of struggles for recognition in the public sphere'.[143] Though constitutionalism was developed in Europe originally to limit the domination of humans over other humans, current visions of modern constitutionalism do not want to create a global, centralised world state after the 'role model' of Western states but rather seek to constitutionalise global, polyarchic and multi-level governance.[144] For the dialogue on global constitutionalism to truly become global, however, it is necessary to strongly include African, Asian and Latin American perspectives on global constitutionalism. Frameworks of global constitutionalism often come with colonial legacies, both as beneficiaries and as vehicles of colonialism, where the modern Western constitutional order and the rule of law went together with colonial political power to justify its prevalence both historically and today. The way global constitutionalism is practised and studied, therefore, needs to be decolonised[145] and the dialogue enriched with non-Western perspectives on global constitutionalism.[146] Walker, thus, summarises the critique as following:

> that constitutionalism remains too state-centered, overstates its capacity to shape political community, exhibits an inherent normative bias against social developments associated with the politics of difference, provides a language easily susceptible to ideological manipulation and, that, consequent upon these challenges, it increasingly represents a fractured and debased conceptual currency.[147]

Therefore, he argues for a model of constitutional pluralism that does not seek to establish a hierarchy but rather a heterarchy. Theories of constitutional pluralism and societal constitutionalism seek to understand the role of non-state actors in constitution-making and find answers beyond the state to these questions.[148] However, the need for democratic legitimacy is and continues to be a challenge

---

[143] Schwöbel (n 71) 150–1.

[144] Peters, 'The Merits of Global Constitutionalism' (n 108) 404.

[145] Jonathan Havercroft and others, 'Decolonising Global Constitutionalism' (2020) 9 Global Constitutionalism 1, 4.

[146] See, for example, the symposium on global constitutionalism in Asia and the Pacific: Ngoc Son Bui, 'Global Constitutionalism: Asia–Pacific Perspectives' (2021) 10 Global Constitutionalism 221.

[147] Neil Walker, 'The Idea of Constitutional Pluralism' [2002] EUI Working Paper LAW No. 2002/1 317.

[148] See Chapter 7.

for global constitutionalism.[149] But this should not necessarily lead legal scholars to abolish the idea of global constitutionalism altogether but rather to democratise it.[150] The problem of (the lack of) democratic legitimacy will be addressed in Chapter 6 in more detail.

3.2.4 Constitutional Quality of IEL Treaties?

In IEL, some documents can be identified that could already possess a certain degree of this normative quality. There is currently no environmental *jus cogens* or customary law (except for the 'no harm' principle[151]) that would qualify for a position at the top of the norm hierarchy.[152] The emergence of *jus cogens* norms is seen as an important step in constitutional development because its strong ethical underpinnings that limit state sovereignty mark the 'transformation of international law from a law of co-operation to a law of community values'.[153] The same function, however, is ascribed to world order treaties[154] that enjoy almost universal membership and are attested to contribute to the emergence of core 'community values' that transcend the interests of individual states.[155] These are 'partial constitutions' (*Teilverfassungen*) because they are treaties of long duration, address important issues and seek to limit any kind of power in their respective fields.[156] Unlike bilateral treaties, they create equal duties for all,[157]

---

[149] Schwöbel (n 71) 150–1; Peters, 'The Merits of Global Constitutionalism' (n 108) 408–9.

[150] Peters, 'The Merits of Global Constitutionalism' (n 108) 409.

[151] Louis J Kotzé and Wendy Muzangaza, 'Constitutional International Environmental Law for the Anthropocene?' (2018) 27 Review of European, Comparative and International Environmental Law 278, 285.

[152] Erika de Wet, 'The Emergence of International and Regional Value Systems as a Manifestation of the Emerging International Constitutional Order' (2006) 19 Leiden Journal of International Law 611.

[153] Kassoti (n 101) 181.

[154] The expression 'world order treaty' was coined by Christian Tomuschat, 'Obligations Arising for States Without or Against Their Will' in Académie de Droit International (The Hague Academy of International Law) (ed), *Recueil des Cours*, vol 241 (Martinus Nijhoff Publishers 1993) 248, 268–71.

[155] Peters, 'Compensatory Constitutionalism: The Function and Potential of Fundamental International Norms and Structures' (n 1) 598; Kassoti (n 101) 182.

[156] Peter Häberle, 'Universaler Konstitutionalismus aus nationalen und völkerrechtlichen Teilverfassungen—Sieben Thesen' in Peter Häberle (ed), *Jahrbuch des Öffentlichen Rechts der Gegenwart* (Mohr Siebeck 2014) 418.

[157] Peters, 'Membership in the Global Constitutional Community' (n 113) 191.

and their structure is not reciprocal.[158] Moreover, since they serve community interests, they have third-party effects and can create rights and obligations for non-members.[159] While a state is not bound by treaties themselves, a treaty might give expression to legal obligations that may have already existed and are merely reinforced by the treaty.[160] Thus, world order treaties are a hybrid of treaty and law[161] and, as such, meet the criteria of modern constitutions, in particular, the cooperative and horizontal mode of creating binding obligations for all.[162] World order treaties encompass 'orientation values, ideals or high texts such as "justice", "world peace", "interests of humankind", "dignity", which partly originate from national constitutional law'.[163] In this sense, they are 'mini-constitutions'.[164]

For some, the UNFCCC (with its Kyoto Protocol and Paris Agreement) is classified as a world order treaty, as it aims to protect nature and the climate as a base for all humans living and generations yet to come, as endorsed by the principle of intergenerational equity (e.g., in the Preamble and Article 3 UNFCCC).[165]

In such a world of public order, international human rights norms are an expression of values and interests that are deemed worthy of particular legal protection by the international community as a whole. Therefore, they would

[158] Kleinlein, *Konstitutionalisierung im Völkerrecht* (n 56) 436.

[159] Thomas Kleinlein, 'Between Myths and Norms: Constructivist Constitutionalism and the Potential of Constitutional Principles in International Law' (2012) 81 Nordic Journal of International Law 79, 90.

[160] Tomuschat (n 154) 269.

[161] Ulrich K Preuss, 'Disconnecting Constitutions from Statehood: Is Global Constitutionalism a Viable Concept?' in Petra Dobner and Martin Loughlin (eds), *The Twilight of Constitutionalism?* (OUP 2010) 45.

[162] Ibid.

[163] Häberle, 'Universaler Konstitutionalismus aus nationalen und völkerrechtlichen Teilverfassungen—Sieben Thesen' (n 156) 418 (tr the author).

[164] Jerzy Zajadło and Tomasz Widłak, 'Constitutionalisation: A New Philosophy of International Law?' in Andrzej Jakubowski and Karolina Wierczyńska (eds), *Fragmentation vs the Constitutionalisation of International Law* (Routledge 2016) 24.

[165] Peters, 'Compensatory Constitutionalism: The Function and Potential of Fundamental International Norms and Structures' (n 1) 604; Häberle, 'Universaler Konstitutionalismus aus nationalen und völkerrechtlichen Teilverfassungen—Sieben Thesen' (n 156) 418. Häberle refers (indirectly) to the Convention on the Conservation of Migratory Species of Wild Animals (1979), the Vienna Convention for the Protection of the Ozone Layer, (1985) and the Montreal Protocol on Substances that Deplete the Ozone Layer (1987), the Convention on Biological Diversity (1992), and the Kyoto Protocol (1997) as world order treaties.

enjoy a superior rank.[166] It remains to be seen if the 2017 Global Pact for the Environment, driven by France and which explicitly recognises the right to an ecologically sound environment, could become such a world order treaty once it comes into force.[167]

3.3 Global Environmental (and Climate) Constitutionalism

The debate surrounding global constitutionalism has been followed with interest by environmental law scholars who seek to make the concept fertile for their area of research. Today, more than 1 300 multilateral agreements are protecting the environment or parts of it.[168] These numbers prove the assumption that environmental protection is a universal issue. However, due to the non-binding character of emissions targets in climate change treaties such as the Paris Agreement and the resulting lack of enforcement mechanisms, the fulfilment of the Agreement's goals depends largely on the will of the ratifying states. This is one of IEL's main struggles: states are either hesitant to subject themselves to binding agreements or do not comply with the obligations of agreements to which they have subjected themselves.[169] Sovereignty, therefore, is 'the largest unresolved problem of political modernity and the biggest impediment to dealing with climate change'.[170] Some scholars argue that the structure of IEL itself helps to foster the status quo. Unequipped with enforcement or sanction instruments and shying away from 'hard law', and giving too much weight to states' sovereignty, IEL is

---

[166] Andrea Bianchi, 'Globalization of Human Rights: The Role of Non-State Actors' in Gunther Teubner (ed), *Global Law without a State* (Dartmouth Publishing 1997) 183.

[167] Sceptical: Louis Kotzé, 'A Global Environmental Constitution for the Anthropocene?' (2019) 8 Transnational Environmental Law 11, 29–32.

[168] See Ronald B Mitchell, 'International Environmental Agreements (IEA) Database Project' < https://iea.uoregon.edu > accessed 31 August 2023.

[169] Louis J Kotzé, 'The Conceptual Contours of Environmental Constitutionalism' (2015) 21 Widener Law Review 187, 202.

[170] Sam Adelman, 'Rethinking Human Rights: The Impact of Climate Change on the Dominant Discourse' in Stephen Humphreys (ed), *Human Rights and Climate Change* (CUP 2009) 166–7.

not capable of dealing with current environmental challenges,[171] despite the huge number of multilateral environmental agreements (MEAs).[172]

> There seems to be both a lack of a dedicated sense of ecological obligation of care and a lack of a sense of being bound by the global rule of environmental law and the obligations such law imposes.[173]

Comparative constitutionalism has analysed that the inclusion of environmental protection in constitutions has proven to be effective. Over recent decades, environmental concerns and protection have increasingly found their way into domestic constitutions.[174] Today, more than three-quarters of the constitutions worldwide include some rights that are related to environmental protection. These rights can vary greatly from state to state, and sometimes, they are composed of traditional human rights that are 'greened' by national judicial bodies.[175] Some constitutions include ecocentric approaches or 'rights for nature', thus, moving away from the current human-focused way of assessing nature's value by its usefulness for humans (anthropocentric approach).[176] Instead, such ecocentric approaches acknowledge that nature has an intrinsic value in itself. Ecuador—so far, uniquely—has adopted rights for 'Pacha Mama' in its constitution ('*derechos de la naturaleza*'). Article 71 allows everybody ('all persons, communities, peoples, and nations') to call upon the public authorities to enforce this right.[177] Bolivia, Colombia, Mexico, Uganda and some communities in the US have adopted similar rules in their regular laws that attribute a special status to the

---

[171] Kotzé and Muzangaza (n 151) 279.

[172] Rakhyun E Kim and Klaus Bosselmann, 'International Environmental Law in the Anthropocene: Towards a Purposive System of Multilateral Environmental Agreements' (2013) 2 Transnational Environmental Law 285, 285–6.

[173] Louis J Kotzé, 'A Global Environmental Constitution for the Anthropocene's Climate Crisis' in Jordi Jaria-Manzano and Susana Borràs (eds), *Research Handbook on Global Climate Constitutionalism* (Edward Elgar Publishing 2019) 55.

[174] For an overview and comparison of European constitutional environmental norms, see Peter Häberle and Markus Kotzur, *Europäische Verfassungslehre* (8th edn, Nomos 2016) 867–78.

[175] Erin Daly and James R May, 'Global Environmental Constitutionalism: A Rights-Based Primer for Effective Strategies', *Elgar Encyclopedia of Environmental Law: Decision Making in Environmental Law (Vol. II)* (2017) 21–22.

[176] See, for example, Christopher D Stone, *Should Trees Have Standing?* (3rd edn, OUP 2010); Cormac Cullinan, *Wild Law: A Manifesto for Earth Justice* (2nd edn, Siber Ink 2011).

[177] Article 71 of the Constitution of Ecuador:

environment against which economic or social interests have to be balanced.[178] While scholarly support for rethinking the position and assessment of nature in our legal systems is increasing, the ecocentric approach is not mirrored in constitutions (yet), except in Ecuador. However, many courts in Latin America have started to consider rights for nature when interpreting the constitution, and by doing so, they demonstrate an openness towards the perceptions and the worth of nature for a people or parts of it, such as indigenous communities.[179]

Moreover, many constitutions already contain a right to a certain quality of environment, mostly those adopted or amended in the 1990s, including, inter alia, those of Armenia, the Dominican Republic (which explicitly addresses climate change), France, Kenya, Madagascar, Myanmar, South Sudan and Turkmenistan.[180] Notably, it appears that—except for France—constitutional environmental rights are a core matter only to states of the Global South. Indeed, it can be observed that mostly older constitutions, such as the US Constitution, are less likely to include environmental protection provisions. The absence of such norms can be explained due to the age of these constitutions and the difficulties that arise with amendment procedures.[181] However, while the constitutional text might lack environmental protection provisions, judges play a key role in interpreting other constitutional provisions in a 'green' and often creative way.[182] The general approval of a rights-based approach to environmental protection has

---

(1) Nature, or Pacha Mama, where life is reproduced and occurs, has the right to integral respect for its existence and for the maintenance and regeneration of its life cycles, structure, functions and evolutionary processes.
(2) All persons, communities, peoples and nations can call upon public authorities to enforce the rights of nature. To enforce and interpret these rights, the principles set forth in the Constitution shall be observed, as appropriate.
(3) The State shall give incentives to natural persons and legal entities and to communities to protect nature and to promote respect for all the elements comprising an ecosystem.

[178] For a comprehensive overview, see UN Harmony with Nature, 'Rights of Nature Law, Policy and Education' < http://www.harmonywithnatureun.org/rightsOfNature/ > accessed 31 August 2023. An example in this sense is the preamble of the constitution of the Free and Hanseatic City of Hamburg. There it reads: "The natural foundations of life are under the special protection of the state. In particular, the Free and Hanseatic City of Hamburg assumes its responsibility for limiting global warming" (tr the author).

[179] On this, see Section 2.3.4.

[180] Daly and May (n 175) 26.

[181] Robert V. Percival, 'The Greening of the Global Judiciary' (2017) 32 Journal of Land Use and Environmental Law 333, 337.

[182] Ibid 336.

led to a United Nations General Assembly (UNGA) resolution that recognises the right to a healthy and clean environment, which was adopted in July 2022: 161 votes in favour, 0 against and 8 abstentions—following the 2021 Human Rights Council Resolution 48/13, which, for the first time, recognised the right to a healthy environment at the international level.[183] Environmental protection has reached the consciousness of law-givers worldwide: a worldwide dialogue of domestic constitution-makers in which academia, national and international courts participate together in an 'open society of constitution-makers'.[184]

The ordinance of environmental protection at the highest level in the national legal system can lead to more environmental protection. Boyd has conducted a comprehensive study on domestic environmental constitutionalism and asserts that those countries that have included environmental provisions in their constitutions indeed made stronger efforts towards the protection of the environment than nations without such provisions, including smaller ecological footprints, higher ranks on comprehensive indices of environmental indicators, an increased likelihood to ratify international environmental agreements and faster progress in reducing emissions of sulphur dioxides, nitrogen oxides and GHGs.[185]

These domestic developments have inspired scholars to identify elements of normative global environmental constitutionalism.[186] Global environmental constitutionalism is seen as a tool for enforcing better environmental protection where IEL has failed to effectively protect humanity from the adverse effects of climate change.[187] As such, it is a relatively recent phenomenon that cross-cuts constitutional law, IL, international human rights law and IEL.[188] Global environmental constitutionalism embraces the idea that the environment is or should be a subject of protection.[189] The duties of governments arising from such constitutional protection are many. They are obliged to:

---

[183] UNGA Resolution „The human right to a clean, healthy and sustainable environment" (A/76/L.75), 26 July 2022; Human Rights Council, Resolution 48/13 "The human right to a clean, healthy and sustainable environment" adopted on 8 October 2021.

[184] Peter Häberle, *Ein afrikanisches Verfassungs- und Lesebuch – mit vergleichender Kommentierung* (Duncker & Humblot 2019) 201, in German: 'offene Gesellschaft der Verfassunggeber'.

[185] Boyd (n 137) 5.

[186] Louis J Kotzé, 'A Global Environmental Constitution for the Anthropocene's Climate Crisis' [2019] Research Handbook on Global Climate Constitutionalism 50.

[187] James R May and Erin Daly, *Global Environmental Constitutionalism* (CUP 2014) 55.

[188] UNEP, 'The Status of Climate Change Litigation—A Global Review' (2017) 5.

[189] Daly and May (n 175) 21.

> ensure intra- and intergenerational equity; to conserve resources, and ensure equitable access to and use of resources; to avoid adverse environmental impacts; to prevent environmental disasters, minimize damage and provide emergency assistance; to compensate for environmental harm; and to ensure environmental justice, access to justice, and sufficient civil society representation and participation.[190]

These duties should not only be recognised by constitutions worldwide but also vindicated by constitutional courts.[191] Global constitutional environmental law would emphasise legal rules over state interests and power. States would no longer be able to base their decisions solely on state consent but would have to consider the separation of powers, the rule of law, democracy and the protection of human rights.[192] This implies 'that while states are the *subjects* of a global constitutional order, they are at once (or at least should be) entirely *subjected* to binding and constraining international 'constitutional' rules that are supported by the majority of states and people within states.'[193]

Global environmental constitutionalism could reform IEL to limit state sovereignty and discourage states' non-compliance with environmental obligations, even when they do not consent to be bound by a norm or deliberately violate binding IEL rules.[194] The first UN Environment Programme (UNEP) Global report on the environmental rule of law seeks to strengthen the environmental rule of law so that states apply, comply with and enforce environmental norms and institutions. States and other entities should be held accountable for non-compliance with their obligations under environmental laws.[195] The environmental rule of law aims to 'integrate critical environmental needs with the elements of rule of law, thus creating a foundation for environmental governance that protects rights and enforces fundamental obligations'.[196]

Therefore, global environmental constitutionalism's greatest potential is seen in its comprehensiveness and its ability to bring certain environmental goals to the top of the norm hierarchy.[197] The fragmented structure of IEL leads to treating

---

[190] Louis J Kotzé, 'Arguing Global Environmental Constitutionalism' (2012) 1 Transnational Environmental Law 199, 208.

[191] James R May and Erin Daly, *Judicial Handbook on Environmental Constitutionalism* (Law Division, UNEP Programme 2017) 1.

[192] Kotzé, 'A Global Environmental Constitution for the Anthropocene?' (n 167) 20.

[193] Ibid (emphasis in original).

[194] Kotzé and Muzangaza (n 151) 282.

[195] UNEP, *Environmental Rule of Law (First Global Report)* (2019) 8.

[196] Ibid (citations omitted).

[197] Kotzé and Muzangaza (n 151) 279.

interdependent environmental matters on an individual issue basis, which results in obstructive or even contradictory norms.[198] And while there is some coherence in the form of general principles, its core system remains vague and weak.[199] Furthermore, IEL lacks a superior goal, as is the case with human security and dignity in international human rights law or free trade in international trade law. These objectives form the normative top of these legal orders in the sense of a normative hierarchy.[200] Global environmental or climate constitutionalism would put the environment and climate at the top position; whenever a conflict between divergent norms or interests arise, environmental and climate concerns would have to be considered.

Global environmental constitutionalism also holds the potential to protect the interests of future generations. It is an opportunity for societies to establish their values that should guide political and social conduct for future generations and protect these values by vesting them into constitutional obligations or rights.[201] According to Häberle, constitutions should be understood as social contracts between generations or society members (*Generationenvertrag* or *Gesellschaftsvertrag*), which necessarily includes future generations: 'Partners of the social contract are therefore not only the living but also the still unborn! A trusteeship exists in their favour.'[202] Constitutions have a temporal element,[203] and the 'very purpose of a constitution is to bind future generations to the values identified by the present one'.[204] This means that they seek not only to protect those living today but to ensure that following generations will also benefit from natural and cultural heritage.[205] While the present generations should not be

---

[198] Kim and Bosselmann (n 172) 286.

[199] Ibid 294.

[200] Ibid.

[201] Richard P Hiskes, *The Human Right to a Green Future: Environmental Rights and Intergenerational Justice* (CUP 2008) 130.

[202] Häberle, 'Verfassungsgerichtsbarkeit in der offenen Gesellschaft' (n 65) 42 (tr the author).

[203] For Habermas, it is a "double temporal reference: as a historic document, it recalls the foundational act that it interprets—it marks a beginning in time. At the same time, its normative character means that the task of interpreting and elaborating the system of rights poses itself anew for each generation; as the project of a just society, a constitution articulates the horizon of expectation opening on an ever-present future", Habermas, *Between Facts and Norms: Contributions to a Discourse Theory of Law and Democracy* (n 49) 384.

[204] May and Daly (n 187) 47–8.

[205] Peter Häberle, 'A Constitutional Law for Future Generations – the "Other" Form of the Social Contract: The Generation Contract' in Jörg Tremmel (ed), *Handbook of Intergenerational Justice* (Edward Elgar Publishing 2006) 218–9, 221–2.

stripped of their hard-earned privileges (e.g., pensions), the young and future generations should not be overburdened.[206] The constitution establishes obligations for the present generations vis-à-vis future generations.[207]

Consequently, while states may be driven by short-term profit thinking, members of the open society of constitutional interpreters can introduce future generations' interests. This is another feature of global constitutionalism in general and global environmental constitutionalism in particular: it could strengthen the participation of non-state actors as it brings together different stakeholders and groups to incorporate their interests and ideas[208]:

> Constitutionalism encompasses law creation, law implementation, and enforcement. And its reach is plenary because it brings together all the constituencies within and sometimes outside the nation: it can speak for one majority or minority group, or speak for the plurality; it can listen to indigenous and marginalized communities, for corporate or development interests, or to lower, middle, or upper classes of the nation.[209]

The open society of constitutional interpreters plays an important part in the shaping of global environmental constitutionalism. The formulation of values of the global legal community and the recognition and consideration of the interests of those who do not have a voice, such as marginalised communities or future generations, cannot depend on the goodwill of states alone. As seen above, constitutionalists have stressed the importance of the individual as the ultimate point of reference. Constitutionalism has to serve the interests of the people, not those of states. This also means that non-state actors should be ascribed a more inclusive role in decision-making and law creation.

---

[206] Häberle, 'Verfassungsgerichtsbarkeit in der offenen Gesellschaft' (n 65) 41–2; see also Häberle, 'A Constitutional Law for Future Generations – the "Other" Form of the Social Contract: The Generation Contract' (n 205) 215.

[207] Another question is who can give future generations a voice in national and international decision-making processes. In this sense, theories of deliberative democracy as a particularly useful tool for considering the interests of future generations but also foreigners will be discussed in Chapter 6.

[208] May and Daly (n 187) 49.

[209] Ibid.

3.4 Conclusions

Global constitutionalism reduces the importance of sovereignty to some extent and binds it to other factors, such as compliance with human rights obligations and the common interest, and includes the protection of the climate. This makes it attractive for environmental law scholars who seek to protect the climate through the medium of (international) law. Another important point that distinguishes global constitutionalism from 'traditional' IL is the role of non-state actors. In the democratic nation-state, the participation of non-state actors, such as individuals, groups and NGOs, is seen as crucial for realising the constitutional project. A constitution will always be an unfinished project.[210] For it to constantly evolve, it depends on the impulses of the open society of constitutional interpreters: the constitutional reality. This also holds for the international realm. Global constitutionalism acknowledges a stronger role and more participation opportunities for non-state actors, but it must address one problem that has been identified in relation to the Westphalian system of IL and remains unresolved: the lack of democratic legitimacy.[211] The following chapters, then, highlight the problem in the specific context of global climate constitutionalism. Climate change is not only an environmental problem but also a major challenge for global justice. The next chapter elaborates on what this means in relation to global democracy and legitimacy, and how visions of global climate constitutionalism can include climate justice. This, it will be argued, requires us to rethink the question of legitimacy. This means turning to 'new types of legitimacy', which can be achieved in the specific context of global climate governance and analysing the role the open society of constitutional interpreters plays in this.[212]

---

[210] Habermas, *Between Facts and Norms: Contributions to a Discourse Theory of Law and Democracy* (n 49) 384.

[211] Peters, 'Compensatory Constitutionalism: The Function and Potential of Fundamental International Norms and Structures' (n 1) 607.

[212] See Chapter 6.

4 Climate Justice and Transnational Climate Constitutionalism

Global constitutionalism offers a way of thinking about IL that finds its raison d'être in the natural human person. Similar to national constitutions, global constitutionalism aims to protect individuals and, therefore, restrains state sovereignty. Due to the failure of states to address climate change as a global problem effectively, the discourse on constitutionalism has also reached the level of seeing IEL as a tool to push states to do more. However, there are some points that the scholarly discourse has tended to ignore. This is especially the case with the question of global democracy. It has often been criticised that IL suffers a legitimacy deficit.[1] Individuals cannot vote or participate in international lawmaking in global assemblies or the like. The members of international organisations are not elected by the global public, and citizens cannot take these global authorities to court.[2] Thus, the central question is whether democratic legitimacy can exist without a democratic system—a democracy—be it global or domestic.[3] This includes, inter alia, questions of the global demos, global collective identity, global solidarity and global decision-making.

Habermas famously developed his co-originality theory according to which the legitimacy of enacted changeable law is derived from both popular sovereignty (public autonomy) and human rights (private autonomy). These pillars are

[1] Anne Peters, 'Compensatory Constitutionalism: The Function and Potential of Fundamental International Norms and Structures' (2006) 19 Leiden Journal of International Law 579, 607.

[2] Jan Aart Scholte, 'Civil Society and Democratically Accountable Global Governance' (2004) 39 Government and Opposition 212; Michael Zürn, 'Global Governance and Legitimacy Problems' (2004) 39 Government and Opposition 260, 260–1.

[3] Martine Beijerman, 'Conceptual Confusions in Debating the Role of NGOs for the Democratic Legitimacy of International Law' (2018) 9 Transnational Legal Theory 147, 162.

M. Niehaus, *Global Climate Constitutionalism "from below"*,
https://doi.org/10.1007/978-3-658-43191-4_4

designed to secure the private and public autonomy of individuals.[4] Drawing on this concept of the constitution as an 'internal connection' between the *Rechtstaat* (or rule of law, including fundamental rights) and democracy, it can be argued that it is not so much the protection of fundamental rights (the private autonomy) that is lacking on the global plane, but how law should be created democratically in a post-national setting (public autonomy).[5] The ever-strengthening of human rights can only realise a half of what the freedom of a democratic constitution entails, while the other half—the political right to democratic self-organisation and self-determination—is becoming ever smaller.[6]

Free elections are the prerequisite for a national government to be considered politically legitimate. However, there is no global discussion on how to resolve the contradiction of being committed to democracy on the one hand and having a deeply undemocratic global order on the other.[7] Of course, it has often been claimed that states are the proxies of their citizens on the international plane, and that, at least in democratic states, citizens are represented at the international level indirectly through their states. Individuals' interests would be enforced more efficiently by their respective states within the complex inter-state relations.[8] Thus,

---

[4] Jürgen Habermas, 'Remarks on Legitimation through Human Rights' in Jürgen Habermas and Max Pensky (eds), *The Postnational Constellation: Political Essays* (Polity Press 2001) 116.

[5] Lars Viellechner, 'Verfassung ohne Staat. Eine Einführung' in Lars Viellechner (ed), *Verfassung ohne Staat* (Nomos 2019) 12.

[6] Hauke Brunkhorst, *Solidarität. Von der Bürgerfreundschaft zur globalen Rechtsgenossenschaft* (Suhrkamp 2002) 201.

[7] Richard Falk and Andrew Strauss, 'Toward Global Parliament' (2001) 80 Foreign Affairs 212, 220. Facing this democratic deficit of international governance, for some commentators such as Carl Schmitt, democracy beyond the nation-state is simply impossible. This is the reason to appeal to the indispensability of the traditional Westphalian model with strong states guaranteeing popular sovereignty. He argues that '[t]he central concept of democracy is people and not humanity.' Democracy cannot exist without and only within the (homogenous) nation-state, see Carl Schmitt, *Constitutional Theory* (1928) (Duke University Press 2008) 261ff (263).

[8] See e.g. Samantha Besson, 'Sovereignty, International Law and Democracy' (2011) 22 European Journal of International Law 373; see also Anne Peters, 'Der Mensch im Mittelpunkt des Völkerrechts', *Lecture given on 27 November 2013 in the context of the farewell of Prof. Dr. Dr. h.c. Rüdiger Wolfrum as Director of the Max Planck Institute for Comparative Public Law and International Law and introduction of Prof. Dr. Anne Peters as new Director* (2013) para 9 < http://www.mpil.de/files/pdf3/Peters_Der_Mensch_im_Mittelpunkt_des_Voelkerrechts._Vortrag_zur_Amtseinfuehrung_als_neue_Direktorin_am_Max_Planck_Institut_fuer_Voelkerrecht_27.11.20131.pdf > accessed 31 August 2023.

citizens in democratic states are participating indirectly in international lawmaking.[9] But since the discourse between states among their representatives is not open to public scrutiny but rather technical, closed and non-transparent, it is not equivalent to an international democratic debate.[10] While not every decision in a nation-state is fully transparent, in many countries, citizens can challenge decisions that disadvantage them by turning to a national court (e.g., through a constitutional complaint) that can review a government decision. This possibility—with the exception of individual complaints to some regional human rights courts—does not exist at the international level. However, this is not the only argument made against the 'democratic by proxy' theory. Many states are not democracies, and citizens cannot have their say. They could benefit from global collective decision-making processes.[11] Even where states fulfil the criterion of a democracy, they potentially do not include the voices of all citizens (e.g., minorities, people who did not vote for the governing parties or those too young to vote). Citizens in high-population countries also tend to be underrepresented.[12]

The argument that the nation-state is best suited to handling all issues concerning its citizens also falls short in transnational and trans-dimensional contexts, such as the climate context. It is precisely the politically supported legitimation process in the nation-state—in particular, elections—that excludes those most affected by climate change from participation. Young people, children and unborn generations cannot vote and are not or are insufficiently represented by their home state. Neither are populations of other countries, for example, those in already heavily affected areas, mostly in the Global South, nor are the unborn generations in other countries represented.[13] Why should a person from, say, Fiji not be allowed to vote in Germany, when decisions on GHG emissions, such as the final date of phasing out coal production, food production or traffic, can influence the continued existence of their home country?

The thought that states are 'trustees of their people' and, as such, have 'fiduciary duties to them and only to them' is deeply rooted in the notion of sovereignty itself.[14] Nonetheless, decisions taken by governments in one state

[9] Peters, 'Der Mensch im Mittelpunkt des Völkerrechts' (n 8) 7.

[10] Anne Peters, 'Dual Democracy' in Jan Klabbers, Anne Peters and Geir Ulfstein (eds), *The Constitutionalization of International Law* (OUP 2009) 332.

[11] Ibid.

[12] Peters, 'Der Mensch im Mittelpunkt des Völkerrechts' (n 8) 7.

[13] Eyal Benvenisti, 'Sovereigns As Trustees of Humanity: On the Accountability of States To Foreign Stakeholders' (2013) 107 The American Journal of International Law 295, 298.

[14] Ibid 296.

can affect the daily lives of individuals in another state far away.[15] Cicero once asked: '*Quae sunt enim patriae commoda, nisi alterius civitatis, aut gentis incommoda*?'[16] Thus, for Kumm, a state's authority can only be legitimate if it exercises its authority over domains in which there are no justice-sensitive externalities. A state cannot exercise authority unilaterally where outsiders of the system are affected by a decision, such as the volume of GHGs it emits into the atmosphere.[17] Rather, sovereigns are 'agents of humanity'[18] who have 'a corollary duty to take account of external interests and even to balance internal against external interests' when managing public affairs within their respective jurisdictions.[19] Precisely against the background of environmental problems travelling abroad, the IACtHR, in its Advisory Opinion of 7 February 2018, affirmed the extra-territoriality of environmental human rights and, therefore, the legal responsibility of states to prevent human rights violations resulting from transboundary pollution.[20]

Economic globalisation that opens and connects the markets leads to shifting powers between states and major transnational corporations, which eventually erodes popular sovereignty and leads to domestic 'de-constitutionalisation', where citizens finditizens find themselves more and more in a 'double-blind', with their possibilities for participation in the democratic process becoming smaller

[15] Ibid 298; David Held, *Democracy and the Global Order: From the Modern State to Cosmopolitan Governance* (Polity Press 1995) 228.

[16] Marcus Tullius Cicero, *De Republica* (Georg Heinrich Moser ed, 1826) 369, 'For what are the advantages of our country if not the disadvantages of another city or nation?' (tr the author).

[17] Mattias Kumm, 'Constituent Power, Cosmopolitan Constitutionalism, and Post-Positivist Law' (2016) 14 International Journal of Constitutional Law 697, 704–5.

[18] Benvenisti (n 13) 300.

[19] Ibid 308.

[20] IACtHR, 'Advisory Opinion OC-23/17—The Environment and Human Rights' (2017); for an analysis see Maria L Banda, 'Inter-American Court of Human Rights' Advisory Opinion on the Environment and Human Rights' *American Society of International Law* (2018) < https://www.asil.org/insights/volume/22/issue/6/inter-american-court-human-rights-advisory-opinion-environment-and-human > accessed 31 August 2023; for an extensive analysis in German see Verena Kahl, 'Ökologische Revolution am Interamerikanischen Gerichtshof für Menschenrechte—Besprechung des Rechtsgutachtens Nr.23 „Umwelt und Menschenrechte " (OC-23/17)' (2019) 17 Zeitschrift für Europäisches Umwelt- und Planungsrecht 110.

in an ever-more limited realm in which self-government can take place.[21] Globalisation is 'unbundling' the relationship between sovereignty, territoriality and political power.[22] The consequences of such one-sided globalisation are state deficits that cannot be compensated for on the domestic plane.[23] State constitutions are no longer 'total constitutions',[24] since the linkage between national constitutional law and democracy has loosened.[25] The nation-state, once the most powerful actor of institutional inclusion, is less and less capable of abolishing inequalities.[26] This becomes extremely clear in the case of environmental problems that are escaping nation-states' borders and control.[27] The traditional Westphalian model cannot guarantee either domestic or global self-determination. It is for global constitutional law to put the exercise of public authority that has escaped the states under a new legal framework to guarantee the effective realisation of human interests.[28]

A narrow definition of global democracy based solely on nation-states and citizenship that excludes those most affected limits the realisation of global self-government: the essence of democracy.[29] Climate change does not fit neatly into

---

[21] See Peters, 'Compensatory Constitutionalism: The Function and Potential of Fundamental International Norms and Structures' (n 1); Christine EJ Schwöbel, *Global Constitutionalism in International Legal Perspective* (Martinus Nijhoff Publishers 2011) 23; Brunkhorst (n 6) 169; Matthias Kumm, 'The Legitimacy of International Law: A Constitutionalist Framework of Analysis' (2004) 15 European Journal of International Law 907, 912–3; Jürgen Habermas, 'The Postnational Constellation and the Future of Democracy' in Jürgen Habermas and Max Pensky (eds), The Postnational Constellation: Political Essays (Polity Press 2001) 78: 'Power can be democratized; money cannot'.

[22] David Held, 'Democratic Accountability and Political Effectiveness from a Cosmopolitan Perspective' (2004) 39 Government and Opposition 364, 367.

[23] Angelika Emmerich-Fritsche, *Vom Völkerrecht zum Weltrecht* (Duncker & Humblot 2007) 304.

[24] Anne Peters, 'Global Constitutionalism Revisited' (2005) 11 Legal Theory 39, 41.

[25] Petra Dobner, 'More Law, Less Democracy? Democracy and Transnational Constitutionalism' in Petra Dobner and Martin Loughlin (eds), *The Twilight of Constitutionalism?* (OUP 2010) 147.

[26] Hauke Brunkhorst, 'Constitutionalism and Democracy in the World Society' in Petra Dobner and Martin Loughlin (eds), *The Twilight of Constitutionalism?* (OUP 2010) 191.

[27] Daniel Bodansky, 'The Legitimacy of International Governance: A Coming Challenge for International Environmental Law' (1999) 93 The American Journal of International Law 596, 362; Emmerich-Fritsche (n 23) 304.

[28] Dobner (n 25) 147; Emmerich-Fritsche (n 23) 300.

[29] Emmerich-Fritsche (n 23) 629.

the Westphalian model of IL, where each state rules over its small piece of territory and regulates the daily lives of its citizens autonomously.[30] The emergence of networks and the rise of non-state actors produce 'global law which addresses or affects citizens directly and which is not restricted to law between states but between different social, economic, or political entities within and outside of states'.[31] Thus, many of these approaches to global constitutionalism have not addressed the problem that this new global public law needs 'full democratic legitimacy for the production process of this law, its application, and its control'[32] but have instead focused (too much) on the promotion of the rule of law.[33]

It has been argued that global constitutionalism would not need to 'copy' all the elements that are essential to a national constitution. Rather, it could be seen in a less 'all-or-nothing' fashion. By 'unpacking' the concept of a constitution down to its constitutional elements, the proper role of each of these elements for international governance could be analysed.[34] Thus, it could be argued that constitutionalism does not really 'need' democracy, since it is not feasible at the international level.[35] However, this work agrees with Peters' point of view, according to which constitutionalism should be understood in a comprehensive and holistic way. Instead of reducing it to some elements, such as the rule of law and separation of powers, all constitutional features (human rights, democracy, judicial review, transparent decision-making and so on) should go hand in hand to understand the normative significance of their interaction and their combination. Global constitutionalism is more than just the sum of its parts.

---

[30] Eric Allen Engle, 'The Transformation of the International Legal System: The Post-Westphalian Legal Order' (2004) 23 Quinnipiac Law Review; Neil Walker, 'Beyond Boundary Disputes and Basic Grids: Mapping the Global Disorder of Normative Orders' (2008) 6 International Journal of Constitutional Law 373.

[31] Dobner (n 25) 148.

[32] Ibid.

[33] Ibid 142.

[34] Daniel Bodansky, 'Is There an International Environmental Constitution?' (2009) 16 Indiana Journal of Global Legal Studies 565, 583.

[35] "[T]o the extent that nonconsensual norms and decision-making processes will need to play a larger role in the future to respond to collective action problems such as climate change, then international law will need some new basis of legitimacy. At first glance, democracy seems like a potential candidate, but it is difficult to conceive how democracy could operate at the global level in the absence of a global demos. As a result, constitutionalism has become an attractive alternative", ibid (citations omitted).

> It [the holistic claim of constitutionalism] reminds us of the interlinkage of the various features of constitutionalism, and calls for complementing the existing constitutional features of international law (such as judicial review of governmental acts) with missing ones, such as democracy and judicial review of acts of international organizations.[36]

Through this form of 'constitutional boot-strapping', elements that are not developed (yet) at the international level can come (to some extent) into existence. For example, a global democracy does not need a 'pre-founded people'. Instead, it can be founded on 'peoples who become continuously more conscious of their common destiny'.[37] These factors, including global solidarity or a global collective identity, do not need to be 'there' a priori to the creation of the polity; they can be developed. 'Boot-strapping is to some extent possible: the democratic process itself can in turn promote and fortify the enabling conditions in a positive loop.'[38]

Consequently, democracy is crucial for theories of constitutionalism. The problem of a lack of legitimacy appears in all versions of constitutionalism, but it is exacerbated in global climate constitutionalism. This is because the constitutionalisation of parts of the international legal order says nothing about the 'justness' of this phenomenon.[39] But climate change is, above all, a question of global justice. Unequally distributed risks and costs both between present and future generations pose some of the main problems of the coming decades.[40] In this sense, questions of the (re)distribution of benefits and burdens of climate change arise.[41] These include especially the historical responsibility of the developed Global North for GHG emissions that have reduced the atmospheric capability so that developing countries will not be able to take the same path that has led the developed countries to wealth (especially by creating cheap energy by

---

[36] Anne Peters, 'The Merits of Global Constitutionalism' (2009) 16 Indiana Journal of Global Legal Studies 397, 403.

[37] Peters, 'Dual Democracy' (n 10) 312–3.

[38] Ibid 278.

[39] Stefan Oeter, 'Regime Collisions from a Perspective of Global Constitutionalism' in Kerstin Blome and others (eds), *Contested Regime Collisions. Norm Fragmentation in World Society* (CUP 2016) 23.

[40] Ulrich Beck, *World at Risk* (Polity Press 2008) 104.

[41] Paul G Harris, *World Ethics and Climate Change: From International to Global Justice* (Edinburgh University Press 2010) 58.

burning fossil fuels). in addition, they have to bear the consequences of dangerous global climate change that disproportionally affects them despite contributing the least to the problem in the first place.

Thus, it will be argued in Section 4.2 that global climate constitutionalism that aims to be more than mere institutionalisation or legalisation[42] must include global climate justice. The basis for this claim lies in the particular nature of climate change as a global problem not only for the environment but also for global justice. Climate justice is not just a question of ethics but a claim that is central to many members of the open society. Many of the recently filed lawsuits concerned with climate protection (which will be analysed throughout the coming chapters) have matters of justice at their heart, for example, the protection of the interests of future generations. Thus, the assumption that questions of justice, including the redistribution of costs and benefits, are considered issues of only domestic democracy needs to be challenged and consequently rejected. Instead, it will be argued that there is a global duty to justice and, consequently, an obligation of the states and populations of the Global North towards the states and populations of the Global South and future generations in both the North and the South to both mitigate emissions and to (financially) share the burdens of climate change. Therefore, in the author's opinion, approaches to global climate constitutionalism cannot ignore climate justice as a central element. Global climate constitutionalism needs to address questions of intra- and intergenerational justice to provide a meaningful response to the challenges of a new era some call the Anthropocene.[43]

4.1 Climate Change as a Justice Problem

Climate justice goes back to theories of environmental justice. In its beginnings, IEL was mostly concerned with environmental standard-setting and implementing standards.[44] The first generation of environmental justice addressed problems concerning unwanted land uses at the national level, for example, waste disposal

[42] Jan Klabbers, 'Setting the Scene' in Jan Klabbers, Anne Peters and Geir Ulfstein (eds), *The Constitutionalization of International Law* (OUP 2009) 8.

[43] Jordi Jaria-Manzano, 'Law in the Anthropocene' in Jordi Jaria-Manzano and Susana Borràs (eds), *Research Handbook on Global Climate Constitutionalism* (Edward Elgar Publishing 2019) 43; Carmen G Gonzalez, 'Global Justice in the Anthropocene' in Louis J Kotzé (ed), *Environmental Law and Governance for the Anthropocene* (Hart/Bloomsbury Publishing 2017) 229ff.

[44] Bodansky (n 27) 596.

or power plants. 'Environmental racism' occurs when a country's entire population benefits from the use of certain facilities, but the burden is borne by the poor and/or people of colour because such locations are often chosen in less affluent neighbourhoods.[45] Distributive justice, thus, refers to 'geographic equity', which means that burdens have to be distributed equally between citizens.[46] The second generation of environmental justice activists moved the discourse from 'not in my backyard' to 'not in anyone's backyard' and demanded the reduction of pollution in general.[47] Climate justice combines both and calls for a reduction of GHG emissions and an equal distribution of the (financial) burdens of climate change, which arise both from historical and current GHG emissions and the costs of combating climate change.[48]

By now, most people understand that GHG emissions emitted in one place can cause global warming and hazardous climate change in other parts of the world; we share the same atmosphere.[49] It has often been claimed that we have entered the era of the Anthropocene: the era of humankind.[50] Accordingly, humankind needs to be seen as a geological agent that has a significant impact on the earth's geology and its ecosystems, including climate change. However, it is not *all* humanity that is responsible for these changes. Instead, 'capitalists in a small corner of the Western world invested in steam, laying the foundation stone for the fossil economy: at no moment did the species vote for it either with feet or ballots, or march in mechanical unison, or exercise any sort of shared authority over its own destiny and that of the Earth System.'[51]

The fossil economy—the major driver of climate change—was not created by all humanity, nor is it upheld by it. One-third of humanity has no access to electricity and instead uses other materials such as firewood, charcoal and organic

[45] Sheila R Foster, 'Vulnerability, Equality and Environmental Justice' in Ryan Holifield, Jayajit Chakraborty and Gordon Walker (eds), *The Routledge Handbook of Environmental Justice* (Routledge 2017) 136.

[46] Robert R Kuehn, 'A Taxonomy of Environmental Justice' (2000) 30 Environmental Law Reporter 10,681, 10,684.

[47] Steve Vanderheiden, 'Environmental and Climate Justice' in Teena Gabrielson and others (eds), *The Oxford Handbook of Environmental Political Theory* (OUP 2016) 323.

[48] Ibid 322–5.

[49] Peter Singer, 'One Atmosphere' in Stephen M Gardiner and others (eds), *Climate Ethics: Essential Readings* (OUP 2010).

[50] Will Steffen and others, 'The Anthropocene: Conceptual and Historical Perspectives' (2011) 369 Philosophical Transactions of the Royal Society 842.

[51] Andreas Malm and Alf Hornborg, 'The Geology of Mankind? A Critique of the Anthropocene Narrative' (2014) 1 The Anthropocene Review 62, 64 (citations omitted).

waste for domestic purposes, which makes their contributions to global GHG emissions close to zero.[52] Thus, a study in 2007 showed that a single average US citizen emitted, on average, as many GHGs as more than 500 citizens of Ethiopia, Chad, Afghanistan, Mali, Cambodia or Burundi:

> The poorest half of the world's population—3.5 billion people—is responsible for just 10 percent of carbon emissions, while the richest 10 percent are responsible for a full half. A person in the wealthiest 1 percent uses 175 times more carbon than one in the bottom 10 percent.[53]

The effect someone has on the atmosphere varies by a factor of more than 1000 depending on where they were born.[54]

Thus, it is not humanity as such that is responsible for causing global warming and climate change, but a rather small group of humans, with consequences for the rest of the world. Everybody will be in some way or another affected by climate change, but the populations of the Global South and vulnerable communities such as indigenous communities, racial and ethnic minorities and the poor, who contributed the least to the problem, will bear the greatest extent of the burdens.[55] Conversely, the developed countries of the Global North, responsible for the major share of historical GHG emissions, have benefited from industrialisation based on the exploitation of the Global South, and are better equipped to deal with hazardous climate change; but, they seem to be reluctant to curb emissions significantly.[56] Thus, environmental and climate justice includes an important North–South dimension. 'Environmental injustice cannot be separated from economic inequality, race and gender subordination, and the colonial and

---

[52] Ibid 65.

[53] Special Rapporteur on Extreme Poverty and Human Rights Philipp Alston, 'Climate Change and Poverty (A/HRC/41/39)' (2019) para 14.

[54] David Satterthwaite, 'The Implications of Population Growth and Urbanization for Climate Change' (2009) 21 Environment and Urbanization 545, 564.

[55] Carmen G Gonzalez, 'Environmental Justice and International Environmental Law' in Alam Shawkat and others (eds), *Routledge Handbook of International Environmental Law* (Routledge 2012) 78ff; (n 53).

[56] Cf. U Thara Srinivasan, 'Economics of Climate Change: Risk and Responsibility by World Region' (2010) 10 Climate Policy 298; Nicolas Stern, 'The Stern Review on Economics of Climate Change' (2006); Sumudu Atapattu, 'Environmental Justice, Climate Justice and Constitutionalism: Protecting Vulnerable States and Communities' in Jordi Jaria-Manzano and Susana Borràs (eds), *Research Handbook on Global Climate Constitutionalism* (Edward Elgar Publishing 2019).

post-colonial domination of the global South.'[57] Colonial ecological violence continues to perpetuate international environmental treaty law in more and less visible dimensions, thereby excluding the perspectives of minorities, indigenous people, women and large parts of the populations of the Global South.[58] Climate change is fundamentally an issue of inequality and global justice. 'In short, we are all on the same boat, but it is not the same to be confined in the hold, the first to drown, or on the first-class bridge, near the lifeboats.'[59] As a result, the principle of climate justice has found its way into international documents. Against the background of the 'norm life cycle' theory, which describes the process of a norm coming into the world and becoming law,[60] it can be ascertained that the principle of climate justice has entered the second stage of the cycle: the norm cascade[61]; thus, the 'active process of international socialization intended to induce norm breakers to become norm followers'.[62] Today, the preamble of the Paris Agreement even makes an explicit reference to climate justice and notes 'the importance for some of the concept of "climate justice", when taking action to address climate change'.[63] It is, by now, a principle that has become increasingly influential at both the international and national levels.[64]

---

57 Gonzalez (n 55) 79.

58 Douglas de Castro, 'The Colonial Aspects of International Environmental Law: Treaties as Promoters of Continuous Structural Violence' (2017) 5 Groningen Journal of International Law 168.

59 Philippe Descola 'Humain. Trop Humain', Esprit 2015 (16–7), quoted and translated by Domenico Branca, 'Humanity in/of the Anthropocene: An Anthropological Perspective' in Elizabeth G Dobbins, Maria Lucia Piga and Luigi Manca (eds), *Environment, Social Justice, and the Media in the Age of the Anthropocene* (Lexington 2020) 24.

60 Martha Finnemore and Kathryn Sikkink, 'International Norm Dynamics and Political Change' (1998) 52 International Organization 887, 895ff.

61 Evan Gach, 'Normative Shifts in the Global Conception of Climate Change: The Growth of Climate Justice' (2019) 8 Social Sciences 12 and 14. He found with respect to the positions of UNFCCC members and non-state actors that a norm of climate justice frames climate change as '(i) a fundamental issue of justice and equality, (ii) a problem that necessitates compensation for loss and damage to those most impacted, (iii) an issue that exacerbates existing gender, racial, social, and economic inequalities, (iv) a human rights issue instead of simply an environmental one, and (v) not an all-encompassing global issue that impacts all countries and peoples, but one of contextual impacts and vulnerabilities'.

62 Finnemore and Sikkink (n 60) 902.

63 UNFCCC Conference of the Parties, Adoption of the Paris Agreement, Dec. 12, 2015. U.N. Doc. FCCC/CP/2015/L.9 (Annex).

64 For an overview of how climate justice was embedded in various environmental treaties, see Harris (n 41) 59–70.

At the heart of climate justice lie three ethical underpinnings: the question of the target (the limit of allowed GHG emissions), allocation (the distribution of costs for meeting the target) and liability (what is owed by whom to those at risk of hazardous climate change in advance [adaptation] or after the fact as compensation?), of which the latter is the most frequently discussed.[65]

More specifically, climate justice addresses a range of issues from the legal status of environmentally induced migration and environmentally displaced persons (so-called 'climate refugees')[66] to questions of whose claims to 'atmospheric security' have to be respected: those of individuals, groups, countries and/or generations?[67] It asks how the 'ecological space' should be equally distributed between emitters[68] and is also concerned with questions of spreading the costs of adaptation and mitigation measures across countries and generations.[69] Sudden events such as hurricanes or floods and the 'slow violence' caused by climate change threaten human's attachment to place and their community, thereby undermining individual and collective identity.[70] These social impacts of climate change as an environmental problem are the subject of climate justice.

Environmental/climate justice means different things to different people and communities.[71] However, the underlying principle is one of equity and

---

65 Paul Baer, 'International Justice' in John S Dryzek, Richard B Norgaard and David Schlosberg (eds), *Oxford Handbook of Climate Change and Society* (OUP 2011) 323.

66 See, for example, Melissa S Knodel, 'Wet Feet Marching: Climate Justice and Sustainable Development for Climate Displaced Nations in the South Pacific' (2012) 14 Vermont Journal of Environmental Law 127; Jeremy M Bellavia, 'What Does Climate Justice Look Like for the Environmentally Displaced in a Post Paris Agreement Environment? Political Questions and Court Deference to Climate Science in the Urgenda Decision' (2016) 4 Denver Journal of International Law and Policy 453.

67 Ludvig Beckman and Edward A Page, 'Perspectives on Justice, Democracy and Global Climate Change' (2008) 17 Environmental Politics 527, 528.

68 Tim Hayward, 'Human Rights Versus Emissions Rights: Climate Justice and the Equitable Distribution of Ecological Space' (2007) 21 Ethics and International Affairs 431.

69 Edward A Page, 'Distributing the Burdens of Climate Change' (2008) 17 Environmental Politics 556.

70 David Schlosberg, 'Disruption, Community, and Resilient Governance—Environmental Justice in the Anthropocene' in Tobias Haller and others (eds), *The Commons in a Glocal World: Global Connections and Local Responses* (Routledge 2019) 64ff.

71 Philip Coventry and Chukwumerije Okereke, 'Climate Change and Environmental Justice' in Ryan Holifield, Jayajit Chakraborty and Gordon Walker (eds), *The Routledge Handbook of Environmental Justice* (Routledge 2017) 365–8; Vanderheiden (n 47).

fairness.[72] Four constituent components of environmental justice can be identified: distributive, procedural, corrective and social justice.[73] These various components—which may overlap—can be described as follows:

> Distributive justice calls for the fair allocation of the benefits and burdens of natural resource exploitation among and within nations. Procedural justice requires open, informed, and inclusive decision-making processes. Corrective justice imposes an obligation to provide compensation for historic inequities and to refrain from repeating the conduct that caused the harm. Social justice, the fourth and most nebulous aspect of environmental justice, recognizes that environmental struggles are inextricably intertwined with struggles for social and economic justice.[74]

So far, climate justice has not drawn the attention of constitutionalists yet. Scholars of (Western) constitutionalism have mostly focused on the rule of law, separation of powers, fundamental rights protection, democracy and solidarity.[75] However, if we recognise that every person should have the same amount of ecological space, but ecological footprint analysis shows that some people have much more,[76] one must ask how global climate constitutionalism should address these imbalances.

In short, since the planet is finite in size, the available environmental space should be shared fairly between *all* people. Thus, global climate constitutionalism has to address questions of justice and fairness. This includes whether rich states would be allowed to choose adaptation over mitigation strategies, and how the costs for mitigation and adaptation measures and the costs for loss and damages should be distributed between countries and citizens while keeping in mind the historical imbalances between developed and developing countries. It seems apt that those states (and their citizens) that caused global warming and climate change in the first place should be the ones who address the climate crisis and finance its consequences. This also includes recognising developing states' desire and urgency to follow the same development path as the industrialised countries.

---

[72] Atapattu (n 56) 201.

[73] Kuehn (n 46).

[74] Gonzalez (n 55) 78–9.

[75] Anne Peters, 'Global Constitutionalism' in Michael Gibbons (ed), *The Encyclopedia of Political Thought* (John Wiley & Sons 2015) 1.

[76] Andrew Dobson, 'Environmental Citizenship: Towards Sustainable Development' (2007) 15 Sustainable Development 276, 281.

These needs must be met by substantial concessions in the form of the distribution of funds and technology to persuade these countries to stop deforestation or abolish heavy fossil fuel use.[77]

The inclusion of climate justice has far-reaching implications. Climate justice imposes obligations on states and possibly individuals. To some degree, forms of financial aid and transfer of knowledge and technologies have already been incorporated into the global climate regime through mechanisms such as the Common but Differentiated Responsibilities and Respective Capabilities principle, the loss and damage principle, and the establishment of the REDD + program, the Clean Development Mechanism and the Green Climate Fund.[78] However, a study of the Organization for Economic Cooperation and Development (OECD) demonstrated that only USD78.9 billion of the goal of raising USD100 billion per year by 2020 had been mobilised by the developed countries to help developing countries tackle and adapt to climate change.[79]

In this context, another issue arises. All these mechanisms address states as duty-bearers. Equally interesting is the question of whether positive obligations of citizens towards other states or their citizens can be identified or established. If a right to not be harmed by hazardous climate change or a right to a stable climate is recognised, it follows that corresponding duties in the form of reducing GHG emissions have to be imposed on the citizens of other countries.[80] Moreover, it could mean that the citizens of rich countries pay for losses and damages induced by climate change in poorer countries. Notably, this debate runs parallel to the debate about cosmopolitanism and communitarianism.

Theories of cosmopolitan climate justice have the universality of principles of justice at their core, whereas criteria such as nationality, race or gender should

---

[77] Harris (n 41) 59; Baer (n 65) 323–4.

[78] For an overview of climate financing and the diverse mechanisms, see Barbara K Buchner and others, 'Global Landscape of Climate Finance' (2019) <https://www.climatepolicyinitiative.org/wp-content/uploads/2019/11/2019-Global-Landscape-of-Climate-Finance.pdf > accessed 31 August 2023; Britta Horstmann and Jonas Hein, 'Aligning Climate Change Mitigation and Sustainable Development under the UNFCCC: A Critical Assessment of the Clean Development Mechanism, the Green Climate Fund and REDD + ' (2017); Lovleen Bhullar, 'REDD + and the Clean Development Mechanism: A Comparative Perspective' [2013] International Journal of Rural Law and Policy; Hayley Stevenson, *Global Environmental Politics. Problems, Policy, and Practice* (CUP 2017); Charlotte Streck, 'Innovativeness and Paralysis in International Climate Policy' (2012) 1 Transnational Environmental Law 137.

[79] OECD, *Climate Finance Provided and Mobilised by Developed Countries in 2013–18* (OECD Publishing 2020) 6.

[80] Baer (n 65) 323.

not matter for the determination of someone's obligations and duties vis-à-vis others.[81] Three elements are shared by all strands of cosmopolitanism:

> First, *individualism*: the ultimate units of concern are *human beings*, or *persons* – rather than, say, family lines, tribes, ethnic, cultural or religious communities, nations, or states. The latter may be the units of concern only indirectly, in virtue of their individual members or citizens. Second, *universality*: the status of ultimate unit of concern attaches to *every* human being *equally*, not only to some sub-set, such as men, aristocrats, Aryans, whites, or Muslims. Third, *generality*: the special status has global force. Persons are ultimate units of concern for *everyone* – not only for their compatriots, fellow religionists, or suchlike.[82]

Much of the current discourse is based on international justice between states rather than global justice that also encompasses individuals.[83] For cosmopolitans, political communities and states matter, but they are not the only ones to play a role in an alternative way of ordering the world.[84] Thus, the discourse should be shifted from 'What do we owe the poor people that suffer from rich states' pollution?' to 'What do we owe the poor people that suffer from rich people's pollution?'[85] Moreover, from a cosmopolitan perspective, concerns of justice can extend to states *and* individuals, since all humans share the same atmosphere. All are citizens of 'one world'.[86]

From these observations on cosmopolitanism, it follows that states and citizens could have obligations towards other citizens than their fellows. These obligations can be of either a negative or positive nature, depending essentially on perspective and framing. Notably, most of the discussion revolves around the question of the nature of different human rights. Even proponents of cosmopolitanism do seem to differentiate between duties and obligations towards others to some degree. For example, Shue differentiates liberty and welfare rights (or subsistence and any other rights).[87] Nussbaum argues that there is a divide between 'first-generation rights'/ 'second-generation rights' that serves as a justification for

[81] Ibid 325.

[82] Thomas Pogge, *World Poverty and Human Rights* (Polity Press 2002) 169 (emphasis in original).

[83] See Chapter 3 'International Environmental Justice' in Harris (n 41) 53–73.

[84] Ibid 100.

[85] Ibid 119.

[86] Ibid 153–4; Peter Singer, *One World: The Ethics of Globalisation* (2nd edn, Yale University Press 2004).

[87] Henry Shue, *Basic Rights: Subsistence, Affluence, and U.S. Foreign Policy* (Princeton University Press 1980) 22ff.

different treatment, such as assistance with material aid.[88] Accordingly, there is a wide consensus on some transnational duties that belong to the category of civil and political rights about, inter alia, torture and the proper conduct of war. Such transnational consensus has not emerged around social and economic rights.[89] Even where these rights found their way into international documents, they are nation-bound insofar as citizens can only claim material entitlement in the state in which they live.[90] To make sure, for both Shue and Nussbaum, the differentiation between 'subsistence' and 'other rights', respectively 'first-generation rights' and 'second-generation rights', is not constructive. Even liberal rights, such as the right to life, can require positive action. For instance, the ECtHR explained in *Tătar v. Romania* that there is 'a positive obligation to adopt reasonable and sufficient measures to protect the rights of the interested parties to respect for their private lives and their home and, more generally, a healthy, protected environment'.[91]

Pogge avoids the problematic nature of positive obligations in the international context altogether by claiming that standards of justice apply to institutions and that the governments of developed countries have violated their negative duties to not harm others.[92] He made this argument in relation to poverty and explained that it is not so much the positive duty of governments and their citizens to aid the poor but their negative duty not to bring poverty over other people independently of their status as fellow citizens or foreigners.[93] People have a negative duty to not participate in or foster unjust socio-economic structures.[94] This argument could be applied to the climate context and hold that governments and citizens do not have a positive duty to contribute to equal burden-sharing and material aid so much as not to violate their duty to not emit more GHGs into the atmosphere than is needed (so-called 'luxury emissions').[95] Furthermore, this argument could

---

[88] Martha C Nussbaum, *The Cosmopolitan Tradition: A Noble but Flawed Ideal* (Harvard University Press 2019) 7–8.

[89] Ibid 18–19.

[90] Ibid 20.

[91] ECtHR, *Tătar v. Romania,* Judgement of 27 January 2009, App. no. 67021/01, para 107, see also Council of Europe, *Manual on Human Rights and the Environment* (2nd edn, 2012) 50.

[92] Pogge (n 82) 23–4, also Chapter 7 'Cosmopolitanism and Sovereignty' (168–95).

[93] Ibid 130ff (133).

[94] Ibid 66.

[95] Simon Caney, 'Cosmopolitanism and the Environment' in Teena Gabrielson and others (eds), *The Oxford Handbook of Environmental Political Theory* (OUP 2016) 246; Henry Shue, 'Subsistence Emissions and Luxury Emissions' (1993) 15 Law & Policy 39.

be underpinned by the 'no harm' principle under which sovereign states are not allowed to use their territory in a way that can lead to transboundary harm.[96]

However, it is apparent that environmental degradation that violates the rights of citizens to life, health, food, water and sanitation, inter alia, is different from the kind of state violence that infringes civil and liberal rights. Rather than simply refraining from violating human rights (e.g., torture or freedom of speech), climate mitigation and adaptation measures require the state to actively do something. Mitigation, for example, requires states to restructure their economy but also the lifestyle of their populations. This can occur through the introduction of a carbon tax, reducing livestock and so on. But the state cannot simply do nothing because unsustainable practices such as cheap flights, cheap meat and ever-bigger cars cannot be adjusted by the markets that work on the maxim of economic growth.[97] Barak noted that:

> Constitutional rights are not merely subjective rights vis-à-vis the state. They also constitute objective constitutional values, which, in turn, may be used as a source for imposing a duty upon the state to act.[98]

The principle of 'sustainable development', which aims to complement economic development with social and environmental concerns developed by the World Commission on Environment and Development in its Brundtland Report, did not challenge this paradigm. Accordingly, '[g]rowth has no set limits in terms of population or resource use beyond which lies ecological disaster'.[99] Such a 'the sky is the limit' approach fosters the paradigm of endless economic growth at the expense of the environment.[100] Thorp, in this sense, identifies both a negative duty not to harm and a positive duty towards each other party to promote or facilitate (economic) development in Article 3 para. 5 UNFCCC.[101]

---

[96] Benoit Mayer, 'Interpreting States' General Obligations on Climate Change Mitigation: A Methodological Review' (2019) 28 Review of European, Comparative and International Environmental Law 107, 108.

[97] Frank Ackerman and Kevin Gallagher, 'Getting the Prices Wrong: The Limits of Market-Based Environmental Policy' [2000] Global Development and Environment Institute Working Paper 00–05.

[98] Aharon Barak, *Proportionality: Constitutional Rights and Their Limitations* (CUP 2012) 427.

[99] UN World Commission on Environment and Development, *Our Common Future (Brundtland Report)* (OUP 1987) 45.

[100] Gonzalez (n 43) 228–9.

[101] Teresa Thorp, 'Climate Justice: A Constitutional Approach to Unify the Lex Specialis Principles of International Climate Law' (2012) 8 Utrecht Law Review 7, 29.

Positive obligations play a major role in environmental and climate protection. In climate matters, it is not enough that states do not actively violate human rights. Instead, they need to fulfil their obligations through positive action so that all other human rights can be enjoyed.[102] Many CCL cases have positive obligations at their heart, in particular those aiming to protect the interests of young people and future generations.[103]

4.2 A (Legal) Duty of Justice towards the Climatically Disadvantaged?

A question that will most likely arise in the (near) future is whether citizens and states of the Global North owe mitigation and financial aid to states and citizens of the Global South. In IL, positive obligations are generally perceived as a matter of internal democracy. A state is 'obligated to take positive measures to promote the interests only of its own nationals', and:

> A state is never bound to act positively to advance the interests of foreigners; for any given foreigner, the task of promoting his or her interests falls upon his or her state. Whatever else is included under the sovereignty of the state, a state is free to ignore the interests of foreigners in the precise sense that it is bound to do nothing at all to advance the interests of foreigners.[104]

In a democratic nation-state based on fundamental rights (*Grundrechtsstaat*), social justice means that fundamental rights need to be accessible to all. The state can achieve this goal by redistributing incomes, assets and decision-making

---

[102] In this sense, UN Special Rapporteur David Boyd points out that "[w]ith respect to substantive obligations, States must not violate the right to a safe climate through their own actions; must protect that right from being violated by third parties, especially businesses; and must establish, implement and enforce laws, policies and programmes to fulfil that right", UN Special Rapporteur on Human Rights and the Environment David Boyd, 'Special Report on Human Rights Obligations Relating to the Enjoyment of a Safe, Clean, Healthy and Sustainable Environment (A/74/161)' (2019) 18 (para 65).

[103] See e.g. Laura Burgers and Tim Staal, 'Climate Action as Positive Human Rights Obligation: The Appeals Judgment in Urgenda v The Netherlands' [2019] Amsterdam Law School Legal Studies Research Paper No. 2019–01.

[104] Henry Shue, *Climate Justice: Vulnerability and Protection* (2014) 144.

powers internally.[105] But can such obligations also exist towards people in other countries or even towards future generations? In other words: is there a global duty of justice?

A philosopher who has intensively researched the nature of justice and positive duties is Thomas Nagel. He discusses in his essay *The Problem of Global Justice* the kind of moral obligations societies and individuals owe to each other.[106] Nagel is a prominent liberal thinker who belongs to the school of communitarianism. As opposed to cosmopolitanism, communitarians argue against the universality of justice.[107] Justice is only possible in a community, for example, the institutional context of the state to which the rights-bearer belongs (although he does not argue that human beings do not have any moral obligations towards each other).[108] Theories of cosmopolitanism are rejected in favour of an approach that is called 'political conception', according to which the existence of states is the prerequisite for any concept of socio-economic justice.[109] The construct of the state puts individual citizens in relation to other citizens of the same state—a relation they do not share with the rest of humanity—and it is only in this relationship that socio-economic justice needs to (and should) be pursued.[110] 'Political conception' is essentially based on Rawls' '*Law of Peoples*'.[111] To the disappointment of cosmopolitans, Rawls did not apply his principles of justice[112] to the global context. Some cosmopolitans have argued that the 'veil of ignorance' could have hidden the most arbitrary factor of all: citizenship.[113] But Rawls held that the principle was applicable within but not across societies.[114] On this account, Nagel

---

105 Josef Isensee, 'Grundrechte und Demokratie' (1981) 20 Der Staat 161, 170. German: 'Soziale Gerechtigkeit des Grundrechtsstaates aber bedeutet: praktische Zugänglichkeit der grundrechtlichen Freiheit für alle in der gesellschaftlichen Realität'.

106 Thomas Nagel, 'The Problem of Global Justice' (2005) 33 Philosophy and Public Affairs 113.

107 David Miller, *On Nationality* (Clarendon Press 1995) 73–80 and Chapter 4.

108 Ibid 75; for an overview of cosmopolitan and communitarian positions, see Ruud Koopmans and Michael Zürn, 'Cosmopolitanism and Communitarianism – How Globalization Is Reshaping Politics in the Twenty-First Century' in Pieter de Wilde and others (eds), *The Struggle Over Borders: Cosmopolitanism and Communitarianism* (CUP 2019) 11–7.

109 Nagel (n 106) 120.

110 Ibid.

111 John Rawls, *The Law of Peoples* (Harvard University Press 1999).

112 John Rawls, *A Theory of Justice (1971)* (Revised Ed, OUP 1999).

113 Charles R Beitz, *Political Theory and International Relations* (Princeton University Press 1979) 151, 176; Gillian Brock, *Global Justice: A Cosmopolitan Account* (OUP 2009) 20.

114 Brock (n 113) 20.

bases his argument on the premise that societies (in Rawls's conception, peoples or societies are such that are organised in a state) have certain obligations towards other societies, but individual citizens do not have such obligations towards other citizens of other states nor within the same society.[115]

Some argue that Rawls's '*Law of Peoples*' is based on an outdated and vanished Westphalian world of sovereign states.[116] The lack of global distributive justice has been sharply criticised, and where elements of such justice have been identified, in particular, the duties of better-off peoples to aid 'burdened societies', it has been argued that these are not far-reaching enough[117] and would need to be extended to grapple with the highly complex problem of climate change.[118] However, the distinction between strict 'duties of justice' that require high moral standards that individuals have to one to another and 'duties of material aid' that they have only towards their 'near and dear' goes back to Cicero's work and has influenced political thought ever since, even the works of cosmopolitans.[119]

Accordingly, the moral presumption against arbitrary inequalities is not a principle of universal application but depends on the societal context.[120] Thus, Nagel differentiates between negative and positive obligations that we owe to others: while the former belong to any human of the world regardless of their membership to any society and have to be respected by everyone, the latter can only be pursued within the closed framework of a state.[121] 'Justice is something we owe through our shared institutions only to those with whom we stand in a strong political relation.'[122]

The unit 'society', which is separable from other societies, is shaped by the paradox of involuntary membership and the engagement of the will to live in this society nonetheless and to follow its rules. Confusingly, it is this incidental

[115] Nagel (n 106) 123–4.

[116] Allen Buchanan, 'Rawls's Law of Peoples: Rules for a Vanished Westphalian World' (2000) 110 Ethics 697.

[117] Ibid 710, arguing that '[t]here is no indication that this duty of aid is to be understood as the collective responsibility of the society of peoples and no mention of a right on the part of "'burdened societies'" to receive it. In other words, the duty as Rawls conceives it seems to resemble an imperfect duty of charity rather than a duty of justice.'; see also Charles R Beitz, 'Rawls's Law of Peoples' (2000) 110 Ethics 669, 689ff.

[118] Hyunseop Kim, 'An Extension of Rawls's Theory of Justice for Climate Change' (2019) 11 International Theory 160.

[119] Nussbaum (n 88) 20ff.

[120] Nagel (n 106) 127–8.

[121] Ibid 127.

[122] Ibid 121.

and, thus, most arbitrary fact—that we are not able to decide by whom or where we are born—that the place we 'arbitrarily find ourselves [in] that gives rise to the special presumption against further arbitrary distinctions within it'.[123] It is because of citizens' active cooperation and their will to live in their society (under strong centralised control and backed by legal force), and their dual role as both a subject of society and as one in whose name its authority is exercised, that the differentiation between members of this society and others can be justified.[124] As Nagel puts it: 'Everyone may have the right to live in a just society, but we do not have an obligation to live in a just society with everyone.'[125]

> Justice [...] requires a collectively imposed social frame-work, enacted in the name of all those governed by it, and aspiring to command their acceptance of its authority even when they disagree with the substance of its decisions.[126]

In this sense, global constitutionalism that seeks not only to guarantee the protection of the most basic human rights but also entails a vision of global socio-economic justice would only be feasible in a world state: the institutional setting that makes everyone a fellow citizen with everyone else.[127] However, it seems neither likely nor desirable that such a world state ever comes into being. As a result, global justice would not be feasible at the global level and, thus, could not possibly be included in a theory of global climate constitutionalism that is supposed to encompass humanity as a whole.

The main idea that underlies the limitedness of a group of people towards whom justice is owed is contractualism. Accordingly, it is only in the national realm that a community can participate in a hypothetical social contract that serves as the basis for the legitimation of the state's authority. Since the group that decides on this hypothetical social contract is not created by a contract itself, it has to be specified and determined prior to the contract.[128] Justice is owned because people have consented to help each other. From the position of contract-based liberalism, justice is 'a matter of social cooperation, that is to say, a voluntary form of interpersonal enterprise. Justice is no more a given

---

[123] Ibid 128.

[124] Ibid.

[125] Ibid 132.

[126] Ibid 140.

[127] Ibid 121, 138.

[128] David Heyd, 'Justice and Solidarity: The Contractarian Case against Global Justice' (2007) 38 Journal of Social Philosophy 112, 113ff.

truth or principle, but a product of a negotiated deal.'[129] Liberalists are quite aware that not every deal is a fair deal, that conditions—called the 'circumstances of justice'[130]—must be in place to guarantee fair outcomes, such as 'moderate scarcity, limited sympathy, mutual vulnerability or interdependence, and rough equality'.[131] The reason why global justice is not possible is shown by the lack of 'limited sympathy': the lack of actual care for others.[132] From this point of view, it could follow in the case of climate change that people of the rich North simply do not care for the populations of the South; therefore, they have no desire to enter a hypothetical social contract with them.

From this contractarian perspective, redistributive justice needs to be domestic. There can be no duty of justice to help either the worst-off societies or the worst-off individuals in the world. The reason for limiting justice to the domestic sphere is seen to be a consequence of the societies that are, to a large extent, responsible for the economic choices they make, including 'demographic planning and other cultural values (such as the rate of savings for future generations, or religious arrangements of property and power distribution)'.[133]

However, this argument largely fails in the face of global climate change because it neglects the historical factors that, to a large extent, are responsible for the current state of affairs, including the fossil fuel industry created and upheld by some countries of the North. It ignores that the Anthropocene has colonial and post-colonial origins[134]:

> The North's control over a large part of the world's resources from the colonial era to the present fuelled the North's industrial development and enabled the North to maintain levels of consumption far beyond the limits of its own natural resource base. [...] The South's economic dependency on export production enabled the North to exploit Southern resources at prices that did not reflect the social and environmental costs of production. Far from producing prosperity, export-led development strategies depleted the South's natural resources, harmed human health and reinforced social and economic inequality by imposing disparate environmental burdens on the communities targeted for petroleum extraction, mining and other forms of resource exploitation. Much of the environmental degradation in the global South has been

---

[129] Ibid 115–6.

[130] John Rawls, *Justice as Fairness—A Restatement* (Erin Kelly ed, Belknap Press 2001) 84–5.

[131] Heyd, 'Justice and Solidarity: The Contractarian Case against Global Justice' (n 128) 116.

[132] Ibid.

[133] Ibid 125.

[134] Gonzalez (n 43) 221ff.

> caused by export-oriented production to satisfy the needs and desires of Northern consumers, rather than local consumption.[135]

Given the long-lasting consequences of colonialism, it is difficult to speak here of developing countries' 'free economic choices'. Rather, they are the unsolicited 'receivers' of the undesirable effects of dangerous climate change caused by countries of the Global North.

The question of justice also arises in the intergenerational context. Rawls discussed the obligation of considering the redistribution of resources between generations under his principle of just savings.[136] 'In following a just savings principle, each generation makes a contribution to those coming later and precedes from its predecessors.'[137] Rawls' complex theory of justice cannot be discussed here in detail. Briefly, for Rawls, a decision on just savings is the outcome of a hypothetical contract between all members in the original position (which refers to a hypothetical situation as 'a status quo in which any agreements reached are fair'[138]). However, present and future generations cannot cooperate with previous generations; their relations are not reciprocal. Reciprocity can only work in one direction, since we do not owe anything to previous generations but also cannot hold them responsible for past choices.[139] Thus, the relations are not conceived as relations characterised by 'circumstances of justice'; there is no cooperation.[140] Moreover, by taking the 'present-time of entry' interpretation, people in the original position may not know to which generation they belong—the 'veil of ignorance' makes them blind to which generation exactly they belong—but they know that they are contemporaries, and, as such, they can refuse to make any savings for their successors.[141]

To solve this problem, Rawls modifies the 'present-time of entry' to the original position by adding a 'motivational aspiration' that makes people save for future generations because they care for their children and grandchildren. The parties of the original position represent family lines that at least care for their immediate descendants; thus, there would be an intergenerational chain that

---

[135] Ibid 223 (citations omitted).

[136] 'The principle of just savings holds between generations, while the difference principle holds within generations', Rawls, *Justice as Fairness—A Restatement* (n 130) 159.

[137] Rawls, *A Theory of Justice (1971)* (n 112) 254.

[138] Ibid 104.

[139] Ibid 254–5.

[140] Ibid 109, 111.

[141] Ibid 121.

covers all generations.[142] Moreover, another constraint can be added insofar as the principle adopted by the parties includes their wish that all earlier generations would have followed the principle of just savings as well.[143] As a result, '[w]hatever a person's temporal position, each is forced to choose for all'.[144]

> The correct principle is that which the members of any generation (and so all generations) would adopt as the one their generation is to follow and as the principle they would want preceding generations to have followed (and later generations to follow), no matter how far back (or forward) in time.[145]

Still, the idea that a duty—in the form of an obligation—can follow from the principle of just savings has been met with criticism. The intergenerational concern for the well-being of one's offspring would not extend beyond one or two generations. Although a parent knows rationally that their grandchildren will likely one day have grandchildren of their own, it seems unlikely that a parent would deeply care about the fate of such 'far-away' relatives.[146] Essentially, the same argument is made in relation to people in other societies: the lack of solidarity. Solidarity is the basis upon which relations of justice can be implemented between generations. Since there is no intergenerational solidarity, there cannot be a duty to uphold justice (as an obligation) between generations.[147] This holds especially for the future generations of other societies or countries. The collective will to preserve the planet is distributed within nations and peoples, 'but rarely shared among them'.[148] This is because every nation or group holds its own cultural identity (language, ideas, history, traditions, values, politics), which makes political cooperation extremely difficult. But within every society, the political will to protect its own future generations is present.[149]

According to such views, 'justice begins at home and ends there'.[150] This does not mean that people and states have no duties towards other members

---

142 Ibid 255.

143 Ibid.

144 Ibid 141.

145 Rawls, *Justice as Fairness—A Restatement* (n 130) 160.

146 David Heyd, 'A Value or an Obligation? Rawls on Justice to Future Generations' in Axel Gosseries and Lukas H Meyer (eds), *Intergenerational Justice* (OUP 2009) 175.

147 Ibid 184–5.

148 Richard P Hiskes, *The Human Right to a Green Future: Environmental Rights and Intergenerational Justice* (CUP 2008) 117.

149 Ibid 118.

150 Heyd, 'Justice and Solidarity: The Contractarian Case against Global Justice' (n 128) 112.

of societies, but '[j]ustice, particularly in its distributive sense, should be kept as a separate category from natural duties, rational ad hoc agreements, impartial solutions of conflicts, and respect for human rights'.[151] Different to justice, which is then understood as purely domestic, charity extends beyond one's home.[152] However, charity is a weak basis for obligation, since it is withdrawn easily, and it reproduces the vulnerability of the recipient. The act of giving out of charity has a paternalistic aspect to it, while justice levels imbalances: the subjects are perceived as putative equals.[153] Justice is something that is owed to the other. 'You can also "not do" justice, of course, just as you can "not do" charity, *but the obligation to do justice remains, even while you are not doing it.*'[154]

In his later writings, Heyd, who rejected a duty of justice in relation to a society's *own* future generations, recognises a global duty of justice towards the future generations of the societies of developing countries based on the global implications of climate change caused by the countries of the Global North. He argues that the present generations of the developed world 'owe a natural duty of care to their own descendants but a duty of justice to the future people of the lower curve [the developing countries]'.[155] This duty of justice entails both intra- and intergenerational implications. Although climate change was not known to industrialists using coal in the 1780s and continued to be unknown until a few decades ago, this knowledge is not required to establish a duty of justice.[156] Such an obligation is not derived from fault but rather from the unjust enrichment that the Global North has achieved by using almost all of the atmospheric capacity and causing harm to countries of the Global South.[157]

From this, it follows that:

1. Past polluters cannot be morally blamed for the current ecological crisis, but we, as beneficiaries of their actions, owe those who have been harmed *restitution.*
2. Present people, who have known for at least a few decades of the risks of continuing pollution, owe developing countries *compensation.*

---

[151] Ibid 127.

[152] Ibid 112.

[153] Dobson (n 76) 281.

[154] Ibid (emphasis in original).

[155] David Heyd, 'Climate Ethics, Affirmative Action, and Unjust Enrichment' in Lukas H Meyer and Pranay Sanklecha (eds), *Climate Justice and Historical Emissions* (CUP 2017) 25.

[156] Ibid 31–2.

[157] Ibid 34ff (36).

3. Future people, after having settled the historical accounts of restitution and compensation, will have to share the burdens of mitigation and adaptation on the basis of *distributive justice*.[158]

The idea of climate justice, including distributive justice among members of the same generation and between generations, thus, has come to the forefront of discourses in ethics, politics and law. Particularly in relation to the latter, members of the open society of constitutional interpreters consequently remind national decision-makers that their interests have to be considered, even though they cannot participate in processes of decision-making such as elections due to their age or nationality.

4.3 A duty to Intra- and Intergenerational Justice? The KSG and the GFCC

The 2021 landmark order of the German Federal Constitutional Court (GFCC) on the (partial) unconstitutionality of the German Climate Protection Act (Klimaschutzgesetz, KSG) of 2019 can be read in this light. Together with 15 claimants from Bangladesh and Nepal, 10 young people from Germany approached the court and asked it to decide whether the state was violating their constitutional rights to life, health and property by not setting sufficient climate goals and, thus, contributing to hazardous climate change.[159]

The Court ruled that it seems 'conceivable in principle' that the state had duties of protection also towards the foreign claimants.[160] However, since the Court already could not find a violation of the fundamental rights to life (Article 2 para. 2 sentence 1 Basic Law, in German: Grundgesetz or GG) of the German claimants,[161] it did not need not to decide whether 'duties of protection arising from fundamental rights also place the German state under an obligation vis-à-vis the complainants living in Bangladesh and in Nepal to take action against

[158] Ibid 43 (emphasis in original).

[159] German Federal Constitutional Court (GFCC), Order of the First Senate of 24 March 2021—1 BvR 2656/18, see also Press Release No. 31/2021 of 29 April 2021 'Constitutional complaints against the Federal Climate Change Act partially successful',<https://www.bundesverfassungsgericht.de/SharedDocs/Pressemitteilungen/EN/2021/bvg21-031.html>accessed 23 August 2023.

[160] GFCC, 1 BvR 2656/18, para 174.

[161] Ibid paras 170, 172.

impairments caused by global climate change'.[162] But even if there was such an obligation, the Court argued that the margin of the duties of protection towards foreign petitioners would be significantly smaller than it is in relation to the German claimants. The Court justified this different treatment with the difference between general climate protection as an objective right on the one hand and the right to life and health as subjective fundamental rights on the other.[163] While climate protection requires necessarily mitigation, the protection of the right to life and health can be ensured by a combination of both mitigation and adaptation. Mitigation is generally understood as involving efforts to curb GHG emissions to slow down or stop. In contrast, adaptation involves strategies to minimise the harm climate change causes.[164] Thus, mitigation measures alone are not sufficient to protect the foreign claimants, since Germany cannot stop climate change on its own. Due to the territorial sovereignty of foreign states, however, the state cannot implement adaptation measures in other countries. 'For this reason alone, a duty of protection could not have the same content as it has vis-à-vis people living in Germany.'[165] Instead, the Court referred to the obligation under IL (including the Paris Agreement) to provide financial assistance to poorer countries suffering from the consequences of climate change for adaptation measures and considered it sufficient that Germany had fulfilled this duty to protect through international advocacy for climate protection and through concrete measures to implement what has been agreed internationally on climate protection.

However, there is an flipside to this argument. The Court modifies the duty of protection towards foreign complainants because the state cannot implement adaptation measures in other countries. The GFCC is right in arguing that both mitigation and adaptation measures are necessary to address climate change. According to the IPCC:

> Many adaptation and mitigation options can help address climate change, but no single option is sufficient by itself. Effective implementation depends on policies and cooperation at all scales and can be enhanced through integrated responses that link mitigation and adaptation with other societal objectives.[166]

[162] Ibid para 174.

[163] Ibid paras 176 ff.

[164] Bert Gordijn and Henk ten Have, 'Ethics of Mitigation, Adaptation and Geoengineering' (2012) 15 Medicine, Health Care and Philosophy 1, 1.

[165] GFCC, 1 BvR 2656/18, para 178.

[166] IPCC, 'Climate Change 2014 Synthesis Report' (2015) 94.

The GFCC took the view that different contents of a possible duty to protect between the German and foreign plaintiffs are based on the grounds that the German state can counter climate change in Germany through a combination of mitigation and adaptation measures, whereas it cannot do so in relation to other countries (such a duty to protect could therefore only be fulfilled through mitigation measures). This view could be seen in a more critical light regarding the nature of mitigation and adaptation. Countries such as Bangladesh and Nepal that barely emit GHGs depend on developed countries such as Germany to mitigate their emissions. In contrast to richer countries that can choose how they want to address climate change (through mitigation or adaptation measures or a combination of both), developing countries have no other choice but to adapt to climate change.

Mitigation can be seen as a global public good that benefits many people in many regions (far away) in the long term, while adaptation can be understood as a local private good that often only brings clear and immediate benefits to local citizens.[167] As a result, developed countries often choose adaptation over mitigation. Having the power of choice, they can either curb GHG emissions to the benefit of the whole world or they can choose adaptation measures to become 'climate-proof' and ensure short-term climate security for their own benefit only:

> So far, many rich countries seem to be unwilling or are unable to carry through radical measures to hold back greenhouse gas emissions. Surely some of them fear mitigation might negatively affect economic growth and material welfare. As a result, many people, especially in the poorest countries in the world, have experienced and will increasingly encounter adverse climate change effects on health, both in terms of morbidity and mortality.[168]

Thus, while both strategies address climate change—and both are necessary to protect people from its adverse effects—the results are different: adaptation protects the people of a particular country only, while mitigation protects possibly everyone.[169]

---

[167] The Climate Reality Project, 'Climate Adaptation vs. Mitigation: What's the Difference, and Why Does It Matter?' (7 November 2019) < https://www.climaterealityproject.org/blog/climate-adaptation-vs-mitigation-why-does-it-matter > accessed 31 August 2023; see also Reviva Hasson, Åsa Löfgren and Martine Visser, 'Climate Change in a Public Goods Game: Investment Decision in Mitigation versus Adaptation' (2010) 70 Ecological Economics 331, 331.

[168] Gordijn and ten Have (n 164) 1.

[169] Cf. Richard JT Klein and others, 'Inter-Relationships between Adaptation and Mitigation' in Martin Parry and others (eds), *Climate Change 2007: Impacts, Adaptation and*

Adaptation alone cannot solve the problem of climate change. It is comparable to removing the water that enters a sinking ship instead of repairing the hole.[170] This hole can only be fixed by those countries that are responsible for the greatest share of GHG emissions by choosing to mitigate instead of only adapting to climate change. To this extent, the order of the GFCC demonstrates how far national law is from considering the interests of others. By stressing the opportunity to protect the right to life not only through mitigation but also through adaptation measures, 'the Court accepts more severe climate change impacts in other countries which result from the fact that the Court grants Germany leeway to emit carbon dioxide because it is able to 'compensate' such emissions by implementing adaptation measures on German territory to reduce national health consequences.'[171]

In short, rich countries such as Germany should recognise a positive duty to mitigate even though it is also possible to address climate change through adaptation (which it cannot implement in other countries). Otherwise, choosing adaptation over mitigation in richer countries could eventually have severe consequences in developing countries, especially since it is not clear yet whether adaptation strategies implemented today can in fact protect those countries against the future effects of climate change, such as stronger storms or more frequent droughts, with a possible 'adaptation limit' looming when no more adaptation measures exist, or the adaptive effort required to sustain a natural system or societal objectives is unacceptable.[172] The Court saw the problem that adaptation alone is not enough but considered it sufficient that Germany had ratified the Paris Agreement, and by doing so, had committed itself to both reducing emissions nationally and providing financial aid to developing countries.[173] Yet, as the developed countries, including Germany, continue to miss these goals, this does little to help the citizens of Bangladesh or Nepal. Nevertheless, the fact that

Vulnerability. Contributions of Working Group II to the Fourth Assessment Report of the Intergovernmental Panel on Climate Change (CUP 2007) 747.

[170] The Climate Reality Project (n 167).

[171] Jasper Mührel, 'All That Glitters Is Not Gold: The German Constitutional Court's Climate Ruling and the Protection of Persons Beyond German Territory Against Climate Change Impacts' *Völkerrechtsblog* (3 May 2021) < https://voelkerrechtsblog.org/all-that-glitters-is-not-gold/ > accessed 31 August 2023.

[172] Richard JT Klein, Guy F Midgley and Benjamin L Preston, 'Adaptation Opportunities, Constraints, and Limits' in Christopher B Field and others (eds), *Climate Change 2014: Impacts, Adaptation, and Vulnerability (Contributions of Working Group II to the Fifth Assessment Report of the Intergovernmental Panel on Climate Change)* (CUP 2014) 907.

[173] GFCC, 1 BvR 2656/18, para 180.

the GFCC found the complaints of the foreign claimants admissible and that it seems 'generally possible' that a duty to protect also exists towards non-German claimants living outside Germany demonstrates that the Court has understood that climate change is a global problem that requires local action, inter alia, in Germany.

While the Court was hesitant to recognise duties of protection in relation to the foreign complainants, it recognised—and in this respect, the Court's order was described as 'historic'[174]—that the state has a duty to protect the fundamental rights of future generations:

> The state's duty of protection arising from Art. 2(2) first sentence GG also includes the duty to protect life and health against the risks posed by climate change [...]. In view of the considerable risks that increasingly severe climate change may also entail for the legal interests protected under Art. 2(2) first sentence GG – for example through heat waves, floods or hurricanes [...] – the state is obliged to afford this protection to the current population and also, in light of objective legal requirements, to future generations.[175]

Rather than relying on the construct of duties of protection, the court recognised that fundamental rights are 'inter-temporal guarantees of freedom'.[176] This means that present generations cannot use almost all the 'climate budget' that is left to achieve climate neutrality in 2050 in the next 10 years as envisioned in the KSG. Instead, fundamental rights protect future generations against threats to their freedoms that are and will be caused by the burdens of reducing GHGs 'being unilaterally offloaded onto the future'. Not curbing enough GHG emissions today has an advanced interference-like effect (*eingriffsähnliche Vorwirkung*) on the fundamental rights of young people tomorrow.[177] Although the Court eventually did not see a violation of the right to life, it made clear that the legislative process cannot ignore the interests of future generations anymore, and that such

---

[174] '"Historic" German Ruling Says Climate Goals Not Tough Enough' *The Guardian* (29 April 2021) < https://www.theguardian.com/world/2021/apr/29/historic-german-ruling-says-climate-goals-not-tough-enough > accessed 31 August 2023.

[175] GFCC, 1 BvR 2656/18, para 148.

[176] Press Release No. 31/2021 of 29 April 2021 in English; see also GFCC, 1 BvR 2656/18, para 48.

[177] GFCC, 1 BvR 2656/18, para 183.

interests find their basis in Article 20a of the Basic Law—an enforceable norm[178]: 'Art. 20a GG is a justiciable legal provision designed to commit the political process to a favouring of ecological interests, partly with a view to future generations who will be particularly affected.'[179]

This case and the attention it received both in and outside Germany show how important matters of climate justice are to people worldwide. Moreover, it demonstrates again how significant the function of the members of the civil society (as constitutional pre-interpreters who engage in a legal discourse with the Constitutional Court) is for the development of the law.[180] The German government sought dismissal of the complaints because Article 20a GG, as a state objective, would not grant any subjective rights.[181] As such, Article 20a GG has often been ridiculed as 'constitutional poetry' since state objectives are generally not enforceable as such.[182] However, the ruling made clear that the norm is not only enforceable but that it even constrains the scope for political decision-making on whether or not to take measures to protect the environment. The legislator cannot ignore these limits that Article 20a GG sets and, thus, also has to consider the interests of future generations that have no say in the formation of the political will today. Additionally, the legislator has to achieve climate neutrality—a concept the Court introduced to Article 20a GG together with the 'inter-temporal guarantees of freedom', which, however, only protect German nationals.

---

[178] Article 20a of the German Basic Law reads: "Mindful also of its responsibility towards future generations, the state shall protect the natural foundations of life and animals by legislation and, in accordance with law and justice, by executive and judicial action, all within the framework of the constitutional order.".

[179] GFCC, 1 BvR 2656/18, para 197.

[180] Peter Häberle, '"The Open Society of Constitutional Interpreters" – A Contribution to a Pluralistic and "Procedural" Constitutional Interpretation (1975)' in Markus Kotzur (ed), *Peter Häberle on Constitutional Theory* (Nomos/Hart 2018) 131.

[181] GFCC, 1 BvR 2656/18, para 51.

[182] „Böse Zungen nennen das Verfassungslyrik" —Interview with Georg Oswald (*Deutschlandfunk*, 29 July 2019) < https://www.deutschlandfunkkultur.de/jurist-oswald-ueber-klimaschutz-im-grundgesetz-boese-zungen.1008.de.html?dram:article_id=455043 > accessed 31 August 2023.

4.4 Constitutionalism and Values

Rather traditional visions of global constitutionalism understand the role of constitutionalism in restraining sovereignty and establishing constitutional elements such as the separation of powers, human rights and democracy at the global level. Including climate justice in such frameworks means analysing whether constitutionalism would be capable of not only binding state powers but also transferring value concepts. In the 'thin' sense of the term 'constitution', it refers to the establishment, definition and organisation of the main organs of the government, their constitution and power.[183] However:

> viable communities need to share values, whether these communities are global, regional, or local. They need to believe that they are linked in common understandings. The global communities, the fragmented communities, and the shifting informal coalitions and multitudinous individuals need to share values, which can be reflected in international, as well as transnational and local, law.[184]

Generally, a constitution in the 'thick' sense, which not only constitutes the state but also a society, transports such values.[185] But it is doubtful whether any international environmental treaty (or all of them combined) could be a constitution in a 'thick' sense. Bodansky, in 2009, rigidly rejected the idea of an international environmental constitution.[186] He argued that the existing elements of IEL (treaties, agreements and institutions) would perhaps classify as constitutions

---

[183] Paul Craig, 'Constitutions, Constitutionalism, and the European Union' (2001) 7 European Law Journal 125, 126.

[184] Edith Brown Weiss, 'International Law in a Kaleidoscopic World' (2011) 1 Asian Journal of International Law 21, 25.

[185] It is less clear how a constitution in the thick sense should be defined but some characteristics could serve for a definition. A constitution in the thick sense (1) incorporates the constitution in the thin sense by establishing and structuring the main organs, (2) it is stable, (3) it is written, (4) it is superior law, (5) it is justiciable, (6) it is entrenched, and (7) it expresses a common ideology, see Joseph Raz, 'On the Authority and Interpretation of Constitutions: Some Preliminaries' in Larry Alexander (ed), *Constitutionalism: Philosophical Foundations* (CUP 1998) 152–3.

[186] Bodansky (n 34).

(with a 'small c') but not as a Constitution (with a 'big C').[187] International documents establish systems of governance and rules of how these systems should work.[188] They fail, however, to establish independent organisations, which is necessary in terms of a 'thick' constitution. Neither is it granted that issues could be taken outside the zone of political influence by implementing effective procedural or substantive constraints on the acting of such organisations, nor do they establish a constitutional order for IEL as a whole.[189] However, the coupling of institutionalisation and constitutionalism has been criticised as too narrow and too close to what resembles domestic constitutionalism.[190] Instead, this work applies an approach that focuses less on legalisation and institutionalisation but understands 'thick' constitutions as 'self-confident assertions of the collective will; they are value-laden and exude numerous characteristics that could legitimize, dignify and improve a legal order.'[191]

A constitution in the 'thick' sense must include the most basic values of a polity to qualify as a constitution at all.[192] Values, in this sense, are the 'beliefs of a person or social group in which they have an emotional investment (either for or against something)'.[193] These values can be found in the small core constitution of both jurists and laypeople, including the principles of dignity, liberty, equality, democracy and the protection of fundamental rights; the 'thin' constitution means the 'jurists' constitution' concerning regulatory and organisational matters.[194] The focus of any constitution is the legal construction of a community

---

[187] Ibid 578; on the small 'c' and big 'C' constitutionalism, see Matthias Kumm, 'The Cosmopolitan Turn in Constitutionalism: On the Relationship between Constitutionalism in and beyond the State' in Jeffrey L Dunoff and Joel P Trachtman (eds), *Ruling the World? Constitutionalism, International Law and Global Government* (CUP 2009) 260; Neil Walker, 'Big "C" or Small "c"?' (2006) 12 European Law Journal 12.

[188] Bodansky (n 34) 578.

[189] Ibid.

[190] Gavin W Anderson, 'Societal Constitutionalism, Social Movements, and Constitutionalism from Below' (2013) 20 Indiana Journal of Global Legal Studies 881.

[191] Louis J Kotzé, 'Arguing Global Environmental Constitutionalism' (2012) 1 Transnational Environmental Law 199, 204 (citations omitted).

[192] Anne van Aaken, 'Defragmentation of Public International Law Through Interpretation: A Methodological Proposal' (2009) 16 Indiana Journal of Global Legal Studies 483, 487.

[193] Margarita Pavlova, *Technology and Vocational Education for Sustainable Development* (Springer 2009) 33.

[194] It has to be noted that Tushnet uses the terms 'thin' and 'thick' oppositely, see Mark Tushnet, *Taking the Constitution Away from the Courts* (Princeton University Press 1999) 9–14; also Uwe Volkmann, 'Der Aufstieg der Verfassung: Beobachtungen zum grundlegenden

of free and equal citizens.[195] But a constitution is much more: it is a society's self-perception; it includes its values and the ideals it applies to itself as a moral yardstick. It contains the (moral) goals and purposes it sets for itself—it is a 'mirror reflecting the national soul'.[196] Among limiting powers, implementing governmental organs, granting basic human rights, establishing democracy and the rule of law, a constitution in the 'thick' sense 'express[es] the deepest, most cherished values of a society'.[197] Lutz uses the term 'culture' (in an overlapping way with other terms such as 'set of values') for these hopes and values. Culture refers to 'a shared set of symbols, used to organize joint behaviour for the solving of common problems, that is passed from generation to generation'.[198] Constitutionalism not only necessarily includes culture but also transcends it: it assumes and uses culture. Understood in this sense, constitutionalism refers not only to the 'classical' functions generally ascribed to constitutions, such as limiting powers, but also to the self-conception a society has of itself and that underlies the formal constitution.[199]

Constitutions, therefore, are also about shaping identity.[200] A legal community, and as such, the constitutional community, is moulded by shared history and culture, which informs their members' value orientations, goals and interest positions.[201] Group identity is related to situations in which the group members

---

Wandel des Verfassungsbegriffs' in Thomas Vesting and Stefan Korioth (eds), *Der Eigenwert des Verfassungsrechts* (Mohr Siebeck 2011) 28.

195 Jürgen Habermas, 'A Political Constitution for the Pluralist World Society?' in Jürgen Habermas (ed), *Between Naturalism and Religion: Philosophical Essays* (Polity Press 2008) 328.

196 Frank I Michelman, 'The Constitution, Social Rights, and Liberal Political Justification' (2003) 1 International Journal of Constitutional Law 13, 13, quoting S v. Acheson 1991 (2) SA 805 (Nm), 813A–B (1991 NR 1, 10A–B) (Mahomed AJ). ('The Constitution of a nation is not simply a statute which mechanically defines the structures of government and the relations between the government and the governed.')

197 David Boyd, *The Environmental Rights Revolution: A Global Study of Constitutions, Human Rights, and the Environment* (UBC Press 2011).

198 Donald S Lutz, 'Thinking About Constitutionalism at the Start of the Twenty-First Century' (2000) 30 Publius: The Journal of Federalism 115, 128.

199 Louis J Kotzé, *Global Environmental Constitutionalism in the Anthropocene* (Bloomsbury Publishing 2016) 48ff.

200 Hans Vorländer, 'Constitutions as Symbolic Orders' in Paul Blokker and Chris Thornhill (eds), *Sociological Constitutionalism* (CUP 2017) 226.

201 Jürgen Habermas, *Between Facts and Norms: Contributions to a Discourse Theory of Law and Democracy* (Polity Press 1996) 156; Vorländer (n 200) 225.

utter an emphatic 'we' that supplements the individual's identity.[202] A constitution is 'a medium for the cultural self-representation of the people, a mirror of their cultural heritage and a foundation of their hopes'.[203] Haltern believes that a constitution embodies the ideals of those who sacrificed themselves in bloody revolutions.[204] A people genuinely 'owns' the constitution because its meaning was transported by the sacrifice they made for it.[205] A constitution ties generations from past to future together:

> The self-constituting of society has three faces – a legal constitution, a real constitution, an ideal constitution. In the legal constitution society sees its total self as it has been, as necessity, as obligation. In the real constitution society sees its total self as it is, as actuality, as action. In the ideal constitution society sees its total self as it might be, as potentiality, as desire.[206]

These three constitutions (past, present and future) make possible the self-constituting of a given society in time and space.[207] A constitution may then act as the guardian and reference point for environment-related fundamental rights. It 'provides an opportunity to memorialize environmental social covenants, symbols, and aspirations' that should have a lasting effect on social norms.[208] In times where all other identifying connections (e.g., religion, fatherland or a 'defining

---

[202] Habermas, *Between Facts and Norms: Contributions to a Discourse Theory of Law and Democracy* (n 201) 160.

[203] Peter Häberle, 'Grundrechte und parlamentarische Gesetzgebung im Verfassungsstaat—Das Beispiel des deutschen Grundgesetzes' (1989) 114 Archiv des öffentlichen Rechts 361, 362 (tr the author); see also Jordi Jaria-Manzano and Susana Borràs, 'Introduction to the Research Handbook on Global Climate Constitutionalism' in Jordi Jaria-Manzano and Susana Borràs (eds), *Research Handbook on Global Climate Constitutionalism* (Edward Elgar Publishing 2019) 6.

[204] Ulrich Haltern, 'Internationales Verfassungsrecht? Anmerkungen zu einer kopernikanischen Wende' (2003) 128 Archiv des öffentlichen Rechts 511, 532–6.

[205] Peters, 'The Merits of Global Constitutionalism' (n 36) 400.

[206] Philip Allott, 'Reconstituting Humanity—New International Law' (1992) 3 European Journal of International Law 219, 225.

[207] Ibid.

[208] Louis J Kotzé, 'The Conceptual Contours of Environmental Constitutionalism' (2015) 21 Widener Law Review 187, 198.

culture') have become brittle, the last resort for identification is the constitution.[209] Habermas coined the expression 'constitutional patriotism' to describe this phenomenon.[210]

Thick constitutionalism is something more than merely a set of rules that organises and structures the architecture of a nation-state, and it is also more than its tasks. It is constitutionalism that transfers ideas, concepts and values into the constitutional text, and it is only through this transfer that the superior position of a constitution in a domestic legal order is legitimised.[211] Thus, '[i]n the background, if not even at the foundations, of any constitutional system are reflections upon the very notion of morality'.[212] A constitution rests on three deeply shared universal human hopes: the hopes of life, liberty and the pursuit of happiness.[213] Some scholars, therefore, believe that a global constitution will always remain utopic, and argue that there is no global civil society as there could be no identity beyond the state. Instead, global society is pluralistic and deeply divided.[214] 'Without a common political identity, why would people feel responsible for one another? What would motivate them to cooperate with one another? Why would they be committed to maintaining a common political enterprise?'.[215]

The answer is that a constitution presupposes and/or promises societal integration in the form of 'a common attachment or common predicament within the putative *demos*'.[216] This means that most members demonstrate the minimum level of sustained mutual respect and concern required to reach and adhere to

---

[209] Volkmann (n 194) 32.

[210] See, for example, Jürgen Habermas, 'The Postnational Constellation and the Future of Democracy' in Jürgen Habermas and Max Pensky (eds), *The Postnational Constellation: Political Essays* (Polity Press 2001) 74.

[211] Kotzé, *Global Environmental Constitutionalism in the Anthropocene* (n 199) 52.

[212] George Anastaplo, 'Constitutionalism and the Good: Explorations' (2003) 70 Tennessee Law Review 738, 738.

[213] Lutz (n 198) 133.

[214] A comprehensive discussion is provided by T Olaf Corry, 'Global Civil Society and Its Discontents' (2006) 17 Voluntas: International Journal of Voluntary and Nonprofit Organizations 303, referring inter alia to Bartelson, 'On the redundancy of civil society', in Jan Hallenberg, Bertil Nygren and Alexa Robertson (eds), Transitions. In Honour of Kjell Goldmann (Stockholm University 2003) 111; see also Jean L Cohen, *Globalization and Sovereignty: Rethinking Legality, Legitimacy, and Constitutionalism* (CUP 2012) 44.

[215] Alex Schwartz, 'Patriotism or Integrity? Constitutional Community in Divided Societies' (2011) 31 Oxford Journal of Legal Studies 503, 504.

[216] Neil Walker, 'Taking Constitutionalism beyond the State' (2008) 56 Political Studies 519, 531.

collective outcomes that may work against their immediate interests in terms of the distribution of common resources and risks.[217]

Moreover, each member should trust all other members to participate in collective decision-making processes and rule-following. Such a community's political culture is characterised by mutual respect and trust that is strong enough to acknowledge and accept differences beyond its core commitment.[218] While there is no global demos, it has been argued in relation to the WTO that informal institutions such as 'a shared history, with its attendant values, concerns, and camaraderie' may well be understood as complements or substitutes for formal constitutional structures, in particular, for the lack of a WTO demos.[219] Even without such a demos, a WTO constitution can or does exist, though it is different from national constitutions.[220]

In this sense, not a demos in the form of a 'nation' but a *civitas* (Kant) is necessary to create and constitute a constitutional order. A *civitas* is composed of many people that have a mutual influence on each other, are in need of a legal status and a constitution and possess a unifying will.[221] A world territorial state is not necessary for a world *civitas,* but representation is, for example, in the form of a world parliament.[222] Conversely, homogeneity or even harmony between humans is not a prerequisite because the *civitas* should enable people to pursue happiness according to their own ethnic, cultural, religious and other ideas of a good life.[223] A political culture does not need to share the same ethnic and cultural roots.[224] Rather, if all members of a polity should be able to identify with it, the majority culture (assuming it is identical to the national culture) has to free itself from its historical identification with a general political culture. If successful—and thus, majority culture is decoupled from political culture—what remains is the more abstract foundation of 'constitutional pluralism' that the members share.[225] It is a shift of understanding from a people's

---

[217] Ibid.

[218] Ibid.

[219] Joel P Trachtman, 'Constitutional Economics of the World Trade Organization' in Jeffrey L Dunoff and Joel P Trachtman (eds), *Ruling the World? Constitutionalism, International Law and Global Government* (CUP 2009) 227.

[220] Ibid 228.

[221] Emmerich-Fritsche (n 23) 631.

[222] Ibid 640.

[223] Ibid 633.

[224] Habermas, *Between Facts and Norms: Contributions to a Discourse Theory of Law and Democracy* (n 201) 500.

[225] Habermas, 'The Postnational Constellation and the Future of Democracy' (n 210) 74.

democracy (*Volksdemokratie*) as absolute in a Rousseauan understanding to a citizens' democracy (*Bürgerdemokratie*).[226] A constitution turns its subjects into citizens,[227] and 'a people is primarily a coalition of citizens'.[228] As such, they are not only citizens of a nation-state but are also members of diverse groups with divergent interests, including religious, ethnic or interest communities.[229] This 'coalition of citizens' operates universally on many planes, in many forms and on many occasions, at least through the everyday application of fundamental rights.[230] The idea of a homogenous people, therefore, is fiction,[231] and so is the idea of a 'collective subject' in the form of a collective identity that connects individuals.[232] Democracy, from such a perspective, is about protecting fundamental rights instead of merely replacing the monarch. 'Fundamental freedoms (pluralism), not "the people" thereby become the point of reference for a democratic constitution.'[233] The constitution is the framework that holds 'the' people together as a pluralistic entity.[234] Thus, it can be assumed that a global community that is held together through a constitution could exist. Constitutions today are not only constituting the state but also society.[235] As such, a constitution needs to include more than merely formal elements, such as a written document or the establishment of its main organs, to justify its position as superior law. Rather, it shapes a polity's identity and perception of self. Thus, although general principles of IEL may still be weak and vague, they could represent a core value

---

[226] Häberle, 'The Open Society of Constitutional Interpreters' (n 180) 147.

[227] Volkmann (n 194) 29.

[228] Häberle, 'The Open Society of Constitutional Interpreters' (n 180) 147; Peter Häberle, *Die Verfassung des Pluralismus* (Athenäum 1980) 89.

[229] Roland Bieber and Markus Kotzur, 'Strukturprinzipen der EU-Verfassung' in Roland Bieber and others (eds), *Die Europäische Union* (14th edn, Nomos 2020) 109; Paul Schiff Berman, 'Global Legal Pluralism' (2007) 80 Southern California Law Review 1155, 1161.

[230] Häberle, 'The Open Society of Constitutional Interpreters' (n 180) 147.

[231] Häberle, *Die Verfassung des Pluralismus* (n 228) 58.

[232] Bieber and Kotzur (n 229) 108–9.

[233] Häberle, 'The Open Society of Constitutional Interpreters' (n 180) 148.

[234] Peter Häberle, 'Verfassungsinterpretation als öffentlicher Prozeß—ein Pluralismuskonzept (1978)', *Verfassung als öffentlicher Prozeß: Materialien zu einer Verfassungstheorie der offenen Gesellschaft* (1st edn, Duncker & Humblot 1978) 141.

[235] Peter Häberle, 'Verfassungsgerichtsbarkeit in der offenen Gesellschaft' in Robert Chr van Ooyen and Martin HW Möllers (eds), *Handbuch Bundesverfassungsgericht im politischen System* (2nd edn, Springer VS 2015) 40.

system for the international community, since they are 'a set of fundamental, substantive rules that might be analogized to a constitution'.[236]

4.5 Concluding Remarks

Global climate constitutionalism is enthusiastically promoted by environmental law scholars as a response to the failure of governments worldwide, particularly those of the Global North, to address the climate crisis efficiently and to push states to enforce their own climate goals. However, by applying ideas of constitutionalism beyond the state, which have been discussed in relation to general IL for some time now, questions of democracy and justice should not be forgotten. One of these is concerned with global climate justice. Although duties of justice have often been treated as an exclusive matter of internal democracy, international climate law will need to address the problem of global justice. The exploitation of the South, the historical imbalances in relation to emitted GHGs and the amount of 'atmospheric capability' that is left lay at the very heart of international climate law. Many IEL principles reflect this: the 'polluter pays' principle, the principle of intergenerational equity and the principle of common but differentiated responsibility (and respective capabilities)[237]—all of these consider in some way the responsibility of 'over-users' both in relation to poorer nations and future generations.

Members of civil society all over the world have made clear how important these questions are to them. They protest in the streets, participate in spectacular actions such as blocking whole cities or sue governments and multinational enterprises to force them to curb their GHG emissions. The order of the German Federal Constitutional Court demonstrates how strongly the problem of climate change is linked to issues of climate justice, in particular intra- and intergenerational justice. The young are especially concerned that the present generations in power are gambling away their future by generating cheap energy from fossil fuels and following individual lifestyles that have serious consequences for the planet. Justice between people of the same generation and towards future generations is now something the courts have to address, since neither people in poorer countries nor future generations have a say in national decision-making processes.

---

[236] Bodansky (n 34) 579–80.

[237] Philippe Sands and Jacqueline Peel, *Principles of International Environmental Law* (4th edn, CUP 2018) 217ff.

From this point of view, climate justice should be central to approaches of global climate constitutionalism. This is because constitutions are not limited to establishing institutions and constraining their powers. Rather, constitutions are mirrors of a society. A constitution is the fabric into which a society weaves its perceptions of self and values that they hold dearest. Thus, if global climate constitutionalism is not only to reduce state sovereignty and increase participation opportunities for non-state actors in IL but also to offer a vision for a better and more just global legal order, then it needs to include climate justice as a guiding principle for both lawmaking and interpretation. Not only because it is morally 'right' to do so but also because the open society of constitutional interpreters has made it clear that they see climate justice (and the possibility that following generations enjoy at least the same quality of life as we do now) as a central element of their respective national constitutions. Members of the open society—including young people and people from countries bearing the brunt of climate change—repeatedly remind the community of states to stop acting short-sightedly by filing lawsuits in domestic and international courts to stress the interests of those not having voices in national decision-making processes.

Placing climate justice at the centre of approaches to global climate constitutionalism implies that states would not only have to refrain from certain behaviours, but they would also have positive duties of justice towards other states and their citizens, including duties of redistribution and mitigation. However, transnational forms of 'increased' democracy—the fulfilment of human rights and global justice—cannot be accomplished through political changes alone, nor by charity.[238] Instead, transnational solidarity is needed to motivate people to commit to the realisation of global justice and to contribute to its construction or constitution.[239] The basis for positive obligations and redistributive justice, thus, is a sense of solidarity among the members of the global legal community. While this global solidarity may not yet exist, the next chapter argues that it can be learned and gradually developed, and that there is already a basis on which such transnational solidarity could emerge.

---

[238] Carol G Gould, *Interactive Democracy. The Social Roots of Global Justice* (CUP 2014) 99.

[239] Ibid 119–20.

Transnational Solidarity 5

Global constitutionalism has been identified as a potential answer to global challenges in IL, but global climate constitutionalism may require thinking further than traditional approaches to global constitutionalism frameworks have done so far. The last chapter argued that approaches to global climate constitutionalism need to take climate justice and, thus, matters of redistribution, recognition and participation seriously. The problem of climate change, besides its environmental side, is its perceived unfairness: it hits those hardest who have contributed the least to the problem: citizens of the Global South and future generations of both the Global North and South.[1] Some states that are already more affected by hazardous climate change stress the issue of loss and damage and of financial distribution. Vanuatu, for example, has recently led a successful campaign to request an Advisory Opinion from the ICJ on the states' climate obligations.[2]

---

[1] World Bank, 'World Development Report: Development and Climate Change' (2010) 5.

[2] While Vanuatu announced at the Climate Vulnerable Forum 2018 that it would consider legal action against developed countries to hold them accountable for loss and damage (cf. 'Low-Lying Vanuatu Threatens to Sue Culprit Countries for Climate Change' *Reuters* (22 November 2018) <https://www.reuters.com/article/vanuatu-climatechange-idINL4N1XX2OW> accessed 31 August 2023), the state later seemed to have changed its strategy. In 2021, Vanuatu announced that it would ask the ICJ for an advisory opinion on climate obligations. Together with 17 other states, including several developed countries, the Core Group drafted a resolution, adopted by the UN General Assembly on 29 March 2023 (A/RES/77/276), to seek an advisory opinion from the ICJ on the following questions:

'(a) What are the obligations of States under international law to ensure the protection of the cli-mate system and other parts of the environment from anthropogenic emissions of greenhouse gases for States and for present and future generations;

(b) What are the legal consequences under these obligations for States where they, by their acts and omissions, have caused significant harm to the climate system and other parts of the environment, with respect to:

M. Niehaus, *Global Climate Constitutionalism "from below"*,
https://doi.org/10.1007/978-3-658-43191-4_5

Many members of the open society of constitutional interpreters, both nationally and internationally, demand, in particular through the use of CCL, that the law finds answers to questions of climate justice. These lawsuits are often concerned with positive obligations of states, for example, obligations to mitigate GHG emissions or enforce adaptation measures under the right to life. Such positive obligations, especially the redistribution of costs and benefits, however, are generally understood as a matter of domestic politics. Addressing these at the international level—as 'world domestic politics'—would require a 'thicker base' in the global community based on the solidarity among its members, as will be discussed in the following section. Solidarity is often understood to be key to redistributive policies. But global solidarity does not exist yet. However, it will be argued here that the global community is capable of gradually developing global solidarity while remaining pluralistic and diverse, and by doing so, it can pave the way for a more just vision of global climate constitutionalism that has climate justice at its heart.

As a first step, this chapter analyses whether a global community exists that is capable of gradually developing global solidarity. It will be analysed in Section 5.1 that constitutions, at least in the nation-state, are not only about creating legal institutions but also about shaping identity and laying the basis for solidarity and redistribution. Given the extreme diversity of people worldwide, it has often been argued that people would not be able to develop a global identity in the same sense that a national identity can be shaped through a constitution. Even if such an identity existed, it could only be 'thin'.[3] A 'thick' identity, however, is the basis on which strangers make sacrifices for one another in the nation-state, for example, through tax distribution, and therefore, is the basis for a constitutional society. Section 5.2 argues that solidarity is not nation-bound, and that the development of global solidarity is generally possible.

Thus, the next sections identify common values or shared risks that can serve as a basis upon which global solidarity can gradually be developed. Finding such a basis can be approached from two different directions. Either common or universal values could serve as a fundament for a global constitutional community (common attachment), or the global community shares a risk that forges them

---

(i) States, including, in particular, small island developing States, which due to their geographical circumstances and level of development, are injured or specially affected by or are particularly vulnerable to the adverse effects of climate change?

(ii) Peoples and individuals of the present and future generations affected by the adverse effects of climate change?'.

[3] Anne Peters, 'Dual Democracy' in Jan Klabbers, Anne Peters and Geir Ulfstein (eds), *The Constitutionalization of International Law* (OUP 2009) 305.

together (common predicament). The latter could be the case with hazardous global climate change that could and eventually will affect all persons in one way or another. It will be claimed here that, with the universal value of caring for one's progeny (common attachment) and the globally shared risk of hazardous climate change (common predicament), such foundations already exist. Section 5.3 then examines whether such values can be identified in relation to climate protection. It is argued here that justice and caring for one's progeny, as embedded in the principle of intergenerational equity, could be global values and motivations deeply rooted in all societies. However, the concept of values is not unproblematic in itself. Another way of 'reading' IL will be presented in Section 5.4 to demonstrate an alternative base on which solidarity could potentially be built in the global constitutional community. Instead of referring to universal values, this second approach seeks to identify common interests and common goals concerning climate protection in the realm of IEL. This section, therefore, analyses global climate change as a shared risk that endangers a common good (the atmosphere). Section 5.5 examines the principle of the 'Common Concern of Humankind' (CCH), a principle of IEL that combines both values and shared risks. Thus, it can be demonstrated that different bases exist upon which global solidarity and a global community could be built as the carrier of this global constitutional climate law.

5.1 A Basic Consensus for Climate Justice?

The last chapter showed that a global constitution can shape the identity of the global legal community. However, given the extreme diversity of people worldwide, it seems unlikely that a bond as strong as the one between the citizens of a nation-state could ever exist. 'Humanity', consisting of multiple *demoi*, seems to be too pluralistic and heterogeneous to be considered *one* community, and a very thin collective identity of humanity would be formed at best.[4] It seems improbable that a societal 'basic consensus' of foundational principles and values could possibly emerge. Such a consensus helps to stabilise institutions; it serves as a guideline when it comes to deciding controversial issues, and it induces diffuse support for the system by its citizens.[5] Due to this pluralistic global population, it seems that nothing more than a merely negative consensus (for example, the

[4] ibid.

[5] ibid 306.

prohibition of committing crimes against humanity or starting wars of aggression) can be achieved at the global level:[6]

> In a pluralistic society, a basic consensus cannot mean agreement on absolute and ultimate values. The basic consensus can at best be general and provisional. It is necessarily vague and only partially articulated. Often it is only a negative consensus, meaning that there is agreement about what is not acceptable. A basic consensus of this type is more easily conceivable on a global scale.[7]

The lack of global solidarity overlaps with these issues. Solidarity has been identified as 'a prerequisite of a viable global democracy, especially when it comes to redistributive policies'.[8] However, it has been argued that the requirements for a basic consensus and global solidarity are much lower than those for national democracies. If the world *civitas* were reduced to global peacekeeping and the protection of basic human rights and, thus, would not pursue world domestic politics (*Weltinnenpolitik*), solidarity between world citizens would not need to be sustained by the same political, cultural or social cohesion that is needed among citizens of a nation-state.[9] A 'consonance of moral indignation' to the violation of negative duties, in particular human rights crimes and the duty to refrain from wars of aggression, would be enough to integrate a society of world citizens. Such shared reactions that extend across different cultures, religions and forms of life, 'including those spawned by sympathy for the victims of humanitarian and natural disasters, gradually produce traces of cosmopolitan solidarity'.[10] Such a model of constitutionalism includes merely negative duties, such as the obligation not to commit crimes against humanity, which has roots in all cultures of the world and is also embedded into the larger UN framework.[11]

While negative human or basic rights obligations consist of merely abstaining from human rights violations, questions of social justice are more difficult to handle and, therefore, are often ignored in the literature on constitutionalism.

---

[6] Jürgen Habermas, 'A Political Constitution for the Pluralist World Society?' in Jürgen Habermas (ed), *Between Naturalism and Religion: Philosophical Essays* (Polity Press 2008) 344.

[7] Peters, 'Dual Democracy' (n 3) 309–10.

[8] ibid 306.

[9] Jürgen Habermas, 'Hat die Konstitutionalisierung des Völkerrechts noch eine Chance?' in Jürgen Habermas (ed), *Der gespaltene Westen* (Suhrkamp 2004) 143 ff.; Angelika Emmerich-Fritsche, *Vom Völkerrecht zum Weltrecht* (Duncker & Humblot 2007) 638.

[10] Habermas, 'A Political Constitution for the Pluralist World Society?' (n 6) 344.

[11] ibid.

However, these questions are particularly interesting and important in relation to the climate crisis. Constitutionalism is often understood as an approach to 'get to grips' with global phenomena such as international trade, international taxation or transnational environmental degradation. However, the constitutionalisation of parts of the international legal order says nothing about the 'justness' of this phenomenon.[12] As argued above, approaches to global climate constitutionalism should centre climate justice to address the major challenges climate change poses not only for the environment but also for global justice.

5.2 Global Solidarity?

Scholars have advanced different ideas on how to distribute burdens or resources.[13] The ideas reach from 'equal per capita' GHG allocations[14] that also include the distinction between luxury and subsistence emissions[15] to a 'you broke it, you fix it' approach based on historical emissions, either on the principle of 'polluter (or beneficiary) pays'[16] or on the ecological respective climate debt of developed countries.[17] Some prefer 'capabilities' approaches[18] and some

---

[12] Stefan Oeter, 'Regime Collisions from a Perspective of Global Constitutionalism' in Kerstin Blome and others (eds), *Contested Regime Collisions. Norm Fragmentation in World Society* (CUP 2016) 23.

[13] For an overview, see Philip Coventry and Chukwumerije Okereke, 'Climate Change and Environmental Justice' in Ryan Holifield, Jayajit Chakraborty and Gordon Walker (eds), *The Routledge Handbook of Environmental Justice* (Routledge 2017); Darrell Moellendorf, 'Climate Change and Global Justice' (2012) 3 WIREs Climate Change Climate Change 131; Paul Baer, 'International Justice' in John S Dryzek, Richard B Norgaard and David Schlosberg (eds), *Oxford Handbook of Climate Change and Society* (OUP 2011) 328 ff.

[14] Peter Singer, 'One Atmosphere' in Stephen M Gardiner and others (eds), *Climate Ethics: Essential Readings* (OUP 2010).

[15] Henry Shue, 'Subsistence Emissions and Luxury Emissions' (1993) 15 Law & Policy 39.

[16] Simon Caney, 'Cosmopolitan Justice, Responsibility, and Global Climate Change' (2005) 18 Leiden Journal of International Law 747.

[17] J Timmons Roberts and Bradley C Parks, 'Ecologically Unequal Exchange, Ecological Debt, and Climate Justice: The History and Implications of Three Related Ideas for a New Social Movement' (2009) 50 International Journal of Comparative Sociology 385; Chukwumerije Okereke, 'Climate Justice and the International Regime' (2010) 1 WIREs Climate Change 462.

[18] Rosie Day, 'A Capabilities Approach to Environmental Justice' in Ryan Holifield, Jayajit Chakraborty and Gordon Walker (eds), *The Routledge Handbook of Environmental Justice* (Routledge 2017); See also Chapter 7 in Martha C Nussbaum, *The Cosmopolitan Tradition: A Noble but Flawed Ideal* (Harvard University Press 2019).

a combination of several approaches.[19] Obligations to reduce GHGs are either directed at states (e.g., through a Greenhouse Development Rights framework)[20] or directly at individuals.[21]

For the Anthropocene, the German Advisory Council on Global Change (an independent, scientific advisory body to the German government) proposes a world social contract for sustainability, based on cosmopolitan theories, between world citizens and future generations.[22] Such a world contract needs to address the major global challenges,[23] and it needs to link 'a culture of attentiveness (born of a sense of ecological responsibility) with a culture of participation (as democratic responsibility) and a culture of obligation towards future generations (future responsibility)'.[24] Also particularly noteworthy is the idea of 'ecological citizenship'. According to its proponents, the world is a global community in which 'global interdependence and responsibility' are acknowledged.[25] The

[19] Simon Caney, 'Human Rights, Responsibilities, and Climate Change' in Charles R Beitz and Robert E Godin (eds), *Global Basic Rights* (OUP 2009).

[20] Paul Baer and others, 'Greenhouse Development Rights: A Framework For Climate Protection That Is "More Fair" Than Equal Per Capita Emissions Rights' in Stephen M Gardiner and others (eds), *Climate Ethics: Essential Readings* (OUP 2010).

[21] Christian Baatz, 'Climate Change and Individual Duties to Reduce GHG Emissions' (2014) 17 Ethics, Policy and Environment 1; Caney (n 16).

[22] WBGU (German Advisory Council on Global Change), 'World in Transition: A Social Contract for Sustainability' (2011) 9.

[23] The WBGU identifies four main challenges: '1. Because of progressive economic and cultural globalisation, the nation state can no longer be considered the sole basis for the contractual relationship. Its inhabitants must responsibly take transnational risks and natural dangers, and the legitimate interests of 'third parties', i. e. other members of the world community, into account.

2. Traditional contract philosophy presupposed the fictitious belief that all members of a society are equal. Considering the disproportionate distribution of resources and capabilities in today's international community of states, we must have effective, fair global compensation mechanisms in place.

3. The natural environment should be given increased consideration when revising the social contract.

4. The contract has to bring two important new protagonists into the equation: the self-organised civil society and the community of scientific experts' (WBGU, 277).

[24] WBGU (n 22) 277; see also Claudius Franzius, 'Klimaschutz im Anthropozän' (2019) 17 Zeitschrift für Europäisches Umwelt- und Planungsrecht 498.

[25] Andrew Dobson, 'Environmental Citizenship: Towards Sustainable Development' (2007) 15 Sustainable Development 276, 284.

post-cosmopolitan[26] idea of 'ecological citizenship' recognises the transnational nature of many environmental problems, including climate change and especially the obligations that people hold towards each other:

> The additional point of ecological citizenship, however, is that we are strangers not only to each other, but to each other's place, and even time. The obligations of the ecological citizen extend through time as well as space, towards generations yet to be born. Ecological citizens know that today's acts will have implications for tomorrow's people, and will argue that 'generationism' is akin to, and as indefensible as, racism or sexism.[27]

'Ecological citizenship' especially recognises the horizontal relationship between citizens rather than the vertical relationship between citizens and the state.[28] Such a concept adds a non-national layer to national citizenship and, thus, imposes obligations on those who use too much of the ecological space that should be fairly distributed among all members of humanity.[29]

However, none of these approaches to distributive justice addresses the problem that 'most regulatory decisions involve normative assumptions and trigger redistributive outcomes that cannot be reduced to seemingly objective scientific inquiries; each time someone wins and someone loses'.[30] Thus, the question is: can distribution face the same solidarity in a global context? As Habermas observes:

> Radical redistributions [...] will meet with resistance from existing interests, value orientations, and property relations; in a national context, they will also have little chance of being realized in a cost-neutral or competition-neutral way.[31]

---

[26] "Post-cosmopolitanism grows out of an understanding of globalization as a producer of inequalities, and consequent relations of injustice", Andrew Dobson, *Citizenship and the Environment* (OUP 2003) 9.

[27] ibid 106–7.

[28] ibid 116.

[29] ibid 118 ff.

[30] Jochen von Bernstorff, 'Procedures of Decision-Making and the Role of Law in International Organizations' (2008) 9 German Law Journal 1939, 1947.

[31] Jürgen Habermas, 'The Postnational Constellation and the Future of Democracy' in Jürgen Habermas and Max Pensky (eds), *The Postnational Constellation: Political Essays* (Polity Press 2001) 92. This point was raised by Habermas in relation to the "labour-based society" which is facing major challenges in times of globalisation such as the end of Keynesian economic policies and heightened global competition, resulting in mass unemployment and the undermining of the public standards of civil solidarity (90–92); see also Ian Gough and James

In a framework developed by Hassoun and Herlitz, this becomes visible. The researchers identified three dimensions regarding equity and distribution: international equality refers to the equal distribution of benefits (and burdens) between countries, intra-national equality means the equal distribution of benefits (and burdens) between individuals within countries, and world equality means the equal distributions of benefits (and burdens) between individuals within the world, irrespective of location.[32] This framework shows how the preference of any model over the others can lead to disadvantages in national, inter-state or global contexts:

> different kinds of inequality (and other things that matter) do not always go hand in hand: good distributions across countries may, for instance, allow for very bad distributions across individuals. Similarly, concern for distribution and total amount of goods can conflict.[33]

It will be argued here that this problem can only be addressed through global solidarity. Conflicts may be unavoidable, but solidarity can help to foster understanding and sympathy when those who have benefited from emitting too much GHG and are the biggest contributors to climate change are asked not only to reduce their ecological footprint but also to (financially) help those more affected by climate change. In this sense, global solidarity is the prerequisite for a viable global democracy that is not only based on a negative consensus on what is not acceptable but also for addressing questions of redistribution.[34] Solidarity is the sine qua non for sustaining and legitimising positively coordinated and effective redistributive policies.[35] In Habermas's words: 'Justice [...] requires solidarity as its reverse side.'[36]

Civic solidarity is rooted in particular collective identities upon which nation-states operate. Accordingly, it is the symbolic construction of 'a people' that leads to the development of national consciousness as the cultural fundament for

---

Meadowcroft, 'Decarbonizing the Welfare State' in John S Dryzek, Richard B Norgaard and David Schlosberg (eds), *Oxford Handbook of Climate Change and Society* (OUP 2011) 494.

32 Nicole Hassoun and Andreas Herlitz, 'Climate Change and Inequity: How to Think about Inequities in Different Dimensions' in Ravi Kanbur and Henry Shue (eds), *Climate Justice: Integrating Economics and Philosophy* (OUP 2018) 99.

33 ibid 109.

34 Peters, 'Dual Democracy' (n 3) 306.

35 Jürgen Habermas, 'Euroskepticism, Market Europe, or a Europe of (World) Citizens?' in Jürgen Habermas, Ciaran Cronin and Max Pensky (eds), *Time of Transitions* (Polity Press 2006) 87.

36 Jürgen Habermas, 'Justice and Solidarity: On the Discussion Concerning "Stage 6"' (1989) 21 The Philosophical Forum 32, 47.

civil solidarity that makes the people of a nation-state feel responsible and make sacrifices for each other while remaining strangers to each other.[37] Financial redistribution (e.g., between federal states) is an example where citizens stand up for their fellow citizens; 'a willingness that an egalitarian, universalistic legal order expects from its citizens'.[38] For global democracy, solidarity would need to be widened to encompass all citizens.[39]

However, it has been questioned whether solidarity could emerge at the global level at all. Accordingly, solidarity is pre-given; it is 'naturally' there (or it is not) since it is the condition on which justice operates.[40] Moreover, it has often been argued that solidarity can only emerge in a single society that is characterised by certain features:

> Solidarity can be based on common cultural heritage, shared aspirations, economic interests and even on unchosen historical contingencies. But it is necessarily 'domestic' or partial, i.e. not extending indefinitely to all human beings, present or future. Unlike respect for human dignity, the protection of human rights, the natural duty to assist a person in distress—which are all universal in some Kantian sense—distributive justice and the principles of fair cooperation are 'local' in their nature, i.e. they apply only within a given society, a particular social practice, institution, etc.[41]

Even for constitutionalists such as Habermas, who argues for constitutionalism without a world state, a cosmopolitan community of world citizens alone cannot be an adequate basis for a global domestic policy that can address issues such as redistribution. Rather, it would call for a closed, demarcated group.[42] To be sure, human rights and popular sovereignty are both essential for the law's legitimacy claim.[43] But the concept of human rights alone cannot substitute for civic solidarity[44]—the 'thick' basis that allows people to make scarifies for one another while remaining strangers. A common ethical-political dimension that is the basis for a collective identity, which would be necessary for a corresponding global society,

---

[37] Habermas, 'The Postnational Constellation and the Future of Democracy' (n 31) 64.

[38] ibid 65.

[39] Habermas, 'Euroskepticism, Market Europe, or a Europe of (World) Citizens?' (n 35) 87.

[40] Cf. David Heyd, 'A Value or an Obligation? Rawls on Justice to Future Generations' in Axel Gosseries and Lukas H Meyer (eds), *Intergenerational Justice* (OUP 2009) 184.

[41] ibid.

[42] Habermas, 'The Postnational Constellation and the Future of Democracy' (n 31) 109.

[43] Jürgen Habermas, 'Remarks on Legitimation through Human Rights' in Jürgen Habermas and Max Pensky (eds), *The Postnational Constellation: Political Essays* (Polity Press 2001) 115.

[44] Habermas, 'The Postnational Constellation and the Future of Democracy' (n 31) 108.

is lacking at the global level.[45] But solidarity does not need to exist before a global community is constituted. Rather, solidarity can and needs to be generated by the political entity.[46] It is something that has been and can be learned.[47] The nation-state is the most obvious example of this. When some argue that solidarity is only possible in the nation-state, they forget that the nation-state is itself the product of artificial conditions, and so is national consciousness. It is 'precisely the artificial conditions in which national consciousness arose' that proves the assumption wrong that solidarity among strangers can only be generated within a nation.[48] In other words: national solidarity did not exist before the nation-state. The historical formation of a collective identity from the local and dynastic to national and then to democratic consciousness indicates that this solidarity-learning process can continue and eventually lead to new forms of solidarity, for example, European or global solidarity.[49]

Thus, civic solidarity is not necessarily bound to the nation-state. This way of understanding solidarity is mostly present in the welfare states of Europe, where its people consented to help the needy among them, regardless of any feelings towards them.[50] However, this is not the only possible use of the term. Three other uses can be identified. The first refers to 'the tie that binds all of us as human beings to one big moral community',[51] thus, universal solidarity. The second use does not refer to all humanity but is constrained to a narrower and more limited community based on a common history, culture and ideals. Solidarity is the 'inner cement' that holds this group together.[52] The third form of solidarity can be identified when individuals form groups to stand up for their common interests.[53] Environmental and social movements fall into this category that generally 'involves a commitment *against* an opponent, from whom positive goals must be wrung'; as such, it is not exclusive but adversative in that it does not

---

[45] ibid.

[46] Samantha Besson, 'Whose Constitution(s)? International Law, Constitutionalism, and Democracy' in Jeffrey L Dunoff and Joel P Trachtman (eds), *Ruling the World? Constitutionalism, International Law and Global Government* (CUP 2009) 397.

[47] Peters, 'Dual Democracy' (n 3) 311.

[48] Habermas, 'The Postnational Constellation and the Future of Democracy' (n 31) 102.

[49] Habermas, 'Euroskepticism, Market Europe, or a Europe of (World) Citizens?' (n 35) 87; Habermas, 'The Postnational Constellation and the Future of Democracy' (n 31) 101–3.

[50] Kurt Bayertz, 'Four Uses of "Solidarity"' in Kurt Bayertz (ed), *Solidarity* (Kluwer Academic Publishers 1999) 21.

[51] ibid 5.

[52] ibid 9.

[53] ibid 16.

exclude certain persons or groups but opposes particular individuals or groups.[54] It is possible that in relation to particular problems ('projected-related-solidarity'), 'one person makes the concerns of another person or group, which faces a special plight, her own'.[55]

This already demonstrates that solidarity can emerge in different contexts. Gould, then, discusses an approach to transnational solidarities. Such transnational networked solidarities are essentially based on social empathy. It is not so much solidarity with every individual person on this planet but solidarity with a specific situation where someone—either an individual or a group of people—suffers harm. Solidarity can extend to relations with groups or associations in other countries or regions.[56] It is an affective feeling towards people that are different from oneself based on the recognition of equal claims to human rights fulfilment and social empathy and entails the readiness to act in support of those suffering harm. In contrast to charity, reciprocity is important, but it is not a characteristic feature once a situation demands better-situated groups to help those worst off.[57] Such a concept of solidarity also includes social critique and attention to institutional processes that may cause or uphold the problem, thus, seeking to improve the situation for those suffering.[58]

Solidarity is not 'naturally' there, but it has to and can be developed. 'The gradually and slowly emerging global solidarity will not be less artificial than national solidarity.'[59] Importantly, there needs to be a certain degree of reciprocal respect and tolerance towards the other members of a pluralistic society.[60] Reciprocal respect, enshrined in Kant's 'universal right to equal liberties',[61] underlies

[54] ibid 17 (emphasis in original).

[55] Klaus Peter Rippe, 'Diminishing Solidarity' (1998) 1 Ethical Theory and Moral Practice 355, 357.

[56] Carol G Gould, *Interactive Democracy. The Social Roots of Global Justice* (CUP 2014) 110.

[57] ibid 113.

[58] ibid 113, 116.

[59] Peters, 'Dual Democracy' (n 3) 311.

[60] Cf. Peter Häberle, 'Verfassungsinterpretation als öffentlicher Prozeß—ein Pluralismuskonzept (1978)', *Verfassung als öffentlicher Prozeß: Materialien zu einer Verfassungstheorie der offenen Gesellschaft* (1st edn, Duncker & Humblot 1978) 123.

[61] Immanuel Kant, *The Metaphysics of Morals* (Lara Denis ed, CUP 2017) 34 (6:237).

not only the idea of solidarity but also the concept of majority decisions and justice.[62] Accordingly, members will accept majority decisions even if they voted against them as legitimate when they know that others take their interests seriously. Consequently, 'sustained mutual respect and concern [are] required to reach and adhere to collective outcomes that may work against their immediate interests in terms of the distribution of common resources and risks'.[63] Democratic solidarity in this transnational context then means sharing resources and methods and engaging in joint projects or activities while respecting the differences and modalities of various groups and communities.[64] It means to limit justice not only to redistribution but also to include recognition as a central element of a framework that fits the 'new' globality.[65] Thus, it becomes clear that transnational solidarities are the basis for global (climate) justice.

> [It is] solidarity that mediates between the more fully particular relations evident on a personal level and the abstract universal principles incorporated in norms of human rights and justice. And solidarity does so [...] by contributing to a more supportive and open, indeed democratic, relationships between people and groups in increasingly transnational contexts.[66]

The next section then seeks to identify a basis on which global solidarity could potentially arise. Solidarity, it has often been claimed, requires a thick identity of the global community, but the people of the world would be too different to form such an identity.[67] However, even in nation-states, individuals are not homogenous and different groups and interests exist. The objective of a constitution, then, is to integrate different and diverse groups into 'one nation'. The state only exists because, and to the extent that, it constantly integrates and is formed of individuals:[68]

---

[62] Peters, 'Dual Democracy' (n 3) 312; Nancy Fraser, 'From Redistribution to Recognition? Dilemmas of Justice in a "Postsocialist" Age' in Steven Seidman and Jeffrey C Alexander (eds), *The New Social Theory Reader* (Routledge 2001) 285–93.

[63] Neil Walker, 'Taking Constitutionalism beyond the State' (2008) 56 Political Studies 519, 531.

[64] Gould (n 56) 115.

[65] Fraser (n 62) 189.

[66] Gould (n 56) 118.

[67] Peters, 'Dual Democracy' (n 3) 311.

[68] Stefan Korioth, 'Rudolf Smend' in Arthur J Jacobson and Bernhard Schlink (eds), *Weimar: A Jurisprudence of Crisis* (University of California Press 2000) 218 (including a translation

> People expect the constitution to unify their society as a polity, thereby transcending the differences of opinion and conflicting interests that exist in all societies. The constitution is regarded as a guarantee of the fundamental consensus that is necessary for social cohesion. If a constitution is successful in this respect, it can even help shape a society's identity.[69]

This is called the integrative function of a constitution.[70] The presupposition or the promise—and often both—of societal integration through a constitution, then, is a 'common attachment or common predicament within the putative *demos*'.[71] But such common attachment or common predicament within the putative demos can also exist beyond the borders of the nation-state. It can also extend to future generations. If constitutions are to be understood as social contracts between generations or society members,[72] present and future generations should be considered as one whole 'world society':

> Perhaps it [the social contract] can even be seen globally today, i.e., to extend to the entire globe of our 'blue planet'. The world society is to be seen in a 'world contract'; even if it does not actually exist, it must behave as if it existed: for the good of all humankind.[73]

This is the starting point for the following section seeking to find the basis on which solidarity could possibly be built. This foundation does not have to be perfect yet, since it can be developed through 'constitutional boot-strapping', in the same way, the global demos, solidarity and other constitutional elements can be developed.[74]

---

of parts of Smend's 'Verfassung und Verfassungsrecht'); for the original work, see 'Verfassung und Verfassungsrecht (1928)' in Rudolf Smend (ed), *Staatsrechtliche Abhandlungen und andere Aufsätze* (4th edn, Duncker & Humblot 2010).

[69] Dieter Grimm, 'Integration by Constitution' (2005) 3 International Journal of Constitutional Law 193, 194.

[70] ibid 195.

[71] Walker (n 63) 531.

[72] Peter Häberle, 'Verfassungsgerichtsbarkeit in der offenen Gesellschaft' in Robert Chr van Ooyen and Martin HW Möllers (eds), *Handbuch Bundesverfassungsgericht im politischen System* (2nd edn, Springer VS 2015) 42.

[73] ibid (tr the author).

[74] Peters, 'Dual Democracy' (n 3) 313; Anne Peters, 'The Merits of Global Constitutionalism' (2009) 16 Indiana Journal of Global Legal Studies 397, 403.

5.3 Approach 1: Global Climate Constitutionalism Based on Values

5.3.1 The Common Values

While no transnational (general or environmental) constitution in the formal sense exists, the concept of constitutionalism allows for identifying constitutional principles and values in the international legal order. This is because constitutions include 'thin' and 'thick' elements. While the thin elements refer to the organisation, establishment and distribution of (governmental) powers, the thick ones describe the core of the constitution—its fabric. A constitution has to hold at least the most basic values of a nation as a society's self-perception. The same holds at the global level. Thus, comprehensive constitutionalisation may require the existence of some sort of basic understanding of universal values.[75] Shared values are defined by Habermas as an expression of 'the preferability of goods that, in specific collectivities, are considered worth striving for and can be acquired or realized through goal-directed action'.[76] Importantly, this approach does not build on (ecological) values held by states but rather those endorsed by individuals in their position as 'universal citizens'.[77] Some states may endorse the same values, but environmental concerns are often not at the forefront, particularly when they may clash with economic interests.[78] States have traditionally been the guardians of such values but they are not the only ones anymore:

> In the kaleidoscopic world, the common values and shared commitments must also flourish from the bottom up. Because local communities, informal or transient groups of participants, or individuals will increasingly be able to influence the development

---

[75] Clemens Mattheis, *Die Konstitutionalisierung des Völkerrechts aus systemtheoretischer Sichtweise* (Springer 2018) 202.

[76] Jürgen Habermas, *Between Facts and Norms: Contributions to a Discourse Theory of Law and Democracy* (Polity Press 1996) 255.

[77] In this sense, the Commission on Global Governance, 'Our Global Neighbourhood' (OUP 1995) 49 states: 'We believe that all humanity could uphold the core values of respect for life, liberty, justice and equity, mutual respect, caring, and integrity. These provide a foundation for transforming a global neighbourhood based on economic exchange and improved communications into a uni-versal moral community in which people are bound together by more than proximity, interest, or identity'.

[78] Cf. Louis J Kotzé, *Global Environmental Constitutionalism in the Anthropocene* (Bloomsbury Publishing 2016) 225.

> and commitment to international agreements and other legal instruments, the sharing of common values becomes essential to effective governance.[79]

If each regime or community contains and must observe certain values, there is a 'value glue' that creates unity.[80] However difficult the identification of common values, in general, might be, there are a few basic environmental values that, according to Peters, seem to have acquired universal acceptance: climate protection and human rights protection (and maybe even free trade).[81] In the same vein, Judge Weeramantry stated in his separate opinion in the *Gabčíkovo-Nagymaros* case:

> The ingrained values of any civilization are the source from which its legal concepts derive, and the ultimate yardstick and touchstone of their validity. This is so in international and domestic legal systems alike, save that international law would require a worldwide recognition of those values. It would not be wrong to state that the love of nature, the desire for its preservation, and the need for human activity to respect the requisites for its maintenance and continuance are among those pristine and universal values which command international recognition.[82]

Environmental consciousness, alongside tolerance, respect for human dignity, sincerity and democratic convictions, culturally ground an open society.[83] The increasing inclusion of moral and natural law norms into positive IL and the legalisation of more global community affairs is seen as a process of constitutionalisation.[84] Such constitutionalisation is not based on form but on substance.[85] IL itself is an 'order of values' (*Werteordnung*) oriented towards the common

---

[79] Edith Brown Weiss, 'Nature and the Law: The Global Commons and the Common Concern of Humankind' [2014] Sustainable Humanity, Sustainable Nature: Our Responsibility. Pontifical Academy of Sciences, Extra Series 41 1, 11.

[80] Andreas L Paulus, 'Commentary to Andreas Fischer-Lescano & Gunther Teubner. The Legitimacy of International Law and the Role of the State' (2004) 25 Michigan Journal of International Law 1047, 1050.

[81] Peters, 'The Merits of Global Constitutionalism' (n 74) 399.

[82] Separate Opinion of Vice-President Weeramantry—*Case Gabcikovo-Nagymaros Project (Hungary vs Slovakia), ICJ Reports 1997* 105.

[83] Peter Häberle, 'The Rationale of Constitutions from a Cultural Science Viewpoint' in Markus Kotzur (ed), *Peter Häberle on Constitutional Theory* (Nomos/Hart 2018) 236.

[84] Thomas Kleinlein, *Konstitutionalisierung im Völkerrecht* (Springer 2012) 12.

[85] See Martti Koskenniemi, 'Constitutionalism as Mindset: Reflections on Kantian Themes about International Law and Globalization' (2006) 8 Theoretical Inquiries in Law 9; Aoife O'Donoghue, *Constitutionalism in Global Constitutionalisation* (CUP 2014) 141.

good of the world community.[86] Constitutional principles, then, would need to represent certain fundamental values that are universally held. Among these are basic democratic principles, human rights and environmental protection.[87] Some core human rights (e.g., the right to life, freedom from torture and slavery) and environmental protection form a 'value glue' that holds the subsystems of the world together.[88]

Human rights are central to any theory of constitutionalism.[89] In a world public order, 'international human rights norms would enjoy a superior rank as they reflect values and interests deemed to be worthy of particular legal protection by the international community as a whole'.[90] They can be understood as a connecting link between nation-states and international (regional) communities, even more so as they are codified in both national and IL.[91] Thus, climate activists, lawyers and judges have tried and continue to try to implement a universal human right to a stable climate, either as a stand-alone right or as a part of a right to a healthy environment.[92] Such a human rights-based approach to climate change highlights the principles of universality and non-discrimination and emphasises that rights of all persons, including those most vulnerable and future generations, are guaranteed.[93]

---

[86] Studies have shown that many U.S. citizens who deny climate change or reject more climate protection score higher in terms of hierarchical and individualist values, seeking to protect either the status quo or to avoid restrictions on the global markets. Those with high scores in relation to egalitarian and cosmopolitan values, on the other hand, can align the value of climate protection with more general values such as the protection of the more vulnerable and restriction of the free markets in favour of the collective goal. See Matthew C Nisbet, 'Public Opinion and Participation' in John S Dryzek, Richard B Norgaard and David Schlosberg (eds), *The Oxford Handbook of Climate Change and Society* (OUP 2011) 361.

[87] Clemens Mattheis, 'The System Theory of Niklas Luhmann and the Constitutionalization of the World Society' (2012) 4 Goettingen Journal of International Law 625, 643–5.

[88] ibid 645.

[89] Ekaterina Yahyaoui Krivenko, *Rethinking Human Rights and Global Constitutionalism* (CUP 2017) 75–6.

[90] Andrea Bianchi, 'Globalization of Human Rights: The Role of Non-State Actors' in Gunther Teubner (ed), *Global Law without a State* (Dartmouth Publishing 1997) 183.

[91] Markus Kotzur, 'Weltrechtliche Bezüge in nationalen Verfassungstexten' (2008) 39 Rechtstheorie 191, 200 (tr the author).

[92] The *Juliana vs United States of America* case case can be understood as an approach to a stand-alone constitutional right to a stable climate, while the latter option is preferred by UN Special Rapporteur on Human Rights and the Environment David Boyd, 'Special Report on Human Rights Obligations Relating to the Enjoyment of a Safe, Clean, Healthy and Sustainable Environment (A/74/161)' (2019) 2.

[93] ibid 27.

The issue of climate change and human rights has been addressed by international documents such as the Malé Declaration[94] and the new UN Global Pact for the Environment,[95] which recognises a right to a healthy environment.[96] In his 2019 report on the issue of human rights obligations relating to the enjoyment of a safe, clean, healthy and sustainable environment, Special Rapporteur Boyd expressed that 'a safe climate is a vital element of the right to a healthy environment and is absolutely essential to human life and well-being'.[97] A safe climate is part of the right to a healthy environment, aside from 'clean air, clean water and adequate sanitation, healthy and sustainably produced food, non-toxic environments in which to live, work, study and play, and healthy biodiversity and ecosystems'.[98] Importantly, such a right should not only benefit present generations but also future generations that are to inherit the earth. As global warming is expected to worsen over the next decades, children, young people and unborn generations have to bear the burden of climate change far more and far longer than adults today will.[99]

However, the globalisation of human rights needs to be anchored in values sufficiently shared among a variety of transnational actors to be effective.[100] Such a value is intergenerational justice, as argued below. Two of the lawsuits that will be examined in greater detail in Chapter 9 (*Juliana v United States* and *Future*

---

[94] Small Island Developing States, 'Male' Declaration on the Human Dimension of Global Climate Change' (2007).

[95] UN General Assembly, Towards a Global Pact for the Environment' (Enabling Resolution), 10 May 2018, A/72/L.51. See also, Yann Aguila and Jorge E Viñuales, 'A Global Pact for the Environment: Conceptual Foundations' (2019) 28 Review of European, Comparative and International Environmental Law 3; Maksim Lavrik, Alicia Jimenez and Mirian Vilela, 'The Global Pact for the Environment As a Next Step on the Way Forward for the Earth Charter' 1; Louis J Kotzé and Duncan French, 'A Critique of the Global Pact for the Environment: A Stillborn Initiative or the Foundation for Lex Anthropocenae?' (2018) 18 International Environmental Agreements: Politics, Law and Economics 811.

[96] "We already have two international (human rights) pacts… The idea is to create a third, for a third generation of rights—environmental rights," former French Prime Minister and current President of the French Constitutional Court Laurent Fabius, see 'Bid for Environmental Rights Pact to Kick off in Paris' (23 June 2017) <https://www.france24.com/en/20170623-bid-environmental-rights-pact-kick-off-paris> accessed 31 August 2023.

[97] UN Special Rapporteur on Human Rights and the Environment David Boyd (n 92) 2.

[98] ibid 13.

[99] Bridget Lewis, 'Human Rights Duties towards Future Generations and the Potential for Achieving Climate Justice' (2016) 34 Netherlands Quarterly of Human Rights 206, 209.

[100] Bianchi (n 90) 203.

Generations v Colombia) established their claims on the adverse effects that climate change will have on the rights of future generations, in particular, the right to life and a healthy environment. In *Juliana*, the plaintiffs seek to establish the right to a stable climate in the US Constitution. These lawsuits demonstrate that the idea of human rights and a healthy environment are inseparably tied to the value of intergenerational justice, which is embodied in the international environmental principle of intergenerational equity or justice. Thus, not only 'hard' human rights, such as the right to life, but also 'soft' international environmental principles could hold important values for global climate constitutionalism.

In this sense, for the present work, IEL principles can be used to identify universal values that could underpin a transnational climate constitution. Of particular importance is the environmental principle of intergenerational equity, which itself is strongly intertwined with a right to a healthy environment and a stable climate. Principles can orientate states and guide action and, thus, are a more suitable instrument for a less densely constituted area such as the international.[101] Different to rules that follow an 'if …, then …' structure that are rather limited to typical hard cases, principles represent general legal standards that need to be specified by interpretation. Their most important function is revealed in difficult lawsuits because they can support a court's judgement about particular rights and obligations.[102]

In the last three decades, there has been a proliferation of environmental principles, and today, there is a multitude of environmental principles belonging to the body of IEL.[103] Not all principles are of the same quality: some enjoy nearly universal support (e.g., those that also belong to the category of general principles of IL as stated in Article 38 para. 1 of the ICJ Statute with which the IEL principles should not be confused[104]), some may point to emerging legal

[101] Markus Kotzur, 'Wechselwirkungen zwischen europäischer Verfassungs- und Völkerrechtslehre' in Alexander Blankenagel, Ingolf Pernice and Helmuth Schulze-Fielitz (eds), *Verfassung im Diskurs der Welt. Liber Amicorum für Peter Häberle* (Mohr Siebeck 2004) 303.

[102] Ronald Dworkin, *Taking Rights Seriously* (Duckworth 1977) 28.

[103] Ludwig Krämer and Emanuela Orlando, 'Introduction to Volume VI' in Ludwig Krämer and Emanuela Orlando (eds), *Elgar Encyclopedia of Environmental Law: Principles of Environmental Law (Vol. VI)* (Edward Elgar Publishing 2018) 1.

[104] For example, the principle of sovereignty of states over their natural resources and the no-harm principle, which reflect customary law; the principle of preventive action, the precautionary principle, the principle of cooperation, the precautionary principle, the polluter-pays principle, the principle of sustainable development, and the principle of common but differentiated responsibilities, see Philippe Sands and Jacqueline Peel, *Principles of International Environmental Law* (4th edn, CUP 2018) 126. Of the general principles of international law,

obligations, and others are less developed.[105] Even if they are not considered sources themselves, environmental principles have a strong influence on the general principles of IL. By 'greening' them, they challenge traditional approaches to sovereignty, in particular the principle of sovereignty over natural resources, to include considerations of environmental protection and the interests of the community as a whole.[106] Thus, '[o]verarching principles establish the relationship between law and justice; they are an expression of the "*ratio constitutionis*", they indicate normative movements and formulate criteria for balancing [constitutional interests]'.[107] Principles are to be observed not because they advance or foster an economic, political or social feature of a community. Instead, a principle is 'a requirement of justice or fairness or some other dimension of morality'.[108] In this sense, the principle of intergenerational equity could not only be relevant in relation to the interpretation of IEL, but it could also include a value that is commonly held by the global community, that is, justice between generations.

5.3.1.1 Intergenerational Equity/Justice

Intergenerational equity or justice has become one of the strongest and most cited environmental principles in international climate change law, and it 'may very well become an intellectual *leitmotif* of the new century'.[109] The term 'intergenerational equity' is often used to refer to both intergenerational justice between members of different generations and intra-generational justice as justice between members of a generation.

What makes the principle of intergenerational equity interesting for the current work is that a strong value-laden base can be identified and, therefore, could serve the notion of a value-constitutionalist principle in IEL. Underlying this principle

---

the principle of faith (including cooperation and consideration of other riparian states' interests when interfering with the flow of rivers, or the legal binding obligation of a universal declaration to abstain from atmospheric nuclear tests), the obligation to make reparations for breaching an agreement, "elementary considerations" of humanity, and "fundamental general principles of humanitarian law", inter alia, may become important in the international environmental context.

[105] ibid 198.

[106] Teresa Fajardo, 'Environmental Principles and General Principles of International Law' in Ludwig Krämer and Emanuela Orlando (eds), *Elgar Encyclopedia of Environmental Law: Principles of Environmental Law (Vol. VI)* (Edward Elgar Publishing 2018) 41.

[107] Kotzur (n 101) 304 (tr the author).

[108] Dworkin (n 102) 22.

[109] Joerg Chet Tremmel, 'Introduction' in Joerg Chet Tremmel (ed), *Handbook of Intergenerational Justice* (Edward Elgar Publishing 2006) 1.

are the values of (social) justice in the form of intergenerational justice (which is another term often used for this principle) and the value of caring for one's poignancy.

The social psychologist and creator of the theory of basic human values, Schwartz, identified social justice as part of the value of universalism that people in all cultures recognise as a value.[110] Similar to the discussion surrounding the inclusiveness of cosmopolitanism, social justice does not have to extend to people outside one's group (e.g., a nation), but it can.[111] Social justice refers to the duty of every member of a given community to contribute to its common good and to the obligation of that community to care and feel responsible for its members, especially those in disadvantaged situations.[112] Due to its distributive element, social justice can be seen as a concept that only applies to the members of a nation within a generation.[113] Many philosophers find it difficult to incorporate environmental goods within theories of social justice, as such theories are often (only) concerned with the distribution of goods to individuals, and as Miller noted, '[n]obody gets a particular share of the ozone layer or the Siberian tiger'.[114] Although everyone may benefit from environmental protection, environmental measures do have a distributive quality of their own, since some will benefit more than others, and their costs will fall more heavily on some.[115] Agius, on the other side, argues that a theory of social justice incorporating ecological elements can or should also extend to future generations and people beyond our borders. He believes that:

> We have an obligation grounded on social justice to share the common heritage with all the present population as well as with future generations.[116]

---

[110] Shalom H Schwartz, 'Universalism Values and the Inclusiveness of Our Moral Universe' (2007) 38 Journal of Cross-Cultural Psychology 711.

[111] ibid 726; Brian Barry, 'Sustainability and Intergenerational Justice' (1997) 89 A Journal of Social and Political Theory 43.

[112] Emmanuel Agius, 'Intergenerational Justice' in Jörg Chet Tremmel (ed), *Handbook of Intergenerational Justice* (Edward Elgar Publishing 2006) 329.

[113] David Miller, *Principles of Social Justice* (Harvard University Press 1999) 19; Tremmel (n 109) 4.

[114] David Miller, 'Social Justice and Environmental Goods' in Andrew Dobson (ed), *Fairness and Futurity: Essays on Environmental Sustainability and Social Justice* (OUP 1999) 154.

[115] ibid 154 f.

[116] Agius (n 112) 330.

The principle of intergenerational equity is based on the idea that Earth is home to all human beings—to past, present and future generations. The present generation holds the planet in trust for future generations, which encompasses both today's children and the unborn, even those to be born in the very far future.[117] At the same time, present generations are beneficiaries with the right to access and benefit from the trust held by previous generations.[118] However, they are not allowed to take advantage of their current possession over Earth but have to act carefully not to disadvantage those following them.[119] Brown Weiss calls this 'planetary rights and obligations'.[120] Planetary rights are held collectively as opposed to traditional human rights, which primarily define the relationships between individuals and the state.[121] In the face of the climate crisis, the current generation cannot simply 'do nothing'[122] and thereby let the planet slip into an 'unsafe operating space'. While climate change may not be inevitable, the international community of states must at least fulfil their legal environmental obligations to keep its effects to a minimum.[123]

What motivates people to care for (far-away) future generations may depend on different factors, but studies have shown that people *do* care about future generations and ecological survival, thus, valuing stewardship and keeping nature intact for future generations.[124] These ideas are strongly intertwined with another

---

[117] Burns H Weston, 'Climate Change and Intergenerational Justice: Foundational Reflections' (2008) 9 Vermont Journal of Environmental Law 375, 384.

[118] Brown Weiss, 'Nature and the Law: The Global Commons and the Common Concern of Humankind' (n 79) 1–2.

[119] Edith Brown Weiss, 'In Fairness To Future Generations and Sustainable Development' (1992) 8 American University International Law Review 19, 20.

[120] ibid 23.

[121] Edith Brown Weiss, *In Fairness to Future Generations: International Law, Common Patrimony, and Intergenerational Equity* (Transnational Publishers/United Nations University 1989) 114.

[122] Eric Biber, 'Law in the Anthropocene Epoch' (2017) 106 Georgetown Law Journal 1, 40.

[123] Jan McDonald, 'A Risky Climate for Decision-Making: The Liability of Development Authorities for Climate Change Impacts' (2007) 24 Environmental and Planning Law Journal 405, 406.

[124] Dieter Birnbacher, 'What Motivates Us to Care for the (Distant) Future?' in Axel Gosseries and Lukas H Meyer (eds), *Intergenerational Justice* (OUP 2009) 229 f.

value identified by Schwartz as being universal: security, including family security/safety for loved ones.[125] Care may be a value, just as justice is.[126] The spatial and temporal limits of care may be unclear, but at least, it seems safe to say that human beings generally care about their own progeny:

> What parent, grandparent, or great-grandparent would disavow a climate legacy beneficial to their descendants? What child, grandchild, or great-grandchild will not feel at least a little resentful if such a legacy is denied them? Somewhere deep inside, all of us know that life is an energetic concurrence of the past, present, and future; that we are a temporary part of it; and that, whatever our past failings, we must reach beyond our egoistic selves to ensure its continuity with fairness to today's children and communities of the future.[127]

These thoughts are buttressed by Passmore's 'chain of love' model, according to which each generation loves and cares deeply for its children and grandchildren, thus, chaining them together through an intergenerational cord.[128]

The concept of intergenerational equity has been known to human civilisation for a long time. Its equivalents can be found in the great world religions and in the everyday life of indigenous people around the world, and it has made its way into both the common and civil law systems. The principle has deep cross-cultural roots.[129] It is also well-represented at the international level. The ICJ stated in its Advisory Opinion on the Legality of the Threat or Use of Nuclear Weapons (1996) that:

> the environment is not an abstraction but represents a living space, the quality of life and the very health of human beings, including generations unborn. The existence of the general obligation of States to ensure that activities within their jurisdiction and control respect the environment of other States or of areas beyond national control is now part of the corpus of international law relating to the environment.[130]

---

[125] Shalom H Schwartz, 'An Overview of the Schwartz Theory of Basic Values' (2012) 2 Online Readings in Psychology and Culture 1, 6; Shalom H Schwartz and others, 'Refining the Theory of Basic Individual Values' (2012) 103 Journal of Personality and Social Psychology 663, 667.

[126] Virginia Held, *The Ethics of Care: Personal, Political, and Global* (OUP 2006) 41.

[127] Weston (n 117) 376.

[128] John Arthur Passmore, *Man's Responsibility for Nature. Ecological Problems and Western Traditions* (2nd ed, Duckworth 1980), 88f.

[129] Brown Weiss, 'Nature and the Law: The Global Commons and the Common Concern of Humankind' (n 79) 3.

[130] ICJ, 'Legality of the Threat of Use of Nuclear Weapons, Advisory Opinion (ICJ Reports 1996)' 241–2.

The preamble of the Paris Agreement demands that states consider intergenerational equity when taking actions to address climate change.[131] And the parties to the UNFCCC are '*[d]etermined* to protect the climate system for present and future generations'.[132] Many domestic constitutions also enshrine the principle. The German constitution provides in Article 20a Basic Law (*Grundgesetz*—GG) that '[m]indful also of its responsibility towards future generations, the state shall protect the natural foundations of life and animals by legislation [...]'. The Constitutional Court (*Bundesverfassungsgericht*—GFCC) recently made clear that the principle is justiciable—Article 20a GG has often been mocked as 'constitutional poetry'[133]—and demands that the legislator respects the interests and rights of future generations by claiming that:

> [as] intertemporal guarantees of freedom, fundamental rights afford the complainants protection against comprehensive threats to freedom caused by the greenhouse gas reduction burdens that are mandatory under Art. 20a GG being unilaterally offloaded onto the future. The legislator should have taken precautionary steps to ensure a transition to climate neutrality that respects freedom – steps that have so far been lacking.[134]

Climate change is expected to have long-term adverse effects on the planet, such as the loss of biodiversity, which will be felt mostly by today's children and the

---

[131] Conference of the Parties, Adoption of the Paris Agreement, Dec. 12, 2015—U.N. Doc. FCCC/CP/2015/L.9/Rev/1 (Dec. 12, 2015).

[132] United Nations Framework Convention on Climate Change, May 9, 1992—1771 U.N.T.S. 107, 165; S. Treaty Doc No. 102–38 (1992); U.N. Doc. A/AC.237/18 (Part II)/Add.1; 31 I.L.M. 849 (1992) (emphasis in original).

[133] „Böse Zungen nennen das Verfassungslyrik"—Interview with Georg Oswald (*Deutschlandfunk*, 29 July 2019) <https://www.deutschlandfunkkultur.de/jurist-oswald-ueber-klimaschutz-im-grundgesetz-boese-zungen.1008.de.html?dram:article_id=455043> accessed 31 August 2023.

[134] Bundesverfassungsgericht (GFCC), 'Constitutional Complaints against the Federal Climate Change Act Partially Successful (Press Release No. 31/2021 of 29 April 2021)' (2021) <https://www.bundesverfassungsgericht.de/SharedDocs/Pressemitteilungen/EN/2021/bvg21-031.html> accessed 31 August 2023.

generations to follow.[135] Thus, intergenerational equity consists of three principles: options, quality and access.[136] The first principle, comparable options, refers to the maintenance of Earth's diverse natural resources so that future generations can satisfy their own needs and values, even if these cannot be predicted today. The second principle, comparable quality, means to ensure the quality of the environment between generations. The world must not be passed to the next generation in a status worse than the one in which it has been received by the present generation. However, the keyword here is 'balance'. Some actions may cause long-term, even irreversible harm to the planet (e.g., the extinction of certain species) or are costly and difficult to remove (e.g., the pollution of groundwater). These actions should be avoided. Others might prejudice the planet in the short term but might equalise or improve the quality of the environment in general (e.g., reforestation to compensate for the clearance somewhere else).[137] As the present generation can ensure neither the comparable options nor their quality, it must at least minimise the predicted harms.[138] The third principle, comparable access, means non-discriminatory access for all generations to Earth and its resources.[139] For the present generation, this means bearing in mind that the resulting benefits and costs from actions or omissions affect not only them but also those to follow. Therefore, long-term goals must not be sacrificed for short-term benefits.[140] These rights of future generations correspond to what Brown Weiss calls 'planetary obligations' or duties of the present generations, including duties of use (duty to conserve resources, ensure equitable use, avoid adverse impacts, prevent disasters, minimise damage and provide emergency assistance) and the duty

---

[135] For example, the future flooding of coastlines may force future generations to abandon properties, even to relocate whole urban areas. By 2050, over 570 low-lying coastal cities will face projected sea level rise by at least 0,5 meters, putting over 800 million people at risk resulting from rising sea-levels and storm surges. The loss of biological diversity is another consequence of changes in the climate, see C40 Cities, 'The Future We Don't Want: Cities and Sea Level Rise' <https://www.c40.org/other/the-future-we-don-t-want-staying-afloat-the-urban-response-to-sea-level-rise> accessed 31 August 2023.

[136] Edith Brown Weiss, 'Climate Change, Intergenerational Equity, and International Law' (2008) 9 Vermont Journal of Environmental Law 615, 616.

[137] Brown Weiss, 'Nature and the Law: The Global Commons and the Common Concern of Humankind' (n 79) 4–5.

[138] Weston (n 117) 376.

[139] Brown Weiss, 'Climate Change, Intergenerational Equity, and International Law' (n 135) 616.

[140] Brown Weiss, 'In Fairness To Future Generations and Sustainable Development' (n 119) 19.

to compensate for environmental harm.[141] The interests of future generations[142] could be safeguarded through the implementation of a High Commissioner for Future Generations,[143] as established by Hungary and Wales.[144]

In the context of climate change, the principle of intergenerational equity goes hand in hand with the concept of intra-generational equity. This means that responsibility not only towards future generations but also towards those already living on Earth exists. While the richest one per cent of the world is responsible for causing more than double the emissions of the poorest half of humanity,[145] the developing countries will bear an estimated 75 to 80 per cent of the costs of climate change.[146] It is known that women, indigenous people, minorities, the old, the young and the disabled are most vulnerable to the effects of climate change.[147] Take the poor, for example. The alleviation of poverty and environmental/climate protection are strongly interlinked: 'Poverty lies at the centre of a number of failures to meet human rights and is a major obstacle to achieving sustainable development.'[148] Many of those living in poverty have no access to the benefits of natural resources and/or limited access to a sustainable way of living (e.g., the lack of waste collection in informal neighbourhoods leading to

---

[141] See Chapter 3 'Planetary Obligations' in Brown Weiss, *In Fairness to Future Generations: International Law, Common Patrimony, and Intergenerational Equity* (n 121) 47–93.

[142] Despite the difficulties for an institution to make assumptions today about something that will occur in the (far) future—Peter Lawrence and Lukas Köhler, 'Representation of Future Generations through International Climate Litigation: A Normative Framework' (2017) 60 German Yearbook of International Law 639, 653.

[143] UN General Assembly, 'Report of the Secretary-General: Intergenerational Solidarity and the Needs of Future Generations (A/68/322)' (2013) para 53 ff.

[144] Éva Tóth Ambrusné, 'The Parliamentary Commissioner for Future Generations of Hungary and His Impact' (2010) 10 Intergenerational Justice Review 18; 'Meet the World's First "Minister for Future Generations"' *The Guardian* (2 March 2019) <https://www.theguardian.com/world/2019/mar/02/meet-the-worlds-first-future-generations-commissioner> accessed 31 August 2023.

[145] Oxfam, 'Confronting Carbon Inequality: Putting Climate Justice at the Heart of the COVID-19 Recovery' (2020) 2 <https://policy-practice.oxfam.org/resources/confronting-carbon-inequality-putting-climate-justice-at-the-heart-of-the-covid-621052/> accessed 31 August 2023.

[146] World Bank (n 1) 5.

[147] UN Special Rapporteur on Human Rights and the Environment John H. Knox, 'Human Rights Obligations Relating to the Enjoyment of a Safe, Clean, Healthy and Sustainable Environment (A/HRC/31/52)' (2016).

[148] John Scanlon, Angela Cassar and Noémi Nemes, *Water as a Human Right?* (IUCN, Gland, Switzerland and Cambridge, UK 2004) 25.

river pollution).[149] The agriculture-based economies and the limited resources for adaptation in the Global South make these populations extremely vulnerable to changes in the climate. The 'energy poor' (those without access to electricity) will have particular difficulties meeting their basic needs (cooking, heating, cooling, sanitation, transportation and so on) and are, therefore, more exposed to death, diseases and dislocation as a consequence of the floods, heatwaves, droughts, rising sea levels and more frequent and severe storms caused by climate change.[150] In his report on extreme poverty and climate change (2019), Special Rapporteur Alston warns that climate change threatens to undo 50 years of progress in development, global health and poverty reduction.[151] He warns of 'a climate apartheid scenario in which the wealthy pay to escape overheating, hunger, and conflict, while the rest of the world is left to suffer'.[152]

The connection between intra- and intergenerational justice also has consequences for the question of 'whose' future generations should be considered. The opinions on this vary according to the communitarianism/cosmopolitism divide, as outlined in the last chapter. Hiskes, for example, argues that the protection of the climate for future generations would be more efficient if every community stayed within its margins (e.g., a state) and focused on its own future generations rather than all future persons. Only within a community are moral agreement and concern possible.[153] But Häberle, in line with his conception of 'International Law as a universal "Law for Humanity"',[154] takes a different stance. Constitutions are to be understood as social contracts between generations or society members,[155] and present and future generations should be considered one whole

[149] Anel du Plessis, 'South Africa's Constitutional Environmental Right (Generously) Interpreted: What Is in It for Poverty?' (2011) 27 South African Journal on Human Rights 279, 290 ff.

[150] Carmen G Gonzalez, 'Global Justice in the Anthropocene' in Louis J Kotzé (ed), *Environmental Law and Governance for the Anthropocene* (Hart/Bloomsbury Publishing 2017) 234.

[151] Special Rapporteur on Extreme Poverty and Human Rights Philipp Alston, 'Climate Change and Poverty (A/HRC/41/39)' (2019) para 13.

[152] ibid 50.

[153] See Chapter 3: Richard P Hiskes, 'Reflexive Reciprocity and Intergenerational Environmental Justice', *The Human Right to a Green Future* (CUP 2008).

[154] Peter Häberle, '"The Open Society of Constitutional Interpreters"—A Contribution to a Pluralistic and "Procedural" Constitutional Interpretation (1975)' in Markus Kotzur (ed), *Peter Häberle on Constitutional Theory* (Nomos/Hart 2018) 164.

[155] Häberle, 'Verfassungsgerichtsbarkeit in der offenen Gesellschaft' (n 72) 42.

'world society'.[156] Such a world social contract links 'a culture of attentiveness (born of a sense of ecological responsibility) with a culture of participation (as democratic responsibility) and a culture of obligation towards future generations (future responsibility)'.[157]

Here, the justice dimension becomes visible again. Future generations in the North would also have obligations towards the other members of their generation.[158] While there may be some areas benefiting in the short term from the effects of climate change, most areas have to expect a poorer climate in the future.[159] Thus, Brown Weiss suggests that those living in 'better' areas help the members of their generation and future generations living or being born in areas with poorer conditions.[160] This becomes even more important as climate change is expected to most egregiously affect impoverished communities that are the most vulnerable to changes in the climate and have the least capacity to adapt.[161]

And while the two elements of intra- and intergenerational equity do not necessarily have to be linked together, Brown Weiss describes the interaction between them as follows:

> [T]he intergenerational element of access gives members of the present generation, defined as living persons, reasonable, nondiscriminatory rights of access to resources to use to improve their own economic and social well-being, with the obligation to respect their obligations to future generations. Thus, in the intragenerational context, the realization of the intergenerational principle of conservation of access means that all peoples should have a minimum level of access to the Earth and its resources today for their own benefit.[162]

For Brown Weiss, the present generation not only acts out of noblesse but is legally obliged to comply with their duties *ante* the unborn. Future generations

---

[156] ibid (tr the author).

[157] WBGU (n 22) 277; see also Franzius (n 24).

[158] Brown Weiss, 'Climate Change, Intergenerational Equity, and International Law' (n 135) 618.

[159] IPCC, 'Climate Change—Impacts, Adaptation, and Vulnerability (Working Group II, Summary for Policymakers)' (2014) 14 ff.

[160] Brown Weiss, 'Climate Change, Intergenerational Equity, and International Law' (n 135) 621.

[161] ibid 618.

[162] Brown Weiss, 'Nature and the Law: The Global Commons and the Common Concern of Humankind' (n 79) 6.

have rights that should be legally enforceable.[163] Following generations are entitled to action being taken today, even if that means a sacrifice on the part of the living: 'the living have to do more than be sorry for the environmental damage we have wrought; we must take steps to alleviate it and its future impact on our successors' human rights'.[164] As the GFCC made clear: the problem cannot be offloaded on the shoulders of future generations. The principle of intergenerational justice, therefore, is one of the most important principles that has found its way into many constitutional and international texts. States must consider their obligations towards future generations when making (international) law. Moreover, the principle incorporates a value that is universal: caring for one's own descendants, regardless of origin, religion, 'race', gender and so on—and as such, it can help to establish solidarity between the people of the world.

5.3.1.2 Excurse: The Rights of Nature?

However, there is an important critique of the principle that also holds for human rights–based approaches to environmental protection. Davies et al. identify that the principle reinforces the anthropocentric view of IEL. Instead of ascribing nature a worth of its own, it seeks to satisfy human needs. The environment is not protected as such but as a basis for humans' 'environmental needs' (Principle 3 of the 1992 Rio Declaration).[165] Current neoliberal climate strategies are more considerate of economic implications and the market than of nature's tipping points or ecological limits. By this, they mute the social and environmental justice aspect of the principle and aggravate the implementation of serious sustainable development policies.[166]

Although this strand of argument cannot be discussed here in length due to space limitations, it is noteworthy that concepts of rights for nature, eco-constitutionalism and Mother Earth/Pachamama, mostly inspired by indigenous peoples' traditional ways of life, have become the subject of a new academic movement. In 2018, the Hague Principles for a Universal Declaration on Human Responsibilities and Earth Trusteeship were launched by 'members of the global

[163] Brown Weiss, 'Climate Change, Intergenerational Equity, and International Law' (n 135) 620.

[164] Richard P Hiskes, *The Human Right to a Green Future: Environmental Rights and Intergenerational Justice* (CUP 2008) 104.

[165] Kirsten Davies and others, 'The Declaration on Human Rights and Climate Change: A New Legal Tool for Global Policy Change' (2017) 8 Journal for Human Rights and the Environment 217, 233.

[166] ibid 234–5.

civil society and representatives of organisations', which moved away from seeing the earth merely as a 'supplier' for human needs but instead understood all humans to be trustees of the whole 'Earth community'.[167] In the same vein, the preamble of the World Charter for Nature claims that '[e]very form of life is unique, warranting respect regardless of its worth to man, and, to accord other organisms such recognition, man must be guided by a moral code of action'.[168] Thus, instead of focusing only on what all should be guaranteed to humans, an 'open, evolving, pluralistic constitution' should be based on fundamental principles of justice and sustainability and strongly rely on the principles of responsibility, precaution and cooperation.[169] Responsibility means that humans are the bearers of rights *and* duties towards the environment and future generations.[170] The effect of such visions, which seek to link inter-species and intergenerational equity with global climate law, remains to be seen, but it holds a certain fascination for researchers and institutions worldwide.[171]

5.3.1.3 Excurse: Can Future Generations Have Rights?

The ideas of Brown Weiss and others consist of conferring rights to future generations instead of them being merely a 'point' considered in legislation-making

---

[167] 'The Hague Principles for a Universal Declaration on Responsibilities for Human Rights and Earth Trusteeship', (2018) See e.g. the preamble:

> *Considering* that the totality of beings and ecosystems on Earth forms a community of life (the 'Earth community'),
> *Realizing* that just as human beings have rights that suit their needs, other beings have the right to exist and flourish according to their specific needs, and that these rights have their source in being part of the Earth community (emphasis in original).

[168] UN General Assembly, World Charter for Nature, 28 October 1982, A/RES/37/7.

[169] Jordi Jaria-Manzano, 'Law in the Anthropocene' in Jordi Jaria-Manzano and Susana Borràs (eds), *Research Handbook on Global Climate Constitutionalism* (Edward Elgar Publishing 2019) 49.

[170] ibid 33 ff; Davies and others (n 164) 240–3 analyse that the idea of human stewardship and responsibility for non-human living beings and entities is as known to the world religions, indigenous traditions and legal systems as is the thought of intergenerational justice.

[171] See, for example, in Europe: Michele Carducci and others, 'Towards an EU Charter of the Fundamental Rights of Nature (Study for the European Economic and Social Committee)' (2019); Marie-Christine Fuchs, 'Rights of Nature Reach Europe: The Mar Menor Case in Spain in the Light of Latin American Precedents' *Verfassungsblog* (24 February 2023) <https://verfassungsblog.de/rights-of-nature-reach-europe/> accessed 31 August 2023; Marie-Christine Fuchs and Levon Theisen, 'Nature—A Legal Subject' [2021], Konrad Adenauer Stiftung, Facts & Findings No. 443.

processes that seek to balance multiple interests. For some scholars, the idea of future generations having rights is not a convincing one. Beckerman and Pasek, for example, distinguish between children (who have rights) and unborn generations. Future persons cannot have rights as they do not exist. Unless one is alive, one cannot possess anything.[172] Future persons are indeterminate in terms of numbers or needs; no one knows if they will exist and what they will need. Consequently, vis-à-vis the lack of ecological rights of the future generation, the present generation would also not have corresponding obligations.[173] However, once future persons are born, they will have full moral status. They have interests that must be respected and create duties for others. It would seem odd that these fundamental interests must be respected by their contemporary peers but not by previous generations that can jeopardise them in exactly the same way.[174] Many domestic institutions (such as the long-term ground lease in the US legal system—generally for 99 years) bear future generations in mind without them being determined. Furthermore, while the identification of the individual members of the group is uncertain, even whether they may exist, it is safe to assume that *a* future generation will exist.[175]

The use of the Public Trust Doctrine (PTD) in the US points in a similar direction. Inherent in the PTD, which antedates the US Constitution, is the idea that the sovereign, be it the federal government or the state governments, are limited in their exercise of sovereignty over natural resources belonging to all persons.[176] In her decision to let the *Juliana* case proceed to trial, Judge Aiken made clear that '[t]he natural resources trust operates according to basic trust principles, which impose upon the trustee a fiduciary duty to "protect the trust property against damage or destruction"', a duty owed 'equally to both current

---

[172] Wilfred Beckerman and Joanna Pasek, *Justice, Posterity, and the Environment* (OUP 2003) 16.

[173] Richard de George, 'The Environment, Rights, and Future Generations' in Ernest Partridge (ed), *Responsibilities to future generations: environmental ethics* (Prometheus Books 1981) 159; Wilfred Beckerman, 'The Impossibility of a Theory of Intergenerational Justice' in Joerg Chet Tremmel (ed), *Handbook of Intergenerational Justice* (Edward Elgar Publishing 2006) 56.

[174] Caney (n 19) 235.

[175] Weston (n 117) 381.

[176] Michael C Blumm and Mary Christina Wood, '"No Ordinary Lawsuit": Climate Change, Due Process, and the Public Trust Doctrine' (2017) 67 American University Law Review 1, 42–53.

and future generations'.[177] Several US courts have invoked the PTD to defend the rights of young people and future generations.[178] Thus, there is a growing precedent that the atmosphere is becoming a PTD resource,[179] which means that the government as a trustee has to protect the atmosphere as a trust 'from damage so that current and future trust beneficiaries will be able to enjoy the benefits of the trust'.[180] Moreover, Hiskes argues that environmental rights, such as the right to a healthy environment and especially the rights of future generations, are primarily group rights.[181] He links his idea to the right of self-determination, another third-generation right, discussing that self-determination also includes the creation of a group's identity. This identity is shaped by the local environment (e.g., the Outback for Australians, the Karoo desert for South Africans) and by past, present and future generations.[182] These group rights exist 'regardless of the number and identity of individuals making up each generation'.[183]

But would future generations even need us to consider their interests? After all, future generations may improve technologies (e.g., renewables) to cope with climate change and, therefore, may not necessarily be worse off than the present generation.[184] It has even been argued that current generations should pay less because future generations would benefit more from climate action taken today.[185] But with IPCC experts warning that global warming has to be limited to 1.5°C by 2030 (instead of holding the increase in the global average temperature to well below 2.0°C, as foreseen by the 2015 Paris Agreement) to avoid the harshest effects of climate change, and as most countries are not on track, this seems unlikely.[186] So far, there is no guarantee that future technologies will

[177] District Court of Oregon, Judge Ann Aiken, 11 October 2016, *Kelsey Cascadia Rose Juliana v United States of America* (Case No. 6:15-Cv-01517-TC) 39.

[178] Blumm and Wood (n 175) 45–6.

[179] ibid 46.

[180] District Court of Oregon, Judge Ann Aiken, 11 October 2016, *Kelsey Cascadia Rose Juliana v United States of America* (Case No. 6:15-Cv-01517-TC) (n 176) 39.

[181] Hiskes (n 163) 122.

[182] ibid 111, 113.

[183] Brown Weiss, 'In Fairness To Future Generations and Sustainable Development' (n 119) 24.

[184] Bjørn Lomborg, *The Skeptical Environmentalist: Measuring the Real State of the World* (CUP 2001) 317.

[185] Gareth Davies, 'Climate Change and Reversed Intergenerational Equity: The Problem of Costs Now, for Benefits Later' (2020) 10 Climate Law 266.

[186] See IPCC, 'Summary for Policymakers of IPCC Special Report on Global Warming of 1.5°C'.

make the planet a more habitable place for future generations. Therefore, current generations must take action to leave behind a planet that sustains life and the needs and aspirations of future people. Although Heyd is sceptical about the concept of a legal obligation to care and save for future generations:

> This does not mean that there is no moral justification for saving for future generations. Justice as fairness is itself a primary *value* in the political life of liberal democratic societies, and hence correctly considered to be worthy of dissemination across all societies in the world and of bequest to future generations.[187]

Thus, it can be concluded that, even if the nature and extent of the obligations that current generations owe (if any) future generations are still controversial from both a moral and legal perspective, there is little doubt that justice is a value that is important to all societies. This includes intergenerational justice, since people care for their progeny, regardless of which nation, religion, ethnicity or else they belong. Despite the criticisms of the anthropocentric focus in the context of climate change and the non-identity problem of future generations, it can be precluded that intergenerational equity is probably one of the few principles whose underlying value (to ensure the planet's future for both present and future generations) deserves the label 'universal'.

In 2018, the Colombian Supreme Court, furthermore, made it clear that eco-centric approaches and intergenerational equity do not need to be exclusive. In *Future Generations*, the Court demonstrated that it is possible to reconcile a rights-based approach and the principle of intergenerational equity with an understanding of human rights as hybrid 'rights-duties' and the concept of rights for nature (in this case, the Colombian Amazon).[188]

5.3.2 Criticism: Universal Values?

For many scholars, constitutionalism is a value-loaded concept.[189] To some, however, the notion of universal values seems at least dubious,[190] if not another result

[187] Heyd (n 40) 186–7 (emphasis in original).

[188] See below Section 9.3.2.

[189] See, for example, Peters, 'The Merits of Global Constitutionalism' (n 74) 409 ('constitutionalism is a value-loaded concept'); Walker (n 63) 528 ('constitutionalism understood as a value-based discourse').

[190] Immanuel Wallerstein, *European Universalism—The Rhetoric of Power* (The New Press 2006) 28: 'It is not that there may not be global universal values. It is rather that we are far

of Eurocentric or Western hegemonic behaviour.[191] There might be universal environmental values incorporated by various (UN) agreements, but they are better dealt with by ethical pluralism according to particular regions, respectively, the four dominant traditions of the world (the Abrahamic, post-Enlightenment, Indic and Confucian traditions).[192] This is because every community has its own goals and understandings of the 'worth' of its environment, its own cultural, historical and political history and a different commitment to development.[193] Alexy doubts that values could serve as a base for the constitutional judiciary, since its judgements have to be justified by rationality to strive for the highest degree of inter-subjective control.[194] Thus, for Habermas, the equation of a value order with the constitution misses its specific legal character (in the same vein, he also rejects the idea of basic rights as principles, in Alexy's sense, as optimisable legal values): 'as legal norms, basic rights are, like moral rules, modeled after obligatory norms of action—and not after attractive goods'.[195] Luhmann argues that '[l]ike stars in the heavens there are countless values' and even the concept of basic values (e.g., freedom, dignity) falls short when it comes to adjudicating them, as there is no value hierarchy.[196] The same holds for the global level. It has been doubted if such a strict value hierarchy could be maintained in the face of the self-referentiality and the resulting indeterminacy of IL.[197] States' consent to a strict hierarchy of values established once and for all hardly

from yet knowing what these values are. Global universal values are not given to us; they are created by us'. He also claims that '[s]o we may start with the paradoxical argument that there is nothing so ethnocentric, so particularist, as the claim of universalism', 39.

191 Martti Koskenniemi, 'Histories of International Law: Dealing with Eurocentrism' (2011) 19 Rechtsgeschichte 152; Thomas Kleinlein, 'Non-State Actors from an International Constitutionalist Perspective' in Jean D'Aspremont (ed), *Participants in the International Legal System: Multiple Perspectives on Non-State Actors in International Law* (Routledge 2011) 48.

192 Jasdev Rai and others, 'Universalism and Ethical Values for the Environment', vol Draft 3/27 (UNESCO 2010) <https://unesdoc.unesco.org/ark:/48223/pf0000188607> accessed 31 August 2023.

193 James R May and Erin Daly, 'The Nature of Environmental Constitutionalism', *Global Environmental Constitutionalism* (2014) 46.

194 Robert Alexy, *A Theory of Constitutional Rights* (OUP 2002) 14.

195 Habermas, *Between Facts and Norms: Contributions to a Discourse Theory of Law and Democracy* (n 76) 256.

196 Niklas Luhmann, 'Are There Still Indispensable Norms in Our Society?' (2008) 14 Soziale Systeme 18, 28–29.

197 Stefan Kadelbach and Thomas Kleinlein, 'International Law—A Constitution for Mankind?' (2007) 50 German Yearbook of International Law 2, 29.

seems conceivable.[198] Instead, in case of value conflicts, community interests rest on 'bilateralist grounding' since there is no international institution that could balance or guide these values in the same way a national constitutional court could.[199] Haltern doubts that international lawmaking could at all address value questions, as it 'stores no memory' or 'deep social meaning'. Unlike domestic constitutional law, IL lacks the 'symbolic-aesthetic' dimension that transfers 'social sense' (*gesellschaftlicher Sinn*). He claims that this dimension is often underestimated by functionalist approaches to constitutionalism.[200]

Indeed, the school of societal constitutionalism explicitly rejects a constitutional order based on allegedly universal values.[201] However, this does not necessarily mean that there is no basis for a world society. Even if one rejects the notion of common values, the concepts of global commons or common interest could help to understand what unites a society.

5.4 Approach 2: Common Interests / Global Commons and Shared Risks

The value-based approach is prevalent mainly in the writings of Western European scholars, whereas their Asian and Eastern European colleagues are rather circumspect to the notion of such a concept and prefer more pragmatic concepts,[202] such as 'usefulness' as expressed by Yasuaki.[203] Even in the EU, with its common values, tensions between states and citizens remain. While they (seeminlgy) share the same values, these can be interpreted in different ways. Values do not necessarily create a 'collective subject'.[204]

---

[198] ibid 30.

[199] ibid 28.

[200] Ulrich Haltern, 'Internationales Verfassungsrecht? Anmerkungen zu einer kopernikanischen Wende' (2003) 128 Archiv des öffentlichen Rechts 511, 525, 556–7.

[201] See, for example, Andreas Fischer-Lescano, 'Die Emergenz der Globalverfassung' (2003) 63 Zeitschrift für ausländisches öffentliches Recht und Völkerrecht 717, 732.

[202] Jean D'Aspremont, 'The Foundations of the International Legal Order' (2009) 18 Finnish Yearbook of International Law 219, 5–6.

[203] Onuma Yasuaki, 'In Quest of Intercivilizational Human Rights: Universal vs. Relative Human Rights Viewed from an Asian Perspective' (2000) 1 Asia-Pacific Journal on Human Rights and the Law 53, 75.

[204] Roland Bieber and Markus Kotzur, 'Strukturprinzipien der EU-Verfassung' in Roland Bieber and others (eds), *Die Europäische Union* (14th edn, Nomos 2020) 107.

However, constitutions do not need to be based on values. They can be thought of as expanding beyond borders and can 'create schemes of cooperation across physical, social, and cultural boundaries because they do not presuppose shared values or shared understandings of social practices'.[205] Instead, they can create a common cognitive and normative horizon, which opens up new possibilities of action for aliens who otherwise would have to organise themselves in less efficient ways, such as purely by voluntary cooperation.[206] Instead of relying on global values that are difficult to determine, such approaches are based on the idea of common interests:

> [C]ommon interests [...] can always be distinguished from global values, since the former are fundamentally relative, context-dependent and ever-evolving. On the contrary, the concept of global values rests on the idea that there is such a thing as an objective truth independent from its factual context of application.[207]

Basing constitutionalist thoughts on common interests rather than global values does not preclude the existence of an international society. Rather, in such a functionalist concept, rules can precisely emerge because they are of benefit to all, and states would cooperate because of the possibility of gains (for both themselves and the whole community).[208]

The constitutional approach could also be reconstructed as a theory of constitutional principles. Contrary to a strict and fixed hierarchy between values—which seems unachievable[209]—the relationship between principles is dynamic, which allows for different outcomes in different settings.[210] Here, constitutional principles are understood as positioning an 'ideal-ought'; their application and balancing depend on the concrete context at hand. This approach aims to gain objectivity through the balancing of adequate principles.[211] It has been argued that *jus cogens* and *erga omnes* norms embody regional or international values

[205] Ulrich K Preuss, 'Disconnecting Constitutions from Statehood: Is Global Constitutionalism a Viable Concept?' in Petra Dobner and Martin Loughlin (eds), *The Twilight of Constitutionalism?* (OUP 2010) 46.

[206] ibid.

[207] D'Aspremont (n 201) 7. This book refers to the page numbers of the text version available at https://pure.uva.nl/ws/files/952445/89866_SSRN_id1265525_1_.pdf.

[208] ibid 12.

[209] Luhmann (n 195) 29.

[210] Kadelbach and Kleinlein (n 196) 30–31.

[211] ibid 35–6, 39.

and, therefore, could serve as constitutional fundamental norms creating a norm hierarchy of IL.[212]

However, norms belonging to these categories cannot be meaningfully understood either *ratione materie* or on the basis of their norm structure as a homogeneous group of fundamental norms.[213] Instead, scholars such as Kleinlein argue for the emergence of an objective universal order for the protection of common goods as an important element for the constitutionalisation of IL.[214] Common interests can be subclassified into common goods and common values. For the latter, the common interest comes from the recognition of a common value (e.g., biodiversity, human rights, indigenous cultures), whereas the former is based on a fact, for example, because certain actions, such as climate change, have transboundary effects. A common good in this sense would be a healthy and intact environment.[215] Norms that protect common goods in a universal objective order are independent of states' consent and could foster, in Hart's sense, the transformation of IL from a 'set of rules' to a 'system of rules'.[216]

The idea of global commons is particularly interesting for constitutionalism because in the same way that values—such as caring for one's progeny—can unite people around the world, so can a shared risk. This refers to the second alternative that has been identified by Walker: the common predicament within the putative demos can be either the presupposition or promise (or both) of constitutional integration.[217] Thus, the protection of the common goods can tie people together and form a base upon which global solidarity could possibly be developed over time.

Using this as a premise, German sociologist Ulrich Beck discusses the emergence of a climate world risk society.[218] Decisions taken in individual enterprises or at the national level can result in global threats that unite all humans in a world

---

[212] Erika de Wet, 'The Emergence of International and Regional Value Systems as a Manifestation of the Emerging International Constitutional Order' (2006) 19 Leiden Journal of International Law 611.

[213] See Chapter 5 'Hierarchisierung im Völkerrecht' in Kleinlein (n 84) 315–426 (425–6).

[214] See Chapter 6 'Völkerrecht als objektive universelle Ordnung zum Schutz von Gemeinschaftsgütern' in ibid 427–509.

[215] ibid 433–4.

[216] ibid 508–9; HLA Hart, *The Concept of Law* (Clarendon Press 1961) 236.

[217] Walker (n 63) 531.

[218] See Chapter 'Global Public Sphere and Global Subpolitics or: How Real is Catastrophic Climate Change?' in Ulrich Beck, *World at Risk* (Polity Press 2008) 82 ff.

risk society.[219] Thus, global threats can lead to a 'cosmopolitan moment'.[220] The impossibility of controlling risks resulting from decisions relating to the environment, such as licensing a new power plant, and ensuring safety and health at the national level, is the 'cosmopolitan moment' of the ecological crisis.[221] Such a sociological concept of cosmopolitanism means dealing with 'cultural others': the inclusion of others being its maxim. It is to recognise that 'through the increased awareness of the dynamics of world risk society, all people have become the immediate neighbours of all others, and thus share the world with non-excludable others, whether they like it, or want to recognize it, or not'.[222] What forces people together are the 'traumatic experiences of the enforced community of global risks that threaten everyone's existence'.[223] Such threats provoke a range of answers, including renationalisation and xenophobia, but also the possibility of recognising that others are equal *and* different.[224] Since everybody is vulnerable to global threats, everybody is responsible for others.[225] 'Enforced cosmopolitanization' is the result of activated global risks that brings people together—across borders—who want to have nothing to do with each other. This is not philosophical or normative but 'real' cosmopolitanism that comes in through the back door of global threats.[226] Therefore, it is not based on values but on real risks. The reliance on values for a world society is impossible, since there cannot be a universal consensus.[227] Rather, 'the faith in the secular religion of threat forces everyone into concerted action'.[228]

Does climate change unite the countries and people of the world? Generally, populations in the Global North are better off than those of the Global South, and they have greater resources to cope with climate change. According to the Global Climate Risk Index of 2021, the countries most affected in 2019 by extreme weather events were Mozambique, Zimbabwe and the Bahamas. 'Eight out of ten countries most affected by the quantified impacts of extreme weather events in 2019 belong to the low- to lower-middle income category. Half of them

219 ibid 91.

220 ibid 56.

221 ibid 91.

222 ibid 56.

223 ibid.

224 ibid 56–7.

225 ibid 57.

226 ibid 61.

227 ibid 64.

228 ibid.

are Least Developed Countries.'[229] In the long-term index (2000–2019), Puerto Rico, Myanmar and Haiti were the countries most affected by extreme weather events.[230] Hazardous climate change seems to unite the poorer countries but does not necessarily include the richer countries of the Global North.

However, in the long run, climate change also will (and already does) affect the Global North both environmentally and economically. The economist Stern calculated in 2006 that 'business as usual' would cost the UK economy at least 5% (and possibly up to 20%) of gross domestic product (GDP) every year.[231] According to the IPCC, the world would suffer socio-economic losses amounting to 13% of global GDP and USD69 trillion in damages from 2°C warming.[232] In total, 1.2 billion jobs (40% of global employment) depend on a sustainable and healthy environment. Heat stress, even in the best-case scenario (the 1.5°C scenario), provides a 2% reduction in global working hours by 2030.[233] Due to the connectedness of global production chains, this also has consequences for countries that may be less affected by the worst effects of climate change so far. However, countries of the Global North must not feel too safe. According to the Global Climate Risk Index, in 2018, the most affected countries were Japan, the Philippines and Germany. Japan and Germany had both experienced severe heatwaves.[234] It becomes clear once more that climate change is a global issue with serious consequences for all areas of social life. In the long run, climate change may put democracy and the rule of law at risk and 'human rights may not survive the coming upheaval'.[235] Thus, the international community of states, but also all human beings, form 'a community of destiny in the sense of a risk society'.[236]

---

229 Germanwatch e.V., 'Global Climate Risk Index 2021', Key Messages.

230 ibid, Key Messages.

231 Nicolas Stern, 'The Stern Review on Economics of Climate Change' (2006).

232 IPCC, 'Special Report on Global Warming of 1.5°C' (2018) 264.

233 ILO, 'Greening with Jobs' (2018) 2, 7, 27.

234 Germanwatch e.V., 'Global Climate Risk Index 2020', Key Messages.

235 Special Rapporteur on Extreme Poverty and Human Rights Philipp Alston (n 150) paras 65, 87.

236 Emmerich-Fritsche (n 9) 304 (tr the author).

The protection of the environment in itself is value-free. It serves the common interest of all to guarantee the survival of humankind.[237] States curb their GHG emissions because they recognise that climate change is a major threat.[238]

Climate change poses a risk to the satisfaction of human physiological needs. According to Maslow's hierarchy of human needs, they are the physical requirements of human survival, and they are universal.[239] They encompass, inter alia, food and water, whose security is likely to be at risk with the increasing frequency and intensity of droughts, floods and heatwaves.[240] It is, therefore, a common interest of humanity to guarantee its survival and the fulfilment of its existential physiological needs. It is against this background, in particular, water scarcity, that the *Leghari* case gains relevance.[241] Justice Biscoe of the Land and Environment Court of New South Wales, Australia, summarises the issue in *Walker vs Minister of Planning*, stating that '[c]limate change presents a risk to the survival of the human race and other species. Consequently, it is a deadly serious issue'.[242]

Thus, it is important to protect the 'ecological global commons'. These are areas to which nobody can prevent access, such as the atmosphere, the oceans, the ocean-atmospheric system with its monsoon system and thermohaline circulation patterns, and the ozone layer.[243] The climate is also a global common good, since

---

237 'An interest is a pattern of value demands on behalf of an individual or a group of identity, supported by expectations that the value demands are advantageous for that identity. [...] In the simplest terms, the common interest is composed of interests widely shared by members of a community. It would benefit the community as a whole and be sup-ported by most community members, if they can find it', Ronald D Brunner and Amanda H Lynch, *Adaptive Governance and Climate Change* (American Meteorological Society 2010) 22–3.

238 D'Aspremont (n 201) 22.

239 AH Maslow, 'A Theory of Human Motivation' (1943) 50 Psychological Review 370, 373: 'Undoubtedly these physiological needs are the most pre-potent of all needs. What this means specifically is, that in the human being who is missing everything in life in an extreme fashion, it is most likely that the major motivation would be the physiological needs rather than any others. A person who is lacking food, safety, love, and esteem would most probably hunger for food more strongly than for anything else.'

240 UN Special Rapporteur on Human Rights and the Environment John H. Knox, 'Special Report on Climate Change and Human Rights' (2015) 5.

241 See Section 9.2 below.

242 NSW Land and Environment Court, *Walker v. Minister for Planning* (NSWLEC 741/ 157 LGERA 124) para 161.

243 Brown Weiss, 'Nature and the Law: The Global Commons and the Common Concern of Humankind' (n 79) 1.

GHG emissions do not know about borders.[244] Once emitted, GHG emissions mix completely with already existing GHGs, which leads to an evenly distributed, measurable amount of GHGs in the atmosphere irrespective of their source of emission.[245]

Preserving the planet and ensuring its survival is a task that no state can do alone. Moreover, with respect to the global commons, the Report of the Commission on Global Governance argues that sovereignty has to be exercised collectively.[246] States should safeguard equal access to the global commons for all.[247] However, viewing the Earth as a global common good that all people share does not mean viewing it as common property.[248] Thus, the idea of global trusteeship is a useful instrument to protect the planet for the community (including future generations) as a whole and to avoid the reference to global values.

5.5 A Hybrid Approach? The Common Concern of Humankind (CCH)

From the foregoing, it could be assumed that these two approaches—common values and shared risks—mutually exclude each other, but this is not necessarily the case. Climate change, in particular, affects both the value of climate justice and, at the same time, poses a shared risk (which threatens the common interest). Thus, it is possible to couple values and shared risks.

Generally, there may be overlaps between the categories of values and common interests. A global interest might be identical to the value it encompasses.[249] Bull speaks of 'maintaining and extending the consensus about common interest *and* global values that provides the foundations of its common rules and institutions'.[250] Thus, values and common interests can go hand in hand. From a

---

[244] ibid.

[245] United States Environmental Protection Agency, 'Overview of Greenhouse Gases' (2016) <https://www.epa.gov/ghgemissions/overview-greenhouse-gases> accessed 31 August 2023.

[246] Commission on Global Governance (n 77) 67, 70.

[247] ibid 57.

[248] Brown Weiss, 'Nature and the Law: The Global Commons and the Common Concern of Humankind' (n 79) para 2.

[249] D'Aspremont (n 201) 7.

[250] Hedley Bull, *The Anarchical Society: A Study of Order in World Politics* (4th edn, Red Globe Press 2012) 303.

constitutionalist perspective, IL represents 'public concerns and community interests on the basis of established constitutional values'.[251] According to Peters, the three 'classical' constitutional values whose implementation depends on states (democracy, the rule of law and human rights) are only tentatively and selectively applied, and human rights come the closest to universal acceptance. However, she sees 'public interest norms' (as 'constitutional norms')[252] emerging from the fundamental provisions of so-called world order treaties as a core element of international constitutionalisation.[253] These treaties embody global community interests, and as such, they overcome the focus on individual states' interests.[254] Furthermore, these 'public interest norms' encompass material values, even if they do not necessarily need to belong to the classic canon of constitutionalism.[255] She concludes that '[t]hese global common interests relate to global goods and/or reflect common assumptions and shared attitudes. At least in part, the relevant norms embody universal values,'[256] among them the value of climate protection.[257]

Climate and environmental protection, therefore, could be such a hybrid. On the one side, IEL encompasses the values of intergenerational justice and environmental protection as such. On the other, from a more pragmatic point of view, the protection of the environment is a community interest: the survival of humanity, regardless of people's origin, religion, gender and so on, which cannot endure without all the components nature provides to satisfy its basic needs. The principle of the CCH serves as an example that encompasses both elements. The CCH principle is one of the manifestations of the concept of solidarity among states and humanity.[258] It incorporates the notion that some ecological concerns are common to all humankind, regardless of physical borders or the fixation on state sovereignty, and that those environmental problems can only be resolved by

[251] Kleinlein (n 190) 47.

[252] Anne Peters, 'Compensatory Constitutionalism: The Function and Potential of Fundamental International Norms and Structures' (2006) 19 Leiden Journal of International Law 579, 601.

[253] ibid 601.

[254] See Section 3.2.3 above.

[255] Peters, 'Compensatory Constitutionalism: The Function and Potential of Fundamental International Norms and Structures' (n 251) 601.

[256] ibid 589.

[257] Peters, 'The Merits of Global Constitutionalism' (n 74) 399.

[258] Kleinlein (n 84) 10 ff.

collective (state) action.[259] These concerns are climate change, loss of biodiversity and—while not explicitly expressed—desertification.[260] The principle seeks to overcome the territorial obsession of both states and IL that has resulted in a binary system categorising natural resources and matters as 'beyond' or 'within national jurisdiction'.[261] Instead, at the fundament of the CCH principle lies the belief that there are certain 'global ecological commons' that have to be addressed by the world community as a whole, regardless of the social, economic, cultural and regional background of its members.[262] As of today, there are two important agreements explicitly proclaiming the CCH principle: the 1992 Convention on Biological Diversity[263] and the UNFCCC.[264] The 1988 UNGA resolution 43/53 recognised 'that climate change is a common concern of mankind, since climate is an essential condition which sustains life on earth'.[265] The 2015 Paris Agreement reaffirmed the principle. Notably, the term 'common concern of *humanity*' does not exclusively refer to the community of states.[266] The idea that common interests could triumph over the interests of individual states has caused slight

---

[259] Jutta Brunnée, 'Common Areas, Common Heritage, and Common Concern' in Daniel Bodansky, Jutta Brunnée and Ellen Hey (eds), *The Oxford Handbook of International Environmental Law* (OUP 2008) 552–3.

[260] See Prue Taylor, 'Common Heritage of Mankind and Common Concern of Humankind', *Elgar Encyclopedia of Environmental Law: Principles of Environmental Law (Vol. VI)* (Edward Elgar Publishing 2018) 303 315. Recently it has been suggested that access to and the quality of fresh water as well as plastic pollution should be added to the list of common concerns, see Edith Brown Weiss, *International Law for a Water-Scarce World* (Brill/ Martinus Nijhoff Publishers 2013); Balraj K Sidhu and Bharat H Desai, 'Plastics Pollution: A New Common Concern of Humankind?' (2018) 48 Environmental Policy and Law 252.

[261] Taylor (n 259) 304.

[262] ibid.

[263] UN General Assembly, UN Conference on Environment and Development: resolution, adopted by the General Assembly, 22 December 1989, A/RES/44/228.

[264] The UNFCCC acknowledges in its preamble that the "change in the Earth's climate and its adverse effects are a common concern of humankind."

[265] UN General Assembly, Protection of global climate for present and future generations of mankind: resolution, adopted by the General Assembly, 6 December 1988, A/RES/43/53.

[266] Though Shelton points out that the restricted terminology referring to the conservation of the biodiversity respectively climate change and its adverse effects instead of declaring the biological diversity or the climate as a whole as common concerns was meant to reach out to the states concerned about their sovereignty and the possibilities of exploiting their territories, see Dinah Shelton, 'Common Concern of Humanity' (2009) 39 Environmental Policy and Law 83, 85.

discomfort to some scholars.[267] However, there are also benefits for all states resulting from commonly taken action, since none of them can solve the problem of climate change by themselves.[268]

Moreover, the term 'humankind' or 'humanity' can also lead to a shift in perspective that moves away from a state-centred focus on IL. Judge Weeramantry suggested in his separate opinion in the *Gabčíkovo-Nagymaro* case that it is possible to understand the principle in a broader sense as a 'common concern of *humanity as a whole*':

> We have entered an era of international law in which international law subserves not only the interests of individual States, but looks beyond them and their parochial concerns to the greater interests of humanity and planetary welfare. [...] International environmental law will need to proceed beyond weighing the rights and obligations of parties within a closed compartment of individual State self-interest, unrelated to the global concerns of humanity as a whole.[269]

To put the CCH principle into perspective, Brown Weiss suggests viewing it through two different lenses: the intergenerational lens, as climate change will affect future generations, and through the kaleidoscopic lens in the form of a bottom-up approach focusing on the actions of those being affected by climate change now and in the future.[270] The individual state's self-interest, and even collectively upon agreed goals in treaties, are not the yardstick for assessing states' actions; rather, it is the question of whether an action can lead to the protection of the interests of humanity and the planet as a whole.[271] Thus, the CCH principle:

> embod[ies] universal solidarity and social responsibility (rather than competitiveness), emanate[s] from human conscience (rather than from the free 'will' of States),

---

[267] See e.g. Brunnée (n 258) 553, stating that 'to address common environmental concerns, international environmental law has not merely had to undergo a significant conceptual expansion, but also had to do so against the grain of the foundational structures of international law.'

[268] Frederiech Soltau, 'Common Concern of Humankind' in Kevin Gray, Richard Tarasofsky and Cinnamon Carlarne (eds), *The Oxford Handbook of International Climate Change Law* (OUP 2016) 206.

[269] Separate Opinion of Vice-President Weeramantry—*Case Gabcikovo-Nagymaros Project (Hungary vs Slovakia), ICJ Reports 1997* (n 82) 115.

[270] Brown Weiss, 'Nature and the Law: The Global Commons and the Common Concern of Humankind' (n 79) 2.

[271] Soltau (n 267) 206.

> reflect[s] basic values of the international community as a whole (rather than State interests), and strengthen[s] the notion of an international *ordre public* (rather than a fragmented contractual vision).[272]

5.6 Conclusion: A Base for Global Solidarity Within the Global Community

In the last chapter, it was argued that climate justice needs to form an important element of global climate constitutionalism. In contrast to forms of constitutionalism beyond the state that have been developed in relation to general IL, global climate constitutionalism has to address questions of global justice and redistribution. A merely negative consensus on what is not acceptable as the minimum of what can be achieved between people worldwide would not be sufficient to address the challenges that climate change poses for IL so far and in the coming decades. In doing so, it needs a 'thicker' base in the global community.

Including climate justice in frameworks of global climate constitutionalism requires solidarity with others—living geographically or temporally far away. This solidarity may not exist yet, but it has been argued in this chapter that the global community is capable of developing global (climate) solidarity. Solidarity 'not only emerges via the opposition of "Us" and "Them", but from compassion for the well-being of other individuals'.[273] Thus, neither homogeneity nor harmony between humans—often seen as the basis of national solidarity—are prerequisites for solidarity to emerge within frameworks of constitutionalism beyond the state. Instead, mutual respect is. A constitution both presupposes and promises the societal integration of different people with different interests into one constitutional society. To adopt this idea at the international level, however, means that a basic minimum of 'a common attachment or common predicament within the putative *demos*' is necessary.[274]

This chapter has argued that the basis of global solidarity and a global constitutional community can be found either in common values or shared risk. In the environmental and climate context, the thick fabric of the global *pouvoir constituent* could be found in the universally shared principle of intergenerational

---

[272] Antônio Augusto Cançado Trindade, *International Law for Humankind: Towards a New Jus Gentium* (3rd edn, Brill/Martinus Nijhoff Publishers 2020) 349 (emphasis in original).

[273] Peters, 'Dual Democracy' (n 3) 312.

[274] Walker (n 63) 531.

equity. The principle of intergenerational equity is inherent to every nation's constitution, as they are made to outlive their creators and to tie a bond between all generations of a community—past, present and future.[275] The concern of how future generations will cope with climate change prompts a transfer to the global realm. It is restricting the sovereign's power today, since the needs of future generations have to be taken into consideration by the governing powers. The idea underpinning this principle has been known to humankind since the beginnings of civilisation and has found its way into a multitude of national and international legal documents. Therefore, it can be argued, intergenerational justice, which is embodied by the principle, is a universal value. However, approaches to constitutionalism based on values are rejected by some, either based on reasons of alleged Western hegemonic tendencies or impracticality, including the impossibility of stratifying values to resolve conflicts between them.[276]

Those who refute the concept of global values can easily identify a common goal in IEL that could present a 'common predicament within the putative *demos*'[277]: to preserve the planet so that humanity—both present and future generations—can survive and flourish.[278] The value and the goal here are identical: they support each other instead of excluding each other.

The CCH principle illustrates that the protection of the climate can be both a universal value and a common interest and that there is not necessarily a 'better' approach towards global environmental constitutionalism. The global civil society is becoming a 'community of fate' (or, in the words of the Committee on Global Governance, an emerging 'global neighbourhood') based on certain universal values and tied together by the global risks of climate change that all members of this global community share.[279]

This development raises the question of the actors in global environmental governance. '[T]he gradual establishment of common values or common concerns' is driven by individuals who 'have emerged as new actors in international society; they stake out demands and raise concerns that are at variance with

[275] Cf. James R May and Erin Daly, *Global Environmental Constitutionalism* (CUP 2014) 47.

[276] Bianchi (n 90) 203.

[277] Walker (n 63) 531 (emphasis in original).

[278] Rakhyun E Kim and Klaus Bosselmann, 'Operationalizing Sustainable Development: Ecological Integrity as a Grundnorm of International Law' (2015) 24 Review of European, Comparative and International Environmental Law 194, 205.

[279] Beck (n 217) 91.

those of states'.[280] Thus, their actions push for the establishment of a community that also protects the interests of non-state actors.[281] This especially includes the interests of future generations.

However, including questions of world domestic politics into frameworks of global (climate) constitutionalism requires us to turn to a problem that has already been identified in relation to IL, understood as *jus gentium* or inter-states law, and has become even more pressing considering the ever-denser quality of IL norms from a constitutionalist perspective: the lack of legitimacy. This problem and the development of possible approaches to the legitimacy of international constitutional law are the subject of the next chapter.

---

280 Antonio Cassese, 'Gathering Up the Main Threads' in Antonio Cassese (ed), *Realizing Utopia: The Future of International Law* (OUP 2012) 653.

281 ibid.

Deliberative Democracy and CCL 6

Climate justice is key for global climate constitutionalism. Redistributive policies can be based on global solidarity that may not exist yet but could be developed. This is because climate change is a problem that concerns humans all over the world who either share common values or the risk of losing their lives, homes, security, livelihoods and traditional ways of life due to the climate crisis. However, one should not forget that climate justice does not only entail distributive policies but also recognition and, especially, participation opportunities for the global community.[1] This is a problem that traditional concepts of IL face: there are no meaningful participation or input opportunities for non-state actors. In other words:

> the kernel of truth in the proposition of the illegitimacy of international law is that the 'old' legitimacy of international law, flowing from the will and consent of sovereign states, no longer satisfies political actors and citizens. What is needed are 'new' types of legitimacy according to 'constitutional' standards. This is indeed what global constitutionalism is about.[2]

Officially, non-state actors cannot participate in international lawmaking because they are not subjects of IL. However, as has already been argued above, if a global constitution should also constitute the world society, then it needs to include

[1] David Schlosberg, 'Reconceiving Environmental Justice: Global Movements and Political Theories' (2004) 13 Environmental Politics 517, 518 ff.

[2] Anne Peters, 'Compensatory Constitutionalism: The Function and Potential of Fundamental International Norms and Structures' (2006) 19 Leiden Journal of International Law 579, 607.

M. Niehaus, *Global Climate Constitutionalism "from below"*,
https://doi.org/10.1007/978-3-658-43191-4_6

citizens as active subjects.[3] Legitimacy, according to constitutional standards, means that citizens need to confer legitimacy to international lawmaking, for example, through elections or referenda, as in the nation-state. This raises the question of how legitimacy should be conferred to international constitutional law. How can citizens have a meaningful say in their own matters and contribute to international lawmaking?

Concepts of constitutionalism that lend themselves stronger to analogies with nation-states either propose a world state or the establishment of a global assembly composed of representatives of individuals and civil society, in which representation would not occur along national lines but rather be based on interests, world-views and political orientation.[4] Many proponents of global constitutionalism propose the constitutionalisation of the world legal system and an ever-densifying quality of international norms but reject a world state.[5] A politically constituted world society would need to be composed of individuals acquiring subject status in IL *and* nation-states.[6] Such visions rely on *demoi-cracy*—a multitude of demos—instead of *one* global demos.[7] It is not possible to abolish the nation-state because there is no turning back to the original state of nature prior to it, a concept appropriate for taming the absolutist state but not nation-states legitimised under the rule of law: '[T]he *political empowerment* of

[3] Peter Häberle, '"The Open Society of Constitutional Interpreters"—A Contribution to a Pluralistic and "Procedural" Constitutional Interpretation (1975)' in Markus Kotzur (ed), *Peter Häberle on Constitutional Theory* (Nomos/Hart 2018) 144.

[4] Richard Falk and Andrew Strauss, 'Toward Global Parliament' (2001) 80 Foreign Affairs 212, 216–7.

[5] Angelika Emmerich-Fritsche, *Vom Völkerrecht zum Weltrecht* (Duncker & Humblot 2007) 596; see also, for example, Mattias Kumm, 'The Cosmopolitan Turn in Constitutionalism: An Integrated Conception of Public Law' (2013) 20 Indiana Journal of Global Legal Studies 605; Jürgen Habermas, 'The Postnational Constellation and the Future of Democracy' in Jürgen Habermas and Max Pensky (eds), *The Postnational Constellation: Political Essays* (Polity Press 2001).

[6] Jürgen Habermas, 'The Constitutionalization of International Law and the Legitimation Problems of a Constitution for World Society' (2008) 15 Constellations 444, 448.

[7] Samantha Besson, 'Institutionalizing Global Demoi-Cracy' in Lukas H Meyer (ed), *Legitimacy, Justice and Public International Law* (CUP 2009) 66 ff.; Anne Peters, 'Dual Democracy' in Jan Klabbers, Anne Peters and Geir Ulfstein (eds), *The Constitutionalization of International Law* (OUP 2009) 304; Andreas L Paulus, 'The International Legal System as a Constitution' in Jeffrey L Dunoff and Joel P Trachtman (eds), *Ruling the world? Constitutionalism, International Law, and Global Governance* (CUP 2009) 109.

a pre-political global civil society composed of citizens from different nations is a different matter from *imposing a constitution* on an existing state power.'[8]

Citizens of democratic states have already gone through the process of legalising an initially unbound acting state power. The emergence of a cosmopolitan legal order, therefore, can only be complementary, not analogous.[9] Not only do states control legitimate means of violence, they can make them available to the international community. Habermas also warns not to underestimate the associated loyalty of citizens to their states insofar as they seek to preserve and improve the national forms of life that they have created, with which they identify and for which they feel responsible.[10] Therefore, while the role of the state is changing—losing somewhat its monopoly in the international legal system[11]—it will most likely remain a core actor.[12] States (including those not democratically legitimised) still constitute 'a crystallisation point for (collective) identity'.[13]

There have been calls for a post-sovereign order in the form of multi-level governance that consists of political institutions at the global, regional, state and substate levels. Authority should be distributed among these levels, with no one being the sovereign.[14] However, such an approach only explains which level should take action, but it cannot answer the question of how highly political

---

[8] Habermas, 'The Constitutionalization of International Law and the Legitimation Problems of a Constitution for World Society' (n 6) 448 (emphasis in original).

[9] Jürgen Habermas, 'Hat die Konstitutionalisierung des Völkerrechts noch eine Chance?' in Jürgen Habermas (ed), *Der gespaltene Westen* (Suhrkamp 2004) 129.

[10] Habermas, 'The Constitutionalization of International Law and the Legitimation Problems of a Constitution for World Society' (n 6) 449.

[11] David Held, *Democracy and the Global Order: From the Modern State to Cosmopolitan Governance* (Polity Press 1995) 233; Thilo Marauhn, 'Changing Role of The State' in Daniel Bodansky, Jutta Brunnée and Ellen Hey (eds), *The Oxford Handbook of International Environmental Law* (OUP 2012).

[12] Anne-Marie Slaughter, *A New World Order* (Princeton University Press 2004) 18.

[13] Anne Peters, 'Membership in the Global Constitutional Community' in Jan Klabbers, Anne Peters and Geir Ulfstein (eds), *The Constitutionalization of International Law* (OUP 2009) 198.

[14] Simon Caney, 'Cosmopolitanism and the Environment' in Teena Gabrielson and others (eds), *The Oxford Handbook of Environmental Political Theory* (OUP 2016) 240; Hayley Stevenson, *Global Environmental Politics. Problems, Policy, and Practice* (CUP 2017) 145, 156 ff.; Eva Sørensen and Jacob Torfing, 'The Democratic Anchorage of Governance Networks' (2005) 28 Scandinavian Political Studies 195, 201.

distribution issues in the global community should be addressed and the need for legitimacy they engender.[15]

The fair allocation of mitigation responsibilities or emission rights between countries is one of the main topics of climate justice, but the matter is far more complex. While it may cause global harm, it is mostly in the interest of the state to exploit its environmental commons and resources.[16] Imbalances also exist within the populations of one country: between the wealthy and the poor. Moreover, countries such as China and India are often perceived as anything but developing, with a fast-growing middle class that is as wealthy or wealthier than average middle-class citizens in some developed countries.[17] It becomes clear that visions of justice differ widely, and legitimacy cannot be measured with output criteria alone. Fair processes of decision-making over societal and common goods are needed, typically in democratic (input) forms.[18] Thus, it is important to remember that, besides distributive justice, recognition and participation are crucial elements for climate justice.[19] The question is how participation in decision-making processes could be enabled at the global level. How could the international global community lend democratic legitimacy to new forms of transnational law?

Different forms of legitimacy need to be discussed in the transnational context. Importantly, such visions have to part from the idea that global democracy would look exactly like domestic democracy. Once the idea of a world state is rejected, voting and representation cannot be established in the same way as in a nation-state. To find such alternatives, this chapter draws on deliberative democracy to consider methods of participation opportunities for non-state actors in IL. The advantage of deliberative democracy lies in its focus on talking instead of voting and, therefore, seems a much better fit for global governance. The chapter then progresses to a discussion of how pluralistic theories increasingly stress the role of disagreement and contestation for the development of a 'true'

---

[15] Jürgen Habermas, 'A Political Constitution for the Pluralist World Society?' in Jürgen Habermas (ed), *Between Naturalism and Religion: Philosophical Essays* (Polity Press 2008) 344 n 41.

[16] Paul G Harris, *World Ethics and Climate Change: From International to Global Justice* (Edinburgh University Press 2010) 99.

[17] Paul Baer, 'International Justice' in John S Dryzek, Richard B Norgaard and David Schlosberg (eds), *Oxford Handbook of Climate Change and Society* (OUP 2011) 324–5; Harris (n 16) 94.

[18] Nico Krisch, *Beyond Constitutionalism: The Pluralist Structure of Postnational Law* (OUP 2010) 265.

[19] Schlosberg (n 1) 518 ff..

democratic discourse. Instead of striving to reach a consensus, the ongoing contesting of norms could help the law to develop in more pluralistic ways that include the perspectives of civil society. In the next step, litigation as a forum for such deliberation and contestation is examined. Finally, it is analysed whether CCL can serve as a 'port of entry'[20] for a dialogue between non-state actors and states in the transnational constitutional climate regime and, thus, a forum for non-state actors to participate in democratic self-government, both nationally and internationally.

Democratic legitimacy is—at least in liberal Western societies—often reduced to voting rights and representation, and sometimes referenda.[21] One could argue that the democratisation of global constitutionalism is impossible without a world parliament. But this gap is not unbridgeable if one stops demanding that global governance has to become a doubleganger of domestic legal orders.[22] In its report *Our Global Neighbourhood*, the Commission on Global Governance claims that 'two minutes in a voting booth every few years does not satisfy [people's] desire for participation' and, thus, calls for decentralisation, new forms of participation and the involvement of more people than traditional democratic systems allow.[23] 'A people' is more than a factor solely appearing on election day to provide democratic legitimacy.[24] Democracy not only expresses itself through elections—as 'the channelled and formalised connection of delegation and responsibility between the people and the state entities'—but also 'in the pluralistic public process of everyday politics and practice, especially with regard to the fulfilment of fundamental rights, often referred to as the "democratic side"'.[25]

Thus, a move away from the idea of traditional political participation and expression of political will, for example, through elections, is necessary. Democracy needs to be uncoupled from its eighteenth-century understanding, and the use of the term 'democracy' extended to refer to any activity in which people assemble and negotiate the way and by whom power is exercised over them, as

[20] Hari M Osofsky, 'Climate Change Litigation as Pluralist Legal Dialogue?' (2007) 26 A Stanford Environmental Law Journal 181, 195.

[21] Balakrishnan Rajagopal, *International Law from Below: Development, Social Movements and Third World Resistance* (CUP 2003) 244; Helle Krunke, 'Courts as Protectors of the People: Constitutional Identity, Popular Legitimacy and Human Rights' in Martin Scheinin, Helle Krunke and Marina Aksenova (eds), *Judges as Guardians of Constitutionalism and Human Rights* (Edward Elgar Publishing 2016) 77–8.

[22] See e.g. Peters, 'Dual Democracy' (n 7) 338.

[23] Commission on Global Governance, 'Our Global Neighbourhood' (OUP 1995) 37.

[24] Häberle, 'The Open Society of Constitutional Interpreters' (n 3) 146.

[25] ibid.

these are also governance struggles in a non-restrictive sense.[26] Democracy can express itself in more forms than the formalised and channelled connection of delegation and responsibility between the people and the state.[27]

6.1 Deliberative Democracy

Cohen describes the basic concept of democracy as follows:

> The fundamental idea of democratic, political legitimacy is that the authorization to exercise state power must arise from the *collective decisions* of the equal members of a society who are governed by that power.[28]

Legitimacy in a state based on fundamental rights dwells from the freedom of the individual (fundamental rights) and the collective will of the people (democracy). In their polarity, they constitute the liberal polity.[29] The power of the state – which emanates from the people and is legitimised by the people – forms the counterpart of the individual, not only as of the most powerful guarantor of fundamental freedom but also its most dangerous adversary.[30] The individual who enjoys the personal liberty to live her life on her terms is also a member of a polity and expected to obey the rules that emerge from the collective will. These can restrict her personal freedom guaranteed by fundamental rights, e.g. in the form of a tax assessment or the granting of a building permit (or not).[31] This is a constitutive feature of the nation-state – the supremacy of state politics over all other societal spheres which can be subject to political intervention.[32] Such intervention is only legitimised through the democratic principle – it is legitimised by the governed people.[33] Political orders need to draw their recognition from the legitimacy claim of the law; the medium through which state power is

---

[26] James Tully, 'The Agonic Freedom of Citizens' (1999) 28 Economy and Society 161, 178.

[27] Häberle, 'The Open Society of Constitutional Interpreters' (n 3) 146.

[28] Joshua Cohen, 'Democracy and Liberty' in Jon Elster (ed), *Deliberative Democracy* (CUP 1998) 185 (emphasis in original).

[29] Josef Isensee, 'Grundrechte und Demokratie' (1981) 20 Der Staat 161, 171.

[30] ibid 165.

[31] ibid 163.

[32] Armin von Bogdandy, 'Globalization and Europe: How to Square Democracy, Globalization, and International Law' (2004) 15 European Journal of International Law 885, 887.

[33] Isensee (n 29) 163.

constituted.[34] Law, then, 'requires more than mere acceptance; besides demanding that its addresses give it de facto recognition, the law claims to deserve their recognition.'[35] An unbroken flow of legitimacy is necessary, and this flow occurs at the national level through proper democratic channels, through what Isensee calls the establishment of power 'from below', through elections, transparency, protection of minorities, and so on.[36] This is the idea of self-determination that is both the basis and the core of the democratic principle.[37] If, for example, a state commits itself to reduce GHG emissions, the final addressees of these regulations are societal actors, such as companies and individuals (e.g. the car industry, the car drivers).[38] Rules that originally impose constraints on states, ultimately constrain its citizens which govern themselves through the institutional framework of the state.[39] Without consent, no free person can be bound against their will.[40] Within society, this is the 'general will' – not everyone has to consent to every law, instead, society as such must be willed to be bound by this law.[41] The sovereignty of the people means nothing else than 'the equal freedom of every person affected by legal norms to do everything that the self-imposed laws do not forbid.'[42] This is the democratic principle – the identity between the authors and the addressees of the law.[43] As such, the democratic principle requires that everybody can have an equal say in decisions that affect her or him– what affects all should be considered and approved by all (quod omnes tangit principle). The content and scope of human rights is not pre-existent to

[34] Jürgen Habermas, 'Remarks on Legitimation through Human Rights' in Jürgen Habermas (ed), The Postnational Constellation: Political Essays (MIT Press 2001) 113.

[35] ibid.

[36] Isensee (n 29) 171.

[37] Emmerich-Fritsche (n 5) 618

[38] Michael Zürn, 'Global Governance and Legitimacy Problems' (2004) 39 Government and Opposition 260, 269.

[39] Mattias Kumm, 'The Legitimacy of International Law: A Constitutionalist Framework of Analysis' (2004) 15 European Journal of International Law 907, 910.

[40] Jean Jacques Rousseau, The Social Contract and Discourses (J M Dent 1913) 93.

[41] ibid 93–4.

[42] Hauke Brunkhorst, Solidarität. Von der Bürgerfreundschaft zur globalen Rechtsgenossenschaft (Suhrkamp 2002) 102. In Article 4 of the 1789 Declaration of Rights of Man and of the Citizen it reads: 'Political liberty consists in the power of doing whatever does not injure another. The exercise of the natural rights of every man has no other limits than those which are necessary to secure to every other man the free exercise of the same rights; and these limits are determinable only by the law.'

[43] Habermas, 'The Postnational Constellation and the Future of Democracy' (n 5) 101.

the constitutive act of a political community but determined by the authors – and addresses – of that law.[44] While this basic claim goes undisputed, scholars distinguish how to achieve a collective decision by basing their claims either on aggregative or deliberative conceptions of democracy. Aggregative forms of democracy are more 'formal' and based on the concept of voting.[45] Such theories depend on the specification of boundaries of the self-governing community, the demos—a requirement that is hardly possible to realise at the international level.[46] Instead, '[d]eliberative democracy should be more at home in the international system' because 'deliberation across boundaries is straightforward'.[47]

The concept of deliberative democracy goes back to the polis of ancient Athens, but it was Habermas's works that largely influenced its modern concept.[48] The basic claim of Habermas's theory of deliberative democracy is that '[j]ust those action norms are valid to which all possibly affected persons could agree as participants in rational discourses'.[49] In a nutshell, deliberative democracy refers to collective decision-making with the participation of all those who will be affected by a decision or their representatives (the democratic element) and to decision-making by means of arguments that are offered *by* and *to* participants who are committed to the values of rationality and impartiality (the deliberative element).[50] Deliberation allows for non-coercive communication, which is capable of connecting expressions of certain interests or positions to more general principles; it initiates reflective processes of those speaking and listening and, thus, seeks to make sense to the other participants that do not share

[44] Jürgen Habermas, The Inclusion of the Other (Pablo De Greiff and Ciaran Cronin eds, Polity Press 1998) 259, 261.

[45] Peters, 'Dual Democracy' (n 7) 269—"Voting means to aggregate preferences or interests of a specific group (normally the 'demos')".

[46] John S Dryzek, *Deliberative Democracy and Beyond* (OUP 2000) 116; Peters, 'Dual Democracy' (n 7) 268.

[47] Dryzek (n 30) 115–16.

[48] John S Dryzek and others, 'Deliberative Democracy', *Encyclopedia of Political Theory* (Sage Publications 2010).

[49] Jürgen Habermas, *Between Facts and Norms: Contributions to a Discourse Theory of Law and Democracy* (Polity Press 1996) 107; Jürgen Habermas, 'Remarks on Legitimation through Human Rights' in Jürgen Habermas (ed), *The Postnational Constellation: Political Essays* (MIT Press 2001) 116.

[50] Jon Elster, 'Introduction' in Jon Elster (ed), *Deliberative Democracy* (CUP 1998) 8.

their conceptual framework.[51] Deliberative democracy is more 'talk-centric' than 'voting-centric'.[52] It is based on the following conditions, among others:

(a) Processes of deliberation take place in argumentative form, that is, through the regulated exchange of information and reasons among parties who introduce and critically test proposals.
(b) Deliberations are inclusive and public. No one may be excluded in principle; all of those who are possibly affected by the decisions have equal chances to enter and take part.
(c) Deliberations are free of any external coercion. The participants are sovereign insofar as they are bound only by the presuppositions of communication and rules of argumentation.
(d) Deliberations are free of any internal coercion that could detract from the equality of the participants. Each has an equal opportunity to be heard, to introduce topics, to make contributions, to suggest and criticize proposals. The taking of yes/no positions is motivated solely by the unforced force of the better argument.[53]

This does not mean that citizens must participate in rational discourse or that everybody has to participate in the same way.[54] Often, participation is left to formal legislative bodies, which takes the cognitive burdens off individuals to form their own moral judgements.[55] These formally organised legislative and quasi-legislative governmental bodies are part of what Habermas calls the 'strong public sphere'. In his two-track model, this strong public sphere is complemented by a 'weak public sphere' where informal opinion formation takes place. 'This "weak" public is the vehicle of "public opinion".'[56] The strong public sphere deals with the problems discovered and identified in the 'weak' public sphere. It

[51] Hayley Stevenson and John S Dryzek, *Democratizing Global Climate Change* (CUP 2014) 12.

[52] Simone Chambers, 'Deliberative Democratic Theory' (2003) 6 Annual Review of Political Science 307, 308.

[53] Habermas, *Between Facts and Norms: Contributions to a Discourse Theory of Law and Democracy* (n 33) 305–6.

[54] ibid 129–30.

[55] 'Parliamentary legislative procedures, judicial decision making, and the doctrinal jurisprudence that precisely defines rules and systematizes decisions represent different ways that law complements morality by relieving the individual of the cognitive burdens of forming her own moral judgments.' The individual is unburdend from all moral choices other than obeying the law, either because she agrees with it or fears sanctions of enforcement in case she disobeys, ibid 115, 118.

[56] ibid 307.

is, therefore, dependent on a constant supply of informal public opinion.[57] Consequently, the existence of a political public sphere where rational discourses by civil society actors *can* take place is crucial.[58] The public sphere is described as 'a network for communicating information and points of view (i.e., opinions expressing affirmative or negative attitudes)'; it is 'the *social space* generated in communicative action'.[59] It is where people engage in discourses of how society should be shaped through all sorts of interactions: on the streets, in bars, but also, and especially, through mass media such as newspapers, television, the internet and social media.[60] In times when the public sphere is at rest, most initiatives to make legal changes lay within the political system; thus, the initiatives come from officeholders or political leaders.[61] In times of mobilisation, that is, 'critical moments of an accelerated history', actors of civil society—despite a lesser degree of organisation, a weaker capacity of action, structural disadvantages and less media coverage—can reverse normal communication processes in the political system and public sphere and shift the entire system's mode of problem-solving.[62]

Ackerman makes a similar distinction with his 'two-track' theory of law-making in the US. While 'normal politics' are mostly left to elected politicians, 'constitutional politics' or 'higher lawmaking' require the people to make fundamental choices on their identity and government. In times of 'normal politics', no 'public interest' grouping is powerful enough to push its agenda to the centre of political attention in a way that turns normal politicians into political leaders to treat '*its* questions as *the* critical questions they *must* answer if they hope to continue to represent the People'.[63] But in times of higher lawmaking, that

---

[57] ibid 306–7; Christopher F Zurn, 'Deliberative Democracy and Constitutional Review' (2002) 4/5 Law and Philosophy 467, 520.

[58] Stevenson and Dryzek dedicated a whole chapter to the importance of the public sphere for the democratisation of global climate governance. See Chapter 3 'Governance with and without institutionalized authority: the importance of public space' Stevenson and Dryzek (n 35) 37–60.

[59] Habermas, *Between Facts and Norms: Contributions to a Discourse Theory of Law and Democracy* (n 33) 360 (emphasis in original).

[60] Laura Burgers, 'Should Judges Make Climate Change Law?' (2020) 9 Transnational Environmental Law 55, 61.

[61] Habermas, *Between Facts and Norms: Contributions to a Discourse Theory of Law and Democracy* (n 33) 379.

[62] ibid 381.

[63] Bruce Ackerman, *We the People: Foundations* (Belknap Press 1991) 272 (emphasis in original).

is, when constitutional issues experience extraordinary support from citizens, the constitution can be changed without any formal amendment. In such rare constitutional moments, 'when political movements succeed in hammering out new principles of constitutional identity that gain the considered support of a majority of American citizens after prolonged institutional testing, debate, decision', a new constitutional regime begins.[64]

Elites begin to listen to the people, and a collective reassessment of values and principles leads to a constitutional paradigm shift.[65] Although elections take place, 'the epicenter of popular sovereignty cannot be identified with one vote. Indeed there is no epicenter'.[66] The civil-social periphery is more sensitive to detecting and identifying new problems, such as world poverty, nuclear energy, climate change and the loss of biodiversity. These topics were not brought up by the political system itself but by the 'outermost periphery': by intellectuals, concerned citizens, professionals or school children, as is the case of Fridays for Future.[67] They force their topics into newspapers, universities, academies, clubs and the like. But only through coverage in the mass media can their topic be made known to a wider public and become part of the public agenda.[68] From there, it can move to the formal agenda, where authorised decision-makers have to seriously consider and decide on the issue.[69] Habermas notes that it is the *crisis consciousness* in the periphery—'activated' once it perceives a social problem—that leads to a shift of power relations.[70] Their authority gains strength in the course of escalating public controversies.[71]

Acts of civil disobedience, in particular, raise attention and can increase media influence. For Habermas, they serve two purposes: on the one hand, they seek to reopen formally concluded political deliberation so that former decisions on certain issues may be reviewed in light of current protests. And they try to appeal

---

[64] Bruce Ackerman, 'Constitutional Politics/Constitutional Law' (1989) 99 The Yale Law Journal 453, 545.

[65] Chambers (n 36) 311.

[66] ibid.

[67] Cf. Habermas, *Between Facts and Norms: Contributions to a Discourse Theory of Law and Democracy* (n 33) 381.

[68] ibid; Roger Cobb, Jennie Keith Ross and Marc Howard Ross, 'Agenda Building as a Comparative Political Process' (1976) 70 American Political Science Review 126.

[69] Cobb, Ross and Ross (n 52) 126, 129.

[70] Habermas, *Between Facts and Norms: Contributions to a Discourse Theory of Law and Democracy* (n 33) 382.

[71] ibid.

'to the sense of justice of the majority of the community' and to mobilise citizens to stand up for their cause.[72] The activities of the grassroots movement Extinction Rebellion, such as blocking roads in cities such as London and Berlin, the protests at airports and open coal mines, and the school strikes organised by Fridays for Future, need to be understood against this background. These actions can also strengthen the self-regulation of transnational regimes. A hybrid constitutionalisation that combines elements of both public—'the exercise of state power, the enforcement of legal rules'—and external factors in the form of 'the strong influence of social countervailing power from other spheres such as the media, public discussion, spontaneous protest, intellectuals, social movements, NGOs, trade unions' that apply massive pressure can limit a system's expansionist tendencies.[73] Grassroots movements and academic circles alike have harshly criticised the prevalence of economic interests in all sorts of transnational regimes (e.g., the WTO or International Organization for Standardization) and their low sensitivity to 'civic concerns'.[74] Thus, a 'radical-democratic change in the process of legitimacy' is necessary to 'erect a democratic dam against the colonializing *encroachment* of system imperatives on areas of the lifeworld'.[75]

The discussion about what the law should look like, therefore, is not only to be carried out in the political centre (e.g., lawmaking bodies) but also in the periphery by civil society actors such as intellectuals or concerned citizens.[76] The political public sphere can be seen as a 'sounding board' for problems that must be dealt with by the political system because they cannot be solved anywhere else. The public sphere is, therefore, a warning system.[77] Public opinion and civil society discussions likely influence views on the legitimacy of organisations[78] or help

[72] ibid 383.

[73] Gunther Teubner, 'Constitutionalizing Polycontexturality' (2011) 20 Social and Legal Studies 209, 225; Gunther Teubner, *Constitutional Fragments: Societal Constitutionalism and Globalization* (OUP 2012) 84.

[74] Oren Perez, 'Normative Creativity and Global Legal Pluralism: Reflections on the Democratic Critique of Transnational Law' (2003) 10 Indiana Journal of Global Legal Studies 25, 26.

[75] Jürgen Habermas, 'Further Reflections on the Public Sphere' in Craig Calhoun (ed), *Habermas and the Public Sphere* (MIT Press 1992) 444 (emphasis in original). Habermas refers to the controlling powers of money (economy) and administrative power.

[76] Habermas, *Between Facts and Norms: Contributions to a Discourse Theory of Law and Democracy* (n 33) 381.

[77] ibid 274.

[78] Ernst Ulrich Petersmann, 'Human Rights, Constitutionalism and the World Trade Organization: Challenges for World Trade Organization Jurisprudence and Civil Society' (2006) 19 Leiden Journal of International Law 633, 666.

to formulate the internal limitation of a regime.[79] Their opinions contribute to the outcomes of institutional will-formation in the political centre. There is a constant flow between formal institutions of decision-making and the non-organised public sphere. For Habermas, this is one of the remaining embodiments of popular sovereignty: 'This sovereignty turned into a flow of communication comes to the fore in the power of public discourses that uncover topics of relevance to all of society, interpret values, contribute to the resolution of problems, generate good reasons, and debunk bad ones.'[80]

6.1.1 Deliberative Democracy for Global Governance

Several scholars have made this idea fertile for concepts of global governance. Nanz and Steffrek, for example, argue that global governance can only be democratically legitimised through the creation of a public sphere in the form of a global arena in which a variety of social actors (e.g., government officials from different national communities, scientific experts, NGOs, individuals) can politically participate through deliberation beyond the limits of national boundaries.[81] In this global public sphere, the existence of public deliberative participation would mean that policy choices would be reported and discussed (e.g., by the national media) and, thus, would be exposed to public scrutiny.[82]

Actors from an organised civil society play an important role in the creation of this global public sphere, in particular, scientific experts and members of NGOs.[83] They can take on the positions of intermediaries: on the one hand, they give a voice to citizens' concerns and channel them into the deliberative process of IOs. On the other, they make the decision-making process in IOs more transparent and 'translate' technical issues into 'easier' language.[84] However, the role of non-experts in deliberative decision-making must not be neglected, and their concerns

---

[79] Andreas Fischer-Lescano and Gunther Teubner, 'Regime-Collisions: The Vain Search for Legal Unity in the Fragmentation of Global Law' (2004) 25 Michigan Journal of International Law 999, 1038; Gunter Teubner, '"Global Bukowina": Legal Pluralism in the World Society' in Gunther Teubner (ed), *Global Law without a State* (Dartmouth Publishing 1997).

[80] Habermas, 'Further Reflections on the Public Sphere' (n 59) 451–2.

[81] Patrizia Nanz and Jens Steffek, 'Global Governance, Participation and the Public Sphere' (2004) 39 Government and Opposition 314, 315.

[82] ibid 316.

[83] Stevenson and Dryzek (n 35) 37.

[84] Nanz and Steffek (n 65) 323.

should be considered in the lawmaking process.[85] The voices of those being affected by a certain decision have to be given extra weight.[86]

> [A]t the international level, the public sphere – conceived as a pluralistic social realm of a variety of sometimes overlapping or contending (often sectoral) publics engaged in transnational dialogue– can provide an adequate political realm with actors and deliberative processes that help to democratize global governance practice.[87]

Deliberation becomes important in another context: the issue of climate justice. As demonstrated, climate justice is the key concept for advancing constitutionalisation in the Anthropocene and crucial for constructing a transnational constitutional order capable of dealing with climate change.[88] However, here it is important to explicitly define the meaning of the term 'climate justice'. As identified above, climate justice does not just entail questions of distribution.[89] Liberal theories of justice that focus exclusively on distributive justice have been criticised for not levelling social and economic differences,[90] and reducing social justice to distribution would be a mistake.[91] Environmental and climate justice has three dimensions: besides the 1) distribution of burdens and costs, 2) the formal and informal procedures through which decisions are made and 3) the recognition of the varying initial positions regarding people's experiences, identities and values are central for a comprehensive concept of climate justice.[92] Liberal justice theory ignores recognition and participation as elements of justice.[93] Recognition—in the form of dignity and respect for the equality of all persons—is both key to and a precondition for participation in democratic

[85] ibid 319–20; see also Vesco Paskalev, 'May Science Be with You: Can Scientific Expertise Confer Legitimacy to Transnational Authority?' (2017) 8 Transnational Legal Theory 202.

[86] Nanz and Steffek (n 65) 323–4.

[87] ibid 321 (citations omitted).

[88] Jordi Jaria-Manzano, 'Law in the Anthropocene' in Jordi Jaria-Manzano and Susana Borràs (eds), *Research Handbook on Global Climate Constitutionalism* (Edward Elgar Publishing 2019) 45, see also Chapter 4 above.

[89] Gordon Walker, *Environmental Justice: Concepts, Evidence and Politics* (Routledge 2012) 42–52; Schlosberg (n 1).

[90] Schlosberg (n 1) 518.

[91] Iris Marion Young, *Justice and the Politics of Difference (1990)* (Princeton University Press 2011) 15.

[92] Walker (n 73) 42–52.

[93] Schlosberg (n 1) 518 ff..

decision-making.[94] One has to be recognised and respected to be included 'behind the veil of ignorance'.[95] Respect for the equality of all persons is itself *the* precondition of deliberative democracy.[96] In this sense, '[d]emocracy is both an element and a condition of social justice'.[97] Moreover, people need to be able to meaningfully participate in decision-making that may affect them. Meaningful involvement means that:

> (1) potentially affected community residents have an appropriate opportunity to participate in decisions about a proposed activity that will affect their environment and/or health; (2) the public's contribution can influence the regulatory agency's decision; (3) the concerns of all participants involved will be considered in the decision-making process; and (4) the decisionmakers seek out and facilitate the involvement of those potentially affected.[98]

6.1.2 Contestation in Deliberative Democracy

Consequently, deliberative democracy based on discourses and more active participation rather than voting has been identified as a good way to democratise and legitimise global climate governance in a way that can also address—at least, partly—concerns of climate justice.[99] In a context that spans the world, however, it seems highly unlikely that everybody would agree to the same interpretation

[94] ibid 519–20.

[95] ibid 520. Here, Schlosberg refers to Rawls's "veil of ignorance", see John Rawls, *A Theory of Justice (1971)* (Revised Ed, OUP 1999) 118. Rawls argues for a procedural theory of justice in which external factors must be nullified to prevent people from exploiting social and natural circumstances to their own advantage. Behind the 'veil of ignorance', people do not know how alternatives will affect their own cases, and they must evaluate and make decisions based solely on general considerations.

[96] Habermas, *Between Facts and Norms: Contributions to a Discourse Theory of Law and Democracy* (n 33) 93–4.

[97] Young (n 75) 91.

[98] United States Environmental Protection Agency, 'Toolkit for Assessing Potential Allegations of Environmental Injustice' (2004) 9; LeRoy C Paddock, 'Environmental Justice' in Lee Paddock, Robert L Glicksman and Nicholas S Bryner (eds), *Elgar Encyclopedia of Environmental Law: Decision Making in Environmental Law (Vol. II)* (Edward Elgar Publishing 2016) 360–3.

[99] Stevenson and Dryzek (n 35) 12 ff., 31; Hayley Stevenson and John S Dryzek, 'The Discursive Democratisation of Global Climate Governance' (2012) 21 Environmental Politics 189.

of what exactly constitutes the 'common good', how to strive for its protection or how to implement climate justice. While this work has analysed that there is a 'common good' in the climate context (the protection of the atmosphere and the Earth to keep it habitable for present and future generations), given the unequally distributed (economic) powers among states, transnational corporations, NGOs and individuals (after all, some 8 billion people) it would seem rather curious that all these participants could be expected to find consensus and accept a particular strategy on how to protect the climate. The UNEP recently identified how difficult it is to translate common but very general goals (such as climate protection) into concrete and enforceable policies. Thus, while all member-states signed and/or ratified the Sustainable Development Goals, there is considerable disagreement on how to achieve these goals.[100]

What do these observations say about Habermas's theory that is oriented towards consensus?[101] Luhmann claims that Habermas's discourse principle is not practicable in the system law because it cannot be tested in the courts. It is impossible to prove whether each norm is valid or not based on the criterion of consensus. Particularly, Luhmann points towards the 'ecologically' mediated involvement of participants to reject Habermas's discourse principle.[102] The old liberal rule according to which everyone can use their freedom (claiming validity) in a way that does not harm others (thus, having no reasonable grounds to object to that claim) is unthinkable given the current conditions of democracy, the redistributive state and ecological sensibilities.[103] Incompatible 'philosophies of life' exist to which reasonable people adhere because they disagree about the relative importance of values such as self-determination and choice, happiness, welfare and self-actualisation, as well as the religious and philosophical backgrounds underpinning these values.[104] Thus, there is no single truth to questions

---

[100] For example, some countries argue for prohibiting all single-use plastic products by 2025, others are against such a ban because they fear of the effects on the economy and the preservation of jobs. See UNEP, 'The Tricky Business of Reaching a Global Consensus on the Environment' (2019) <https://www.unenvironment.org/news-and-stories/story/tricky-business-reaching-global-consensus-environment> accessed 31 August 2023.

[101] William Rehg, 'Translator's Introduction', *Between Facts and Norms. Contributions to a Discourse Theory of Law and Democracy* (Polity Press 1996) 18.

[102] Niklas Luhmann, *Law as a Social System (1993)* (Fatima Kastner and others eds, OUP 2004) 123.

[103] ibid 123 n 114.

[104] Cohen (n 28) 187–8.

of how reasonable people want to live and how they want to regulate their life as a political community.[105]

Some scholars, therefore, seek to enrich theories of deliberation with the idea of contestation. This seems paradoxical at first, since Habermas's discourse principle aims to reach consensus through free and equal participation in the discourse. Participants of a rational discourse would adopt an 'attitude oriented toward reaching an understanding'.[106] However, the role of dissent and contestation is crucial and consistent with deliberative democracy.[107] Proponents of 'reasonable interpretive pluralism'[108] believe that agreement or consensus is utopic even in the smaller realm of the nation-state; that it is a superficial and deceptive phenomenon. Instead, they employ the idea that reasonable interpretive pluralism does not mean that people have to overcome their differences. Rather, it is a peaceful coexistence of different visions regulated through radical democracy.[109] Democratic will-formation occurs 'through argument, contestation, revision and rejection'.[110] Conflict and dissent are expressions of the *res publica.*[111]

For proponents of interpretive pluralism, '[p]rinciples do not possess stable meanings beyond, and independent of, their application to concrete cases'.[112] While there may be a truth (or a single right answer) to a subject matter, the persistence of actual disagreement indicates that this truth is simply not available to anybody participating in the system 'interpretation' because nobody inside the system can occupy the position of an impartial observer.[113] Epistemic pluralists, thus, argue that 'participants cannot reasonably hope to surmount the pluralism

---

[105] Cf. ibid 188.

[106] Habermas, *Between Facts and Norms: Contributions to a Discourse Theory of Law and Democracy* (n 33) 247.

[107] Stevenson and Dryzek (n 35) 24.

[108] See, for example, Frank I Michelman, 'Human Rights and the Limits of Constitutional Theory' (2000) 13 Ratio Juris 63, 70; Cohen (n 28); Jeremy Waldron, *Law and Disagreement* (OUP 1999).

[109] Nanette Funk, 'Habermas and the Social Goods' (1987) 18 Social Text 19, 24.

[110] Seyla Benhabib, 'Twilight of Sovereignty or the Emergence of Cosmopolitan Norms? Rethinking Citizenship in Volatile Times' (2007) 11 Citizenship Studies 19, 32.

[111] Peter Häberle, 'Verfassungsinterpretation als öffentlicher Prozeß—ein Pluralismuskonzept (1978)', *Verfassung als öffentlicher Prozeß: Materialien zu einer Verfassungstheorie der offenen Gesellschaft* (1st edn, Duncker & Humblot 1978) 150.

[112] Jürgen Habermas, 'On Law and Disagreement. Some Comments on "Interpretative Pluralism"' (2003) 16 Ratio Juris 187, 188.

[113] ibid 189; David Kennedy, 'One, Two, Three, Many International Legal Orders: Legal Pluralism and the Cosmopolitan Dream' (2008) 31 N.Y.U. Review of Law & Social Change 641,

of conflicting views, since nobody can be certain of whether somebody gets it right or of who that somebody is'.[114]

The debate goes on and on without the possibility of there ever being a result achieved in public that everyone can rationally be expected to accept.[115] The deliberative process needs to be ended by vote and majority decision at some point, but these are no final points: 'a fallible and reversible majority vote is perceived as the interruption of an ongoing discourse' that for the time being enjoys 'the presumption of rational acceptability without thereby imposing on the minority any change of mind'.[116] The next round, then, could be the opportunity for the minority to shift the wheel around.[117] This also holds for dissenting opinions in court rulings, which can one day turn into majority decisions and through which the normative force of the public may unfold in the longer term.[118] This is observable even at the international level. An example, in this case, is ICJ Judge Weeramantry's separate opinion in the *Gabčíkovo–Nagymaros Project* case. He argued that the environmental impact principle is dynamic, and, thus, an environmental impact assessment should not only be undertaken before the commencement of the project but rather continue as long as the project is in operation.[119] This view was later adopted by the ICJ in its *Pulp Mills* case decision.[120]

644: 'We know it is legal pluralism when we have to admit under the canons of professional interpretation that either of us could be right-that there is, in fact, a conflict, a gap, or an ambiguity in the legal fabric that cannot be definitively closed by the routines of legal argument. It is legal pluralism when we have to put something on the map that doesn't fit.'

[114] Habermas, 'On Law and Disagreement. Some Comments on "Interpretative Pluralism"' (n 96) 190.

[115] ibid.

[116] ibid 192.

[117] ibid.

[118] Häberle, 'The Open Society of Constitutional Interpreters' (n 3) 136, 160; Peter Häberle, *Die Verfassung des Pluralismus* (Athenäum 1980) 52.

[119] ICJ, Separate Opinion of Judge Weeramantry in the *Gabčíkovo-Nagymaros Project (Hungary v Slovakia)* case, Judgment of 25 September 1997, ICJ Reports 1997, 111.

[120] ICJ, *Pulp Mills Case (Argentina v Uruguay)*, Judgment of 20 April 2010, ICJ Reports 2010, 73: "The Court also considers that an environmental impact assessment must be conducted prior to the implementation of a project. Moreover, once operations have started and, where necessary, throughout the life of the project, continuous monitoring of its effects on the environment shall be undertaken."

No one is ever required to accept a certain legal or political decision. The availability of, inter alia, constitutional amendments, juridical review, appeal and elections opens the decision process to a multitude of actors.[121]

> Contestedness thus reflects the central assumption that is common to the range of approaches to democratic constitutionalism, namely, that in principle, the norms, rules and principles of governance ought to be contestable at any time by those governed by them.[122]

For Wiener, they even require regular contestation to work.[123] Since 'contestedness both indicates and generates legitimacy',[124] she attempts to fill the legitimacy gap between what she identifies as widely respected fundamental norms at the meta-level (so-called Type-1 norms) on the one hand, and highly contested standards and regulations at the micro-level (so-called Type-3 norms) on the other—in other words, between the general agreement to and the specific interpretation of an international treaty[125]—based on the principle of contestedness.[126] Contestedness is the normative meta-organising principle at an imagined intermediary level (so-called Type-2 norms) between the two categories that allow for facilitated access to regulated (rather than ad hoc) contestation for all involved stakeholders, that is, those who claim a legitimate interest in a policy.[127] The legitimation of the principle of contestedness as a meta-organising principle, however, depends on the specific circumstances of every sector of global governance.[128] Contestation is norm-generative and, thus, a sine qua non for legitimacy

[121] Though Waldron argues that most decisions deserve some respect as they demonstrate what the community considers relevant and which should not simply be ignored or appealed just because those disagreeing are capable of doing so, Waldron (n 92) 100. This reveals the deep tensions between deliberative democracy and constitutional review at the national level—a bank of constitutional judges, remotely elected without direct participation of the citizens, having the power in the name of the constitution to overturn a decision made by a body that is legitimized—through periodical elections—by the people, see Zurn (n 41).

[122] Antje Wiener, *A Theory of Contestation* (Springer 2014) 4.

[123] ibid 3.

[124] ibid 5.

[125] ibid 34.

[126] ibid 4–5.

[127] ibid 3.

[128] ibid 5, 65. For the climate sector, Wiener identifies sustainability at the meta-level and emission standards at the micro-level. Organizing principles at the imagined intermediary level are the—somewhat outdated—CBDR principle and the newer principle of "equitable access to sustainable development" (65–69).

in any context, including global governance.[129] Striving for consensus and harmony could even lead to de-democratisation when conflicts remain but are no longer open to debate.[130]

In this sense, many scholars have argued for a broader understanding of democracy in global constitutionalism of which contestation is an essential part. This is also the essence of Teubner's approach to legitimacy in transnational regimes. For him, the problem of traditional notions of constitutionalism lies in the uncritical transfer of the '*Quod omnes tangit, ab omnibus tractari et approbari debet*' principle (what touches all should be considered and approved by all) to the transnational level.[131] The principle describes that the identity of the authors of the law is the same as that of their addressees.[132] Teubner explains that the democratic principle in the nation-state has been able to combine two contradictory elements: identitarian consensus-building (consent) and the enlargement of internal dissent (contestation).[133] While this particular combination makes the nation-state successful, it is impossible to strive for consent at the transnational level. This does not mean that the element of identitarian consensus should be given up, but it should be reduced to local and national levels.[134] Legitimacy in transnational regimes, instead, is bestowed through organised dissent, which 'needs to be supported by a high learning capacity in collective decisions and vice versa.'[135] The element of organised dissent needs to be advanced and strengthened. The institutions of political representation of the nation-state (elections, representation and organised opposition) should be replaced by the principle of self-contestation in transnational regimes.[136] Teubner, thus, agrees

---

[129] ibid 13.

[130] Christoph Möllers, *The Three Branches: A Comparative Model of Separation of Powers* (OUP 2013) 76.

[131] Gunther Teubner, 'Quod Omnes Tangit: Transnational Constitutions without Democracy?' (2018) 45 Journal of Law and Society S5, S11.

[132] ibid.

[133] ibid S12.

[134] ibid.

[135] ibid S13.

[136] ibid S14. Given the extreme epistemic diversity among issue-specific transnational regimes, this self-contestation cannot follow a one-size-fits-it-all approach for all regimes.

with deliberative democracy theories that claim justification once classical democratic processes no longer function at the transnational level. However, instead of striving for consensus, a stronger orientation towards dissent is necessary.[137]

The positive role of insurmountable disagreements is also important for critical and inclusive democratic discourses. Every agreement is non-consensual to some point, given that every agreement is tied to a specific spatial-temporal field of power and norms, but the best agreements are those that remain 'potentially open to reasonable disagreement and dissent':[138]

> Participation is a strategic-communicative game in which citizens struggle for recognition and rule, negotiate within and sometimes over the rules, bargain, compromise, take two steps back, start over again, reach a provisional agreement or agree to disagree, and learn to govern and be governed in the context of relatively stable irresolution where the possibility of dissent is an implicit 'permanent provocation' which affects the negotiations. What shapes and holds individuals and groups together as 'citizens' and 'peoples' is not this or that agreement but the free agonic activities of participation themselves.[139]

The best theories of deliberation take disagreement seriously and incorporate it. Such a theory is presented by Gutmann and Thompson, who argue that the hope to resolve moral disagreements lies in the nature of the claim itself. Both the problem and the resolution of disagreement lie partly in morality itself. Thus, when citizens publicly appeal to reasons shared (or such that could be shared) by their fellow citizens, and if they consider the reasons brought by similarly motivated citizens, then they are already engaged in a discourse that aims at a justifiable resolution of disagreements.[140] Nonetheless, some moral conflicts cannot be solved and, therefore, must be lived with. Deliberation can be the answer to these unresolved disagreements: 'By making democracy more deliberate, citizens stand a better chance of resolving some of their moral disagreements, and living with those that inevitably persist, on terms that all can accept.'[141] This also

[137] ibid S26. Teubner refers to Rainer Forst, *Transnationale Gerechtigkeit und Demokratie: Zur Überwindung von drei Dogmen der politischen Theorie in Peter Niesen ed. Transnationale Gerechtigkeit und Demokratie* (Campus Verlag 2012) 29 (44).

[138] Tully (n 26) 170–1.

[139] ibid 171.

[140] Amy Gutmann and Dennis Thompson, *Democracy and Disagreement* (Belknap Press 1996) 25.

[141] ibid 51.

means that principles and values are provisional; they are formed and revised continually and respond to the moral claims of the public.[142] While consensus might not be achievable through deliberation, at least understanding and mutual respect are.[143]

Disagreement should not be seen as 'incompleteness' or the politically unsatisfactory character of deliberation but as a part of complex societies.[144] Contestation is one of the keys to legitimacy; the constitutional quality of norms develops through regime collisions.[145] Contestation can relativise the election mechanisms in democratic theory (which will remain central in some form) and assume some of their functions in a post-national global order.[146] Therefore, the central point of a theory of deliberative democracy is not consensus but participation. The ability to participate in rational discourses (what Habermas calls 'political' autonomy) is crucial. The openness and fairness of the process is guaranteed through the tolerance that is expected from participants.[147]

6.2 Participation through Interpretation

Participation in the form of 'rights of communication and participation',[148] therefore, is one of the most important aspects of a normative theory of global climate constitutionalism. This is already highlighted by many international environmental treaties. In 1992, procedural rights (usually defined as the rights to access information, to participate in decision-making and access to justice rights) were incorporated into Principle 10 of the Rio Declaration.[149] From there, they made

---

142 ibid 26.

143 Dryzek (n 30) 17.

144 Waldron (n 92) 91.

145 Stefan Oeter, 'Regime Collisions from a Perspective of Global Constitutionalism' in Kerstin Blome and others (eds), *Contested Regime Collisions. Norm Fragmentation in World Society* (CUP 2016) 30–5.

146 Krisch (n 18) 271.

147 Häberle, 'Verfassungsinterpretation als öffentlicher Prozeß—ein Pluralismuskonzept (1978)' (n 95) 123; Peter Häberle, 'Demokratische Verfassungstheorie im Lichte des Möglichkeitsdenkens' (1977) 102 Archiv des öffentlichen Rechts 27, 56.

148 Jürgen Habermas, *The Inclusion of the Other* (Pablo De Greiff and Ciaran Cronin eds, Polity Press 1998) 259.

149 Principle 10 of the Rio Declaration: "Environmental issues are best handled with the participation of all concerned citizens, at the relevant level. At the national level, each individual shall have appropriate access to information concerning the environment that is held

their way into a multitude of international documents, including the Aarhus Convention,[150] the Escazú Agreement[151] and domestic constitutions. The principle explicitly recognises the link between public participation and democratic decision-making on the one hand and a quality environment on the other.[152] Where these rights do not formally exist, international courts have created them. The IACtHR, for example, interprets Art. 13 ACHR broadly, which protects the freedom of expression, including the freedom to seek, receive and impart information. In *Claude Reyes et al v Chile*, by referring to international instruments such as the Aarhus Convention and Principle 10 of the Rio Declaration,[153] the Court stated that, for this purpose, public bodies must disclose the information they are holding upon request without the inquirer needing to demonstrate direct interest or personal involvement.[154]

All of this points to the importance of being able to participate in environmental discourses. A discourse is 'by definition a shared set of assumptions and capabilities embedded in language that enables its adherents to assemble bits of sensory information that come their way into coherent wholes'.[155] In IL, discourses take on the form of 'institutional software', while formal rules constitute the hardware. The software becomes even more important given the poorly developed hardware in the international legal system.[156] In discourses, the pluralistic public can issue their interpretations on particular matters. Every constitutional norm depends on and refers to the activities of its addressees. Since no rule is

by public authorities, including information on hazardous materials and activities in their communities, and the opportunity to participate in decision-making processes. States shall facilitate and encourage public awareness and participation by making information widely available. Effective access to judicial and administrative proceedings, including redress and remedy, shall be provided" (Rio Declaration on Environment and Development, June 14, 1992, U.N. Doc. A/CONF.151/5/Rev. 1 (1992), 31 I.L.M. 876).

[150] UNECE Convention on Access to Information, Public Participation in Decision-Making and Access to Justice in Environmental Matters, Aarhus, 25 June 1998, UNTS 2161, 447.

[151] Regional Agreement on Access to Information, Public Participation and Justice in Environmental Matters in Latin America and the Caribbean, Escazú, 4 March 2018, C.N.195.2018.TREATIES-XXVII.18 of 9 April 2018.

[152] David A Wirth, 'Reexamining Decision-Making Processes in International Environmental Law' (1994) 79 Iowa Law Review 769, 772.

[153] Sophie Thériault, 'Environmental Justice and the Inter-American Court of Human Rights' in Anna Grear and Louis J Kotzé (eds), *Research Handbook on Human Rights and the Environment* (Edward Elgar Publishing 2015) 319–20.

[154] IACtHR, *Claude Reyes et al vs Chile*, Judgement of 19 September 2006, para 77.

[155] Dryzek (n 30) 121.

[156] ibid 122.

self-executing, the given situation must be checked against a particular rule of action[157] because any action—and the very concept of action—emerges from ideas: 'Without language, ideas, abstractions, comparisons, interpretation, there can be no human action, or at least none that is recognizably human.'[158] Before any action can be carried out, a norm has to be interpreted.[159] This concerns not only the meaning of the norm but also, for example, whether a rule should be applied or not and whether exceptions should be made. Rules need constant monitoring and checking whether they fit a given situation. Different mindsets and interpretations of both the addressees and the applicators of a rule have to be compared, which, thereby, generates an ongoing 'judicial dialogue'.[160]

This is a deliberative process in itself.[161] A rule is a starting point for deliberation rather than a product of it. The rule is a vital but not conclusive part of a deliberative process that needs to address questions such as whether the rule meets the situation, the consideration of related rules and so on. Thus, 'the action taken is the result of deliberation on the circumstances, the rule, and the contingencies'.[162] Every rule needs to go through this deliberative process, not only concerning uncertain meaning but also whether it applies to a given situation or what its weight is in relation to other rules.[163] From this, it follows that interpretation is itself a form of deliberation. Interpretation of rules becomes a core element of constitutional self-government.[164] The competition of opinions, ideas and interpretations of the pluralistic public is what integrates the people.[165] As Lhotta and Zucca-Soest identify in relation to Europe, integration and legitimacy can meaningfully be created only in the competing 'arenas of citizenship' rather than through a merely declaratory constitutional consensus.[166] It is 'not so much

[157] Roland Lhotta and Sabrina Zucca-Soest, 'Legitimation und Integration durch Verfassung in einem Mehrebenensystem' in Christoph Hönninge, Sascha Kneip and Astrid Lorenz (eds), *Verfassungswandel im Mehrebenensystem* (VS Verlag für Sozialwissenschaften 2011) 369.

[158] Jennifer Hochschild, 'How Ideas affect Actions', in Robert E. Goodin and Charles Tilly (eds), Oxford Handbook of Contextual Political Analysis (Oxford University Press 2006), 284 (291), cited after ibid.

[159] ibid.

[160] ibid 370.

[161] Denis Galligan, *Law in Modern Society* (OUP 2006) 57.

[162] ibid.

[163] ibid 60, 68.

[164] Christopher L Eisgruber, *Constitutional Self-Government* (Harvard University Press 2001) 41; Lhotta and Zucca-Soest (n 141) 369.

[165] Lhotta and Zucca-Soest (n 141) 369.

[166] ibid 382.

consent as contestability' that generates legitimacy because it allows people to fight interferences with their rights:[167]

> What makes [the demos or the people] self-ruling or democratic is the fact that they are not exposed willy-nilly to that pattern of decision-making: they are able to contest decisions at will and, if the contestation establishes a mismatch with their relevant interests or opinions, able to force an amendment.[168]

Therefore, it is not so much the substantive outcome of a rational discourse but the specific process of democratic will-formation through deliberation itself—of course, this says nothing of the justness of the deliberative process, and the 'tyranny of the majority' remains a problem.[169] The essence of democracy for a theory of deliberative democracy is in the content and style of interaction.[170] It is this a 'genuinely procedural understanding of democracy'.[171] When consent is not possible, a majority rule allows for equally distributed decision-making.[172] Thus, even when someone disagrees with a particular decision, they endorse the process of decision-making as such. This is why the outcome can be accepted even if it is disagreed with:

> Even though [...] the adversary process of an open-ended exchange of competing arguments does not carry the promissory note of final agreement, the performance as such seems to create the kind of authority that explains why participants accept outcomes with which they disagree.[173]

Accordingly, the involvement of the pluralistic public with its diverse ideas and interests is essential. Constitutional interpretation without the participation of

---

[167] Philip Pettit, *Republicanism: A Theory of Freedom and Government* (OUP 1998) 185.

[168] ibid 186.

[169] Though Habermas makes clear that '[t]he ethical-political process of coming to an understanding about how, as members as a particular collectivity, we want to live must at least not be at odds with moral norms', Habermas, 'Further Reflections on the Public Sphere' (n 59) 448, see also Chapter 10.

[170] Dryzek (n 30) 153.

[171] See the Chapter 'Deliberative Politics: A Procedural Concept of Democracy' in Jürgen Habermas (ed), *Between Facts and Norms: Contributions to a Discourse Theory of Law and Democracy* (Polity Press 1997) 226ff (esp. 236ff).

[172] Möllers (n 114) 71.

[173] Habermas, 'On Law and Disagreement. Some Comments on "Interpretative Pluralism"' (n 96) 190.

active citizens and public participants is impossible.[174] Häberle's theory could, therefore, be understood as the 'democratisation of constitutional interpretation'.[175]

The pluralistic public is composed of many interests: some are powerful and organised (such as strong environmental movements), while others are not organised or not organisable (e.g., persons displaced by climate change, future generations, animals or nature[176]) and strongly rely on being considered by and in constitutional interpretation as minorities but also as 'common interests'.[177] As part of the pluralistic public that is essentially involved in constitutional interpretation—protest groups, for example, in the form of citizen's initiatives—should be considered when, for example, environmental issues are discussed.[178]

By arguing that everybody interprets the constitution, the question of legitimacy arises for any power that is not 'formally', 'officially' or by virtue of their 'jurisdiction' 'called upon' to conduct constitutional interpretation.[179] Actors—the courts—that are authorised to interpret the constitution are directly bound to and by it. Citizens and groups are bound as well, although by a weaker bound and only indirectly through the sanctioning authority of the state.[180] Does a weaker bond equal a lower degree of legitimacy when interpreting the law? After all, 'citizens and groups have no democratic legitimacy to conduct constitutional interpretation in a conventional sense'[181] since nobody voted for them and no constitution bestows them with constitutional interpretive authority.

Ultimately, the final decision-making rests with the constitutional judiciary.[182] However, in the formal process of interpretation before a constitutional court, the pluralistic public can (and often must) explicitly issue its own interpretations (since in many civil-law countries, plaintiffs must justify their claims in order for

---

[174] Häberle, 'The Open Society of Constitutional Interpreters' (n 3) 131.

[175] ibid.

[176] Randall S Abate, *Climate Change and the Voiceless* (CUP 2019).

[177] Häberle, *Die Verfassung des Pluralismus* (n 102) 50; see Peter Lawrence and Lukas Köhler, 'Representation of Future Generations through International Climate Litigation: A Normative Framework' (2017) 60 German Yearbook of International Law 639, 645ff.

[178] Häberle, *Die Verfassung des Pluralismus* (n 102) 51.

[179] Häberle, 'The Open Society of Constitutional Interpreters' (n 3) 140.

[180] ibid 141.

[181] ibid 145.

[182] ibid 131.

them to be admissible[183]). This public process is safeguarded by the possibility of lodging a constitutional complaint and forcing the court to engage in a legal dialogue (*Rechtsgespräch*).[184] They act as 'productive powers of interpretation' (*interpretatorische Produktivkräfte*), and at least they are 'pre-interpreters'.[185] By the same token, the constitutional judiciary cannot simply issue an interpretation; it has to be approached by someone who claims their rights have been violated—'the decisions of the judiciary are based on the initiative and the will of the individual—the judiciary neither forms its own institutional will nor does it act upon its own initiative'.[186]

'Informal' or 'implicit' interpretation, conversely, occurs everywhere, all the time, by everybody.[187] Nobody needs to be authorised to do so: by simply living in the fundamental right, citizens interpret and publicly update the content of the constitution.[188] A person does not necessarily need to understand that they are interpreting the constitution; most of the time, the realisation of fundamental rights occurs through 'existential interpretation'.[189] Most of these constitutional interpretations never reach a court because no constitutional complaint was filed. Nevertheless, these 'implicit' interpretations create and develop autonomous substantive constitutional law.[190] Explicit or implicit interpretations by 'ordinary' people makes constitutional interpretation a public process. It is a public process through constitutional interpretation.[191] The interplay between 'lived' and 'knowing' interpretation by laypeople on one hand and experts such as lawyers and judges on the other results in pluralistic constitutional interpretations.[192]

---

[183] See, for example, §§ 92 and 93 para. 1 of the Act on the Federal Constitutional Court (Bundesverfassungsgerichtsgesetz—BVerfGG). § 93 para. 1 reads: 'The constitutional complaint shall be lodged and reasons stated within one month.' § 92 specifies that 'The reasons of the [constitutional] complaint shall specify the right which has allegedly been violated, as well as the act or omission of the organ or authority by which the complainant claims his or her rights have been violated.'

[184] Häberle, 'The Open Society of Constitutional Interpreters' (n 3) 136.

[185] ibid 131.

[186] Möllers (n 114) 89.

[187] Ernst Forsthoff, *Der Staat der Industriegesellschaft* (CH Beck 1971) 69.

[188] Häberle, 'The Open Society of Constitutional Interpreters' (n 3) 131.

[189] Josef Isensee, *Wer definiert die Freiheitsrechte?* (CF Müller Juristischer Verlag 1980) 20.

[190] Häberle, 'The Open Society of Constitutional Interpreters' (n 3) 150.

[191] Häberle, *Die Verfassung des Pluralismus* (n 102) 50.

[192] Häberle, 'Verfassungsinterpretation als öffentlicher Prozeß—ein Pluralismuskonzept (1978)' (n 95) 124.

The 'living' constitution is open to change over time.[193] A constitution can adapt to new (social and political) realities without the need to amend its text. Instead, different factors can lead to a change in its reference framework, among them political and social developments but also judicial activism.[194] This informal constitutional change (or *Verfassungswandel*) can be caused both by external and internal factors.[195] External factors, such as the embedding of national law in a net of international and supranational (EU) norms, the decisions of international courts and tribunals, and trends in global lawmaking, can influence constitution-building, constitutional amendments and constitutional change, particularly due to the challenges of globalisation and global governance. Inextricable links between formerly autochthonous nation-states, emerging multi-level constitutionalism, global pluralism and fragmentation also have to be taken into account.[196] Internal factors are mainly the actors themselves—ordinary people bringing their cases to the courts and judges with their given power of judicial review that can help to develop the law and influence the authorised lawmakers. Citizens, in particular, have the opportunity to indicate constitutional change by filing cases that become 'precedent', 'leading' or 'landmark' cases insofar as they create new insights, interpretations or legal techniques.[197]

However, interpretation is not equally open for all norms. Some norms exclude certain developments per se. In the area of organisation and competence norms, interpretation is not 'open'; here, change occurs through formal constitutional amendment.[198] Contrastingly, fundamental rights—as part of the 'citizen's conscience'—with their vague and open terms can be subject to constitutional amendment through interpretation without the need for formal amendment procedures to further develop and preserve the constitution.[199]

---

[193] Peter Häberle, 'Zeit und Verfassung: Prolegomena zu einem "zeit-gerechten" Verfassungsverständnis' (1974) 21 ZfP 111, 121 ff.; see also Bruce Ackerman, 'The Living Constitution (2006 Oliver Wendell Holmes Lectures)' (2007) 120 Harvard Law Review 1737.

[194] Markus Kotzur, 'Constitutional Amendments and Constitutional Changes in Germany' in Xenophon Contiades (ed), *Engineering Constitutional Change* (Routledge 2013) 134.

[195] ibid 136.

[196] ibid 136–7.

[197] ibid 140.

[198] Häberle, 'Zeit und Verfassung: Prolegomena zu einem "zeit-gerechten" Verfassungsverständnis' (n 177) 122.

[199] ibid 136.

Each interpretation includes a moment of constituting the constitution.[200] The differentiation between constitutional interpretation and constitutional lawmaking disappears.[201] The task of constitutional interpretation is to prepare and follow up on the act of constitutional legislation and to update it.[202] The constitution is, after all, an unfinished project:

> The constitutional state does not represent a finished structure but a delicate and sensitive—above all fallible and revisable—enterprise, whose purpose is to realize the system of rights anew in changing circumstances, that is, to interpret the system of rights better, to institutionalize it more appropriately, and to draw out its contents more radically. This is the perspective of citizens who are actively engaged in realizing the system of rights.[203]

Thus, no interpretation can ever claim to be permanent or decisive. The constitutional practice—understood as *law in public action*—excludes such an assumption. Instead, an interpretation that is the result of constitutional reality today can become history tomorrow—a constant story of 'trial and error'.[204] Interpretation, thus, should not be bound to one moment of history (when the constitution was formally drafted) but to a process of time, if only because the constitutional legislators suffer from an information deficit. They cannot foresee the future and are not prepared for new developments.[205] This stresses again the importance of litigation for members of civil society to fight unjust practices or as a channel to pursue their political and social interests.[206]

The inclusion of the pluralistic public into everyday practices and politics, in particular the fulfilment of the 'democratic side' of fundamental rights, is how democracy expresses itself in an open polity. According to Häberle's understanding, every act interprets the constitution anew, even without formal recognition

---

[200] Peter Häberle and Markus Kotzur, *Europäische Verfassungslehre* (8th edn, Nomos 2016) 471.

[201] Peter Häberle, 'Verfassungsinterpretation und Verfassunggebung (Berner Gastvortrag 1977)', *Verfassung als öffentlicher Prozeß: Materialien zu einer Verfassungstheorie der offenen Gesellschaft* (Duncker & Humblot 1978) 209.

[202] ibid 210.

[203] Habermas, *Between Facts and Norms: Contributions to a Discourse Theory of Law and Democracy* (n 33) 384.

[204] Häberle, 'Zeit und Verfassung: Prolegomena zu einem "zeit-gerechten" Verfassungsverständnis' (n 177) 125.

[205] ibid.

[206] Habermas, 'On Law and Disagreement. Some Comments on "Interpretative Pluralism"' (n 96) 188.

as an interpretation. However, to convince others of one's interpretation, it needs to be articulated.[207] In an ideal deliberative discourse, the best argument—not power or money—wins:

> Deliberation, understood as reasoning that is aimed at best addressing practical problems, focuses political debates on the common good: interests, preferences and aims that comprise the common good are those that 'survive' deliberation.[208]

The chances of the recognition of a particular interpretation (both among the courts and the public) increase if a particular interpretation concerns a generalisable self-image.[209] Environmental associations and citizens' initiatives take advantage of this when they represent the individual basic rights of citizens and also strive for a concentrated, group-conform self-understanding. To assert their interpretation, they must present a united front to the outside world and to other competing groups. Thus, the 'exegesis of fundamental rights has become the (indispensable) weapon of social conflict of interest and political dissent'.[210]

But no matter how strong public opinion is, civil society can only acquire influence, not political power: 'Discourses do not govern.'[211] Civil society's influence is limited to the procurement and withdrawal of legitimation.[212] For it to turn into political power, civil society depends on processes of institutionalisation, either in parliamentary bodies or the courts that decide political cases.[213] Public opinion represent political potentials that can be used by the official organs of the state.[214] The decision about the validity of a norm is made in the courts, not by the members of civil society.[215] This becomes clear when comparing the interpretation of law either by a court or a scholar. Kelsen argues that the law-applying organ can combine the cognitive interpretation of the law to be applied with an

---

[207] Wolfram Höfling, *Offene Grundrechtsinterpretation* (Duncker & Humblot 1987) 21.

[208] Nanz and Steffek (n 65) 318.

[209] Höfling (n 191) 21.

[210] Isensee (n 173) 22 (tr the author).

[211] Habermas, 'Further Reflections on the Public Sphere' (n 59) 452.

[212] ibid.

[213] Habermas, *Between Facts and Norms: Contributions to a Discourse Theory of Law and Democracy* (n 33) 371.

[214] ibid 364.

[215] Andreas Fischer-Lescano, *Globalverfassung—Die Geltungsbegründung der Menschenrechte* (Velbrück 2005) 127–8; Andreas Fischer-Lescano, 'Die Emergenz der Globalverfassung' (2003) 63 Zeitschrift für ausländisches öffentliches Recht und Völkerrecht 717, 739–41, 760.

act of will by which the organ chooses among the possible cognitive interpretations. This act of will creates a norm at the lower level or executes a coercive act stipulated in the legal norm that is to be applied.[216] Consequently, the interpretation of law by scholars or citizens—who can choose between different possible interpretations but lack the act of will—cannot create law.[217]

Here, the importance of litigation as a driver of global environmental and climate constitutionalism becomes apparent. 'Constitutionalisation from below' can be promoted in several ways. Four legal mobilisation tactics (that can be combined) can be identified: 1) litigation, 2) advocacy campaigns, lobbying and engaging political institutions, 3) mobilisation and claim-making and 4) constitutional contestation and resistance as actions.[218] Of these, litigation is key for the emergence of a transnational climate constitution.

This focus on ligation has been criticised. Theories of constitutionalism, and societal constitutionalism in particular, would consequently neglect non-legal forms of public participation.[219] Rajagopal and Anderson, for example, discuss the importance of social movements as extra-institutional forms of collective action to renew democratic ideals and the emergence of a 'constitutionalism from below'.[220] Groups, such as Extinction Rebellion, Just Stop Oil or Letzte Generation (Last Generation) are raising public awareness through spectacular actions.[221] Fridays for Future[222] unites students all over the globe and is supported by scientists and experts worldwide.[223] Over 4 million people in an estimated 185 countries joined a global climate strike on 20 September 2019 to

---

[216] Hans Kelsen, *Pure Theory of Law. Translation from the Second (Revised and Enlarged) German Edition* (University of California Press 2005) 354.

[217] ibid.

[218] Paul Blokker, 'Constitutional Mobilization and Contestation in the Transnational Sphere' (2018) 45 Journal of Law and Society S52, S60.

[219] ibid S54, S57ff.

[220] Rajagopal (n 21) 258; Gavin W Anderson, 'Societal Constitutionalism, Social Movements, and Constitutionalism from Below' (2013) 20 Indiana Journal of Global Legal Studies 881.

[221] Matthew Todd, 'Extinction Rebellion's Tactics Are Working. It Has Pierced the Bubble of Denial' *The Guardian* (10 June 2019) <https://www.theguardian.com/commentisfree/2019/jun/10/extinction-rebellion-bubble-denial-climate-crisis> accessed 31 August 2023.

[222] 'Fridays for Future' <https://fridaysforfuture.org> accessed 31 August 2023.

[223] Scientists for Future, 'Statement of Scientists and Scholars Concerning the Protests for More Climate Protection' (12 March 2019) <https://www.scientists4future.org/stellungnahme/statement-text/> accessed 31 August 2023. Over 26.800 scientists, mainly from Germany, Austria and Switzerland, signed the statement to support the Fridays for Future movement.

protest for effective climate policies.[224] The President of the European Commission has openly acknowledged the influence of climate activists such as Greta Thunberg and the Fridays for Future movement in shaping the 'New Green Deal'.[225]

Several environmental law scholars have employed theories of deliberative democracy to think about how to democratise global climate governance.[226] They discuss participatory models such as the implementation of mini-assemblies similar to the constitutional assemblies held in Ireland and France.[227] The World Wide Views (WWViews) is an example of a deliberative forum at the global level. In 2009, it involved around 10 000 citizens from 76 countries to deliberate in the run-up of the 21st UNFCCC Conference of the Parties (COP21) in 2015. The results showed strong support for more aggressive climate regulation and deep climate action and have helped to pave the way for the Paris Agreement. UNFCCC Spokesperson and Director of Communications and Outreach, Nuttall, said about the impact of WWViews on Climate and Energy that:

> The results were indeed useful, because in 2015 we were making efforts to engage with new sections of society beyond governments to achieve a supportive environment in the run up to Paris, to achieve a supportive environment that would give governments the confidence to do the right thing. The supportive input from citizens through WWViews – together with input from cities, investors and many more – was part of the reason why we got a good outcome in Paris.[228]

---

[224] Sandra Laville and Jonathan Watts, 'Across the Globe, Millions Join Biggest Climate Protest Ever' *The Guardian* (21 September 2019) <https://www.theguardian.com/environment/2019/sep/21/across-the-globe-millions-join-biggest-climate-protest-ever> accessed 31 August 2023.

[225] European Commission, 'Press Remarks by President von Der Leyen on the Occasion of the Adoption of the European Climate Law' (4 March 2020) <https://ec.europa.eu/commission/presscorner/detail/en/statement_20_381> accessed 31 August 2023.

[226] See, for example, Stevenson and Dryzek (n 35); Michael Ray Harris, 'Environmental Deliberative Democracy and the Search for Administrative Legitimacy: A Legal Positivism Approach' (2011) 44 University of Michigan Journal of Law Reform 343; Karin Bäckstrand, 'Democratizing Global Environmental Governance? Stakeholder Democracy after the World Summit on Sustainable Development' (2006) 12 European Journal of International Relations 467.

[227] Leslie Anne Duvic-Paoli, 'Re-Imagining the Making of Climate Law and Policy in Citizens' Assemblies' (2022) 11 Transnational Environmental Law 235; Laura Devaney and others, 'Ireland's Citizens' Assembly on Climate Change: Lessons for Deliberative Public Engagement and Communication' (2020) 14 Environmental Communication 141.

[228] Nick Nuttall, available at <http://wwviews.org/why-world-wide-views> accessed 31

Similarly, the Draft General Comment No. 26 on Children's rights and the environment with a special focus on climate change, adopted by the Committee on the Rights of the Child in February 2023, was strongly influenced by the opinions and views of 7416 children from 103 countries that were consulted in the run-up to the drafting process of the General Comment in 2016 via an online survey, in focus groups and in-person national and regional consultations.[229] Moreover, the first successful non-legal European Citizens' Initiative of the European water movement ('Right2Water') collected over 2 million signatures and moulded new European policies against the privatisation of water services.[230] These examples demonstrate that non-legal tactics employed by non-state actors can influence and shape international lawmaking. They allow for a multitude of different actors to participate in transnational discourses on global common goods (such as the atmosphere or water) and, thus, can foster and strengthen the idea of global (climate) constitutionalism.

However, while non-legal forms are important, litigation is still (one of) the most efficient tool(s). It has been identified as one of the ten dominant social drivers of deep decarbonisation.[231] The UN High Commissioner for Human Rights explicitly recognised the role of litigation—besides the millions of people joining climate marches—as an important tool for striving for better climate protection and a response to slow and hesitant governments.[232] In the absence of effective climate policies, economist Sachs urges rethinking climate justice from a legal perspective and introducing climate rights through the use of public nuisance and the PTD. If governments are unwilling to act, citizens need to

---

August 2023, see also Ryan Gunderson, 'Global Environmental Governance Should Be Participatory: Five Problems of Scale' (2018) 33 International Sociology 715, 726–7.

[229] Committee on the Rights of the Child, 'Draft General Comment No. 26—Children's Rights and the Environment with a Special Focus on Climate Change' para 2ff.

[230] Blokker (n 202) S68–70.

[231] The other dominant societal factors identified by the Cluster of Excellence 'Climate, Climate Change and Society (CLICCS)' at the University of Hamburg are UN climate governance, transnational initiatives, climate-related regulation, climate protests and social movements, corporate responses, fossil-fuel divestment, consumption patterns, media, and knowledge production, see the report by Anita Engels and others, 'Hamburg Climate Futures Outlook 2023—The Plausibility of a 1.5°C Limit to Global Warming' (2023).

[232] 'Statement by United Nations High Commissioner for Human Rights, Michelle Bachelet', *Human Rights for the Planet—High-Level International Conference on Human Rights and Environmental Protection, 5 October 2020* <https://www.ohchr.org/EN/NewsEvents/Pages/DisplayNews.aspx?NewsID=26343&LangID=E> accessed 31 August 2021. She refers explicitly to the Urgenda case as a role model for rights-based approaches to climate protection.

'flood the courts with lawsuits' to implement a human right to a healthy environment.[233] It becomes apparent that law is central to the struggle for human rights.[234] But it is also a tool to incorporate scientific findings by expert committees such as the IPCC into social reality, for example, in the form of the 2°C and 1.5°C targets. The vindication of environmental protection by (constitutional) courts is an important feature of global environmental constitutionalism.[235] Thus, '[l]aw is the bridge between scientific knowledge and political action',[236] and litigation is meant to push policymakers to implement effective climate mitigation and adaptation measures.[237]

6.3 Climate Change Litigation (CCL)

CCL is a form of strategic litigation.[238] The term refers to an increasing number of lawsuits concerned with climate matters that are filed by members of civil society (such as NGOs and individuals) and other actors (e.g., substate agents) against supranational organisations (e.g., the EU), transnational companies and especially national governments. These lawsuits are directed at implementing international treaty provisions or enforcing them 'at home'.[239] Litigants use a variety of legal instruments to broaden the scope of existing law by introducing new interpretations or create new rights, such as the right to a stable climate. Most of these interpretations focus on domestic fundamental rights or international human rights

---

233 Jeffrey Sachs, 'A Proposal for Climate Justice' (*Lecture delivered at London School of Economics and Political Science (3 October 2017)*) <http://www.lse.ac.uk/Events/2017/10/20171003t1830vOT/a-proposal-for-climate-justice> accessed 31 August 2023.

234 Jack Donnelly, 'The Virtues of Legalization' in Saladin Meckled-García and Başak Çalı (eds), *The Legalization of Human Rights: Multidisciplinary Perspectives on Human Rights and Human Rights Law* (Routledge 2006) 67.

235 James R May and Erin Daly, *Global Environmental Constitutionalism* (CUP 2014) 1.

236 Sultan Azlan Shah, The New Millennium: Challenges and Responsibilities, lecture at Universiti Kebangsaan Malaysia, 23 August 1997, cited by 'Commentary on the Oslo Principles on Global Climate Change Obligations'.

237 UNEP, 'Global Climate Litigation Report (2023 Status Review)' (2023) 4; UNEP, 'The Status of Climate Change Litigation—A Global Review' (2017) 8.

238 Jacqueline Peel and Hari M Osofsky, 'Litigation as a Climate Regulatory Tool' in Christina Voigt (ed), *International Judicial Practice on the Environment: Questions of Legitimacy* (CUP 2019) 311.

239 See Jacqueline Peel and Hari M Osofsky, 'Litigation as a Mitigation Tool', *Climate Change Litigation: Regulatory Pathways to Cleaner Energy* (CUP 2015).

law, or a combination of both, and they rely heavily on science.[240] Today, there are more climate laws than ever, and their importance is growing as they recognise new rights and duties.[241] However, implementation has been unsatisfying so far.[242] Litigation seeks to transform these pieces of paper into effective climate policies by pushing policymakers, particularly governments, to meet their climate targets.[243] As of August 2023, the Sabin Center listed 1627 cases concerned with climate change in the U.S. alone.[244] Another 775 cases (since 2011) have been filed in another 55 countries before national, regional and international courts or tribunals.[245]

CCL can take on diverse forms. The Grantham Research Institute on Climate Change and the Environment provides an overview of strategic litigation. Accordingly, litigation against governments and public bodies seeks to increase mitigation ambition (*Urgenda, Juliana*), enforce existing mitigation and adaptation goals (*Future Generations, Leghari*) or to consider climate change as part of environmental review and licensing.[246] Six elements can be identified that plaintiffs use to hold governments accountable for their climate policies. These are 1) the use of public interest litigation as a means to overcome standing requirements obstacles, 2) the use of climate science to prove the links between GHG emissions to climate change and the damages that the latter causes, 3) the use of unusual mixes of innovative arguments and sources such as human rights law, 4) public negligence and 5) the PTD, all accompanied by 6) the support of fundamental principles and treaties of IL.[247] When taking a closer look at *Urgenda, Leghari, Juliana* and *Future Generations* in Chapter 9, we see that these factors

---

[240] For a detailed description and analysis of the cases of *Urgenda v the Netherlands, Asghar Leghari v Pakistan, Juliana v the United States*, and *Future Generations v Colombia*, see Chapter 9.

[241] UNEP, 'The Status of Climate Change Litigation—A Global Review' (n 221) 4.

[242] Rakhyun E Kim and Klaus Bosselmann, 'International Environmental Law in the Anthropocene: Towards a Purposive System of Multilateral Environmental Agreements' (2013) 2 Transnational Environmental Law 285, 285–6.

[243] UNEP, 'The Status of Climate Change Litigation—A Global Review' (n 221) 6, 14 ff.

[244] To access data on litigation in the U.S., see http:// climatecasechart.com/us-climate-change-litigation/. This database is maintained by the Sabin Center at Columbia Law School and the Arnold and Porter law firm.

[245] For the Sabin Center database on non-U.S. climate change litigation, see http://climatecasechart.com/non-us-climate-change-litigation/.

[246] Joana Setzer and Rebecca Byrnes, 'Global Trends in Climate Change Litigation: 2019 Snapshot' (2019) 6.

[247] Giulio Corsi, 'A Bottom-up Approach to Climate Governance: The New Wave of Climate Change Litigation' [2017] ICCG Reflection No. 57 1, 2.

apply to almost all of them.

CCL is more than just the enforcement of individuals' rights. It is a response to the failed attempts of the international community of states to effectively establish a climate change regime. It seeks to bridge the gaps between hesitant and insufficient state action and the goal of a sustainable future for the planet.[248] Litigation is a strategy of 'attempting to control, order or influence the behaviour of others'—in this case, governmental actors—and seeks to have a regulatory effect on targeted rules, policies or decision-making procedures.[249]

6.4 Litigation as Participation in Self-Government

It is for these reasons that litigation is not only a tool through which non-state actors make themselves heard, but it can also inform new ways of thinking about legitimacy in transnational constitutional law. In her study on litigation, Lahav worked out different functions of litigation that are generally underrepresented in legal discourse. She argues that litigation can help to enforce the law, that it increases transparency because it can reveal information that is essential for decision-making, and that it can promote social equality by giving litigants the opportunity to speak and be heard.[250] Jhering believed that every claim made by an individual is also made on behalf of society as a whole. Whoever defends one's rights defends the ideas of the whole society.[251] Claims of law—unlike claims of privilege or interest—constitute the claimants as members of a legal (and thus, political) community. Individuals recognise others as carriers of rights they are entitled to: rights and duties they owe to others 'not because of charity or interest but because such rights and duties belong to every member of the community in that position'.[252] Law universalises benefits and burdens that belong to one particular person or group to all members of that community: 'What otherwise would be a mere private violation, a wrong done to *me*, a violation of *my interest*,

[248] Jacqueline Peel and Hari M Osofsky, *Climate Change Litigation: Regulatory Pathways to Cleaner Energy* (CUP 2015) 52; UNEP, 'The Status of Climate Change Litigation—A Global Review' (n 221) 6.

[249] Peel and Osofsky, *Climate Change Litigation: Regulatory Pathways to Cleaner Energy* (n 232) 33.

[250] Alexandra Lahav, *In Praise of Litigation* (OUP 2017) 1–2.

[251] Rudolf von Jhering, *The Struggle for Law (Translated from the Fifth German Edition)* (2nd edn, Callaghan and Company 1915) 77, 'Every man is a born battler for the law in the interest of society.'

[252] Martti Koskenniemi, *The Politics of International Law* (Hart Publishing 2011) 239.

is transformed by law into a violation against *everyone in my position*, a matter of concern for the political community itself.'[253] Thus, the 'struggle for law' can strengthen the community in this way.

Above all, however, litigation can be understood as a form of participation in self-government.[254] Deliberation can occur in many areas, including court procedures.[255] 'Litigation serves the democratic value of participation by enabling individuals to engage directly in the process of lawmaking and law enforcement.'[256]

As such, litigation is complementary to traditional democratic procedures such as voting or standing for election. But its advantage is that it comes closer to the deliberative ideal than voting does.[257] Litigation requires that participants present their positions based on arguments and proofs. The positions are tested against each other in court, with the impartial judge deciding who has the better arguments and corresponding evidence. However, these arguments are not only made for the judge but also for the public at large, which can build its opinions based on the deliberation in the courtroom.[258] Public interest litigation is a tool that helps actors who are unable or unwilling to pursue their political goals through majoritarian decision-making processes to use alternative forums.[259] CCL is never seen as 'the' only tool but as one among many to achieve better climate protection.[260] Rather, it forms an 'integral part of the multilevel climate governance system that creates fluid pathways for interactions among regulation at subnational, national, and international levels'.[261] Often, CCL is combined with traditional campaigning techniques and a strong media presence.[262] Litigation can influence the choices key actors make, especially when this means increasing costs or reputational risks

---

253 ibid (emphasis in original).

254 See Chapter 3 'Participation in Self-Government' in Lahav (n 234).

255 Bernhard Peters, 'On Public Deliberation and Public Culture—Reflections on the Public Sphere' [1997] InIIS-Arbeitspapier Nr. 7/97 13.

256 Lahav (n 234) 84.

257 ibid 95.

258 ibid 85.

259 Ran Hirschl, 'The Judicialization of Politics' in E Goodin (ed), *The Oxford Handbook of Political Science* (OUP 2011) 269.

260 Peel and Osofsky, *Climate Change Litigation: Regulatory Pathways to Cleaner Energy* (n 232) 28.

261 ibid 53.

262 ibid 51.

that come with particular projects or when public opinion shifts through climate awareness.[263]

Many of the cases filed in recent years have been brought with the specific goal of social norm changing, for example, the Inuit petition with the Inter-American Commission on Human Rights (IAComHR).[264] The petitioners were aware of the little chance their case would have in court. However, the main objective of the petition was to relate human rights to climate change and to start a public discourse that could potentially influence future decisions and outcomes, and in this, they were successful.[265] In Australia and the U.S., where political conflict and negative media reporting by conservative media in the past have impeded efficient climate change action, CCL plays three roles that can help to change and form the public's opinion on the issue:

> (1) making the political culture and public debate more climate-informed; (2) supporting and galvanizing grassroots climate campaigns; and (3) translating abstract scientific concepts into tangible impacts that the general public can understand and relate to better.[266]

Litigation, therefore, is one of the measures that are deemed necessary to ensure sustainable development for present and future generations. Climate change is seen as the dominator of the environmental agenda, whether explicitly or inexplicitly, and brings together many different actors.[267] Courts can be accessed by a wider range of actors than international negotiation forums, which are often limited to states and IOs. They can also be approached by foreign claimants whose human rights may be violated by certain political decisions.[268] Thus,

---

[263] ibid 47.

[264] Petition to the Inter-American Commission on Human Rights Seeking Relief from Violations Resulting from Global Warming Caused by Acts and Omissions of the United States, submitted by Sheila Watt-Cloutier, with the support of the Inuit Circumpolar Conference, on behalf of all Inuit of the Arctic regions of the United States and Canada (2005).

[265] Peel and Osofsky, *Climate Change Litigation: Regulatory Pathways to Cleaner Energy* (n 232) 50.

[266] ibid 224.

[267] Edith Brown Weiss, 'Nature and the Law: The Global Commons and the Common Concern of Humankind' [2014] Sustainable Humanity, Sustainable Nature: Our Responsibility. Pontifical Academy of Sciences, Extra Series 41 1, 2.

[268] In Germany, 15 plaintiffs from Bangladesh and Nepal asked the German Federal Constitutional Court to declare the German Climate Protection Law as "unconstitutional" because it would violate their rights to life, health, and property, see GFCC, Order of 24 March 2021, 1 BvR 2656/18, see also in greater detail Section 4.3.

courts are bringing various actors, such as states, NGOs and private sector actors, together that would usually not participate in the same forum and have their voices heard.[269] The courtroom, then, works similarly to a local marketplace. The combination of bringing together key stakeholders at multiple levels and accessibilities has made, and likely will continue to make, courts an important place for shaping climate change regulation.[270] It is for this reason that CCL is perceived as a bottom-up approach that uses the judiciary to shape climate change policy[271] by focusing on the actions of those affecting the commons (the climate) and those being affected by these actions.[272] In this sense, adjudication is a form of climate change governance. It is 'judicialization from below'.[273]

Litigation is not (only) about winning. Rather, litigants often seek to attract attention to their concerns through spectacular cases and to influence public opinion. This has consequences for how the role of the court for litigation is perceived. Lobel identifies three perspectives.[274] First, the traditional view reduces the courts to the role of neutral arbiters of disputes or, quoting Fried: '[c]ourts should be the impartial tool for doing justice between man and man'.[275] The second view assumes that courts are being used to implement social changes, with legal proceedings going beyond ordering private relationships (reform-oriented litigation). Both have in common that victory in court is seen as an indicator of success.[276] In contrast, Lobel develops a third perspective. He argues that courts are also forums for protest:

> [C]ourts not only function as adjudicators of private disputes, or institutions that implement social reforms, but as arenas where political and social movements agitate for, and communicate, their legal and political agenda.[277]

Victory is seen as a 'by-product'. It is not the yardstick against which the success of a case is measured. Neither is the role of the judge—which is key for

---

[269] Peel and Osofsky, *Climate Change Litigation: Regulatory Pathways to Cleaner Energy* (n 232) 15.

[270] ibid.

[271] Corsi (n 231) 2.

[272] Brown Weiss (n 251) 2.

[273] Hirschl (n 243) 263.

[274] Jules Lobel, 'Courts as Forums for Protest' (2004) 52 UCLA Law Review 477, 479.

[275] ibid citing Charles Fried, *Order and Law: Arguing the Reagan Revolution—A Firsthand Account* (Simon & Schuster 1991) 57.

[276] ibid 480.

[277] ibid 479.

the traditional and the reform-oriented perspectives of litigation—central to the determination of successful litigation. Rather, the court serves as a bottom-up forum where different actors in the case interact with each other and with society, mainly through the media. Without the concern of possibly losing the case, the judge ceases to be the epicentre of litigation.[278] Instead, the court works as an arena of policy disputation where the court, activists and other branches of the government are seen as interdependent to achieve meaningful law reform.[279] This does not mean that plaintiffs seeking to educate the public or mobilise social and political movements may not also have the desire to gain relief for injustices suffered.[280] The main goal, however, is often to cause a ripple effect arising from the doctrine of precedent. 'After all, historic cases matter because they change the hierarchy of legal rules and set up default principles that apply to all future matters that come within its domain.'[281] They encourage plaintiffs in other countries to try 'at home' what has been successful elsewhere:[282]

> Climate change litigation – whether successful or not – thus has important indirect influences on the regulatory landscape through the role it plays in shaping social norms, including public perceptions of climate change, accepted understandings of climate science, and views on the appropriate regulatory response.[283]

It becomes clear that through litigation, '[t]hese actors engage in through courts, rather than simply with the courts, at multiple levels of government'.[284] Through litigation, the stories 'behind' ecological sensibilities can be told. Traditional IL focusing exclusively on formal decision-making by states easily misses the

---

[278] ibid 489–90.

[279] ibid 490.

[280] ibid. The case of Saúl Luciano Lliuya against the German energy company RWE is illustrative in this sense. While he and his lawyer Roda Verheyen are trying to hold large GHG emitters such as RWE responsible for the climate damage and thus to show the consequences of the energy policy pursued so far, Lluyia is also calling for intervention to prevent the violation of his rights. If the dam breaks, his family, his home and the city of Huaraz would be in danger. Further information can be found on the homepage of the NGO Germanwatch which orchestrates the case: <https://rwe.climatecase.org/de> accessed 31 August 2023.

[281] Parvez Hassan and Azim Azfar, 'Securing Environmental Rights Through Public Interest Litigation in South Asia' (2004) 22 Virginia Environmental Law Journal 215, 216.

[282] Oliver A Houck, *Taking Back Eden: Eight Environmental Cases That Changed the World* (Island Press 2010) 3.

[283] Peel and Osofsky, *Climate Change Litigation: Regulatory Pathways to Cleaner Energy* (n 232) 223.

[284] Osofsky, 'Climate Change Litigation as Pluralist Legal Dialogue?' (n 20) 194.

multi-level dimensions of litigation. For example, in the case of the Inuit petition before the IAComHR, the Inuit are not 'only' indigenous people but also citizens, members of longstanding communities whose existence is threatened and members of the Inuit Circumpolar Conference.[285] Harms to their traditional way of life, their understanding of who they are, and their relationships with each other occur at multiple levels of governance—individual, cooperative and governmental decision-making. Thus, more and more narratives join a mix that has fundamental ties to place and identity besides citizenship but is ignored by a traditional perspective that focuses only on the formal aspects of decision-making.[286] CCL, therefore, can be perceived as a form of dialogue among multiple levels of governance that is crucial for shaping transnational regulatory governance.[287]

However, it is important to note that not all cases that belong to the broader category of CCL can be perceived as forms of self-government or rational discourses. Climate activists use lawsuits to protect a common good (the atmosphere). Conversely, corporations, especially those belonging to 'Big Oil' have 'discovered' anti-climate lawsuits as a way to fight stricter regulations, especially via so-called SLAPPs (strategic lawsuits against public participation), which aim to silence climate activists and NGOs when it comes to issues that are controversial in society, such as genetically modified organisms, 'fracking' and stronger climate regulation.[288] Unlike the lawsuits that belong to the category of CCL analysed in this work that aim to open up more arenas for deliberation where the voices of the 'voiceless' can be heard, SLAPPs seek to achieve the exact opposite: to exclude public participation as much as possible to push through (infrastructural) projects, even if residents or society in general are opposed to them.[289]

Peters has argued that deliberative democracy in the form of 'presence, observation, notice and comment, and hearing' cannot be called democracy because it does not empower participants to block a decision or to disempower law- and policymakers.[290] Litigation proves another advantage in this context. It is a

---

[285] ibid 221.

[286] ibid 220–1.

[287] ibid 221.

[288] Chris Hilson, 'Law, Courts and Populism: Climate Change Litigation and the Narrative Turn' in Susan Sterett and Lee Walker (eds), *Research Handbook on Law and Courts* (Edward Elgar Publishing 2019) 82; Christopher J Hilson, 'Environmental SLAPPs in the UK: Threat or Opportunity?' (2016) 25 Environmental Politics 248.

[289] George (Rock) Pring and Catherine (Kitty) Pring, 'Greening Justice—Creating and Improving Environmental Courts and Tribunals' (The Access Initiative 2009) 53.

[290] Peters, 'Dual Democracy' (n 7) 339; also Paulus (n 7) 96.

way in which ordinary citizens—even if it is only in an indirect manner through the institution of a court—can enforce the law (e.g., the objectives of the Paris Agreement) and force governments to change their route.[291]

Many scholars, therefore, are convinced that the courts play an important role in fostering global climate governance and the establishment of global climate constitutionalism.[292] What is more, CCL can even be understood as a form of informal lawmaking. Under a traditional Westphalian model of IL, only states can make IL. From a modified Westphalian perspective[293]—which recognises a stronger role of non-state actors but still sees states as the main actors of IL—non-state actors can engage in lawmaking in the national, but not in the international sphere. Their influence can only be indirect: through the actions of states in international lawmaking. Instead, CCL should be understood as a pluralist dialogue among several actors, including states but also other normative communities. A pluralist vision that recognises the existence of a multitude of normative areas covering the same social field claims that non-state actors are directly engaging in international lawmaking through litigation.[294] Litigants are international lawmakers in their own right and participate in the transnational climate change regime alongside other actors. The initiation of a climate suit, then, can help to create the contours of this regime,[295] and it helps to democratise it:

> Through the interpretational development of constitutional norms, a piece of citizen's democracy is realised. The possibilities and reality of the free discourse of individuals and groups 'on' and 'under' the constitutional law norms and their pluralistic influence 'within' them are diversely conveyed to the interpretational process.[296]

---

[291] Lahav (n 234) 32.

[292] See, for example, James R May and Erin Daly, 'Global Climate Constitutionalism and Justice in the Courts' in Jordi Jaria-Manzano and Susana Borràs (eds), *Research Handbook on Global Climate Constitutionalism* (Edward Elgar Publishing 2019); Sumudu Atapattu, 'Environmental Justice, Climate Justice and Constitutionalism: Protecting Vulnerable States and Communities' in Jordi Jaria-Manzano and Susana Borràs (eds), *Research Handbook on Global Climate Constitutionalism* (Edward Elgar Publishing 2019); May and Daly (n 219) 87ff.; Tim Stephens, *International Courts and Environmental Protection* (CUP 2009) 116.

[293] See Hari M Osofsky, 'The Geography of Climate Change Litigation: Implications for Transnational Regulatory Governance' (2005) 83 Washington University Law Review 1789; Hari M Osofsky, 'The Geography of Climate Change Litigation Part II: Narratives of Massachusetts v. EPA' (2008) 8 Chicago Journal of International Law 573.

[294] Osofsky, 'Climate Change Litigation as Pluralist Legal Dialogue?' (n 20) 227.

[295] ibid 209.

[296] Häberle, 'The Open Society of Constitutional Interpreters' (n 3) 148–9.

In this sense, can litigation be understood as a form of international lawmaking? The answer is a 'yes, but':

> These suits serve in part as 'ports of entry' – and perhaps ports of exit as well – for a dialogue among a range of governmental and nongovernmental actors operating at multiple scales about climate change. Many of the petitioners and respondents are directly engaged in, or at least linked to those directly engaged in, formulating climate policy. So, even when its formal relevance to international law is limited, this litigation serves as a form of international lawmaking.[297]

Litigation can serve in the process of norm internalisation.[298] The many efforts of climate activists, including litigation, can help to shape transnational norms about climate change. From a pluralistic view, however, litigation can do even more: the transnational regime can be seen as a space that not only belongs exclusively to governmental actors and is shaped through legislative efforts and executive behaviour but is also shared with civil society actors.[299]

Several normative orders cover the same social field, and the state is just one—albeit a very important—actor among others.[300] Accordingly, such a model decentres international lawmaking to include the multi-scalar interactions of non-state actors.[301] From such a point of view, the formal treaties—the UNFCC, the Kyoto Protocol and the Paris Agreement—cease to be the centre of attention in international lawmaking regarding climate matters.[302]

Instead of engaging in international lawmaking only through the mediation of the nation-state as understood from the classical Westphalian view (refusing to treat anything but the nation-state's consensus to treaty regimes as a relevant act under IL), non-state actors filing an extensive amount of CCL suits can be seen as lawmakers in their own right.[303] Therefore, non-state actors, although not possessing recognised lawmaking capacity, through strategic litigation and introducing interpretations of their own, can participate (although informally) in the creation and development of IEL.

A traditional view of IL misses how important informal acts can be for the development of IL, for example, supranational petitions backed by intense civil

[297] Osofsky, 'Climate Change Litigation as Pluralist Legal Dialogue?' (n 20) 195–6.

[298] ibid 208, referring to Koh's theory on Transnational Legal Processes.

[299] ibid 208–9.

[300] ibid 227.

[301] ibid 228.

[302] ibid 209.

[303] ibid.

society engagement.[304] From a pluralist view, the multiple communities engaged with these petitions should be recognised as informal lawmakers and the petition consequently as lawmaking in a broader sense, as '[t]hey have the potential to create obligations for nation-states, but as importantly, they pressure and/or support "lawmakers" responding to the problem of climate change'.[305] States have to respond to these petitions and justify their positions in court.[306]

However, such a pluralistic approach towards international lawmaking might be too vague and bottomless and, therefore, needs to be limited to some degree in relation to both the relevant CCL cases and the actors—normative communities that should be included—even if this contradicts the very idea of pluralism as being as inclusive as possible.[307] Osofsky suggests limiting the amount of litigation that counts as international lawmaking according to two criteria: first, limiting the scope of litigation to those cases that include 'actions in any kind of formally-constituted tribunals that specifically focus on the phenomenon of climate change' as relevant to international lawmaking.[308] Second, as a matter of the 'who', only those should be regarded as international lawmakers 'who participate directly by formally filing or by adjudicating' the lawsuit.[309] This shows that, again, the role of the plaintiffs should not be underestimated.[310] It is only because they are the ones initiating a lawsuit—'forcing the court to engage (in a legal dialogue)'[311]—that the court can rule on climate matters. The judiciary cannot act on its own: it depends on the will of the plaintiffs.[312]

[304] ibid 223.

[305] ibid.

[306] ibid 224.

[307] ibid 233.

[308] ibid.

[309] ibid 234.

[310] Häberle, 'The Open Society of Constitutional Interpreters' (n 3) 131, 160.

[311] ibid 136.

[312] Möllers (n 114) 89, in more detail see Section 10.5 below.

6.5 Conclusion

Traditional democratic concepts focusing exclusively on voting rights and representation fail to recognise the many ways in which civil society actors can become involved and could lend democratic legitimacy to international constitutional law.[313] While for Falk and Strauss, institutionalisation is key, and, thus, their ideas are limited to reforming and democratising international institutions,[314] others believe that global democratisation could occur in the informal realm of global public spheres and its discourses.[315]

Conferring legitimacy will depend on 'the general accessibility of a deliberative process whose structure grounds an expectation of rationally acceptable results'.[316] Due to the lack of a world state, humans are not 'world citizens' (*Weltstaatsbürger/innen*) but can be seen as 'universal citizens' of both their state and global civil society. Contrary to the domestic sphere, their participation in civil society is not manifested through elections and votes but through their contribution to the world discourse (*Weltdiskurs*) and the world public (*Weltöffentlichkeit*).[317] A discourse-oriented approach with a focus on talking rather than voting is key to a concept aiming to achieve a high(er) level of democratic legitimacy in the pursuit of a world domestic policy without a world government. A truly democratic and open transnational process of constitutionalism, therefore, has to be open to the participation of everyone potentially affected by climate change. A constitution that not only incorporates the state but also structures the public and constitutes society may not only act passively upon them, treating the societal and private powers as objects, but must also include them actively as subjects.[318] This does not mean that the participants necessarily have to come to a consensus about what constitutes good climate policies. Rather, dissent is necessary for a pluralistic discourse that helps to shape a transnational climate regime and its boundaries. 'The democratic process depends on a consensus on

[313] Cf. Häberle, 'The Open Society of Constitutional Interpreters' (n 3) 148.

[314] Falk and Strauss (n 4).

[315] Cf. Stevenson and Dryzek (n 83) 190; Nanz and Steffek (n 65); Claudia Kissling, 'The Evolution of CSO's Legal Status in International Governance and Its Relevance for the Legitimacy of International Organizations' in Jens Steffek, Claudia Kissling and Patrizia Nanz (eds), *Civil Society Participation in European and Global Governance* (Palgrave Macmillan 2008) analyses how conferring legal status to NGOs in/by IOs could help to overcome the democratic deficit.

[316] Habermas, 'The Postnational Constellation and the Future of Democracy' (n 5) 110.

[317] Emmerich-Fritsche (n 5) 605.

[318] Häberle, 'The Open Society of Constitutional Interpreters' (n 3) 144.

the procedure, but also on dissent on the merits.'[319] Deliberation and contestation are the two pillars of democratic practice in a transnational order,[320] and it is this interplay in an open society of constitutional interpreters through which 'the productive power of pluralism arises'.[321] However, discourses alone can only influence public opinion, but they cannot govern. Some form of institutionalisation is necessary.[322] Using the courts offers this possibility to litigants. By forcing the court to engage in a legal dialogue,[323] litigants can present arguments and respond to those of the defendants before an impartial judge who decides whose interpretations of the law are more convincing. Climate litigation can foster and strengthen climate justice as a guiding and interpreting principle for global climate constitutionalism. From this point of view, litigation, both before national and international courts, can be seen as a form of self-government and possibly also a form of international constitution-making; this is analysed through the lens of societal constitutionalism in the next chapter.

[319] Möllers (n 114) 76 (citations omitted).

[320] Krisch (n 18) 270.

[321] Häberle, 'Verfassungsinterpretation als öffentlicher Prozeß—ein Pluralismuskonzept (1978)' (n 95) 151 (tr the author).

[322] Krisch (n 18) 270; Habermas, 'Further Reflections on the Public Sphere' (n 59) 452.

[323] Häberle, 'The Open Society of Constitutional Interpreters' (n 3) 136.

Societal Constitutionalism 7

Chapter 6 concluded that CCL can be understood as a form of participation in self-government and, consequently, as a form of international lawmaking. Global constitutionalism generally welcomes a more active role of individuals and other non-state actors; however, their role as potential lawmakers has not been subject to much discussion yet. Instead, it seems that discourses on global constitutionalism are generally concerned with identifying elements of domestic constitutions (such as the rule of law, judicial review, democracy or fundamental rights) at the international level or comparing which IOs or norms of customary law, *jus cogens*, could potentially belong to a global constitutional order. Less attention has been paid to the '*who*'—the question of who makes this transnational climate law.

For a long time, scholarship has focused almost exclusively on states as the only formal lawmakers.[1] Based on the principle of sovereignty, according to which states have to consent to the norms by which they want to be bound, international lawmaking law is—at least formally—reserved for states alone:[2]

> Non-state actors may and certainly do contribute to the elaboration of international texts and influence state behavior in ways that may contribute to the development of international custom, but *they do not as such make public international law*.[3]

---

[1] Alan Boyle and Christine Chinkin, *The Making of International Law* (OUP 2007) 10 ff (12).

[2] Ingo Venzke, *How Interpretation Makes International Law: On Semantic Change and Normative Twists* (OUP 2012) 1–2.

[3] Alexandre Kiss and Dinah Shelton, *Guide to International Environmental Law* (Martinus Nijhoff Publishers 2007) 2–3 (emphasis added).

M. Niehaus, *Global Climate Constitutionalism "from below"*,
https://doi.org/10.1007/978-3-658-43191-4_7

However, the ongoing domestic de-constitutionalisation, as outlined in Chapter 3, requires us to take a closer look at the question of the actors.[4] Several instruments already support the participation of civil society in lawmaking processes at both the national and international levels.[5] The extent to which non-state actors, such as NGOs or individuals, should be involved *de lege ferenda* in IL in general and in international lawmaking in the UN bodies,[6] in particular, vary.[7] Especially the treaties on environmental matters recognise the importance of procedural rights.[8] The constitutionalist perspective, which has emerged as a contrast to the state-centred and sovereignty-oriented theory of IL, goes further.[9] Natural persons should not only be better represented at the global level but also have (limited)

[4] On this, see Boyle and Chinkin (n 1).

[5] Cf. Barbara B Woodward, 'International Lawmaking and Civil Society' in Catherine Brölmann and Yannick Radi (eds), *Research Handbook on the Theory and Practice of International Lawmaking* (Edward Elgar Publishing 2016).

[6] The Cardoso Report, for example, examined the possibilities for greater civil society participation in the UN system, see Fernando Henrique Cardoso, 'We the Peoples: Civil Society, the United Nations and Global Governance—Report of the Panel of Eminent Persons on United Nations–Civil Society Relations (Cardoso Report)' (2004); see also Peter Willetts, 'The Cardoso Report on the UN and Civil Society: Functionalism, Global Corporatism, or Global Democracy?' (2006) 12 Global Governance 305.

[7] Ideas in this sense are the participation of individuals as representatives of the civil society in international forums and the institutionalisation of (separate voting) chambers of civil society (e.g. businesses, NGOs) in intergovernmental decision-making, see Frank Biermann, 'New Actors and Mechanisms of Global Governance' in John S Dryzek, Richard B Norgaard and David Schlosberg (eds), *Oxford Handbook of Climate Change and Society* (OUP 2011) 693; Christine EJ Schwöbel, *Global Constitutionalism in International Legal Perspective* (Martinus Nijhoff Publishers 2011) 21.

[8] See, in particular, the Convention on Access to Information, Public Participation in Decision-making and Access to Justice in Environmental Matters (Aarhus Convention) and the Regional Agreement on Access to Information, Public Participation and Justice in Environmental Matters in Latin America and the Caribbean (Escazu Agreement). Chapter 27 of the Agenda 21 emphasises the importance of NGOs and proposes that society, governments, and international bodies 'should develop mechanisms to allow non-governmental organizations to play their partnership role responsibly and effectively in the process of environmentally sound and sustainable development' (United Nations Conference on Environment & Development Rio de Janeiro, 1992, Agenda 21, Chapter 21, para 5).

[9] Thomas Kleinlein, 'Non-State Actors from an International Constitutionalist Perspective' in Jean D'Aspremont (ed), *Participants in the International Legal System: Multiple Perspectives on Non-State Actors in International Law* (Routledge 2011) 41.

lawmaking powers[10] since 'the process of empowerment is a core element of the constitutionalisation of the international legal system'.[11]

Proponents of societal constitutionalism, therefore, argue that (regime) constitutions are not only the product of states but also of non-state actors who create their own 'civil' constitutional law or help to develop new human rights. Such approaches to global constitutionalism depart from the idea that the law made by states is supposed to cover every legal situation and that it applies to everyone in the same way (in the limited territories of states). Societal constitutionalism, as will be shown below, argues that a multitude of normative orders coexists, which are important for people because they belong to different communities due to their interests or affiliation. So-called 'legal pluralism' cannot be captured by the idea of global constitutionalism as one world constitution in the same sense that a domestic constitution forms the top of the norm pyramid in a nation-state. Instead, proponents of societal constitutionalism argue that non-state actors can participate in shaping the constitutional rules of specific normative orders. This idea is particularly useful in relation to the creation of constitutional climate rules by non-state actors, since, as it is argued here, although not formally authorised to participate in international decision-making, through their roles as plaintiffs, defendants, or amicus curiae in CCL, non-state actors bring their own interpretations of the black letter law before the courts and, thus, engage in international constitution-making. By being discussed and perhaps recognised by the court, these interpretations can become enforceable law that binds the state, often against its will, and might lead to stronger and better climate policies. Thus, non-state actors can help to develop and shape the norms that belong to the constitution of the international climate regime. As outlined earlier, the inclusion of climate justice is of particular importance to the members of the international open society of constitutional interpreters and, thus, is repeatedly the subject matter of court decisions on CCL cases.[12]

However, given the centrality of the state in IL, such a new role for private lawmakers seems bold, to say the least, and would need to be analysed with some care. After exploring the general positions of societal constitutionalism, this chapter examines the ideas of two influential proponents of societal constitutionalism. The first is Gunther Teubner, who developed the idea of a

---

[10] Anne Peters, 'Membership in the Global Constitutional Community' in Jan Klabbers, Anne Peters and Geir Ulfstein (eds), *The Constitutionalization of International Law* (OUP 2009) 155.

[11] ibid 155ff (166).

[12] See Chapter 4.

'Global Bukovina'—the coexistence of a multitude of legal orders—and argued that such orders can develop their own constitutional law. The second is Andreas Fischer-Lescano, who discusses the development of a human right to be free from enforced disappearance as part of the *lex humana* through scandalisation by the global civil society. Both scholars demonstrate how non-state actors play an important role in shaping normative orders. These theories underpin the idea that CCL is a form of (international) lawmaking through interpretation—although activists need a court to accept their ideas.

The second part of this chapter focuses on the question of the unity of (international) constitutional law. If everybody was recognised as a constitutional interpreter—and therefore, a lawmaker to a certain degree—would this not lead to increased fragmentation of IL, and even chaos? This question may not be related directly to the question of whether non-state actors can be considered interpreters. However, by acknowledging such a position, several 'follow-up' questions arise, such as how to solve regime clashes between the environmental and the economic regime, and it is important to understand what they and their answers mean for this claim. Here, it will be demonstrated that, again, the theory of the open society of constitutional interpreters provides a useful tool. By formulating its own expectations and focusing on public interests such as environmental protection, the open society can help to shape the contours of specific regimes.

7.1 Participation of Non-State Actors

In formal processes of negotiation and lawmaking, non-state actors play no or only a small role, with some exceptions for NGOs. The Aarhus Convention is particularly noteworthy in this respect. NGOs can participate in the Meeting of the Parties and even nominate candidates for elections to the Convention's implementation committee.[13] One of the most advanced MEAs in this respect is the Convention on International Trade in Endangered Species, which grants NGOs that are 'technically qualified in protection, conservation or management of wild fauna and flora' an observer status at the Conference of the Parties, as long as at least one-third of the member-states do not object (Article IX). Once admitted, they enjoy the right to participate but are not allowed to vote.[14] Generally,

[13] Philippe Sands and Jacqueline Peel, *Principles of International Environmental Law* (4th edn, CUP 2018) 90.

[14] Jonas Ebbesson, 'Public Participation' in Daniel Bodansky, Jutta Brunnée and Ellen Hey (eds), *The Oxford Handbook of International Environmental Law* (OUP 2008) 691.

there are many hurdles for NGOs to formally participate in institutional settings, including the possibility of member-states' vetos and the requirement of proof of expertise in the relevant field.[15] The accreditation requirement ultimately 'makes states the gatekeepers of NGO involvement'.[16] Their participation is often limited to the provision of information, political pressure and campaigning instead of contributing with their expertise.[17] NGOs can promote certain legal action through extensive lobbying and campaigning, which may be adopted by a multitude of states.[18] But, in short, NGO participation is mostly reduced to the role of watchdogs over the implementation of environmental treaties. As of today, Mbengue sees only a few options of what a 'global environmental partnership' between states and non-state actors look like or could look like.[19] It becomes clear that 'equal' participation opportunities for non-state actors are quite limited under the traditional concept of IEL.

---

[15] Kal Raustiala, 'States, NGOs, and International Environmental Institutions' (1997) 41 International Studies Quarterly 719, 721–2.

[16] Peters, 'Membership in the Global Constitutional Community' (n 10) 223.

[17] Kal Raustiala, 'The "Participatory Revolution" in International Environmental Law' (1997) 21 Harvard Environmental Law Review 537, 556.

[18] Andrea Bianchi, 'Globalization of Human Rights: The Role of Non-State Actors' in Gunther Teubner (ed), *Global Law without a State* (Dartmouth Publishing 1997) 186.

[19] Makane Moïse Mbengue, 'Non-State Actors in International Environmental Law. A Rousseauist Perspective' in Jean D'Aspremont (ed), *Participants in the International Legal System Multiple Perspectives on Non-State Actors in International Law* (Routledge 2011) 379. Accordingly, the "model of surveillance" means that non-state actors (e.g. businesses) subscribe to rules and principles of treaty law and customary law. The "model of transparency" describes the contribution of non-state actors to define issues that should be dealt with at the international stage. Both models have in common that the "last word" lays with the states. The "model of mutuality" refers to an equal partnership between state and non-state actors in public-private-partnerships, such as the World Bank/WWF Alliance for Forest Conversation and Sustainable Use (380–3).

7.2 Who makes IL?

But 'law-creation is not only a question of threshold'.[20] Legal scholarship is increasingly concerned with the role of non-state actors as informal lawmakers[21] since '[n]ow, all you need to create rules is a well-organised group of people and a website. Such a body can set rules for others and try to gain legitimacy, often with rather minimal control by national lawmakers'.[22] Rather than participating in formal decision-making forums, it is argued here that non-state actors can participate in international lawmaking through the interpretation of (already existing) norms and principles. As seen above,[23] interpretative practice covers the space between the text and the law. It is this space where all great changes in IL have taken place in recent decades.[24]

In the context of climate change, individuals, NGOs, sub-states and regional governments, indigenous groups and communities bring their own interpretations of climate change issues, human/fundamental rights, the PTD, environmental principles such as climate justice or intergenerational equity, science and political statements before the courts.[25] CCL aims to achieve protection from hazardous climate change through the interpretation of human rights law (and other laws) by introducing climate concerns in a way that judicially establishes the obligations

---

[20] Georges Abi-Saab, 'Are We Heading for a New Normativity in the International Community? Contribution to the Discussion', *Change and Stability in International Law-Making* (de Gruyter 1988) 76; see also Manfred Lachs, 'The Threshold in Law-Making' in Rudolf Bernhardt and others (eds), *Völkerrecht als Rechtsordnung, Internationale Gerichtsbarkeit, Menschenrechte (FS f. Hermann Mosler)* (Springer 1983).

[21] See, inter alia, Eva Kassoti, 'Beyond State Consent? International Legal Scholarship and the Challenge of Informal International Law-Making' (2016) 63 Netherlands International Law Review 99; Ramses A Wessel, 'Informal International Law-Making as a New Form of World Legislation?' (2011) 8 International Organizations Law Review 253; Boyle and Chinkin (n 1).

[22] Maurits Barendrecht and others, 'Rulejungling—When Lawmaking Goes Private, International and Private' (2012) 3 <https://www.hiil.org/wp-content/uploads/2018/09/Rulejungling-When-lawmaking-goes-private-international-and-informal.pdf> accessed 31 August 2023.

[23] See Section 2.1 and 2.2.

[24] Venzke (n 2) 197.

[25] On Children and youth-led claims and future generations, see UNEP, 'Global Climate Litigation Report (2023 Status Review)' (2023), see also UNEP, 'The Status of Climate Change Litigation—A Global Review' (2017).

of states to act in the form of mitigation and adaptation measures.[26] Often, this occurs against the political will of the state, which raises questions of the separation of powers, legitimacy and the unity of IL. The following chapters will take a closer look at these questions. The present chapter, however, lays the theoretical fundaments for the assumption that non-state actors are engaged in the creation of private and public constitutional law.

7.3 The Positions of Proponents of Societal Constitutionalism

Heyvaert describes the relationship between law and society as follows:

> law (i) is a territorial concept, which (ii) emanates from the state; (iii) it is divided into a public and a private sphere; (iv) it has a constitutive, regulating and communicative function, and (v) is cohesive and comprehensive in its coverage.[27]

This idea is radically challenged by proponents of societal constitutionalism, who argue that there is a global constitutional order based on certain social relationships between the subjects of this order.[28] Rather than applying a state-centred focus, societal constitutionalism employs the idea of a global legal order that seeks to organise social behaviour through the participation of constitutional subjects.[29] In this sense, Teubner analyses how law is created by actors other than states. His starting point is the idea that self-regulatory regimes develop their own constitutions that are emerging and becoming entrenched in the global legal order. 'Constitutions' are not exclusively assigned to the public sector but can also develop in the private sectors, such as economic enterprises or universities.[30]

[26] Brian J Preston, 'The Influence of Climate Change Litigation on Governments and the Private Sector' (2011) 2 Climate Law 485.

[27] Veerle Heyvaert, 'The Transnationalization of Law: Rethinking Law through Transnational Environmental Regulation' (2017) 6 Transnational Environmental Law 205, 205–6.

[28] Schwöbel (n 7) 14.

[29] Christine EJ Schwöbel, 'Organic Global Constitutionalism' (2010) 23 Leiden Journal of International Law 529, 530.

[30] Gunther Teubner, 'Societal Constitutionalism: Nine Variations on a Theme by David Sciulli' in Paul Blokker and Chris Thornhill (eds), *Sociological Constitutionalism* (CUP 2017) 314.

Thus, Teubner focuses on global constitutionalism from a socio-legal perspective and the emergence of a global legal order driven by civil society.[31]

7.3.1 Legal Pluralism

Teubner's theory on societal constitutionalism has its roots in theories of legal pluralism. More precisely, societal constitutionalism is one of several international legal pluralism approaches.[32] Legal pluralism seeks to challenge what has been called 'legal centralism', according to which, 'law is and should be the law of the state, uniform for all persons, exclusive of all other law, and administered by a single set of state institutions'.[33] Legal centralism implies that where other normative orders (e.g., the church, family, voluntary or economic associations) exist, they are of a lesser hierarchical rank and are supposed to subordinate themselves to the law and institutions of the state.[34] Legal pluralism, therefore, deals with and acknowledges the existence of multiple overlapping normative communities or with 'situation[s] in which two or more legal systems coexist in the same social field'.[35] These can be tied to territory in the form of nation-states or municipal communities.[36] But besides such territorial bonds, people can also belong to and feel affiliated with multiple other communities that do not need to be territory-based, including ethnic, religious, epistemic, transnational, subnational or international communities.[37] Despite their lack of formal legal authority, these communities produce norms. Moore emphasises that 'not all the phenomena

[31] Gunter Teubner, '"Global Bukowina": Legal Pluralism in the World Society' in Gunther Teubner (ed), *Global Law without a State* (Dartmouth Publishing 1997) 3 ff.

[32] Rachel J Anderson, 'Theoretical Approaches to Global Regulation of Transnational Corporations' in Alice de Jonge and Roman Tomasic (eds), *Research Handbook on Transnational Corporations* (Edward Elgar Publishing 2017) 45.

[33] John Griffiths, 'What Is Legal Pluralism?' (1986) 18 Journal of Legal Pluralism and Unofficial Law 1, 3.

[34] ibid.

[35] Sally Engle Merry, 'Legal Pluralism' (1988) 22 Law and Society Reivew 869, 870.

[36] Paul Schiff Berman, *Global Legal Pluralism—A Jurisprudence of Law beyond Borders* (CUP 2012) 3.

[37] Paul Schiff Berman, 'Global Legal Pluralism' (2007) 80 Southern California Law Review 1155, 1161.

related to law and not all that are law-like have their source in government'.[38] It is a 'jurisgenerative' process in which 'communities do create law and do give meaning to law through their narratives and precepts'.[39] Contemporary scholarship focuses on 'solid authority' in terms of domestic governmental authority that is capable of creating legal obligations and has binding powers.[40] But by looking for something on the global plane that resembles domestic government, one could lose sight of 'softer' forms of authority whose impact can be the same or even stronger than those of traditional powers.[41] The creation of legal meaning requires not necessarily the state but a creative social or collective process.[42] Such bottom-up rules can pass from being 'informal' to 'law' and can even trump state law or treaties that initiate top-down processes in terms of effectiveness.[43]

Proponents of legal pluralism acknowledge the importance of state law but argue that state law does not or only partially penetrates certain areas. In such places, alternative forms of ordering are taking place, and they provide opportunities for resistance, contestation and alternative vision.[44] IL 'is part of a larger world social process that comprehends all the interpenetrating and interstimulating communities on the planet'.[45] This, in return, means that multiple sites of normative authority exist—beyond the nation-state—and that pluralism has to manage them instead of eliminating them.[46]

---

[38] Sally Falk Moore, 'Legal Systems of the World: An Introductory Guide to Classifications, Typological Interpretations, and Bibliographical Resources' in Leon Lipson and Stanton Wheeler (eds), *Law and the Social Sciences* (Russell Sage Foundation 1987) 15.

[39] Robert M Cover, 'The Supreme Court, 1982 Term—Foreword: Nomos and Narrative' (1983) 97 Harvard Law Review 4, 40.

[40] Nico Krisch, 'Authority, Solid and Liquid, in Postnational Governance' in Roger Cotterrell and Maksymilian del Mar (eds), *Authority in Transnational Legal Theory: Theorising Across Disciplines* (Edward Elgar Publishing 2016) 26.

[41] ibid.

[42] Cover (n 39) 11.

[43] Janet Koven Levitt, 'A Bottom-up Approach to International Lawmaking: The Tale of Three Trade Finance Instruments' (2017) 30 The Globalization of International Law 125, 126.

[44] Paul Schiff Berman, 'The New Legal Pluralism' (2009) 5 Annual Review of Law and Social Science 225, 237.

[45] Myres S McDougal, W Michael Reisman and Andrew R Willard, 'World Community: A Planetary Social Process' (1987) 1 U.C. Davis Law Review 808, 808.

[46] Berman, 'The New Legal Pluralism' (n 44) 237.

7.3.2 Is it Really Law, and Does it Matter?

Proponents of legal pluralism have cheered the overcoming of legal centralism. The debate about the status of IL—is it law or is it not?—can finally be left behind because what matters are the interactions of normative communities and normative commitments resulting from such action.[47] But two major problems can be identified in this regard: firstly, there is no agreed-upon definition of what is law, and secondly, those provided definitions fail to distinguish legal norms from social norms.[48] Presuming that non-state actors are engaged in lawmaking (at least in their very own *nomos*), '[w]here do we stop speaking of law and find ourselves simply describing social life?'[49] Can law created by non-state actors be classified as law, and does such a distinction even matter?

The literature is divided on this point. Klabbers, for example, argues in favour of a presumptive lawmaking thesis. Whether something is law is determined by its addressees: 'normative utterances should be presumed to give rise to law, unless and until the opposite can somehow be proven'.[50] The circle of those who make IL is broadened to all those who are affected by the law. Actors usually heard and followed, such as states, will have some prima facie lawmaking capacity.[51] This approach has been fiercely criticised. An infinite number of lawmakers could arise, as well as legal insecurity as to whether a particular action could be labelled law or not. The lack of a conflict-settling legal framework would further foster legal insecurity.[52] It also does not address the problem of democratic accountability.[53] Rather, a distinction should be made between formal and informal participation.[54] Individuals would only participate '*besides* states where appropriate'.[55]

---

[47] ibid.

[48] Brian Z Tamanaha, 'A Non-Essentialist Version of Legal Pluralism' (2000) 27 Journal of Law and Society 296, 298–9.

[49] Merry (n 35) 878.

[50] Jan Klabbers, 'Law-Making and Constitutionalism' in Jan Klabbers, Anne Peters and Geir Ulfstein (eds), *The Constitutionalization of International Law* (OUP 2009) 115 (–21).

[51] ibid 119.

[52] Eva Kassoti, 'The Constitutionalization of International Law and the Challenge of Non-State Actors' (2017) 11 ICL Journal 177, 199–200.

[53] Thomas Kleinlein, 'On Holism, Pluralism, and Democracy: Approaches to Constitutionalism beyond the State' (2010) 21 European Journal of International Law 1075, 1077.

[54] Peters, 'Membership in the Global Constitutional Community' (n 10) 156.

[55] Anne Peters, 'Dual Democracy' in Jan Klabbers, Anne Peters and Geir Ulfstein (eds), *The Constitutionalization of International Law* (OUP 2009) 265 (emphasis in original).

The introduction or alteration of social norms can be quite powerful, but some would disagree with calling such norms law. The relations in businesses, neighbourhoods and families are (often) not governed by formalised rules but are shaped by informal social norms and voluntary, non-contractual understandings. While lacking formal force, non-binding norms and informal social norms can be just as effective. They are a flexible and efficient response to common problems. They do not need to be law to influence behaviour in the desired way.[56] As Weber famously identified, it is not only the law but also conventions, customs and mores that can order societies.[57] On this account, it does not really matter whether something is called law or not, nor which criteria one adopts to classify a norm. 'The universe of norms is larger than the universe of law.'[58] Soft law, for example, often has higher compliance rates than hard law, and courts of other fields tend to refer to non-binding instruments in any case.[59]

For constitutionalism, however, there are several reasons why the distinction between law and non-law provides useful guidance. Legal certainty, stability and predictability in international relations depend on the distinction *lege lata/lege ferenda.*[60] A state's legal accountability, according to the ILC Draft Articles on State Responsibility, relies on the dichotomy between legal and non-legal obligations. Turning away from a clear differentiation between law and non-law could carry the risk of losing a lingua franca in international legal scholarship.[61] More important, however, is the point that constitutionalism is concerned with legal and not social norms.[62] While other forms can also order society, only the law is backed up by state coercion, and through its legitimacy and normativity, it is always stronger than the other bases of action.[63] Recent developments can lead

---

[56] Dinah Shelton, 'Normative Hierarchy in International Law' (2006) 100 American Journal of International Law 291, 322.

[57] Max Weber, *Wirtschaft und Gesellschaft* (JCB Mohr (Paul Siebeck) 1922) 15.

[58] Joost Pauwelyn, 'Is It International Law or Not, and Does It Even Matter?' in Joost Pauwelyn, Ramses Wessel and Jan Wouters (eds), *Informal International Lawmaking* (OUP 2013) 125.

[59] ibid 160.

[60] Kassoti (n 52) 191.

[61] ibid 191–2.

[62] Bernhard Zangl and Michael Zürn, 'Make Law, Not War: Internationale und transnationale Verrechtlichung als Baustein für Global Governance' in Michael Zürn and Bernhard Zangl (eds), *Verrechtlichung—Baustein für Global Governance?* (Stiftung Entwicklung und Frieden 2004) 18.

[63] Weber (n 57) 17 ff; Andreas Maurer, 'Transnationales Recht' in Lars Viellechner (ed), *Verfassung ohne Staat* (Nomos 2019) 190.

to legalisation (*Verrechtlichung*) and even constitutionalisation, where superior rules are developed that decide how to resolve conflicts between legal systems (e.g., trade and environment) or between levels of governance (e.g., national/ international) and if these rules are themselves bound to general and public fundamental values.[64] Constitutionalisation is the link between socialisation and legalisation.[65]

For the research objective of this book, therefore, it is important to understand, from the viewpoint of societal constitutionalism, that non-state actors are not only forming social norms and behaviours, but that they also seek to create (constitutional) law that is binding, even against the will of states.

7.3.2.1 Teubner: Global Law without a State

Teubner argues that many ideas of constitutionalism are still state-centred by defining 'constitution' as both a liberation and restriction of state political action.[66] The oscillation between the institutionalisation of politics (*Politikverfassung*, political constitution) and the demand to constitute the (nation) society as a whole (*Gesellschaftsverfassung*, societal constitution) is already highly problematic in the nation-state context and cannot be simply transferred to the international plane[67] (Allott refers to these attempts as 'naïve constitutional extrapolationism'[68]). Rather, Teubner seeks to make the concept of 'constitution' fruitful for the international legal order by generalising it (disconnecting it from the state) and re-specifying it (adapting it to global conditions).[69]

Teubner expands on Luhmann's system theory and pioneering work on the law of societies[70] to describe how functional systems constitute themselves according to their inner logic (the economy, science, law and so on) as the result of a

---

[64] Zangl and Zürn (n 62) 17–8.

[65] ibid 18.

[66] Gunther Teubner, 'Globale Zivilverfassungen: Alternativen zur staatszentrierten Verfassungstheorie' (2003) 63 Zeitschrift für ausländisches öffentliches Recht und Völkerrecht 1, 5.

[67] ibid 5–6.

[68] Philip Allott, 'The Emerging Universal Legal System' (2001) 3 International Law Forum du droit international 12, 14.

[69] Gunther Teubner, *Constitutional Fragments: Societal Constitutionalism and Globalization* (OUP 2012) 132.

[70] Niklas Luhmann, *Soziale Systeme* (Suhrkamp 1984); Niklas Luhmann, *Das Recht der Gesellschaft* (Suhrkamp 1993); Niklas Luhmann, *Die Gesellschaft der Gesellschaft* (Suhrkamp 1997), translated into English: *Theory of Society, Vol. I* (2012) and *Theory of Society, Vol. II* (2013), Stanford University Press.

functional differentiation of society, which is not based on political decisions but complex evolutionary processes.[71] They are constituted as 'communication systems' which themselves define their elements—communications[72]—and reproduce them.[73] Different approaches to post-national constitutionalism focus on the role of relations, networks or private orders that are not embedded in a policy- or institution-centred order.[74] Teubner, therefore, argues in the sense of *ubi societas, ibi constitutio*[75] that wherever certain social formations in the world society develop (e.g., transnational regimes, functional systems, formal organisations), they have their own constitutions, which enter into competition with the constitutions of nation-states.[76] Thereby, he breaks free from the conviction that supranational constitutional law can only be created by states derived from their consent, given that there is no global (or even regional) constituent power.[77] Instead, he discusses the emergence of a multitude of civil constitutions, identifying that:

> [t]he constitution of world society is not realized exclusively in the representative institutions of international politics, nor can it take place in a global constitution that encompasses all areas of society, but it arises incrementally in the constitutionalisation of a multitude of autonomous subsystems of world society.[78]

---

[71] For the differences and further development of Luhmann's theory by Teubner, see Lars Viellechner, 'Verfassung ohne Staat. Eine Einführung' in Lars Viellechner (ed), *Verfassung ohne Staat* (Nomos 2019) 14 ff.

[72] Niklas Luhmann, *Ökologische Kommunikation (1986)* (4th edn, VS Verlag für Sozialwissenschaften 2004). Communication, in this sense, is not understood as an act of communication that 'transmits' information, but as an independent autopoietic operation that combines three different selections, namely information, communication and understanding, into an emergent entity to which further communications can connect.

[73] Klaus Kraemer, *Die soziale Konstitution der Umwelt* (VS Verlag für Sozialwissenschaften 2008) 91.

[74] Neil Walker, 'The Idea of Constitutional Pluralism' (2002) 65 Modern Law Review 317, 324.

[75] Latin: "Where there is society, there is a constitution."

[76] Teubner, 'Societal Constitutionalism: Nine Variations on a Theme by David Sciulli' (n 30) 313.

[77] Cf. Mattias Kumm, 'Constituent Power, Cosmopolitan Constitutionalism, and Post-Positivist Law' (2016) 14 International Journal of Constitutional Law 697, 702.

[78] Teubner, 'Globale Zivilverfassungen: Alternativen zur staatszentrierten Verfassungstheorie' (n 66) 6 (tr the author).

Constitutionalism occurs in both public and private law regimes. This has become apparent in the construction of the *lex mercatoria*,[79] the *lex sportiva*[80] or the *lex digitalis/lex cybertoria*,[81] which are not the result of state-centred decisions but processes inside these regimes. Transnational regimes, different to nation-states, usually focus on one certain social problem, for example, child labour, technical standards, food security, the protection of virgin forests or climate change, and its members are determined and willing to work on finding solutions for these problems. A regime exists where the people and organisations working together create self-organising, permanent and problem-oriented communities.[82] Such regimes have their own secondary rules on lawmaking, law recognition and legal sanctions.[83] The idea of regimes should not be reduced to public discourses preparing and criticising legislation, administration and adjudication of external state (based) authorities. Rather:

> Transnational regimes consist of the full range of regulatory forms—legislation, public discourse, administration, adjudication and constitution—that were invented in nation-states, and are now being adapted to the specific social nature of transnational regimes.[84]

It was Eugen Ehrlich, a law professor from the multi-cultural Bukovina, who wrote in 1936:

---

[79] See, for example, Hans-Joachim Mertens, 'Lex Mercatoria—A Self-Applying System Beyond National Law?' in Gunther Teubner (ed), *Global Law without a State* (Dartmouth Publishing 1997); Stephan W Schill, 'Lex Mercatoria', *Max Planck Encyclopedia of Public International Law [MPEPIL]* (OUP 2014); Gralf-Peter Calliess, 'Reflexive Transnational Law' (2016) 23 Zeitschrift für Rechtssoziologie 185, 196 ff.

[80] Robert CR Siekmann and Janwillem Soek (eds), *Lex Sportiva: What Is Sports Law?* (TMC Asser Press/Springer 2012); Ken Foster, 'Lex Sportiva and Lex Ludica: The Court Of Arbitration for Sport's Jurisprudence' (2005) 3 The Entertainment and Sports Law Journal 2.

[81] Myriam Senn, *Non-State Regulatory Regimes* (Springer 2011) 166–71; on the ICANN Domain Name Dispute Resolution Process, see Calliess (n 79) 201–6.

[82] Wil Martens, 'Demokratie für transnationale Regimes' in Kornelia Hahn and Andreas Langenohl (eds), *Kritische Öffentlichkeiten—Öffentlichkeiten in der Kritik* (Springer 2017) 28.

[83] Andreas Fischer-Lescano and Gunther Teubner, 'Regime-Collisions: The Vain Search for Legal Unity in the Fragmentation of Global Law' (2004) 25 Michigan Journal of International Law 999, 1015; the concept of primary and secondary rules goes back to HLA Hart, *The Concept of Law* (Clarendon Press 1961) 94ff.

[84] Wil Martens, 'Democracy for Transnational Regimes' in Bas Leijssenaar, Judith Martens and Evert Van der Zweerde (eds), *Futures ofDemocracy* (Wilde Raven Publishing 2014) 134.

> The center of gravity of legal development therefore from the time immemorial has not lain in the activity of the state, but in society itself, and must be sought there at the present time.[85]

Teubner takes this further with his 'Global Bukovina',[86] which resembles a fragmented world society that creates its own (fragmented) law. Various sectors of the world society are developing a global law on their own 'in relative insulation from the state, official international politics and international public law'.[87] The constitution of the global society, therefore, is not driven by international politics but rather occurs due to polycentric circles of globalisation in which different areas of life are breaking through their regional barriers and are constituting autonomous global sectors for themselves, for example, the ecological sector.[88] This leads to the constitution of a multitude of global villages, each with its own dynamics that cannot be influenced from outside[89] and with their own constitutions because 'not every polity has a written constitution, but every polity has constitutional norms'.[90]

Crucially, there is no structural coupling in the form of a 'constitution' between the system 'law' and the system 'politics'. This 'autonomous' law, therefore, does not (primarily) depend on political processes.[91] It will not be created in the political centre (e.g., negotiations between states or in the national parliament) or by courts authorised to create law emerging from conflict.[92] Instead, global constitutional law will mainly grow from the social peripheries—beyond the state or political institutions.[93] The periphery of the legal regimes or global villages is populated by 'political, economic, religious etc. organizational or spontaneous, collective or individual subjects of law', who, at the borders of the law, establish

---

[85] Eugen Ehrlich, *Fundamental Principles of the Sociology of Law* (Harvard University Press 1936) 390.

[86] Teubner, '"Global Bukowina": Legal Pluralism in the World Society' (n 31).

[87] ibid 3.

[88] Teubner, 'Globale Zivilverfassungen: Alternativen zur staatszentrierten Verfassungstheorie' (n 66) 11.

[89] ibid 11–2.

[90] Robert Uerpmann, 'Internationales Verfassungsrecht' (2001) 56 Juristenzeitung 565, 566 (tr the author).

[91] Teubner, '"Global Bukowina": Legal Pluralism in the World Society' (n 31) 7.

[92] Teubner, 'Globale Zivilverfassungen: Alternativen zur staatszentrierten Verfassungstheorie' (n 66) 14.

[93] Teubner, '"Global Bukowina": Legal Pluralism in the World Society' (n 31) 7; Teubner, 'Globale Zivilverfassungen: Alternativen zur staatszentrierten Verfassungstheorie' (n 66) 15.

close connections to other autonomous social sectors.[94] They are the members of the open society that offer their own interpretations on particular subject matters, and they can be quite influential. Due to the lack of global central instances, transnational law develops in the peripheries of the law through the structural couplings with other functional systems, for example, the economy, in the form of the *lex mercatoria*.[95] Besides the economy, science, culture, technology, health, military, transportation, tourism, sports and—with some delay—law, welfare and politics are examples of such autonomous global villages that operate freely from territorial borders and are constituting themselves worldwide.[96]

The globalisation of the legal system is driven by civil society, without the state.[97] Moreover, this constitutionalisation can establish binding norms even against the expressed will of states, as their legitimacy is not derived from state consent (in the form of an international treaty) but from the orientation towards the public interest.[98] New global law is influenced by both internal and external factors; however, the legal system is always involved as this process occurs both in the social sub-system and on the peripheries of the law.[99] Teubner identifies this phenomenon as 'a self-reproducing, worldwide legal discourse which closes its meaning boundaries by the use of the legal/illegal binary code and reproduces itself by processing a symbol of global (not national) validity'.[100] Essential in his understanding is a 'linguistic turn' from sanctions, rules and social control to the binary code legal/illegal.[101] This shift from function to code seeks to avoid

---

94 Fischer-Lescano and Teubner (n 83) 1012–3.

95 Teubner, '"Global Bukowina": Legal Pluralism in the World Society' (n 31) 3; see also Mertens (n 79).

96 Andreas Fischer-Lescano and Gunther Teubner, 'Fragmentierung des Weltrechts: Vernetzung globaler Regimes statt etatistischer Rechtseinheit' in Mathias Albert and Rudolf Stichweh (eds), *Weltstaat und Weltstaatlichkeit* (VS Verlag für Sozialwissenschaften 2007) 41; Teubner, 'Globale Zivilverfassungen: Alternativen zur staatszentrierten Verfassungstheorie' (n 66) 12–3. Teubner argues that these processes have barely touched the political: "world politics" (e.g. in UN institutions) are still "international politics" made by autonomous nation-states. Therefore, these institutions cannot constitute society as a whole.

97 Teubner, '"Global Bukowina": Legal Pluralism in the World Society' (n 31) 3.

98 Teubner, *Constitutional Fragments: Societal Constitutionalism and Globalization* (n 69) 50.

99 Teubner, 'Globale Zivilverfassungen: Alternativen zur staatszentrierten Verfassungstheorie' (n 66) 15.

100 Teubner, '"Global Bukowina": Legal Pluralism in the World Society' (n 31) 12.

101 ibid 12–4, 'Legal pluralism is then defined no longer as a set of conflicting social norms but as a multiplicity of diverse communicative processes in a given social field that observe social action under the binary code of legal/illegal. Purely economic calculations are

the problem many proponents of legal pluralism are struggling with: the distinction of economic and other social processes from law, as discussed above.[102] Teubner's approach refuses to label social conventions and moral norms as 'law', for they are not based on the legal/illegal code.[103] Furthermore, this approach can accommodate the various functions of law, including 'social control, conflict regulation, reaffirmation of expectations, coordination of behaviour or the disciplining of bodies and souls'.[104] For international constitutional law, this means that it can be identified, first according to its code 'constitutional/unconstitutional' (in the form of a hybrid binary meta-code) that is given precedence over the legal/illegal binary, which distinguishes it from ordinary law,[105] and second, the criterion 'global validity' that delineates global law from national law.[106] The so-emerging constitutional processes do not require a codified text[107] nor a constitutional moment.[108] Instead of coming into existence with a big bang, sectorial constitutions, such as the environmental,[109] are the product of slow, long-term evolutionary processes.[110]

---

excluded from it as are the sheer pressures of power and merely conventional or moral norms, transactional patterns or organizational routines' (14).

102 Cf. Tamanaha (n 48) 307.

103 Teubner, '"Global Bukowina": Legal Pluralism in the World Society' (n 31) 14.

104 ibid 14–5.

105 Teubner, *Constitutional Fragments: Societal Constitutionalism and Globalization* (n 69) 110.

106 Teubner, '"Global Bukowina": Legal Pluralism in the World Society' (n 31) 12.

107 Andreas Fischer-Lescano, 'Global Constitutional Struggles: Human Rights between Colère Publique and Colère Politique' in Wolfgang Kaleck and others (eds), *International Prosecution of Human Rights Crimes* (Springer 2007) 17: 'So the thesis seems justified: a constitution is not a text, but a form of structural coupling. A constitution emerges from the processes of law and politics, in the hypercircles of their operation.'

108 Anne Peters, 'Compensatory Constitutionalism: The Function and Potential of Fundamental International Norms and Structures' (2006) 19 Leiden Journal of International Law 579, 584. Peters describes that a characteristic of domestic codified constitutions is that 'they are made by a pouvoir constituant in a kind of constitutional big bang'; on the relevance of constitutional moments for IL, see Markus Kotzur, '„Constitutional Moments" in globaler Perspektive—Eine noch zeitgemäße völkerrechtliche Spurensuche?' in Ewald Grothe and Arthur Schlegelmilch (eds), *Constitutional Moments* (Berliner Wissenschafts-Verlag 2019).

109 Louis J Kotzé, 'Arguing Global Environmental Constitutionalism' (2012) 1 Transnational Environmental Law 199, 229; Louis J Kotzé, 'The Anthropocene's Global Environmental Constitutional Moment' (2015) 25 Yearbook of International Environmental Law 24.

110 Teubner, 'Globale Zivilverfassungen: Alternativen zur staatszentrierten Verfassungstheorie' (n 66) 15.

The concept of societal constitutionalism as such does not assess whether the creation of (constitutional) law by the members of the regimes is necessarily 'good' for (global) society. Rather, it takes the differentiation in functional systems that may develop their own law as a fact. But this differentiation has its problems: each system strives for self-maximisation and displays totalising (and self-destructive) tendencies.[111] The economic system, for example, according to its code, strives for the maximisation of profit. The clash of the economic system with environmental protection becomes visible here.[112] This raises the question of how the economic system (and every other sub-system) in a functionally differentiated society can assume responsibility for (the common interests of) society as a whole.[113] Here, one of the great achievements of state constitutionalism becomes visible: its ability to limit the totalisation of power by means of political power itself (especially through the use of human rights as protections against the state).[114] The nation-state has the advantage that it does not strictly follow the rationality criterion of a functional system; therefore, it does not have the tunnel vision of a functional regime that acts only according to its own logic. This makes it easier to orient it towards the public interests of a polity.[115]

Functional regimes, therefore, must limit their own maximising tendencies. Each sub-system needs to be open for its own constitutional moment—a decision

[111] Cf. Teubner, *Constitutional Fragments: Societal Constitutionalism and Globalization* (n 69) 10; Fischer-Lescano, 'Global Constitutional Struggles: Human Rights between Colère Publique and Colère Politique' (n 107) 27.

[112] ILC, 'Report of the Study Group of the International Law Commission (Finalized by Martti Koskenniemi) on "Fragmentation of International Law: Difficulties Arising from the Diversification and Expansion of International Law" (A/CN.4/L.682)' (2006) 34; Joanna Gomula, 'Environmental Disputes in the WTO' in Malgosia Fitzmaurice, David M Ong and Panos Merkouris (eds), *Research Handbook on International Environmental Law* (Edward Elgar Publishing 2010); Daniel C Esty, 'Bridging the Trade-Environment Divide' (2001) 15 Journal of Economic Perspectives 113.

[113] Leonie Breunung and Joachim Nocke, 'Environmental Officers: A Viable Concept for Ecological Management?' in Gunther Teubner, Lindsay Farmer and Declan Murphy (eds), *Environmental Law and Ecological Responsibility. The Concept and Practice of Self-Organization* (Wiley 1994) 269.

[114] Teubner, 'Societal Constitutionalism: Nine Variations on a Theme by David Sciulli' (n 30) 319; Christian Walter, 'Constitutionalizing (Inter)National Governance—Possibilities for and Limits to the Development of an International Constitutional Law' (2001) 44 German Yearbook of International Law 170, 193.

[115] Teubner, *Constitutional Fragments: Societal Constitutionalism and Globalization* (n 69) 156.

needs to be made 'between the total destruction of the energy [its growth-energies] and its self-limitation'.[116] The political and economic systems, for example, would need to constrain their inherent totalising tendencies to protect the interests of other regimes, such as the climate. This point will be discussed in greater detail below.[117]

Thus, the existence of a multitude of societal constitutions can institutionalise the completely different and incompatible rationalities of their respective systems (the economic, political, legal systems and so on) alongside one another, while at the same time, they can constrain their totalising tendencies with which they endanger each other.[118] The creation of new instruments in IEL, such as the new Global Pact for the Environment, demonstrates that constitutionalist ideas are being present to counter political and economic resistance against more comprehensive means to respond to the climate crisis.[119] Environmental protection is an emerging hybrid transnational regime that has begun to develop constitutional structures of its own.[120] Such hybrid regimes are simultaneously composed of public and private, and vertical and horizontal law.[121] So far, however, the climate regime is not comparable to comprehensive, integrated regimes such as the Forest Stewardship Council, the Marine Stewardship Council or the Global Good Agricultural Practices.[122] Rather, the 'regime complex for climate change' is 'a loosely coupled system of institutions; it has no clear hierarchy or core, yet many of its elements are linked in complementary ways'.[123] There are at least four cooperation problems among the members of the regime complex, including 1) the coordination of emission regulations, 2) compensation, including financial

---

[116] Gunther Teubner, 'A Constitutional Moment? The Logics of "Hitting the Bottom"' in Poul F Kjaer, Gunther Teubner and Alberto Febbrajo (eds), *The Financial Crisis in Constitutional Perspective: The Dark Side of Functional Differentiation* (Hart Publishing 2011) 12.

[117] See Section 7.4.2.

[118] Teubner, 'Societal Constitutionalism: Nine Variations on a Theme by David Sciulli' (n 30) 324.

[119] Louis J Kotzé, 'A Global Environmental Constitution for the Anthropocene's Climate Crisis' in Jordi Jaria-Manzano and Susana Borràs (eds), *Research Handbook on Global Climate Constitutionalism* (Edward Elgar Publishing 2019) 73.

[120] Teubner, 'Societal Constitutionalism: Nine Variations on a Theme by David Sciulli' (n 30) 315; referring to Kotzé, 'Arguing Global Environmental Constitutionalism' (n 109).

[121] Chris Thornhill, 'Constitutional Law from the Perspective of Power: A Response to Gunther Teubner' (2011) 20 Social and Legal Studies 244, 244.

[122] Martens (n 82) 29.

[123] Robert O Keohane and David G Victor, 'The Regime Complex for Climate Change' (2011) 9 Perspectives on Politics 7, 9.

aid, 3) the coordinating efforts (how to address the problem, including aspects of adaptation and geoengineering) and 4) the coordination of common scientific assessments to increase the public knowledge about climate change.[124]

Thus, it would be difficult for a single institution to address all these points comprehensively, especially since the members' motifs to do something against climate change and the strategies they employ are not congruent. The weaknesses of IEL are well known.[125] Integrated 'core treaties' such as the UNFCCC/Paris Agreement are unlikely to succeed when interests differ widely and there is high uncertainty about which measures states are willing and able to implement to address the climate crisis.[126] A more promising idea, therefore, could be the inclusion of ecological considerations into other existing fields of law by way of interpretation.[127] One of the most prominent examples of ecological considerations that have 'eaten' their way in is the area of human rights law.[128] The focus on human rights is quite useful for bringing climate and environmental matters to the forefront. Fundamental rights support the inclusion of the whole population in the relevant social sphere, but they also have constraining functions on functional

---

124 ibid 13.

125 Rakhyun E Kim and Klaus Bosselmann, 'International Environmental Law in the Anthropocene: Towards a Purposive System of Multilateral Environmental Agreements' (2013) 2 Transnational Environmental Law 285, 286.

126 Keohane and Victor (n 123) 14–5.

127 Luhmann, *Ökologische Kommunikation (1986)* (n 72) 131.

128 Ground-breaking: "Man has the fundamental right to freedom, equality and adequate conditions of life, in an environment of a quality that permits a life of dignity and well-being, and he bears a solemn responsibility to protect and improve the environment for present and future generations." (Principle 1 UN Conference on the Human Environment, 'Stockholm Declaration of the United Nations Conference on the Human Environment' ['Stockholm Declaration']), see also, Alan Boyle, 'Environment and Human Rights', *Max Planck Encyclopedia of Public International Law* (OUP 2009) and the reports of the Special Rapporteur on Human Rights and the Environment on this issue, inter alia, UN Special Rapporteur on Human Rights and the Environment John H. Knox, 'Human Rights Obligations Relating to the Enjoyment of a Safe, Clean, Healthy and Sustainable Environment (A/HRC/31/52)' (2016); UN Special Rapporteur John H. Knox, 'Framework Principles on Human Rights and the Environment—Report of the Special Rapporteur on the Issue of Human Rights Obligations Relating to the Enjoyment of a Safe, Clean, Healthy and Sustainable Environment (A/HRC/37/5)' (2018); UN Special Rapporteur on Human Rights and the Environment David Boyd, 'Special Report on Human Rights Obligations Relating to the Enjoyment of a Safe, Clean, Healthy and Sustainable Environment (A/74/161)' (2019).

systems. Fundamental rights 'serve to secure boundaries, giving individuals and institutions guarantees of autonomy against expansionist tendencies'.[129]

The next sub-section, thus, analyses Fischer-Lescano's theory on the global constitution. Fischer-Lescano discusses, from a societal constitutionalist perspective, the emergence and development of a human right by global civil society. Against this work's focus on non-state actors as international climate lawmakers, it provides an innovative approach that could help to understand how human rights are created and charged with meaning and by whom.

7.3.2.2 Fischer-Lescano: A global constitution

Fischer-Lescano discusses how civil society actors can participate in making law in an autopoietic, politically supported 'world law'. His work draws intensely on the ideas of Luhmann and Teubner to explain the emergence of a 'global constitution' in world law as a structural coupling of the functionally differentiated global legal and the global political system into one decision-making unit: the international community.[130] This world law can be constituted by both politically supported actors (e.g., governments) and members of civil society. An important part of this theory is concerned with the making of human rights law by non-state actors. This could potentially serve as an interesting starting point for the discussion on the creation of rights such as the 'right to a stable climate', a 'right to future' or 'an ecological existence minimum', and other versions of environmental rights (for future generations) as proposed by social movements, NGOs and individuals, in cases such as *Juliana v the United States* or the GFCC's order.[131]

IL is still understood in the sense of traditional *jus gentium*—law between and made by states. Fischer-Lescano describes this as *colère politique*.[132] However, even if not formally vested with lawmaking powers, civil society possesses 'normative power'.[133] The *colère publique*—a term coined by Durkheim that could be translated to 'public temper'[134]—refers to what could be described as the

[129] Teubner, *Constitutional Fragments: Societal Constitutionalism and Globalization* (n 69) 134.

[130] Andreas Fischer-Lescano, 'Die Emergenz der Globalverfassung' (2003) 63 Zeitschrift für ausländisches öffentliches Recht und Völkerrecht 717, 759.

[131] See Sections 4.3 above and 9.3.1 below.

[132] Andreas Fischer-Lescano, *Globalverfassung—Die Geltungsbegründung der Menschenrechte* (Velbrück 2005) 119.

[133] ibid 271.

[134] Emile Durkheim, *The Division of Labor in Society (1933)* (4th edn, The Macmillan Company 1960) 102.

'conscience of the world' or sentiments that are common to everybody.[135] It describes normative expectations that are formed through the activities of actors other than states, for example, NGOs and mass media.[136] It means lawmaking through scandalisation in the face of human rights violations such as slavery or torture.[137]

Scandalisation can trigger legal instauration processes by global civil society: the creation of the so-called *lex humana*.[138] This law can be formulated in organised or spontaneous ways by civil society actors in cooperation with the media and become 'global customary law' in a postmodern *jus gentium*.[139] Rules belonging to the *lex humana* are valid even if they are not created according to the traditional legal sources theory (Article 38 ICJ Statute) or by IL subjects.[140] The question of whether the *colère publique* can set law or whether such rules are valid (according to the binary code valid/void) depends on the communication process about law itself. This methodological approach, therefore, does not seek to identify the sources of law (Why is the law valid?—'Validity can only be explained by validity'[141]) and, therefore, also does not rely on the Article 38 ICJ Statute but asks 'How are normative—and thus counterfactual—legal expectations changing in society?'[142] Law is not identical to the politically supported legal systems but contains normative expectations regardless of origin.[143] Therefore, beside the *jus gentium* exists another law-production operation: 'the political instauration process of the lex humana, world society's customary law, Eugen Ehrlich's "living law"'.[144] The *colère publique mondiale* can establish the

---

[135] ibid 102–03.

[136] Fischer-Lescano, 'Global Constitutional Struggles: Human Rights between Colère Publique and Colère Politique' (n 107) 20.

[137] Fischer-Lescano, 'Die Emergenz der Globalverfassung' (n 130) 732.

[138] Fischer-Lescano, 'Global Constitutional Struggles: Human Rights between Colère Publique and Colère Politique' (n 107) 20 Fischer-Lescano clarifies that the lex humana "does not refer to scholastic concepts of lex aeterna/lex naturalis/lex humana, but points to 'global law without a state,' and to legal pluralistic sources of law in civil society."

[139] Fischer-Lescano, 'Die Emergenz der Globalverfassung' (n 130) 751.

[140] Fischer-Lescano, *Globalverfassung—Die Geltungsbegründung der Menschenrechte* (n 132) 118.

[141] ibid 119, German: 'Geltung ist nur mit Geltung begründbar' (tr the author).

[142] ibid 118.

[143] ibid.

[144] ibid 119 (tr the author).

lex humana as law without it having to be recognised as law by 'official' IL or its subjects.[145]

Importantly, at the heart of the pluralistic global civil society is conflict and contestation instead of consensus; the *colère publique* is not harmonious, and there are no 'global core values'.[146] Rather, human rights law is the result of long processes that depend on operations in the centre or periphery of the global communication system 'law' and result in a difference between the 'before' and 'after'.[147] This difference changes the human rights law of world society. Not every claim or mere legal assertion can have such an effect, and the factuality of a global feeling of injustice cannot itself lead to the creation of law.[148] The valid law only changes if normative expectations are changing operationally.[149] Consequently, the protest needs to reach the level of a *colère publique mondiale:* global law can only be created by a *global colère publique.* An assumed global consensus is required; a regional one (Asian, European, etc.) is not sufficient.[150] This *colère publique mondiale* is what distinguishes a mere appellate claim from a normative expectation in which the 'symbol of validity' (*Geltungssymbol*) is processed.[151] This is decisive for whether a claim can become part of the *lex humana.*[152] It depends on the intensity of the scandal, the quantity and quality of the actors involved and the reporting by the media.[153] This leads to a '[g]lobal law [that] finds itself caught between civil society's colère publique and a colère politique of the states' world'.[154]

The question then arises of how such laws made by the *colère publique* can become 'law' in the *colère politique*—in the *jus gentium.*

---

[145] ibid 122.

[146] Fischer-Lescano, 'Die Emergenz der Globalverfassung' (n 130) 732.

[147] Fischer-Lescano, *Globalverfassung—Die Geltungsbegründung der Menschenrechte* (n 132) 68.

[148] Andreas Fischer-Lescano, 'Globalverfassung: Los Desaparecidos und das Paradox der Menschenrechte' (2002) 23 Zeitschrift für Rechtssoziologie 217, 225.

[149] Fischer-Lescano, *Globalverfassung—Die Geltungsbegründung der Menschenrechte* (n 132) 118.

[150] ibid 96.

[151] ibid 271.

[152] Fischer-Lescano, 'Globalverfassung: Los Desaparecidos und das Paradox der Menschenrechte' (n 148) 228.

[153] ibid.

[154] Fischer-Lescano, 'Global Constitutional Struggles: Human Rights between Colère Publique and Colère Politique' (n 107) 24.

Article 38 ICJ Statute mentions the sources of IL. These are international treaties, customary law, general IL principles and—as subsidiary means—the 'judicial decisions and the teachings of the most highly qualified publicists of the various nations'.[155] However, it has been identified that the listed sources are not exhaustive, and that Article 38 was never meant to be a quasi-constitutional provision on lawmaking in the global community.[156] Fischer-Lescano argues that the *lex humana* can become part of 'traditional' IL by the detour of the Martens clause, which by now has become part of customary law.[157] The Martens clause, introduced to the preamble of the 1899 Hague Convention II on the Laws and Customs of War on Land and named after Russian delegate Fyodor Fyodorovich Martens, states:

> Until a more complete code of the laws of war is issued, the High Contracting Parties think it right to declare that in cases not included in the Regulations adopted by them, populations and belligerents remain under the protection and empire of the principles of international law, as they result from the *usages established between civilized nations, from the laws of humanity and the requirements of the public conscience.*[158]

While the clause belongs to international humanitarian law, today, scholars discuss its impact and importance on the sources of IL in general. Some argue that the inclusion of 'usages established between civilized nations, from the laws of humanity and the requirements of the public conscience' paves the way for including more sources than those postulated by Article 38 ICJ Statute.[159] The Martens clause and its elements form values that underpin the whole of IL and should inform a decision on how to deal with identified legal gaps. Thus, IL rules today must be understood as the work of the elements of the Martens clause 'not as if the individual norms were to be derived logically from them, but as if they

---

[155] Article 38 of the Statute of the International Court of Justice.

[156] Klabbers (n 50) 87, 89.

[157] Fischer-Lescano, *Globalverfassung—Die Geltungsbegründung der Menschenrechte* (n 132) 121, quoting ICTY, The Proescutor v Zoran Kupreskic, (IT-95-16): 'More specifically, recourse might be had to the celebrated Martens Clause which, in the authoritative view of the International Court of Justice, has by now become part of customary international law.'

[158] Emphasis added.

[159] Antonio Cassese, 'The Martens Clause: Half a Loaf or Simply Pie in the Sky?' (2018) 11 The Development and Principles of International Humanitarian Law 373, 189–92, discussing the various interpretations of the clause propounded in legal literature, in particular footnote 5.

were the expression of humanity, civilization and conscience. It follows from this that a transformation of these three elements transforms law'.[160]

In this sense, the '*colère publique* sets law, even without international law accepting it',[161] which, however, has to be taken into account via the Martens clause by postmodern *jus gentium,* even if such world social law is not produced according to the norm-setting norms postulated in Article 38 ICJ Statute. The Martens clause, then, is an example of how civil society works as a catalyst for the formation of IL in relation to all traditional legal sources.[162]

7.3.3 Who Acts?

According to Teubner, transnational regimes do not have one demos, but three *demoi*: members, rule addressees and affected outsiders. They form the three action arenas of the regime: its centre, where members prepare, produce and implement the regime rules; the regime periphery, which consists of interactions of the centre with its constituencies; and the group of outsiders that are affected negatively by the regime's decisions.[163] Belonging to one of these groups depends less on the individual than on their actions. They can fluctuate between these categories ('fuzzy citizenship').[164]

Not only can the centre and the periphery have considerable influence on a regime, but so can outsiders. This group is composed of actors who are not part of a regime but are affected negatively by its decisions.[165] Social movements fall into this category. Protest groups around the world—such as the Italian *beni comuni* movement—act from below as oppositional forces to the process of economic constitutionalism imposed by globalisation from above.[166] Such outsiders

---

160 Friedrich Münch, 'Die Martenssche Klausel und die Grundlagen des Völkerrechts' (1976) 36 Zeitschrift für ausländisches öffentliches Recht und Völkerrecht 347, 371 (tr the author).

161 Fischer-Lescano, *Globalverfassung—Die Geltungsbegründung der Menschenrechte* (n 132) 122 (tr the author).

162 Peters, 'Dual Democracy' (n 55) 315.

163 Gunther Teubner, 'Quod Omnes Tangit: Transnational Constitutions without Democracy?' (2018) 45 Journal of Law and Society S5, S17.

164 ibid.

165 ibid S17–9.

166 Saki Bailey and Ugo Mattei, 'Social Movements as Constituent Power: The Italian Struggle for the Commons' (2013) 20 Indiana Journal of Global Legal Studies 965, 986, 1012.

can appear as 'irritants' in the broader *pouvoir constitué* of global governance,[167] and rather than re-articulating, they seek to refuse the forces of neoliberalism. Contestation, not foundation, is at their centre.[168] These movements form an essential part of 'constitutionalism from below'.[169] They are an important part of the open society because they formulate their interpretations with which they want to be heard and change the status quo.

The issue of outsiders can also be observed in relation to the climate. Decisions made in states that emit high amounts of GHGs can affect the populations in far-away countries.[170] However, Luhmann explains that the imperative of consideration in the form of a reciprocal consensus (as you to me, so I to you) is an exclusively societal concept and does not work in the context of a global environment where our activities have consequences for people living far away. All that can be achieved in the global society is a 'negative' consensus: that damages should be kept away.[171] However, he is sceptical that individuals can live according to this negative consensus and concludes that:

> Under these circumstances, the exhortation of political activity, social solidarity, and just problem-solving remain as abstract as it is inconsequential. A legal categorization of commandments of consideration for the environment will only be able to introduce them into the law, if at all, with other terms. Legal-dogmatic learning processes are slow and take decades, if not centuries, to condense case experiences into terms and maxims and to reorganize the law accordingly.[172]

Less radical contestation, which, at the same time, is more effective, is to be expected by the second group: the norm addressees in the spontaneous sectors of the regime. Amicus curiae and group action in court proceedings fall under this category.[173] Their interests need to be articulated by associations of directly affected persons and by experts or organisations acting on behalf of

[167] Nico Krisch, 'Pouvoir Constituant and Pouvoir Irritant in the Postnational Order' (2016) 14 International Journal of Constitutional Law 657, 673.

[168] ibid 676.

[169] Gavin W Anderson, 'Societal Constitutionalism, Social Movements, and Constitutionalism from Below' (2013) 20 Indiana Journal of Global Legal Studies 881.

[170] Eyal Benvenisti, 'Sovereigns As Trustees of Humanity: On the Accountability of States To Foreign Stakeholders' (2013) 107 The American Journal of International Law 295, 298.

[171] Luhmann, *Ökologische Kommunikation (1986)* (n 72) 154; see also Fischer-Lescano and Teubner (n 96) 54.

[172] Luhmann, *Ökologische Kommunikation (1986)* (n 72) 146 (tr the author).

[173] Teubner, 'Quod Omnes Tangit: Transnational Constitutions without Democracy?' (n 163) S20.

those affected.[174] In this sense, Luhmann argues that the courts would need to be called upon to initiate legal-dogmatic learning processes to introduce environmental protection. In 1986, he saw little movement in this regard.[175] Today, CCL has become a phenomenon that has gained momentum around the world. How strategic litigation can introduce environmental concerns to other areas of law will be analysed in Chapter 9.

The (final) decision on legal validity, the decision of whether the symbol of validity is transferred and whether it is a norm-projection or a norm, can only be made in the centres of the legal system, namely the courts[176] responsible for the management of paradoxes.[177] The court decides in cases of the divergent norm-setting between the *colère politique* and the *colère publique* whether they seek to establish new law or confirm the old one.[178] The centre of the system 'law' is composed of politically supported legal bodies, the *global remedies*: international courts, human rights tribunals and domestic courts.[179] These courts are central to NGO action, especially for strategic litigation.

The periphery includes all other non-judicial working areas of the legal system and is also the contact zone to the other social functional areas.[180] It protects the centre of the legal system by deciding which irritations it brings into legal form and, therefore, which it allows to pass through to the political centre and which it does not. Which cases are brought to court in the first place depends on the political environment—whether public opinion is supportive or divided.[181]

However, '[i]t would be an inadmissible reduction to view the activities of civil society groups solely in terms of mobilizing the world public'.[182] This may be accurate for the first phase of their activity, but a second phase is characterised by the effort that characterises all protest movements and serves as proof

---

174 Martens (n 84) 130; Teubner, 'Quod Omnes Tangit: Transnational Constitutions without Democracy?' (n 163) S20.

175 Luhmann, *Ökologische Kommunikation (1986)* (n 72) 146.

176 Fischer-Lescano, 'Die Emergenz der Globalverfassung' (n 130) 760.

177 Fischer-Lescano, *Globalverfassung—Die Geltungsbegründung der Menschenrechte* (n 132) 61.

178 ibid 127–8.

179 Fischer-Lescano, 'Die Emergenz der Globalverfassung' (n 130) 739.

180 Fischer-Lescano, 'Globalverfassung: Los Desaparecidos und das Paradox der Menschenrechte' (n 148) 231–2.

181 Jacqueline Peel and Hari M Osofsky, *Climate Change Litigation: Regulatory Pathways to Cleaner Energy* (CUP 2015) 223.

182 Fischer-Lescano, 'Globalverfassung: Los Desaparecidos und das Paradox der Menschenrechte' (n 148) 233 (tr the author).

of the differentiation between the centre and the periphery.[183] 'The periphery protests, but not against itself. The center is expected to listen and take the protest into account.'[184] The constitutional complaints against data retention filed by over 35 000 citizens before the GFCC could be read in this sense: as a mass petition.[185] Illustrative of this point are also the *madres* (mothers) of the *desaparecidos* (disappeared persons) who protested wearing white veils during the Argentinian dictatorship against the enforced disappearance of their children, spouses and relatives. The Argentinian practice provoked a global outcry from civil society. Moreover, it was addressed and condemned by several courts in, inter alia, Spain, Sweden, Germany, France and the U.S.[186] The *madres*, thus, created a human right by generating (or at least effectively confirming[187]) the norm 'disappearance is injustice' in world law and by communicating a decision about whether to tolerate or not (tolerance/*colère*) such practice to the world within the framework of a social procedure mediated by the media and NGOs.[188]

Through the spread of information, particularly due to technological developments such as the internet, email and social media,[189] and raising awareness, NGOs can create 'an aura of hostility'.[190] The distinction between soft law and hard law is blurred in these cases; rather, the conduct of states is assessed in terms of the binary code of legal/illegal, regardless of whether any IL obligations have been breached, in a communicative process activated by NGOs.[191] These communicative processes of NGOs, interest groups and networks operating in

---

183 ibid.

184 Niklas Luhmann, *Theory of Society (Vol. 2)* (Stanford University Press 2013) 157.

185 Uwe Volkmann, 'Der Aufstieg der Verfassung: Beobachtungen zum grundlegenden Wandel des Verfassungsbegriffs' in Thomas Vesting and Stefan Korioth (eds), *Der Eigenwert des Verfassungsrechts* (Mohr Siebeck 2011) 23.

186 Hauke Brunkhorst, 'Die Legitimationskrise der Weltgesellschaft. Global Rule of Law, Global Constitutionalism und Weltstaatlichkeit' in Mathias Albert and Rudolf Stichweh (eds), *Weltstaat und Weltstaatlichkeit* (VS Verlag für Sozialwissenschaften 2007) 89.

187 The Nuremberg Tribunal had already found "that the Nazi practice of enforced disappearance constituted a crime against humanity", see Darryl Robinson, 'Defining "Crimes Against Humanity" at the Rome Conference' (1999) 93 American Journal of International Law 43, 56, footnote 76; see Fischer-Lescano, 'Globalverfassung: Los Desaparecidos und das Paradox der Menschenrechte' (n 148) 228.

188 Fischer-Lescano, 'Globalverfassung: Los Desaparecidos und das Paradox der Menschenrechte' (n 148) 228.

189 Bianchi (n 18) 193.

190 ibid 191.

191 ibid.

civil society can lead to alterations in the environment in which state actors operate and gradually change human rights practices and introduce new modalities to IL.[192] Similarly, Judge van den Wyngaert stated in her dissenting opinion in the Arrest Warrant case:

> Advocacy organizations [...] have taken clear positions on the subject of international accountability. This may be seen as the opinion of civil society, an opinion that cannot be completely discounted in the formation of customary international law today.[193]

The massive influence of articulations of (global) civil society can be observed by taking a closer look at cases that seem 'hopeless'.[194] The Guantanamo litigation, for example, 'started as a lonely protest', was rejected by the lower courts and did not receive much support from the legal community. However, due to the publicity and global public outcry, the Supreme Court took the case seriously and ruled for the plaintiffs. More important than the victory in the Supreme Court was the fundamental lesson drawn from the 'decision of a dedicated group of lawyers to litigate the case in order to protest the administration's policy despite the seemingly difficult odds of success'.[195] It becomes clear that public opinion represents political potentials that can be used by the courts (and by parliaments and administrative agencies). It is important to note, however, that actors of civil society can only acquire influence but not political power.[196] As already outlined in Chapter 6, the transformation from political influence or political potentials into political power can only happen through institutionalised procedures: either by democratically elected assemblies or by the courts that decide political cases.[197] This is what motivates activists to pursue their climate goals through strategic litigation which gives institutional authority to their interpretations.

From this, it follows that lawmaking processes not only occur in the political centre of the system law but also in the strong peripheries where the world civil society formulates its normative expectations. NGOs can set law by consequently appealing to the validity of certain human rights, even where no positive

---

[192] ibid 194.

[193] Dissenting Opinion of Judge van den Wyngaert in *Arrest Warrant of 1 April 2000 (Democratic Republic of the Congo v. Belgium)*, Judgment, I.C.J. Reports 2002, 3, 154–5.

[194] Jules Lobel, 'Courts as Forums for Protest' (2004) 52 UCLA Law Review 477, 560.

[195] ibid.

[196] Jürgen Habermas, *Between Facts and Norms: Contributions to a Discourse Theory of Law and Democracy* (Polity Press 1996) 364.

[197] ibid 283.

obligations exist (e.g., in the form of customary law or international treaties).[198] In this sense, the protest of the *madres* can be understood as the initiation of a process that led to the creation of a new human right to be free from enforced disappearance, enshrined in the 2006 International Convention for the Protection of All Persons from Enforced Disappearance.[199]

However, assuming that everybody could engage in international constitution-making raises some questions. If everybody was a constitutional interpreter—and as such, a potential lawmaker—how is it possible to maintain a certain unity of IL? The international legal order already struggles with fragmentation.[200] More actors involved in international constitutional interpretation means more interpretations, and more interpretations signify greater conflict potential, thereby, a greater risk of destabilising the international legal order. The inclusion of more actors could also lead to a lack of transparency.[201]

Häberle's theory of the open society of constitutional interpreters faces similar points of critique. The assumption that everybody interprets the constitution all the time would lead to the emergence of a multitude of interpreters and interpretations and, consequently, endanger constitutional unity.[202] Such an approach could increase the risk of a fragmented constitution.[203] The search for a compromise or consensus on a single interpretation might become increasingly difficult. However, the following section will show that this fear of fragmentation may be unnecessary. Instead, it is argued that the differentiation into highly specific regimes that have greater expertise in regulating specific issues is the result of a continuous proliferation of IL. The resolution of conflicts between competing interests—for example, between the environment and international trade—need not be resolved by a single authority or a single hierarchical international legal order. Instead, the following section illustrates that regimes can consider the interests of other regimes and thereby limit their own maximising tendencies.

---

198 Fischer-Lescano, 'Globalverfassung: Los Desaparecidos und das Paradox der Menschenrechte' (n 148) 227.

199 UN General Assembly, International Convention for the Protection of All Persons from Enforced Disappearance, 20 December 2006, adopted by General Assembly Resolution 61/177 on 12 January 2007, also Peters, 'Dual Democracy' (n 55) 315.

200 ILC (n 112) 11.

201 Clemens Mattheis, *Die Konstitutionalisierung des Völkerrechts aus systemtheoretischer Sichtweise* (Springer 2018) 350.

202 Peter Häberle, '"The Open Society of Constitutional Interpreters"—A Contribution to a Pluralistic and "Procedural" Constitutional Interpretation (1975)' in Markus Kotzur (ed), *Peter Häberle on Constitutional Theory* (Nomos/Hart 2018) 140.

203 ibid.

Consequently, a multitude of constitutional orders coexist at different levels—there are local, national and global constitutions, which may be private, public or hybrid in nature. Such constitutional pluralism is more realistic and better suited to addressing the challenges of the twenty-first century than 'world order constitutionalism' for the whole of IL.

7.4 Endangered Constitutional Unity? Constitutional Pluralism in a Fragmented International Legal Order

Unity is seen as such an important aspect of national constitutions because they claim to subject all state activity to their regulatory demands.[204] The state constitution possesses a holistic quality. The authority and meaning of the various parts are understood and treated as dependent on the integrity of the whole constitution.[205] It is this interwovenness that gives constitutions their overall texture and, therefore, is a defining characteristic of modern state constitutions.[206] The constitutional norms are the 'rules of the game' that all involved actors share. Even where they disagree on the 'meaning-in-use' of a particular constitutional norm, they consent to the norm as such.[207] Through this 'latent' consensus, constitutional integration creates legitimacy because the addressees perceive constitutional rules as meaningful.[208] Since such normative consensus in the international legal order is absent, the emerging transnational law will essentially be of a contested nature.[209]

Until the end of the nineteenth century, IL was concerned with the limits of state jurisdiction and how to conduct diplomatic relations. Since the end of the Second World War, it has expanded in scope and today covers more areas than

[204] Teubner, 'Societal Constitutionalism: Nine Variations on a Theme by David Sciulli' (n 30) 329.

[205] Neil Walker, 'Beyond the Holistic Constitution?' in Petra Dobner and Martin Loughlin (eds), *The Twilight of Constitutionalism?* (OUP 2010) 297–8.

[206] ibid 298.

[207] Stefan Oeter, 'Regime Collisions from a Perspective of Global Constitutionalism' in Kerstin Blome and others (eds), *Contested Regime Collisions. Norm Fragmentation in World Society* (CUP 2016) 29–30.

[208] Roland Lhotta and Sabrina Zucca-Soest, 'Legitimation und Integration durch Verfassung in einem Mehrebenensystem' in Christoph Hönninge, Sascha Kneip and Astrid Lorenz (eds), *Verfassungswandel im Mehrebenensystem* (VS Verlag für Sozialwissenschaften 2011) 368.

[209] Oeter (n 207) 30.

ever, inter alia, those that were formerly dealt with by international politics.[210] This expansion has led to the emergence of functional areas such as environmental law, trade law, European law or the law of the seas.[211] Highly specialised 'boxes' are the response to new technical and functional progress.[212]

Fragmentation generally occurs in terms of functional specialisation of whole areas that are composed of specific rules and principles, for example, principles of IEL, and differ from both the principles or rules of other functional areas and from what general IL provides for analogous situations.[213] Lawyers and other keyholders of epistemic communities[214] and interpretive communities[215] operating in such systems claim priority when issues arise that are concerned with their particular regime.[216] The common denominator of special regimes can be an institution (e.g., the WTO), common framework treaties (e.g., the UNFCCC) or a shared ethos (e.g., human dignity in human rights law).[217]

These specific regimes are considered forms of *lex specialis*.[218] The commentary to Article 55 of the ILC Draft Articles on State Responsibility mentions both

---

[210] Mario Prost, *The Concept of Unity in Public International Law* (Hart Publishing 2012) 4.

[211] ILC (n 112) 11.

[212] ibid 14.

[213] ibid 68. 'What once appeared to be governed by "general international law" has become the field of operation for such specialist systems as "trade law", "human rights law", "environmental law", "law of the sea", "European law" and even such exotic and highly specialized knowledges as "investment law" or "international refugee law" etc.—each possessing their own principles and institutions' (11).

[214] See e.g. Peter M Haas, 'Epistemic Communities and International Environmental Law', *Epistemic Communities, Constructivism, and International Environmental Politics* (Routledge 2015).

[215] Seminal: Ian Johnstone, 'Treaty Interpretation: The Authority of Interpretive Communities' (1990) 12 Michigan Journal of International Law 371; Ian Johnstone, 'The Power of Interpretive Communities' in Michael Barnett and Raymond Duval (eds), *Power in Global Governance* (CUP 2005).

[216] ILC (n 112) 68.

[217] Michael Waibel, 'Interpretive Communites in International Law' in Andrea Bianchi, Daniel Peat and Matthew Windsor (eds), *Interpretation in International Law* (OUP 2015) 148.

[218] Commentary to Article 55 (*lex specialis*) of the ILC Draft Articles on Responsibility of States for Internationally Wrongful Acts, Report of the International Law Commission on the work of its 35th session, A/56/10, 140.

'weaker' and 'stronger' forms of specialisation.[219] The stronger forms of specialisation include the so-called self-contained regimes, a term coined by the Permanent Court of International Justice in the *S.S. Wimbledon* case in 1923.[220] Understandings of what constitutes a self-contained regime vary, but in a narrower sense, it is required that these regimes create not only highly specialised primary norms but also their own secondary rules as understood by Hart (rules of recognition, change and adjudication).[221] Instead of falling back to general IL, these systems produce their own norms on lawmaking, law recognition and legal sanctions.[222] A self-contained regime, then, is 'a certain category of subsystems, namely those embracing, in principle, a full (exhaustive and definite) set of secondary rules'.[223]

While some scholars argue that fragmentation is just a sign of maturity and a normal step in the evolution of a complex system, most scholars fear that fragmentation is a threat to the unity of IL. Whether someone accepts or rejects fragmentation is also important for the debate on global constitutionalism. For those who fear fragmentation, constitutionalism is supposed to establish international legal unity and coherence through a hierarchy of norms.[224] For those who, on the other side, argue that fragmentation is a natural phenomenon of a system that has evolved over the decades and is here to stay, rather than searching in vain for legal unity, constitutionalism is supposed to define the constitutional norms of each (self-contained) regime.[225] Roughly speaking, these strands of constitutionalism can be classified as 'world order constitutionalism' and 'sectoral constitutionalism'.[226] World constitutionalism aims to constitutionalise the

---

[219] Malgosia Fitzmaurice, 'Responsibility and Climate Change' (2010) 53 German Yearbook of International Law 89, 131.

[220] Permanent Court of International Justice, *S.S. Wimbledon (U.K. v. Japan)*, 1923 P.C.I.J. (ser. A) No. 1 (Aug. 17), para 32.

[221] Hart (n 83) 91 ff (94 ff); Lars Viellechner, 'Responsive Legal Pluralism: The Emergence of Transnational Conflicts Law' (2015) 6 Transnational Legal Theory 312, 320.

[222] Bruno Simma, 'Self-Contained Regimes' (1985) 16 Netherlands Yearbook of International Law 111; Fischer-Lescano and Teubner (n 83) 1015.

[223] Simma (n 222) 117.

[224] Karolina Milewicz, 'Emerging Patterns of Global Constitutionalization: Toward a Conceptual Framework' (2014) 16 Indiana Journal of Global Legal Studies 413, 424, see also Stefan Kadelbach and Thomas Kleinlein, 'International Law—A Constitution for Mankind?' (2007) 50 German Yearbook of International Law 2.

[225] Fischer-Lescano and Teubner (n 83).

[226] Aoife O'Donoghue, *Constitutionalism in Global Constitutionalisation* (CUP 2014) 141.

whole of IL, or, at least, its crucial norms and principles should achieve constitutional status to create a sophisticated legal system.[227] Therefore, constitutionalism necessarily needs to be perceived as a higher form of IL to 'fulfil its purpose as a normative regulator of the governance order'.[228] For sectorial constitutionalism, which argues that different regimes (*lex mercatoria, lex digitalis* and so on) can be constitutionalised, this is not necessary. Each regime develops its own constitutional rules at its own speed.[229]

Against the latter, it has been argued that if lawyers and scholars are exclusively operating and researching in their fields, they may lose sight of the whole. The specialisation of the different regimes is accompanied by epistemological 'tunnel vision'.[230] The large number of international juridical bodies operating without a hierarchical order—most of them are closely coupled with their own specialised regimes—results in the unsatisfying consequence of one treaty regime frustrating the goal of another, for example, the proliferation of free trade may contradict the ultimate goal of the UNFCCC to curtail GHG emissions.[231] Constitutionalisation of the whole of IL, conversely, could bestow the international legal order with greater predictability and legal certainty for those subject to the rules.[232] The ILC Report on the Fragmentation of International Law has outlined different interpretation tools that could help to prevent fragmentation and resolve conflicts, including interpretative maxims and conflict-solution techniques such as *lex posterior* or *lex specialis*.[233] Moreover, *jus cogens* and *erga omnes* norms can serve as collision rules that already establish some fragments of hierarchy.[234] The principles of balancing and proportionality could help to achieve fair results

---

[227] ibid 148.

[228] ibid 138.

[229] Teubner, *Constitutional Fragments: Societal Constitutionalism and Globalization* (n 69) 42.

[230] Horatia Muir Watt, 'Private International Law Beyond the Schism' (2011) 2 Transnational Legal Theory 347, 374.

[231] Anne Peters, 'The Refinement of International Law: From Fragmentation to Regime Interaction and Politicization' (2017) 15 International Journal of Constitutional Law 671, 679.

[232] Jeffrey L Dunoff and Joel P Trachtman, 'A Functional Approach to International Constitutionalization' in Jeffrey L Dunoff and Joel P Trachtman (eds), *Ruling the World? Constitutionalism, International Law, and Global Governance* (CUP 2009) 8.

[233] ILC (n 112) 25.

[234] For *jus cogens* and *erga omnes* norms in international environmental law, see Louis J Kotzé and Wendy Muzangaza, 'Constitutional International Environmental Law for the Anthropocene?' (2018) 27 Review of European, Comparative and International Environmental Law 278.

of interpretation by identifying and balancing constitutional principles of each area against each other.[235]

From this point of view, there would be no such thing as a specific climate or environmental regime that has its own rules. IL would need to consider environmental aspects as well. An instrument for balancing different interests against each other is the principle of sustainable development.[236] In his separate opinion on the *Gabčíkovo-Nagymaros Project* case, Judge Weeramantry argued that both economic development and environmental protection are protected under IL but might collide. It is then for sustainable development—which, for him, is not just a mere concept but a principle that has normative value—to balance environmental rights and competing economic law against each other and to resolve the conflict.[237] Sustainable development is particularly useful, as it can encompass a multitude of different factors and interests, such as human rights, state responsibility, environmental rights, economic and industrial law, equity, territorial sovereignty, the abuse of rights and good neighbourliness.[238] The connection between environmental protection and human rights is a 'natural' one; it is required and justified that they are interpreted together,[239] for example, by recognising a Grundnorm of environmental protection (more from a Kantian than Kelsian understanding) that underpins legal reasoning and, thus, binds and guides all governmental power.[240]

---

235 Anne van Aaken, 'Defragmentation of Public International Law Through Interpretation: A Methodological Proposal' (2009) 16 Indiana Journal of Global Legal Studies 483, 492.

236 Marie-Claire Cordonier Segger, 'Sustainable Development in International Law' in David Armstrong and others (eds), *Routledge Handbook of International Law* (Routledge 2009) 369ff.

237 Separate Opinion of Judge Weeramantry in the *Gabčíkovo-Nagymaros Project case*, Judgment of 25 September 1997, ICJ Reports 1997, 88–9; on sustainable development as a normative principle, see Paulo Canelas de Castro, 'The Judgment in the Case Concerning the Gabčíkovo-Nagymaros Project: Positive Signs for the Evolution of International Water Law' (1997) 8 Yearbook of International Environmental Law 21; see also Marie-Claire Cordonier Segger and Judge CG Weeramantry, *Sustainable Development Principles in the Decisions of International Courts and Tribunals: 1992–2012* (Routledge 2017) 271.

238 Separate Opinion of Judge Weeramantry in the *Gabčíkovo-Nagymaros Project* case, ICJ Reports 1997, 95.

239 Nina Mileva and Marina Fortuna, 'Environmental Protection as an Object of and Tool for Evolutionary Interpretation' in Georges Abi-Saab and others (eds), *Evolutionary Interpretation and International Law* (Hart/Bloomsbury Publishing 2019) 136.

240 Rakhyun E Kim and Klaus Bosselmann, 'Operationalizing Sustainable Development: Ecological Integrity as a Grundnorm of International Law' (2015) 24 Review of European, Comparative and International Environmental Law 194, 205.

However, it seems doubtful that unity can be created through interpretation.[241] Even where interpretation principles and rules can be identified that potentially could help to develop a coherent body of principles, none of these can claim absolute validity.[242] While principles such as the *lex specialis* and *lex posterior* rules may help to resolve conflicts between IL and the legal order of a specific regime, their usefulness is limited when it comes to inter-regime conflicts, for example, an assessment of climate mitigation measures under the UNFCCC and the WTO regime.[243] Therefore, from the perspective of societal constitutionalism, '[a]ny aspiration to the organizational and doctrinal unity of law is surely a chimera'.[244] Global society is 'a society without an apex or a center'.[245] Fragmentation in law is largely the result of fragmentation in society, which not only stems from economic globalisation but is also the result of the differentiation of society into autonomous social systems crossing territorial borders and constituting itself globally.[246] In the era of globalisation, people do not identify themselves only as citizens of nation-states, but they also belong to (or feel affiliated with) multiple groups that can be classically territory-centred such as nations, states and towns but also transnational or subnational ethnic groups, religious institutions, trade organisations or environmental protest groups.[247] Different communities (e.g., judges or a religious community, such as the Amish) are engaging in constitutional understanding, and their legal meanings are interdependent. But as each has different starting points and identifications (e.g., state law, religion), a unitary law is impossible,[248] which leads to a replacement of state-oriented values by community-oriented values.[249]

The logical consequence of such functional thinking is that a uniform global constitution for the whole of IL is impossible.[250] These views focus on the plurality of both legal claims and society's complexity and draw intensively on

---

[241] ILC (n 112) 20.

[242] ibid; C Wilfred Jenks, 'The Conflict of Law-Making Treaties' (1953) 30 Brit. Y.B. Int'l L. 401, 407.

[243] Margaret A Young, 'Climate Change Law and Regime Interaction' (2017) 5 Carbon & Climate Law Review 147, 150–1.

[244] Fischer-Lescano and Teubner (n 83) 1017.

[245] Niklas Luhmann, *Political Theory in the Welfare State* (de Gruyter 1990) 31.

[246] Fischer-Lescano and Teubner (n 83) 1006.

[247] Berman, 'The New Legal Pluralism' (n 44) 227.

[248] Cover (n 39) 33.

[249] Walter (n 114) 182.

[250] Teubner, *Constitutional Fragments: Societal Constitutionalism and Globalization* (n 69) 13.

concepts of 'global legal pluralism' that understand IL as a non-hierarchal system of autonomous, pluralist legal systems based upon democratic institutional orders.[251] Today, pluralism is mostly concerned with 'the multiplicity of overlapping normative orders, the cacophony of actors, and functional differentiation'.[252] Crucially, for legal pluralism, the recognition of a plurality of sources that are incommensurable to some extent and do not allow for a categorical ranking is not seen as a problem but merely as a fact.[253] What is more, legal pluralism acknowledges the ability of normative communities outside formal lawmaking to engage in (international) lawmaking.[254]

7.4.1 Constitutional Pluralism

From the foregoing, the concepts of global legal pluralism and global constitutionalism seem to present alternative but opposite solutions of how to reduce complexity in a transformative period in IL.[255] While global legal pluralism stands for the 'disorder of normative orders',[256] constitutionalism is understood to create a coherent, comprehensive, exclusive and hierarchical global legal system,[257] or in Koskenniemi's words: 'the need for centralism and control on the one hand, diversity and freedom on the other'.[258] But this does not necessarily need to be the case. This work draws on theories of 'constitutional pluralism', which seeks to overcome the notion that constitutionalism and pluralism are necessarily mutually exclusive and, rather, acknowledges the existence of a multitude of (international) constitutions:

> Where there is a plurality of institutional normative orders, each with a functioning constitution (at least in the sense of a body of higher-order norms establishing

---

[251] O'Donoghue (n 226) 90.

[252] Ingo Venzke, 'Semantic Authority' [2016] ACIL Research Paper 2016–03 5.

[253] Victor M Muniz-Fraticelli, *The Structure of Pluralism* (OUP 2014) 11.

[254] Berman, 'The New Legal Pluralism' (n 44) 231; Cover (n 39) 40.

[255] In this sense, Martin Loughlin, 'Constitutional Pluralism: An Oxymoron?' (2014) 3 Global Constitutionalism 9.

[256] Neil Walker, 'Beyond Boundary Disputes and Basic Grids: Mapping the Global Disorder of Normative Orders' (2008) 6 International Journal of Constitutional Law 373.

[257] Aydin Atilgan, *Global Constitutionalism* (Springer 2018) 69; Paul Blokker and Chris Thornhill, 'Sociological Constitutionalism: An Introduction' in Paul Blokker and Chris Thornhill (eds), *Sociological Constitutionalism* (CUP 2017) 16.

[258] Martti Koskenniemi, *The Politics of International Law* (Hart Publishing 2011) 354.

> and conditioning relevant governmental powers), it is possible that each acknowledge the legitimacy of every other within its own sphere, while none asserts or acknowledges constitutional superiority over another. In this case, 'constitutional pluralism' prevails.[259]

This approach is based on one of the key insights of pluralism: the 'recognition that multiple normative orders exist and a focus on the dialectical interaction between and among these normative orders'.[260] These normative orders, both state-based and private, exist side by side.[261] Transnational legal pluralism, then, seeks to identify emerging constitutional processes and sites that are realised in elements of sectorial constitutionalism.[262] It addresses both vertical (e.g., between national and international) and horizontal (between functionally diverse legal orders) aspects of constitutionalism.[263]

Consequently, a multitude of constitutions exists alongside state constitutions. The latter are not disappearing, but they are no longer total constitutions that can claim to regulate all public issues. Instead, they have to be understood as 'partial constitutions' (*Teilverfassungen*) in a broader global legal order and on which (other) partial constitutions (e.g., the ECHR, the UN Convention of the Law of the Seas (UNCLOS) and the General Agreement on Tariffs and Trade (GATT)/ WTO law[264] but also 'private constitutions' of institutions such as ICANN or

---

[259] Neil MacCormick, *Questioning Sovereignty. Law, State, and Nation in the European Commonwealth* (OUP 1999) 104.

[260] Berman, 'The New Legal Pluralism' (n 44) 228.

[261] Cf. Joel P Trachtman, 'Constitutional Economics of the World Trade Organization' in Jeffrey L Dunoff and Joel P Trachtman (eds), *Ruling the World? Constitutionalism, International Law and Global Government* (CUP 2009).

[262] O'Donoghue (n 226) 143.

[263] Ernst Ulrich Petersmann, *Multilevel Constitutionalism for Multilevel Governance of Public Goods* (Hart Publishing 2017) 10; Teubner, 'Societal Constitutionalism: Nine Variations on a Theme by David Sciulli' (n 30) 314.

[264] Oliver Diggelmann and Tilmann Altwicker, 'Is There Something Like a Constitution of International Law? A Critical Analysis of the Debate on World Constitutionalism' (2008) 68 Zeitschrift für ausländisches öffentliches Recht und Völkerrecht 623, 627–8.

the Global Covenant of Mayors for Climate and Energy[265] and indigenous law/ constitutions[266] have an increasing impact.[267]

These orders or organisations can overlap, 'as they are involved in solving the same constitutional problem'.[268] This poses one of the biggest problems with theories of sectorial and societal constitutionalism: which order of which regime's constitution prevails when conflict arises between them? Constitutional pluralism recognises the existence of different constitutional sites and processes that operate in a rather heterarchical than hierarchical order.[269] Importantly, it is one of the characterising features of legal pluralism that it will not provide any yardsticks against which the prevailing norm in a messy hybrid world should be determined. Rather, there cannot ever be one single answer to this question.[270] This concerns both the interpretation of the contested norm and the authority of the interpreter. (Constitutional) authority is perceived as a fluid concept rather than a fixed one.

Instead of establishing a hierarchy among norms, multi-level constitutionalism in the form of 'nested constitutional orders'[271] is a better solution to deal with multi-level governance.[272] Multi-level constitutionalism, as a horizontal rather than a vertical principle of coherence based upon values rather than hierarchy, can describe how different regimes can coexist and regulate themselves.[273] These 'constitutional fragments' can be compared to federal systems where local communities or states within federal states have their substate constitutions.[274] There, society is organised in a two-level system, and power and competencies are shared

---

[265] Sigrid Boysen, 'Entgrenzt—pluralistisch—reflexiv—polyzentrisch—kontestiert: Das Transnationale am transnationalen Klimaschutzrecht' (2018) 29 Zeitschrift für Umweltrecht 643, 645 ff.

[266] Teubner, *Constitutional Fragments: Societal Constitutionalism and Globalization* (n 69) 162 ff.

[267] Häberle (n 202) 161, 165; Peter Häberle and Markus Kotzur, *Europäische Verfassungslehre* (8th edn, Nomos 2016) 314ff; Walter (n 114) 194; Lars Viellechner, 'Constitutionalism as a Cipher: On the Convergence of Constitutionalist and Pluralist Approaches to the Globalization of Law' (2012) 4 Goettingen Journal of International Law 599, 605–6; Diggelmann and Altwicker (n 264) 627ff.

[268] Marcelo Neves, 'From Constitutionalism to Transconstitutionalism' in Paul Blokker and Chris Thornhill (eds), *Sociological Constitutionalism* (CUP 2017) 293.

[269] Walker, 'The Idea of Constitutional Pluralism' (n 74) 337.

[270] Berman, 'Global Legal Pluralism' (n 37) 1165.

[271] Peters, 'Membership in the Global Constitutional Community' (n 10) 202.

[272] ibid.

[273] Neil Walker, 'Taking Constitutionalism beyond the State' (2008) 56 Political Studies 519, 539–40.

[274] Peters, 'Membership in the Global Constitutional Community' (n 10) 202.

between the nation-state and subnational states.[275] Multi-level constitutionalism must not be misunderstood as establishing a system of subordination. Instead, the different constitutions are equal 'partial constitutions'. Principles such as the primacy of federal law over state law (e.g., Article 31 of the German Basic Law), the primacy of EU law over national law, the principle of subsidiarity, covenant loyalty and the European duty of cooperation aim to ensure consideration between equal partners and to avoid conflicts.[276]

Resolving conflicts becomes more difficult when rules of conflict management are lacking, for example, in the case of conflicts between different regimes, such as the economic and the environmental/climate law regimes. Importantly, for proponents of societal constitutionalism, international constitutional law can only be perceived as a 'global collision law' (*globales Kollisionsverfassungsrecht*[277]), which connects the constitutional fragments: of nations, transnational regimes and regional cultures.[278] Instead of being tied to territorial borders, jurisdiction is determined both nationally and internationally according to who has the closest connection to the functional regime.[279]

One way to resolve conflicts among a variety of different actors and regimes is the 'compatibilization technique'.[280] In the 'strange legal Esperanto of regimes', the courts, both national and international, would need to create transnational substantive norms out of this chaos by identifying the appropriate norms 'beyond their territorial, organizational and institutional legal spheres' for the case at hand and thereby combine these norms in a way that they develop a transnational body of law.[281] It is not 'policies' that clash, but there are rationality collisions because many of the colliding units are autonomous private governance regimes that are not based on the state (those producing global law without the state) and have their roots in a variety of non-political sectors of the world society. Conflicts, then, essentially have to be understood as social conflicts, and the law should be directly concerned with these social issues.[282] It should aim to be 'its main

[275] Ingolf Pernice, 'Multilevel Constitutionalism and the Treaty of Amsterdam: European Constitution-Making Revisited?' (1999) 36 Common Market Law Review 703, 709.

[276] Häberle and Kotzur (n 267) 312.

[277] See the German edition, Gunther Teubner, *Verfassungsfragmente* (Suhrkamp 2012) 31.

[278] Teubner, *Constitutional Fragments: Societal Constitutionalism and Globalization* (n 69) 13.

[279] ibid 155.

[280] Fischer-Lescano and Teubner (n 83) 1030.

[281] ibid 1022–3.

[282] ibid 1023.

objective to establish a compatibility between colliding rationality principles of global sectors'.[283] Thus, instead of creating a hierarchy within the fragmentation of global law, each regime must develop its own internal logic and evolve its own *jus non dispositivum*.[284] As such, each *jus non dispositivum* will mirror the specific needs of the regime (e.g., the *lex mercatoria*). However, each regime will also have to take the *jus non dispositivum* of other regimes not only into consideration but take parts of them into their *jus non dispositivum* and, thus, create an internal limitation in its own logic.[285] For example, WTO law clashed with the national health laws of Brazil that ignored rules concerning the rights of patent-holders in favour of producing '*generica*' to bring the AIDS epidemic under control. In this case, economic and health interests collided. The WTO, driven by the desire of the U.S. to protect the intellectual property of its pharmaceutical companies, gave in to the pressure of massive protests by civil society and stressed in its Doha Declaration that it would implement and interpret the Agreement on Trade-Related Aspects of Intellectual Property Rights (TRIPS) 'in a manner supportive of public health […]'.[286] This means that the economically-driven WTO regime has created an internal limitation on its logic through the re-formulation of a principle of health protection (of another regime), which it then incorporated as its own.[287] The long-term effect of this could be observed in the COVID-19 pandemic: interestingly, it was WTO Director-General Ngozi Okonjo-Iweala who 'warmly welcomed' (against the opposition from European countries) proposals by some countries (including the U.S.) for a temporary vaccine patent waiver under the TRIPS Agreement.[288]

A regime is, thus, capable of solving conflicts arising from the collision of different regimes through the re-entry of the interests of other regimes. Hybrid constitutionalisation means the combination of both state power and external pressure from civil society through the media, spontaneous protest and so on so that

---

[283] ibid 1024.

[284] ibid 1037.

[285] Teubner, *Constitutional Fragments: Societal Constitutionalism and Globalization* (n 69) 84.

[286] WTO Ministerial Conference, 4th Sess., Ministerial Declaration, WT/MIN(01)/Dec/1, para. 17. (Nov. 20, 2001); see Fischer-Lescano and Teubner (n 83) 1028.

[287] ibid 1030.

[288] WTO, 'Statement of Director-General Ngozi Okonjo-Iweala on USTR Tai's Statement on the TRIPS Waiver' <https://www.wto.org/english/news_e/news21_e/dgno_06may21_e.htm> accessed 31 August 2023.

a system will build up its own internal self-limitations as part of its own logic.[289] No regime can be completely self-sufficient and ignore the demands of other regimes.

Viellechner's approach to 'responsive pluralism' goes in the same direction. For him, however, it is not external pressure that leads systems to consider interests and concerns other than their own as part of their logic. Rather, the different legal orders are capable of and willing to take each other into account of their own volition.[290] Legal systems constrain themselves because they are aware that each of them regulates a particular subject area. They acknowledge that none of them would be able to regulate all subject areas.[291] Responsive pluralism demands that legal orders reflect on their own identity and, thus, find themselves between independence and interdependence and assess their influence and effects on other legal orders.[292] Central to Viellechner's idea are the principles of complementary and subsidiarity. Legal orders can expand in scope if gaps are found in foreign law (complementary), but they must confine their scope where they overlap with other legal orders.[293] At the same time, each legal order has to define its identity from which it may not be compelled to relinquish.[294]

In the climate context, the Stern Review gives a good example of how climate change concerns can be incorporated to define the limits of the economic regime. The 2006 report warned that the costs of taking action today are minor in comparison to the costs of doing nothing, the latter of which would cost the global economy 20 per cent of its performance every year. By using the logic of the regime (profit maximisation), it sought to limit unconstrained and unsustainable economic activities that harm the environment as 'acceptable costs of business'.[295] Ultimately, a 'green capitalism' regime can emerge that does not formulate economics and ecology as opposites but as 'a direct route to profits'.[296]

It follows that rather than establishing a hierarchy between different legal orders, these approaches are informed by the structure of international private

[289] Teubner, *Constitutional Fragments: Societal Constitutionalism and Globalization* (n 69) 84.

[290] Viellechner, 'Responsive Legal Pluralism: The Emergence of Transnational Conflicts Law' (n 221) 323.

[291] ibid 324.

[292] ibid.

[293] ibid.

[294] ibid.

[295] Nicolas Stern, 'The Stern Review on Economics of Climate Change' (2006) 6; Ulrich Beck, *World at Risk* (Polity Press 2008) 102.

[296] Beck (n 295) 103.

law (including the horizontal effects of human rights)[297] based on horizontal coordination rather than hierarchy.[298] The application of horizontal methods of international private law would lead to clear and predictable results, unlike public law mechanisms such as the balancing of interests. General clauses under private law could serve as conflict rules, which, in this respect, are seen as substantive constitutional rules.[299] These approaches certainly seem to be more realistic than a universal constitution for the global community. However, some scholars point out that the recourse to private law tools may lack the complexity for questions that overreach the scope of a particular regime. In this sense, while hierarchical and unitary concepts are no longer convincing in a time where a multitude of different governance actors act beyond the state, and often informally,[300] private actors are not capable of resolving all their conflicts:

> The claim for the desirability of a 'public' dimension expresses the awareness and conviction that social interactions are, and should be, regulated by rules that emerge from discourses about common interests. Neither the ambitious political vision for peace and justice, nor the articulation and promotion of more specific common interests can be achieved by regimes based solely on spontaneous private ordering.[301]

This becomes evident in relation to the worldwide economy/climate change nexus (but also in the area of labour rights/human rights). These conflicts are typically framed as clashes between 'private' interests (such as property and contract) and (global) public interests, such as the use and protection of common goods.[302] Not all conflicts should be left to the goodwill of private regimes, especially when fundamental rights, the protection of common goods (e.g., the atmosphere)

[297] Cf. Florian Rödl, 'Fundamental Rights, Private Law, and Societal Constitution: On the Logic of the so-Called Horizontal Effect' (2013) 20 Indiana Journal of Global Legal Studies 1015.

[298] Viellechner, 'Responsive Legal Pluralism: The Emergence of Transnational Conflicts Law' (n 221) 323.

[299] Viellechner, 'Verfassung ohne Staat. Eine Einführung' (n 71) 18.

[300] Armin Von Bogdandy, Matthias Goldmann and Ingo Venzke, 'From Public International to International Public Law: Translating World Public Opinion into International Public Authority' (2017) 28 The European Journal of International Law 115, 120–1.

[301] ibid 121.

[302] Peters, 'The Refinement of International Law: From Fragmentation to Regime Interaction and Politicization' (n 231) 676.

or third-party interests are involved.[303] But societal constitutionalism is not blind to this problem. Teubner, for example, is aware that a purely horizontal perspective—as in international private law—could lead to inadequate and unjust results.[304] Generally, in a conflict, regime constitutions must, under the principle of 'constitutional tolerance', reciprocally acknowledge the other constitution and directly apply their rules.[305] However, pluralist approaches should not be misunderstood to mean that the state has to accept (or even enforce) every claim made by non-state authorities.[306] Constitutional pluralism, after all, does not mean that each (sometimes illiberal) agenda of every normative community must be accepted in the same way if this means risking the fundamental values of another (the state's) community:

> Just because one embraces insights from legal pluralism, after all, does not mean that the values of pluralism must necessarily and always trump any other values a community might hold. It simply cannot be that legal pluralism is only a true normative position if it is pursued to the exclusion of all other values, interests, and commitments.[307]

For transnational constitutionalism, this means that one transnational constitution can (and must) refuse to recognise another transnational constitution if the latter contravenes its fundamental norms; in the same way, a domestic constitutional court can refuse to accept the priority of a foreign norm. This *ordre public transnational* (which has yet to be developed) should be a leading principle of transnational law with an orientation towards a global public interest.[308] This observation is particularly important for international human rights, which enjoy an '*ex ovo* constitutional status'.[309] Importantly, each regime must internally

---

303 Mattheis (n 201) 355; Lixinski, on the other side, argues for more "blurring" of the public/private divide in international law, see Lucas Lixinski, 'Across the Public/Private International Legal Divide in the Governance of Global Public Goods' (2020) 47 Denver Journal of International Law and Policy 1.

304 Teubner, *Constitutional Fragments: Societal Constitutionalism and Globalization* (n 69) 157.

305 ibid 158.

306 Paul Schiff Berman, 'The Evolution of Global Legal Pluralism' in Roger Cotterrell and Maksymilian del Mar (eds), *Authority in Transnational Legal Theory: Theorising Across Disciplines* (Edward Elgar Publishing 2016) 158–60.

307 ibid 159.

308 Teubner, *Constitutional Fragments: Societal Constitutionalism and Globalization* (n 69) 157.

309 ibid 124.

formulate its own overarching *ordre public transnational* from its own perspective.[310] Here, the open society of constitutional interpreters becomes important again. Not only states but also members of civil society help to formulate the *ordre public transnational.* As outlined above, litigation can help to shape the contours of the international climate regime, including the recognition of the interests of future generations.

7.4.2 Authority

Who would decide on the last word when multiple (transnational) communities ascertaining jurisdiction over the same subject matter are engaged in a 'dialectical dance'?[311] From a pluralist view, it is certainly not the states (alone) that get to decide. A formal approach to IL, which relies on who has the formal authority to articulate norms or to enforce them coercively, is rejected[312] in favour of a 'jurisgenerative' approach 'that focuses on the creative interventions made by various normative communities drawing on a variety of normative sources in ongoing political, rhetorical, and legal iterations'.[313] Importantly, pluralism, as a descriptive and not a normative framework, does not decide on the 'who'.[314] 'Radical pluralism' assumes that there is no common legal framework for different legal systems, each with its own rules of recognition from which authority is derived.[315] Authority itself is contested as there is no final answer to the question of who is authorised to issue a binding decision. While some actors might be able to wield coercive power and, through their powerful status, are more likely to answer the question of authority in their favour, a decision cannot be perceived as a full stop. Competing silenced voices might raise again and change a formerly taken decision over time.[316] This fluidity of authority also holds true for the courts deciding such cases. Here, 'constitutional heterarchy' describes how a multitude of constitutional actors engage with each other in lieu of explicit

[310] ibid 161.

[311] Berman, 'The New Legal Pluralism' (n 44) 235.

[312] ibid 237.

[313] Berman, 'Global Legal Pluralism' (n 37) 1166.

[314] Paul Schiff Berman, 'A Pluralist Approach to International Law' (2007) 32 Yale Journal of International Law 301, 327.

[315] Nico Krisch, 'Who Is Afraid of Radical Pluralism? Legal Order and Political Stability in the Postnational Space' (2011) 24 Ratio Juris 386, 388.

[316] Berman, 'Global Legal Pluralism' (n 37) 1165–66.

collision rules.[317] In many states, the federal constitutions regulate which norm prevails.[318] Such collision rules are absent at the European and international levels. Thus, in systems such as the EU (between the EU and its member-states) and the U.S. (between the institutions Congress, President and Supreme Court), an unsettled relationship concerning powers and final legal authority remains.[319] This constitutional pluralism is not seen as a flaw but forms an essential characteristic of these legal systems.[320] The absence of hierarchy, however, does not lead to chaos but constitutes a system of order of its own where various constitutional actors can be accommodated in a spontaneous and decentralised way.[321]

Heterarchy allows for constitutional conflicts and coordination among various actors to be managed by turning to constitutional considerations.[322] Three factors are decisive as primary values of constitutionalism: voice, expertise and rights.[323] Whether actors can claim constitutional superiority depends on their ability to invoke these values. Halberstam defines these values as:

> the first [voice] as asking which actor has the better claim of representing the relevant political will; the second [expertise] as asking which actor has the better claim of knowledge or instrumental capacity; and the third [rights] as asking which actor has the better claim of protecting individual rights.[324]

None of these values is uniquely associated with any particular level, unit or institution of governance, and actors present competing claims based on one or a combination of these values.[325] 'The organization of contestation in each system is the result of concrete actions and interactions of the competing institutions, each drawing on the primary values of constitutionalism to support their stance

---

[317] Daniel Halberstam, 'Constitutional Heterarchy: The Centrality of Conflict in the European Union and the United States' in Jeffrey L Dunoff and Joel P Trachtman (eds), *Ruling the World? Constitutionalism, International Law, and Global Governance* (CUP 2011) 326–55.

[318] For example, Article 31 of the German Basic Law; Article 49 para. 1 of the Swiss Constitution.

[319] Halberstam (n 317) 329–36.

[320] Neil Walker, 'Constitutional Pluralism Revisited' (2016) 22 European Law Journal 333, 333–34.

[321] Halberstam (n 317) 328. 'Constitutional heterarchy is therefore not a principle of disorder but a principle of organization' (at 354).

[322] ibid 337.

[323] ibid 328.

[324] ibid 337.

[325] ibid 354.

of authority or deference.'[326] In doing so, a 'community of courts'[327] is built, in which courts can enter into dialectic relationships that exist without an official hierarchical relationship based on coercive power.[328] 'Legal pluralism', therefore, not only describes the plurality of public and private sources of law but is also used as a normative legal term to challenge the binary conceptions of 'national law' and 'international law'.[329] Notably, the courts play a crucial role in the development and establishment of constitutional pluralism.[330]

So far, constitutionalisation occurs only *within* the regimes but not among them; there is no international constitutional law.[331] This means that '(inter)national governance may have constitutional elements and consist of regimes with partial constitutions but it is difficult to speak of a constitution of the international community. (Inter)national governance remains "hybrid governance"'.[332] But this hybridity is not necessarily a problem. Instead, it could provide the answer to managing legal conflicts.[333] The reality of the hybridity of IL—in terms of shared authority by both national and international courts and the addition of non-state legal norms created by multiple communities (e.g., ethnic, religious, epistemic, transnational, subnational, international)—in scholarly discourse leads either to excluding any international or transnational influences and to resorting to national authority ('sovereigntist territorialism') or calling for extreme harmonisation of the international legal order (so-called 'universalism').[334] But the hybridity is impossible to escape, and none of these approaches can provide satisfying answers. Legal pluralism, instead, attempts to address the fragmentation of society into a variety of regimes, each with its own normative order, without seeking to assimilate or dissolve the differences between the regimes but searching for modes of cooperation, mainly through the design of

---

[326] ibid.

[327] Anne-Marie Slaughter, *A New World Order* (Princeton University Press 2004) 68–9.

[328] Berman, 'The New Legal Pluralism' (n 44) 233–4.

[329] Petersmann (n 263) 114.

[330] See Section 9.5.

[331] Walter (n 114) 201.

[332] ibid.

[333] Berman, *Global Legal Pluralism—A Jurisprudence of Law beyond Borders* (n 36).

[334] Berman, 'Global Legal Pluralism' (n 37) 1163; for an extensive analysis on 'sovereignitist territorialism', see Chapter 3 'The Limits of Sovereigntist Territoriality' in Paul Schiff Berman (ed), *Global Legal Pluralism—A Jurisprudence of Law beyond Borders* (2012); and for universalism, see Chapter 4 in the same book.

procedural mechanisms and institutions.[335] These procedures can help to resolve conflicts as they bring together several actors in a shared social space.[336]

7.5 Criticism of Societal Constitutionalism

Theories on societal constitutionalism were well-received in legal scholarship but the idea that non-state actors could be involved in international lawmaking has also been met with criticism.[337] Accordingly, non-state actors might have some influence in advocating global constitutionalisation by stimulating the content of IL, setting the international legal agenda, promoting human rights and environmental law or mobilising states and leveraging public opinion, but 'it is the states that produce international law'.[338]

An important critique that has been raised is that societal constitutionalism could be problematic for democracy. '[T]he move from territoriality to functionality' could put democracy in danger if such a move is accompanied by a shift 'from democracy to technocracy',[339] as the democratisation of such regimes is impossible.[340] However, it has been argued that many of these criticisms are still strongly tied to ideas of national democracy, which they unsuccessfully seek to copy transnational regimes one-to-one:[341]

> The difference between issue-based transnational regimes and nation states makes an adoption of models that were developed in the latter impossible. An issue-based regime attempting to realize a default value in a social space that is populated by several values needs to invent new forms of (a) representation and (b) public discourse and decision-making.[342]

---

[335] Berman, 'Global Legal Pluralism' (n 37) 1165.

[336] Berman, 'A Pluralist Approach to International Law' (n 314) 327.

[337] See, for example, Dieter Grimm, *Constitutionalism. Past, Present, and Future* (OUP 2016) 342 ff; Mattheis (n 201) 340 ff.

[338] Milewicz (n 224) 425–6; Jean L Cohen, 'Whose Sovereignty? Empire Versus International Law' (2004) 3 Ethics & International Affairs 1, 13.

[339] Andreas L Paulus, 'International Law and International Community' in David Armstrong and others (eds), *Routledge Handbook of International Law* (Routledge 2008) 52.

[340] See, for example, Julia Black, 'Constructing and Contesting Legitimacy and Accountability in Polycentric Regulatory Regimes' (2008) 2 Regulation & Governance 137.

[341] Teubner, 'Quod Omnes Tangit: Transnational Constitutions without Democracy?' (n 163) S26.

[342] Martens (n 84) 128.

Democracy in transnational constitutions will depend mostly on contestation, as outlined in Chapter 6. But self-contestation in transnational constitutions will be fundamentally different from resistance against state power in nation-states. Each regime's constitution is unique and needs its own forms of contestation. This requires knowledge and expertise: 'a transnational regime dealing with issues of science and technology, medicine, or education cannot be successfully contested via countervailing power; rather, it requires a specific counter-expertise that challenges effectively the dominant knowledge patterns.'[343]

Another problem is the exclusion of the regime's outsiders from its decision-making processes. Paulus, for example, argues that states must remain core actors in IL as they are the only ones legitimised to represent the people and, thus, take actions that can potentially affect all citizens.[344] Questions on fundamental issues can only be answered by 'general international law which bases its legitimacy on decisions of, ideally democratic, national processes of decision-making'.[345] Paulus provides an example to stress this point: a French court ruled that Yahoo! had to block a racist webpage offering World War II memorabilia as far as it can be seen in France because the display of these contents violates the French Criminal Code.[346] Who should decide on questions of accessibility and the banning of such webpages? Should the 'web community' (e.g., ICANN) be allowed to regulate itself, as argued by proponents of societal constitutionalism? Or is the French court the legitimate actor? Paulus argues in favour of the latter, discussing that an 80-year-old (French) Holocaust victim, without internet access, reading about the webpage in her local newspaper would not be represented by the 'web community' if it was allowed to self-regulate.[347] Only the state can represent every citizen affected and society as a whole, and thus, only the state can be legitimised to act. Throughout history, since nation-states became democratised, they have been perceived as having the power to exclude inequality and

[343] Teubner, 'Quod Omnes Tangit: Transnational Constitutions without Democracy?' (n 163) S26.

[344] Andreas L Paulus, 'Commentary to Andreas Fischer-Lescano & Gunther Teubner. The Legitimacy of International Law and the Role of the State' (2004) 25 Michigan Journal of International Law 1047, 1049.

[345] ibid 1050.

[346] Tribunal de Grande Instance, RG 05308—UEJF and Licra v Yahoo! Inc v Yahoo France. For an analysis of the case, see Mathias Reimann, 'Introduction: The Yahoo! Case and Conflict of Laws in the Cyberage' (2003) 24 Michigan Journal of International Law 663.

[347] Paulus (n 344) 1054–5.

include the 'other'.[348] Theories of societal constitutionalism would not consider the outsiders of a system, and consequently, are undemocratic.[349]

It holds true that only those who want to work on the solutions to a specific social problem (e.g., sustainability or child labour) and are willing to be bound by the regimes' rules are considered members of the regime, and thus, the only ones able to engage in the regime's decision- and rule-making processes. Nevertheless, their decisions can potentially affect the outsiders of the regime negatively, as seen above. This problem is not limited to transnational cases, though. The exclusion of potentially affected persons can also occur in nation-states, for example, where decisions of how to address the climate crisis has also consequences for people living in other countries, as has been argued in Chapter 4. Another exampele are associations setting standards that have to be followed by companies to receive certain certificates that are required by their clients.[350]

Moreover, the danger of excluding the interests of the outsiders of the system can be countered by applying concepts of deliberative democracy, as outlined in Chapter 6. While a regime necessarily needs to be 'closed' to permanently exist as a collective actor and, thus, cannot include potentially everyone that is affected by its decisions in its democratic self-governing processes, it also cannot simply ignore the justified claims and interests of the regime's outsiders. Instead, the members of the regime—its demos—must consider the consequences of certain outcomes and make these a basis for their decisions.[351] Here, the 'talking instead of voting' approach of deliberative democracy becomes practical again. But not only is the exclusion of outsiders problematic, the idea of regimes making their own law that may have consequences beyond the regime itself also raises the question of the legitimacy of its members. Their members are not elected, and some have been criticised for not acting democratically themselves. This becomes particularly important in relation to (powerful) NGOs, a point that will be analysed in more detail in the next chapter.[352]

---

[348] Hauke Brunkhorst, 'Constitutionalism and Democracy in the World Society' in Petra Dobner and Martin Loughlin (eds), *The Twilight of Constitutionalism?* (OUP 2010) 181, 191.

[349] Paulus (n 344) 1055.

[350] Martens (n 82) 41.

[351] ibid 41–2.

[352] See Section 8.1.3.

7.6 Conclusion

Non-state actors are not formally authorised to make 'official' IL. However, proponents of societal constitutionalism argue that non-state actors, such as individuals, NGOs and transnational corporations, are engaged in transnational constitutional lawmaking, which encompasses both private transnational constitutions and international human rights law. Non-state actors formulate their own *lex humana*, even against the expressed will of nation-states. This opens up the possibility that members of the global civil society could create a human right to a stable climate by calling upon such a right and by seeking to implement it through litigation. Global pressure in the form of protests against climate inaction (e.g., by the Fridays for Future movement) could foster and strengthen the development of a transnational constitutional climate regime that can put limits on the expansionist tendencies of other regimes, such as the economic.

Societal constitutionalism that supports the independent constitutionalisation of different regimes by a multitude of private actors may lead to increased fragmentation of IL with severe consequences for subject matters such as authority, hierarchy and unity. In this chapter, the concept of unity was rejected as unrealistic for any vision of transnational legal orders. Instead of hierarchy and subordination, a relation of mutual communication characterises visions of twenty-first-century constitutionalism.[353] The idea of a global climate constitution could act as a 'matrix' for mediation between the different constitutional fragments: 'the constitutional discourse must serve as the field in which different approaches can build a dialogue to define common goals, particularly with regard to the protection of nature'.[354]

It is against this background that interpretation needs to be understood as an open process, neither passive submission nor subordination.[355] 'The "unity of the constitution" ("*Einheit der Verfassung*") develops, if at all, through the "combination" of procedures and functions of many constitutional interpreters [...].'[356] Accepting the plurality of actors and options—and the fact that some disagreements are unavoidable and insurmountable—provides the basis for a truly open

[353] Thomas Cottier and Maya Hertig, 'The Prospects of 21st Century Constitutionalism' (2003) 7 Max Planck UNYB 261, 328.

[354] José Rubens Morato Leite and Patryck de Araujo Ayala, 'Global Environmental Constitutionalism as a Constitutionalism of the Earth' in Jordi Jaria-Manzano and Susana Borràs (eds), *Research Handbook on Global Climate Constitutionalism* (Edward Elgar Publishing 2019) 100.

[355] Häberle (n 202) 141.

[356] ibid 143.

process of interpretation, since 'consensus arises from conflict and compromise between participants with divergent opinions and self-serving interests. Constitutional law is, after all, conflict and compromise law.'[357] Transnational climate law, all the more, is delimited, pluralistic, reflexive, polycentric and contested.[358] After analysing that non-state actors can engage in international constitution-making and the creation of human rights, the next chapter turns to the question of who these actors are that participate in constitutional discourses.

[357] ibid 155.

[358] Boysen (n 265) 645.

8 The Actors

The last chapter demonstrated that non-state actors, at least from the perspective of societal constitutionalism, can be considered constitutional lawmakers in their own right. Thus, one could argue that individuals and NGOs have had a strong influence on the constitutionalisation processes of the international legal order. However, most of these processes are imposed in a top-down manner. This holds particularly for the EU:

> In the member states of the EU, these processes have not been triggered 'from below' by civic protest or even revolutionary movements, or as a result of the intervention of foreign powers—rather, parliamentarization and the institutionalization of human rights are élite-driven processes.[1]

Other institutions and their founding treaties (which could be considered regime constitutions), such as the WTO, are also the result of a 'top-down economic constitutionalism' and are criticised for their lack of democratic legitimacy.[2] Therefore, many scholars call for an open and pluralist version of global constitutionalism, which includes meaningful participation opportunities for civil society.[3] For Häberle, it is constitutionalism that makes a society an open society. Constitutionalism can guide, frame and safeguard pluralistic ideas and interests.[4]

---

[1] Berthold Rittberger and Frank Schimmelfennig, 'Explaining the Constitutionalization of the European Union' (2006) 13 Journal of European Public Policy 1148, 1150.

[2] Saki Bailey and Ugo Mattei, 'Social Movements as Constituent Power: The Italian Struggle for the Commons' (2013) 20 Indiana Journal of Global Legal Studies 965, 1001 ff.

[3] ibid 1004.

[4] Peter Häberle, *Ein afrikanisches Verfassungs- und Lesebuch—mit vergleichender Kommentierung* (Duncker & Humblot 2019) 282.

M. Niehaus, *Global Climate Constitutionalism "from below"*,
https://doi.org/10.1007/978-3-658-43191-4_8

A society is formed by 'potentially all state entities, all public entities, all citizens and groups', which are engaging in the processes of constitutional interpretation.[5] This is the main point of his theory: the enhancement of the circle of constitutional interpreters to include potentially everybody. This is the mutually enforced bond between constitutionalism and an open and pluralistic society.

Similarly, societal constitutionalism argues that new actors, especially non-state actors, have to be considered when it comes to international lawmaking, recognising that 'the center of lawmaking has moved away from the state and into the periphery of transnational actors'.[6] Transnational law is becoming increasingly important and offers novel perspectives on matters and problems of a global scale. Scholars of societal constitutionalism have noted that law exists beyond the state and can be created independently of states, but such law is not community-based. Based on discourses—the use of the binary code legal/illegal combined with an institutional element (institutionalised processes of secondary rule-making by each regime)—rather than communities, these forms of constitutionalism demonstrate only a 'weak social embeddedness'.[7] Although societal constitutionalism embraces the participation of non-state actors in the creation of the *lex mercatoria* or *lex digitalis*, the result is a global legal pluralism from the top down instead of pointing towards a constitutionalisation from below.[8]

Moreover, even societal constitutionalism is still bound to the ideas of Western societies and their pictures of constitutionalism. While it has been claimed that global law can only be explained by a theory of legal pluralism turning away from colonial societies' law to the laws of diverse ethnic, cultural and religious communities,[9] and, thus, losing the focus on nation-states, (societal) constitutionalism still clings to institutions that resemble the Western nation-state (e.g., the WTO for the economic regime/*lex mercatoria*, ICANN for the internet regime/*lex digitalis*).[10] Such a perspective narrowed down to institutionalisation neglects the

---

[5] Peter Häberle, '"The Open Society of Constitutional Interpreters"—A Contribution to a Pluralistic and "Procedural" Constitutional Interpretation (1975)' in Markus Kotzur (ed), *Peter Häberle on Constitutional Theory* (Nomos/Hart 2018) 130.

[6] Ralf Michaels, 'Global Legal Pluralism' (2009) 5 Annual Review of Law and Social Science 1, 7.

[7] ibid.

[8] ibid.

[9] Gunter Teubner, '"Global Bukowina": Legal Pluralism in the World Society' in Gunther Teubner (ed), *Global Law without a State* (Dartmouth Publishing 1997) 4.

[10] Gavin W Anderson, 'Societal Constitutionalism, Social Movements, and Constitutionalism from Below' (2013) 20 Indiana Journal of Global Legal Studies 881, 886.

effect of social movements on constitutionalism.[11] Therefore, Blokker criticises Teubner, who interprets civil society actors and social movements as corrections to the expansionist tendencies of transnational regimes, as failing to recognise societal calls for comprehensive *political constitutional* orders in the transnational domain.[12] In short, while societal constitutionalism offers perspectives of how non-state actors could participate in international lawmaking, this approach may nevertheless focus too narrowly on institutionalisation[13] and ignores the dimensions of democratic input, self-governance and contestation.[14] Instead, in the constitutional state, legitimacy depends on the inclusion of those who are subject to its norms:

> A constitution that not only incorporates the state in a narrow sense, but also structures the public and constitutes society, while directly including the private realm, may not only act passively upon them, treating the societal and private powers as objects. It must actively include them: as subjects.[15]

Solidarity and democratic legitimacy require 'constitutionalism from below', which considers the interests of individuals and groups. Not only states but also members of civil society must be involved in decision-making processes on the norms and principles relevant to them. Therefore, this present chapter takes a closer look at the actors standing behind CCL. Who interprets in a transnational open society of constitutional interpreters?

In the context of climate change, and CCL in particular, this chapter looks at different actors who are interpreting and articulating their interpretations through litigation. Non-state actors are not (yet) formally recognised as legal subjects in IL. Thus, the group of non-state actors is often defined negatively by describing what they are not: neither states nor state-empowered bodies (such as IOs), and they have no recognised lawmaking capacity.[16] Nevertheless, they play a central but informal role in the development and application of IL in practice.[17]

---

[11] ibid 887 and passim.

[12] Paul Blokker, 'Constitutional Mobilization and Contestation in the Transnational Sphere' (2018) 45 Journal of Law and Society S52, S59 (emphasis in original).

[13] See Anderson (n 10).

[14] Blokker (n 12) S54.

[15] Häberle, 'The Open Society of Constitutional Interpreters' (n 5) 143.

[16] Eva Kassoti, 'The Constitutionalization of International Law and the Challenge of Non-State Actors' (2017) 11 ICL Journal 177, 190.

[17] Philippe Sands and Jacqueline Peel, *Principles of International Environmental Law* (4th edn, CUP 2018) 164.

Besides the sovereign states, which are front and centre of IL, other actors must be considered today. Apart from the UN, Häberle names NGOs and citizens as the beneficiaries of human rights and, through its denomination in Article 38 of the ICJ Statute, scholarship of IL.[18] Additionally, the nominative power of the international public (and the regional public) should not be underestimated.[19] Häberle's list is not exhaustive. In the field of international climate law, highly specialised lawyers, indigenous groups and local communities, sub-states and local governments filed important cases. However, for reasons of space, this work cannot comprehensively address all actors and, therefore, will focus on NGOs and individuals, the amicus curiae, the media and legal scholarship. All of these actors played important roles in the success of CCL cases, as will be shown in more detail in Chapter 9.

8.1 Individuals and (Environmental) NGOs

Probably the most visible groups of non-state actors are individuals and (environmental) NGOs. Most of the high-profile cases[20] against national governments or major private GHG emitters that gained attention worldwide were filed by NGOs or individuals.[21] NGOs seek to draw attention to issues such as the climate crisis by creating publicity, informing citizens and governments, enhancing knowledge and making their expertise and research available, contributing to (global) capacity building and giving expert advice.[22] CCL is another approach to creating awareness. Although questions concerning legitimacy and accountability have to

---

[18] Häberle, 'The Open Society of Constitutional Interpreters' (n 5) 164.

[19] ibid 165.

[20] David Markell and JB Ruhl, 'An Empirical Assessment of Climate Change in the Courts: A New Jurisprudence or Business as Usual' (2012) 64 Florida Law Review 15, paras 17–8.

[21] See, for example, in Switzerland: *Union of Swiss Senior Women for Climate Protection v. Swiss Federal Council and Others* (No. A-2992/2017); in Norway: *Greenpeace Nordic Association and Nature and Youth v. Ministry of Petroleum and Energy* (16-166674TVI-OTIR/06); in Australia: *Ironstone Community Action Group Inc. v. NSW Minister for Planning and Duralie Coal Pty. Ltd.* ([2011] NSWLEC 195); in Pakistan: *Maria Khan et al. v. Federation of Pakistan et al.* (No. 8960 of 2019); in South Africa: *EarthLife Africa Johannesburg v. Minister of Environmental Affairs and Others* (Case no. 65662/16); in New Zealand: *Thomson v. Minister for Climate Change Issues* ([2017] NZHC 733).

[22] Cathrin Zengerling, *Greening International Jurisprudence* (Martinus Nijhoff Publishers 2013) 22.

be raised, NGOs are generally seen as possible stakeholders of environmental interests in juridical proceedings and enforcement procedures.[23]

8.1.1 NGOs in IL

NGOs are 'groups of individuals organized for the myriad of reasons that engage human imagination and aspiration'.[24] The term 'NGO' could, in a broader sense, also include business associations; however, for this purpose, the term will only refer to organisations that are freely created by private initiative, are state-independent and are non-profit-seeking. They can emerge at all levels of governance—local, national or global.[25]

Political processes at the international level can benefit from NGO participation as they hold specialised information, resources and policy power. Important domestic NGOs, for instance, could help to reduce the possibility of failure of an achieved treaty, since they have a greater knowledge of domestic affairs.[26] Furthermore, global and local NGOs, well-funded and staffed with experts in their respective fields, often put considerable effort into researching environmental (policy) issues and developing technical and applied expertise.[27] Such independent knowledge could close the gap and complete the expertise that governments have themselves.[28]

NGOs have a long history of introducing social change to legal frameworks. Some of the oldest civil society movements include the transnational abolition of slavery and the fight for women's rights, in particular, suffrage.[29] British and American abolitionist networks frequently exchanged letters, publications and visits about tactics such as the filing of petitions, the publishing of newspaper

---

[23] ibid 40.

[24] Steve Charnovitz, 'Two Centuries of Participation: NGOs and International Governance' (1997) 18 Michigan Journal of International Law 183, 185.

[25] Cf. Christine Fuchs, 'Environment, Role of Non-Governmental Organizations', *Max Planck Encyclopedias of International Law* (OUP 2009) para 3; Stephan Hobe, 'Non-Governmental Organizations', *Max Planck Encyclopedias of International Law* (OUP 2010) paras 1–5.

[26] Kal Raustiala, 'The "Participatory Revolution" in International Environmental Law' (1997) 21 Harvard Environmental Law Review 537, 563.

[27] ibid 559.

[28] ibid 560.

[29] Manuela Niehaus and Kirsten Davies, 'Voices for the Voiceless—Climate Protection from the Streets to the Courts' (2021) 12 Journal for Human Rights and the Environment 228.

articles and pamphlets and boycotting goods produced by slaves.[30] The International Committee of the Red Cross, an institution founded by Henry Dunant after witnessing the horrors of the Battle of Solferino in 1859, was essentially involved in shaping the contours of modern international humanitarian law.[31] The involvement of NGOs in environmental protection started as early as 1860, with the first international meeting of the Society for the Protection of Animals.[32] Several other issues, such as the protection of birds, the regulation of fishing activities or the protection of marine mammals, have been discussed in international meetings in which both NGOs and governmental actors participated.[33] Today, their most significant impacts occur in the field of human rights and environmental law.[34] Their activities in the latter are manifold: they 'discover' environmental problems or provide scientific evidence, raise awareness of environmental problems, prepare and participate in negotiations of MEAs and the ratification processes at home and influence states on their decisions to join treaties or IOs.[35] In judicial proceedings, NGOs can typically participate as amicus curiae (see Section 8.2) or parties.[36]

The *Urgenda* case is named after the NGO that filed the claim. The Urgenda Foundation (a contraction of 'urgent agenda') is a Dutch environmental organisation that aims for a more sustainable society by focusing on the transition towards a circular (world) economy using only renewable energy, starting in the Netherlands.[37] *Juliana v United States* was indicated by the NGO Our Children's Trust with the support of experts such as leading climate scientist James Hansen, the director of the U.S.'s NASA Goddard Space Institute, whose granddaughter is one of the 21 plaintiffs.[38] The case of *Future Generations* against the Colombian

---

[30] Jenny S Martinez, 'The Anti-Slavery Movement and the Rise of Non-Governmental Organizations' in Dinah Shelton (ed), *The Oxford Handbook of Human Rights Law* (OUP 2013) 236.

[31] ibid 246.

[32] Charnovitz (n 24) 206.

[33] ibid 206–08.

[34] Fuchs (n 25) para 3.

[35] ibid 10–30.

[36] ibid 54.

[37] Urgenda Foundation Homepage, available at <http://www.urgenda.nl/en/> accessed 31 August.

[38] Katherine Ellison, 'An Inconvenient Lawsuit: Teenagers Take Global Warming to the Courts' *The Atlantic* (9 May 2012) <https://www.theatlantic.com/national/archive/2012/05/an-inconvenient-lawsuit-teenagers-take-global-warming-to-the-courts/256903/> accessed 31 August 2023; Umair Irfan, 'Pay Attention to the Growing Wave of Climate Change

Republic has been brought forward by 25 children and young people ranging in age from 7 to 26 and was decided in April 2018 by Colombia's Supreme Court. The complaint was organised by Dejusticia, a Colombia-based advocacy and research organisation 'dedicated to the strengthening of the rule of law and the promotion of social justice and human rights in Colombia and the Global South'.[39] Dejusticia aims to achieve its advocacy goals through communications, education, capacity building and particularly litigation as a core strategy.[40]

Thus, NGOs play an important role in CCL. However, there have been some difficulties identified around their participation. One of them is a technical problem: do NGOs have legal standing in climate change cases? This depends largely on the legal system at hand, as will be outlined in Section 8.1.2. Another question that is more difficult to answer is whether NGOs are legitimised to engage in international lawmaking through litigation at all. NGOs are not elected, but some hold great political power that they are not hesitant to use. Section 8.1.3 analyses the dangers and benefits that the participation of NGOs holds for transnational governance.

8.1.2 Excurse: *Locus Standi* in CCL

Häberle stresses the importance of procedural constitutional law and argues that its possibilities lie in creating opportunities for pluralism and participation, especially in the 'legal dialogue' (*Rechtsgespräch*).[41] As identified above, non-state actors depend on institutions, such as the courts, since discourses do not govern. To turn political pressure into political power, they require a court decision. This requires that non-state actors bring their complaints before a legal body in the first place. Thus, standing is the prerequisite to 'force the court to engage (in a legal dialogue)'[42] and to present one's interpretation of the subject matter. Without

---

Lawsuits' *Vox* (4 June 2019) <https://www.vox.com/energy-and-environment/2019/2/22/17140166/climate-change-lawsuit-exxon-juliana-liability-kids> accessed 31 August 2023.

[39] See Dejusticia, 'About Us' <https://www.dejusticia.org/en/about/> accessed 31 August 2023.

[40] ibid.

[41] Peter Häberle, 'Verfassungsgerichtsbarkeit in der offenen Gesellschaft' in Robert Chr van Ooyen and Martin HW Möllers (eds), *Handbuch Bundesverfassungsgericht im politischen System* (2nd edn, Springer VS 2015) 37.

[42] Häberle, 'The Open Society of Constitutional Interpreters' (n 5) 136.

legal standing, a court often will not rule on the merits.[43] This does not necessarily mean that a case is 'useless' if CCL is understood as a climate governance tool that, above all, seeks to raise awareness.[44] The *Juliana* case is a good example in this regard.[45] But it shows that protecting nature and the climate in court has been proven difficult in the past, mainly due to the prererquisites of standing in national and (regional) international legal orders. While some are putting their hopes on new approaches, such as granting standing to nature itself,[46] NGOs and individuals attempted to overcome the hurdles of admissibility by demonstrating a surprising amount of legal creativity.[47] The access to justice, in particular the right to initiate juridical proceedings, gives the courts the ability to decide on breaches of domestic and IEL in the first place.[48] The principle of '*nullum ius sine actione*'[49] applies to many legal orders, for instance, in Germany and Brazil, whereas in some states, Green Benches exist that can initiate proceedings *suo motu*, as in India.[50] Standing issues can emerge on both the (regional) international and the domestic levels.

8.1.2.1 Domestic Jurisdiction

In the U.S., 'citizen suits' became possible after Congress adopted or amended environmental acts in the 1970s that authorised 'any person' to sue without having to prove an 'injury in fact'.[51] This 'open standing' came to an end when the Supreme Court decided in *Lujan* that the courts' role was 'solely, to decide on the rights of the individual' and where there is no individual 'injury in fact', the two other branches of government were the ones to address such questions of public

---

[43] James R May and Erin Daly, *Judicial Handbook on Environmental Constitutionalism* (Law Division, UNEP Programme 2017) 131–7.

[44] See Section 6.4 above.

[45] See Section 9.3.1 below.

[46] See e.g. Christopher D Stone, 'Should Trees Have Standing? Towards Legal Rights for Natural Objects' (1972) 45 Southern California Law Review 450.

[47] See the selected cases in Chapter 9.

[48] Zengerling (n 22) 14.

[49] The principle of "*nullum ius sine actione*" provides that a court may not initiate proceedings of its own motion without a claimant or plaintiff having filed a claim.

[50] Sridhar Rengarajan and others, 'National Green Tribunal of India—an Observation from Environmental Judgements' (2018) 25 Environmental Science and Pollution Research 11313, 11317, although the Madras High Court challenged the Indian Green National Tribunal's suo motu act in 2015, arguing that the court overstepped its jurisdiction.

[51] Cass R Sunstein, 'What's Standing after Lujan? Of Citizen Suits, "Injuries," and Article III' (1992) 91 Michigan Law Review 163, 165–6.

interest.[52] The question of legal standing in the U.S. is strongly intertwined with the doctrine of the separation of powers. However, the decision (which, after all, invalidated a legislative decision) was and is subject to fierce criticism.[53] Nonetheless, the Supreme Court is unyielding on the doctrine of the separation of powers:

> No principle is more fundamental to the judiciary's proper role in our system of government than the constitutional limitation of federal court jurisdiction to actual cases or controversies. […] The concept of standing is part of this limitation.[54]

There are many uncertainties around CCL cases. For example, in its *Massachusetts v EPA* decision, the Supreme Court allowed state petitioners to file climate change cases to some extent but rejected standing for non-state petitioners in *AEP v Connecticut*.[55] In *Massachusetts v EPA*, the Court held that the state had standing due to its special position and interest in protecting its citizens and territory ('entitled to special solicitude'), and while not being able to protect itself from GHG emissions as it had transferred its 'sovereign prerogatives' to the powers of the federal government, it was the U.S. Environmental Protection Agency's (EPA) duty to protect it.[56] The question remains unanswered whether a petition brought only by non-state actors would find standing today.[57] In the *Juliana* case, the back and forth concerning whether the case may proceed to trial or not has been going on for 8 years now, and there is still no end in sight.[58]

The situation is—in theory—different in Europe. The Aarhus Convention was meant to lower standing requirements and open the doors to the domestic judiciaries for NGOs without having to demonstrate a specific interest in the case

---

[52] U.S. Supreme Court, *Lujan v. Defenders of Wildlife* (1992), 504 U.S. 555.

[53] See e.g. Sunstein (n 51).

[54] U.S. Supreme Court, *Simon v. Eastern Kentucky Welf. Rights. Org.*, 426 U.S. 26 (1976), at IV. On the separation of powers, see Section 10.1.2 below.

[55] Jacqueline Peel and Hari M Osofsky, *Climate Change Litigation: Regulatory Pathways to Cleaner Energy* (CUP 2015) 269.

[56] U.S. Supreme Court, *Massachusetts v. EPA*, 549 U.S. 497 (2007); Mia Hammersley, 'The Right to a Healthy and Stable Climate: Fundamental or Unfounded?' (2016) 7 Arizona Journal of Environmental Law and Policy 117, 127.

[57] Patrick Parenteau, 'Some Observations on How Courts in the United States and European Union View Their Role in Adjudicating Climate Litigation' (2023) 26 Environmental Liability: Law, Policy, and Practice 138, 143; Peel and Osofsky (n 55) 273f.

[58] For an overview over the history of the case see Sabin Center for Climate Change Law, 'Juliana v United States' <http://climatecasechart.com/case/juliana-v-united-states/> accessed 31 August 2021, see also Section 9.3.1 below.

(Article 9 para. 2 Aarhus Convention). However, many states were hesitant to implement the provisions into their domestic legal orders. The Cout of Justice of the European Union (CJEU), subsequently, in a handful of cases, reminded the member-states that the Aarhus Convention is 'an instrument which forms an integral part of the EU legal order'[59] and that Article 9 para. 2:

> limits the discretion available to the Member States when determining the detailed rules for the legal actions which it envisages inasmuch as that provision has the objective of granting 'wide access to justice' to the public concerned, which includes environmental organisations meeting the conditions laid down in Article 2(5) of the convention.[60]

Furthermore, Article 9 para. 3 reads:

> In addition and without prejudice to the review procedures referred to in paragraphs 1 and 2 above, each Party shall ensure that, where they *meet the criteria, if any*, laid down in its national law, *members of the public* have access to administrative or judicial procedures to challenge acts and omissions by private persons and public authorities which contravene provisions of its national law relating to the environment.[61]

The paragraph sparked another debate in Europe, namely the question of who is included as 'members of the public' and if this could even require the implementation of *actio popularis* (popular action) complaint mechanisms—unwanted by most member-states—in environmental matters.[62] Latvia did so by implementing a new Law on Environmental Protection in 2006, which granted legal standing to 'each private person, also associations, organisations and groups of persons'.[63] Germany, instead, tried to hold on to a subject interest approach despite ratifying the Aarhus Convention. Germany implemented Directive 2003/35/EC, which should safeguard the implementation of the Aarhus Convention in the national jurisdictions, inadequately. Only after two CJEU decisions in cases filed by

---

[59] CJEU, C-243/15, *Lesoochranárske zoskupenie VLK*, (ECLI:EU:C:2016:838) para 45.

[60] ibid para 58.

[61] Emphasis added.

[62] Žaneta Mikosa, 'Implementation of the Aarhus Convention through Actio Popularis' in Jerzy Jendrośka and Magdalena Bar (eds), *Procedural Environmental Rights: Principle X in Theory and Practice* (Intersentia 2017) 264–6.

[63] ibid 275–6.

NGOs[64] and the initiation of infringement proceedings by the European Commission did Germany adopt in 2016/2017 the new *Umwelt-Rechtsbehelfsgesetz* (Environmental Legal Assistance Act) that grants standing to environmental NGOs without the need to prove a direct interest in the case.[65]

In *Urgenda v The Netherlands*, the District Court of The Hague (DC) granted standing according to Book 3, Art. 305a of the Dutch Civil Code, which states that:

> A foundation or association with full legal capacity may initiate an action seeking to protect similar interests of other persons, provided that it advances those interests in accordance with its articles of association and that those interests are adequately safeguarded.[66]

The judges argued that the claim was an extension of Urgenda's objectives as formulated in its by-laws and that Urgenda was allowed to represent the interests of at least current generations.[67] The Supreme Court later argued that this argumentation was in line with the Aarhus Convention.[68] The District Court did not explicitly answer the question of whether Urgenda could represent future generations but referred to intergenerational equity as an element of sustainability, which was an interest that Urgenda was allowed to defend in court.[69] The Court

---

[64] CJEU, C-115/09, *Trianel (Bund für Umwelt und Naturschutz Deutschland, Landesverband Nordrhein- Westfalen eV v Bezirksregierung Arnsberg),* (ECLI:EU:C:2011:289); CJEU, C-72/12, *Gemeinde Altrip and Others v Land Rheinland-Pfalz* (ECLI:EU:C:2013:712).

[65] See also Karl-Peter Sommermann, 'Transformative Effects of the Aarhus Convention in Europe' (2017) 77 Zeitschrift für ausländisches öffentliches Recht und Völkerrecht 321. However, the German Federal Administrative Court (Bundesverwaltungsgericht) until today still finds provisions of the Umwelt-Rechtsbehelfsgesetz not to be compatible with the Aarhus Convention, see e.g. German Federal Administrative Court, Judgement of 26 January 2023, BVerwG 10 CN 1.23.

[66] Translation provided by the Netherlands Commercial Court, see <https://www.rechtspraak.nl/SiteCollectionDocuments/New-dutch-legislation-on-collective-actions.pdf> accessed 31 August 2023.

[67] District Court of The Hague, Urgenda v The Netherlands'[2015] (ECLI:NL:RBHDHA:2015:7196) para 4.8; see also KJ de Graaf and JH Jans, 'The Urgenda Decision: Netherlands Liable for Role in Causing Dangerous Global Climate Change' (2015) 27 Journal of Environmental Law 517, 519.

[68] Supreme Court of the Netherlands, Urgenda v The Netherlands [2019] ECLI:NL:HR:2019:2007 para 5.9.2.

[69] District Court of The Hague (n 67) para 4.8.

rejected the standing of the claim on behalf of the 886 plaintiffs as 'the individual claimants do not have sufficient (own) interests besides Urgenda's interests'.[70]

Leghari, *Juliana* and *Future Generations* are cases filed by individuals, but the latter two were orchestrated by NGOs. Asghar Leghari filed a public interest claim. The issue of standing was not addressed in the Court's decision, but, according to May and Daly, the courts in Pakistan, Nepal, India and Bangladesh seem to have recognised a form of open standing for actions concerning environmental impacts on behalf of the public.[71] Different from Western societies, Southern Asian countries do not rely on the (possible) violation of individual rights but follow a duty-based indigenous jurisprudential approach, which allows for public interest litigation as a less expensive tool for litigation.[72] The reason is seen in the material difference regarding prosperity and literacy between developed and developing countries.[73] Not only has access to the courts been facilitated but also the rules of procedure been relaxed. The courts, for example, in India, are not holding adherently to the adversarial procedure to allow for the 'poor and weak' to approach the courts.[74] For China, Gao and Whittaker note a shift from rights-based litigation to an 'objective reality' model that allows individuals to defend common goods, such as the protection of the environment.[75]

Such class action is also possible under many statutes in Latin America. However, in *Future Generations*, the plaintiffs made no use of this option and instead filed an individual *acción de tutela*. Art. 86 of the Colombian Constitution constitutes that:

> Every individual may claim legal protection before the judge, at any time or place, through a preferential and summary proceeding, for himself/herself or by whoever acts in his/her name, the immediate protection of his/her fundamental constitutional

---

[70] ibid 4.109.

[71] James R May and Erin Daly, *Global Environmental Constitutionalism* (CUP 2014) 278.

[72] Parvez Hassan and Azim Azfar, 'Securing Environmental Rights Through Public Interest Litigation in South Asia' (2004) 22 Virginia Environmental Law Journal 215, 224, citing Werner Menski and others, Public Interest Litigation in Pakistan (Platinum Publishing 2000) 109.

[73] ibid 225.

[74] Supreme Court of India, *Bandhua Mukti Morcha vs Union of India and Others*, 1984 AIR 802, 1984 SCR (267), para 9.

[75] Qi Gao and Sean Whittaker, 'Standing to Sue beyond Individual Rights: Who Should Be Eligible to Bring Environmental Public Interest Litigation in China?' (2019) 8 Transnational Environmental Law 327, 331; see also Yue Zhao, Shuang Lyu and Zhu Wang, 'Prospects for Climate Change Litigation in China' (2019) 8 Transnational Environmental Law 349.

> rights when the individual fears the latter may be jeopardized or threatened by the action or omission of any public authority.

Generally, when collective interests are at stake, the admissible type of complaint is the 'popular action' (*actio popularis*). Only in rare cases, when at the same time individual rights are at risk, an *acción de tutela* can be admissible.[76] While the right to a healthy environment generally belongs to the category of collective interests, the Colombian Supreme Court made it clear that:

> [w]ithout a healthy environment, subjects of rights and sentient beings in general will not be able to survive, let alone safeguard those rights, for our children or for future generations. Nor can the existence of the family, society or the State itself be guaranteed.[77]

The connection between the environment and fundamental rights was, therefore, established and the *acción de tutela* admissible.[78]

8.1.2.2 International Jurisdiction

At the international level, access to justice in the past had been granted almost exclusively to states. Today, these juridical and quasi-juridical bodies have become more accessible to non-state actors such as individuals and NGOs.[79] But some courts, such as the ICJ[80] and the WTO settlement bodies, are still closed to NGOs as parties.[81] The same holds in principle for the CJEU, where NGOs as non-privileged plaintiffs (Article 263 para. 4 of the Treaty on the Functioning of the European Union [TFEU]) can only bring an action if they are the addressees of that act, which means that their members must be directly affected by the

[76] This is the case when a) the transgression of collective rights causes the affection of fundamental individual rights [connection between the rights], b) the claimant is directly affected by the action in her rights, c] the violation is real and must be proved throughout the proceedings and d) the claim must aim at restoring individual rights, and not the collective rights considered, even when these are implicitly safeguarded in the decision, see the ruling of the Corte Suprema de Justicia de Colombia, *Future Generations v Colombia* (2018), STC4360-2018, para 1.

[77] ibid para 2.

[78] ibid para 3.

[79] Zengerling (n 22) 10.

[80] See Article 34 para. 1 of the ICJ Statute: "Only States may be parties in cases before the court".

[81] Ulrich Beyerlin, 'The Role of NGOs in International Environmental Litigation' (2001) 81 Zeitschrift für ausländisches öffentliches Recht und Völkerrecht 356, 358–9.

act. In its *Plaumann* decision, the CJEU made clear that 'individual concern' means that a person has to be affected by the questioned decision because of their individuality, their special position or certain attributes peculiar to them and differentiates them from all other persons.[82] The Aarhus Convention, to which the EU is a member, should facilitate access for NGOs to the CJEU.[83] However, the Court continues to apply the Plaumann test and generally dismisses environmental cases as inadmissible due to the lack of direct concern, even when the applicants have suffered harm.[84] Neither the entry into force of the Lisbon treaty nor the findings of the Aarhus committee, according to which the EU failed to implement effective access to justice and, therefore, breached its obligations under Article 9 para. 3 of the Aarhus Convention, lead to a significant change in the CJEU's criteria of assessing standing.[85]

The Plaumann test also has implications for actions brought by individuals, as a recent decision by the CJEU illustrates.[86] The Carvalho case (or the 'People's Climate Case') was the first attempt at a CCL case at the European level. The Portuguese Carvalho and nine other plaintiffs (seven from Europe, including a Swedish association representing the Indigenous Sami youth [Sáminuorra], one from Kenya and one from Fiji), supported by an alliance of (European) NGOs, urged the EU to take action and to protect their homes, livelihoods, traditional family occupation, culture and the rights of future generations.[87] On 8 May 2019, the General Court of the EU rejected the case on grounds of a lack of 'individual concern'. The applicants had argued that the Plaumann test leads to paradoxical results: the more widespread the harmful effects of an act are, the more restricted the access to the courts is and, therefore, argued for a more flexible application of the Plaumann formula.[88] The Court, however, did not follow this argumentation:

---

[82] CJEU, Case 25–62, *Plaumann & Co. v Commission of the European Economic Community* (ECLI:EU:C:1963:17), para 100.

[83] Nicola Notaro and Mario Pagano, 'The Interplay of International and EU Environmental Law' in Inge Govaere and Sasha Garben (eds), *The Interface Between EU and International Law—Contemporary Reflections* (Hart Publishing 2019) 163.

[84] See EU GC, T-219/95, *Danielsson and Others v Commission* (ECLI:EU:T:1995:219), at 71.

[85] Notaro and Pagano (n 83).

[86] EU GC, T-330/18, *Carvalho and Others v Parliament and Council* (ECLI:EU:T:2019:324).

[87] 'The People's Climate Case' <https://peoplesclimatecase.caneurope.org> accessed 31 August 2023.

[88] Application Carvalho and Others, T-330/18, 19–20, available at <https://peoplesclimatecase.caneurope.org/wp-content/uploads/2018/08/application-delivered-to-european-general-court.pdf> accessed 31 August 2023.

> It is true that every individual is likely to be affected one way or another by climate change [...]. However, the fact that the effects of climate change may be different for one person than they are for another does not mean that, for that reason, there exists standing to bring an action against a measure of general application. [...] a different approach would have the result of rendering the requirements of the fourth paragraph of Article 263 TFEU meaningless and of creating locus standi for all without the criterion of individual concern [...] being fulfilled.[89]

The CJEU upheld this decision and declared the case inadmissible.[90] Although the Aarhus Compliance Committee had already criticised the criteria of the Plaumann test as being too strict in 2011, stating that '[t]he consequences of applying the Plaumann test to environmental and health issues is that in effect no member of the public is ever able to challenge a decision or a regulation in such case before the ECJ',[91] the Court has not yet changed its jurisprudence on legal standing. However, the EU legislative bodies decided to address this problem. In 2021, the Regulation (EC) No 1367/2006 on the application of the provisions of the Aarhus Convention to EU institutions and bodies was amended through Regulation (EC) No 2021/1767. Article 11 now provides that, in addition to NGOs, individuals can also submit an application for internal review of administrative acts of the EU organs. They either need to 1) demonstrate the impairment of their rights caused by the alleged contravention of EU environmental law and that they are directly affected by such impairment in comparison with the public at large (in this case, they have to be represented by a NGO or a lawyer authorised to practise before a court of a Member State; or 2) demonstrate a sufficient public interest and that the request is supported by at least 4 000 members of the public residing or established in at least five EU Member States, with at least 250 members of the public coming from each of those Member States. The effect of this new regulation yet remains to be seen.

The International Tribunal for the Law of the Sea (ITLOS) is closed to individuals and organisations other than those who have an interest in research and exploitation of the seabed (Articles 87, 153 para. 2 UNCLOS and Article 37 of the Statute of the Court). Non-profit NGOs, therefore, are not allowed to

---

[89] EU GC, T-330/18, *Carvalho and Others v Parliament and Council, Judgement of 8 May 2019* (ECLI:EU:T:2019:324), para. 50.

[90] CJEU, C-565/19 P, *Carvalho and Others v Parliament and Council, Judgement of 25 March 2021* (ECLI:EU:C:2021:252).

[91] Report of the Aarhus Convention Compliance Committee—Findings and Recommendations with Regard to Communication ACCC/C/2008/32 (Part I) Concerning Compliance by the European Union, 14 April 2011, para 86. Both 'ECJ' and 'CJEU' are abbreviations for the European Court of Justice.

participate as parties.[92] However, it seems that the ITLOS in the *Arctic Sunrise case*, while not relaxing standing requirements, was at least partially receptive to hearing NGO views.[93]

Among those courts that allow NGOs to participate are the human rights tribunals in Europe, America and Africa.[94] Individuals can also approach these tribunals (Art. 34 ECHR; Articles 45(3), 55 African Charter on Human and Peoples' Rights (AfCHPR); Article 44 ACHR). The AfCHPR (Article 24) and the ACHR (Article 11 of the Protocol of San Salvador) even include a human right to a healthy environment. Although individuals are not able to claim a violation of Article 11 IACHR before the Inter-American Commission or Court due to a restriction in Article 19 para. 6 of the Protocol of San Salvador, by recognising an autonomous right to a healthy environment in Article 26 ACHR, the IACtHR has made this right justiciable.[95] So far, there has been one successful case invoking Art. 24 of the AfCHPR.[96] While the Arab Charter of Human Rights recognises a right to a healthy environment (Article 38), the Statute of the Arab Court of Human Rights (which has not yet entered into force at the time of writing) does not include individual complaint mechanisms.

8.1.2.3 Concluding Remarks

It seems that courts are becoming more open to CCL, with standing rules are being relaxed to some extent at both the national and the international levels.[97] This has benefited NGOs and individuals who are the main drivers of CCL and, thus, opens the doors for the open society of constitutional interpreters to articulate their interpretations of fundamental rights before domestic and international courts. In this sense, the GFCC surprised many when it declared the constitutional complaints of the Bangladeshi and Nepali claimants against the KSG admissible. Consequently, this allows non-citizens to articulate their interests and

---

[92] Astrid Epiney, 'The Role of NGOs in the Process of Ensuring Compliance with MEAs' in Ulrich Beyerlin, Peter-Tobias Stoll and Rüdiger Wolfrum (eds), *Ensuring Compliane with Multilateral Environmental Agreements: Academic Analysis and Views from Practice* (2006).

[93] Anna Dolidze, 'The Arctic Sunrise and NGOs in International Judicial Proceedings' (2014) 18 ASIL Insights <https://www.asil.org/insights/volume/18/issue/1/arctic-sunrise-and-ngos-international-judicial-proceedings> accessed 31 August 2023.

[94] Beyerlin (n 81) 359.

[95] IACtHR, Advisory Opinion OC-23/17—The Environment and Human Rights (2017) para 56 ff., see also IACtHR, *Caso Comunidades indígenas miembros de la asociación Lhaka Honhat (Nuestra Tierra) vs. Argentina*, Judgement of 6 February 2020, para 203.

[96] African Commission, *SERAC and CESR v. Nigeria* (2001), Communication 155/96.

[97] May and Daly (n 71) 278.

helps to raise awareness for their concerns before Germany's highest court. In this sense, the question of having standing is the very starting point of national court proceedings, which may result in transnational dialogues between citizens, scholarship and the courts.

8.1.3 Legitimacy of NGOs

As outlined above, in transnational regimes, lawmaking occurs in a decentralised way and through protests of the international public (*colère publique*), even against the will of official policymakers.[98] Such global law can even 'overrun the constitutional autarky of every single state and [...] therefore can claim constitutional quality itself'.[99]

Thus, in the same way, IOs are often not deemed legitimate, the engagement of NGOs raises questions of democratic legitimacy. The *Brent Spar* case, for example, has highlighted the (economic) power NGOs hold even over multinational oil companies when they manage to channel and aggressively promote their objectives, for example, by calling for boycotts.[100]

The majority of CCL suits have been filed or orchestrated by NGOs. Unlike most individuals and local or indigenous communities, NGOs enjoy great political influence on IL and society and are backed by financial resources.[101] Even individual cases are often embedded in NGO action. For NGOs, strategic litigation is also one of the tools they use to pursue their social, political or environmental goals.[102]

For Zengerling, NGOs engaged in litigation do not need to prove legitimacy, as they are not taking any decisions that are legally binding on any citizen. Their roles are limited to being the initiators of juridical processes and amici curiae.

---

98 See Section 7.3.2.2 above.

99 Petra Dobner, 'More Law, Less Democracy? Democracy and Transnational Constitutionalism' in Petra Dobner and Martin Loughlin (eds), *The Twilight of Constitutionalism?* (OUP 2010) 148.

100 Ulrich Beck, *World at Risk* (Polity Press 2008) 96.

101 Ann Marie Clark, 'Non-Governmental Organizations and Their Influence on International Society' (1995) 48 Journal of International Affairs 507; Peter Spiro, 'Non-Governmental Organizations and Civil Society' in Daniel Bodansky, Jutta Brunnée and Ellen Hey (eds), *The Oxford Handbook of International Environmental Law* (OUP 2008).

102 Peel and Osofsky (n 55) 95.

Thus, NGOs engage in law enforcement and compliance control but not in international lawmaking, where representation and legitimacy matter.[103] However, such an approach may not be comprehensive enough to address the specific phenomenon of CCL. As identified already, litigation can serve as a 'port of entry' for a dialogue between various governmental stakeholders and non-state actors in the field of climate change.[104] Such an analysis is supported by Häberle's approach, who argues that '[a]nyone who lives within the scope and with the circumstances governed by the norm is indirectly, and possibly directly, a norm interpreter'.[105] NGOs are at least 'pre-interpreters' ('*Vorinterpreten*').[106] The case of *Juliana v United States* shows clearly how NGOs not only enforce existing norms but seek to re-interpret them or introduce new normative concepts such as the 'right to a stable climate'.[107] At best, CCL, from this point of view, could be described as a hybrid: while NGOs seek to enforce international climate law, such as the Paris Agreement, some cases may well have been conspiring to attempt to engage in international lawmaking.[108]

Membership in an NGO, unlike citizenship, is voluntary. The 'authority' of NGOs is a moral rather than a legal authority.[109] Sometimes, their inner organisation is neither democratic nor transparent. Some NGOs, such as Extinction Rebellion, Just Stop Oil or the Last Generation (*Letzte Generation*) explicitly call for civil disobedience to overturn or block laws that are the result of a legitimate majority-driven process.[110]

The lack of internal democracy in many NGOs has been addressed by some scholars who call for stronger democratisation of internal NGO processes and increasing transparency and argue that NGOs should 'practise what they preach'

---

[103] Zengerling (n 22) 37 (also fn. 90).

[104] Hari M Osofsky, 'Climate Change Litigation as Pluralist Legal Dialogue?' (2007) 26 A Stanford Environmental Law Journal 181, 195.

[105] Häberle, 'The Open Society of Constitutional Interpreters' (n 5) 131.

[106] ibid.

[107] See, for example, Mary Christina Wood, 'Atmospheric Trust Litigation: Securing a Constitutional Right to a Stable Climate System' (2018) 29 Colorado Natural Resources, Energy, and Environmental Law Review 321; Hammersley (n 56); Michael C Blumm and Mary Christina Wood, '"No Ordinary Lawsuit": Climate Change, Due Process, and the Public Trust Doctrine' (2017) 67 American University Law Review 1.

[108] Osofsky (n 104) 196.

[109] Steve Charnovitz, 'Nongovernmental Organizations and International Law' (2006) 100 The American Journal of International Law 348, 348.

[110] Zengerling (n 22) 37.

and prove that they have the authority to speak for those they intend to represent.[111] Anderson and Rieff, for example, argue that NGOs do not represent the whole of the population and especially not 'the' global civil society.[112] They differ between domestic and international NGOs. They claim that NGOs in the domestic realm are not taken as the only actors speaking for the nation, while international NGOs would claim to represent global society and try to be the intermediaries between the people of the world and international institutions. International NGO action, therefore, is illegitimate.[113] Indeed, it has been noticed that Urgenda sought to represent not only the current Dutch population but also the people of other countries and future generations both in the Netherlands and abroad, thus, literally everybody.[114] However, the differentiation between domestic and international NGOs fails to recognise that while NGOs are not elected by the concerned public, the same is true for foreign governments participating in multilateral negotiation processes whose outcomes may affect the people of other states. NGO participation can help to amplify individual voices in seeking the support or opposition of other governments on whose election they have no influence.[115]

For others, the lack of internal democracy in many NGOs does not automatically lead to less legitimacy. Peters points out that undemocratic states are allowed to vote at the international level without restrictions. Moreover, NGO members can 'vote with their feet' if they feel the NGO's policies are wrong or undesirable and, thus, leave an organisation they no longer want to belong to, something members of a state cannot (easily) do. These more direct ways of participating and leaving replace, to some extent, internal democratic control.[116]

---

[111] See Martine Beijerman, 'Practice What You Preach? Limitations to Imposing Democratic Norms on NGOs' (2018) 20 International Community Law Review 3; Martine Beijerman, 'Conceptual Confusions in Debating the Role of NGOs for the Democratic Legitimacy of International Law' (2018) 9 Transnational Legal Theory 147, 158.

[112] Kenneth Anderson and David Rieff, '"Global Civil Society": A Sceptical View' in Helmut Anheier, Marlies Glasius and Mary Kaldor (eds), *Global Civil Society* (Sage Publications 2005) 1.5.

[113] ibid 1.6–1.7.

[114] Otto Spijkers, 'Pursuing Climate Justice through Public Interest Litigation: The Urgenda Case' *Völkerrechtsblog* (29 April 2020) <https://voelkerrechtsblog.org/articles/pursuing-climate-justice-through-public-interest-litigation-the-urgenda-case/> accessed 31 August 2023. The court limited itself to establishing standing on behalf of the (current) residents of the Netherlands.

[115] Charnovitz (n 109) 366.

[116] Anne Peters, 'Dual Democracy' in Jan Klabbers, Anne Peters and Geir Ulfstein (eds), *The Constitutionalization of International Law* (OUP 2009) 317.

A democratic mandate would not only be unnecessary but even contradictory, as NGOs do not seek to represent whole societies but to pursue single issues or specific interests by (claiming to be) speaking for minorities and the 'voiceless'.[117] 'It is precisely a feature of pluralist law-making processes to offer interest groups the opportunity to participate and give input into the process without requiring any democratic mandate.'[118]

It has also been doubted whether NGO participation in international lawmaking is efficient. Accordingly, NGOs would often underestimate the complexity of transnational participation, deliberation and checks and balances. Their sometimes quite rigid positions can make it difficult to enter an open debate and can provoke unwillingness to listen to other actors.[119] Furthermore, international governance focuses strongly on the concerns of 'Northern' NGOs and does not sufficiently include the voices of 'Southern' NGOs.[120] Moreover, the growth in numbers of NGOs participating in international lawmaking leads to the so-called 'openness dilemma'—more openness for civil society participation means not only more information that needs to be absorbed and channelled by formal institutions but also fierce competition among NGOs.[121]

Another point of critique is the so-called 'second bite of the apple' thesis.[122] In the international context, governments negotiate on behalf of the entire nation, including the political minority defeated in democratic elections. NGO participation in international governance, thus, 'provides a second opportunity for intrastate advocates to reargue their positions, thus advantaging them over their opponents who are either unwilling or unable to reargue their cases in international fora'.[123]

But despite all the criticism, there are many benefits of NGO participation. People no longer determine their identity only by belonging to a particular territory but also as members of different functional communities. NGOs defining and defending community interests, such as the protection of human rights or the environment, can offer alternative forms of 'representation' by providing a more

---

[117] ibid 316.

[118] ibid 317.

[119] Beijerman, 'Conceptual Confusions in Debating the Role of NGOs for the Democratic Legitimacy of International Law' (n 111) 154.

[120] ibid 154–5.

[121] ibid 155.

[122] JR Bolton, 'Should We Take Global Governance Seriously?' (2000) 1 Chicago Journal of International Law 205, 217.

[123] ibid.

refined reflection of individuals' views than their governments could.[124] As such, they are members of the complex regime of climate change. To this regime's legitimacy, NGOs can contribute through their voice, knowledge and social engagement.[125] They are supposed to serve as a 'connective tissue' between the global and the local.[126] In pluralist models, agendas and formal communications of international lawmaking are opened up for broader participation of different actors, thus, expanding the opportunities for affected people to participate and make their voices heard at the international level. In this sense, NGOs can introduce minority views marginalised by states into the discourse.[127] Thus, NGOs are not the representatives of *the* global civil society. But they are critical watchdogs over the activities of governments, and they can help to defend the claims of those without a voice in will-formation processes (such as future generations, nature, foreigners) against majority decisions and the interests of economically and politically powerful players.[128]

Brunkhorst, who argues that human rights operate in the grey area between morals and law, believes that the great advantage of NGOs lies in their ability to speak 'the *still* moral but *already* legal "language of human rights"', which is understandable for both civil society and politicians.[129] 'In their function as a placeholder of democratic legitimacy, human rights constitute a strong public sphere in the making due to their—deeply ambivalent—moral and legal dual character.'[130] NGOs could be seen as the first kernels of a strong public in the making and, thus, the vanguard of a transnational 'people'. However, they are not constituent representative bodies and, therefore, do not represent *the* people. All they can do in a weak global public sphere is to represent a 'global' people in counterfactual and advocacy ways, with engagement and transparency being the only criteria of legitimacy.[131] Through their engagement, they fulfil the same

[124] Daniel C Esty, 'Non-Governmental Organizations at the World Trade Organization: Cooperation, Competition, or Exclusion' (1998) 1 Journal of International Economic Law 124, 131–2.

[125] Beijerman, 'Conceptual Confusions in Debating the Role of NGOs for the Democratic Legitimacy of International Law' (n 111) 151.

[126] For the WTO, see Esty (n 124) 125–6.

[127] Beijerman, 'Conceptual Confusions in Debating the Role of NGOs for the Democratic Legitimacy of International Law' (n 111) 151.

[128] Zengerling (n 22) 218.

[129] Hauke Brunkhorst, *Solidarität. Von der Bürgerfreundschaft zur globalen Rechtsgenossenschaft* (Suhrkamp 2002) 210 (tr the author, emphasis in the German original).

[130] ibid 211.

[131] ibid 213.

constitutional functions political parties serve in the nation-state. They can give those who cannot or are not (yet) willing to articulate themselves a voice. Transparency means inclusive openness. If NGOs started to exclude anybody, they would exclude themselves from the global legitimation process.[132] This openness offers a 'compensatory channel' for citizens' influence at the transnational level.[133] Even when NGOs cannot claim to represent *the* global society, more inclusive, open, transparent, and deliberative processes of international lawmaking, which include NGO participation, could reduce the legitimacy gap at the international level.[134]

8.2 Amicus Curiae

While the access to international juridical proceedings for NGOs is somewhat limited, their opportunities to agitate as amici curiae are broader. Originating in Roman law and established early in common-law traditions,[135] the amicus curiae is a 'friend of the court' who—through the instrument of the so-called amicus curiae brief—can provide information to the court to deal with an issue at hand. The instrument of the amicus curiae has become well established on the international plane in the past decades and recently, even in civil-law jurisdictions.[136] One of the most illustrative examples in this regard is Brazil, a civil-law country, where Häberle's theory of the open society of constitutional interpreters has influenced the implementation of this figure in the domestic legal order, not only in constitutional proceedings but also for the courts of appeal (*Tribunais de Justiça*).[137]

---

[132] ibid 213–4.

[133] Magdalena Bexell and others, 'Democracy in Global Governance: The Promises and Pitfalls of Transnational Actors' (2010) 16 Global Governance 81, 86.

[134] Charnovitz (n 109) 365.

[135] On the origin of the amicus curiae, see Frank Covey Jr., 'Amicus Curiae: Friend of the Court' (1959) 9 DePaul Law Review 30, 33–5.

[136] Steven Kochevar, 'Amici Curiae in Civil Law Jurisdictions' (2013) 122 Yale Law Journal 1653, 1653–4.

[137] Gilmar Mendes, 'A influência de Peter Häberle no constitucionalismo brasileiro' (2016) 2 Journal of Institutional Studies 30, 33–4.

8.2.1 Amici in International Proceedings

The ICJ allows for briefs to be submitted on their own initiative by 'public international organisations'. Despite scholars arguing for a broad interpretation, the ICJ identified that the term refers to 'international organization[s] of States' (Article 69 para. 2 of the Rules of the Court) only. However, NGOs can participate indirectly as their briefs occasionally are integrated into parties' memorials.[138] In the *Gabčikovo-Nagymaros Project* case, for example, the brief was referred to as part of the annex of the memorial.[139]

The international human rights tribunals are more open towards NGOs as amici curiae. In this sense, the IACtHR welcomes the receiving of amicus briefs under Article 44 ACHR, and so does the ECtHR under Article 36 of ECHR. Particularly in the European human rights system, NGOs have made intensive use of this instrument.[140]

8.2.2 The Changing Role of the Amicus Curiae

The role of the amicus curiae is to provide neutral, useful information to the court. In 1879, an amicus curiae was described as:

> a bystander, who without having an interest in the cause, of his own knowledge makes a suggestion on a point of law or of fact, for the information of the presiding judge.[141]

The amicus was conceived as someone who brought up cases not known to the judge, and the court welcomed the amicus' help kindly, as 'it is for the honor of a court of justice to avoid error'.[142] The amicus should attempt to help the court

[138] Saratoon Santivasa, 'The NGOs' Participation in the Proceedings of the International Court of Justice' (2012) 5 Journal of East Asia and International Law 377, 390.

[139] ibid 390–1.

[140] Andrea Bianchi, 'Globalization of Human Rights: The Role of Non-State Actors' in Gunther Teubner (ed), *Global Law without a State* (Dartmouth Publishing 1997) 187.

[141] Benjamin Vaughan Abbott, 'Amicus Curiae', *Dictionary of terms and phrases used in American or English jurisprudence* (Little, Brown, and Company 1879) 62.

[142] The Protector v. Geering, 145 Eng. Rep. 394 (Ex. 1656), cited by Samuel Krislov, 'The Amicus Curiae Brief: From Friendship to Advocacy' (1963) 72 Yale Law Journal 694, 695.

rather than the parties:[143] 'he acts for no one'.[144] Throughout the years, the amicus has been a highly adaptable instrument also due to the lack of precise rules around the scope of its acting and, therefore, provides a very useful tool for third parties to participate in lawsuits and call attention to collective lawsuits.[145] But in 1963, Krislov noticed a shift in the amicus' position from neutrality to advocacy. A reason for this could be the strict American participation system in juridical proceedings where third-party interests were potentially underrepresented.[146] The amicus has become a lobbyist, an advocate and a defender of the politically powerless.[147] With the help of creative judges and litigants, amici overcame the role of merely briefing the court and, today, perform activities that had formerly been limited to the parties of a case, such as engaging in oral argument, introducing physical evidence and even enforcing previous court decisions upon the parties of the lawsuit.[148]

Now, the brief serves as both an endorsement and as an instrument to introduce (new) legal interpretations to the court.[149] The position of the amicus is quite favourable: as a non-participant, the amicus can bring emotional and questionable arguments that might be successfully considered by the court but are too risky to be brought up by litigants themselves:

> Arguments that might anger the Justices, doctrines that have not yet been found legally acceptable, and emotive presentations that have little legal standing can best be utilized in most instances by the amicus rather than by the principal.[150]

If the argument fails, conversely, it attaches only a minimum of disapprobation to the cause.[151]

While the amicus is an instrument of the common-law circle, it has now made its way into civil jurisdictions. Many Latin American countries have

---

[143] Covey Jr. (n 135) 30.

[144] Supreme Court of Indiana, Campbell v. Swasey, 12 Ind. 70, 72 (1859), cited by Krislov (n 142) 697.

[145] ibid 696.

[146] ibid 697.

[147] Michael K Lowman, 'The Litigating Amicus Curiae: When Does the Party Begin After the Friends Leave?' (1991) 41 American University Law Review 1243, 1245.

[148] ibid 1246.

[149] Krislov (n 142) 713.

[150] ibid 712.

[151] ibid 711.

approved the use of amicus briefs.[152] Prior to the formal recognition either by the legislator (Brazil) or the courts (Argentina), amicus briefs were already informally accepted.[153] In Europe, some countries, such as France, the Netherlands and Poland, have implemented the figure in their jurisdictions.[154] According to Kochevar, one reason why many civil-law countries have adopted the amicus is that 'pushy' NGOs submitted briefs even to jurisdictions that would not have recognised them or published their own editorials on controversial subject matters dealt with by a court.[155] Additionally, he names the influence of IL on domestic legal systems[156] and that the amicus curiae fits quite well into civil-law jurisdictions due to the comparability of the brief to civil-law techniques, such as the judge's ability to refer to expert witnesses for gathering information.[157] Thus, Henríquez-Prieto and Miranda-Nigro analysed in their study that almost all countries of the world fulfil at least one or more of the seven criteria that make the participation of amici curiae possible or more likely in the future.[158]

In environmental adjudication, the amicus fulfils another important task. A judge having to balance different interests against each other may face challenges when it comes to evaluating the consequences for whole ecosystems when interfering with one of its components. Amici of the scientific community can introduce scientific findings in highly complex cases that might help judges to

[152] Latin America Subcommittee—International Trademark Association, Alvaro Correa-Ordoñez and Sasha Mandakovic, 'Report: A Guide to Filing Amicus Curiae Briefs in Latin America' (2014). It is possible to file a brief in Argentina, Brazil, Costa Rica, Ecuador, Mexico, Panama, Paraguay, and Peru. It is not officially possible but briefs are considered by the courts in three countries (Colombia, Uruguay, and Venezuela). Briefs cannot be filed in Bolivia, Chile, El Salvador, and Honduras.

[153] Kochevar (n 136) 1660, 1662.

[154] M Francisca Henríquez-Prieto and Pablo Miranda-Nigro, 'Amicus Curiae and Ecosystem Services: On Public Interest Interventions to Help Resolve Environmental Controversies' (2018) 36 Journal of Energy and Natural Resources Law 209, 213.

[155] Kochevar (n 136) 1664.

[156] ibid 1665–7.

[157] ibid 1667–8.

[158] See Appendix I, Henríquez-Prieto and Miranda-Nigro (n 154) 225–31. Those criteria include whether a country belongs to the common law legal systems or non-pure common law based legal systems, where 'Common law jurisprudence retains its character as the fundamental law' (e.g. mixed with Sharia Law), whether it supports Principle 10 of the Rio Declaration (attendance at the Earth Summit), whether it ratified the Aarhus Convention or the Escazú Agreement, and whether specialised environmental courts exist.

understand what is at risk.[159] In *Future Generations*, for example, leading scientist Hansen filed an amicus brief supporting the plaintiffs' action by offering his scientific expertise.[160]

The amicus instrument can, therefore, help to open the doors for more actors. In Chile, for example, members of the civil society (of all nationalities) can participate as amici curiae in the proceedings before the three specialised environmental courts when they aim to protect a public interest.[161] Furthermore, from a socio-legal perspective, amici curiae can bridge the gap between the centre (the courts) and the periphery (the global and national public) of the system 'law' and, therefore, confer legitimacy to these procedures in the courts:[162]

> They can also introduce additional perspectives and might be able to trigger processes of scandalisation that contribute to discussions and mobilize the general public. Civil society at the periphery of international processes tends to show a greater sensibility for social and ecological questions when compared with actors at the centre of international political decision-making.[163]

8.3 The Media

CCL is often perceived as one tool among many to raise awareness.[164] Therefore, most cases initiated by NGOs are embedded in massive media campaigning, such as classic campaigning tools (press releases) but also digital platforms, especially social media, petition websites or crowdfunding platforms.[165] Attracting public attention is often more important to litigators than winning in court.[166] Even an

---

[159] ibid 217.

[160] Amicus Brief filed by Dr James E. Hansen (13 June 2018), available at <https://climatecasechart.com/non-us-case/future-generation-v-ministry-environment-others> accessed 31 August 2023.

[161] Maite Aguirrezábal Grünstein, 'Participación de La Sociedad Civil En El Proceso a Través Del Amicus Curiae' (*Instituto Chileno de Derecho Procesal*, 29 June 2016) <https://www.ichdp.cl/participacion-de-la-sociedad-civil-en-el-proceso-a-traves-del-amicus-curiae/> accessed 31 August 2023.

[162] Teubner (n 9), see also Chapter 7.

[163] Armin von Bogdandy and Ingo Venzke, 'On the Democratic Legitimation of International Judicial Lawmaking' in Armin von Bogdandy and Ingo Venzke (eds), *International Judicial Lawmaking* (Springer 2012) 504.

[164] Peel and Osofsky (n 55) 31.

[165] ibid 51.

[166] See also Section 6.5.

unsuccessful case can reveal weaknesses in the law that the media can expose to the public, which can promote legal change.[167] Successful cases, conversely, can have a ripple effect leading to new cases in other countries.

8.4 Scholarship

Article 38 of the ICJ Statute refers to 'the teachings of the most highly qualified publicists of the various nations' as one source of law. According to Häberle, constitutional law scholarship 'holds a special status, as it examines the other participant powers and is nonetheless itself a participant on several levels'.[168] The role of constitutional scholarship is not limited to analysing (constitutional) jurisdiction, which 'is a defining, albeit not the sole catalyst of constitutional legal scholarship in constitutional interpretation'.[169] Scholars also present their ideas in academia and practice, sometimes in a very progressive and creative manner. Thus, 'the writing of jurists appears to have had a remarkable influence on the shaping and gradual emergence of the idea of a world public order'.[170] Scholars contribute to the development of IL by discussing judicial decisions and by framing theories that can guide interpretation.[171] Their ideas have 'long-term' effects that can gradually (albeit slowly) influence lawmaking.[172]

In South Africa, for example, du Plessis discusses the interconnectedness of the right to a healthy environment (Section 24 of the South African Constitution)[173] and socio-economic rights. She argues for a generous interpretation so

---

[167] Brian J Preston, 'Characteristics of Successful Environmental Courts and Tribunals' (2014) 26 Journal of Environmental Law 365, 387.

[168] Häberle, 'The Open Society of Constitutional Interpreters' (n 5) 137.

[169] ibid 139–40.

[170] Bianchi (n 140) 183.

[171] Ingo Venzke, *How Interpretation Makes International Law: On Semantic Change and Normative Twists* (OUP 2012) 65.

[172] Cf. Peter Häberle, 'Universaler Konstitutionalismus aus nationalen und völkerrechtlichen Teilverfassungen—Sieben Thesen' in Peter Häberle (ed), *Jahrbuch des Öffentlichen Rechts der Gegenwart* (Mohr Siebeck 2014) 418.

[173] Section of the South African Constitution reads:
Everyone has the right –

1. (a) to an environment that is not harmful to their health or well-being; and
2. (b) to have the environment protected, for the benefit of present and future generations, through reasonable legislative and other measures that –
   1. (i) prevent pollution and ecological degradation;

that other constitutional issues, such as poverty, can be considered under the environmental right. Since there is no jurisdiction around the term 'well-being' in Section 24 yet, it has been argued that, as opposed to the explicitly named health, well-being could also refer to social, economic, mental and emotional factors.[174] Feris embraces the idea of a 'sense of place' in terms of a sense of belonging,[175] which can be violated through environmental degradation, for example, through fracking in the semi-desert Karoo.[176] The idea is informed by what Australian environmental philosopher Albrecht termed 'solastalgia',[177] which refers to 'homesickness': mental and existential distress due to environmental degradation, in particular through climate change.[178] The New South Wales Land and Environmental Court used solastalgia to analyse the possible negative social

2. (ii) promote conservation; and
   (iii) secure ecologically sustainable development and use of natural resources while promoting justifiable economic and social development.

[174] Anel du Plessis, 'South Africa's Constitutional Environmental Right (Generously) Interpreted: What Is in It for Poverty?' (2011) 27 South African Journal on Human Rights 279; Anel du Plessis, 'The Promise of "Well-Being" in Section 24 of the Constitution of South Africa' (2018) 34 South African Journal on Human Rights 191, arguing that 'underdevelopment is unsustainable'.

[175] Loretta Feris, 'Loss of Sense of Place as Displacement—New Frontiers for Environmental Rights' in Erin Daly and others (eds), *New Frontiers in Environmental Constitutionalism* (UNEP 2017).

[176] Ambre Nicolson, 'A Sense of Place: New Frontiers for the Law (Inaugural Lecture of Prof Loretta Feris at University of Cape Town on 8 October 2014)' (16 October 2014) <https://www.news.uct.ac.za/article/-2014-10-16-a-sense-of-place-new-frontiers-for-the-law> accessed 31 August 2023.

[177] Glenn Albrecht and others, 'Solastalgia: The Distress Caused by Environmental Change' (2007) 15 Australasian Psychiatry.

[178] G. Albrecht, *Expert Report (Case Milbrodale Progress Association v Minister for Planning and Infrastructure, Land and Environmental Court of New South Wales)* (2012). 'I therefore describe solastalgia as the pain or sickness caused by the ongoing loss of solace and the sense of desolation connected to the present state of one's home and territory. It is the "lived experience" of negative environmental change manifest as an attack on one's sense of place. It is characteristically a chronic condition tied to the gradual erosion of the sense of belonging (identity) to a particular place and a feeling of distress (psychological desolation) about its transformation (loss of wellbeing). In direct contrast to the dislocated spatial and temporal dimensions of nostalgia, it is the homesickness you have when you are still located within your home environment.'

effects of a planned extension of a coal mine on a local community, the latest in its landmark case on the Gloucester mine.[179]

In the same way, the concept of future generations having rights has been introduced to jurisprudence. Brown Weiss developed the idea in her book *In Fairness to Future Generations: International Law, Common Patrimony, and Intergenerational Equity* (1989). Oposa, who sought a way to protect the virgin rainforests of the Philippines, heard of the idea that the rights and interests of future generations should be considered when making decisions today while he was studying in Oslo. Back home in the Philippines, he tested these ideas in court and filed a claim on behalf of 43 children, including his own, and 'generations unborn'. The Trial Court dismissed the case. Oposa appealed the decision to the Supreme Court, but the solicitor general questioned whether Oposa could sue on behalf of generations unborn and found that the claim had no basis in law.[180] By then, Oposa had come across the works of Brown Weiss. He sent her books to the court.[181] The Supreme Court ruled for Oposa on every argument.[182]

While the influence of meanings and theories of individual scholars is quite limited, they gain weight and authority when acting collectively or in an institutionalised form such as the ILC. As such, they were capable of introducing scholarly ideas such as the concept of *jus cogens* or the law on state responsibility into IL.[183] This interconnectedness of theory and practice can be observed in the creation of the Oslo Principles on global climate change obligations, which was adopted by a group of experts from all over the world with different backgrounds in law. Besides university scholars, judges and advocates are members of the group. They aimed to create principles and a legal commentary 'that draws on the best joint interpretation of international law, human rights law, national

---

[179] Land and Environment Court New South Wales, *Bulga Milbrodale Progress Association Inc v Minister for Planning and Infrastructure and Warkworth Mining Limited* (2013) NSWLEC 48, para. 420–430; NSW Land and Environment Court, *Gloucester Resources Limited v Minister for Planning* (2019) NSWLEC 7, para 313.

[180] Oliver A Houck, *Taking Back Eden: Eight Environmental Cases That Changed the World* (Island Press 2010) 52.

[181] Emily Newburger, 'Visionary of the Visayan Sea' *Harvard Law Today* (28 July 2008) <https://today.law.harvard.edu/feature/visionary-of-the-visayan-sea/> accessed 31 August 2023.

[182] Supreme Court of the Philippines, *Minors Oposa v Factoran* (1993) 224 SCRA 792.

[183] Venzke (n 171) 66.

environmental law and tort law' and could help judges to address climate change issues.[184]

According to some legal scholars, these developments demonstrate that a new field of law is emerging: international climate change law.[185] It is 'a dynamic, multidisciplinary field of law, covering many jurisdictions with different economies (which also change over time), and many specific issues, with connections to many other legal fields' and is cross-cutting many different areas of law, climate science, economics, cultural and social science.[186] Cooperation and exchange are necessary, since the new discipline is too comprehensive to be mastered by individual scholars alone.[187] Legal scholarship can help to shape the values of IEL, not only in theory but also practice, since 'a self-reproductive legal discourse, elaborated by a restricted intellectual community when coupled with social processes that give support to the basic tenets of the discourse, may ultimately affect state behaviour'.[188] In doing so, 'jurists set the stage for the development of a new world order based on shared values and common interests'.[189]

8.5 Other Actors

Häberle's theory was designed for German constitutional law and later modified to fit European particularities. IL, of course, has its own characteristics to which the theory needs to be adapted. One of those points where such a modification—or rather, an enhancement—is necessary is the question of who interprets and further develops IL.[190] Häberle lists the sovereign states, the UN (including the

---

[184] See 'Oslo Principles on Global Climate Change Obligations' (*Global Justice Program (Yale University)*) <https://globaljustice.yale.edu/oslo-principles-global-climate-change-obligations> accessed 31 August 2023.

[185] Jacqueline Peel, 'Climate Change Law: The Emergence of a Legal Discipline' (2008) 32 Melbourne University Law Review 922; Thijs Etty and others, 'The Maturing of Transnational Environmental Law' (2017) 6 Transnational Environmental Law 193; Thijs Etty and others, 'Transnational Climate Law' (2018) 7 Transnational Environmental Law 191.

[186] Daniel A Farber and Marjan Peeters, 'The Emergence of Global Climate Law' in Michael G Faure (ed), *Elgar Encyclopedia of Environmental Law: Climate Change Law (Vol. I)* (Edward Elgar Publishing 2015) 691.

[187] ibid.

[188] Bianchi (n 140) 185.

[189] ibid.

[190] Häberle, 'The Open Society of Constitutional Interpreters' (n 5) 164.

Security Council, the General Assembly, the tribunals), the ICJ, NGOs and the international public. Additional actors have important roles in an open society in international climate constitutional law.

There are, for example, highly specialised environmental lawyers. Cities and sub-states in the US play a central role in developing climate policies (one only has to think of *EPA v Massachusetts*). Further to mention are indigenous groups and local communities. National judges and courts also play a special role, as will be analysed below in Section 9.5. Some of the most important cases have been filed on behalf of future generations (see *Juliana* and *Future Generations*). Private business actors and corporations engaging in anti-regulatory litigation may also shape climate policies.[191] Due to a limitation of space and a focus on pro-regulatory litigation, business actors will not be covered by this work. However, their influence on climate law as both an obstacle and a social driver for deep decarbonisation must not be overlooked.[192]

8.5.1 Cities, Local Governments and States

Local governments and states also play a role in CCL in the U.S. Their policies sometimes are more progressive and far-reaching than those of the Federal State. Some cities such as Los Angeles or Minneapolis have signed up to comply with the Kyoto Protocol, which has not been ratified by the U.S.[193] Since 2019, 24 cities and one state (Hawai'i) so far have declared a climate emergency—among them New York City and San Francisco[194]—because they fear the costs climate change will cause due to the necessity of constructing higher dams or the re-construction of whole cities after extreme weather events such as hurricanes.[195]

---

[191] Peel and Osofsky (n 55) 52.

[192] Corporate responses have been identified as one of the ten dominant social drivers for deep decarbonisation by Anita Engels and others, 'Hamburg Climate Futures Outlook 2023—The Plausibility of a 1.5°C Limit to Global Warming' (2023).

[193] Tomas Alex Tizon, 'Mayor Is on a Mission to Warm U.S. Cities to the Kyoto Protocol' *Los Angeles Times* (22 February 2005) <https://www.latimes.com/archives/la-xpm-2005-feb-22-na-greenteam22-story.html> accessed 31 August 2023.

[194] Chris Mills Rodrigo, 'New York City Officials Declare Climate Emergency' *The Hill* (26 June 2019) <https://thehill.com/policy/energy-environment/450506-new-york-city-officials-declare-climate-emergency> accessed 31 August 2023.

[195] For an overview, see David Hasemyer, 'Fossil Fuels on Trial: Where the Major Climate Change Lawsuits Stand Today' *Inside Climate News* (17 January 2020) <https://insideclimatenews.org/news/04042018/climate-change-fossil-fuel-company-lawsuits-timeline-exxon-children-california-cities-attorney-general> accessed 31 August 2023.

Sub-entities such as states and local communities have increasingly started to take action in the U.S., mostly by filing claims against the auto industry and energy companies.[196] The City of New York, for example, has filed a lawsuit against major oil and gas companies, which seeks to hold the defendants liable for damages stemming from domestic and foreign GHGs.[197]

While these complaints are filed against private actors in the industry and, therefore, are not the focus of this work, the case is notable insofar as the federal government intervened as an amicus curiae in support of the defendants. The brief argues that the City's claims, inter alia, are inconsistent with the system of the separation of powers and are 'all the more out of place in the international context, where the risk that courts and litigants will encroach on the proper functions of Congress and the Executive Branch is acute'.[198] It also repeats the Supreme Court's *AEP* decision, according to which '[f]ederal judges lack the scientific, economic, and technological resources an agency can utilize in coping with issues of this order'.[199] Although the case was ultimately dismissed, several other states and cities are still trying to make oil companies pay for losses.[200] After *West Virginia v EPA*, it remains to be seen whether the courts will uphold their jurisprudential line considering the conservative majority in the U.S. Supreme Court.[201]

8.5.2 Environmental Lawyers

Important in this regard is the role of environmental lawyers. Generally, people look for lawyers' advice or help when they suffer harm or seek to prevent a violation of their rights. However, in CCL, it is often the other way around:

[196] For some of the suits California filed, see Osofsky (n 104) 197–202.

[197] Southern District Court of New York, *City of New York v. BP p.l.c.*, 1:18-cv-00182; for an overview of the case, see <https://climatecasechart.com/case/city-new-york-v-bp-plc/> accessed 31 August 2023.

[198] 'Brief of the United States as Amicus Curiae in Support of Appellees (Case City of New York v BP P.L.C., et Al., No. 1:18-Cv-00182)' (2019) 27 <https://climatecasechart.com/case/city-new-york-v-bp-plc/> accessed 31 August 2023.

[199] ibid 28–9.

[200] For an overview, see <https://climatecasechart.com/case-category/actions-seeking-money-damages-for-losses/> accessed 31 August 2023.

[201] Mark A Lemley, 'The Imperial Supreme Court' (2023) 136 Harvard Law Review 97, 114; Rachael Lyle, 'A Reckless Decision' [2022] *Verfassungsblog* <https://verfassungsblog.de/a-reckless-decision/> accessed 31 August 2023.

lawyers reach out to potential plaintiffs. Equipped with environmental activism and ambition, highly specialised environmental lawyers are creating their own cases to test unusual legal techniques, challenge legal hurdles such as the doctrines of standing and test the limits of adjudication. The *Urgenda* case, for example, was supported by lawyer Roger J. Cox. Himself the founder of an NGO called Planet Prosperity Foundation, Cox is the author of a book named *Revolution Justified* (2012), in which he outlines ideas for bringing climate issues before the courts.[202] According to Cox, Urgenda's director Minnesma decided to realise Cox's ideas after reading the book and to initiate the first CCL case in Europe with his help.[203] Attorney Julia Olsen founded Our Children's Trust after watching Al Gore's movie *An Inconvenient Truth* while she was pregnant. Her colleague, Mary Wood, director of the Environmental and Natural Resources Law Program at the University of Oregon, mentioned the *Oposa Minors* case, which inspired Olsen to file a suit on behalf of children—the *Juliana* case.[204] Different to 'ordinary' lawsuits, there is no specific violation of anyone's rights or any concrete indication as known from 'classical' lawsuits. Instead, the cases are designed in a way that they would fit the claim: the requirements of its advocacy that had been prepared.[205] According to Cox, Urgenda aimed to take his theories to court and test their foundations against possible legal hurdles.[206] After a successful outcome, Cox helped to shape the Belgium Klimaatzaak.[207] In this sense, it becomes quite apparent why public interest litigation is referred to as *strategic* litigation. However, current CCL has been criticised for not addressing the needs of marginalised communities.[208] The 'interests of white, middle-class people determine the movement's priorities and activities' when white, middle-class lawyers develop strategies for courts staffed with white judges, and these

---

202 Planet Prosperity Foundation, 'Revolution Justified—About the Book' <https://www.revolutionjustified.org> accessed 31 August 2023.

203 Planet Prosperity Foundation, 'Bringing Government to Court. Claiming a Green Energy Revolution' <http://www.planetprosperity.org/news/3-revolution-justified> accessed 31 August 2023.

204 Ellison (n 38).

205 Planet Prosperity Foundation, 'Revolution Justified—About the Book' (n 202).

206 Planet Prosperity Foundation, 'The Climate Case' <https://www.planetprosperity.org/news/15-the-climate-case> accessed 31 August 2023.

207 vzw Klimaatzaak asbl (Association without lucrative purpose), 'Klimaatzaak (Belgium)' <https://www.klimaatzaak.eu/en> accessed 31 August 2023.

208 Systemic Justice, 'Our Vision for Community-Driven Litigation' (2023) <https://systemicjustice.ngo/2023/02/our-vision-for-community-driven-litigation/?trk=feed_main-feed-card_feed-article-content> accessed 31 August 2023.

strategies are not necessarily community driven or giving affected communities a voice.[209] They can even foster racist paradigms. For example, when indigenous peoples are portrayed in CCL cases as merely passive elements of nature rather than active managers of their own affairs, including their economic interests in the exploitation of natural resources, they are assigned an exclusive role as guardians of nature that is not necessarily compatible with indigenous sovereignty and can lead to a neo-colonial mischaracterisation of indigenous peoples in the imagination of other environmental activists.[210] Community-driven approaches to litigation, therefore, stress the need to include climate justice for BIPoC (Black people, Indigenous people, People of Colour) in ways that address not only the negative effects of climate change that these groups and communities strongly experience but also the injustices they suffer due to systemic racism.[211]

8.5.3 Indigenous People

Indigenous people, both in the Global South and the Global North, are among those expected to experience the worst effects of climate change as they tend to live in the most vulnerable places of the world (such as the Amazon rainforest or the Arctic ice sheet)[212] and are strongly related to their lands. Understanding themselves as the guardians of the land[213] and, thus, having a legal connection to the land, indigenous tribes cannot just move somewhere else. Instead, they rely

[209] Nani Jansen Reventlow, 'The Climate Movement's Racial Blind Spots' *Project Syndicate* (2 November 2022) <https://www.project-syndicate.org/commentary/european-climate-movement-racial-blind-spots-by-nani-jansen-reventlow-2022-11> accessed 31 August 2023; Dylan Asafo, 'The Racism in Climate Change Law: Critiquing the Law on Climate Change-Related Displacement with Critical Race Theory' (2021) 39 Berkeley Journal of International Law 249.

[210] Sam Bookman, 'Indigenous Climate Litigation in Anglophone Settler-Colonial States' *Verfassungsblog/Völkerrechtsblog* (25 March 2022) <https://verfassungsblog.de/indigenous-climate-litigation-in-anglophone-settler-colonial-states/> accessed 31 August 2023.

[211] See, for example, the climate justice-based approach by the NGO Systematic Justice, <https://systemicjustice.ngo/climatejustice/> accessed 31 August 2023.

[212] Randall Abate and Elizabeth Ann Kronk, 'Commonality among Unique Indigenous Communities: An Introduction to Climate Change and Its Impacts on Indigenous Peoples' (2013) 26 Tulane Environmental Law Journal 179, 182.

[213] Catherine Iorns Magallanes, 'Using Human Rights to Recognize Human Responsibilities toward Nature' in Erin Daly and others (eds), *New Frontiers in Environmental Constitutionalism* (UNEP 2017) 238: 'Traditional indigenous views of the environment consider humans as being part of nature and acknowledge and reflect humankind's interdependence with nature. Importantly, these indigenous cultures' connections with nature are so deep that the nature

on intact ecosystems to live according to their traditional beliefs, which includes the presence of certain endangered species.[214] The preamble of the Anchorage Declaration, drafted from the Indigenous People's Global Summit on Climate Change, states:

> We are experiencing profound and disproportionate adverse impacts on our cultures, human and environmental health, human rights, well-being, traditional livelihoods, food systems and food sovereignty, local infrastructure, economic viability, and our very survival as Indigenous People.[215]

Climate change threatens indigenous culture in its most basic aspects, such as indigenous languages[216] and their understanding of who they are. For indigenous people living in the Arctic, for example, the permanence of the frozen climate is essential to identify themselves.[217] Petitions such as the Inuit petition[218] were unsuccessful in the end; however, they were:

> filed to raise the profile of the marginalised concerns of the victims of climate change, such as indigenous peoples, and to articulate important values such as equity and justice which are basic principles of international environmental law, but which tend to receive less attention in the dominant climate change discourse because of the latter's regulatory and economic focus.[219]

Participation of indigenous communities should, however, not only be limited to their status as 'victims of climate change'. Rather, humanity would benefit from their ancestral knowledge of living in harmony with nature. The participants in the

---

is imbued with personality and viewed as kin—it is regarded as a true living ancestor of the people. This view corresponds with responsibilities to protect nature as guardians, as they would in respect to a family member.'

214 Abate and Kronk (n 212) 184.

215 Indigenous People's Global Summit on Climate Change, The Anchorage Declaration (2009).

216 Robert Melchior Figueroa, 'Indigenous Peoples and Cultural Losses' in John S Dryzeck, Richard B Norgaard and David Schlossberg (eds), *The Oxford Handbook of Climate Change and Society* (OUP 2011) 240.

217 Osofsky (n 104) 220.

218 Petition to The Inter-American Commission on Human Rights Seeking Relief from Violations Resulting from Global Warming Caused by Acts and Omissions of the United States (*Sheila Watt-Cloutier v United States*, "Inuit" petition), Petition No. P-1413–05 (2006).

219 Jolene Lin, 'Climate Change and the Courts' (2012) 32 Legal Studies 35, 40.

Indigenous Peoples' Global Summit on Climate Change in Anchorage explicitly expressed this:

> We offer to share with humanity our Traditional Knowledge, innovations, and practices relevant to climate change, provided our fundamental rights as intergenerational guardians of this knowledge are fully recognized and respected. We reiterate the urgent need for collective action.[220]

8.6 New Points of Reference: International Agreements and Climate Science

Almost every CCL case cites the findings of the IPCC or national science agencies, particularly in combination with international treaties such as the Paris Agreement, which itself is based on IPCC data. Climate science has become a powerful tool for litigants. This is because the global consensus that global warming is a human-made problem is extremely high,[221] and even some major GHG emitters do not even try to disagree with climate science anymore.[222]

Science has been underestimated by some defendants. In *Urgenda*, for example, the government had freely admitted that its mitigation effects as of 2015 would only achieve a 17% reduction of GHG emissions and argued that an increase to a 25% reduction would be just a 'drop in the ocean' and, therefore, 'negligible'.[223] The Dutch courts fully rejected this line of argumentation, as will be shown in Chapter 9. Instead, the courts made specific references to scientific findings. The courts in *Urgenda* and *Leghari*[224] relied on data provided by the IPCC and national scientific agencies. In *Future Generations*, the court used

[220] Indigenous People's Global Summit on Climate Change (n 215).

[221] IPCC, 'Sixth Assessment Report' (2023).

[222] Debra Kahn, 'Oil Giant Accepts Climate Consensus, Denies Responsibility for Warming' *Scientific American* (22 March 2018) <https://www.scientificamerican.com/article/oil-giant-accepts-climate-consensus-denies-responsibility-for-warming/> accessed 31 August 2023.

[223] Benoit Mayer, 'The State of the Netherlands v. Urgenda Foundation: Ruling of the Court of Appeal of the Hague (9 October 2018)' (2019) 8 Transnational Environmental Law 167, 179–80.

[224] Lahore High Court, Asghar Leghari v Federation of Pakistan, Judgement of 25 January 2018 (W.P. No. 25501/2015) para 9.

findings of the national science agency IDEAM (Institute of Hydrology, Meteorology and Environmental Studies).[225] A judge presiding over lawsuits filed by Oakland and San Francisco against Big Oil scheduled a five-hour tutorial on climate science to prepare himself for the trial;[226] this and the many amicus briefs filed by leading scientists seem to underline the assumption that climate science has become an important weapon for litigants that can help to decide cases in their favour.[227] But a group of researchers in the U.S. found that '[t]here was no association between the mention of climate science and more favourable outcome for proregulatory litigants'.[228] However, they put their findings in context:

> Despite these findings, both litigant types often said that science was important to their cases. Therefore, it is likely that the coding of decisions alone does not fully capture the role of science in cases, perhaps because we coded the text of judicial decisions, but not the pleadings and other documents filed by the litigants.[229]

Two problems usually occurred when courts were requested to consider scientific data. The first argument, often brought by private business actors of the oil and gas industry, is that GHG emissions grew historically and are not quantifiable due to their diffuse and transboundary character. Courts, therefore, were reluctant to assume causation.[230] However, newer research has shown that 90 carbon majors (the 90 companies that have historically produced two-thirds of human-caused global GHG emissions[231]) are responsible for nearly two-thirds of historic CO_2

---

[225] Corte Suprema de Justicia de Colombia (n 76) 35–7.

[226] Warren Cornwall, 'In a San Francisco Courtroom, Climate Science Gets Its Day on the Docket' *Science* (22 March 2018) <https://www.sciencemag.org/news/2018/03/san-francisco-court-room-climate-science-gets-its-day-docket> accessed 31 August 2023.

[227] See e.g., the amicus brief by Dr James E. Hansen (13 June 2018) in *Future Generations v Colombia*, available at <https://climatecasechart.com/non-us-case/future-generation-v-ministry-environment-others/> accessed 31 August 2023.

[228] Sabrina McCormick and others, 'Strategies in and Outcomes of Climate Change Litigation in the United States' [2018] Nature Climate Change 1, 3.

[229] ibid 4.

[230] Geetanjali Ganguly, Joana Setzer and Veerle Heyvaert, 'If at First You Don't Succeed: Suing Corporations for Climate Change' (2018) 38 Oxford Journal of Legal Studies 841, 852.

[231] Suzanne Goldenberg, 'Just 90 Companies Caused Two-Thirds of Man-Made Global Warming Emissions' *The Guardian* (20 November 2013) <https://www.theguardian.com/environment/2013/nov/20/90-companies-man-made-global-warming-emissions-climate-change> accessed 31 August 2023.

and methane emissions.[232] At least two cases were built on these findings.[233] The second obstacle is the attributability of extreme weather events, such as hurricanes, to climate change. It concerns both causation and foreseeability and the question of whether weather events are unpredictable— therefore, non-justiciable. On these grounds, many courts have dismissed CCL cases.[234] But attribution science has improved since the early CCL lawsuits, which has increased 'the foreseeability of certain climatic events and patterns in specific locations, and in identifying increasing risks of consequential impacts on property, physical assets and people'.[235]

Paskalev claimed that law was not properly taking scientific findings into account and that scientists' voices should be heard in juridical proceedings.[236] But a shift is notable. In *Leghari*, Chief Judge Syed Mansoor Ali Shah stated that '[c]limate justice is informed by science, responds to science and acknowledges the need for equitable stewardship of the world's resources.'[237]

However, a too-heavy reliance on science also seems undesirable. Mayer claimed that the court in *Urgenda* had adopted the scientific findings of the IPCC (a necessary reduction of GHG emissions by 25 per cent compared to 1990 levels by 2020) without reflection.[238] He argues that it is not for climate science to determine which is the most important objective in a pluralistic society. Instead, value-based rulings must determine what societies should strive for.[239] Technocratic approaches to climate change based solely on the expertise of climate scientists would most likely face resistance from the public and potentially make it more difficult to convince people to adopt truly sustainable climate policies. This means that voices other than those of scientific experts, including those of

232 Richard Heede, 'Tracing Anthropogenic Carbon Dioxide and Methane Emissions to Fossil Fuel and Cement Producers, 1854–2010' (2014) 122 Climatic Change 229, 238.

233 Ganguly, Setzer and Heyvaert (n 230) 853 mention the petition filed in September 2015 by the Philippines Reconstruction Movement and Greenpeace Southeast Asia with the Philippines' Commission on Human Rights and Saul Luciano Lliuya v RWE.

234 Sophie Marjanac and Lindene Patton, 'Extreme Weather Event Attribution Science and Climate Change Litigation: An Essential Step in the Causal Chain?' (2018) 36 Journal of Energy and Natural Resources Law 265, 266.

235 Sophie Marjanac, Lindene Patton and James Thornton, 'Acts of God, Human Infuence and Litigation' (2017) 10 Nature Geoscience 616, 616.

236 Cf. Vesco Paskalev, 'May Science Be with You: Can Scientific Expertise Confer Legitimacy to Transnational Authority?' (2017) 8 Transnational Legal Theory 202.

237 Lahore High Court (n 224) para 21.

238 See, for example, Mayer (n 223) 181 ff.

239 ibid 182.

the 'voiceless' (future generations and nature), must be heard and their interests considered when it comes to addressing climate change.

8.7 Conclusion

An open society of constitutional interpreters of IL recognises the multitude of interpretations by many different actors. Non-state actors, particularly NGOs and individuals, interpret domestic law in light of IEL principles and introduce these interpretations to the courts. This is possible because standing has been facilitated to a certain extent, and the introduction of the amicus curiae in some civil-law countries has allowed broader and different participation of non-state actors. Alongside individuals and NGOs, international scholarship plays an important role in the interpretation and development of international climate law. Media coverage can help to expose gaps in the legal system, which makes the opinions of legal scholars and climate scientists available to a large public and exercises public pressure on responsible governmental actors. These actors are participating in lawmaking through litigation by articulating their interpretations before the courts. This indicates that global climate constitutionalism from below is possible if one considers interpretation as a tool for changing (international) constitutional law—as has been argued in the previous chapters—in the form of (evolutionary) constitutional change rather than constitutional amendment. CCL is one of the most effective tools to make the voices of those who do not have an 'original' voice in IL heard, and this even includes future generations and people in other countries. Therefore, '[t]he question is not whether there will be another wave of climate-related litigation, but when it will occur and whether it will be more successful than prior efforts'.[240] Four of these successful (and not so successful) cases of this new wave—*Urgenda v the Netherlands*, *Leghari v Pakistan*, *Juliana v the United States* and *Future Generations v Colombia*—will be analysed in the next chapter.

[240] Marjanac and Patton (n 234) 266.

Interpretation by Non-State Actors in CCL Cases

9

The spectacular case of *Urgenda* belongs to a new, third wave of climate litigation, which began in 2015.[1] The first wave of climate litigation focused on individual cases, such as *EPA v Massachusetts*, directed to compliance with environmental and planning laws.[2] The second wave then created typologies and classified cases according to these.[3] The third wave is more concerned with the role the courts play 'in helping to create and develop regulatory responses to the complex climate change problem'.[4] However, these waves overlap and coexist, and there are still cases filed today that would belong to the first or second wave.[5]

A UNEP report lists five trends within the third wave of CCL. These are:

> holding governments to their legislative and policy commitments; linking the impacts of resource extraction to climate change and resilience; establishing that particular emissions are the proximate cause of particular adverse climate change impacts;

[1] Giulio Corsi, 'A Bottom-up Approach to Climate Governance: The New Wave of Climate Change Litigation' [2017] ICCG Reflection No. 57 1, 2.

[2] Lauren Musgrave, 'Turning a Ripple into a Torrent: Riding the Waves of Climate Litigation' [2021] Paper presented at Clayton Utz seminar, Sydney, 16 March 2021 para 6 ff.

[3] Jacqueline Peel and Hari M Osofsky, *Climate Change Litigation: Regulatory Pathways to Cleaner Energy* (CUP 2015) 14–5; on the first and second wave in private climate litigation against transnational corporations, see Geetanjali Ganguly, Joana Setzer and Veerle Heyvaert, 'If at First You Don't Succeed: Suing Corporations for Climate Change' (2018) 38 Oxford Journal of Legal Studies 841, 846 ff.

[4] Peel and Osofsky (n 3) 14–5 (citations omitted).

[5] Jacqueline Peel and Hari M Osofsky, 'Climate Change Litigation' (2020) 16 Annual Review of Law and Social Science 21, 30.

M. Niehaus, *Global Climate Constitutionalism "from below"*,
https://doi.org/10.1007/978-3-658-43191-4_9

establishing liability for failures (or efforts) to adapt to climate change; and applying the public trust doctrine to climate change.[6]

The 2023 UNEP status review report, further specified that climate cases would often fall in one or several of six categories: 1) the use of "climate rights" in climate litigation, 2) domestic enforcement, 3) keeping fossil fuels and carbon sinks in the ground, 4) corporate liability and responsibility, 5) climate disclosures and greenwashing and 6) failure to adapt and the impacts of adaptation.[7]

Plaintiffs and their lawyers have been quite innovative in seeking legal concepts that can push boundaries concerning standing, causation or accountability, as well as the introduction of new concepts such as intergenerational justice or rights for nature to (constitutional) lawsuits. These efforts can be observed in the cases of *Urgenda*, *Leghari*, *Juliana* and *Future Generations*, which will be analysed in the following sections. Moreover, this chapter seeks to answer the question of whether CCL cases filed with domestic courts can influence and develop IL or whether their rulings are only relevant to the nation-state in whose jurisdiction it was issued.

9.1 *Urgenda v the Netherlands*: Duty of Care and Human Rights

Urgenda v the Netherlands was the first successful (explicit) CCL case worldwide. In 2012, Urgenda sent a letter to the Dutch government requesting a 40% reduction in Dutch GHG emissions by 2020 compared to 1990 levels. By then, Dutch climate policies were merely aiming at a 14–17% reduction compared to 1990 levels.[8] This request was denied. Together with 886 Dutch citizens, Urgenda brought the case before the DC, claiming that the state would be acting unlawfully if it failed to reduce its annual GHGs by 40%, or at least by 25%, compared with 1990 levels, by the end of 2020. The DC decided on 24 June 2015 in favour of the plaintiffs and ordered the state to reduce its GHG emissions by at least 25% by 2020 below 1990 levels. The Dutch government appealed the decision later, but the Appeal Court (CA) upheld the decision in 2018. Following this judgement, the state appealed to the Hoge Raad (Supreme Court, SC), the highest

[6] UNEP, 'The Status of Climate Change Litigation—A Global Review' (2017) 14.

[7] UNEP, 'Global Climate Litigation Report (2023 Status Review)' (2023) 26.

[8] UNEP, *Environmental Rule of Law (First Global Report)* (2019) 165 (case study—*Urgenda v The Netherlands*).

court in the Netherlands. In September 2019, the Procurator General and Advocate General to the Supreme Court published an opinion to uphold the judgement of the CA. On 20 December 2019, the SC upheld the judgement of the CA, thus, confirming that the Netherlands must reduce its emissions by a minimum of 25% before the end of 2020 compared to 1990 levels.[9]

The *Urgenda* case can be viewed from two different perspectives: one is a tort law perspective and the other a human rights law perspective. The reason for this is a shift in the legal basis of the rulings. In 2015, the DC focused on the unwritten duty to care established in civil law, whereas the CA in 2018 turned the case into a human rights case with a focus on Articles 2 and 8 ECHR. The Supreme Court judgement subsequently relied on human rights.

9.1.1 *Urgenda I*: Unwritten Duty of Care

The District Court (partly) followed Urgenda's argumentation and ruled that the Netherlands was acting unlawfully due to their lax mitigation policies. What surprised many was the way the court determined this unlawfulness. Urgenda had based its claim, inter alia, on Article 21 of the Dutch Constitution, which imposes a duty on the state 'to keep the country habitable and to protect and improve the environment'. However, the court found that the way the government carries out this task is covered by its discretionary powers.[10] Furthermore, the state was not acting unlawfully towards Urgenda under IEL—neither with regard to the international agreements ratified by the Netherlands, such as the UNFCCC or the Kyoto Protocol, nor with regard to the 'no harm' principle in combination with Article 93 of the Constitution[11]—as these obligations are only binding between states and not vis-à-vis citizens (private individuals and legal persons).[12] The court also did not follow Urgenda's argumentation on Article 2 (right to life) and Article 8 (family and private life) ECHR due to Article 34 ECHR. Urgenda, as

---

[9] For an overview of the case history, see Urgenda, 'Climate Case Explained' <https://www.urgenda.nl/en/themas/climate-case/climate-case-explained/> accessed 31 August 2023.

[10] District Court of The Hague, *Urgenda v The Netherlands* [2015] (ECLI:NL:RBHDHA:2015:7196) para 4.36.

[11] Article 93 of the Constitution of the Netherlands: "Provisions of treaties and of resolutions by international institutions which may be binding on *all* persons by virtue of their contents shall become binding after they have been published" (emphasis added).

[12] District Court of The Hague (n 10) para 4.42.

a legal entity, could neither be violated in its physical integrity nor in its privacy and, therefore, cannot directly rely on those articles.[13]

At the heart of the court's argumentation lay the interpretation of the unwritten standard of due care. The negligence provision of Article 162 of Book 6 of the Dutch Civil Code states in para. 2 that '[a]s a tortious act is regarded a violation [...] of what according to unwritten law has to be regarded as proper social conduct [...]'. The court had to define the scope of the unwritten and vague concept of due care. The DC stated that while the government has wide discretionary powers to organise its climate policies:

> the court is of the opinion that due to the nature of the hazard (a global cause) and the task to be realised accordingly (shared risk management of a global hazard that could result in an impaired living climate in the Netherlands), the objectives and principles, such as those laid down in the UN Climate Change Convention and the TFEU, should also be considered in determining the scope for policymaking and duty of care.[14]

The court invoked the principle of fairness (in particular towards future generations), the precautionary principle and the sustainability principle.[15] While not having a direct effect, they are 'important viewpoints' in assessing whether the state acted wrongfully towards Urgenda or whether it had taken sufficient measures to prevent hazardous climate change to humankind and the environment.[16] It established six criteria to determine the scope of due care owed by the state: 1) the nature and extent of climate change damage; 2) the foreseeability of such damage; 3) the chance that hazardous climate change will occur; 4) the nature of the acts or omissions of the state; 5) the onerousness of taking precautionary measures; and 6) the extent of the state's discretionary powers with due regard to public law principles in light of the latest scientific knowledge, the available (technical) option to take security measures and the cost-benefit ratio of the security measures to be taken.[17] It took the court less than half a page to stress the hazardous risk of climate change and the state's serious duty of care to take measures to prevent it.[18] The court—with regard to the fourth factor—rejected the Netherlands' argument, according to which it cannot be seen as one of the perpetrators of climate change as it does not emit GHG itself. Instead, the DC

[13] ibid 4.45.

[14] ibid 4.55.

[15] ibid 4.56.

[16] ibid 4.63.

[17] ibid.

[18] ibid 4.64–4.65.

claimed that the state had the power to control the collective Dutch emission level and also had expressively accepted this responsibility by becoming a signatory of international treaties such as the UNFCCC and the Kyoto Protocol.[19] Concerning the fifth factor, the court found that mitigation measures, as requested by Urgenda, are the most efficient methods of prevention, given the latest scientific findings, and that it would be more cost-effective to take adequate action rather than to postpone measures to prevent hazardous climate change.[20] The discretionary powers of the state (the sixth factor) are wide but not limitless. Instead, the state must protect its citizens by taking appropriate and effective measures.[21] Adaptation measures would not be sufficient, and therefore, 'the State has limited options: mitigation is vital for preventing dangerous climate change'.[22] The state also must take into account that the costs have to be 'distributed reasonably' between current and future generations and '[i]f according to the current insights it turns out to be cheaper on balance to act now, the State has a serious obligation, arising from due care, towards future generations to act accordingly'.[23] In particular, the court rejected the state's argument according to which the amount of its GHG emissions was negligible, as they account for only 0.5% of worldwide emissions ('drop in the ocean' argument):[24]

> The fact that the amount of the Dutch emissions is small compared to other countries does not affect the obligation to take precautionary measures in view of the State's obligation to exercise care. After all, it has been established that any anthropogenic greenhouse gas emission, no matter how minor, contributes to an increase of CO2 levels in the atmosphere and therefore to hazardous climate change.[25]

Thereby, causality was established.[26] The court also affirmed—against the state's argument—that the possibility of damages (which is sufficient for a tort claim under Book 6 Article 162 of the DCC)

> for those whose interests Urgenda represents, including current and future generations of Dutch nationals, is so great and concrete that given its duty of care, the State

[19] ibid 4.66.

[20] ibid 4.73.

[21] ibid 4.74.

[22] ibid 4.75.

[23] ibid 4.76.

[24] ibid 4.78.

[25] ibid 4.79.

[26] ibid 4.90.

> must make an adequate contribution, greater than its current contribution, to prevent hazardous climate change.[27]

Interestingly, the court followed Urgenda's argumentation in large part, even though it had rejected the possibility of binding obligations stemming from international treaties towards citizens. However, through a 'back door', it introduced the principles of IEL invoked by Urgenda and interpreted the state's obligations in light of international treaties. By using the latest scientific knowledge on climate change, it defined the scope of the open term 'due care'. According to Dutch scholars De Graaf and Jans, such considerations of IL is not uncommon in Dutch law when a court needs to interpret and apply an open or vague norm. IL can have a 'reflex effect' in national law.[28] They argued, however, that by using principles and norms of IEL, the court was bypassing Articles 93 and 94 of the Dutch Constitution and doubted that the decision would survive appeal.[29] The judgement was upheld by the CA on 9 October 2018, which did not address the question again.

9.1.2 *Urgenda II*: Human Rights (Articles 2 and 8 ECHR)

The state appealed the DC decision on 29 grounds (which were all rejected). Initially content with the decision of the DC, due to the state's appeal, Urgenda cross-appealed on one ground (which was successful). Urgenda claimed that it could rely directly on Articles 2 and 8 ECHR.[30] The CA found that Article 34 ECHR is only concerned with access to the ECtHR (legal standing) and cannot serve as a base for denying Urgenda the possibility to rely on Articles 2 and 8 ECHR.[31] This argumentation was meant to strengthen the legal basis of the claim.[32]

---

[27] ibid 4.89.

[28] KJ de Graaf and JH Jans, 'The Urgenda Decision: Netherlands Liable for Role in Causing Dangerous Global Climate Change' (2015) 27 Journal of Environmental Law 517, 525.

[29] ibid 525–6.

[30] Benoit Mayer, 'The State of the Netherlands v. Urgenda Foundation: Ruling of the Court of Appeal of the Hague (9 October 2018)' (2019) 8 Transnational Environmental Law 167, 167–8.

[31] The Hague Court of Appeal, *Appeal Decision Urgenda v The Netherlands* [2018] (ECLI:NL:GHDHA:2018:2610) para 35.

[32] *Urgenda v The Netherlands*, 'Respondent's Notice on Appeal Including Notice of Cross-Appeal (2017)' para 11.3.

These 'newly admitted' provisions allowed the CA to take a whole new perspective on the case and essentially turn it into a human rights case without further reliance on tort law.[33] Notably, the court was not allowed to offer a different legal basis for the case unless the legal basis of the first judgement was mistaken. However, the state did not raise this point.[34]

On this new basis, the CA recognised a positive human rights obligation under the ECHR. Thus, the court framed that:

> the State has a positive obligation to protect the lives of citizens within its jurisdiction under Article 2 ECHR, while Article 8 ECHR creates the obligation to protect the right to home and private life. This obligation applies to all activities, public and non-public, which could endanger the rights protected in these articles, and certainly in the face of industrial activities which by their very nature are dangerous. If the government knows that there is a real and imminent threat, the State must take precautionary measures to prevent infringement as far as possible.[35]

The CA then assessed the severity of climate change according to IPCC and UNEP statements and whether the state acted unlawfully in the face of these findings knowing that there is a real and imminent threat.[36] The court rejected all grounds brought by the State, in particular, the 'drop in the ocean' argument, remarking that the Netherlands is one of the biggest per-capita emitters in the world, with CO_2 rates increasing instead of decreasing over the past few years.[37] The court also did not allow the state to rely on more lax EU policies (a 20% reduction target) since the latest Dutch policy goals were even aiming at a 49% reduction.[38] Thus, it found that the state was acting unlawfully by infringing its duty of care under Articles 2 and 8 ECHR.[39]

---

[33] Jonathan Verschuuren, 'The State of the Netherlands v Urgenda Foundation: The Hague Court of Appeal Upholds Judgment Requiring the Netherlands to Further Reduce Its Greenhouse Gas Emissions' (2019) 28 Review of European, Comparative and International Environmental Law 94, 96.

[34] Jaap Spier, '"The 'Strongest' Climate Ruling Yet": The Dutch Supreme Court's Urgenda Judgment' (2020) 67 Netherlands International Law Review 319, 322 (esp. Fn. 10).

[35] The Hague Court of Appeal (n 31) para 43.

[36] ibid 44–53.

[37] ibid 26.

[38] See Verschuuren (n 33) 97.

[39] The Hague Court of Appeal (n 31) para 76.

9.1.3 *Urgenda III*: Human Rights

The positive human rights obligations that the CA had already identified were accepted by the SC: the Netherlands not only have an obligation to not violate the right to life (Article 2 ECHR) and the right to private and family life (Article 8 ECHR) but also to prevent future violations of these rights. The state must safeguard the lives of those within its jurisdiction under Article 2 and 'to take reasonable and appropriate measures to protect individuals against possible serious damage to their environment' under Article 8,[40] especially in hindsight of the precautionary principle.[41]

The reliance on the 25% target has been criticised as somewhat arbitrary;[42] however, the Court accepted it based on the 'common ground' method.[43] This approach has been developed by the ECtHR to interpret the ECHR in the light of international treaties if these form 'common ground' among the member-states of the Council of Europe, even if a particular member-state is not a party to that treaty.[44] The CA, thus, had rightly applied the 25% target (and did not aim at a lower objective), particularly as the Netherlands is among the countries with the highest per-capita emissions in the world.[45] Following the other instances, the SC rejected the Netherlands' argument, according to which its GHG emissions would be negligible given the total historical and current emissions. Instead, the Court was convinced that every state is responsible for its share of emissions, even if it is comparatively minor.[46]

The Urgenda ruling has been named the '"Strongest" Climate Ruling Yet'.[47] What makes the case so special is not only that it was the first successful case

---

[40] Supreme Court of the Netherlands (Hoge Raad), *Urgenda v The Netherlands* [2019] ECLI:NL:HR:2019:2007 para 5.2.

[41] ibid 5.3.2.

[42] Mayer (n 30) 185.

[43] Supreme Court of the Netherlands (n 40) para 7.2.11.

[44] ibid 5.4.2, referring to ECtHR, *Demir and Baykara v. Turkey*, Judgement of 12 November 2008, App. No. 34503/97, para 86; see also André Nollkaemper and Laura Burgers, 'A New Classic in Climate Change Litigation: The Dutch Supreme Court Decision in the Urgenda Case' *Blog of the European Journal of International Law* (2020) <https://bit.ly/38h3WEa> accessed 31 August 2023. See also Section 2.3.4 above.

[45] Supreme Court of the Netherlands (n 40) para 7.3.4.

[46] ibid 5.7.5.

[47] 'In "Strongest" Climate Ruling Yet, Dutch Court Orders Leaders to Take Action' *The New York Times* (20 December 2019) <https://nytimes.com/2019/12/20/climate/netherlands-climate-lawsuit.html?smid=url-share> accessed 31 August 2023.

belonging to the third wave of CCL, but that all three courts decided in favour of Urgenda. The courts presented a unified front in the fight against climate change.

However, not everyone thinks that Urgenda has done a service to the fight against climate change. For Mayer, the ruling is a merely symbolic success that has not only not led to a decrease but actually to an increase of 0.3 $MtCO_2eq$, cumulatively, between 2020 and 2029 in global emissions mostly because the implementation measurements have displaced the sources of emissions to other countries.[48] Unlike international climate treaties, which have a larger timeframe of 10–15 years in which certain outcomes must be achieved, the courts gave the legislator only 5 years to reach the 25% reduction target. This would have led the government to take quick reduction implementation measures, such as introducing a tax on the disposal of foreign waste, with the result that some of the waste would be landfilled in the UK instead of being incinerated in the Netherlands, thereby shifting the problem instead of solving it.[49] Mayer noted:

> While the case has raised public awareness, it is not clear that this has led to an enhanced political support for mitigation action; it could just as well have hindered international cooperation and eroded political support for action on climate change mitigation. Altogether, Urgenda has likely caused more harm than good from the perspective of international action on climate change mitigation.[50]

Courts would be ill-equipped to substitute comprehensive policies on climate change.[51] Parenteau disagrees with Mayer and argues that the Netherlands's annual budget would now include a category of 'Urgenda measures' to incentivise the necessary action to achieve the 49% reduction target for 2030.[52] And though it may be disputed whether the case really has spurred climate action in the Netherlands in a meaningful way, and the problem of enforcement remains,[53] the case has significantly contributed to legal reasoning.

---

[48] Benoit Mayer, 'The Contribution of Urgenda to the Mitigation of Climate Change' (2023) 35 Journal of Environmental Law 167, 169.

[49] ibid 183 f.

[50] ibid 184.

[51] ibid.

[52] Patrick Parenteau, 'Some Observations on How Courts in the United States and European Union View Their Role in Adjudicating Climate Litigation' (2023) 26 Environmental Liability: Law, Policy, and Practice 138, 138.

[53] Cf. Diederik Baazil, 'After Climate Court Victories Comes the Problem of Enforcement' *Bloomberg* (18 August 2023) <https://www.bloomberg.com/news/articles/2021-08-18/climate-litigation-victories-face-enforcement-problems> accessed 31 August 2023.

The ruling rebutted one of the main arguments of the defendants, that is, the 'drop in the ocean' argument. According to this argument, the effect of a single project or country would be so small that it would not make much of a difference in global overall GHG emissions. Consequently, in the past, it was difficult to establish the causality between the emissions of, for example, a coal mine or power plant and the effects of global climate change.[54] The Dutch courts put an end to this argument by clarifying that all emissions, no matter how small a country's contribution to the mix of GHGs in the atmosphere is, contribute to dangerous climate change and, therefore, matter. Other courts, including the Lahore High Court (discussed in the next paragraph),[55] the Ninth Circuit Court of Appeals in *Juliana* (see Section 9.3.1),[56] the High Court of New Zealand[57] and the GFCC[58] have rejected the 'drop in the ocean' argument on the same basis and sometimes by directly referring to the *Urgenda* judgement.[59]

This demonstrates that courts have entered a transnational dialogue on climate matters. Judges examine the courts's rulings in other jurisdictions to find inspiration on how to decide on climate cases at home. In the past, it has been difficult to establish the causality between the emissions of a particular source and damages attributable to climate change. However, it took only one case to grapple with this problem by arguing that no contribution to climate change is negligible to show that this hurdle can partly be overcome. This shows how big an impact a single case and a progressive court can have.

9.2 *Leghari v Pakistan*: Climate Justice

Leghari, different from the other cases analysed in this chapter, is an 'adaptation' lawsuit. Pakistan is one of the smallest GHG emitters in the world but will be highly affected by climate change; frequent floods and droughts are already a challenge for the country. Pakistan, as well as other countries of South

[54] J Peel, 'Issues in Climate Change Litigation' (2011) 5 Carbon & Climate Law Review 15, 16.

[55] Lahore High Court, *Asghar Leghari v Federation of Pakistan*, Judgement of 25 January 2018 (W.P. No. 25501/2015) para 7.

[56] Ninth Circuit Court of Appeals, *Juliana v United States*, No. 18–36082 (17 January 2020) 19 f.

[57] High Court of New Zealand, *Thomson v The Minister for Climate Change Issues*, Judgement of 2 November 2017 para 133.

[58] GFCC, 1 BvR 2656/18 (2021) para 203.

[59] ibid.

Asia, has an extensive environmental legislative framework,[60] including the 1997 Environment Protection Act, the 2012 National Climate Change Policy and the Framework for Implementation of Climate Change Policy 2014–2030 ('Framework'). The Framework identifies various goals that should be achieved in four different timeframes. The 242 Priority Actions should have been achieved within 2 years, by 2016, to make Pakistan 'climate-proof'. Farmer and law student Leghari sought protection from the adverse effects of climate change, in particular, on Pakistan's scarce water resources, which affect his agricultural activities. He claimed that Pakistan violated his fundamental rights to life and human dignity (Articles 9 and 14 of Pakistan's constitution) by not implementing and enforcing the Priority Actions regulating water, food and energy security. He argued 'that international environmental principles like the doctrine of public trust, sustainable development, precautionary principle and intergenerational equity form part of the abovementioned fundamental rights also stand offended'.[61] While Pakistan's constitution does not mention environmental rights, the Supreme Court interpreted in *Shehla Zia* (1994) the right to life in Article 9 as entailing a right to a healthy environment.[62] The Lahore High Court took the present case to reassess the concept of environmental protection through constitutional provisions.

> Fundamental rights, like the right to life (Article 9) which includes the right to a healthy and clean environment and right to human dignity (Article 14) read with constitutional principles of democracy, equality, social, economic and political justice include within their ambit and commitment, the international environmental principles of sustainable development, precautionary principle, environmental impact assessment, inter and intra-generational equity and public trust doctrine.

The court had, in former cases, established the concept of 'environmental justice', which it would now further develop into a concept of 'climate justice':[63]

> Climate Justice links human rights and development to achieve a human-centered approach, safeguarding the rights of the most vulnerable people and sharing the burdens and benefits of climate change and its impacts equitably and fairly.[64]

---

[60] Parvez Hassan and Azim Azfar, 'Securing Environmental Rights Through Public Interest Litigation in South Asia' (2004) 22 Virginia Environmental Law Journal 215, 221.

[61] Lahore High Court (n 55) para 3.

[62] Supreme Court of Pakistan, *Shehla Zia and others v. WAPDA, (PLD 1994 SC 693)*, 1994.

[63] Lahore High Court (n 55) para 12.

[64] ibid 21.

Furthermore, the court argued that water justice is a sub-part of climate justice.[65] Water justice means the access of individuals to clean water, both for survival and recreational purposes, as a human right. Stressing the importance of interconnectedness between water with the environment, land and other ecosystems, the court held that:

> Climate Justice and Water Justice go hand in hand and are rooted in articles 9 and 14 of our Constitution and stand firmly on our preambular constitutional values of social and economic justice.[66]

Adaptation needs to cover many different sectors.[67] Therefore, the court ordered the creation of a Climate Change Commission (CCC) with members of ministries, provincial governments, think tanks and environmental NGOs to effectively implement the National Climate Change Policy and the Framework. In its judgement sheet of 2018, the court assessed the work of the CCC and deemed it satisfactory, with 66,1% of Priority Actions under the Framework had been successfully implemented. It dissolved the CCC and left it to the respective governments to 'implement the Framework, formulate the National Water Policy and ensure that the new Act is actualized and given effect to in letter and spirit'.[68] A Standing Committee on Climate Change was constituted that should act as a link between the court and the executive.[69] In the meantime, in 2017, the Government issued a new Climate Change Act that has been received with scepticism but also hope, as it recognised the extreme vulnerability of the country and demonstrated a new will of the political actors.[70] This could be a sign that litigation and regulative processes can enter a cooperative partnership.[71]

---

[65] ibid 23.

[66] ibid.

[67] ibid 22. 'Climate Justice covers agriculture, health, food, building approvals, industrial licenses, technology, infrastructural work, human resource, human and climate trafficking, disaster preparedness, health, etc.'

[68] ibid 19, 24.

[69] ibid 25.

[70] 'Pakistan Passes Climate Change Act, Reviving Hopes—and Skepticism' *Reuters* (24 March 2017) <https://www.reuters.com/article/us-pakistan-climatechange-lawmaking/pakistan-passes-climate-change-act-reviving-hopes-and-skepticism-idUSKBN16V19N> accessed 31 August 2023.

[71] Joana Setzer and Lisa Benjamin, 'Climate Litigation in the Global South: Constraints and Innovations' (2020) 9 Transnational Environmental Law 77, 98.

Leghari was the first successful case from the Global South that has also attracted attention in the Global North. Due to its relevance, therefore, it has great symbolic value for CCL in the Global South. Many countries of the Global South are already more strongly affected by the effects of climate change, including crop failure, territory loss and the loss of life.[72] The judiciary's recognition of the urgency to adapt to climate change, thus, comes closer to the realities experienced in the Global South than rulings from the Global North, such as *Urgenda*, can. This is all the more the case because of the similarity of the Global South's legal systems, where courts generally play a more significant role when governments fail to address economic, ecological and social problems effectively.[73] However, its importance goes far beyond its symbolic value for the Global South. If global climate constitutionalism is meant to secure climate justice for people in the most climate-vulnerable situations, it needs to include the perspectives of the Global South and understand the different ways in which they are approaching CCL and also learn from them. In the Global South, a 'justice-centred approach to climate change seeks to […] foster a more human-rights and equity-conscious perspective in climate change responses'.[74] Many cases in the Global North follow(ed) a more technocratic, science-based approach, such as *EPA v Massachusetts* in the US or *the Rocky Hill Coal Mine* case in Australia.[75] Only recently has CCL in the Global North started to connect rights with climate concerns. Such rights-based approaches are quite common in the legal systems in the Global South. Many (not only environmental) issues are framed in the language of human and constitutional rights. This more active approach of 'transformative adjudication' is an important (constitutional) element in many countries of the Global South.[76] Thus, *Leghari* is 'a bold example of transformative adjudication in pursuit of climate justice and is emblematic of the "rights turn" in climate change litigation'.[77]

---

[72] Emily Barritt and Boitumelo Sediti, 'The Symbolic Value of Leghari v Federation of Pakistan: Climate Change Adjudication in the Global South' (2019) 30 King's Law Journal 203, 208.

[73] ibid.

[74] International Bar Association, 'Achieving Justice and Human Rights in an Era of Climate Disruption' (2014) 46.

[75] Jacqueline Peel and Jolene Lin, 'Transnational Climate Litigation: The Contribution of the Global South' (2019) 113 American Journal of International Law 679, 721.

[76] Barritt and Sediti (n 72) 208.

[77] ibid 204 (citations omitted).

9.3 The Future Generations Lawsuits

Many spectacular CCL cases in domestic courts are based on the principle of intergenerational equity and constructed around the idea that future generations have rights, or at least interests, that have to be protected by the present generation holding the planet in trust for generations yet to come.

Young people have started to 'try' the principle of intergenerational equity not only in domestic courts (such as the *Juliana* and *Future Generations* cases) but also in international judicial bodies. In September 2019, a communication was filed by 16 children (including Swedish activist Thunberg) against five countries (Argentina, Brazil, France, Germany and Turkey as the five largest GHG emitters that have ratified the UN Convention on the Rights of the Child[78]) with the Committee on the Rights of the Child. They claim that the climate crisis is essentially a children's rights crisis, since policymakers' choices and inactions result in harms that are predicted to become more intense and hazardous in the future and, thus, violate the petitioners' rights to life, health, the prioritisation of the child's best interests, and the cultural rights of the petitioners from indigenous communities.[79] In its decision, the Committee employed the approach designed by the IACtHR in its Advisory Opinion 23/17 on the Environment and Human Rights, which 'implies that when transboundary harm occurs, children are under the jurisdiction of the State on whose territory the emissions originated for the purposes of article 5 (1) of the Optional Protocol if there is a causal link between the acts or omissions of the State in question and the negative impact on the rights of children located outside its territory, when the State of origin exercises effective control over the sources of the emissions in question' and when the harm is 'reasonably foreseeable' by the state. While the Committee cautiously affirmed that these requirements were met, it dismissed the petition for failure to exhaust domestic remedies.[80] Notably, two amicus curiae briefs submitted by the former and the present UN Special Rapporteur on Human Rights and the Environment, John Knox and David Boyd, respectively, supported the case. They argued that in 'the unique circumstances of the climate crisis, the pursuit of domestic remedies

---

[78] UN Commission on Human Rights, Convention on the Rights of the Child, 7 March 1990, E/CN.4/RES/1990/74.

[79] Chiara Sacchi and others, Communication to the Committee on the Rights of the Child (2019) para 33.

[80] Committee on the Rights of the Child, Decision adopted by the Committee on the Rights of the Child under the Optional Protocol to the Convention on the Rights of the Child on a communications procedure in respect of Communication No. 104/2019, 22 September 2021, paras 10.7ff, 10.15ff.

would be futile'[81] and that a decision by an international body would send an important message to all children. In their opinion, '[c]limate justice delayed is climate justice denied'.[82]

In another case, six children and young adults from Portugal filed an application in September 2020 with the ECtHR against 33 states, including the members-states of the EU, Norway, Russia, Switzerland, Turkey, the UK and Ukraine (the latter later being withdrawn by the plaintiffs due to the Russian war of aggression against Ukraine), after the disastrous wildfires and severe heat-waves led to the deaths of 120 people in Portugal in 2017.[83] They claim that these countries are violating their human rights to life (Article 2 ECHR), the right to a private and family life (Article 8) and the prohibition of discrimination on reasons of age (Article 14 ECHR). On 30 November, the ECtHR announced that the case was 'important' and 'urgent' and, thus, granted it priority status.[84] Furthermore, the court took an unusual step: it expanded the scope of the case and asked each of the 33 defendants to respond to the question of whether climate change may constitute an 'inhuman or degrading treatment or punishment' due to anxiety and mental issues that the young people would suffer because of its adverse effects. This point was not even raised by the applicants.[85] In June 2022, the Chamber of the ECtHR relinquished jurisdiction in favour of the Grand Chamber. According to Article 30 ECHR, the Grand Chamber decides in cases that raise a serious question affecting the interpretation of the Convention, demonstrating once again the controversy around CCL.

Juliana v the United States and *Future Generations v Colombia* were some of the first cases in which the principle of intergenerational equity in relation to climate change was put to the test in court. While the Supreme Court in *Future Generations* ruled on the arguments of the plaintiffs, *Juliana*'s long journey seemed to be over before it even started, since the case could not proceed to trial. However, *Future Generations* and *Juliana* have not only sparked discussion

---

[81] Amici Curiae Brief of Special Rapporteurs on Human Rights and the Environment in Support of Admissibility, C.S. et al.v. Argentina, Brazil, France, Germany and Turkey, para 53.

[82] ibid para 49.

[83] ECtHR, *Duarte Agostinho and Others v. Portugal and 32 Other States*, App. No. 39371/20 (pending).

[84] 'European States Ordered to Respond to Youth Activists' Climate Lawsuit' *The Guardian* (30 November 2020) <https://www.theguardian.com/environment/2020/nov/30/european-states-ordered-respond-youth-activists-climate-lawsuit> accessed 31 August 2023.

[85] 'Does Climate Change Violate Children's Human Rights? A European Court May Soon Decide' *Time* (30 November 2020) <https://time.com/5916362/climate-change-human-rights-portugal/> accessed 31 August 2023.

on how to safeguard the interests of future generations, but they have also served as a precedent for many lawsuits that have been filed subsequently and strongly focus on intergenerational justice.

9.3.1 *Juliana v the United States*: The Right to a Stable Climate and ATL

Juliana v the United States is a constitutional rights suit that seeks to advance the concept of a 'right to a healthy environment' to a 'right to a stable climate'.[86] The lawsuit is orchestrated by Our Children's Trust and was filed in the District Court of Oregon in 2015 by 21 plaintiffs, then aged between 8 and 19 years, against the federal government. The plaintiffs argue that the government, despite knowing for over 50 years that CO_2 pollution from burning fossil fuels is causing global warming and dangerous climate change, continued their policies and practices of allowing the exploitation of fossil fuels[87] and are continuing to do so.[88] These policies and practices would violate the plaintiffs' fundamental rights. They presented four claims for relief: 1) violation of the Due Process Clause of the Fifth Amendment, 2) violation of equal protection principles embedded in the Fifth Amendment, 3) violation of the unenumerated rights preserved for the People by the Ninth Amendment and 4) violation of the PTD.

The Due Process Clause of the Fifth Amendment guarantees that no one shall be 'deprived of life, liberty, or property, without due process of law'.[89] Those 'inherent and inalienable' rights 'reflect the basic societal contract of the Constitution to protect citizens and posterity from government infringement upon basic freedoms and basic (or natural) rights'.[90] The plaintiffs argue that these rights have evolved (and continue to evolve) and belong to both present and future generations. However, they are endangered by the accumulated actions of the government that have resulted in dangerous levels of CO_2,[91] thus, harming '[o]ur nation's climate system, including the atmosphere and oceans, [that] is critical

[86] Mia Hammersley, 'The Right to a Healthy and Stable Climate: Fundamental or Unfounded?' (2016) 7 Arizona Journal of Environmental Law and Policy 117, 124.

[87] *Kelsey Cascadia Rose Juliana et al. v United States*, First Amendment Complaint for Declaratory and Injunctive Relief (Case No. 6:15-Cv-01517-TC) para 1.

[88] ibid 9.

[89] ibid 277.

[90] ibid 278.

[91] ibid 280.

to Plaintiffs' rights to life, liberty, and property'.[92] The plaintiffs then express that 'without a stable climate system, both liberty and justice are in peril': the fundaments of the 'scheme of ordered liberty'.[93] According to the plaintiff's interpretation, the U.S. Constitution, therefore, includes the unenumerated right to a stable climate (as both a consequence of the Fifth Amendment and as an unenumerated right under the Ninth Amendment, as stated in Claim 3).[94] In the second claim for relief (violation of the equal protection principle embedded in the Fifth Amendment), the plaintiffs argue that the same protection of fundamental rights afforded to prior and present generations of adult citizens is denied to them by the government,[95] and that they suffer indiscrimination as they lack political power or influence over the government due to their age, which keeps them from voting.[96] Accordingly, they should be treated as 'protected classes'.[97]

Finally, in their fourth claim, the plaintiffs claimed that the government violated their rights under the PTD by not refraining from 'substantial impairment' of essential natural resources,[98] inter alia, the air (atmosphere), water, seas, the shores of the sea and wildlife. They argue that they are the beneficiaries of these rights that 'protect the rights of present and future generations to those essential natural resources that are of public concern to the citizens of our nation'.[99] The case, according to Blumm and Wood, is to be categorised as Atmospheric Trust Litigation (ATL), which describes the many lawsuits in different forums that are concerned with the connection between science and law.[100] ATL applies public trust principles to the atmosphere and demands that the law should reflect the actual physical, chemical and biological requirements of the planet.[101] A

---

92 ibid 279.

93 ibid 303.

94 See, for example, ibid 279, 282, 283 and 304.

95 ibid 292.

96 ibid 294, 295.

97 ibid 297.

98 ibid 309.

99 ibid 308.

100 Michael C Blumm and Mary Christina Wood, '"No Ordinary Lawsuit": Climate Change, Due Process, and the Public Trust Doctrine' (2017) 67 American University Law Review 1, 21.

101 ibid 23. "The basic ATL case applies public trust principles to the atmosphere, making the following claims: (1) the air and atmosphere, along with other vital natural resources, are within the res of the public trust, and therefore subject to special sovereign obligations; (2) the legislature and its implementing agencies are public trustees; (3) both present and future generations of the public are beneficiaries of the public trust; (4) the government trustees owe

fundamental rights approach should be applied in the face of the climate crisis to set firm boundaries on political discretion and to foster 'broad, enduring, system-changing solutions that hold the promise of protecting life, liberty, and property'.[102]

The federal government filed a motion to dismiss the case, arguing that the plaintiffs lacked Article III standing after *Lujan.*[103] The alleged injuries were not 'particular and concrete' and did not affect them in a 'personal and individual way'.[104] Instead, the plaintiffs are 'in no different a position than any other person when it comes to climate change impacts'.[105]

Three factors need to be present to have standing: injury in fact that is fairly traceable to the defendant's allegedly unlawful conduct, causality and redressability.[106] The government argued that there was no link between the government's actions to the asserted harms presented 'except through vague and generalized assertions that those acts contribute to global climate change' and, therefore, no causation.[107] Furthermore, future generations could not have suffered any harm as they do not exist yet, referring to the rejection of other cases brought on behalf of non-persons.[108] The plaintiffs could also not be redressed by the court as the complaint 'presents a generalized attack on government action and inaction regarding climate change, rather than a challenge to specifically identifiable violations of law that can be concretely rectified by a favorable decision'.[109] Moreover, the government argued that the plaintiffs failed to state a claim under the constitution because there is no constitutional right to be free of carbon dioxide emissions, and that the court lacked jurisdiction over PTD suits. Courts should

---

a fiduciary duty of protection against "substantial impairment" of the air, atmosphere, and climate system, which amounts to an affirmative duty to restore its balance; and (5) courts have a duty to enforce these trust obligations.".

102 ibid 24.

103 For the *Lujan* decision, see Section 8.1.2.1 above.

104 Federal Defendants' Memorandum of Points and Authorities in Support of Their Motion to Dismiss (Case No. 6:15-Cv-01517-TC) 10.

105 ibid 17.

106 U.S. Supreme Court, *Allen v. Wright*, 468 U.S. 737 (1984) 468.

107 'Federal Defendants' Memorandum of Points and Authorities in Support of Their Motion to Dismiss (Case No. 6:15-Cv-01517-TC)' (n 104) 12.

108 ibid 16.

109 ibid 14.

respect the separation of powers. If they wanted to consider the Ninth Amendment, they would need to, citing the Supreme Court, 'exercise the utmost care whenever we are asked to break new ground in this field'.[110]

However, in her 2016 decision, Judge Aiken of the District Court in Oregon allowed the *Juliana* case to proceed to trial. She agreed with Magistrate Judge Coffin, who had held in his order that the plaintiffs met the requirements of standing at the pleading stage, with causality being an issue that would have to be addressed thoroughly at the summary judgement stage. In her decision, she referred to *Minors Oposa* (Philippines), the first successful future generations lawsuit ('without "a balanced and healthful ecology," future generations "stand to inherit nothing but parched earth incapable of sustaining life"'[111]), and she explicitly recognised a right to a stable climate:

> I have no doubt that the right to a climate system capable of sustaining human life is fundamental to a free and ordered society. Just as marriage is the 'foundation of the family,' a stable climate system is quite literally the foundation 'of society, without which there would be neither civilization nor progress.'[112]

Such a right to a healthy environment or stable climate—similar to the right to life, liberty or the pursuit of happiness—would not need to be created by the constitution. Instead, the constitution has to protect and promote these already existing rights. Referring again to *Minors Oposa*, Aiken stressed that 'the right of future generations to a "balanced and healthful ecology" is so basic that it "need not even be written in the Constitution for [it is] assumed to exist from the inception of humankind"'.[113]

She expressed that this does not mean that every governmental action would constitute a violation of constitutional rights, but that:

> where a complaint alleges governmental action is affirmatively and substantially damaging the climate system in a way that will cause human deaths, shorten human lifespans, result in widespread damage to property, threaten human food sources,

110 ibid 22.

111 District Court of Oregon, Judge Ann Aiken, 11 October 2016, *Kelsey Cascadia Rose Juliana v United States of America* (Case No. 6:15-Cv-01517-TC) 32, referring to Supreme Court of the Philippines, Minors Oposa v. Secretary of the Department of Environment and Natural Resources (DENR), 33 ILM 173 (1994).

112 ibid.

113 ibid 50.

> and dramatically alter the planet's ecosystem, it states a claim for a due process violation.[114]

Even if an injury was widely shared, as long as it was not abstract or indefinite, it could not be automatically rendered a generalised grievance. Furthermore, the plaintiffs' injuries were sufficiently imminent given the present level of CO_2 in the atmosphere and warming trends.[115] She rejected the government's reliance on the *Bellon* case, in which a court had denied standing as it saw the causal link between the plaintiff's injuries and the agencies' regulatory decisions as 'too attenuated'. Even if the chain between the government's actions and the youth's injuries was complex, this alone would not mean that causation could not be established, even more so because the U.S.'s emissions make up a significant share of global emissions. She did not want 'to forever close the courthouse doors to climate change claims'.[116] Regarding redressability, she ruled that the declaratory and injunctive relief requested by the plaintiffs would 'slow or reduce the harm'.[117]

Since the utterance of this decision, the admissibility of the case has been disputed for more than 8 years now. The U.S. government has filed several motions to prevent the case from going to trial and being decided on the merits. The courts received more than 53 declarations and amicus briefs to support the plaintiffs by, inter alia, the states of New York, Delaware, Hawai'i, Minnesota, Oregon and Vermont, law professors, religious, women's and children's associations and environmental NGOs.[118]

On 17 January 2020, in a split decision, the Ninth Circuit Court of Appeals confirmed their scepticism regarding the separation of powers[119] and ruled that the young plaintiffs did not have Article III standing. While at least some of the plaintiffs could prove that they met the injury and causation requirements, the plaintiffs were not able to establish the redressability requirement. The court

---

114 ibid 33.

115 ibid 21.

116 ibid 24.

117 ibid 26–8.

118 These can be accessed at Our Children's Trust, 'Juliana v United States (Major Court Orders and Filings)' <https://www.ourchildrenstrust.org/court-orders-and-pleadings> accessed 31 August 2023.

119 Carolyn Kormann, 'The Right to a Stable Climate Is the Constitutional Question of the Twenty-First Century' [2019] *The New Yorker* <https://www.newyorker.com/news/daily-comment/the-right-to-a-stable-climate-is-the-constitutional-question-of-the-twenty-first-century> accessed 31 August 2023.

noted that although the plaintiffs 'challenge only affirmative activities by the government, an order simply enjoining those activities will not, according to their own experts' opinions, suffice to stop catastrophic climate change or even ameliorate their injuries.[120]

Rather, a fundamental transformation of the U.S.'s (if not of the whole industrialised world's) energy system would be required to reduce the global consequences of climate change. This, however, was beyond the powers of an Article III court. Climate change would 'require a host of complex policy decisions entrusted, for better or worse, to the wisdom and discretion of the executive and legislative branches'.[121] The judges found that the issuance of a declaratory judgement as sought by the plaintiffs would not help them to mitigate their asserted concrete injuries.

> A declaration, although undoubtedly likely to benefit the plaintiffs psychologically, is unlikely by itself to remediate their alleged injuries absent further court action.[122]

In her dissenting opinion, Judge Staton agreed with the majority that a single court order would not be enough to combat the consequences of climate change. Nevertheless, this alone would not mean that the suit presents no claim suitable for judicial resolution.[123]

> Plaintiffs bring suit to enforce the most basic structural principle embedded in our system of ordered liberty: that the Constitution does not condone the Nation's willful destruction. So viewed, plaintiffs' claims adhere to a judicially administrable standard. And considering plaintiffs seek no less than to forestall the Nation's demise, even a partial and temporary reprieve would constitute meaningful redress.[124]

Furthermore, she noted:

> The majority portrays any relief we can offer as just a drop in the bucket. [...] In a previous generation, perhaps that characterization would carry the day and we would hold ourselves impotent to address plaintiffs' injuries. But we are perilously close to an overflowing bucket. These final drops matter. *A lot*. Properly framed, a court order—even one that merely postpones the day when remedial measures become

[120] Ninth Circuit Court of Appeals (n 56) 23.

[121] ibid 25.

[122] ibid 22.

[123] Dissent by Judge Staton, ibid 33.

[124] ibid.

> insufficiently effective—would likely have a real impact on preventing the impending cataclysm. Accordingly, I conclude that the court could do something to help the plaintiffs before us. And 'something' is all that standing requires.[125]

The plaintiff's counsel requested that the Ninth Circuit re-hear the decision *en banc*, but the petition was rejected in February 2021.[126] The plaintiffs announced that they would appeal the decision to the Supreme Court but would also be open to settlement negotiations. It has been feared that with today's Supreme Court being extremely conservative, standing could be narrowed and by this, future climate cases made impossible.[127] Settlement processes between the plaintiffs and the U.S. Department of Justice ended without resolution. After another two-and-a-half years,[128] in June 2023, the federal District Court for the District of Oregon allowed the plaintiffs to amend their suit to address the deficiency identified by the Ninth Circuit Court and, thereby, cleared the way for the case to go to trial (though the defendants try to prevent this by filing motions to dismiss the plaintiffs' amended complaint). With their amended complaint, the plaintiffs are now no longer pushing for a change in climate policy but for a decision declaring the country's fossil fuel-based energy system unconstitutional.[129]

At the same time, *Held v Montana* was the first constitutional climate case in the U.S. to go on trial. The case was filed by 16 young Montana residents who argued that Montana's fossil fuel policies would violate Article 9 para. 1 of Montana's Constitution, according to which 'the state and each person shall maintain and improve a clean and healthful environment in Montana for present and future generations.' On 14 August 2023, Judge Kathy Seeley ruled in the

---

[125] ibid 45 f, emphasis in original.

[126] Our Children's Trust, 'Juliana v United States—Youth Climate Lawsuit' <https://www.ourchildrenstrust.org/juliana-v-us> accessed 31 August 2023.

[127] Sarah Brunswick, 'Not a Kid Anymore: What's Next for Juliana v. United States' *Arizona State Law Journal* (6 April 2021) <https://arizonastatelawjournal.org/2021/04/06/not-a-kid-anymore-whats-next-for-juliana-v-united-states/> accessed 31 August 2023.

[128] The plaintiffs had referred to the U.S. Supreme Court's opinion in *Mississippi v. Tennessee* (November 2021) in which it had supported "the broad principle that even after a case is dismissed for failing to plead a viable remedy, a motion to amend could be brought to cure the pleading deficiency" to substantiate Plaintiffs' Motion for Leave to File Amended Complaint. Notice of supplemental authority filed by plaintiffs, 29 November 2021, available at <https://climatecasechart.com/case/juliana-v-united-states/> accessed 31 August 2023.

[129] 'Youth Climate Lawsuit Against Federal Government Headed for Trial' *YaleEnvironment360* (2 June 2023) <https://e360.yale.edu/digest/juliana-youth-climate-lawsuit-trial> accessed 31 August 2023.

plaintiffs' favour.[130] She found that a provision of the Montana Environmental Policy Act which forbids Montana and its agents to consider the impacts of GHG emissions or climate change in their environmental reviews violated the right to a clean and healthful environment granted to Montana's children and future generations in Montana's constitution, and, therefore, is unconstitutional.[131] With the success of *Held v Montana* and *Juliana* (maybe) going to trial, it seems that youth-led climate litigation has, again, gained momentum in the US.

Juliana has gained attention worldwide and inspired people in other countries to file lawsuits on behalf of future generations. Although the case itself had not (yet) had a favourable outcome for the plaintiffs, their strategy to build on the rights of future generations has been successful, for example, in Colombia (see below), Ireland and Germany. Moreover, the recognition of a right to a stable climate is discussed by legal scholars and has influenced other cases.

Even though *Juliana* has not (yet) enshrined the right to a stable climate in the U.S. Constitution and is unlikely to do so in the near future given the current conservative makeup of the Supreme Court,[132] the idea is out in the world and might be more successful somewhere else with scholars continuing to push for it. While the Alaska Supreme Court affirmed the dismissal of a climate case of young people, dissenting Justice Maassen would have found that Alaskans had an individual constitutional right to a liveable climate.[133] The Special Rapporteur on the issue of human rights obligations has acknowledged a right to a safe climate as part of a human right to a healthy environment.[134]

Another important lesson can be learned from this case: it demonstrates the limits of private constitutional lawmaking and why it is so important that a court accepts such a claim. Although the case has been heavily supported by scientists, experts and an array of NGOs of all fields all over the world have demonstrated that there could be a basis for the recognition of a right to a stable climate in civil society: this interpretation needs to be 'anchored' in the U.S. Constitution

---

[130] Kate Selig, 'Judge Rules in Favor of Montana Youths in Landmark Climate Decision' *The Washington Post* (14 August 2023) <https://www.washingtonpost.com/climate-environment/2023/08/14/youths-win-montana-climate-trial/> accessed 31 August 2023.

[131] First Judicial District Court, Lewis and Clark County, *Held et al. v. State of Montana*, CDV-2020-307 (2023), para 37ff.

[132] Parenteau (n 52) 149.

[133] Alaska Supreme Court, *Sagoonick v. State*, Opinion of 28 January 2022, Supreme Court No. S-17297.

[134] UN Special Rapporteur on Human Rights and the Environment David Boyd, 'Special Report on Human Rights Obligations Relating to the Enjoyment of a Safe, Clean, Healthy and Sustainable Environment (A/74/161)' (2019) para 43.

by a court. The decision of the District Court, which had recognised the right to a stable climate, was cheered by many climate activists precisely for this reason. Political potentials, in Habermas's sense, cannot govern; they need to be turned into political power by a governmental institution.[135] Where this does not happen, as with the overturning of the decision by the Ninth Circuit Court, such an interpretation has no legally binding force on the state.

9.3.2 *Future Generations v Colombia*: Environmental Rights for Future Generations

The 2018 *Future Generations* case against the Colombian government in the Colombian Supreme Court is another important intergenerational CCL case. In the first instance, the Higher Tribunal of Bogotá declared the claim inadmissible, but the Supreme Court not only took a different view on the case's admissibility but also followed the plaintiffs' argumentation to protect the Amazon rainforest.

The Amazon as the main environmental axis of the planet is often called the 'lung of the world'. It is one of the largest carbon sinks[136] and counts for one-quarter of all species existing in this world.[137] Despite the Colombian government's commitment to reach zero deforestation during the Paris Agreement negotiations, deforestation rates were 44% higher in 2016 compared to 2015.[138] According to Dejustica, the NGO behind the case, the government failed to present significant and effective actions to stop deforestation. The 25 plaintiffs, therefore, argued that, as part of the future generations who will spend most of their adult lives in the period between 2041–2070 (a period in which the annual temperature of Colombia is expected to gradually increase by 1.6 °C) and part of their old age after that time (expected increase by 2.14 °C),[139] they will be adversely affected by such governmental inaction:

> There is a threat to the rights of all Colombians because there is a causal relationship between the violation of the right to a healthy environment due to deforestation in the

[135] Jürgen Habermas, *Between Facts and Norms: Contributions to a Discourse Theory of Law and Democracy* (Polity Press 1996) 364.

[136] RJW Brienen and others, 'Long-Term Decline of the Amazon Carbon Sink' (2015) 519 Nature 344.

[137] Corte Suprema de Justicia de Colombia, *Future Generations v Colombia* para 10.

[138] ibid 11, 11.3.

[139] *Demanda Tutela Amazonía Colombia* [4.3.2], available at < https://www.dejusticia.org/wp-content/uploads/2018/01/TutelaCambioClimático.pdf?x54537 > accessed 31 August.

> Colombian Amazon and the threat to our fundamental rights as future generations to a dignified life, health, food, and water.[140]

Unlike the other countries in the CCL cases presented here, Colombia recognises in its constitution a right to a healthy environment (Article 79) and a corresponding duty for the government 'to plan the handling and use of natural resources in order to guarantee their sustainable development, conservation, restoration, or replacement' (Article 80).

The plaintiffs asked the Court to interpret these rights in such a way that climate change, even if unknown 25 years ago when the articles were drafted, would now be considered a threat to their right to a healthy environment.[141] They then presented those environmental principles of 'the constitution and constitutional jurisprudence, in harmony with international instruments ratified by Colombia' that the judges should consider when interpreting the right to a healthy environment,[142] including the precautionary principle and the principle of '*in dubio pro natura*',[143] the principle of intergenerational equity,[144] the principle of solidarity between generations and species and with the countries with whom Colombia shares the Amazon,[145] the principle of participation in environmental matters that demands real opportunities for democratic and pluralistic participation,[146] and the consideration of interests of children being superior[147]—topics that have rarely, if ever, been discussed by the Supreme Court.[148]

The Court echoed the thoughts brought forward by the plaintiffs and, in its decision, demanded that humans stop thinking selfishly only of their own interests. It found that a shift from 'private ethics' focussing only on individual goods to a form of 'public ethics' which is concerned with the implementation of moral values that seek to advance social justice in general, is necessary. As a consequence, fundamental rights should be understood as not only recognising individual rights but also as entailing duties, in the form of 'rights-duties'

---

140 ibid 5 (tr the author).

141 ibid 5.1.

142 ibid 5.

143 ibid 5.1.1.

144 ibid 5.1.2.

145 ibid 5.1.3.

146 ibid 5.1.4.

147 ibid 5.1.5.

148 Paola Andrea Acosta Alvarado and Daniel Rivas-Ramírez, 'A Milestone in Environmental and Future Generations' Rights Protection: Recent Legal Developments before the Colombian Supreme Court' (2018) 30 Journal of Environmental Law 519, 522.

('*derechos-deberes*').[149] As such, the Constitution, 'recognises, on the one hand, the protection of the environment as a constitutional *right*, closely linked to life, health and physical, spiritual and cultural integrity; and on the other, as a *duty*, because it demands from the authorities and the private actions aimed at its protection and safeguarding'.[150] This duty does not only extend to future generations but also encompasses nature and non-humans beings:

> the scope of protection of the fundamental rights is each person, but also the 'other.' The 'fellow' is otherness; its essence, the other people that inhabit the planet, also encompassing the other animal and plant species. But, in addition, it includes the subjects not yet born, who deserve to enjoy the same environmental conditions experienced by us.[151]

The court exclaimed that future generations have environmental rights and that these are based on two fundaments: a) the ethical duty of solidarity of the species and b) the intrinsic value of nature.[152]

The Court elaborates in relation to the first fundament that all persons, born or not yet born, share the same natural resources. Future generations do not have access to these resources yet but they will be the tributaries, recipients and owners of them, and these resources become increasingly limited.[153] Thus, solidary between generations is indispensable to a point where solidarity and environmentalism '*relate to becoming the same*'.[154] The 'obligation of human solidarity with nature' then 'constitutes the essential content of "the true values that daily facilitate life", both in its present and future dimensions'.[155] The second fundament is the shift from an anthropocentric to an ecocentric approach. Nature has an intrinsic value of its own, and, therefore, is worth to be protected. Humans do not stand 'outside' of the environment—the German term *Umwelt* ('*surrounding world*') illustrates this quite well[156]—but are part of it.[157]

---

[149] Corte Suprema de Justicia de Colombia (n 137) para 5.1.

[150] Constitutional Court of Colombia, *Tierra Digna v Presidencia de La República (T-622), 2016* para 5.5 (tr the author, emphasis added).

[151] Corte Suprema de Justicia de Colombia (n 137) para 5.2 (tr the author).

[152] ibid 5.3.

[153] ibid.

[154] ibid (emphasis in the Spanish original).

[155] ibid (tr the author).

[156] Cf. Frank Biermann, *Earth System Governance* (MIT Press 2014) 1.

[157] Corte Suprema de Justicia de Colombia (n 137) para 5.3.

The Supreme Court underpinned this by referring to several international agreements and constitutional provisions. The 'national ecological public order' is constituted not only through 'classical' environmental norms but also, inter alia, by the primacy of the general interest (Article 1), education that 'will train the Colombian [...] for the protection of the environment' (Article 67), the creation of the popular action 'for the protection of collective rights and interests related [...] to the environment' (Article 88) and the state's obligation to promote the internationalisation of ecological relations (Article 226) as norms being part of the of the so-called Ecological Constitution (*Constitución Ecológica*).[158] The fundamental rights of present and, in particular, of future generations, are at risk as the (illegal) logging activities in the Amazon forest continue to unleash huge amounts of CO_2 that are fuelling the greenhouse effect, which leads to increasing temperatures and transformations in the ecosystems and water resources.[159]

The most notable issue of this case is that the Supreme Court granted the Amazon River ecosystem rights. The plaintiffs had relied on several rulings of the Constitutional Court (CC)—Colombia's apex court—to stress the importance of a quality environment. The CC analyses 'the constitutional postulates from a "green" perspective, cataloguing the Political Charter as an "Ecological Constitution" and elevating the "environment" to the category of fundamental rights'.[160] In May 2017, the CC recognised the Atrato River in a landmark case as a subject of rights.[161] Notably, the plaintiffs in that case had claimed the violation of their rights to 'life, health, water, food security, a healthy environment, the culture and territory of the active ethnic communities, and consequently, a series of orders and measures are issued to articulate structural solutions to the serious health, socio-environmental, ecological and humanitarian crisis in the Atrato river basin, its tributaries and surrounding territories.'[162]

But, they had not made a claim that the Atrato River should become the subject of rights.[163] However, the CC referred to the Colombian ecoconsciousness and 'Colombia's cultural and ethnical pluralism as well as the ancestral knowledge, uses and customs bequeathed by indigenous and tribal peoples' to explore 'an alternative vision of the collective rights of ethnic communities in relation to

[158] ibid 7.

[159] ibid 11.

[160] ibid 7.

[161] Constitutional Court of Colombia (n 150).

[162] ibid 5.5.

[163] ibid 7.

their natural and cultural environment', so-called 'biocultural rights'.[164] The CC saw this broad interpretation of the Constitution as justified because of

> the superior interest of the environment which has been widely developed by constitutional jurisprudence and which is made up of numerous constitutional clauses that constitute what has been called the 'Ecological Constitution' or 'Green Constitution'.[165]

In *Future Generations*, the plaintiffs asked the Supreme Court to interpret the principle of solidarity in a broad manner, not only towards humans but also embracing all other organisms 'with whom we share our planet since the existence of these is worthy of protection in itself'.[166] Even though they clearly showed some preference for the ecocentric approach, the plaintiffs used and analysed all three approaches (anthropocentric, bio-centric and ecocentric) to demonstrate that their claim was justified.[167] They did not raise the issue to declare the Amazon a subject of rights.[168] However, by identifying that deforestation even occurred in protected national parks and that '[h]umanity is the main actor responsible' for degrading ecosystems since 'its planetary hegemonic position led to the adoption of an anthropocentric and selfish model, whose characteristic features are harmful to environmental stability',[169] the Supreme Court recognised the Colombian Amazon 'as a "subject of rights", entitled to protection, conservation, maintenance and restoration under the responsibility of the State and the territorial agencies that comprise it'.[170] In addition to establishing monitoring and reporting obligations in the affected areas, the court ordered the government to establish a 'Pact for Generations in the Life of the Colombian Amazon' with the active participation of the plaintiffs, communities, scientific organisations, environmental research groups and affected populations.[171]

This ruling was remarkable in many ways. Not only did it grant the Amazon legal status, but it also recognised 'environmental rights for future generations'. These, however, are not only benefiting humans since they come with a duty to respect and protect the 'otherness', which includes nature. Human rights law,

---

[164] ibid 43.

[165] ibid 138.

[166] *Demanda Tutela Amazonía Colombia* (n 139) para 5.1.3 (tr the author).

[167] ibid 5.1.

[168] See 'Peticiones', ibid 7.

[169] Corte Suprema de Justicia de Colombia (n 137) para 4 (tr the author).

[170] ibid 14 (tr the author).

[171] ibid.

with its focus on 'absolutes and universals rather than contingencies and compromises', has been criticised as a concept too narrow for the protection of the environment in the twenty-first century. Instead, human rights law should also be moderated by an idea of responsibility towards other species and future generations.[172] The decision of the Colombian Supreme Court, based on inter-species and inter-temporal solidarity, can be read as a step in this direction.

9.4 CCL as a Form of International Lawmaking?

The cases examined in this chapter all contributed in one way or another to legal thought through their interpretative innovations. In *Urgenda*, the courts interpreted the unwritten duty to include the state's obligation to protect its citizens from the adverse effects of climate change. Moreover, the CA and the SC expanded the positive obligation under Articles 2 and 8 ECHR from individual sites of pollution, such as a waste site, to global climate change. In *Leghari*, the concept of environmental justice was further developed into a concept of climate justice that includes water justice. *Juliana* was the first lawsuit to test a right to a stable climate in court, which was at least accepted by one court. And in *Future Generations*, the Colombian Supreme Court recognised the environmental rights of future generations based on the solidarity between generations and species and fostered the ecocentric approach by declaring the Amazon a subject of rights. It managed, in a unique way, to reconcile a human rights-based approach to environmental protection with rights for nature itself.

The potential of litigation for self-government and participation in lawmaking processes was discussed in Chapter 6. Since this work is concerned with *global* climate constitutionalism, however, it has to be asked whether CCL can be understood as a form of *international* lawmaking. The cases analysed in this chapter were all filed with domestic courts. While they fulfil the two criteria Osofsky had laid out for cases to count as lawmaking under a pluralist perspective—according to which 1) cases must focus on climate change and be filed with formally-constituted tribunals and 2) only those who file or adjudicate the case can be considered international lawmakers—her model is only concerned with supranational petitions such as the Inuit petition with the Inter-American

[172] Jordi Jaria-Manzano, 'Law in the Anthropocene' in Jordi Jaria-Manzano and Susana Borràs (eds), *Research Handbook on Global Climate Constitutionalism* (Edward Elgar Publishing 2019) 39; for a general critique of the use of human rights law in climate litigation, see Fanny Thornton, 'The Absurdity of Relying on Human Rights Law to Go After Emitters' in Benoit Mayer and Alexander Zahar (eds), *Debating Climate Law* (CUP 2021).

Commission on Human Rights or a petition filed with the World Heritage Committee.[173] Accordingly, it is *international* litigation that can be understood as a form of international lawmaking. From this point of view, the application filed by six Portuguese children with the ECtHR can be understood as relevant to international lawmaking but not the cases filed with domestic courts. While those cases were innovative, and the courts used a large amount of creativity to protect the environment, this raises the question of whether *domestic* litigation is relevant to IL.

9.5 Influence of Domestic CCL Cases on IL

It is somewhat apparent that international courts develop IL and are important drivers of global constitutionalism.[174] However, most CCL cases are filed with national, often constitutional, courts. The question this raises is whether domestic courts can also contribute to the development of a transnational legal order or if they—as organs of a state—can merely influence domestic policy.

In regard to the latter, it could be said that the system of courts forms the judicial branch and, thus, belongs to the government. Consequently, its influence is limited to interpreting, concreting and applying domestic law. Therefore, national courts would have internal but no external influence, since they are only part of a particular state and do not themselves play a role in the development of IL. For dualistic models of the law, national and international courts operate in separate legal spheres.[175] Under such a perspective, the role of domestic courts is

[173] Hari M Osofsky, 'Climate Change Litigation as Pluralist Legal Dialogue?' (2007) 26A Stanford Environmental Law Journal 181, 210.

[174] Armin von Bogdandy and Ingo Venzke, *International Judicial Lawmaking* (Springer 2012); Ingo Venzke, 'The Role of International Courts as Interpreters and Developers of the Law: Working Out the Jurisgenerative Practice of Interpretation' (2011) 34 Loyola of Los Angeles International and Comparative Law Review 99; Marc Jacob, 'Lawmaking Through International Adjudication' (2011) 12 German Law Journal 1005; for an overview of how international and regional courts have ruled on matters of climate change, see Mehrdad Payandeh, 'The Role of Courts in Climate Protection and the Separation of Powers' in Wolfgang Kahl and Marc-Philippe Weller (eds), *Climate Change Litigation—A Handbook* (Beck/Hart/Nomos 2021).

[175] Shany Yuval, 'Should the Implementation of International Rules by Domestic Courts Be Bolstered?' in Antonio Cassese (ed), *Realizing Utopia: The Future of International Law* (2012) 201.

limited to the enforcement of IL due to the absence of a central law-enforcement mechanism.[176]

However, according to Scelle, their role is double-functional. In his theory of *dédoublementfonctionnel*, he argued that national agents not only perform the role intended for them in domestic settings but that they are also international agents. As such, they act as international organs for the international community.[177] In Falk's words:

> the decentralized quality of international law places a special burden upon all legal institutions at the national level. Domestic courts are agents of a developing international legal order, as well as servants of various national interests.[178]

Institutions and individuals form part of the government's branches as independent actors engaging in the interpretation of IL, especially the ever more significant domestic courts.[179] While international courts are restricted to interpreting IL, national courts can interpret and apply domestic law *and* IL.[180] This frequently occurs when a court determines a government's obligation under international or regional human rights law, as the cases of *Urgenda, Leghari* and *Future Generations* have demonstrated. From such a view, national courts not only function as law enforcers but also as law creators.[181]

In the context of the U.S., Osofsky identifies that the EPA's obligation to regulate GHG emissions of motor vehicles shapes the national base on which the U.S. acts on the international plane. As a member of the UNFCCC, the U.S. has to aim to stabilise and reduce GHG emissions under the good faith obligation. The successful suit influenced how the EPA formulates federal policy and, thus, how the U.S. government regulates GHG emissions.[182] But even unsuccessful cases

---

[176] Anthea Roberts, 'Comparative International Law? The Role of National Courts in Creating and Enforcing International Law' (2011) 60 International and Comparative Law Quarterly 57, 60; Anne Peters, 'Rechtsordnungen und Konstitutionalisierung: Zur Neubestimmung der Verhältnisse' (2010) 65 Zeitschrift für öffentliches Recht 3, 22.

[177] Georges Scelles, 'Le phénomène juridique du dédoublement fonctionnel' in Walter Schätzel and Hans-Jürgen Schlochauer (eds), *Rechtsfragen der internationalen Organisation (FS f. Hans Wehberg)* (Vittorio Klostermann 1956) 324.

[178] Richard A Falk, *The Role of Domestic Courts in the International Legal Order* (Syracuse University Press 1964) 65.

[179] Ingo Venzke, *How Interpretation Makes International Law: On Semantic Change and Normative Twists* (OUP 2012) 67–8.

[180] Payandeh (n 174) para 22.

[181] Roberts (n 176) 60.

[182] Osofsky (n 173) 203.

can spur debate on how to address climate concerns and, thus, formulate national policy answers in a broader context of IL. Litigation can help to determine the extent to which states are meeting their obligations.

Under a traditional Westphalian understanding, litigation can only influence national decision-making and would certainly not fall into the rubric of IL.[183] Under a more pluralist understanding of IL, however, both domestic and international cases can influence international lawmaking.

Moreover, national courts play an important role in the generalising of expectations on the global level.[184] Especially in the field of human rights law, domestic courts have implemented international human rights law and have used particular interpretative and legal argumentation techniques, even when this has caused international embarrassment to their own state (or foreign states).[185] Domestic courts are not 'only' organs of their state but instead are quasi-independent players in IL.[186] 'In this respect, judges seem to act more as the law-enforcement officers of a global order than as mere instrumentalities of national legal systems.'[187]

From an IL sources perspective, national court decisions provide evidence of the practices of the forum state and thereby contribute to the interpretation of international treaties and customs and, consequently, engage in IL creation.[188]

Domestic courts cannot ignore IL because they need to react to the pressures of globalisation. However, it has been argued that courts are merely resorting to international rules to uphold national powers and expand national spaces. Domestic courts would see themselves firstly as national agents and be reluctant to apply IL, especially those norms that could clash with their domestic government's

---

[183] ibid 184.

[184] Andreas Fischer-Lescano, 'Global Constitutional Struggles: Human Rights between Colère Publique and Colère Politique' in Wolfgang Kaleck and others (eds), *International Prosecution of Human Rights Crimes* (Springer 2007) 17.

[185] Andrea Bianchi, 'Globalization of Human Rights: The Role of Non-State Actors' in Gunther Teubner (ed), *Global Law without a State* (Dartmouth Publishing 1997) 194. Bianchi names the F*ilartiga v Pena Irala* case in the U.S., in which the Court of Appeals resorted to the 1789 Alien Tort Claims Act allowing foreign citizens to bring a legal actions before U.S. courts for a tort committed in violation of the law of nations.

[186] André Nollkaemper, 'Internationally Wrongful Acts in Domestic Courts' (2007) 101 American Journal of International Law 760, 799.

[187] Bianchi (n 185) 195.

[188] Roberts (n 176) 59.

positions.[189] Domestic courts monitor and observe the decision of foreign courts only because they want to take external pressures off their executives and make space for domestic deliberation. This, however, can be achieved more effectively when courts ensure that their judgements complement rather than contradict or conflict with each other.[190] Whether this is the courts' main motivation remains doubtful. Slaughter points out that rather than seeing themselves as governmental actors, domestic courts seek to correspond to the ethos of their juridical profession—which is formed by international networks of courts and agencies[191]—in a 'disaggregated' state.[192] These networks would be formed because judges talk to each other in seminars, organise summits with their counterparts or negotiate with each other, facilitated by the internet.[193] Judges would see each other as participants in the enterprise of a global judicial enterprise: 'not only as servants and representatives of a particular government or polity, but also as fellow members of a profession that transcends national borders'.[194] Judges would create horizontal and vertical networks by communicating with each other. Juridical interaction of courts, then, can occur on many levels, for example, through constitutional cross-fertilisation, the construction of a global community of human rights law, relations between national courts and the CJEU, private transnational litigation, but also in face-to-face meetings of judges around the world.[195] The creation of global networks such as the UNEP Global Judges program, which developed a series of environmental law training materials for judges or the International Union for Conservation of Nature (IUCN) Global Judicial Institute on Environmental Law, which is organised by judges for judges seeking to support them to handle cases concerning the environment, demonstrate the emergence of a dialogue among judges for the global environmental realm.[196]

---

[189] Eyal Benvenisti, 'Reclaiming Democracy: The Strategic Uses of Foreign and International Law by National Courts' (2008) 102 The American Journal of International Law 241, 241 ff.

[190] Eyal Benvenisti and George W Downs, 'National Courts, Domestic Democracy, and the Evolution of International Law' (2009) 20 European Journal of International Law 59, 61.

[191] Anne-Marie Slaughter, *A New World Order* (Princeton University Press 2004) 65.

[192] ibid 12.

[193] ibid 65.

[194] ibid 68.

[195] ibid 69.

[196] IUCN World Commission on Environmental Law, 'Global Judicial Institute on the Environment' <https://www.iucn.org/our-union/commissions/group/iucn-wcel-global-judicial-institute-environment-task-force> accessed 31 August 2023.

Judges often examine other jurisdictions to learn from their counterparts, especially in new and emerging legal areas such as environmental rights and climate law.[197] Judge Aiken, for example, cited directly from the Filipino *Minors Oposa* case to prove that a right to a stable climate existed.[198] The GFCC, too, has cited and referred to *Urgenda, Juliana,* a 2017 climate decision of the High Court New Zealand and the 2020 ruling of the Irish Supreme Court in which the National Mitigation Plan was quashed.[199] Unfortunately, the (sometimes far more innovative and progressive) rulings of the Global South have not yet attracted the attention of the courts of the Global North that they deserve. The cases cited above by the GFCC were all filed with courts in the Global North.[200] Similarly, the High Court of New Zealand in 2017 did not cite the *Leghari* decision but merely found support for its position (that CCL cases have a judicial role) by referring to a number of cases from the Global North.[201] The courts missed an opportunity here to enter a truly transnational, unbiased dialogue. By ignoring the Global South's perspective, the transnational discourse on litigation as a driver for global climate constitutionalism, however, would remain one-sided and incomplete.

'Interpretive communities' of judges evolve over time together with their respective regimes.[202] Thus, CCL is an example of the trans-governmental networks in which IL needs to operate in the future. Strategic lawsuits and the (domestic) courts who adjudicate them are participating in these networks.[203] In South Asia, judiciaries have been drawing on each other's decisions and have built a strong body of environmental constitutional rights despite the lack of both a regional human rights mechanism and the absence of a right to a healthy environment in domestic constitutions.[204] In South Africa, judges must consider

[197] Sumudu Atapattu, 'Environmental Justice, Climate Justice and Constitutionalism: Protecting Vulnerable States and Communities' in Jordi Jaria-Manzano and Susana Borràs (eds), *Research Handbook on Global Climate Constitutionalism* (Edward Elgar Publishing 2019) 197.

[198] District Court of Oregon, Judge Ann Aiken, 11 October 2016, *Kelsey Cascadia Rose Juliana v United States of America* (Case No. 6:15-Cv-01517-TC) (n 111) 50.

[199] GFCC, 1 BvR 2656/18, para 203 passim.

[200] ibid para 203 passim.

[201] High Court of New Zealand (n 57) paras 105–32.

[202] Michael Waibel, 'Interpretive Communites in International Law' in Andrea Bianchi, Daniel Peat and Matthew Windsor (eds), *Interpretation in International Law* (OUP 2015) 152. He names the interpretive community of European judges as a prominent example.

[203] Osofsky (n 173) 229.

[204] Atapattu (n 197) 207.

IL and may consider foreign law when interpreting the South African Bill of Rights.[205] The South African Constitutional Court has made extensive use of this possibility. For instance, in its decision on the unconstitutionality of the death penalty, the court referred to several foreign documents and court rulings, inter alia, those of Canada, Germany and India.[206] The courts have also considered IL, including international environmental obligations, to interpret domestic laws.[207] But not only can ideas of constitutional law cross borders, but so can constitutional personnel. In at least 27 states, foreign judges work in courts of constitutional jurisdiction. In the Pacific region, this has led constitutional judges to cite and apply foreign law in constitutional courts.[208] According to Peel and Lin, courts in the Global South have generally not been relying on each other's climate change judgements (yet). NGOs and private actors seek to establish and foster such a dialogue, for example, by filing amicus briefs.[209]

However, not every court expressively cites foreign sources; instead, they sometimes absorb legal ideas silently. The 'foreign' sources become 'lost in translation', and such newly created rights are perceived as constitutive parts of the nation's identity.[210] Häberle describes, under the term '*Textstufen*' paradigm, from a historical viewpoint, how scholarly writings and court decisions are subsequently incorporated into legal and constitutional texts. This not only includes the incorporation of theory, practices, scholarship and court decisions of one's

[205] Constitution of South Africa, Section 39 para. 1 (b) (c), see also Dire Tladi, 'Interpretation of Treaties in an International Law-Friendly Framework—The Case of South Africa' in Helmut Aust and Georg Nolte (eds), *The Interpretation of International Law by Domestic Courts—Unity, Diversity, Convergence* (OUP 2016).

[206] Constitutional Court of South Africa, *The State v T Makwanyane and M Mchunu*, Case No. CCT/3/94 (Judgement of 6 June 1995), para 16.

[207] In Earthlife Africa, the South African High Court considered the UNFCCC and the Paris Agreement, stating that the National Environmental Management Act 'must also be interpreted consistently with international law. Section 233 of the Constitution provides that when interpreting any legislation, every court must prefer any reasonable interpretation of the legislation that is consistent with international law over any alternative interpretation that is inconsistent with international law', see High Court of South Africa, *Earthlife Africa Johannesburg v Minister of Environmental Affairs and Others*, Judgement of 6 March 2017 (Case No. 65662/16) 33–4.

[208] Anna Dziedzic, 'Foreign Judges of the Pacific as Agents of Global Constitutionalism' (2021) 10 Global Constitutionalism 351, 352.

[209] Peel and Lin (n 75) 710.

[210] Judith Resnik, 'Law's Migration: American Exceptionalism, Silent Dialogues, and Federalism's Multiple Ports of Entry' (2006) 115 Yale Law Journal 1564, 1564.

national jurisdiction, but also those of other countries, which results in an 'open society of constitutional legislators'.[211]

Moreover, domestic courts' decisions can influence the rulings of international tribunals in a cosmopolitan pluralist jurisprudence.[212] Trachtman, for example, observes an inter-constitutional dialogue between the supranational CJEU and the constitutional courts of the member-states of the EU as well as between the US Constitution and international constitutions, such as the WTO constitution.[213] In *Urgenda*, the CA and the SC applied Articles 2 and 8 of the ECHR in quite a broad fashion, which went far beyond the criteria that the ECtHR's authoritative interpretations have set in a multitude of decisions, according to which the presence of a real, imminent and foreseeable threat to identifiable victims is crucial.[214] It remains to be seen how the ECtHR will react to the Dutch way of interpreting the Convention, but it will certainly foster a judicial dialogue between the national courts and the regional human rights court, in particular when the ECtHR decides upon admissibility and merits of several climate cases pending before its chambers and the Grand Chamber.[215] Thus, not only international tribunals but also national courts contribute to the development of international constitutional law.

> Apart from developing domestic environmental jurisprudence, these courts also contribute, through processes of trans-jurisdictional comparison, to the steady growth of transnational comparative environmental constitutionalism [...]. In doing so, some latent degree of uniformity is developing globally with respect to the interpretation,

[211] Peter Häberle, 'The Jurisprudence of European Law—Viewed as a Cultural Study' in Markus Kotzur (ed), *Peter Häberle on Constitutional Theory: Constitution as Culture and the Open Society of Constitutional Interpreters* (Nomos/Hart 2018) 312 (tr the author); Peter Häberle, *Ein afrikanisches Verfassungs- und Lesebuch—mit vergleichender Kommentierung* (Duncker & Humblot 2019) 11.

[212] Paul Schiff Berman, *Global Legal Pluralism—A Jurisprudence of Law beyond Borders* (CUP 2012) 154.

[213] Joel P Trachtman, 'The Constitutions of the WTO' (2006) 17 European Journal of International Law 623, 627; T Alexander Aleinikoff, 'Thinking Outside the Sovereignty Box: Transnational Law and the U.S. Constitution' (2004) 82 Texas Law Review 1989.

[214] Nina Mileva and Marina Fortuna, 'Environmental Protection as an Object of and Tool for Evolutionary Interpretation' in Georges Abi-Saab and others (eds), *Evolutionary Interpretation and International Law* (Hart/Bloomsbury Publishing 2019) 137.

[215] Cases at the time of writing pending before the Grand Chamber of the ECtHR: *KlimaSeniorinnen Schweiz and Others v. Switzerland* (application no. 53600/20), *Carême v. France* (application no. 7189/21), *Duarte Agostinho and Others v. Portugal and 32 Other States* (application no. 39371/20), see ECtHR, 'Climate Change (Factsheet)' (2023) <https://www.echr.coe.int/documents/d/echr/FS_Climate_change_ENG> accessed 31 August 2023.

> application and development of environmental law, including constitutional aspects such as environmental rights.[216]

'Constitutional moments' can be drawn from both international and domestic law. International and national law have to be considered complementary.[217]

Such a perspective also conforms to an understanding of climate governance as polycentric.[218] Instead of waiting for a global response to climate change, the problem needs to be addressed by a multitude of public and private actors at different levels of government.[219] While climate change is a global problem, it also has a local component. After all, its energy producers, food industry and transportation sectors and, in particular, millions of consumers (especially in the Global North) that emit GHG emissions are based in states and regions.[220] Climate change is a 'glocal' problem and requires responses on the international, subcontinental, national and local levels.[221]

Courts have begun to consider the global consequences of local GHG emissions. In Australia, the New South Wales Land and Environment Court dismissed an appeal against refusal of consent to the issuance of a licence for a planned open-cut coal mine because of the high CO_2 emissions that were to be expected. It saw the mine as a project coming at 'the wrong place at the wrong time'.[222] A polycentric understanding of climate governance aligns it in a coherent way with postmodern concepts of constitutional pluralism. The inter-judicial dialogues between national courts and supranational judicial bodies foster

---

216 Louis J Kotzé, *Global Environmental Constitutionalism in the Anthropocene* (Bloomsbury Publishing 2016) 230–1.

217 Häberle, *Ein afrikanisches Verfassungs- und Lesebuch—mit vergleichender Kommentierung* (n 211) 297.

218 Elinor Ostrom, 'A Polycentric Approach for Coping with Climate Change' [2009] The World Bank—Policy Research Working Paper 5095; Hari M Osofsky, 'Polycentrism and Climate Change' in Daniel A Farber and Marjan Peeters (eds), *Elgar Encyclopedia of Environmental Law: Climate Change Law (Vol. I)* (Edward Elgar Publishing 2015).

219 Ostrom (n 218) 4ff.

220 ibid 5.

221 Joyeeta Gupta, Kim van der Leeuw and Hans de Moel, 'Climate Change: A "Glocal" Problem Requiring "Glocal" Action' (2007) 4 Environmental Sciences 139.

222 NSW Land and Environment Court, *Gloucester Resources Limited v Minister for Planning* (2019) NSWLEC 7, at para. 699, 'In short, an open cut coal mine in this part of the Gloucester valley would be in the wrong place at the wrong time. Wrong place because an open cut coal mine in this scenic and cultural landscape, proximate to many people's homes and farms, will cause significant planning, amenity, visual and social impacts. Wrong time because the GHG emissions of the coal mine and its coal product will increase global total concentrations

'the imagery of a heterarchy of diverse legal discourses'.[223] As shown above,[224] transnational law comprises many partial constitutions, including nation-state constitutions and regime constitutions that are increasingly shaped by non-state actors. There is no strict legal hierarchy corresponding to a pyramid structure in the same way that domestic law is organised in the nation-state.

> Law unfolds as a network: one with stronger, weaker and even missing links—maybe a patchwork more than a network. The law that feeds into and emanates from transnational regulatory decision making does not self-organize into a monolithic structure; it is fragmented and polycentric.[225]

Climate governance is pluralistic; it is multi-scalar and involves multiple actors, including domestic courts. Their role should not be neglected. First, because, in an emerging multi-level system, the principle of subsidiarity and practical considerations make national courts the primary forums.[226] The direct applicability of IL in national forums 'empowers individuals and elevates them to the quality of an active legal subject of the relevant regime's legal order'.[227] Second, '[t]he future of international law is domestic'.[228] National courts are the forums that are approached by those who have the greatest interests in governments complying with their environmental and climate laws and human rights obligations: the stakeholders in that country.[229]

---

of GHGs at a time when what is now urgently needed, in order to meet generally agreed climate targets, is a rapid and deep decrease in GHG emissions. These dire consequences should be avoided. The Project should be refused.'

[223] Gunther Teubner, 'The Two Faces of Janus: Rethinking Legal Pluralism' in Kaarlo Tuori, Zenon Bankowski and Jyrki Uusitalo (eds), *Law and Power: Critical and Socio-Legal Essays* (Deborah Charles Publications 1997) 128.

[224] See Chapter 7 above.

[225] Veerle Heyvaert, 'The Transnationalization of Law: Rethinking Law through Transnational Environmental Regulation' (2017) 6 Transnational Environmental Law 205, 221.

[226] Anne Peters, 'Membership in the Global Constitutional Community' in Jan Klabbers, Anne Peters and Geir Ulfstein (eds), *The Constitutionalization of International Law* (OUP 2009) 162.

[227] ibid 207.

[228] Anne Marie Slaughter and William Burke-White, 'The Future of International Law Is Domestic (or, The European Way of Law)' (2006) 47 Harvard International Law Journal 327.

[229] Johan Karlsson Schaffer, 'The Co-Originality of Human Rights and Democracy in an International Order' (2015) 7 International Theory 96, 117.

It is important not to underestimate the domestic realm, as it continues to be the 'main battleground for social change'.[230] Precisely when people are personally affected they start fearing the consequences for their homes and neighbourhood; they experience 'environmental injustice', and they eventually stand up for themselves.[231] If 'local' people would do this all over the globe, they would make small contributions to the scholarly discourses on global climate constitutionalism by 'providing' the cases that, in return, will be discussed by national and international courts and whose legal findings eventually become part of the international climate constitution.

This became recently visible in the Human Rights Committee's decision in *Billy v. Australia.* The plaintiffs argued that Australia was in violation of Article 6 ICCPR (right to life) by failing to prevent a foreseeable loss of life from the effects of climate change and referred directly to the *Urgenda* decision.[232] Australia countered that the *Urgenda* decision was based on the Dutch Civil Code provisions on negligence (overlooking the fact that the legal basis had changed from civil law to human rights in the 2019 Supreme Court decision on which the claimants had relied).[233] While the Committee ultimately did not find a violation of the right to life, in his individual opinion, Committee Member Duncan Laki Muhumuza found that 'as highlighted by the Urgenda Foundation v. the State of Netherlands case, the State Party is tasked with an obligation to prevent a foreseeable loss of life from the impacts of climate change, and to protect the authors' right to life with dignity'.[234] By quoting directly from the *Urgenda* ruling, he argued that climate change was such a real and imminent threat that requires states to take precautionary measures to prevent the infringement of rights 'as far as possible'.[235] These referrals show that the dialogue of the courts is indeed not a monologue:

---

[230] Hans Peter Schmitz, 'Domestic and Transnational Perspectives on Democratization' (2004) 6 International Studies Review 403, 409.

[231] David Schlosberg, 'Disruption, Community, and Resilient Governance—Environmental Justice in the Anthropocene' in Tobias Haller and others (eds), *The Commons in a Glocal World: Global Connections and Local Responses* (Routledge 2019) 63–5.

[232] UN Human Rights Committee, *Daniel Billy et al v Australia*, Views adopted on 21 July 2022, CCPR/C/135/D/3624/2019, para 3.4.

[233] ibid para 4.7.

[234] Individual opinion by Committee Member Duncan Laki Muhumuza, Annex I, Human Rights Committee, Daniel Billy et al v Australia, para 10.

[235] ibid para 14.

> New international law is made in countless international forums, implemented through countless international agencies, interpreted and applied by countless new international courts and tribunals. And new international law is re-enacted by national legislatures, implemented by national executive branches of government, enforced in national courts. We are now beginning to see that old international law was essentially a rudimentary international constitutional law, providing the fundamental structures of a primitive form of international society.[236]

9.6 Concluding Remarks

The cases analysed in this chapter demonstrate how important judicial decisions are for the development of global climate constitutionalism. They have introduced new interpretive concepts, including the right to a stable climate or the unwritten duty of care to protect citizens from climate change's adverse effects. From this point of view, the plaintiffs of all four cases examined above could be seen as international lawmakers in their own right by initiating cases with a focus on climate change. Non-state actors engaging in (domestic) litigation present bottom-up approaches to global climate constitutionalism. 'Top-down political processes could then be increasingly replaced by bottom-up judicial actions. On this view, every legal case *counts*. Every judicial initiative *matters*.'[237] While social movements and international protests are important for shaping ecological consciousness in discourses, it is only for the courts to accept the argumentation of climate activists as legally binding and enforceable law. Both international and domestic courts are key players in global climate governance that contribute through ongoing judicial dialogues to the sharpening of the climate regime.

However, using the courts to pursue certain social and political goals raises pressing questions about the separation of powers. It has been claimed, including by several courts, that the courts are the wrong arenas for climate concerns (the keyword here is 'judicial activism') and that questions of climate policies should

[236] Philip Allott, 'The Emerging Universal Legal System' (2001) 3 International Law Forum du droit international 12, 16. Allott refers to old international law as 'the modest self-limiting of the potentially conflictual behaviour of governments in relation to each other, as they recognise the emergence of new "states", settle the limits of each other's land and sea territory and the limits of their respective national legal systems, resolve disputes and disagreements which may arise in their everyday "relations".'

[237] Carlo Vittorio Giabardo, 'Climate Change Litigation, State Responsibility and the Role of Courts in the Global Regi' in Barbara Pozzo and Valentia Jacometti (eds), *Environmental Loss and Damage in a Comparative Law Perspective* (Intersentia 2021) 401 (emphasis in original).

be addressed by the elected legislators.[238] This problem will be discussed in the next chapter.

[238] See, for example, Lucas Bergkamp, 'The Urgenda Judgment: A "Victory" for the Climate That Is Likely to Backfire' *Energypost.eu* (9 September 2015) <https://energypost.eu/urgenda-judgment-victory-climate-likely-backfire/> accessed 31 August 2023.

10 The Role of the Courts in CCL

Civil society is a driving force of the processes of transnational constitutionalisation. Social movements, protests in the form of rallies and boycotts, and petitions (such as the Right2Water petition in Europe) all influence and shape policies.[1] Giving these actors more opportunities for participation and deliberation could help to overcome the democratic deficit that scholars have identified with the ongoing de-constitutionalisation of the nation-state,[2] international organisations with no direct legitimacy[3] and the power drift from states to transnational regimes and civil actors such as ICANN.[4] However, talking and listening alone do not empower civil society actors to participate in decision-making.[5] This is, from the litigants' perspective, where the courts come into play. Courts have proven to be an efficient tool in pursuing social and legal change.[6]

---

[1] Jonathan Pickering, Karin Bäckstrand and David Schlosberg, 'Between Environmental and Ecological Democracy: Theory and Practice at the Democracy-Environment Nexus' (2020) 22 Journal of Environmental Policy & Planning 1, 7.

[2] Anne Peters, 'Compensatory Constitutionalism: The Function and Potential of Fundamental International Norms and Structures' (2006) 19 Leiden Journal of International Law 579.

[3] Robert A Dahl, 'Can International Organizations Be Democratic? A Skeptic's View' in Ian Shapiro and Casiano Hacker-Cordón (eds), *Democracy's Edges* (CUP 1999) 19.

[4] Paul Schiff Berman, 'The Globalisation of Jurisdiction' (2002) 151 University of Pennsylvania Law Review 311, 352, 405; Milton L Mueller, *Ruling the Root: Internet Governance and the Taming of Cyberspace* (MIT Press 2002) 211 calls ICANN a 'global regulatory regime'.

[5] Anne Peters, 'Dual Democracy' in Jan Klabbers, Anne Peters and Geir Ulfstein (eds), *The Constitutionalization of International Law* (OUP 2009) 339.

[6] Jacqueline Peel and Hari M Osofsky, 'Litigation as a Climate Regulatory Tool' in Christina Voigt (ed), *International Judicial Practice on the Environment: Questions of Legitimacy* (CUP 2019) 335.

M. Niehaus, *Global Climate Constitutionalism "from below"*,
https://doi.org/10.1007/978-3-658-43191-4_10

However, rulings such as *Urgenda* have had a mixed response. Besides worldwide enthusiasm, they have also been criticised for allegedly violating the principle of the separation of powers. Climate change is a complex political problem that, as we have seen, raises many questions. As Chapter 4 demonstrated, climate change requires us to address the problem of global climate justice: who must reduce GHG emissions? Who has to pay for loss and damage or provide financial aid to help those worse off? How much do we have to save for future generations? Who in the state is allowed to 'spend' what percentage of the remaining carbon budget?

Climate rulings result in a series of complex consequences. If a state is required to curtail GHGs, this will, in some way, affect industry, transport, energy generation and consumption. States try to reduce environmentally unfriendly behaviour mainly through monetary burdens.

However, these hit the lower middle class and the poorest citizens the hardest (while they are responsible for less GHG emissions than the wealthiest parts of the population[7]), as many of them cannot afford to switch to more sustainable but more expensive technologies such as electric cars. These questions and problems are strongly intertwined with the question of *who* decides what climate obligations exist or whether they exist at all. In most states in which the principle of the separation of powers is included in the constitution, it is the (elected) legislative's competence to regulate political subject matters. The role of the courts, conversely, is strictly limited to judicial review (whether a certain measure is compatible with the constitution), but they must not participate in politics. However, CCL precisely aims to change the law via court decisions. This raises the question of whether CCL is an illegitimate form of lawmaking and violates the principle of the separation of powers. The present chapter analyses the importance of case-law for the development of the law and considers what role the courts should play when confronted with 'super wicked' cases that may also raise political questions (Sections 10.1-10.3). Drawing on Habermas's co-originality thesis, Section 10.4 sheds light on the tensions between democracy and the protection of human rights that the courts face. Sections 10.4.1 und 10.4.2 explore issues raised in relation to CCL, namely the recognition of positive obligations under human rights law to protect citizens against the adverse impacts of climate change and, by comparing the constitutions of the U.S. and Germany, the creation of new constitutional rights, such as the right to a stable

---

[7] For Europe, cf. Oxfam, 'Confronting Carbon Inequality in the European Union' (2020) <https://www.oxfam.org/en/research/confronting-carbon-inequality-european-union> accessed 31 August 2023.

climate or the concept of an ecological subsistence minimum. Section 10.5 and 10.06 take a critical look at the role of judicial lawmaking in relation to legislative lawmaking and its limits. Section 10.7 closes with some concluding remarks.

10.1 The Importance of Case-Law

Interpretation by non-state actors needs to be institutionalised by the courts to produce legal effects that can regulate and guide the actions of the 'target person', for example, the government. Every norm addressee is called to first interpret a norm on their own; everybody is a co-interpreter in Häberle's sense.[8] Someone may think that their right to life or health should be protected from the adverse effects of climate change; however, it is only when this interpretation reaches a court that it can become vested in legal and enforceable claims.

Not all interpretations are equal. Different interpreters enjoy varying degrees of legitimacy and authority regarding their interpretations.[9] A juridical ruling possesses more legal force than any other interpretation:

> The judgment represents the quintessential form of authorized, public, official speech which is spoken in the name of and to everyone. These performative utterances, substantive—as opposed to procedural—decisions publicly formulated by authorized agents acting on behalf of the collectivity, are magical acts which succeed because they have the power to make themselves universally recognized. They thus succeed in creating a situation in which no one can refuse or ignore the point of view, the vision, which they impose.[10]

Another characteristic is the jurispathic function of courts. Since 'interpretation always takes place in the shadow of coercion', judges 'do not create law, but kill' competing legal orders.[11] Thus, even if every community and every individual

[8] Mehrdad Payandeh, *Judikative Rechtserzeugung* (Mohr Siebeck 2017) 278; Peter Häberle, '"The Open Society of Constitutional Interpreters"—A Contribution to a Pluralistic and "Procedural" Constitutional Interpretation (1975)' in Markus Kotzur (ed), *Peter Häberle on Constitutional Theory* (Nomos/Hart 2018) 131.

[9] Payandeh (n 8) 278.

[10] Pierre Bourdieu, 'The Force of Law: Toward a Sociology of the Juridical Field' (1987) 7 Hastings Law Journal 805, 838.

[11] Robert M Cover, 'The Supreme Court, 1982 Term—Foreword: Nomos and Narrative' (1983) 97 Harvard Law Review 4, 40, 53.

can interpret and further develop the law, it is only for the courts to discard interpretations.[12]

Both international and domestic courts play crucial roles in the creation of the autopoietic system 'law'.[13] As seen above, non-state actors can make law without the *jus gentinum* accepting it. But to introduce the so-emerging *lex humana* into the politically supported 'traditional' law, the use of the courts as the centre of the system 'law' is necessary.[14] Activists seeking to introduce new interpretational concepts in IEL, either by broadening ('greening') the scope of rights already existing, such as the right to life, or by introducing new rights, such as the right to a stable climate, need to test these concepts in court. Only the courts are responsible for the management of paradoxes and can decide on the divergence of norms between the *colère publique* and the *colère politique.* It is up to them to decide whether a norm of the *lex humana* is valid and thereby binding for the *colère politique.*[15]

10.1.1 The Role of the Courts

The judicialisation of highly contentious political and moral questions ('mega-politics') that have been framed as constitutional issues and brought before High and Constitutional Courts has significantly increased throughout the last three decades.[16] Many actors see courts as better suited for decision-making on key issues concerning moral and political questions than politicians or the demos itself.[17] Hirschl sees three factors as decisive for the 'judicialization of politics': the existence of a written constitutional framework featuring a bill of rights, a

---

[12] ibid 40; in another essay, Cover also attests courts a 'homicidal potential'. Their legal interpretations generate 'credible threats and actual deeds of violence, in an effective way', for example, when the interpretation of a text by a judge results in the loss of freedom of somebody, see Robert M Cover, 'Violence and the Word' (1986) 95 The Yale Law Journal 1601, 1610.

[13] Clemens Mattheis, *Die Konstitutionalisierung des Völkerrechts aus systemtheoretischer Sichtweise* (Springer 2018) 387.

[14] Andreas Fischer-Lescano, *Globalverfassung—Die Geltungsbegründung der Menschenrechte* (Velbrück 2005) 128.

[15] ibid.

[16] Ran Hirschl, 'The Judicialization of Politics' in E Goodin (ed), *The Oxford Handbook of Political Science* (OUP 2011) 256.

[17] 'Not a single week passes by without a national high court somewhere in the world releasing a major judgment pertaining to the scope of constitutional rights protections or the limits on legislative or executive powers', ibid 254–5.

relatively autonomous judiciary willing to engage in public policy-making and, above all, a political environment that is conducive to the judicialisation of politics ('judicialization from below').[18] The courts are used as 'forums of protest' where litigants engage in discourses with various stakeholders and build political movements.[19]

Cases are perceived as opportunities to influence national and international policy[20] and as an important component of law enforcement.[21] Many plaintiffs see the courts as impartial actors in a 'dirty' game of politics and economic interests.[22] The strength of adjudication is that it can address environmental concerns through a process divorced from political disputation.[23] A court decision, above all, is effective. Because the juridical language bears 'all the marks of a rhetoric of impersonality and of neutrality', the decision of the court as an actor that is independent of the social groups in conflict and, thus, represents the public, is accepted as impartial and, therefore, can obtain and sustain general social consent.[24]

Litigation has been criticised from different angles. Rosenberg claims that courts act as 'fly-paper' for social reformers who succumb to the 'lure of litigation'.[25] Litigation would waste precious resources in harmless legal battles, whereas more than symbolic success can only be won in battles in the political arena.[26] Litigation is expensive, especially in countries where the 'loser pays' system demands the unsuccessful party to pay the costs. Since climate change is mostly affecting the poor, there are vast majorities that might be excluded from

[18] ibid 272, 269.

[19] Jules Lobel, 'Courts as Forums for Protest' (2004) 52 UCLA Law Review 477, 480.

[20] As one of the interviewees of Peel and Osofsky's study explained, litigation enables people of 'actually doing something to try and deal with a massive issue that at an individual level is hard to [do] because the decisions are made by government and internationally that individuals can't influence very much. But two or three, or maybe half a dozen key people can run a really good court case. Half a dozen people can't normally influence national policy or international policy', Jacqueline Peel and Hari M Osofsky, *Climate Change Litigation: Regulatory Pathways to Cleaner Energy* (CUP 2015) 15.

[21] Alexandra Lahav, *In Praise of Litigation* (OUP 2017) 34.

[22] Cf. Jolene Lin, 'Climate Change and the Courts' (2012) 32 Legal Studies 35, 37.

[23] Tim Stephens, *International Courts and Environmental Protection* (CUP 2009) 116.

[24] Bourdieu (n 10) 819, 830, see also the translator's introduction by Richard Terdiman, 810.

[25] Gerald N Rosenberg, *The Hollow Hope: Can Courts Bring About Social Change?* (2nd edn, University of Chicago 2008) 427.

[26] ibid.

using CCL as a tool for advancing climate protection.[27] And where such cases are successful, the outcome is a paradox in the Global South: while courts may protect citizens from the adverse effects of climate change, the result is that taxpayers of the countries that contributed least to climate change in the first place have to pay for climate action.[28] But by far the most important argument brought against CCL is the alleged violation of the separation of powers if a court rules on environmental matters.

10.1.2 The Separation of Powers and Legitimacy of the Actors

The separation of powers—or horizontal structuring—goes back to Montesquieu[29] and is a vital element of democratic governance. Accordingly, some branches are better suited to deal with certain subject matters than others. The main objective of separating governmental power into three branches, however, is to prevent the encroachment of one branch onto the competencies of the other branches and, thus, prevent the tyranny of one branch over the others.[30] Thus, the separation of powers is an important element in democratic states.[31]

For many, climate change is first and foremost a policy problem that should be dealt with by democratically elected governmental organs.[32] This leads straight to the core of the debate: the question of adjudication, that is, how judges decide

---

[27] James R May and Erin Daly, *Global Environmental Constitutionalism* (CUP 2014) 90.

[28] Juan Auz, 'Global South Climate Litigation versus Climate Justice: Duty of International Cooperation as a Remedy?' *Völkerrechtsblog* (28 April 2020) <https://voelkerrechtsblog.org/de/global-south-climate-litigation-versus-climate-justice-duty-of-international-cooperation-as-a-remedy/> accessed 31 August 2023.

[29] Montesquieu, *Complete Works, Vol. 1 (The Spirit of Laws) [1748]* (T Evans 1777) 198ff.

[30] Jenny S Martinez, 'Horizontal Structuring' in Michel Rosenfeld and András Sajó (eds), *The Oxford Handbook of Comparative Constitutional Law* (OUP 2012) 548.

[31] Christoph Möllers, *The Three Branches: A Comparative Model of Separation of Powers* (OUP 2013) 108. It has to be mentioned, though, that this view is not shared by all. Kelsen even claimed that the principle of the separation of powers is undemocratic and would only strengthen the powers of the executive—the monarchy, see Hans Kelsen, *The Essence and Value of Democracy (1920)* (Nadia Urbinati and Carlo Invernizzi Accetti eds, Rowmann and Littlefield Publishers 2013) 89ff.

[32] For example, in *Juliana*, defendants argued that "[p]laintiffs seek a comprehensive national climate policy, overseen by a single federal district court that would require wholesale changes to energy production and consumption in this country. [...] Formulating and enforcing this expansive relief lies outside this Court's competence and jurisdiction", Federal

cases or how they ought to decide them.[33] What is the role of the judge in climate cases? 'Should' judges make climate law?[34] This debate is strongly intertwined with (but not identical to) the discussion on the interpretation of the law.

10.1.3 Adjudication

The debate as to whether judges may decide climate policy questions runs along the front lines of the discussion of what kind of role the (constitutional) judge should play: whether a constitution should be interpreted as intended by its drafters ('originalists') or whether it is seen as a living instrument that can accommodate social change.[35] The role of a judge whose job is seen as 'merely' applying the law is naturally more limited than that of a judge whose task is seen as using creativity to develop the law and to take on a more active role. Roughly, these different approaches divide under the adjudication theories of 'realism' and 'formalism'.

Realism describes that judges are influenced by the underlying facts of a case that they are deciding and on which they (unconsciously) base their decisions.[36] Realists' ideas about these underlying facts differ, with Dworkin remarking ironically that the outcome of a case depends on what the judge had had for breakfast.[37] As long as the result 'tastes' good, it does not matter how judges reached their conclusion.[38] Bourdieu, who uses the term instrumentalism instead,

---

Defendants' Memorandum of Points and Authorities in Support of Their Motion to Dismiss (Case No. 6:15-Cv-01517-TC) 14.

[33] Brian Leiter, 'Positivism, Formalism, Realism. Review Essay on Anthony Sebok's "Legal Positivism in American Jurisprudence"' (1999) 99 Columbia Law Review 1138, 1199.

[34] Laura Burgers, 'Should Judges Make Climate Change Law?' (2020) 9 Transnational Environmental Law 55.

[35] See Chapter 2.

[36] Leiter (n 33) 1148; for a general overview see Michael Steven Green, 'Legal Realism as Theory of Law' (2005) 46 William & Mary Law Review 1915.

[37] Ronald Dworkin, *Law's Empire* (Belknap Press 1986) 36.

[38] "[R]ealism views a court not as a syllogism machine, but as a sausage factory, where it doesn't much matter what goes into the product as long as it tastes good. Under a sausage factory view of adjudication, a judge is not a skilled mechanic [as for formalists], but a short order cook. The value of her work is measured, not by the rigor of the search for proper ingredients, but by the extent to which the final product conforms to the tastes of the best customers", Burt Neuborne, 'Of Sausage Factories and Syllogism Machines: Formalism, Realism, and Exclusionary Selection Techniques' (1992) 67 New York University Law Review 419, 420.

warns that, in this way, interpretation becomes an instrument of domination. Law and jurisprudence are direct reflections of social power relations dominated by the expressions of certain groups.[39] Driven to the extreme, the law loses its neutrality and becomes the playball of various interest groups. The idea of the rule of law and its impartiality is at risk if the law could be bent in ways that serve special interests, many of which are supported by various groups with resources in the form of legal skills and financial means. The closeness of interests and parallelism of habitus between judges as members of the dominant class and those holding political or economic power means that the latter are unlikely to be disadvantaged as a result.[40]

Formalism, conversely, argues that law is a closed system untouched by external facts, social or historical backgrounds and, especially, morality.[41] Developments occur in an 'internal[ly] dynamic' way within the legal system.[42] Legal reasoning, therefore, has to be austerely simple to not let discretion sneak into adjudication through interpretation.[43] The role of judges, in this view, takes on the role of historians.[44] Their job is to identify the 'right' externally-mandated rule, but they have little legitimate discretion over the choice of the rule. Judges have to feed the 'true' facts into the machine 'judicial system', and the correct conclusion will emerge autonomously as a matter of logic.[45] The meaning of the rule is frozen and has to be applied in exactly the same manner to the next case.[46] The interpretation of a norm should not be influenced by external factors such as public opinion. In *South Africa v Makwanyane*, Judge Chaskalson P argued that '[p]ublic opinion may have some relevance to the enquiry, but in itself, it is no substitute for the duty vested in the Courts to interpret the Constitution and to uphold its provisions without fear or favour'.[47]

---

[39] Bourdieu (n 10) 814.

[40] ibid 842.

[41] Not to be confused with positivism, which is a theory of law, whereas formalism refers to a theory of adjudication, see Leiter (n 33) 1144.

[42] Bourdieu (n 10) 814.

[43] Leiter (n 33) 1144–9, referring to Justice Scalia's radical understanding of formalism, see Antonin Scalia, *A Matter of Interpretation* (Princeton University Press 1997).

[44] Pierre-Marie Dupuy, 'Evolutionary Interpretation of Treaties: Between Memory and Prophecy' in Enzo Cannizzaro (ed), *The Law of Treaties Beyond the Vienna Convention* (OUP 2011) 128.

[45] Neuborne (n 38) 421.

[46] HLA Hart, *The Concept of Law* (Clarendon Press 1961) 129.

[47] Constitutional Court of the Republic of South Africa, *The State v Makwanyane and Another* (CCT3/94) [1995] ZACC 3; 1995 (6) BCLR 665; 1995 (3) SA 391; [1996] 2

However, it is not clear how the formalist approach could respond to the vagueness of most legal norms, especially human rights law and constitutional rights. Instead, the 'open texture of law leaves a vast field for a creative activity'.[48] A norm needs to be 'filled' by interpretation, or as Häberle stated: 'There are no legal norms, there are only interpreted legal norms'.[49] But even *after* interpreting a norm, there is not only *one* correct interpretation. A judge always has to choose among different options (see Section 10.5) and, thus, needs to make a personal contribution to a norm's understanding.

In this context, it should be noted that the judge—who is simultaneously a citizen—does not operate 'outside' of reality.[50] Besides observing the activities of their professional peers, courts are also able to mirror and respond to public opinions, which can also include changing perceptions of the science in both ways—either towards more or less regulation.[51] Even formally independent and impartial judges are making their decisions 'within the framework of the public and the reality of the constitution'.[52] Interferences, expectations and social 'constraints' should not be perceived merely as perils for judicial independence but rather as containing a core of legitimacy because they prevent arbitrary judicial interpretation.[53]

Dworkin's role model of a perfect judge who is knowing, capable, patient and equipped with superhuman spirit, 'Hercules',[54] is ultimately very lonely in

---

CHRLD 164; 1995 (2) SACR 1 (6 June 1995). Judge Chaskalson P argued that he was 'prepared to assume that [...] the majority of South Africans agree that the death sentence should be imposed in extreme cases of murder. The question before us, however, is not what the majority of South Africans believe a proper sentence for murder should be. It is whether the Constitution allows the sentence. Public opinion may have some relevance to the enquiry, but in itself, it is no substitute for the duty vested in the Courts to interpret the Constitution and to uphold its provisions without fear or favour. If public opinion were to be decisive there would be no need for constitutional adjudication. The protection of rights could then be left to Parliament, which has a mandate from the public, and is answerable to the public for the way its mandate is exercised, but this would be a return to parliamentary sovereignty, and a retreat from the new legal order established by the 1993 Constitution' (paras 87–88).

48 Hart (n 46) 204.

49 Peter Häberle, 'Zeit und Verfassung: Prolegomena zu einem "zeit-gerechten" Verfassungsverständnis' (1974) 21 Zeitschrift für Politik 111, 127 (tr the author, citations omitted).

50 Häberle, 'The Open Society of Constitutional Interpreters' (n 8) 142.

51 Peel and Osofsky (n 20) 223.

52 Häberle, 'The Open Society of Constitutional Interpreters' (n 8) 142.

53 ibid.

54 Ronald Dworkin, *Taking Rights Seriously* (Duckworth 1977) 105 ff.; Dworkin (n 37) 239 ff.

his judicial monologue.[55] Judicial independence only becomes bearable because the judge does not interpret in a vacuum. Instead, the other state functions and the pluralistic public deliver material 'to' the law.[56] For Habermas, therefore, the 'open society of constitutional interpreters' is better suited as an anchoring point for legal theory than the idealised personality of a judge.[57] Courts should be open for the inputs of the 'open society of constitutional interpreters':

> The essential ideas behind the social theory of law are to keep a close eye on what people—legal actors and non-legal actors—are actually doing relative to law, and to discover and pay attention to the ideas that inform their actions. These ideas, beliefs, and actions give rise to law, determine the uses to which law is put, and constitute the reactions to, and consequences of, law.[58]

For Fischer-Lescano's model of a global constitution, this means that the new global law should observe 'the droit naturel, reformulated [...] as *lex humana*'.[59] Global law operating outside its social environment loosens its legitimacy and the attention of its social and individual substrata.[60] It is the open society of constitutional interpreters that constantly readjusts the basic consensus on which a constitutional society is based.[61] Judges need to balance the values and (short-term) interests and expectations of society against each other.[62] Constitutional

[55] Frank I Michelman, 'The Supreme Court, 1985 Term—Foreword: Traces of Self-Government' (1986) 100 Harvard Law Review 4, 76: 'Hercules, Dworkin's mythic judge, is a loner. He is much too heroic. His narrative constructions are monologues. He converses with no one, except through books. He has no encounters. He meets no otherness. Nothing shakes him up. No interlocutor violates the inevitable insularity of his experience and outlook. Hercules is just a man, after all. He is not the whole community. No one man or woman could be that.'

[56] Häberle, 'The Open Society of Constitutional Interpreters' (n 8) 142.

[57] Jürgen Habermas, *Between Facts and Norms: Contributions to a Discourse Theory of Law and Democracy* (Polity Press 1996) 223.

[58] Brian Tamanaha, *A General Jurisprudence of Law and Society* (OUP 2001) 165–6.

[59] Andreas Fischer-Lescano, 'Global Constitutional Struggles: Human Rights between Colère Publique and Colère Politique' in Wolfgang Kaleck and others (eds), *International Prosecution of Human Rights Crimes* (Springer 2007) 24 (emphasis in original).

[60] ibid.

[61] Andreas Voßkuhle, 'Verfassungsstil und Verfassungsfunktion: Ein Beitrag zum Verfassungshandwerk' (1994) 119 Archiv des öffentlichen Rechts 35, 38.

[62] As Christopher L Eisgruber, *Constitutional Self-Government* (Harvard University Press 2001) 5 puts it: 'The psychology of a community, like the psychology of an individual, is complex. People have views about how they ought to behave, and views about what they want or desire. These views sometimes tug in different directions. Our interests are not always in

interpretation has to find the middle way between withstanding the pressures of the public and opening itself to innovative impulses from the outside, which it has to 'implement'.[63]

However, it is not all black and white, and formalism and realism can overlap. An example in this sense is Hart's approach. He argues that the law, due to its open texture, is composed of a 'core of certainty' and a 'penumbra of doubt'.[64] He is a formalist when it comes to cases concerning the 'settled meaning', such cases where the facts of the case fall easily within the pattern of those keywords in the applicable legal rule. In these cases, a judge should not have discretion. If a case cannot easily be assigned to a keyword in the legal rule, it is considered a hard case, drifting into the 'penumbral area'. In this case, judges have to be realists and must exercise their discretion.[65] This is the inevitable result of a complex legal system that welcomes both informed—that is to say, context sensitive—and individualised decision-making.[66]

Thus, every norm needs to be interpreted, but not all norms are equally open for judicial creativity. As shown in Chapter 2, the vague language of human rights law, on which many cases of CCL are based, requires the judge to consider other legal texts such as international agreements (see Article 31 para. 3 (c) of the VCLT) and extra-textual factors such as climate science to give meaning to the relevant norms.

---

harmony with our values: we sometimes desire things that we not ought to have. Under these circumstances, most of us hope that we will be faithful to our values, not our interests: we hope, in other words, that we will do the right thing. A good representative government must take these complexities into account. It must be able to represent the people's convictions about what is right and what is in their interest, and it must also reflect the people's judgment that values should take priority over interests. Congress and the president, because they must please voters to get re-elected, are likely to represent people's interests. But Supreme Court justices, because they have both a democratic pedigree and the freedom to behave disinterestedly, are better positioned to represent the people's convictions about what is right. The justices thereby make a distinctive contribution to representative democracy'.

[63] Peter Häberle, 'Verfassungsinterpretation als öffentlicher Prozeß—ein Pluralismuskonzept (1978)', *Verfassung als öffentlicher Prozeß: Materialien zu einer Verfassungstheorie der offenen Gesellschaft* (1st edn, Duncker & Humblot 1978) 135.

[64] HLA Hart, 'Positivism and the Separation of Law and Morals' (1958) 71 Harvard Law Review 593, 607ff.; Hart (n 46) 123.

[65] Hart (n 46) 124ff. (135).

[66] ibid 204, 'the open texture of law leaves a vast field for a creative activity which some call legislative'; Leiter (n 33) 1150.

10.2 Separation of Powers in 'Super Wicked' Climate Cases

It is important to notice, however, that climate cases are not only 'hard cases' but are far more complex. Environmental matters cross-cutting various legal areas could be described as 'polycentric tasks', which can be seen as spider-webs.[67] Pulling one string affects another and can likely lead to outcomes that are undesirable or unintended. Adjudication is not suited to solve these problems.[68]

Climate change as a 'super wicked problem'[69] is such a polycentric task. Both the adverse effects of climate change and mitigation and adaptation measures will have enormous effects on the daily life of all actors. As mentioned above, it is not the state that would need to curtail GHG emissions but, for example, the car industry and car drivers in its jurisdiction.[70] For Fuller, therefore, polycentric tasks should be solved by parliamentary bodies in the form of political 'deals' based on negotiation and compromise rather than through 'all-or-nothing' decisions by the judiciary.[71]

The courts have reacted in different ways. A divide between hesitant judges refusing to rule on matters that touch climate policies and those profiling themselves through spectacular climate lawsuits has become visible. Benjamin, a Justice of the Brazilian Supreme Court, calls them 'spectator judiciary' and 'protagonist judiciary'.[72] The first is 'an institutional "non-actor" or peripheral actor' with a hands-off approach whenever it comes to environmental matters.[73] Accordingly, judges should 'stay in their lane' and handle only those matters that have traditionally been dealt with by the judiciary: the protection and enforcement of contracts, property and family relationships. Everything else is too complex to be decided by the judiciary and should, therefore, be reserved for public policy and the administrative sector. Judges would lack the experience it takes to make

---

[67] Lon L Fuller, 'The Forms and Limits of Adjudication' (1978) 92 Harvard Law Review 353, 394ff. (395).

[68] ibid 394.

[69] Richard J Lazarus, 'Super Wicked Problems and Climate Change: Liberate the Future' (2009) 1234 Cornell Law Review 1153.

[70] Michael Zürn, 'Global Governance and Legitimacy Problems' (2004) 39 Government and Opposition 260, 269.

[71] Fuller (n 67) 400.

[72] Antonio Herman Benjamin, 'We, the Judges, and the Environment' (2011) 29 Pace Environmental Law Review 582.

[73] ibid 584.

well-informed decisions on environmental issues.[74] Benjamin counters this argument by pointing out that judges traditionally would deal with complex social and technical questions, such as the beginning and end of life. They can appoint experts or conduct studies to make these highly sensitive decisions.[75]

10.3 The Active Role of Courts in CCL Cases

Judges of the first category identified by Benjamin are afraid 'to enter the murky and judicially prohibited waters of political confrontation and policy-making, which are the exclusive provinces of other state actors—namely, those elected directly by the people—which cannot be labelled (as judges can) as democratically illegitimate.'[76]

However, these concerns can be defused and even dismissed for several reasons. In those cases where the courts ruled in favour of the plaintiffs, their decisions to force governments to do more against climate change were not issued in a 'climate law-free' vacuum. In *Leghari*, the Lahore High Court found a violation of the plaintiff's rights because the Pakistani government was not fulfilling its obligations under its own 2012 National Climate Change Policy and the Framework for Implementation of Climate Change Policy (2014–2030).[77] The Colombian Supreme Court pointed to the declaration to reach zero deforestation made by the Colombian government in the run-up to the Paris Agreement negotiations.[78] In *Urgenda*, the government's self-imposed obligations to curtail GHG emissions by 25% was the result of the Netherland's membership in the UNFCCC and its ratification of the Kyoto Protocol/Paris Agreement and from European law, which enjoys priority over national law in member-states of the EU.[79] The cases where such laws are absent are more difficult to assess, with courts using a mixture of fundamental rights, IL and science to decide climate cases. Here, the question arises whether judges are illegally engaging in the creation of law.[80] For

[74] ibid.

[75] ibid 585.

[76] ibid 584.

[77] Lahore High Court, *Asghar Leghari v Federation of Pakistan*, Judgement of 25 January 2018 (W.P. No. 25501/2015) para 13.

[78] Corte Suprema de Justicia de Colombia, *Future Generations v Colombia* para 11.3.

[79] District Court of The Hague, *Urgenda v The Netherlands* [2015] (ECLI:NL:RBHDHA:2015:7196) para 2.34ff.

[80] Burgers (n 34).

example, if a state such as the Netherlands decides to curb its GHG emissions by 14–17% until the year 2020—a decision made by the directly elected legislator—how can a body of the third branch claim that such a target would not be sufficient? What justifies a decision such as *Urgenda* in which the government has been ordered to do more against climate change? The same problem arose in the German case. The GFCC declared the Climate Protection Act—an Act implemented by the democratically elected German Parliament—unconstitutional because it violated the fundamental rights of a handful of individuals.[81] The consequence is that Germany must curb more GHG emissions until 2030, and this means more constraints on the freedoms of all people living in Germany, since their climate budget just became smaller.

This points to the tension between democratic decisions on the one hand and human rights on the other—and the role of the courts between these poles. This tension not only arises in CCL cases, but it becomes extremely clear when litigants, often by referring to their human rights, seek to force unwilling states to adopt stricter climate policies. This problem is particularly relevant in relation to the argument presented here. It has been argued so far that non-state actors can engage in (international) lawmaking through climate litigation. The role of the courts is essential, since it is up to them to accept the litigants' arguments and by doing so, incorporate an interpretation into enforceable law. However, the latter is the result of a democratic lawmaking process as well. It seems at least somewhat questionable that the court is the legitimate actor to make such a decision.

This problem will be analysed through the lens of Habermas' co-originality theory. Habermas' work, in particular his Critical Theory and the co-originality theory, have been made fertile by environmental law and policy scholars to understand the need for the creation of ecological norms or the role judges play in the creation of climate change law.[82] The co-originality theory is concerned with the fundamental problem at the core of the tensions between majority decision-making and the protection of the rights of individuals. It seeks to give an answer to the question of under which circumstances a court can 'overrule' the explicit will of the legislator and protect human rights without violating the principle of the separation of powers.

[81] See in detail Section 4.3.

[82] For example, Robert J Brulle, 'Habermas and Green Political Thought: Two Roads Converging' (2002) 11 Environmental Politics 1, 5; and especially Burgers (n 34).

10.4 The Tension Between Democracy and Human Rights

According to Habermas' co-originality theory, there is a tension between a 'liberal' and a 'republican' understanding of politics, between private and public autonomy, and between human rights and popular sovereignty:

> The principle of popular sovereignty is expressed in rights of communication and participation that secure the public autonomy of citizens; the rule of law is expressed in those classical basic rights that guarantee the private autonomy of members of society. Thus the law is legitimated as an instrument for the equal protection of private and public autonomy.[83]

For liberalists, private autonomy means that everyone is free to do whatever they want as long as this does not interfere with the rights of others. The right is intended to secure the free exercise of the individual will. Rights are primarily understood as defensive rights that are intended to protect individuals from unlawful interference with their lives, liberty and property by tyrannical majority decisions.[84] Conversely, the republican view gives the highest priority to public autonomy. By public autonomy, Habermas means the possibility of participating in discourses of self-government, that is, of participating in the collective self-determination of a political community that lives according to the laws it has given itself.[85] These laws can, in turn, lead to the restriction of the private autonomy of individuals. This tension is also evident in climate lawsuits: on one hand are the protection of the fundamental rights of individuals from the effects of climate change and on the other are the climate targets set by the legislator by majority vote.

It is important to understand that this is the conflict at the heart of many of the 'political' cases that constitutional courts often have to decide about. The question is: what is more important—the will of the legislator (the public autonomy) or the protection of human rights (the private autonomy)?

---

83 Jürgen Habermas, *The Inclusion of the Other* (Pablo De Greiff and Ciaran Cronin eds, Polity Press 1998) 258.

84 Habermas, *Between Facts and Norms: Contributions to a Discourse Theory of Law and Democracy* (n 57) 85; Habermas, *The Inclusion of the Other* (n 83) 258.

85 Habermas, *The Inclusion of the Other* (n 83) 258.

For Habermas, however, these concepts do not exclude each other. Rather, 'private and public autonomy, human rights and popular sovereignty, mutually presuppose one another'.[86] They are co-original—and, thus, equal in status.

On the one hand, the will of the legislator expresses the deliberative process of decision-making among citizens. As (co-)legislators, citizens cannot choose the medium through which they want to realise their autonomy. They can participate in legislation only as legal subjects. Hence, democratic self-legalisation can only be realised through the medium of law.[87] Self-legislation by citizens means that the addressees of law can understand themselves as simultaneously being the authors of that law.[88] From this point of view, if '[j]ust those action norms are valid to which all possibly affected persons could agree as participants in rational discourses',[89] and if only those laws are legitimate to which all of those who are possibly affected could consent,[90] then this means that citizens must be able to participate in rational discourses in which, according to the deliberative ideal, they see one another as free, equal and reasonable.[91] This—in a Kantian sense—refers to the most basic right: the universal right to equal liberties, which is the one right that is owed to each human being 'by virtue of his humanity'.[92] This single 'right to equal liberties' needs to differentiate itself into a *system of rights* in which both 'the freedom of every member of society as a human being' and the 'equality of each member with every other as a subject' can be acknowledged and translated into positive law.[93] The system of rights secures for everybody who has an interest or is affected by a decision the possibility of equal participation in processes of rational opinion- and will-formation.[94]

Human rights, therefore, are not only constraints. They also enable the legal conditions for participating in rational discourses, for they make the exercise

---

[86] Habermas, *Between Facts and Norms: Contributions to a Discourse Theory of Law and Democracy* (n 57) 84.

[87] ibid 116; Habermas, *The Inclusion of the Other* (n 83) 260.

[88] Habermas, *Between Facts and Norms: Contributions to a Discourse Theory of Law and Democracy* (n 57) 120.

[89] ibid 107.

[90] Jürgen Habermas, 'Remarks on Legitimation through Human Rights' in Jürgen Habermas (ed), *The Postnational Constellation: Political Essays* (MIT Press 2001) 116.

[91] Joshua Cohen, 'Democracy and Liberty' in Jon Elster (ed), *Deliberative Democracy* (CUP 1998) 193–4.

[92] Immanuel Kant, *The Metaphysics of Morals* (Lara Denis ed, CUP 2017) 34 (6:237).

[93] Habermas, *Between Facts and Norms: Contributions to a Discourse Theory of Law and Democracy* (n 57) 93–4.

[94] ibid 105.

of popular sovereignty possible.[95] 'Hence the principle of democracy can only appear as the heart of a *system* of rights.'[96] The system of rights must contain these basic rights, which citizens must grant each other if they wish to legitimately regulate their life in common through positive law.[97] This includes the rights that guarantee participation and communication[98] but also all other 'classical' rights (to life, liberty and so on) as interpretations of a 'general right to individual liberties', in other words, citizen's private autonomy. Private autonomy needs to be protected so that citizens can participate equally in rational discourses on how they want to live, thus, public autonomy. Someone who cannot freely express their opinion without the fear of being prosecuted, who is tortured, who is without a home, might find it impossible or difficult to participate in discussions about new laws, including climate statutes.[99] Human rights, therefore, are meant to protect the possibility of participating in rational discourses. They depend on each other.[100]

Thus, put shortly: human rights are not 'given' to citizens prior to defining their scope and content of these rights in rational discourses through which citizens can see themselves as the authors of the law. But this participation itself needs to be enabled and protected through legal institutionalisation in the form of human rights (a system of rights). This is why human rights and democracy are co-original; none can claim primacy over the other:[101]

> Therefore, if constitutional review is to be oriented towards protecting and promoting participatory opinion- and will-formation, it will need to be much more than an impartial referee between voters and their representative bodies: it will have to ensure that the 'sluice-gates' through which public opinion gets channeled into the legally structured strong public sphere remain unobstructed.[102]

For the courts, this means that they have to uphold both public and individual autonomy. The people do not want to be ruled by judges. The courts have to

---

[95] Habermas, *The Inclusion of the Other* (n 83) 259.

[96] Habermas, *Between Facts and Norms: Contributions to a Discourse Theory of Law and Democracy* (n 57) 121.

[97] ibid 111.

[98] Habermas, *The Inclusion of the Other* (n 83) 259–60.

[99] Burgers (n 34) 63.

[100] Habermas, *The Inclusion of the Other* (n 83) 257 ff.

[101] ibid 261.

[102] Christopher F Zurn, 'Deliberative Democracy and Constitutional Review' (2002) 4/5 Law and Philosophy 467, 520.

respect the outcome of rational discourses through which citizens decide how they want to regulate their daily lives. It is for them to create the laws, not the judges.[103] If judges 'discover' extra-textual fundamental values that guide their jurisprudence, they would violate the democratic ideal of the constitutional project, according to which the people would want to determine these values themselves.[104] Thus, the judiciary is bound by the *applicable* law.

However, this does not mean that judges merely 'apply' the law. They can affirm values already held by society and introduce new values into the legal order by drawing attention to interests that would likely go unprotected because they are either diffuse and vague, such as environmental rights, or do not have a powerful lobby (e.g., poor and marginalised communities, future generations, animals and nature). For even if the people do not want to be ruled by courts, they are not under the 'government by the dead'.[105] Courts, especially constitutional courts, should be able to react to social, technical, economic and ecological changes.[106]

By doing this, in Habermas' sense, the courts are not creating but merely 'finding' the law that is already there. This is because the legitimacy of the law is not derived from the institutions of the legislature or judiciary (which only produce the most authoritative interpretations of the law) but from inter-subjective discourses between citizens. The courts can 'update' the law where there is already a public consensus about the law, but the legislator has not changed that law yet.[107] This 'information deficit' by the (constitutional) legislator can be addressed by the courts responding to new developments through case law.[108] Thus, the legislative and societal consensus is also decisive for how dynamic the jurisprudence will be. In the European context, this means:

> When the [European] Convention [of Human Rights] itself refers to those extra-legal concepts that are intrinsically dynamic, such as the majority views in a national society, they are necessarily meant to be interpreted in an evolutionary manner. In those cases, evolution is taking place not within the law, but outside it, and through normative references it is incorporated into the law. And the Court is expected to

[103] Burgers (n 34) 62.

[104] See Chapter 3 'Discovering Fundamental Values' in John Hart Ely, *Democracy and Distrust: A Theory of Judicial Review* (Harvard University Press 1980) 43–72; Zurn (n 102) 481.

[105] Eisgruber (n 62) 40.

[106] May and Daly (n 27) 87–8.

[107] Burgers (n 34) 63–4.

[108] Häberle, 'Zeit und Verfassung: Prolegomena zu einem "zeit-gerechten" Verfassungsverständnis' (n 49) 125.

> implement this development by interpreting the extra-legal concepts in accordance with the changes that have taken place in society.[109]

However, the courts can rule (only) against majority decisions where fundamental rights are at stake or violated. Habermas outlines that 'the constitutional court should keep watch over just that system of rights that makes citizens' private and public autonomy equally possible'.[110] If fundamental rights are violated, a majority decision may endanger private autonomy and, thus, democracy in general. Rights are, in Dworkin's sense, 'trumps' held by individuals that can be played in a game where individuals defend their interests against disadvantages that are the result of majority policy decisions.[111] Not every right will trump every collective decision, but the limits on such decisions ultimately follow from the principle of equal respect for each person.[112] Judge Chaskalson P made this point clear by framing the task of the South African Constitutional Court in the field of tension between majority decisions and human rights:

> The very reason for […] vesting the power of judicial review of all legislation in the courts, was to protect the rights of minorities and others who cannot protect their rights adequately through the democratic process. Those who are entitled to claim this protection include the social outcasts and marginalised people of our society. It is only if there is a willingness to protect the worst and the weakest amongst us, that all of us can be secure that our own rights will be protected.[113]

Thus, where fundamental rights are violated, a court may rule against the applicable law as a majority decision. Burgers analysed how the *Urgenda* decisions fit into this paradigm. Given that the Dutch government—elected by the Dutch people to represent them—had decided to reduce GHG emissions by 14–17%,

---

109 Oliver Dörr, 'The Strasbourg Approach to Evolutionary Interpretation' in Georges Abi-Saab and others (eds), *Evolutionary Interpretation and International Law* (Hart Publishing 2019) 117.

110 Habermas, *Between Facts and Norms: Contributions to a Discourse Theory of Law and Democracy* (n 57) 263.

111 Dworkin (n 54) xi; Habermas, *Between Facts and Norms: Contributions to a Discourse Theory of Law and Democracy* (n 57) 204.

112 Habermas, *Between Facts and Norms: Contributions to a Discourse Theory of Law and Democracy* (n 57) 204.

113 Constitutional Court of the Republic of South Africa, *S v Makwanyane and Another* (CCT3/94) [1995] ZACC 3; 1995 (6) BCLR 665; 1995 (3) SA 391; [1996] 2 CHRLD 164; 1995 (2) SACR 1 (6 June 1995), para 88.

the DC ruled against a majority decision.[114] The DC had not directly based its justifications on human rights law but on the civil-law doctrine of an unwritten duty of care (thereby invoking human rights only indirectly). Accordingly, the decision has been criticised for lacking democratic legitimacy.[115] The subsequent decisions were based on the violation of human rights law. The CA explained in a Habermasian fashion that:

> The State argues that [...] the system of the separation of powers should not be interfered with, because it is not up to the courts but to the democratically legitimised government as the appropriate body to make the attendant policy choices. This argument is rejected in this case, also because the State violates *human rights*, which calls for the provision of measures.[116]

This decision gained more approval from legal scholars.[117] Both the court and scholars' positions seem to support Habermas's theory, according to which the violation of human rights allows the overturning of majority decisions without the accusation of breaching the principle of the separation of powers. This could be a reason why many CCL cases of the third wave are based on human rights law. Nevertheless, rights-based litigation has been problematic in at least two other ways in relation to the principle of the separation of powers. The first issue arises in the context of what a court can impose on the state, given its discretionary power. The second issue is about the creation of new rights, as envisaged in some lawsuits such as *Juliana* (the right to a stable climate) or in *Neubauer et al. v Germany* (ecological subsistence minimum).

10.4.1 Positive Obligations and the Margin of Appreciation

In *Urgenda*, the Court of Appeal and the Supreme Court argued that the Dutch government had violated its positive obligations under Article 2 and Article 8 of

---

[114] Burgers (n 34) 65.

[115] See, for example, Lucas Bergkamp, 'The Urgenda Judgment: A "Victory" for the Climate That Is Likely to Backfire' *Energypost.eu* (9 September 2015) <https://energypost.eu/urgenda-judgment-victory-climate-likely-backfire/> accessed 31 August 2023.

[116] The Hague Court of Appeal, Appeal Decision *Urgenda v The Netherlands* [2018] (ECLI:NL:GHDHA:2018:2610) para 67 (emphasis added).

[117] Burgers (n 34) 65.

the ECHR.[118] The main criticism of the application of the doctrine of positive obligations to climate change is its unclear scope. Positive obligations can be fulfilled in many ways and require a balance and prioritisation between competing interests. Therefore, they include a deeply political component that must be left untouched by the courts.[119] It has been discussed whether the doctrine of positive obligations should not be applied to complex cases that differ from the original context for which it was developed (cases in which an individual suffers harm from a single source, such as pollution from a leather factory).[120] However, the fact that a case touches political questions does not mean that a court should refrain from issuing effective human rights protection. While there are differences concerning the scope and scale of the environmental problem, it seems paradoxical that the court should refrain from ruling on an issue that is potentially more dangerous and of a larger scale. In such cases, it seems that more rather than less protection is needed.[121]

Thus, the court may declare that the state violated its positive obligations under national or IL. This point was enforced by the Dutch CA.[122] It stressed, furthermore, that it did not intend to create legislation (which is forbidden under Dutch law) and that it was obliged to apply IL in case it had a direct effect on the Netherlands, since such law forms part of Dutch jurisdiction and even prevails over national law.[123] But it is for the other two branches of government to determine the measures they wish to take to resolve the problem.[124] The margin of appreciation is limited insofar as the state *must* choose to address the problem, but it has discretionary powers of *how* to achieve the target of a 25% GHG emissions reduction.[125]

---

[118] The Hague Court of Appeal (n 116) para 29; Supreme Court of the Netherlands, *Urgenda v The Netherlands* [2019] ECLI:NL:HR:2019:2007 paras 5.1–5.10.

[119] Ingrid Leijten, 'Human Rights v. Insufficient Climate Action: The Urgenda Case' (2019) 37 Netherlands Quarterly of Human Rights 112, 119; Mehrdad Payandeh, 'The Role of Courts in Climate Protection and the Separation of Powers' in Wolfgang Kahl and Marc-Philippe Weller (eds), *Climate Change Litigation—A Handbook* (Beck/Hart/Nomos 2021) para 29.

[120] Laura Burgers and Tim Staal, 'Climate Action as Positive Human Rights Obligation: The Appeals Judgment in Urgenda v The Netherlands' [2019] Amsterdam Law School Legal Studies Research Paper No. 2019–01 6.

[121] ibid 14.

[122] The Hague Court of Appeal (n 116) para 67.

[123] ibid 68–9.

[124] Payandeh (n 119) para 29.

[125] Leijten (n 119) 117; Burgers and Staal (n 120) 10.

10.4.2 Recognition of New Rights: The Examples of the U.S. and German Constitutions

Equally difficult is the judicial creation or recognition of new rights. Courts may only employ already existing laws: 'In any event, rulings on constitutional complaints and the concrete constitutional review initiated by individual cases are both *limited* to the *application* of (constitutional) norms presupposed as valid.'[126] However, besides the re-interpretation of already existing laws, litigants sometimes seek to introduce new rights, such as the right to a stable climate.

Given the courts' limitation to applying the existing law, it is questionable whether they can create or 'find' new law. However, in case of a 'gap' in legislation that leaves the interests and dignity of citizens unprotected, courts may 'find' new rights.[127] This practice will be illustrated here by means of two constitutions: the constitutions of the U.S. and Germany. In both countries, citizens have approached (constitutional) courts to introduce new constitutional rights. In the US, the plaintiffs sought to establish the 'right to a stable climate'; in Germany, they claimed that a 'right to future' and an 'ecological subsistence minimum' exist.

10.4.2.1 The U.S. Constitution

In *Juliana*, the plaintiffs based their claims on a right to a stable climate—a right that was recognised by Judge Aiken as an unenumerated right.[128] She argued that such a right was inherent to the U.S. Constitution and based on the Fifth and Ninth Amendments. In over 250 years of jurisprudence, however, the

[126] Habermas, *Between Facts and Norms: Contributions to a Discourse Theory of Law and Democracy* (n 57) 261 (emphasis in original).

[127] Jürgen Habermas, 'The Concept of Human Dignity and the Realistic Utopia of Human Rights' (2010) 41 Metaphilosophy 464, 467.

[128] District Court of Oregon, Judge Ann Aiken, 11 October 2016, *Kelsey Cascadia Rose Juliana v United States of America* (Case No. 6:15-Cv-01517-TC): 'Because the public trust is not enumerated in the Constitution, substantive due pro-cess protection also derives from the Ninth Amendment. […]. But it is the Fifth Amendment that provides the right of action. Plaintiffs" claims rest "directly on the Due Process Clause of the Fifth Amendment." Davis, 442 U.S. at 243 (1979); see also Carlson v. Green, 446 U.S. 14, 18 (1980) ("[T]he victims of a constitutional violation by a federal agent have a right to recover damages against the official in federal court despite the absence of any statute conferring such a right.") They may, therefore, be asserted in federal court.'

Supreme Court found only five rights not enumerated in the Constitution to be fundamental.[129]

The U.S. Constitution does not include a right to a healthy environment. Judges have relied on the commerce clause to protect the environment, which has been criticised for overstretching the term 'commerce'.[130] Activists had sought to implement a right to a healthy environment (e.g., in the form of a right to be free from toxic chemicals) under the Ninth Amendment but ultimately failed.[131] While the Ninth Amendment of the U.S. Constitution and its recognition of unenumerated rights seem to give some leeway to the development and recognition of new rights that were not considered at the moment of drafting the constitutional Bill of Rights, legal scholars and judges seem reluctant to see the norm as a standalone base for the inclusion of new rights.[132] Justice Bork, for example, argued that the Ninth Amendment would be comparable to an inkblot in a text. The Supreme Court should not make something up that might be under the ink if it cannot be read. Thus, 'if the Supreme Court makes up a new right for which there is not historical evidence, then I think it has exceeded its powers under the Constitution'.[133] Conversely, it has been argued that the Ninth Amendment means to protect so-called natural rights in addition to positive rights. People

---

[129] These are are the right to control the upbringing of one's children, the right to marry, the right to access contraception, the right to have an abortion pre-viability and later in the pregnancy to save the life of the mother, and the right to engage in private, consensual sexual conduct, see Mia Hammersley, 'The Right to a Healthy and Stable Climate: Fundamental or Unfounded?' (2016) 7 Arizona Journal of Environmental Law and Policy 117, 118–9.

[130] Robert V. Percival, 'The Greening of the Global Judiciary' (2017) 32 Journal of Land Use and Environmental Law 333, 336–7.

[131] Though one court stated that "[s]uch claims, even under our present Constitution, are not fanciful and may, indeed, some day, in one way or another, obtain judicial recognition" (US District Court for the Eastern District of Arkansas, *Environmental Defense Fund, Inc. v. Corps of Eng. of US Army*, [325 F. Supp. 728] [1971]), cf. also Caleb Hall, 'A Right Most Dear: The Case for a Constitutional Environmental Right' (2016) 30 Tulane Environmental Law Journal 85, 105.

[132] Richard Kay, 'Adherence to the Original Intentions in Constitutional Adjudication: Three Objections and Responses' (1987) 82 Northwestern University Law Review 226, 269 ff.; Earl M Maltz, 'Unenumerated Rights and Originalist Methodology: A Comment on the Ninth Amendment Symposium' (1988) 64 Chicago-Kent Law Review 981; Nomination of Robert H. Bork to Be Associate Justice of the Supreme Court of the United States: Hearings Before the Committee on the Judiciary US Senate (Testimony of Robert Bork) (1989).

[133] Nomination of Robert H. Bork to Be Associate Justice of the Supreme Court of the United States: Hearings Before the Committee on the Judiciary US Senate (Testimony of Robert Bork) (n 132) 249–50; see also Raoul Berger, 'The Ninth Amendment' (1980) 66 Cornell Law Review 1, 2 who claims that such activity would transform the Ninth Amendment 'into

have these natural rights independently of what rights are granted to them by the government. They are unenumerated because they are so self-evident that they do not need to be written into the Constitution and include every possible freedom to do whatever one wishes to do unless this violates the rights of others. Instead of cluttering the constitution with all sorts of rights, the Ninth Amendment is meant to guarantee all these 'inalienable rights' that were never to be called into question (such as wearing a hat or drinking a sip of water). Since the human imagination is limitless, it would be impossible to enumerate all these rights.[134]

In *Juliana*, Judge Aiken attempted to fill this gap of the lack of environmental protection in the constitution by recognising a right to a stable climate (initially based on the Fifth and Ninth Amendments, but eventually limiting herself to the Fifth Amendment[135]). She argued that such a right is a preposition for the enjoyment and exercise of all other rights to life, liberty and property.[136] Other courts still seem hesitant or outright reject such an interpretation. In a similar lawsuit filed by 13 young people under the age of 18, the Superior Court of Washington for King County rigidly rejected a right to a healthy environment or stable climate. The plaintiffs had asked the court to follow Judge Aiken's decision, but the court dismissed this request.[137] Judge Scott criticised the *Juliana* case for comparing the right to a stable climate as equally fundamental for an ordered scheme of liberty as marriage.[138] He claims that, unlike the right to marry, a right to

---

a bottomless well in which the judiciary can dip for the formation of undreamed of "rights" in their limitless discretion'.

[134] Randy E Barnett, 'A Ninth Amendment for Today's Constitution' (1991) 26 Valparaiso University Law Review 419, 422–6.

[135] District Court of Oregon, Judge Ann Aiken, 11 October 2016, *Kelsey Cascadia Rose Juliana v United States of America* (Case No. 6:15-Cv-01517-TC) (n 128) 51. On 30 July 2018, the Supreme Court remarked in a short note that "the breadth of respondents' claims is striking […] and the justiciability of those claims presents substantial grounds for difference of opinion" and that the DC 'should take these concerns into account in assessing the burdens of discovery and trial' (U.S. Supreme Court, United States v. United States District Court for the District of Oregon, Application for stay denied, 30 July 2018). Back before Judge Ann Aiken, she dismissed the plaintiff's Ninth Amendment claim (along with their equal protection claim) on 15 October 2018, arguing that the Ninth Amendment has never been 'recognized as independently securing any constitutional right', Federal District Cout for the District of Oregon, 'Opinion and Order (Case No. 6:15-Cv-01517-AA), 15 October 2018' 65, citing *Strandberg v. City of Helena*, 791 F.2d 744, 748 (9th Cir. 1986).

[136] District Court of Oregon, Judge Ann Aiken, 11 October 2016, *Kelsey Cascadia Rose Juliana v United States of America* (Case No. 6:15-Cv-01517-TC)' (n 128) 32.

[137] Superior Court of Washington for King County, *Aji P v State of Washington*, Case No. 18-2-04448-1 SEA (14 August 2018), 1, 7–9.

[138] ibid 8.

a stable climate would be a mere aspiration, similar to economic prosperity or world peace, but not an individual right that could be enforced by a court and should be left to the governmental branches.[139] Conversely, in a recent case, the dissenting Justice Maassen would have found that Alaskans had an individual constitutional right to a liveable climate (although the majority did not).[140]

It becomes apparent that this question is not resolved yet. Thus, it remains to be seen whether the idea can take root in the U.S. American legal system. However, in the eyes of May and Daly, there are good reasons why a right to a stable climate should be enshrined in the constitution and, thus, should be recognised by the courts:

> The Constitution protects what is of fundamental importance and what cannot be relegated to protection in the political branches alone. A stable climate system satisfies both of these and does so, arguably more than anything else in history. Protection against the degradation of the environment is precisely the kind of problem that the political branches are *least* likely to be able to protect: it requires long-term thinking for the benefit of those who have no political voice, including children and future generations.[141]

10.4.2.2 Germany

In Germany, the German Federal Constitutional Court has recognised a number of fundamental rights—particularly the general right of personality—that are not included in the written German Basic Law *(Grundgesetz*, GG) of 1949. But the general right of personality had a long history in German legal thought[142] before it was recognised in 1954 by the GFCC.[143] The GFCC combined the right to the free development of one's personality as laid down in Article 2 para. 1 GG and

---

[139] ibid 9.

[140] Alaska Supreme Court, *Sagoonick v. State*, Opinion of 28 January 2022, Supreme Court No. S-17297.

[141] James May and Erin Daly, 'Can the U.S. Constitution Encompass a Right to a Stable Climate? (Yes, It Can.)' (2021) 39 UCLA Journal of Environmental Law and Policy 39, 45–6 (emphasis in original).

[142] The general right to privacy (Allgemeines Persönlichkeitsrecht) was formulated by Otto von Giercke, *Deutsches Privatrecht Band 1: Allgemeiner Teil und Personenrecht* (Duncker & Humblot 1895) 702ff.

[143] Bundesverfassungsgericht, Veröffentlichung von Briefen (Publication of letters), Judgement of 25 May 1954, BGHZ 13, 334, para 15. An English translation is available at https://germanlawarchive.iuscomp.org/?p=108.

human dignity (Article 1 GG) to explain the existence of such a right.[144] Over time, the court developed several rights within the scope of the general right of personality, among them the right to protection of the private, confidential and intimate spheres, the right to an identity, the right to social respect, the right to self-presentation and the right to informational self-determination.[145] These rights contain the idea of human dignity and are, therefore, the result of human dignity.[146]

The right to informational self-determination, in particular, can be seen as the GFCC's reaction to social and technological developments, which the authors of the Basic Law could not have foreseen in 1949. The constitutional legislator remained inactive in the following decades and did not address emerging concerns by introducing a formal basic right to protect the citizens' data privacy. In its 'census' decision, the GFCC recognised the 'fundamental right to informational self-determination as an outflow of the general right of personality and human dignity'.[147] The Court argued that such a right is part of everyone's self-determination to decide which information they want to reveal to the public. Moreover, the protection of personal data from being accessed by authorities is necessary to guarantee that citizens can make use of their other fundamental rights, for example, the freedom of assembly (Article 8 GG) or the freedom of association (Article 9 GG). Thus, this right has a collective dimension, and besides individuals' interests, protects 'the common good, since self-determination is an elementary functional condition of a free democratic community founded on the capacity of its citizens to take action and participate'.[148]

---

[144] Jon A Lehmann, 'The Right to Privacy in Germany' (1968) 1 N.Y.U. Journal of International Law and Politics 113.

[145] Christian Bumke and Andreas Voßkuhle, *German Constitutional Law: Introduction, Cases, and Principles* (OUP 2019) 109–14.

[146] Claudia Kodde, 'Germany's "Right to Be Forgotten"—between the Freedom of Expression and the Right to Informational Self-Determination' (2016) 30 International Review of Law, Computers and Technology 17, 19.

[147] 25 Jahre 'Volkszählungsurteil' des Bundesverfassungsgerichts (*Press Release No. 106/2008 of 11 December 2008*) <https://www.bundesverfassungsgericht.de/SharedDocs/Pressemitteilungen/DE/2008/bvg08-106.html> accessed 31 August 2023 (tr the author).

[148] German Federal Constitutional Court, BVerfGE 65, 1 (43)—Volkszählung (Census) (tr. Bumke and Voßkuhle [n 145] 111).

In further decisions, the GFCC strengthened and specified the scope of the new right, and it has been implemented by a series of state constitutions (*Länderverfassungen*).[149] Today, the right to self-determination is based on other sources as well, but the census decision can be seen as the *Magna Carta* for data protection in Germany.[150] In 2008, the GFCC recognised another right based on the general right to personality—the fundamental right to the confidentiality and integrity of information systems.[151] This right is intended to close the gaps left open by the right to informational self-determination (e.g., mass storage of data).[152] In 2021, the GFCC recognised a right to school education based on Article 2 para. 1 and Article 7 GG (school system) and, in their climate complaint, the plaintiffs sought to introduce an 'ecological subsistence minimum' under the general right of personality based on Article 1 and 2 para. 1 (and Article 20a GG).[153] Thus, it seems that Article 2 para. 1 GG serves as the anchor for the creation and development of unnamed liberty rights (*unbenannte Freiheitsrechte*).[154] The GFCC held that:

> the doctrine of the general right to personality guarantees elements of the human personality that are not the subject of particular rights guarantees in the Grundgesetz, but which are no less important in their constitutive importance of for the personality [...]. Such a gap-filling rights guarantee is important particularly to deal with new dangers which can arrive as a result of scientific progress and changed life circumstances.[155]

---

[149] Andreas Busch and Tobias Jakobi, 'Die Erfindung eines neuen Grundrechts. Zu Konzept und Auswirkungen der „informationellen Selbstbestimmung"' in Christoph Hönnige, Sascha Kneip and Astrid Lorenz (eds), *Verfassungswandel im Mehrebenensystem* (VS Verlag für Sozialwissenschaften 2011) 304.

[150] Wolfgang Hoffmann-Riem, 'Informationelle Selbstbestimmung in der Informationsgesellschaft—Auf dem Wege zu einem neuen Konzept des Datenschutzes' (1998) 123 Archiv des öffentlichen Rechts 513, 515.

[151] Bumke and Voßkuhle (n 145) 112.

[152] ibid 114.

[153] GFCC, Order of 24 March 2021, 1 BvR 2656/18 (2021), para 40, see also in greater detail Section 4.3.

[154] Werner Heun, *The Constitution of Germany—A Contextual Analysis* (Hart Publishing 2011) 205.

[155] German Federal Constitutional Court, BVerfGE 120, 274 (303)—Online-Durchsuchung (Online Search), (tr Bumke and Voßkuhle [n 145] 112).

Article 2 para. 1 GG transforms the unsystematic Bill of Rights into a closed and coherent system of fundamental rights.[156] Only by means of broad interpretation can these gaps be filled, and thereby, the catalogue of rights turned into a comprehensive system of rights protection without any loopholes.[157]

The recognition and vindication of the fundamental right to informational self-determination marked an 'axial moment' in the history of the GFCC. It sharpened its profile as the guardian of the people that left the leading political parties looking out of time and touch.[158] Today, over 35 years after the census decision, the 'new' fundamental right to informational self-determination has been accepted as part of Germany's constitutional Bill of Rights.[159] The need to guarantee the general right to privacy, including informational self-determination, as a prerequisite for the enjoyment of all other human rights has also been acknowledged by the Council of Europe.[160] Furthermore, the GFCC's creation of a right to self-determination has influenced European legislation, the jurisprudence of the ECtHR[161] and scholarship all over the world.[162] It has, in large part, been codified in European law. Additionally, the right to informational self-determination has become somewhat 'autonomous', as it has been further developed by legislative

[156] Heun (n 154) 207.

[157] ibid.

[158] Justin Collings, *Democracy's Guardians: A History of the German Federal Constitutional Court, 1951–2001* (OUP 2015) 196–7.

[159] Walter Rudolf, '§ 90: Recht auf Informationelle Selbstbestimmung' in Detlef Merten and Hans-Jürgen Papier (eds), *Handbuch der Grundrechte in Deutschland und Europa*, vol IV (CF Müller 2011) para 16.

[160] Antoinette Rouvroy and Yves Poullet, 'The Right to Informational Self-Determination and the Value of Self-Development: Reassessing the Importance of Privacy for Democracy' in Serge Gutwirth and others (eds), *Reinventing Data Protection?* (Springer Sciene + Business Media 2009) 76.

[161] Cécile de Terwangne, 'The Right to Be Forgotten and Informational Autonomy in the Digital Environment' in Alessia Ghezzi, Ângela Guimarães Pereira and Lucia Vesnić-Alujević (eds), *The Ethics of Memory in a Digital Age* (Palgrave Macmillan 2014) 86.

[162] See, for example, a discussion of a right to self-determination in Brazil: Rafael Copetti and Marcel Andreata de Miranda, 'Autodeterminação informativa e proteção de dados: Uma ánalise crítica da jurisprudência brasileira (Informational Self-Determination and Data Protection: A Critical Analysis of the Brazilian Jurisprudence)' (2015) 1 Revista de Direito, Governança e Novas Tecnologias 28, 31ff.; in the United States: Paul Schwartz, 'The Computer in German and American Constitutional Law: Towards an American Right of Informational Self-Determination' (1989) 37 The American Journal of Comparative Law 675; in Australia: Åste Corbridge, 'Responding To Doxing in Australia: Towards a Right To Informational Self-Determination?' (2018) 3 UniSA Student Law Review 1.

and judicial bodies outside Germany. The European Commission, for example, based a 'right to be forgotten' on a European right to self-determination.[163]

Something similar could happen to the concept of an 'ecological subsistence minimum'. The plaintiffs in *Neubauer et al. v Germany* claimed that the 'subsistence minimum' as recognised in German law would also entail an ecological component. The GFCC argued that this component is already protected by other fundamental rights, such as the right to property, but:

> a mechanism for safeguarding the ecological minimum standard could indeed acquire its own independent validity if, in an environment transformed to the point of being toxic, adaptation measures [...] would still be capable of protecting life, physical integrity and property but not the other prerequisites for social, cultural and political life. Another conceivable scenario is that adaptation measures would have to be so extreme that they would no longer allow for meaningful social, cultural and political interaction and participation.[164]

However, as of today, no such 'existential threats of catastrophic or even apocalyptic proportions' can be identified.[165]

The recognition of such new rights, however, does not go smoothly. The census ruling prompted a fierce debate among legal scholars on whether the GFCC had or had not created a new fundamental right.[166] Krause argued that the creation of a new right was not the GFCC's intention and that even the idea that it could do so demonstrates 'signs of crisis for our constitutional awareness'.[167] Regulations based on case law (*einfaches Richterrecht*) are already highly problematic, but the creation of constitutional law through the adjudication of constitutional judges (*Richterverfassungsrecht*) would be forbidden, despite the dictum of the 'living constitution'.[168] Most scholars followed this strand of

---

[163] de Terwangne (n 161) 87–9.

[164] GFCC, 1 BvR 2656/18 (2021), para 114.

[165] Ibid para 115.

[166] In this sense, Friedrich Karl Fromme, 'Ein neues Grundrecht ist erfunden' *Frankfurter Allgemeine Zeitung* (17 December 1983) 12; Spiros Simits, 'Das Volkszählungsurteil oder der lange Weg zur Informationsaskese—(BVerfGE 65, 1)' (2000) 83 Kritische Vierteljahresschrift für Gesetzgebung und Rechtswissenschaft 359, 365.

[167] Peter Krause, 'Das Recht auf informationelle Selbstbestimmung—BVerfGE 65, 1' [1984] Juristische Schulung 268, 268 (tr the author).

[168] ibid 268, fn. 3.

thought and stress that the court merely found what was already there[169]and that the GFCC had only fulfilled its judicial duty to solidify the general right to personality under changing social and technical circumstances.[170] The idea that a court could have created new law contradicts the traditional idea of its task to merely apply the law and was consequently denied.[171] This is part of the legacy of the Weimar Republic: in the 1920s, politics and law were understood as absolutely irreconcilable, antagonistic concepts. There was to be a sphere of state leadership—untouchable by the legislative and judicial branches—in which politics were to be made.[172] However, this conception changed throughout the following years, particularly after the establishment of the GFCC in 1951 with its broader competencies than those of the former State Court for the German Reich. Political parties started using constitutional complaints as a tool to force legal decisions on subject matters with underlying existential political questions, which made it impossible for the GFCC to withdraw from touching political aspects.[173]

While the GFCC is concerned with the limitations of further development of the law by judges (*richterliche Rechtsfortbildung*), for example, by limiting interpretation with a reliance on the wording and will of the legislator (the 'how'), the GFCC does not seem to question whether it has such competences at all (the

[169] However, Bernhard Schlink, 'Das Recht der informationellen Selbstbestimmung' (1986) 25 Der Staat 233 noted that 'It is a certainty behind which the question of whether a new fundamental right has been found, a new meaning of a fundamental right has been discovered or an old effect of a fundamental right has been put into a new light, fades away. It is not only fading away in practice. The difference between the invention of new fundamental rights, the discovery of new fundamental rights meanings and the new illumination of old fundamental rights effects can also be neglected in theory. It only proves the same process of judicial creation of law with different terms. The process is inevitable and indispensable as such; there is no way back to the idea of the judge as the mouth of the law' (tr. the author).

[170] Herman Heußner, 'Datenverarbeitung und die Rechtsprechung des Bundesverfassungsgerichts im Spannungsfeld zwischen Recht und Politik' (1985) 33 Arbeit und Recht 309, 313.

[171] In this sense, ibid; Krause (n 167) 268; for the creation of a new right, see Fromme (n 166) 12; Busch and Jakobi (n 149); Claudio Franzius, 'Das Recht auf informationelle Selbstbestimmung' [2015] ZJS 259, 260; Simits (n 166) 365.

[172] Frieder Günther, 'Wer beeinflusst hier wen? Die westdeutsche Staatsrechtslehre und das Bundesverfassungsgericht während der 1950er und 1960er Jahre' in Robert Chr van Ooyen and Martin HW Möllers (eds), *Handbuch Bundesverfassungsgericht im politischen System* (2nd edn, Springer VS 2015) 206.

[173] Günther mentions, inter alia, the accession to the European Defense Community or rearmament in 1952/53, the Saar Statute in 1954/55, and the ban of the KPD (Communist Party of Germany) from 1951 to 1956, ibid 207–8.

'if'). Rather, it seems that the GFCC takes this for granted.[174] The argument goes that the legislative branch increasingly employs general clauses and blanket terms that need to be filled with content by the courts. The development of the law by jurisprudence is the consequence of the legislator's recourse to open and general norms and is, therefore, a genuine judicial activity.[175] The GFCC made clear that the development of the law by the judges is 'indispensable' because:

> developments in fact or in law may make a previously clear and complete regulation incomplete, in need of supplementation and at the same time capable of being supplemented. The constitutional legitimacy of the search for and closure of gaps is justified, inter alia, by the fact that laws are subject to an ageing process. They stand in an environment of social conditions and socio-political views, the change in which the content of the norm can also change [...]. To the extent that gaps in the provisions are created as a result of such changes, the law loses its ability to provide a fair solution for all cases at which its provisions are aimed. The courts are therefore authorised and obliged to examine what constitutes 'law' within the meaning of Article 20 paragraph 3 of the Basic Law under the changed circumstances.[176]

Thus, by recognising the competence to further develop the law through its jurisprudence, the GFCC emphasised that it sees the judicial creation of law as an original task of the third branch.[177]

10.5 Judicial Lawmaking

Traditional scholarship assumes that there is a difference between will and application. The legislature 'wills' and the courts 'apply' what has been 'willed' without the need to add any personal contribution to the self-explanatory rule.[178]

In 1928, Kelsen coined the term 'negative legislator', which means that a constitutional court itself becomes a legislator by overturning norms, since its

[174] Payandeh (n 8) 321.

[175] ibid 322.

[176] 'BVerfG: Anwendung der §§ 569a, 569b BGB auf nichteheliche Lebensgemeinschaften (German Federal Constitutional Court, Judgement of 3 April 1990—1 BvR 1186/89)' [1990] Neue Juristische Wochenschrift 1593, paras 1593–4 (tr the author).

[177] Payandeh (n 8) 327.

[178] Möllers (n 31) 82–3.

judgement has the character of legislation.[179] In her comparative study of the decisions of the European courts (the CJEU, the General Court and the ECtHR) and the European constitutional courts, Florczak-Wątor found that these courts today not only fall solely in the category of negative legislators but that they are creating law at the level of both the provisions of the constitution and statutory norms, for example, by correcting, supplementing and developing the wording of statutes as a result of creative interpretation.[180] Five other functions of constitutional jurisdiction in constitutions worldwide have been identified: positive legislation as entailed by negative legislation (concerning the question of whether previous statutes will be revoked after nullifying a statute), pre-enactment scrutiny, legislative proposals, substitute and mandated legislation, and legislation through interpretation.[181]

As a result, the traditional understanding of the principle of separation of powers should be re-defined and enhanced. For Möllers, for example, the task of the three branches is not the exercise of powers but the *creation of law*.[182] The founders of the Vienna school of legal theory, Merkl and Kelsen,[183] did also not believe that the powers were so different in nature and had already questioned the separation of branches such as jurisdiction and administration. Accordingly, every legal act is Janus-faced[184]: each comprises law application and law creation at the same time and, therefore, contains both a legal and a political element. Merkl called this the *double legal appearance* (*doppeltes Rechtsantlitz*).[185] Kelsen clarified that any final court decision can become enforceable law:

---

[179] Hans Kelsen, 'Wesen und Entwicklung der Staatsgerichtsbarkeit', *Verhandlungen der Tagung der Deutschen Staatsrechtslehrer zu Wien am 23. und 24. April 1928* (De Gruyter 1929) 54, 87.

[180] Monika Florczak-Wątor, *Judicial Law-Making in European Constitutional Courts* (Routledge 2020) 264.

[181] Anna Gamper, 'Constitutional Courts and Judicial Law-Making: Why Democratic Legitimacy Matters' (2015) 4 Cambridge International Law Journal 423.

[182] Möllers (n 31) 81.

[183] András Jakab, 'Problems of the Stufenbaulehre: Kelsen's Failure to Derive the Validity of a Norm from Another Norm' (2007) 20 Canadian Journal of Law and Jurisprudence 35, 36.

[184] Adolf Merkl, *Die Lehre von der Rechtskraft entwickelt aus dem Rechtsbegriff* (Franz Deuticke 1923) 216.

[185] See Adolf Merkl, 'Das doppelte Rechtsantlitz' [1918] Juristische Blätter paras 425–7, 444–7, 463–6; see also Thomas Olechowski, 'Legal Hierarchies in the Works of Hans Kelsen and Adolf Julius Merkl' in Ulrike Müßing (ed), *Reconsidering Constitutional Formation II Decisive Constitutional Normativity* (Springer International Publishing 2018) 356ff.

> The interpretation by the law-applying organ is always authentic. It creates law. To be sure, we speak of 'authentic interpretation' only if this interpretation assumes the form of a statute or an international treaty and has general character, that is, if it creates law not only for a concrete case but for all similar cases—in other words, if the act described as authentic has the character of the creation of a general norm. However, the interpretation by a law-applying organ is authentic (law-creating) also if it creates law only for a concrete case, that is, if the organ creates only an individual norm or executes a sanction. Here it is to be noted: By way of authentic interpretation (that is, interpretation of a norm by the law-applying organ) not only one of the possibilities may be realized that have been shown by the cognitive interpretation of the norm to be applied; but also a norm may be created which lies entirely outside the frame of the norm to be applied.[186]

The political and constitutional legal processes are much more intertwined than many assume. Häberle claims that politics is a strong part of constitutional interpretation, as 'politics through constitutional interpretation'.[187] Constitutional jurisprudence is also constitutional creation.[188] Each constitutional interpretation includes a moment of constituting the constitution.[189] Even if a legal provision may prohibit certain courses of action, it does not determine which of several possible alternatives a court should choose.[190] Kelsen claims that the cognitive process seeking to fill this space is not based on positive law alone but can take other norms into account, including morals, justice and constituting social values, such as 'the good of the people'.[191] It is precisely this undetermined space where conflicts arise about how courts *ought* to decide:

> Taking new situations and their consequences into account to avoid unreasonable judgments produces indeterminacy that must be closed by 'interpretative reasoning' of judges. This leads to the creation of new rules and therefore to uncertainty for cases that must be adjudicated. Habermas diagnoses this tension, and concludes that judges cannot avoid being legislators who make political choices. This is why courts come up with justifications for their legislative decisions, which can become elements of

186 Hans Kelsen, *Pure Theory of Law. Translation from the Second (Revised and Enlarged) German Edition* (University of California Press 2005) 354.

187 Häberle, 'The Open Society of Constitutional Interpreters' (n 8) 138 fn. 37.

188 Tamara Ehs, 'Horizontgericht—Das Politische in der Verfassungsgerichtsbarkeit' in Martin Möllers and Robert van Ooyen (eds), *Verfassungs-Kultur. Staat, Europa und pluralistische Gesellschaft bei Peter Häberle* (Nomos 2016) 113.

189 Peter Häberle and Markus Kotzur, *Europäische Verfassungslehre* (8th edn, Nomos 2016) 471.

190 Alexander Stark, *Interdisziplinarität der Rechtsdogmatik* (Mohr Siebeck 2020) 95 ff.

191 Kelsen, *Pure Theory of Law. Translation from the Second (Revised and Enlarged) German Edition* (n 186) 353.

> public discourses. Public discussion about case law made by the courts democratizes this kind of legislation.[192]

From such a perspective, the difference between constitutional interpretation and constitutional lawmaking becomes increasingly blurry.[193] Constitutional jurisprudence, which entails the creation of constitutional law, makes apex courts such as the GFCC 'as-well-as' organs ('*sowohl-als-auch Organ*'), which are neither purely legal nor purely political organs.[194] Parliament and the Constitutional Court are not competing for political power. Rather, both are constitutional bodies that make policies and implement the constitution.[195]

There is no hierarchy between the constitutional organs, and thus, there is neither *the* one institution that makes law nor *the* one institution that has the last word on interpretation.[196] Consequently, there is not *the* one representative legislative body. For Eisgruber, the logic that 'the electorate represents "the people"' is too simple to fully grasp the concept of democratic legitimacy. This is because 'the voter' itself is an abstract concept that is limited to very reduced actions—in this case, the vote itself, without any explanation. Voters know that their individual vote has no influence on the outcome of the election, and that it will neither influence their reputation nor the government's policy. 'The voter' might, therefore, act differently in a different setting, for example, as a testimony at a public hearing.[197] It follows that those who would be the best representatives are not necessarily the ones who attract majority votes, as the very little number of Black or female electorates in the U.S. Congress would demonstrate.[198] Instead, unelected (constitutional) judges would have some abilities and features that the electorates naturally do not have, such as life tenure. Courts combine 'a democratic pedigree with disinterestedness and moral responsibility'.[199] Judges

192 Wil Martens, 'Democracy for Transnational Regimes' in Bas Leijssenaar, Judith Martens and Evert Van der Zweerde (eds), *Futures of Democracy* (Wilde Raven Publishing 2014) 5 (citations omitted).

193 Peter Häberle, 'Verfassungsinterpretation und Verfassunggebung (Berner Gastvortrag 1977)', *Verfassung als öffentlicher Prozeß: Materialien zu einer Verfassungstheorie der offenen Gesellschaft* (Duncker & Humblot 1978) 209.

194 Ehs (n 188) 111, 113; following Peter Häberle, 'Demokratische Verfassungstheorie im Lichte des Möglichkeitsdenkens' (1977) 102 Archiv des öffentlichen Rechts 27, 39.

195 Ehs (n 188) 113.

196 ibid 114.

197 Eisgruber (n 62) 50–1.

198 ibid 51.

199 ibid 78.

who have reached the peak of their careers are more likely to engage in moral issues in a disinterested fashion without having to fear disadvantages for their professional paths.[200] Moreover, history has shown that the judicial branch is less influenced by the interests of strong industries.[201] Thus, judges might be 'better positioned to represent the people's convictions about what is right' and 'thereby making a distinctive contribution to representative democracy'.[202] As judges are indirectly elected (through the nomination of the elected politicians), they are also representatives of the people[203] and Eisgruber concludes that:

> Large-scale polities can pursue democratic ideals only by choosing among a variety of institutions, all of which are imperfect representatives of the people. Neither 'voters' nor 'legislators' nor 'judges' are the same thing as 'the people'; each is a political office, subject to particular incentives, constructed in order to provide a representation of the people.[204]

Instead of privileging one of the branches over the others, all three branches are 'in equal distance to the people, no institution or procedure is taken to represent the people as a whole'.[205]

From a rule-of-law perspective, judicial law creation is not only necessary but it is democratically legitimised because it strengthens the legitimation context between the norm and the decision and brings out the normativity of statutory law in reality.[206] Thus, Benjamin believes that the concept of the 'protagonist judiciary' (not to be confused with the activist judiciary) as opposed to the 'spectator judiciaries' with their 'hands-off' approach gains relevance, particularly in environmental matters.[207] This view is supported by cases that have been decided by apex courts in countries where environmental protection norms are enshrined

---

[200] ibid.

[201] Katherine Ellison, 'An Inconvenient Lawsuit: Teenagers Take Global Warming to the Courts' *The Atlantic* (9 May 2012) <https://www.theatlantic.com/national/archive/2012/05/an-inconvenient-lawsuit-teenagers-take-global-warming-to-the-courts/256903/> accessed 31 August 2023.

[202] Eisgruber (n 62) 5.

[203] ibid 78.

[204] ibid 205–6.

[205] Hauke Brunkhorst, 'Constitutionalism and Democracy in the World Society' in Petra Dobner and Martin Loughlin (eds), *The Twilight of Constitutionalism?* (OUP 2010) 197.

[206] Payandeh (n 8) 250.

[207] Benjamin (n 72) 585.

in the national constitution. The South African Constitutional Court, for example, stated that:

> the role of the courts is especially important in the context of the protection of the environment and giving effect to the principle of sustainable development. The importance of the protection of the environment cannot be gainsaid. Its protection is vital to the enjoyment of the other rights contained in the Bill of Rights; indeed, it is vital to life itself. It must therefore be protected for the benefit of the present and future generations. The present generation holds the earth in trust for the next generation. This trusteeship position carries with it the responsibility to look after the environment. It is the duty of the court to ensure that this responsibility is carried out.[208]

Today, many judges see themselves as important keyholders in climate change governance. Chief Justice Syed Mansoor Ali Shah, for example, noted in *Leghari* that '[o]n a jurisprudential plane, a judge today must be conscious and alive to the beauty and magnificence of nature, the interconnectedness of life systems on this planet and the interdependence of ecosystems'.[209] It can be noted that constitutional courts are co-legislators, if not in name, then at least through their decisions on values and directions that have impacts for more than just the case at hand.[210] Consequently, a strict separation between the powers becomes impossible. But this does not necessarily need to be a bad thing, as Feris notes:

> While the ideal of a strict separation of powers may be a noble one, it is unattainable in a modern democracy in an absolute form and it is also not necessarily desirable. The emphasis should rather be on developing an appropriate system of checks and balances to ensure accountability, responsibility and transparency as well as an interaction among the different organs of state. Constitutions charge judiciaries, as guardians of the Bill of Rights, with a variety of duties. The Constitution, for example, does not require the rights it entrenches only to be respected, but also to be protected, promoted and fulfilled. The courts are therefore also required to safeguard and facilitate these 'active' duties assigned to the state. This necessarily entails an expansion of the powers of the judiciary and enhances its influence in political matters.[211]

---

[208] Constitutional Court of South Africa, *Fuel Retailers Association of Southern Africa v Director-General Environmental Management, Department of Agriculture, Conservation and Environment, Mpumalanga Province and Others,* Case CCT 67/06 [2007] ZACC 13, para 102.

[209] Lahore High Court (n 77) para 20.

[210] Kelsen, *Pure Theory of Law. Translation from the Second (Revised and Enlarged) German Edition* (n 186) 354.

[211] Loretta Feris, 'Constitutional Environmental Rights' (2008) 24 South African Journal on Human Rights 29, 34.

10.6 Limitations of Judicial Law Creation

However, if all three powers are creating law, where should the line be drawn between them? Given that the courts—instead of parliaments—are increasingly deciding on values and directions for the political community,[212] 'the "politicisation of law" must have limits and controls'.[213] Although the idea that no branch has a hierarchy over the other may, in some ways, be convincing, it overlooks the fact that the final say usually rests with the constitutional judiciary.[214] The Constitution of Eswatini, for example, states in its preamble that 'whereas all the branches of government are the Guardians of the Constitution, it is necessary that the Courts be the ultimate Interpreters of the Constitution'. In this sense, constitutional courts can become 'dangerous' from the perspective of the other branches.[215]

Coming back to Habermas, a court must generally respect the decision made by citizens in rational discourses. Thus, it is necessary to redefine the issue from a different perspective. Instead of asking what the powers of each branch are, we need to analyse how the forms of lawmaking by each branch differ from each other. By drawing on Möllers's theory of the three branches, it becomes clear that legislative and judicial lawmaking is different in both nature and objective.

Möllers addresses these concerns by putting forward a theory of different types of legitimacy. He draws on Habermas's co-originality thesis to emphasise the different functions of the branches in relation to legitimacy. A legal system must protect both individual and democratic self-determination. Processes that protect the first can claim individual legitimacy; processes protecting the latter, democratic legitimacy.[216] Individual legitimacy refers to individual self-determination, defined as a strictly personal action by a specific individual in a specific context.[217] It requires that substantive rights exist that protect this self-determination both from public authority (e.g., the enforcement of a right against the state) and

---

[212] Ehs (n 188) 107.

[213] See concluding words by Peter Häberle, 'Grundrechte im Leistungsstaat' (1972) 30 Veröffentlichungen der Vereinigung der Deutschen Staatsrechtslehrer 7, 188; for an English translation of his report, see Peter Häberle, 'Fundamental Rights in the Welfare State. Second Co-Report of Professor Dr. Peter Häberle, Marburg on Lahn' in Markus Kotzur (ed), *Peter Häberle on Constitutional Theory* (Nomos/Hart 2018) 17.

[214] Häberle, 'The Open Society of Constitutional Interpreters' (n 8) 131.

[215] Anna Gamper, 'Dangerous or Endangered Constitutional Courts? A View from among and within the Branches of Power' (2021) 76 Zeitschrift für öffentliches Recht 331.

[216] Möllers (n 31) 67.

[217] ibid 69.

other individuals (e.g., a claim to fulfilment of a contract).[218] It is the initiation of legal procedures by the affected and entitled person before the courts that justifies the whole process. However, individual legitimacy depends only on the procedure itself, not on the outcome. Not every single majority decision can be overturned in favour of an individual interest.[219] Democratic legitimacy refers to the equal opportunity for all members of a community to participate in a collective expression.[220] For an act of public authority to be legitimate, it must satisfy both individual and democratic legitimacy.[221] The branches' competencies vary according to criteria of legal determination, the scope of their decisions and their temporal aspect.

The legislative protects democratic self-determination and, thus, institutes democratic legitimacy.[222] The initiative comes from within, and it must be open in its results (similar to what Häberle calls 'thinking in alternatives').[223] Moreover, the legislative must be authorised to make general decisions.[224] Generally, legislative decisions are future-oriented. Both single-case legislation and retrospective laws are forbidden in many constitutional systems.[225] Judicial lawmaking, conversely, is constrained to a particular case.[226] The judiciary derives its justification to decide a case from an individual claim to self-determination. It acts on external initiative and in a retrospective fashion; cases are oriented to the past.[227] It is the plaintiff's will that carries—and is carried through—the whole process.[228]

In Möllers' view, thus, the separation of powers is a procedural principle. A court does not overstep its competencies just because it interprets a constitutional provision in an 'anomalous' fashion. Even if it may seem that the court acts as a legislator by reinterpreting a statute and, therefore, could be accused of

[218] ibid 68.

[219] ibid 71.

[220] ibid.

[221] ibid 79.

[222] ibid 84.

[223] Häberle, 'Demokratische Verfassungstheorie im Lichte des Möglichkeitsdenkens' (n 194).

[224] Möllers (n 31) 86.

[225] ibid. Möllers points out that there are expectations to these general rules.

[226] Payandeh (n 8) 247 ff.

[227] Möllers (n 31) 89–90; Habermas, *Between Facts and Norms: Contributions to a Discourse Theory of Law and Democracy* (n 57) 245.

[228] Möllers (n 31) 71.

judicial activism, 'not even fatuous, nonsensical, or anomalous interpretations' constitute a violation of the separation of power 'as long as the court still acts as a court within a judicial procedure'.[229] A violation in this sense would be if a court initiated a case on its own or without a plaintiff to interfere with ongoing executive or legislative affairs.[230]

Whether such a procedural approach alone would be sufficient to safeguard the essence of the principle of the separation of powers remains doubtful. A constitutional court is bound to the constitution and even ordinary law where it is compatible with constitutional review, but due to the desired independence of constitutional courts, there is no supervision of their jurisprudence nor an examination of whether their verdicts comply with the rule of law, which makes this obligation a *lex imperfecta*.[231] However, various mechanisms flank the procedural prerequisites identified by Möllers to protect the competencies of the powers: judgements of constitutional courts look to the past rather than the future. When reviewing draft legislation prior to entry into force, another constitutional organ must expressly empower the constitutional court to do so.[232] Its interpretations have to be consistent with existing laws and it is not allowed to interpret *contra legem*. Unwritten law (usually) cannot claim prevalence over written constitutional law.[233] The 'consistency method' (*verfassungskonforme Auslegung*) is an interpretational approach that requires a constitutional court to uphold a legal statute by interpreting it in a way that is consistent with the constitution instead of declaring it unconstitutional and, therefore, void due to its ambiguity.[234]

Yet, the question of the separation of powers is far more complex than the often-invoked fear of one branch taking over the others. Gamper argues that 'the judiciary cannot truly be described as a monolith vis-à-vis the other two branches' since this ignores the 'internal' separation of powers among constitutional courts and national courts on the one hand and constitutional courts and supranational

[229] ibid 95.

[230] ibid.

[231] Gamper (n 181) 438.

[232] ibid 437.

[233] Heinrich Amadeus Wolff, *Ungeschriebenes Verfassungsrecht unter dem Grundgesetz* (Mohr Siebeck 2000) 359 ff.

[234] Horst Ehmke, 'Prinzipien der Verfassungsinterpretation', *Prinzipien der Verfassungsinterpretation. Gefährdungshaftung im öffentlichen Recht: Aussprache zu den Berichten in den Verhandlungen der Tagung der deutschen Staatsrechtslehrer zu Freiburg vom 4. bis 7. Oktober 1961* (De Gruyter 1971) 74ff.; see also the Chapter 'Consistent Interpretation' in André Nollkaemper, *National Courts and the International Rule of Law* (OUP 2011) 139ff.

courts such as the CJEU on the other.[235] What is more, the legal historical scholar van den Berge points out that Montesquieu never indented to advocate for a full separation of powers in which a strict line between the powers could be drawn that ascribes to each its own well-defined domain that could be neatly separated from the other two branches. While this was the result of subsequent writings by other scholars, Montesquieu's own ideas of constitutional architecture were based on shared sovereignty that is distributed among several actors and balanced among the powers, in which no one had the final say.[236] This said, the principle of the separation of powers is not as clear-cut as it has been described by many scholars, including those that argue that courts should not rule on climate cases. Instead, the idea of the intertwined *trias politica* has consequently been stressed by several courts that have ruled in climate cases. The DC elaborated on this point in its *Urgenda* decision by arguing that, under Dutch law, there is no full separation of powers. Instead of being sharply separated from one another, the *trias politica* must attempt to establish a balance.[237] Restraint is required when a case involves policy-related considerations of different interests that could have consequences for the structure or organisation of society.[238] However, the court identifies that '[i]t is an essential feature of the rule of law that the actions of [...] political bodies, such as the government and parliament can—and sometimes must—be assessed by an independent court'.[239] Legislation itself enables the judge to do so by authorising and ensuring 'power' to decide legal disputes.[240] And while climate cases touch political matters, they are still legal cases ruled under existing laws—a competence that is assigned to the courts by legislation, in particular, constitutional provisions. The courts' role has often been described as the 'guardians of the constitution'; as such, they protect the citizen's rights enshrined in the constitution.[241] Bearing in mind Ackerman's note of the court as representation and trace of the people's absent self-government, for Habermas,

[235] Gamper (n 215) 347f.

[236] Lukas van den Berge, 'Montesquieu and Judicial Review of Proportionality in Administrative Law: Rethinking the Separation of Powers in the Neoliberal Era' (2017) 10 European Journal of Legal Studies 203, 206, 212.

[237] District Court of The Hague (n 79) para 4.95.

[238] ibid.

[239] ibid.

[240] ibid 4.97.

[241] Gamper (n 181) 438; see also Helle Krunke, 'Courts as Protectors of the People: Constitutional Identity, Popular Legitimacy and Human Rights' in Martin Scheinin, Helle Krunke and Marina Aksenova (eds), *Judges as Guardians of Constitutionalism and Human Rights* (Edward Elgar Publishing 2016).

the 'constitutional court thus assumes the role of republican guardian of positive liberties that the citizens themselves, as nominal bearers of these liberties, fail to exercise'.[242]

For Grimm, democracies do not necessarily need constitutional review to protect citizens' rights.[243] But it can prove useful to compensate for democratic deficits. Thus, he sees a major danger for democracies in the 'professionalization of party politics'. Where political parties are only interested in winning elections and gaining power, they tend to concentrate on short-term success, which, as a downside, leads to the neglect of long-term issues and side effects occurring in the not-so-near future.[244] This problem becomes more than obvious in the case of the climate crisis. The GFCC addressed it as follows:

> The Constitution sets limits here on the leeway enjoyed in the political decision-making process to determine whether environmental protection measures should be taken or not. In Art. 20a GG, environmental protection is elevated to a matter of constitutional significance because the democratic political process is organised along more short-term lines based on election cycles, placing it at a structural risk of being less responsive to tackling the ecological issues that need to be pursued over the long term. It is also because future generations – those who will be most affected – naturally have no voice of their own in shaping the current political agenda. In view of these institutional conditions, Art. 20a GG imposes substantive constraints on democratic decision-making ([...]). This binding of the political process as envisaged by Art. 20a GG would be in danger of being lost if the material content of Art. 20a GG were fully determined by the day-to-day political process with its more short-term approach and its orientation towards directly expressible interests.[245]

In a nutshell, for Barak, there is no fault if a court decides a 'political' case according to legal standards. The principle of the separation of powers does not even justify refraining from adjudicating state acts, including those that are by their very nature political. If the third branch refused to adjudicate such cases, it would itself violate the rule of law and the separation of powers by recognising the political branches' power to decide political disputes illegally.[246] According to the concept of functional democracy, this means that where a constitution

[242] Habermas, *Between Facts and Norms: Contributions to a Discourse Theory of Law and Democracy* (n 57) 278.

[243] Dieter Grimm, *Constitutionalism. Past, Present, and Future* (OUP 2016) 217f.

[244] ibid 229.

[245] GFCC, Order of the First Senate of 24 March 2021—1 BvR 2656/18, para 206.

[246] Aharon Barak, 'On Judging' in Martin Scheinin, Helle Krunke and Marina Aksenova (eds), *Judges as Guardians of Constitutionalism and Human Rights* (Edward Elgar Publishing 2016) 43f.

has established courts, including a constitutional court or a supreme court, the courts derive their democratic legitimacy from their function of protecting the constitution.[247]

Where courts found a violation of the plaintiffs' fundamental or human rights, they made clear that they would leave full discretionary powers to the respective branches to decide how to comply with their obligations under national and IL. The GFCC, therefore, limited its role to determining that the KSG had violated the fundamental rights of the plaintiffs, but it was up to the legislative branch to decide how to address the problem:

> Art. 20a GG does leave the legislator considerable leeway to design. It is not, in principle, for the courts to translate the open wording of Art. 20a GG into quantifiable global warming limits and corresponding emission amounts or reduction targets. At the same time, however, Art. 20a GG may not be drained of substance as an obligation to take climate action. In this respect too, it remains for the Federal Constitutional Court to review whether the boundaries of Art. 20a GG are respected ([...]). There is nothing to indicate that Art. 20a GG – as a singular exception among the provisions of the Basic Law – is beyond the scope of judicial review with regard to how its regulatory content is interpreted and applied.[248]

Although the waters of constitutional jurisprudence in environmental and climate change cases can be somewhat murky,[249] the courts have shown great sensitivity to the dangers and pitfalls that can arise from accusations of judicial activism and violation of the principle of separation of powers and have, therefore, exercised their authority with great restraint so far.

10.7 Concluding Remarks

The role of the courts in CCL cases remains disputed under the separation of powers doctrine. Many fear that judges are bypassing the legislative branch when deciding on highly disputed subject matters such as climate mitigation. Climate change is a particularly complex problem, a 'polycentric task', where a court decision can lead to unintended consequences for the economy and citizens. Accordingly, it has been argued that judges should merely apply the law as

[247] Gamper (n 181) 438.

[248] GFCC,1 BvR 2656/18, para 206.

[249] Benjamin (n 72) 588.

it stands and withdraw from deciding cases that have a political component; otherwise, they would illegally engage in lawmaking.

However, this chapter has demonstrated that all three branches are involved in law creation, albeit to varying degrees. Judicial decisions also create law. The invention of the general right to privacy and the right to informational self-determination by the GFCC are particularly illustrative of this point. In most constitutional systems, the powers are not strictly separated but need to be balanced. The competencies of the legislative are safeguarded through the restrictions that are imposed on the third branch. While judges create law, too, they are not as free as legislators.[250] As protectors of individual legitimacy—instead of democratic legitimacy—courts are case-bound, restricted to the plaintiffs' will and decide in a retrospective fashion.

The court's role is complex due to the tension between popular sovereignty and human rights mutually presupposing each other.[251] While a court should generally respect a legislative outcome that citizens have consented to as participants of rational discourses, a majority decision can be 'trumped' by human rights when these could be violated through that decision. The creation of new rights and the extension of existing rights is justified when unforeseen challenges require the courts to protect human dignity.[252]

Courts increasingly seek to protect people from environmental degradation where it endangers their human rights and, therefore, can meet the demands of the public to 'update' the law on issues on which the legislative has been hesitant or slow. Many policy changes are the direct result of court rulings that obliged the legislative to change the existing laws, for example, to protect the right to marry for same-sex couples.[253] By doing so, judges act as 'guardians of the people'.[254]

---

[250] Kelsen, *Pure Theory of Law. Translation from the Second (Revised and Enlarged) German Edition* (n 186) 353.

[251] Zurn (n 102) 485.

[252] Christopher McCrudden, 'Human Dignity and Judicial Interpretation of Human Rights' (2008) 19 European Journal of International Law 655, 721; Habermas, 'The Concept of Human Dignity and the Realistic Utopia of Human Rights' (n 127) 467.

[253] See, for example, Avril Rushe, 'Same-Sex Marriage under the Grundgesetz and the European Convention on Human Rights' (2017) 60 German Yearbook of International Law 711.

[254] Krunke (n 241) 71.

Conclusion 11

Climate change is 'the defining challenge of our era'.[1] GHG emissions must be curbed now to keep global warming under 1.5–2°C compared to 1990 levels. Given the latest scientific data and appeals by climate experts, many people, especially the young, realise that their future is at risk when states are not meeting their climate commitments.

Climate change is not only an environmental problem but also an issue of global social justice. It hits those hardest that have contributed least to the problem: the populations of the Global South and future generations—not yet born or those who are children today—and indigenous peoples both in the Global North and South. But voluntary climate action by the countries of the Global North, which caused the problem in the first place and are better suited to address it, so far has been hesitant, slow and not far-reaching enough. Voluntary cooperations between states fall short when they do not feel bound by the environmental rule of law.

Against these backgrounds, this book has argued that litigation by non-state actors strengthens and develops global climate constitutionalism. Global climate constitutionalism aims to govern the relationships between the actors of climate governance, including states and non-state actors, such as NGOs, individuals, transnational corporations, local and indigenous communities, and also sub-states and local governments, which are not recognised as legal subjects under the Westphalian model of IL. Climate governance is pluralistic and polycentric. As a 'glocal' problem, climate change requires the global community to give a global response and to take local action to effectively curb GHG emissions.

---

[1] 'Climate Change Poses "Defining Challenge" of Our Time, Ban Says' *UN News* (7 October 2008) < https://news.un.org/en/story/2008/10/276912-climate-change-poses-defining-challenge-our-time-ban-says > accessed 31 August 2023.

M. Niehaus, *Global Climate Constitutionalism "from below"*,
https://doi.org/10.1007/978-3-658-43191-4_11

According to the Westphalian model of IL, states govern their relations with each other but also within their territories without any interference and with equal respect for each other's autonomy, thus, enjoying internal and external sovereignty. This model has come under pressure with challenges that have come alongside globalisation. Transnational problems, such as climate change, require global solutions. No state can be forced to comply with its climate obligations against its will due to the absence of a central enforcement mechanism in IL. On the downside, however, no state can solve the problem on its own. States cannot or can only to a certain degree protect their territories from the adverse effects that climate change has on the fundamental rights of their citizens, such as the right to life, health, water and food. Global climate constitutionalism, therefore, aims to constrain state sovereignty in matters that affect all persons and make states' non-compliance with (environmental) norms more difficult or unlikely.

Based on theories of legal pluralism and societal constitutionalism, it was analysed that ragimes, such as the climate regime, can or could possess their own constitution, which have to respect the principles of general constitutionalism (such as fundamental rights and the rule of law) but also have their very own constitutional norms. These constitution are not only developed by states but also by a multitude of non-state actors.

Many of the changes in IL are not the result of formal amendments or the implementation of new human rights. Rather, IL is further developed through interpretation. For many legal institutions, an evolutionary and dynamic approach allows them to take into account factors external to the law, including technological, social and environmental developments. Interpretation, then, 'occupies the space between the norm texts and the law'[2] and changes of meaning occur by 'constitutional change' instead of 'constitutional amendment'. The result can be just the same, especially when courts include factors that have not been considered by the constitution's drafters or even find new rights, such as the right to a stable climate, environmental rights for future generations or an ecological subsistence minimum.

In an open society of constitutional interpreters, however, it is not the courts alone that interpret the constitution. Instead, everybody is a constitutional interpreter: all citizens, groups, NGOs and communities are interpreters. They can interpret the constitution by simply living in the fundamental right or by articulating their interpretations. This can take the form, for example, of public outrage in the face of human rights violations, through mass protests or mass petitions.

[2] Ingo Venzke, *How Interpretation Makes International Law: On Semantic Change and Normative Twists* (OUP 2012) 197.

Another important form of articulation are constitutional complaints and other lawsuits in which plaintiffs force the court to engage in a legal dialogue. Although they are not officially authorised to interpret the constitution, they are at least constitutional pre-interpreters who offer their interpretations to the court. Both domestic and international courts have been open to the inclusion of environmental aspects in their interpretation of civil and political human rights, otherwise known as the 'greening' of human rights; the connection between a quality environment and the enjoyment of human rights has long been acknowledged.

Therefore, strategic litigation has become an important tool for environmental and climate activists. An array of different actors, including individuals, NGOs, local and indigenous communities, but also sub-states and local governments, have formulated their own interpretations of constitutional law, international (environmental) law, human rights law and science. Relaxed standing requirements, the influence of amici curiae and judges that see themselves as 'protagonists' in the wake of environmental degradation have contributed to the success of CCL cases.

Litigation cannot only lead to more climate protection. Instead, it has been argued that CCL can be perceived as a form of self-government in the face of governmental failure to address climate change. Litigation can help to reduce the gaps that scholars have identified in relation to global climate constitutionalism. It can include the voices of those who are silent in national will-formation processes because they cannot vote due to their age or nationality. Litigation can help to establish climate justice in constitutionalist frameworks and, by doing so, create more just visions of IL. Moreover, it can help civil society to transform its interpretations into legally binding and enforceable law, even against the will of states.

The lack of democratic legitimacy and opportunities for public participation is one of the biggest problems in relation to global constitutionalism. Many visions of global constitutionalism lack a deeper engagement with democratic questions and meaningful concepts for the participation of non-state actors. And although some scholars of global constitutionalism have come forward with ideas of how to give individuals a greater say in international lawmaking, most of these approaches limit themselves to forms of 'constitutionalism lite'.

By now, it seems that the global community cannot achieve anything more than a minimal basic consensus in a Habermasian fashion: the negative consensus of what people do not accept, for example, refraining from human rights violations. However, the relevance of the scholarly discourse of global climate constitutionalism will also be measured by its ability to address the 'super wicked' challenges of the climate crisis, which, besides its ecological dimensions, are its impacts on (global) social justice. Climate justice, including intra- and intergenerational justice, needs to become central to approaches of global climate constitutionalism.

Climate justice requires, inter alia, the redistribution of burdens and benefits, including the costs caused by climate change, not only among states but also between generations, since it is expected that the worst effects of climate change will only manifest in the future. However, a model of global constitutionalism that also encompasses distribution and other issues of world domestic politics—thereby, positive obligations towards other members of a society—needs something more than a merely negative agreement. But global viable democracy that also includes redistributive policies requires solidarity among its members.

Such global solidarity may not exist yet; however, it can be gradually developed in a global constitutional 'community of fate'. Solidarity is not citizenship-bound. Rather, the artificial making of nation-states demonstrates that it is possible (and necessary) to actively construct and foster solidarity within a polity. Solidarity depends on 'identity-building', for example, of groups, interests or nations. It can develop transnationally when people feel empathy towards other groups of people affected by a certain situation.

Although the populations of the world are very different from each other, people are realising that climate change affects them all in some way or another. Catastrophes such as the recent heatwaves and floodings in North America and large parts of Europe show the populations of the Global North that climate change is no longer a problem only of the Global South. After all, we all 'sit in the same boat'—a boat that is currently sinking. Climate change is a global problem and, therefore, has global effects on the lives of potentially everybody.

In a nation-state, a constitution not only restricts governmental powers but also aims to integrate the people into one nation ('We the people') in which citizens make sacrifices for one another. A national constitution that aims to socially integrate those in whose name it is promulgated and to whom it is directed requires a 'common attachment or common predicament within the putative *demos*'.[3] However, such a common attachment in the form of commonly held values and a common predicament in the form of a shared risk can also be identified at the international level. One value that is commonly shared is the hope that one's children will be better off in the future or at least enjoy the same preconditions. This idea is equally present in religions, philosophy, indigenous cultures

[3] Neil Walker, 'Taking Constitutionalism beyond the State' (2008) 56 Political Studies 519, 531.

and both common and civil law systems all over the world. It has been translated into the principle of intergenerational equity, of which intra-generational equity is an essential part. A global community could also be based on the idea of a 'world risk society'. Since all people share the same Earth, it is in the interest of all to save this planet for the survival of humanity. Thus, there exists a—albeit yet weak—bond on which a global community could develop global solidarity.

However, climate justice, besides redistribution, requires mutual recognition and meaningful participation possibilities. People must recognise each other as equals and grant each other the same liberties in a global community as a requirement to participate in common decision-making. All people that are potentially affected by a particular decision have to have the opportunity to participate in rational discourses about this decision. This is the idea underpinning deliberative democracy as the most promising form of democracy for legitimising global climate governance. Deliberation, instead of voting, is meant to come to fairer outcomes because it can consider the interests of those that cannot vote, including non-citizens, future generations and nature.

Deliberation can occur in specifically designed assemblies similar to the Irish Constitutional Assembly or 'mini-publics' such as the WWViews. But deliberation can also take place in the courts. Plaintiffs and defendants have to present their arguments and evidence, and their interpretations are put to the test in the courtroom. Litigation can serve as a forum in which stakeholders come together to deliberate and negotiate over a particular subject matter. While winning is a plus, for many litigants, it is more important to reach a broader public than merely the judges deciding the case. Courts are used as forums of protest.

Litigation, then, can be understood as one opportunity for people to engage in self-government. Unlike voting, courts can be accessed by minors and non-citizens. In many jurisdictions, the participation of both national and foreign NGOs and individuals is possible through the instrument of the amicus curiae brief. Moreover, many courts, including the Colombian Supreme Court, the District Court of Oregon, the GFCC and the European Court of Human Rights, have also shown themselves open to considering the interests of future generations and, in the cases of Germany and Colombia, of foreigners and even nature.

Thus, litigation can develop and shape global climate constitutionalism. Transnational climate law is interpreted and thereby created by both international and domestic courts. Domestic courts do not see themselves only as state agents but as representatives of the global judiciary. Judges participate in a global judicial dialogue that shapes and fosters their understanding as participants of transnational judicial networks. Some networks have officially been established, such as the IUCN Global Judicial Institute on Environmental Law, but sometimes, courts simply let themselves be inspired by other courts' decisions.

In pluralistic and polycentric governance, a multitude of actors offer interpretations on the same subject matter. Sometimes, their interpretations are at 'war'; other times, they complement rather than compete with each other. This fluidity of authority between various actors is the consequence of an understanding that multi-level constitutionalism is composed of 'nested constitutional orders' at various levels. This 'law in public action' is shaped by a multitude of interpretations. No interpretation may ever claim absolute validity. Each interpretation can be contested again; there are no final points. The majority decisions of today can become history tomorrow when minority views turn the wheel around. Contestation, both in courts and on the streets by grassroots movements through civil disobedience—skipping school, blocking cities, airports or highways—seek to reopen formally concluded political deliberation. Former decisions should be reviewed, and the concerns of the protesters and litigants should be considered. The constitution is understood as an unfinished project that is meant to be interpreted anew and better in changing circumstances. Contestation, therefore, is crucial for deliberative democracy.

In an open society of constitutional interpreters, these interpretations can be offered by everybody. However—here lies another advantage of litigation—some interpreters have more power than others. Civil society does exercise public pressure through street rallies, internet petitions and social media. Groups such as Fridays for Future and Extinction Rebellion made the issue of climate change visible to the global public and influenced the implementation of stronger climate policies, including the EU New Green Deal. Despite such influence and public pressure ('naming and shaming'), they have no means to enforce their interpretations. Rather, their interpretations need to become institutionalised, either by the parliament in the form of statutes or by a court in the form of a judicial decision.

Individuals or NGOs cannot issue a legally binding interpretation of a norm, but courts can. The interpretation by a court, particularly an apex court, holds greater authority than the interpretation of a single citizen because it is only for the courts to decide whether a norm of civil society's *lex humana* is also valid in the politically supported system law. Courts can transform political potentials, such as civil society pressure, into political power. Litigation precisely aims to make use of this transformative potential and to change the law through interpretation. Decisions such as *Urgenda*, *Leghari* or *Future Generations* have given climate activists' interpretations of the law an aura of legitimacy that street protests alone cannot achieve.

However, the role of the courts in strategic climate lawsuits has been questioned as violating the principle of the separation of powers. Accordingly, 'polycentric tasks' such as climate change should be left to the directly elected, thereby democratically legitimised, branches of government. Once the legislator has decided whether and how to address climate change, for example, through mitigation or adaptation measures or a combination of both or to decide to do nothing at all, a court generally has to accept such existing laws as majority decisions and as such, an expression of the people's will. Only where human rights are at stake may courts declare that such majority decisions are unconstitutional.[4] Rights are 'trumps' that can even override majority decisions. Thus, many CCL cases are based on human rights claims. Where existing climate policies have been declared too weak, as in the case of *Urgenda,* courts have resolved the tension between majority voting and human rights in favour of the latter. This includes 'greening' already existing rights, but also the creation of new rights, such as environmental rights for future generations (*Future Generations*) and a right to a stable climate (*Juliana*).

Interpretation always includes an element of norm creation. Every constitutional interpretation—by whomever—constitutes the constitution anew. Although the law may prohibit certain choices, by not telling the courts exactly what to do and, therefore, opening the space to 'think in alternatives and possibilities',[5] it even expects the judiciary to exercise judicial creativity. This is all the more important when a norm is vague, such as the unwritten 'duty of care' in the *Urgenda* case before the DC, which it interpreted as including the state's obligation to protect its citizens from the adverse effects of climate change. Thus, courts play an important role in protecting the climate because they can consider external factors important to society when choosing between the alternative possibilities the interpretation of a norm offers.

Thus, the powers of government are far less separated than it is often claimed. Instead, all branches are engaging in lawmaking. A court creates new law once its legal action cannot be rescinded because it has become binding and final. The competencies of the branches, therefore, cannot be sharply differentiated from one another but are intertwined and require balancing. The core of the principle of the separation of powers needs to be guaranteed. However, the perceived danger of the judiciary overstepping its competence can be tamed by turning towards

4 Jürgen Habermas, *Between Facts and Norms: Contributions to a Discourse Theory of Law and Democracy* (Polity Press 1996) 204.

5 Peter Häberle, 'Demokratische Verfassungstheorie im Lichte des Möglichkeitsdenkens' (1977) 102 Archiv des öffentlichen Rechts 27.

procedural requirements: litigation must be initiated by plaintiffs and their (and the defendants) will carries the whole process. Courts are limited to rule in a retrospective fashion—on matters in the past—whereas the other branches can direct their decisions towards the future. The court is generally not allowed to interfere with ongoing legislation processes. But the courts are constitutionally called upon to decide on the legality of all state action—even in political cases, which they may, however, only judge according to legal standards. The judgements in *Urgenda*, *Leghari*, *Juliana* and *Future Generations* are spectacular and so innovative they were called 'landmark' decisions but also labelled as 'judicial activism'. However, none of the courts exceeded their powers. Instead, they left it to the legislator to decide *how* to remedy the identified violation of human or fundamental rights.

Yet, while litigation holds great chances, it is important to note that it is quite limited as a form of self-government. Unlike voting, litigation is expensive. This excludes many people, particularly people in the Global South, from accessing the courts. Moreover, lawsuits can address the problem of climate justice only to a very limited degree. For example, CCL directed against governments in the Global South would make those pay for mitigation or adaptation measures that have not caused climate change in the first place.

It is not as democratic: litigation only represents the interpretations of the (few) litigants engaged in a single lawsuit. It cannot be measured whether their lawsuit would enjoy public support, particularly if the consequences of a decision are likely to have major impacts on the daily lives of citizens, for example, in the form of CO_2 taxes or speed limits. Even where people would like to have access to the courts, they can be denied such access: In many countries, there is no free and independent judiciary, and it can be dangerous for plaintiffs to fight for environmental protection in court against powerful political and economic interests. Environmentalists are among the most vulnerable activists and are threatened, tortured and killed for their causes in many countries.[6]

An increase in "backlash" litigation may diminish the judicial success activists have fought for. Investor-state settlements and cases belonging to the category of so-called "just transition" litigation may dismantle or delay climate action. In times of the ongoing Russian war of aggression against Ukraine and the resulting inflation, many people are demanding that climate protection should not be a

---

[6] According to a report of the NGO Global Witness, over 1.700 environmental activists were killed during the last decade, see Global Witness, 'Decade of Defiance: Ten Years of Reporting Land and Environmental Activism Worldwide' (2022).

burden on the purse, making it difficult for governments to implement aggressive and far-reaching climate-regulating measures.[7]

As an enforcement tool, litigation depends on political will. Litigation can, at best, push more or less willing states to comply with their international climate obligations. The NGO Dejusticia, for example, claims that the Colombian government had done nothing to stop deforestation and that rates of deforestation were even reaching new peaks after the Supreme Court's judgement in *Future Generations*.[8] The effectiveness of litigation is limited because states can refuse to comply with judicial decisions (which, however, is not a problem of environmental lawsuits alone).

Nevertheless, it can also be seen as a forum through which the environmental rule of law can be strengthened. Most governments respect decisions issued by their apex courts. The German government raised its climate target for 2030 from a 55 to a 65% GHG reduction compared to 1990 levels and decided to achieve climate neutrality by 2045 instead of 2050.[9] While the Dutch government appealed the first decision through all instances, it is now complying with the Supreme Court's judgement and aims to achieve a 25% reduction of GHG emissions by, inter alia, limiting livestock, scaling back coal and providing subsidies for homeowners to use plant-based materials instead of concrete.[10] From Urgenda's perspective, however, these measures are not ambitious enough or have not been efficiently implemented, and they announced that they will go back to court to demand penalties from the state for non-compliance.[11]

CCL can only complement regulatory efforts, but it cannot substitute them. Large-scale measures that are much needed to effectively address climate change, including a change in the attitude towards climate change, cannot be imposed by the courts. Litigation can only set small sections of the frame for a politically

---

[7] UNEP, 'Global Climate Litigation Report (2023 Status Review)' (2023) 70 ff.

[8] Dejusticia, '¿Qué le hace falta al gobierno para implementar la sentencia contra el cambio climático y la deforestación?' (2 December 2020) < https://www.dejusticia.org/que-le-hace-falta-al-gobierno-para-implementar-la-sentencia-contra-el-cambio-climatico-y-la-deforestacion/ > accessed 31 August 2023.

[9] 'Germany Sets Ambitious New Carbon Emissions Target' *Financial Times* (5 May 2021) < https://www.ft.com/content/75956e41-57b1-4c55-981e-aec7a21560a0 > accessed 31 August 2023.

[10] 'Dutch Officials Reveal Measures to Cut Emissions after Court Ruling' *The Guardian* (24 April 2020) < https://www.theguardian.com/world/2020/apr/24/dutch-officials-reveal-measures-to-cut-emissions-after-court-ruling > accessed 31 August 2023.

[11] 'Urgenda Opnieuw Naar Rechter in Klimaatzaak, Nu Om Dwangsom Te Eisen van Staat' *NOS News* (27 June 2021) < https://nos.nl/artikel/2386855-urgenda-opnieuw-naar-rechter-in-klimaatzaak-nu-om-dwangsom-te-eisen-van-staat > accessed 31 August 2023.

constituted world society that makes individuals the front and centre of IL. This requires the inclusion and participation of both individuals acquiring subject status in IL *and* nation-states. Litigation, therefore, offers one (not *the*) opportunity for the pluralistic and open society to articulate its interpretations. Deliberation in both domestic and international courts can be understood as one (again, not *the*) way for non-state actors to participate meaningfully in the processes of deciding on climate policies and strengthening the global environmental rule of law. This, in consequence, can densify the quantity and quality of international climate law and thus, shaping and fostering global climate constitutionalism 'from below'. Non-state actors as constitutional interpreters are part of an international 'open society of constitution-makers'.[12]

[12] Peter Häberle, *Ein afrikanisches Verfassungs- und Lesebuch – mit vergleichender Kommentierung* (Duncker & Humblot 2019) 257.

Bibliography

Abate R and Kronk EA, 'Commonality among Unique Indigenous Communities: An Introduction to Climate Change and Its Impacts on Indigenous Peoples' (2013) 26 Tulane Environmental Law Journal 179

Abate RS, *Climate Change and the Voiceless* (CUP 2019)

Abbott BV, 'Amicus Curiae', *Dictionary of terms and phrases used in American or English jurisprudence* (Little, Brown, and Company 1879) 62

Abi-Saab G, 'Are We Heading for a New Normativity in the International Community? Contribution to the Discussion', *Change and Stability in International Law-Making* (de Gruyter 1988)

Ackerman B, 'Constitutional Politics/Constitutional Law' (1989) 99 The Yale Law Journal 453

Ackerman B, *We the People: Foundations* (Belknap Press 1991)

Ackerman B, 'The Living Constitution (2006 Oliver Wendell Holmes Lectures)' (2007) 120 Harvard Law Review 1737

Ackerman F and Gallagher K, 'Getting the Prices Wrong: The Limits of Market-Based Environmental Policy' [2000] Global Development and Environment Institute Working Paper 00–05

Adelman S, 'Rethinking Human Rights: The Impact of Climate Change on the Dominant Discourse' in Stephen Humphreys (ed), *Human Rights and Climate Change* (CUP 2009)

Agius E, 'Intergenerational Justice' in Jörg Chet Tremmel (ed), *Handbook of Intergenerational Justice* (Edward Elgar Publishing 2006)

Aguila Y and Viñuales JE, 'A Global Pact for the Environment: Conceptual Foundations' (2019) 28 Review of European, Comparative and International Environmental Law 3

Albrecht G, 'Expert Report (Case Milbrodale Progress Association v Minister for Planning and Infrastructe, Land and Environmental Court of New South Wales)' (2012)

Albrecht G, 'Solastalgia: The Distress Caused by Environmental Change' (2007) 15 Australasian Psychiatry

Aleinikoff TA, 'Thinking Outside the Sovereignty Box: Transnational Law and the U.S. Constitution' (2004) 82 Texas Law Review 1989

Alexy R, *A Theory of Constitutional Rights* (OUP 2002)

Allott P, 'Reconstituting Humanity – New International Law' (1992) 3 European Journal of International Law 219

M. Niehaus, *Global Climate Constitutionalism "from below"*,
https://doi.org/10.1007/978-3-658-43191-4

Allott P, 'The Concept of International Law' in Michael Byers (ed), *The Role of Law in International Politics: Essays in International Relations and International Law* (OUP 2001)

Allott P, 'The Emerging Universal Legal System' (2001) 3 International Law Forum du droit international 12

Allott P, 'Interpretation — An Exact Art' in Andrea Bianchi, Daniel Peat and Matthew Windsor (eds), *Interpretation in International Law* (OUP 2015)

Alvarado PAA and Rivas-Ramírez D, 'A Milestone in Environmental and Future Generations' Rights Protection: Recent Legal Developments before the Colombian Supreme Court' (2018) 30 Journal of Environmental Law 519

Ambrusné ÉT, 'The Parliamentary Commissioner for Future Generations of Hungary and His Impact' (2010) 10 Intergenerational Justice Review 18

Anastaplo G, 'Constitutionalism and the Good: Explorations' (2003) 70 Tennessee Law Review 738

Anderson GW, 'Societal Constitutionalism, Social Movements, and Constitutionalism from Below' (2013) 20 Indiana Journal of Global Legal Studies 881

Anderson K and Rieff D, '"Global Civil Society": A Sceptical View' in Helmut Anheier, Marlies Glasius and Mary Kaldor (eds), *Global Civil Society* (Sage Publications 2005)

Anderson RJ, 'Theoretical Approaches to Global Regulation of Transnational Corporations' in Alice de Jonge and Roman Tomasic (eds), *Research Handbook on Transnational Corporations* (Edward Elgar Publishing 2017)

Armstrong D and Gilson J, 'Introduction: Civil Society and International Governance' in David Armstrong and others (eds), *Civil Society and International Governance. The Role of Non-State Actors in Global and Regional Regulatory Frameworks* (Routledge 2011)

Asafo D, 'The Racism in Climate Change Law: Critiquing the Law on Climate Change-Related Displacement with Critical Race Theory' (2021) 39 Berkeley Journal of International Law 249

Atapattu S, 'Environmental Justice, Climate Justice and Constitutionalism: Protecting Vulnerable States and Communities' in Jordi Jaria-Manzano and Susana Borràs (eds), *Research Handbook on Global Climate Constitutionalism* (Edward Elgar Publishing 2019)

Atilgan A, *Global Constitutionalism* (Springer 2018)

Baatz C, 'Climate Change and Individual Duties to Reduce GHG Emissions' (2014) 17 Ethics, Policy and Environment 1

Backer LC, 'Theocratic Constitutionalism: An Introduction to a New Global Legal Ordering' (2009) 16 Indiana Journal of Global Legal Studies 85

Bäckstrand K, 'Democratizing Global Environmental Governance? Stakeholder Democracy after the World Summit on Sustainable Development' (2006) 12 European Journal of International Relations 467

Baer P, 'International Justice' in John S Dryzek, Richard B Norgaard and David Schlosberg (eds), *Oxford Handbook of Climate Change and Society* (OUP 2011)

Baer P, 'Greenhouse Development Rights: A Framework For Climate Protection That Is "More Fair" Than Equal Per Capita Emissions Rights' in Stephen M Gardiner and others (eds), *Climate Ethics: Essential Readings* (OUP 2010)

Bailey S and Mattei U, 'Social Movements as Constituent Power: The Italian Struggle for the Commons' (2013) 20 Indiana Journal of Global Legal Studies 965

Barak A, *Purposive Interpretation in Law* (Princeton University Press 2005)
Barak A, *Proportionality: Constitutional Rights and Their Limitations* (CUP 2012)
Barak A, 'On Judging' in Martin Scheinin, Helle Krunke and Marina Aksenova (eds), *Judges as Guardians of Constitutionalism and Human Rights* (Edward Elgar Publishing 2016)
Barendrecht M and others, 'Rulejungling – When Lawmaking Goes Private, International and Private' (2012) <https://www.hiil.org/wp-content/uploads/2018/09/Rulejungling-When-lawmaking-goes-private-international-and-informal.pdf>
Barnett MN and Finnemore M, 'The Politics, Power, and Pathologies of International Organizations' (1999) 53 International Organization 699
Barnett RE, 'A Ninth Amendment for Today's Constitution' (1991) 26 Valparaiso University Law Review 419
Barritt E and Sediti B, 'The Symbolic Value of Leghari v Federation of Pakistan: Climate Change Adjudication in the Global South' (2019) 30 King's Law Journal 203
Barry B, 'Sustainability and Intergenerational Justice' (1997) 89 A Journal of Social and Political Theory 43
Baude W and Sachs SE, 'The Law of Interpretation' (2017) 130 Harvard Law Review 1079
Bayertz K, 'Four Uses of "Solidarity"' in Kurt Bayertz (ed), *Solidarity* (Kluwer Academic Publishers 1999)
Beck U, *World at Risk* (Polity Press 2008)
Beckerman W, 'The Impossibility of a Theory of Intergenerational Justice' in Joerg Chet Tremmel (ed), *Handbook of Intergenerational Justice* (Edward Elgar Publishing 2006)
Beckerman W and Pasek J, *Justice, Posterity, and the Environment* (OUP 2003)
Beckman L and Page EA, 'Perspectives on Justice, Democracy and Global Climate Change' (2008) 17 Environmental Politics 527
Beijerman M, 'Conceptual Confusions in Debating the Role of NGOs for the Democratic Legitimacy of International Law' (2018) 9 Transnational Legal Theory 147
Beijerman M, 'Practice What You Preach? Limitations to Imposing Democratic Norms on NGOs' (2018) 20 International Community Law Review 3
Beitz CR, *Political Theory and International Relations* (Princeton University Press 1979)
Beitz CR, 'Rawls's Law of Peoples' (2000) 110 Ethics 669
Bellamy R, *Political Constitutionalism: A Republican Defence of the Constitutionality of Democracy* (CUP 2007)
Bellavia JM, 'What Does Climate Justice Look Like for the Environmentally Displaced in a Post Paris Agreement Environment? Political Questions and Court Deference to Climate Science in the Urgenda Decision' (2016) 4 Denver Journal of International Law and Policy 453
Benhabib S, 'Twilight of Sovereignty or the Emergence of Cosmopolitan Norms? Rethinking Citizenship in Volatile Times' (2007) 11 Citizenship Studies 19
Benjamin AH, 'We, the Judges, and the Environment' (2011) 29 Pace Environmental Law Review 582
Benvenisti E, 'Reclaiming Democracy: The Strategic Uses of Foreign and International Law by National Courts' (2008) 102 The American Journal of International Law 241
Benvenisti E, 'Sovereigns As Trustees of Humanity: On the Accountability of States To Foreign Stakeholders' (2013) 107 The American Journal of International Law 295
Benvenisti E and Downs GW, 'National Courts, Domestic Democracy, and the Evolution of International Law' (2009) 20 European Journal of International Law 59

Berger R, 'The Ninth Amendment' (1980) 66 Cornell Law Review 1

Berman PS, 'The Globalisation of Jurisdiction' (2002) 151 University of Pennsylvania Law Review 311

Berman PS, 'A Pluralist Approach to International Law' (2007) 32 Yale Journal of International Law 301

Berman PS, 'Global Legal Pluralism' (2007) 80 Southern California Law Review 1155

Berman PS, 'The New Legal Pluralism' (2009) 5 Annual Review of Law and Social Science 225

Berman PS, *Global Legal Pluralism – A Jurisprudence of Law beyond Borders* (CUP 2012)

Berman PS, 'The Limits of Sovereigntist Territoriality' in Paul Schiff Berman (ed), *Global Legal Pluralism – A Jurisprudence of Law beyond Borders* (2012)

Berman PS, 'Universalism and Its Discontents' in Paul Schiff Berman (ed), *Global Legal Pluralism – A Jurisprudence of Law beyond Borders* (2012)

Berman PS, 'The Evolution of Global Legal Pluralism' in Roger Cotterrell and Maksymilian del Mar (eds), *Authority in Transnational Legal Theory: Theorising Across Disciplines* (Edward Elgar Publishing 2016)

Berner K, 'Authentic Interpretation in Public International Law' (2016) 76 Zeitschrift für ausländisches öffentliches Recht und Völkerrecht 845

Besson S, 'Institutionalizing Global Demoi-Cracy' in Lukas H Meyer (ed), *Legitimacy, Justice and Public International Law* (CUP 2009)

Besson S, 'Whose Constitution(s)? International Law, Constitutionalism, and Democracy' in Jeffrey L Dunoff and Joel P Trachtman (eds), *Ruling the World? Constitutionalism, International Law and Global Government* (CUP 2009)

Besson S, 'Sovereignty, International Law and Democracy' (2011) 22 European Journal of International Law 373

Bexell M and others, 'Democracy in Global Governance: The Promises and Pitfalls of Transnational Actors' (2010) 16 Global Governance 81

Beyerlin U, 'The Role of NGOs in International Environmental Litigation' (2001) 81 Zeitschrift für ausländisches öffentliches Recht und Völkerrecht 356

Bhullar L, 'REDD+ and the Clean Development Mechanism: A Comparative Perspective' [2013] International Journal of Rural Law and Policy

Bianchi A, 'Globalization of Human Rights: The Role of Non-State Actors' in Gunther Teubner (ed), *Global Law without a State* (Dartmouth Publishing 1997)

Bianchi A, 'The Game of Interpretation in International Law' in Andrea Bianchi, Daniel Peat and Matthew Windsor (eds), *Interpretation in International Law* (OUP 2015)

Biber E, 'Law in the Anthropocene Epoch' (2017) 106 Georgetown Law Journal 1

Bieber R and Kotzur M, 'Strukturprinzipen der EU-Verfassung' in Roland Bieber and others (eds), *Die Europäische Union* (14th edn, Nomos 2020)

Biermann F, 'New Actors and Mechanisms of Global Governance' in John S Dryzek, Richard B Norgaard and David Schlosberg (eds), *Oxford Handbook of Climate Change and Society* (OUP 2011)

Biermann F, *Earth System Governance* (MIT Press 2014)

Birnbacher D, 'What Motivates Us to Care for the (Distant) Future?' in Axel Gosseries and Lukas H Meyer (eds), *Intergenerational Justice* (OUP 2009)

Bjorge E, *The Evolutionary Interpretation of Treaties* (OUP 2014)

Bjorge E, 'The Convergence Methods of Treaty Interpretation: Different Regimes, Different Methods of Interpretation?' in Mads Adenas and Eirik Bjorge (eds), *A Farewell to Fragmentation* (CUP 2015)

Bjorge E, 'The Vienna Rules, Evolutionary Interpretation, and the Intentions of the Parties' in Andrea Bianchi, Daniel Peat and Matthew Windsor (eds), *Interpretation in International Law* (OUP 2015)

Black J, 'Constructing and Contesting Legitimacy and Accountability in Polycentric Regulatory Regimes' (2008) 2 Regulation & Governance 137

Blokker P, 'Constitutional Mobilization and Contestation in the Transnational Sphere' (2018) 45 Journal of Law and Society S52

Blokker P and Thornhill C, 'Sociological Constitutionalism: An Introduction' in Paul Blokker and Chris Thornhill (eds), *Sociological Constitutionalism* (CUP 2017)

Blumm MC and Wood MC, '"No Ordinary Lawsuit": Climate Change, Due Process, and the Public Trust Doctrine' (2017) 67 American University Law Review 1

Bodansky D, 'The Legitimacy of International Governance: A Coming Challenge for International Environmental Law' (1999) 93 The American Journal of International Law 596

Bodansky D, 'Is There an International Environmental Constitution?' (2009) 16 Indiana Journal of Global Legal Studies 565

Bodansky D, Brunnée J and Rajamani L, *International Climate Change Law* (OUP 2017)

Bogdandy A Von, Goldmann M and Venzke I, 'From Public International to International Public Law: Translating World Public Opinion into International Public Authority' (2017) 28 The European Journal of International Law 115

Bolintineanu A, 'Expression of Consent to Be Bound by a Treaty in the Light of the 1969 Vienna Convention' (1974) 68 American Journal of International Law 672

Bolton JR, 'Should We Take Global Governance Seriously?' (2000) 1 Chicago Journal of International Law 205

Bourdieu P, 'The Force of Law: Toward a Sociology of the Juridical Field' (1987) 7 Hastings Law Journal 805

Bouwer K, 'The Unsexy Future of Climate Change Litigation' (2018) 30 Journal of Environmental Law 483

Boyd D, *The Environmental Rights Revolution: A Global Study of Constitutions, Human Rights, and the Environment* (UBC Press 2011)

Boyd DR, 'The Constitutional Right to a Healthy Environment' (2012) 54 Environment: Science and Policy for Sustainable Development 3

Boyle A, 'Environment and Human Rights', *Max Planck Encyclopedia of Public International Law* (OUP 2009)

Boyle A and Chinkin C, *The Making of International Law* (OUP 2007)

Boysen S, 'Entgrenzt – pluralistisch – reflexiv – polyzentrisch – kontestiert: Das Transnationale am transnationalen Klimaschutzrecht' (2018) 29 Zeitschrift für Umweltrecht 643

Branca D, 'Humanity in/of the Anthropocene: An Anthropological Perspective' in Elizabeth G Dobbins, Maria Lucia Piga and Luigi Manca (eds), *Environment, Social Justice, and the Media in the Age of the Anthropocene* (Lexington 2020)

Brandom RB, 'Some Pragmatist Themes in Hegel's Idealism: Negotiation and Administration in Hegel's Account of the Structure and Content of Conceptual Norms' (1999) 7 European Journal of Philosophy 164

Breunung L and Nocke J, 'Environmental Officers: A Viable Concept for Ecological Management?' in Gunther Teubner, Lindsay Farmer and Declan Murphy (eds), *Environmental Law and Ecological Responsibility. The Concept and Practice of Self-Organization* (Wiley 1994)

Brienen RJW and others, 'Long-Term Decline of the Amazon Carbon Sink' (2015) 519 Nature 344

Brock G, *Global Justice: A Cosmopolitan Account* (OUP 2009)

Brown GW, 'The Constitutionalization of What?' (2012) 1 Global Constitutionalism 201

Brown Weiss E, *In Fairness to Future Generations: International Law, Common Patrimony, and Intergenerational Equity* (Transnational Publishers/United Nations University 1989)

Brown Weiss E, 'In Fairness To Future Generations and Sustainable Development' (1992) 8 American University International Law Review 19

Brown Weiss E, 'Climate Change, Intergenerational Equity, and International Law' (2008) 9 Vermont Journal of Environmental Law 615

Brown Weiss E, 'International Law in a Kaleidoscopic World' (2011) 1 Asian Journal of International Law 21

Brown Weiss E, 'Nature and the Law: The Global Commons and the Common Concern of Humankind' [2014] Sustainable Humanity, Sustainable Nature: Our Responsibility. Pontifical Academy of Sciences, Extra Series 41 1

Brugger W, 'Legal Interpretation, Schools of Jurisprudence, and Anthropology: Some Remarks from a German Point of View' (1994) 2 The American Journal of Comparative Law 395

Brulle RJ, 'Habermas and Green Political Thought: Two Roads Converging' (2002) 11 Environmental Politics 1

Brunkhorst H, *Solidarität. Von der Bürgerfreundschaft zur globalen Rechtsgenossenschaft* (Suhrkamp 2002)

Brunkhorst H, 'Die Legitimationskrise der Weltgesellschaft. Global Rule of Law, Global Constitutionalism und Weltstaatlichkeit' in Mathias Albert and Rudolf Stichweh (eds), *Weltstaat und Weltstaatlichkeit* (VS Verlag für Sozialwissenschaften 2007)

Brunkhorst H, 'Constitutionalism and Democracy in the World Society' in Petra Dobner and Martin Loughlin (eds), *The Twilight of Constitutionalism?* (OUP 2010)

Brunnée J, 'Common Areas, Common Heritage, and Common Concern' in Daniel Bodansky, Jutta Brunnée and Ellen Hey (eds), *The Oxford Handbook of International Environmental Law* (OUP 2008)

Brunner RD and Lynch AH, *Adaptive Governance and Climate Change* (American Meteorological Society 2010)

Buchanan A, 'Rawls's Law of Peoples: Rules for a Vanished Westphalian World' (2000) 110 Ethics 697

Bui NS, 'Global Constitutionalism: Asia-Pacific Perspectives' (2021) 10 Global Constitutionalism 221

Bull H, *The Anarchical Society: A Study of Order in World Politics* (4th edn, Red Globe Press 2012)

Bumke C and Voßkuhle A, *German Constitutional Law: Introduction, Cases, and Principles* (OUP 2019)

Burgers L, 'Should Judges Make Climate Change Law?' (2020) 9 Transnational Environmental Law 55

Burgers L and Staal T, 'Climate Action as Positive Human Rights Obligation: The Appeals Judgment in Urgenda v The Netherlands' [2019] Amsterdam Law School Legal Studies Research Paper No. 2019–01

Busch A and Jakobi T, 'Die Erfindung eines neuen Grundrechts. Zu Konzept und Auswirkungen der „informationellen Selbstbestimmung"' in Christoph Hönnige, Sascha Kneip and Astrid Lorenz (eds), *Verfassungswandel im Mehrebenensystem* (VS Verlag für Sozialwissenschaften 2011)

'BVerfG: Anwendung der §§ 569a, 569b BGB auf nichteheliche Lebensgemeinschaften (German Federal Constitutional Court, Judgement of 3 April 1990 – 1 BvR 1186/89)' [1990] Neue Juristische Wochenschrift 1593

Çalı B, 'Specialized Rules of Treaty Interpretation: Human Rights' in Duncan B Hollis (ed), *The Oxford Guide to Treaties* (OUP 2012)

Calliess G-P, 'Reflexive Transnational Law' (2016) 23 Zeitschrift für Rechtssoziologie 185

Cançado Trindade AA, *International Law for Humankind: Towards a New Jus Gentium* (3rd edn, Brill/Martinus Nijhoff Publishers 2020)

Caney S, 'Cosmopolitan Justice, Responsibility, and Global Climate Change' (2005) 18 Leiden Journal of International Law 747

Caney S, 'Human Rights, Responsibilities, and Climate Change' in Charles R Beitz and Robert E Godin (eds), *Global Basic Rights* (OUP 2009)

Caney S, 'Cosmopolitanism and the Environment' in Teena Gabrielson and others (eds), *The Oxford Handbook of Environmental Political Theory* (OUP 2016)

Cardoso FH, 'We the Peoples: Civil Society, the United Nations and Global Governance – Report of the Panel of Eminent Persons on United Nations–Civil Society Relations (Cardoso Report)' (2004)

Carducci M and others, 'Towards an EU Charter of the Fundamental Rights of Nature (Study for the European Economic and Social Committee)' (2019)

Cassese A, 'Gathering Up the Main Threads' in Antonio Cassese (ed), *Realizing Utopia: The Future of International Law* (OUP 2012)

Cassese A, 'The Martens Clause: Half a Loaf or Simply Pie in the Sky?' (2018) 11 The Development and Principles of International Humanitarian Law 373

Chambers S, 'Deliberative Democratic Theory' (2003) 6 Annual Review of Political Science 307

Charney J, 'Universal International Law' (1993) 87 The American Journal of International Law 529

Charnovitz S, 'Two Centuries of Participation: NGOs and International Governance' (1997) 18 Michigan Journal of International Law 183

Charnovitz S, 'Nongovernmental Organizations and International Law' (2006) 100 The American Journal of International Law 348

Chynoweth P, 'Legal Research' in Andrew Knight and Les Ruddock (eds), *Advanced Research Methods in the Built Environment* (Wiley-Blackwell 2008)

Cicero MT, *De Republica* (Georg Heinrich Moser ed, 1826)

Clark AM, 'Non-Governmental Organizations and Their Influence on International Society' (1995) 48 Journal of International Affairs 507

Cobb R, Ross JK and Ross MH, 'Agenda Building as a Comparative Political Process' (1976) 70 American Political Science Review 126

Coelho IM, 'As idéias de Peter Häberle e a abertura da interpretação constitucional no direito brasileiro' (1998) 35 Revista de Informação Legislativa 157

Cohen J, 'Democracy and Liberty' in Jon Elster (ed), *Deliberative Democracy* (CUP 1998)

Cohen JL, 'Whose Sovereignty? Empire Versus International Law' (2004) 3 Ethics & International Affairs 1

Cohen JL, *Globalization and Sovereignty: Rethinking Legality, Legitimacy, and Constitutionalism* (CUP 2012)

Collings J, *Democracy's Guardians: A History of the German Federal Constitutional Court, 1951–2001* (OUP 2015)

Commission on Global Governance, 'Our Global Neighbourhood' (OUP 1995)

Committee on the Rights of the Child, 'Draft General Comment No. 26 – Children's Rights and the Environment with a Special Focus on Climate Change'

Copetti R and Miranda MA de, 'Autodeterminação informativa e proteção de dados: Uma ánalise crítica da jurisprudência brasileira (Informational Self-Determination and Data Protection: A Critical Analysis of the Brazilian Jurisprudence)' (2015) 1 Revista de Direito, Governança e Novas Tecnologias 28

Corbridge Å, 'Responding To Doxing in Australia: Towards a Right To Informational Self-Determination?' (2018) 3 UniSA Student Law Review 1

Correa-Ordoñez A and Mandakovic S, 'Report: A Guide to Filing Amicus Curiae Briefs in Latin America' (2014)

Corry TO, 'Global Civil Society and Its Discontents' (2006) 17 Voluntas: International Journal of Voluntary and Nonprofit Organizations 303

Corsi G, 'A Bottom-up Approach to Climate Governance: The New Wave of Climate Change Litigation' [2017] ICCG Reflection No. 57 1

Cottier T and Hertig M, 'The Prospects of 21st Century Constitutionalism' (2003) 7 Max Planck UNYB 261

Council of Europe, *Manual on Human Rights and the Environment* (2nd edn, 2012)

Coventry P and Okereke C, 'Climate Change and Environmental Justice' in Ryan Holifield, Jayajit Chakraborty and Gordon Walker (eds), *The Routledge Handbook of Environmental Justice* (Routledge 2017)

Cover RM, 'The Supreme Court, 1982 Term – Foreword: Nomos and Narrative' (1983) 97 Harvard Law Review 4

Cover RM, 'Violence and the Word' (1986) 95 The Yale Law Journal 1601

Covey Jr. F, 'Amicus Curiae: Friend of the Court' (1959) 9 DePaul Law Review

Craig P, 'Constitutions, Constitutionalism, and the European Union' (2001) 7 European Law Journal 125

Crawford J, 'A Consensualist Interpretation of Article 31(3) of the Vienna Convention on the Law of Treaties' in Georg Nolte (ed), *Treaties and Subsequent Practice* (OUP 2013)

Crawford J, 'Foreword' in Eirik Bjorge (ed), *The Evolutionary Interpretation of Treaties* (OUP 2014)

Cullinan C, *Wild Law: A Manifesto for Earth Justice* (2nd edn, Siber Ink 2011)

Curtis CP, 'A Better Theory of Legal Interpretation' (1950) 3 Vanderbilt Law Review 407

D'Aspremont J, 'The Foundations of the International Legal Order' (2009) 18 Finnish Yearbook of International Law 219

Dahl RA, 'Can International Organizations Be Democratic? A Skeptic's View' in Ian Shapiro and Casiano Hacker-Cord6n (eds), *Democracy's Edges* (CUP 1999)

Daly E and May JR, 'Global Environmental Constitutionalism: A Rights-Based Primer for Effective Strategies', *Elgar Encyclopedia of Environmental Law: Decision Making in Environmental Law (Vol. II)* (2017)

Davies G, 'Climate Change and Reversed Intergenerational Equity: The Problem of Costs Now, for Benefits Later' (2020) 10 Climate Law 266

Davies K and others, 'The Declaration on Human Rights and Climate Change: A New Legal Tool for Global Policy Change' (2017) 8 Journal for Human Rights and the Environment 217

Day R, 'A Capabilities Approach to Environmental Justice' in Ryan Holifield, Jayajit Chakraborty and Gordon Walker (eds), *The Routledge Handbook of Environmental Justice* (Routledge 2017)

de Castro D, 'The Colonial Aspects of International Environmental Law: Treaties as Promoters of Continuous Structural Violence' (2017) 5 Groningen Journal of International Law 168

de Castro PC, 'The Judgment in the Case Concerning the Gabčíkovo-Nagymaros Project: Positive Signs for the Evolution of International Water Law' (1997) 8 Yearbook of International Environmental Law 21

de George R, 'The Environment, Rights, and Future Generations' in Ernest Partridge (ed), *Responsibilities to future generations: environmental ethics* (Prometheus Books 1981)

de Graaf KJ and Jans JH, 'The Urgenda Decision: Netherlands Liable for Role in Causing Dangerous Global Climate Change' (2015) 27 Journal of Environmental Law 517

de Terwangne C, 'The Right to Be Forgotten and Informational Autonomy in the Digital Environment' in Alessia Ghezzi, Ângela Guimarães Pereira and Lucia Vesnić-Alujević (eds), *The Ethics of Memory in a Digital Age* (Palgrave Macmillan 2014)

de Wet E, 'The Emergence of International and Regional Value Systems as a Manifestation of the Emerging International Constitutional Order' (2006) 19 Leiden Journal of International Law 611

De Wet E, 'The International Constitutional Order' (2006) 55 International and Comparative Law Quaterly 51

Devaney L and others, 'Ireland's Citizens' Assembly on Climate Change: Lessons for Deliberative Public Engagement and Communication' (2020) 14 Environmental Communication 141

Diggelmann O and Altwicker T, 'Is There Something Like a Constitution of International Law? A Critical Analysis of the Debate on World Constitutionalism' (2008) 68 Zeitschrift für ausländisches öffentliches Recht und Völkerrecht 623

Dobner P, 'More Law, Less Democracy? Democracy and Transnational Constitutionalism' in Petra Dobner and Martin Loughlin (eds), *The Twilight of Constitutionalism?* (OUP 2010)

Dobson A, *Citizenship and the Environment* (OUP 2003)

Dobson A, 'Environmental Citizenship: Towards Sustainable Development' (2007) 15 Sustainable Development 276

Donnelly J, 'The Virtues of Legalization' in Saladin Meckled-García and Başak Çalı (eds), *The Legalization of Human Rights: Multidisciplinary Perspectives on Human Rights and Human Rights Law* (Routledge 2006)

Dörr O, 'The Strasbourg Approach to Evolutionary Interpretation' in Georges Abi-Saab and others (eds), *Evolutionary Interpretation and International Law* (Hart Publishing 2019)

Dryzek JS, *Deliberative Democracy and Beyond* (OUP 2000)

Dryzek JS, 'Deliberative Democracy', *Encyclopedia of Political Theory* (Sage Publications 2010)
du Plessis A, 'The Promise of "Well-Being" in Section 24 of the Constitution of South Africa' (2018) 34 South African Journal on Human Rights 191
Du Plessis L, 'Legal Academics and the Open Community of Constitutional Interpreters' (1996) 12 South African Journal on Human Rights 214
Dunoff JL and Trachtman JP, 'A Functional Approach to International Constitutionalization' in Jeffrey L Dunoff and Joel P Trachtman (eds), *Ruling the world? Constitutionalism, International Law, and Global Governance* (CUP 2009)
Dupuy P-M, 'Evolutionary Interpretation of Treaties: Between Memory and Prophecy' in Enzo Cannizzaro (ed), *The Law of Treaties Beyond the Vienna Convention* (OUP 2011)
Durkheim E, *The Division of Labor in Society (1933)* (4th edn, The Macmillan Company 1960)
Duvic-Paoli LA, 'Re-Imagining the Making of Climate Law and Policy in Citizens' Assemblies' (2022) 11 Transnational Environmental Law 235
Dworkin R, *Taking Rights Seriously* (Duckworth 1977)
Dworkin R, *Law's Empire* (Belknap Press 1986)
Dziedzic A, 'Foreign Judges of the Pacific as Agents of Global Constitutionalism' (2021) 10 Global Constitutionalism 351
Ebbesson J, 'Public Participation' in Daniel Bodansky, Jutta Brunnée and Ellen Hey (eds), *The Oxford Handbook of International Environmental Law* (OUP 2008)
ECtHR, 'Environment and the European Convention on Human Rights (Factsheet)' (2021) <http://www.echr.coe.int/Documents/FS_Environment_ENG.pdf> accessed 31 August 2023
ECtHR, 'Climate Change (Factsheet)' (2023) <https://www.echr.coe.int/documents/d/echr/FS_Climate_change_ENG> accessed 31 August 2023
Ehmke H, 'Prinzipien der Verfassungsinterpretation', *Prinzipien der Verfassungsinterpretation. Gefährdungshaftung im öffentlichen Recht: Aussprache zu den Berichten in den Verhandlungen der Tagung der deutschen Staatsrechtslehrer zu Freiburg vom 4. bis 7. Oktober 1961* (De Gruyter 1971)
Ehrlich E, *Fundamental Principles of the Sociology of Law* (Harvard University Press 1936)
Ehs T, 'Horizontgericht – Das Politische in der Verfassungsgerichtsbarkeit' in Martin Möllers and Robert van Ooyen (eds), *Verfassungs-Kultur. Staat, Europa und pluralistische Gesellschaft bei Peter Häberle* (Nomos 2016)
Eisgruber CL, *Constitutional Self-Government* (Harvard University Press 2001)
Ekardt F and Lessmann V, 'EuGH, EGMR und BVerfG: Die dritte Gewalt im transnationalen Mehrebenensystem' [2006] Kritische Justiz 381
Elster J, 'Introduction' in Jon Elster (ed), *Deliberative Democracy* (CUP 1998)
Ely JH, *Democracy and Distrust: A Theory of Judicial Review* (Harvard University Press 1980)
Emmerich-Fritsche A, *Vom Völkerrecht zum Weltrecht* (Duncker & Humblot 2007)
Engels A and others, 'Hamburg Climate Futures Outlook 2023 – The Plausibility of a 1.5°C Limit to Global Warming' (2023)
Engle EA, 'The Transformation of the International Legal System: The Post-Westphalian Legal Order' (2004) 23 Quinnipiac Law Review

Epiney A, 'The Role of NGOs in the Process of Ensuring Compliance with MEAs' in Ulrich Beyerlin, Peter-Tobias Stoll and Rüdiger Wolfrum (eds), *Ensuring Compliane with Multilateral Environmental Agreements: Academic Analysis and Views from Practice* (2006)

Esty DC, 'Non-Governmental Organizations at the World Trade Organization: Cooperation, Competition, or Exclusion' (1998) 1 Journal of International Economic Law 124

Esty DC, 'Bridging the Trade-Environment Divide' (2001) 15 Journal of Economic Perspectives 113

Etty T and others, 'The Maturing of Transnational Environmental Law' (2017) 6 Transnational Environmental Law 193

Etty T and others, 'Transnational Climate Law' (2018) 7 Transnational Environmental Law 191

Fajardo T, 'Environmental Principles and General Principles of International Law' in Ludwig Krämer and Emanuela Orlando (eds), *Elgar Encyclopedia of Environmental Law: Principles of Environmental Law (Vol. VI)* (Edward Elgar Publishing 2018)

Falk R and Strauss A, 'Toward Global Parliament' (2001) 80 Foreign Affairs 212

Falk RA, *The Role of Domestic Courts in the International Legal Order* (Syracuse University Press 1964)

Farber DA and Peeters M, 'The Emergence of Global Climate Law' in Michael G Faure (ed), *Elgar Encyclopedia of Environmental Law: Climate Change Law (Vol. I)* (Edward Elgar Publishing 2015)

Fassbender B, 'Sovereignty and Constitutionalism in International Law' in Neil Walker (ed), *Sovereignty in Transition* (Hart 2003)

Feris L, 'Constitutional Environmental Rights' (2008) 24 South African Journal on Human Rights 29

Feris L, 'Loss of Sense of Place as Displacement – New Frontiers for Environmental Rights' in Erin Daly and others (eds), *New Frontiers in Environmental Constitutionalism* (UNEP 2017)

Figueroa RM, 'Indigenous Peoples and Cultural Losses' in John S Dryzeck, Richard B Norgaard and David Schlossberg (eds), *The Oxford Handbook of Climate Change and Society* (OUP 2011)

Finnemore M and Sikkink K, 'International Norm Dynamics and Political Change' (1998) 52 International Organization 887

Fischer-Lescano A, 'Globalverfassung: Los desaparecidos und das Paradox der Menschenrechte' (2002) 23 Zeitschrift für Rechtssoziologie 217

Fischer-Lescano A, 'Die Emergenz der Globalverfassung' (2003) 63 Zeitschrift für ausländisches öffentliches Recht und Völkerrecht 717

Fischer-Lescano A, *Globalverfassung – Die Geltungsbegründung der Menschenrechte* (Velbrück 2005)

Fischer-Lescano A, 'Global Constitutional Struggles: Human Rights between Colère Publique and Colère Politique' in Wolfgang Kaleck and others (eds), *International Prosecution of Human Rights Crimes* (Springer 2007)

Fischer-Lescano A and Teubner G, 'Regime-Collisions: The Vain Search for Legal Unity in the Fragmentation of Global Law' (2004) 25 Michigan Journal of International Law 999

Fischer-Lescano A and Teubner G, 'Fragmentierung des Weltrechts: Vernetzung globaler Regimes statt etatistischer Rechtseinheit' in Mathias Albert and Rudolf Stichweh (eds), *Weltstaat und Weltstaatlichkeit* (VS Verlag für Sozialwissenschaften 2007)

Fitzmaurice M, 'Responsibility and Climate Change' (2010) 53 German Yearbook of International Law 89

Florczak-Wątor M, *Judicial Law-Making in European Constitutional Courts* (Routledge 2020)

Forsthoff E, *Der Staat der Industriegesellschaft* (CH Beck 1971)

Foster K, 'Lex Sportiva and Lex Ludica: The Court Of Arbitration for Sport's Jurisprudence' (2005) 3 The Entertainment and Sports Law Journal 2

Foster SR, 'Vulnerability, Equality and Environmental Justice' in Ryan Holifield, Jayajit Chakraborty and Gordon Walker (eds), *The Routledge Handbook of Environmental Justice* (Routledge 2017)

Franzius C, 'Das Recht auf Informationelle Selbstbestimmung' [2015] ZJS 259

Franzius C, 'Klimaschutz im Anthropozän' (2019) 17 Zeitschrift für Europäisches Umwelt- und Plannungsrecht 498

Fraser N, 'From Redistribution to Recognition? Dilemmas of Justice in a "Postsocialist" Age' in Steven Seidman and Jeffrey C Alexander (eds), *The new Social Theory Reader* (Routledge 2001)

Fromme FK, 'Ein Neues Grundrecht Ist Erfunden' *Frankfurter Allgemeine Zeitung* (17 December 1983) 12

Fuchs C, 'Environment, Role of Non-Governmental Organizations', *Max Planck Encyclopedias of International Law* (OUP 2009)

Fuchs M-C and Theisen L, 'Nature – A Legal Subject' [2021]

Fuller LL, 'The Forms and Limits of Adjudication' (1978) 92 Harvard Law Review 353

Funk N, 'Habermas and the Social Goods' (1987) 18 Social Text 19

Gach E, 'Normative Shifts in the Global Conception of Climate Change: The Growth of Climate Justice' (2019) 8 Social Sciences

Galligan D, *Law in Modern Society* (OUP 2006)

Gamper A, 'Constitutional Courts and Judicial Law-Making: Why Democratic Legitimacy Matters' (2015) 4 Cambridge International Law Journal 423

Gamper A, 'Dangerous or Endangered Constitutional Courts? A View from among and within the Branches of Power' (2021) 76 Zeitschrift für öffentliches Recht 331

Ganguly G, Setzer J and Heyvaert V, 'If at First You Don't Succeed: Suing Corporations for Climate Change' (2018) 38 Oxford Journal of Legal Studies 841

Gao Q and Whittaker S, 'Standing to Sue beyond Individual Rights: Who Should Be Eligible to Bring Environmental Public Interest Litigation in China?' (2019) 8 Transnational Environmental Law 327

Gardbaum S, 'Human Rights and International Constitutionalism' in Jeffrey L Dunoff and Joel P Trachtman (eds), *Ruling the World? Constitutionalism, International Law and Global Government* (CUP 2009)

Gardiner R, 'The Vienna Convention Rules on Treaty Interpretation' in Duncan B Hollis (ed), *The Oxford Guide to Treaties* (OUP 2012)

Gardiner R, *Treaty Interpretation* (2nd edn, OUP 2015)

Germanwatch e.V., 'Global Climate Risk Index 2020'

Germanwatch e.V., 'Global Climate Risk Index 2021'

Giabardo CV, 'Climate Change Litigation, State Responsibility and the Role of Courts in the Global Regi' in Barbara Pozzo and Valentia Jacometti (eds), *Environmental Loss and Damage in a Comparative Law Perspective* (Intersentia 2021)

Global Witness, 'Decade of Defiance: Ten Years of Reporting Land and Environmental Activism Worldwide' (2022)

Gomula J, 'Environmental Disputes in the WTO' in Malgosia Fitzmaurice, David M Ong and Panos Merkouris (eds), *Research Handbook on International Environmental Law* (Edward Elgar Publishing 2010)

Gonzalez CG, 'Environmental Justice and International Environmental Law' in Alam Shawkat and others (eds), *Routledge Handbook of International Environmental Law* (Routledge 2012)

Gonzalez CG, 'Global Justice in the Anthropocene' in Louis J Kotzé (ed), *Environmental Law and Governance for the Anthropocene* (Hart/Bloomsbury Publishing 2017)

Gordijn B and ten Have H, 'Ethics of Mitigation, Adaptation and Geoengineering' (2012) 15 Medicine, Health Care and Philosophy 1

Gough I and Meadowcroft J, 'Decarbonizing the Welfare State' in John S Dryzek, Richard B Norgaard and David Schlosberg (eds), *Oxford Handbook of Climate Change and Society* (OUP 2011)

Gould CG, *Interactive Democracy. The Social Roots of Global Justice* (CUP 2014)

Gould SJ, *Hen's Teeth and Horse's Toes: Further Reflections in Natural History* (WW Norton & Company 1984)

Gourgourinis A, 'The Distinction between Interpretation and Application of Norms in International Adjudication' (2011) 2 Journal of International Dispute Settlement 31

Green MS, 'Legal Realism as Theory of Law' (2005) 46 William & Mary Law Review 1915

Griffiths J, 'What Is Legal Pluralism?' (1986) 18 Journal of Legal Pluralism and Unofficial Law 1

Grimm D, 'Integration by Constitution' (2005) 3 International Journal of Constitutional Law 193

Grimm D, *Constitutionalism. Past, Present, and Future* (OUP 2016)

Gross L, 'States as Organs of International Law and the Problem of Autointerpretation', *Essays on International Law and Organization* (Springer 1984)

Gunderson R, 'Global Environmental Governance Should Be Participatory: Five Problems of Scale' (2018) 33 International Sociology 715

Günther F, 'Wer beeinflusst hier wen? Die westdeutsche Staatsrechtslehre und das Bundesverfassungsgericht während der 1950er und 1960er Jahre' in Robert Chr van Ooyen and Martin HW Möllers (eds), *Handbuch Bundesverfassungsgericht im politischen System* (2nd edn, Springer VS 2015)

Gupta J, van der Leeuw K and de Moel H, 'Climate Change: A "Glocal" Problem Requiring "Glocal" Action' (2007) 4 Environmental Sciences 139

Gutmann A and Thompson D, *Democracy and Disagreement* (Belknap Press 1996)

Haas PM, 'Introduction: Epistemic Communities and International Policy Coordination' (1992) 46 International Organization 1

Haas PM, 'Epistemic Communities and International Environmental Law', *Epistemic Communities, Constructivism, and International Environmental Politics* (Routledge 2015)

Häberle P, 'Grundrechte im Leistungsstaat' (1972) 30 VVDStRL 7

Häberle P, 'Zeit und Verfassung: Prolegomena zu einem "zeit-gerechten" Verfassungsverständnis' (1974) 21 Zeitschrift für Politik 111

Häberle P, 'Die offene Gesellschaft der Verfassungsinterpreten: Ein Beitrag zur pluralistischen und „prozessualen" Verfassungsinterpretation' (1975) 30 Juristenzeitung 297

Häberle P, 'Demokratische Verfassungstheorie im Lichte des Möglichkeitsdenkens' (1977) 102 Archiv des öffentlichen Rechts 27

Häberle P, 'Verfassungsinterpretation als öffentlicher Prozeß – Ein Pluralismuskonzept (1978)', *Verfassung als öffentlicher Prozeß: Materialien zu einer Verfassungstheorie der offenen Gesellschaft* (1st edn, Duncker & Humblot 1978)

Häberle P, 'Verfassungsinterpretation und Verfassunggebung (Berner Gastvortrag 1977)', *Verfassung als öffentlicher Prozeß: Materialien zu einer Verfassungstheorie der offenen Gesellschaft* (Duncker & Humblot 1978)

Häberle P, *Die Verfassung des Pluralismus* (Athenäum 1980)

Häberle P, 'Grundrechte und parlamentarische Gesetzgebung im Verfassungsstaat – Das Beispiel des deutschen Grundgesetzes' (1989) 114 Archiv des öffentlichen Rechts 361

Häberle P, *Verfassung als öffentlicher Prozess. Materialien zu einer Verfassungsheorie der Offenen Gesellschaft* (3rd edn, Duncker & Humblot 1998)

Häberle P, *Verfassungslehre als Kulturwissenschaft* (2nd edn, Duncker & Humblot 1998)

Häberle P, 'A Constitutional Law for Future Generations – the "Other" Form of the Social Contract: The Generation Contract' in Jörg Tremmel (ed), *Handbook of Intergenerational Justice* (Edward Elgar Publishing 2006)

Häberle P, 'Universaler Konstitutionalismus aus nationalen und völkerrechtlichen Teilverfassungen – Sieben Thesen' in Peter Häberle (ed), *Jahrbuch des Öffentlichen Rechts der Gegenwart* (Mohr Siebeck 2014)

Häberle P, 'Verfassungsgerichtsbarkeit in der offenen Gesellschaft' in Robert Chr van Ooyen and Martin HW Möllers (eds), *Handbuch Bundesverfassungsgericht im politischen System* (2nd edn, Springer VS 2015)

Häberle P, 'Fundamental Rights in the Welfare State. Second Co-Report of Professor Dr. Peter Häberle, Marburg on Lahn' in Markus Kotzur (ed), *Peter Häberle on Constitutional Theory* (Nomos/Hart 2018)

Häberle P, 'The Jurisprudence of European Law – Viewed as a Cultural Study' in Markus Kotzur (ed), *Peter Häberle on Constitutional Theory: Constitution as Culture and the Open Society of Constitutional Interpreters* (Nomos/Hart 2018)

Häberle P, '"The Open Society of Constitutional Interpreters" – A Contribution to a Pluralistic and "Procedural" Constitutional Interpretation (1975)' in Markus Kotzur (ed), *Peter Häberle on Constitutional Theory* (Nomos/Hart 2018)

Häberle P, 'The Rationale of Constitutions from a Cultural Science Viewpoint' in Markus Kotzur (ed), *Peter Häberle on Constitutional Theory* (Nomos/Hart 2018)

Häberle P, *Ein Afrikanisches Verfassungs- und Lesebuch – Mit vergleichender Kommentierung* (Duncker & Humblot 2019)

Häberle P and Kotzur M, *Europäische Verfassungslehre* (8th edn, Nomos 2016)

Habermas J, 'Justice and Solidarity: On the Discussion Concerning "Stage 6"' (1989) 21 The Philosophical Forum 32

Habermas J, 'Further Reflections on the Public Sphere' in Craig Calhoun (ed), *Habermas and the Public Sphere* (MIT Press 1992)

Habermas J, *Between Facts and Norms: Contributions to a Discourse Theory of Law and Democracy* (Polity Press 1996)

Habermas J, 'Deliberative Politics: A Procedural Concept of Democracy' in Jürgen Habermas (ed), *Between Facts and Norms: Contributions to a Discourse Theory of Law and Democracy* (Polity Press 1997)

Habermas J, *The Inclusion of the Other* (Pablo De Greiff and Ciaran Cronin eds, Polity Press 1998)

Habermas J, 'Remarks on Legitimation through Human Rights' in Jürgen Habermas and Max Pensky (eds), *The Postnational Constellation: Political Essays* (Polity Press 2001)

Habermas J, 'Remarks on Legitimation through Human Rights' in Jürgen Habermas (ed), *The Postnational Constellation: Political Essays* (MIT Press 2001)

Habermas J, 'The Postnational Constellation and the Future of Democracy' in Jürgen Habermas and Max Pensky (eds), *The Postnational Constellation: Political Essays* (Polity Press 2001)

Habermas J 'On Law and Disagreement. Some Comments on "Interpretative Pluralism"' (2003) 16 Ratio Juris 187

Habermas J, 'Hat die Konstitutionalisierung des Völkerrechts noch eine Chance?' in Jürgen Habermas (ed), *Der gespaltene Westen* (Suhrkamp 2004)

Habermas J, 'Euroskepticism, Market Europe, or a Europe of (World) Citizens?' in Jürgen Habermas, Ciaran Cronin and Max Pensky (eds), *Time of Transitions* (Polity Press 2006)

Habermas J, 'A Political Constitution for the Pluralist World Society?' in Jürgen Habermas (ed), *Between Naturalism and Religion: Philosophical Essays* (Polity Press 2008)

Habermas J, 'The Constitutionalization of International Law and the Legitimation Problems of a Constitution for World Society' (2008) 15 Constellations 444

Habermas J, 'The Concept of Human Dignity and the Realistic Utopia of Human Rights' (2010) 41 Metaphilosophy 464

Hailbronner M, 'Hierarchical Authority in German Constitutional Law: The Constitutional Court between Law and Politics', *Traditions and Transformations. The Rise of German Constitutionalism* (2015)

Halberstam D, 'Constitutional Heterarchy: The Centrality of Conflict in the European Union and the United States' in Jeffrey L Dunoff and Joel P Trachtman (eds), *Ruling the world? Constitutionalism, International Law, and Global Governance* (CUP 2011)

Hall C, 'A Right Most Dear: The Case for a Constitutional Environmental Right' (2016) 30 Tulane Environmental Law Journal 85

Haltern U, 'Internationales Verfassungsrecht? Anmerkungen zu einer kopernikanischen Wende' (2003) 128 Archiv des öffentlichen Rechts 511

Hammersley M, 'The Right to a Healthy and Stable Climate: Fundamental or Unfounded?' (2016) 7 Arizona Journal of Environmental Law and Policy 117

Harlow C, 'Global Administrative Law: The Quest for Principles and Values' (2006) 17 The European Journal of International Law 187

Harris MR, 'Environmental Deliberative Democracy and the Search for Administrative Legitimacy: A Legal Positivism Approach' (2011) 44 University of Michigan Journal of Law Reform 343

Harris PG, *World Ethics and Climate Change: From International to Global Justice* (Edinburgh University Press 2010)

Hart HLA, 'Positivism and the Separation of Law and Morals' (1958) 71 Harvard Law Review 593

Hart HLA, *The Concept of Law* (Clarendon Press 1961)

Hassan P and Azfar A, 'Securing Environmental Rights Through Public Interest Litigation in South Asia' (2004) 22 Virginia Environmental Law Journal 215

Hasson R, Löfgren Å and Visser M, 'Climate Change in a Public Goods Game: Investment Decision in Mitigation versus Adaptation' (2010) 70 Ecological Economics 331

Hassoun N and Herlitz A, 'Climate Change and Inequity: How to Think about Inequities in Different Dimensions' in Ravi Kanbur and Henry Shue (eds), *Climate Justice: Integrating Economics and Philosophy* (OUP 2018)

Havercroft J and others, 'Decolonising Global Constitutionalism' (2020) 9 Global Constitutionalism 1

Hayward T, 'Human Rights Versus Emissions Rights: Climate Justice and the Equitable Distribution of Ecological Space' (2007) 21 Ethics and International Affairs 431

Heede R, 'Tracing Anthropogenic Carbon Dioxide and Methane Emissions to Fossil Fuel and Cement Producers, 1854–2010' (2014) 122 Climatic Change 229

Held D, *Democracy and the Global Order: From the Modern State to Cosmopolitan Governance* (Polity Press 1995)

Held D, 'Democratic Accountability and Political Effectiveness from a Cosmopolitan Perspective' (2004) 39 Government and Opposition 364

Held V, *The Ethics of Care: Personal, Political, and Global* (OUP 2006)

Hennig Leal MC, 'As audiências públicas no âmbito do Supremo Tribunal Federal brasileiro: Uma nova forma de participação?' (2014) 19 Novos Estudos Jurídicos 327

Hennig Leal MC and Müller Bittencourt C, 'Jurisdição constitucional aberta: Democratizando interpretação constitucional para a sociedade pluralista com a proposta hermenêutica de Peter Häberle' in Clovis Gorczevski and Jorge Renato dos Reis (eds), *Constitucionalismo Contemporâneo* (Norton 2008)

Henríquez-Prieto MF and Miranda-Nigro P, 'Amicus Curiae and Ecosystem Services: On Public Interest Interventions to Help Resolve Environmental Controversies' (2018) 36 Journal of Energy and Natural Resources Law 209

Heun W, *The Constitution of Germany – A Contextual Analysis* (Hart Publishing 2011)

Heußner H, 'Datenverarbeitung und die Rechtsprechung des Bundesverfassungsgerichts im Spannungsfeld zwischen Recht und Politik' (1985) 33 Arbeit und Recht 309

Heyd D, 'Justice and Solidarity: The Contractarian Case against Global Justice' (2007) 38 Journal of Social Philosophy 112

Heyd D, 'A Value or an Obligation? Rawls on Justice to Future Generations' in Axel Gosseries and Lukas H Meyer (eds), *Intergenerational Justice* (OUP 2009)

Heyd D, 'Climate Ethics, Affirmative Action, and Unjust Enrichment' in Lukas H Meyer and Pranay Sanklecha (eds), *Climate Justice and Historical Emissions* (CUP 2017)

Heyne L, 'Globalisierung und Demokratie – Führt Denationalisierung zu einem Verlust an Demokratiequalität?' in Wolfgang Merkel (ed), *Demokratie und Krise – Zum schwierigen Verhältnis von Theorie und Empirie* (Springer VS 2015)

Heyvaert V, 'The Transnationalization of Law: Rethinking Law through Transnational Environmental Regulation' (2017) 6 Transnational Environmental Law 205

Heyvaert V and Duvic-Paoli L-A, *Research Handbook on Transnational Environmental Law* (Veerle Heyvaert and Leslie-Anne Duvic-Paoli eds, Edward Elgar Publishing 2020)

Heyvaert V and Etty T, 'Introducing Transnational Environmental Law' (2012) 1 Transnational Environmental Law 1
Hilson C, 'Law, Courts and Populism: Climate Change Litigation and the Narrative Turn' in Susan Sterett and Lee Walker (eds), *Research Handbook on Law and Courts* (Edward Elgar Publishing 2019)
Hilson CJ, 'Environmental SLAPPs in the UK: Threat or Opportunity?' (2016) 25 Environmental Politics 248
Hirschl R, 'The Judicialization of Politics' in E Goodin (ed), *The Oxford Handbook of Political Science* (OUP 2011)
Hiskes RP, 'Reflexive Reciprocity and Intergenerational Environmental Justice', *The Human Right to a Green Future* (CUP 2008)
Hiskes RP, *The Human Right to a Green Future: Environmental Rights and Intergenerational Justice* (CUP 2008)
Hobe S, 'Non-Governmental Organizations', *Max Planck Encyclopedias of International Law* (OUP 2010)
Hoffmann-Riem W, 'Informationelle Selbstbestimmung in der Informationsgesellschaft – Auf dem Wege zu einem neuen Konzept des Datenschutzes' (1998) 123 Archiv des öffentlichen Rechts 513
Höfling W, *Offene Grundrechtsinterpretation* (Duncker & Humblot 1987)
Hollis DB, 'Interpretation and International Law' [2015] Legal Studies Research Paper Series, No. 42
Hollis DB, 'The Existential Function of Interpretation in International Law' in Andrea Bianchi, Daniel Peat and Matthew Windsor (eds), *Interpretation in International Law* (OUP 2015)
Holmes OW, 'Law in Science and Science in Law' (1899) 13 Harvard Law Review 443
Horstmann B and Hein J, 'Aligning Climate Change Mitigation and Sustainable Development under the UNFCCC: A Critical Assessment of the Clean Development Mechanism, the Green Climate Fund and REDD+' (2017)
Houck OA, *Taking Back Eden: Eight Environmental Cases That Changed the World* (Island Press 2010)
Human Rights Committee, 'General Comment No. 36 (2018) on Article 6 of the International Covenant on Civil and Political Rights, on the Right to Life – (CCPR/C/GC/36)' (2018)
Huntington SP, 'The Clash of Civilizations?' (1993) 72 Foreign Affairs 22
Iacovino A, 'Constitucionalismo ecológico en América Latina: De los derechos ambientales a los derechos de La naturaleza' (2020) 31 Cultura Latinoamericana 266
IBGE, 'Censo demográfico 2010' (2011)
ILC, 'Draft Articles on the Law of Treaties with Commentaries' (1966) 2 Yearbook of the International Law Commission 187
ILC, 'Report of the Study Group of the International Law Commission (Finalized by Martti Koskenniemi) on "Fragmentation of International Law: Difficulties Arising from the Diversification and Expansion of International Law" (A/CN.4/L.682)' (2006)
ILC, 'Draft Articles on the Law of Transboundary Aquifers (Report of the International Law Commission on the Work of Its Sixtieth Session, UN Doc. A/CN.4/L.724)' (2008)
ILO, 'Greening with Jobs' (2018)
Indigenous People's Global Summit on Climate Change, 'The Anchorage Declaration' (2009)

International Bar Association, 'Achieving Justice and Human Rights in an Era of Climate Disruption' (2014)
IPCC, 'Climate Change – Impacts, Adaptation, and Vulnerability (Working Group II, Summary for Policymakers)' (2014)
IPCC, 'Climate Change 2014 Synthesis Report' (2015)
IPCC, 'Special Report on Global Warming of 1.5°C' (2018)
IPCC, 'Summary for Policymakers of IPCC Special Report on Global Warming of 1.5°C'
IPCC, 'Special Report: The Ocean and Cryosphere in a Changing Climate – Summary for Policymakers'
IPCC, 'Sixth Assessment Report' (2023)
Isensee J, *Wer definiert die Freiheitsrechte?* (CF Müller Juristischer Verlag 1980)
Isensee J, 'Grundrechte und Demokratie' (1981) 20 Der Staat 161
Jacob M, 'Lawmaking Through International Adjudication' (2011) 12 German Law Journal 1005
Jacobs FG, 'Varieties of Approach to Treaty Interpretation: With Special Reference to the Draft Convention on the Law of Treaties before the Vienna Diplomatic Conference' (1969) 18 International and Comparative Law Quarterly 318
Jakab A, 'Problems of the Stufenbaulehre: Kelsen's Failure to Derive the Validity of a Norm from Another Norm' (2007) 20 Canadian Journal of Law and Jurisprudence 35
Jaria-Manzano J, 'Law in the Anthropocene' in Jordi Jaria-Manzano and Susana Borràs (eds), *Research Handbook on Global Climate Constitutionalism* (Edward Elgar Publishing 2019)
Jaria-Manzano J and Borràs S, 'Introduction to the Research Handbook on Global Climate Constitutionalism' in Jordi Jaria-Manzano and Susana Borràs (eds), *Research Handbook on Global Climate Constitutionalism* (Edward Elgar Publishing 2019)
Jaria-Manzano J and Borràs S, *Research Handbook on Global Climate Constitutionalism* (Jordi Jaria-Manzano and Susana Borràs eds, Edward Elgar Publishing 2019)
Jellinek W, *Allgemeine Staatslehre* (O Härig 1914)
Jendrośka J and Reese M, 'The Courts as Guardians of the Environment – New Developments in Access to Justice and Environmental Litigation' in Jonathan Isted (ed), *Environment & Climate Change 2019 (International Comparative Legal Guides)* (Global Legal Group 2019)
Jenks CW, 'The Conflict of Law-Making Treaties' (1953) 30 Brit. Y.B. Int'l L. 401
Jhering R von, *The Struggle for Law (Translated from the Fifth German Edition)* (2nd edn, Callaghan and Company 1915)
Johnston K, 'Public Governance: The Government of Non-State Actors in "Partnerships"' (2015) 35 Public Money and Management 15
Johnstone I, 'Treaty Interpretation: The Authority of Interpretive Communities' (1990) 12 Michigan Journal of International Law 371
Johnstone I, 'The Power of Interpretive Communities' in Michael Barnett and Raymond Duval (eds), *Power in Global Governance* (CUP 2005)
Kadelbach S and Kleinlein T, 'International Law – A Constitution for Mankind?' (2007) 50 German Yearbook of International Law 2
Kahl V, 'Ökologische Revolution am Interamerikanischen Gerichtshof für Menschenrechte – Besprechung des Rechtsgutachtens Nr.23 „Umwelt und Menschenrechte" (OC-23/17)' (2019) 17 Zeitschrift für Europäisches Umwelt- und Plannungsrecht 110

Kant I, *Project for a Perpetual Peace: A Philosophical Essay. Translated from the German* (Vernor & Hood 1796)

Kant I, *The Metaphysic of Morals, Vol. I* (1799)

Kant I, *The Metaphysics of Morals* (Lara Denis ed, CUP 2017)

Kassoti E, 'Beyond State Consent? International Legal Scholarship and the Challenge of Informal International Law-Making' (2016) 63 Netherlands International Law Review 99

Kassoti E, 'The Constitutionalization of International Law and the Challenge of Non-State Actors' (2017) 11 ICL Journal 177

Kay R, 'Adherence to the Original Intentions in Constitutional Adjudication: Three Objections and Responses' (1987) 82 Northwestern University Law Review 226

Keller H and Grover L, 'General Comments of the Human Rights Committee and Their Legitimacy' in Helen Keller and Geir Ulfstein (eds), *UN Human Rights Treaty Bodies: Law and Legitimacy* (CUP 2012)

Kelsen H, 'Wesen und Entwicklung der Staatsgerichtsbarkeit', *Verhandlungen der Tagung der Deutschen Staatsrechtslehrer zu Wien am 23. und 24. April 1928* (De Gruyter 1929)

Kelsen H, *Pure Theory of Law. Translation from the Second (Revised and Enlarged) German Edition* (University of California Press 2005)

Kelsen H, *The Essence and Value of Democracy (1920)* (Nadia Urbinati and Carlo Invernizzi Accetti eds, Rowmann and Littlefield Publishers 2013)

Kelsey Cascadia Rose Juliana et al. v United States, 'First Amendment Complaint for Declaratory and Injunctive Relief (Case No. 6:15-Cv-01517-TC)'

Kennedy D, 'One, Two, Three, Many International Legal Orders: Legal Pluralism and the Cosmopolitan Dream' (2008) 31 N.Y.U. Review of Law & Social Change 641

Kennedy D, 'The Mystery of Global Governance' in Jeffrey L Dunoff and Joel P Trachtman (eds), *Ruling the world? Constitutionalism, International Law, and Global Governance* (CUP 2009)

Keohane RO and Victor DG, 'The Regime Complex for Climate Change' (2011) 9 Perspectives on Politics 7

Kim H, 'An Extension of Rawls's Theory of Justice for Climate Change' (2019) 11 International Theory 160

Kim RE and Bosselmann K, 'International Environmental Law in the Anthropocene: Towards a Purposive System of Multilateral Environmental Agreements' (2013) 2 Transnational Environmental Law 285

Kim RE and Bosselmann K, 'Operationalizing Sustainable Development: Ecological Integrity as a Grundnorm of International Law' (2015) 24 Review of European, Comparative and International Environmental Law 194

Kirchhof P, 'Kompetenzaufteilung zwischen den Mitgliedstaaten der EU' in Vertretung der Europäischen Kommission in der Bundesrepublik Deutschland (ed), *Europäische Gespräche 2/94. Europäisches Forum: Die künftige Verfassungsordnung der Europäischen Union* (1994)

Kiss A and Shelton D, *Guide to International Environmental Law* (Martinus Nijhoff Publishers 2007)

Kissling C, 'The Evolution of CSO's Legal Status in International Governance and Its Relevance for the Legitimacy of International Organizations' in Jens Steffek, Claudia Kissling and Patrizia Nanz (eds), *Civil Society Participation in European and Global Governance* (Palgrave Macmillan 2008)

Klabbers J, 'On Rationalism in Politics: Interpretation of Treaties and the World Trade Organization' (2005) 74 Nordic Journal of International Law 405

Klabbers J, 'Law-Making and Constitutionalism' in Jan Klabbers, Anne Peters and Geir Ulfstein (eds), *The Constitutionalization of International Law* (OUP 2009)

Klabbers J, 'Setting the Scene' in Jan Klabbers, Anne Peters and Geir Ulfstein (eds), *The Constitutionalization of International Law* (OUP 2009)

Klein RJT and others, 'Inter-Relationships between Adaptation and Mitigation' in Martin Parry and others (eds), *Climate Change 2007: Impacts, Adaptation and Vulnerability. Contributions of Working Group II to the Fourth Assessment Report of the Intergovernmental Panel on Climate Change* (CUP 2007)

Klein RJT, Midgley GF and Preston BL, 'Adaptation Opportunities, Constraints, and Limits' in Christopher B Field and others (eds), *Climate Change 2014: Impacts, Adaptation, and Vulnerability (Contributions of Working Group II to the Fifth Assessment Report of the Intergovernmental Panel on Climate Change)* (CUP 2014)

Kleinlein T, 'On Holism, Pluralism, and Democracy: Approaches to Constitutionalism beyond the State' (2010) 21 European Journal of International Law 1075

Kleinlein T, 'Non-State Actors from an International Constitutionalist Perspective' in Jean D'Aspremont (ed), *Participants in the International Legal System: Multiple Perspectives on Non-State Actors in International Law* (Routledge 2011)

Kleinlein T, 'Between Myths and Norms: Constructivist Constitutionalism and the Potential of Constitutional Principles in International Law' (2012) 81 Nordic Journal of International Law 79

Kleinlein T, *Konstitutionalisierung im Völkerrecht* (Springer 2012)

Klenert D and others, 'Five Lessons from COVID-19 for Advancing Climate Change Mitigation' (2020) 76 Environmental and Resource Economics 751

Knodel MS, 'Wet Feet Marching: Climate Justice and Sustainable Development for Climate Displaced Nations in the South Pacific' (2012) 14 Vermont Journal of Environmental Law 127

Kochevar S, 'Amici Curiae in Civil Law Jurisdictions' (2013) 122 Yale Law Journal 1653

Kodde C, 'Germany's "Right to Be Forgotten" – between the Freedom of Expression and the Right to Informational Self-Determination' (2016) 30 International Review of Law, Computers and Technology 17

Koh HH, 'Transnational Legal Process' (1996) 75 Nebraska Law Review 181

Koh HH, *The Trump Administration and International Law* (OUP 2018)

Kolb R, *Interprétation et Création Du Droit International* (Bruylant (Editions de l'Université de Bruxelles) 2006)

Kolb R, 'Is There a Subject-Matter Ontology in Interpretation of International Legal Norms?' in Mads Andenas and Eirik Bjorge (eds), *A Farewell to Fragmentation* (CUP 2015)

Koopmans R and Zürn M, 'Cosmopolitanism and Communitarianism – How Globalization Is Reshaping Politics in the Twenty-First Century' in Pieter de Wilde and others (eds), *The Struggle Over Borders: Cosmopolitanism and Communitarianism* (CUP 2019)

Korioth S, 'Rudolf Smend' in Arthur J Jacobson and Bernhard Schlink (eds), *Weimar: A Jurisprudence of Crisis* (University of California Press 2000)

Koskenniemi M, *From Apology to Utopia: The Structure of International Legal Argument* (CUP 2005)

Koskenniemi M, 'Constitutionalism as Mindset: Reflections on Kantian Themes about International Law and Globalization' (2006) 8 Theoretical Inquiries in Law 9
Koskenniemi M, 'Histories of International Law: Dealing with Eurocentrism' (2011) 19 Rechtsgeschichte 152
Koskenniemi M, *The Politics of International Law* (Hart Publishing 2011)
Kotzé LJ, 'A Global Environmental Constitution for the Anthropocene?' (2019) 8 Transnational Environmental Law 11
Kotzé LJ, 'Arguing Global Environmental Constitutionalism' (2012) 1 Transnational Environmental Law 199
Kotzé LJ, 'The Anthropocene's Global Environmental Constitutional Moment' (2015) 25 Yearbook of International Environmental Law 24
Kotzé LJ, 'The Conceptual Contours of Environmental Constitutionalism' (2015) 21 Widener Law Review 187
Kotzé LJ, *Global Environmental Constitutionalism in the Anthropocene* (Bloomsbury Publishing 2016)
Kotzé LJ, 'Global Environmental Constitutionalism in the Anthropocene' in Louis J Kotzé (ed), *Environmental Law and Governance for the Anthropocene* (Hart/Bloomsbury Publishing 2017)
Kotzé LJ, 'A Global Environmental Constitution for the Anthropocene's Climate Crisis' in Jordi Jaria-Manzano and Susana Borràs (eds), *Research Handbook on Global Climate Constitutionalism* (Edward Elgar Publishing 2019)
Kotzé LJ, 'A Global Environmental Constitution for the Anthropocene's Climate Crisis' [2019] Research Handbook on Global Climate Constitutionalism 50
Kotzé LJ and French D, 'A Critique of the Global Pact for the Environment: A Stillborn Initiative or the Foundation for Lex Anthropocenae?' (2018) 18 International Environmental Agreements: Politics, Law and Economics 811
Kotzé LJ and Muzangaza W, 'Constitutional International Environmental Law for the Anthropocene?' (2018) 27 Review of European, Comparative and International Environmental Law 278
Kotzur M, 'Wechselwirkungen zwischen europäischer Verfassungs- und Völkerrechtslehre' in Alexander Blankenagel, Ingolf Pernice and Helmuth Schulze-Fielitz (eds), *Verfassung im Diskurs der Welt. Liber Amicorum für Peter Häberle* (Mohr Siebeck 2004)
Kotzur M, 'Weltrechtliche Bezüge in nationalen Verfassungstexten' (2008) 39 Rechtstheorie 191
Kotzur M, 'Overcoming Dichotomies: A Functional Approach to the Constitutional Paradigm in Public International Law' (2012) 4 Goettingen Journal of International Law 585
Kotzur M, 'Constitutional Amendments and Constitutional Changes in Germany' in Xenophon Contiades (ed), *Engineering Constitutional Change* (Routledge 2013)
Kotzur M, '„Constitutional Moments" in globaler Perspektive – Eine noch zeitgemäße völkerrechtliche Spurensuche?' in Ewald Grothe and Arthur Schlegelmilch (eds), *Constitutional Moments* (Berliner Wissenschafts-Verlag 2019)
Kraemer K, *Die soziale Konstitution der Umwelt* (VS Verlag für Sozialwissenschaften 2008)
Krämer L and Orlando E, 'Introduction to Volume VI' in Ludwig Krämer and Emanuela Orlando (eds), *Elgar Encyclopedia of Environmental Law: Principles of Environmental Law (Vol. VI)* (Edward Elgar Publishing 2018)

Krasner SD, *Sovereignty: Organized Hypocrisy* (Princeton University Press 1999)

Krause P, 'Das Recht auf informationelle Selbstbestimmung – BVerfGE 65, 1' [1984] Juristische Schulung 268

Krisch N, *Beyond Constitutionalism: The Pluralist Structure of Postnational Law* (OUP 2010)

Krisch N, 'Who Is Afraid of Radical Pluralism? Legal Order and Political Stability in the Postnational Space' (2011) 24 Ratio Juris 386

Krisch N, 'Authority, Solid and Liquid, in Postnational Governance' in Roger Cotterrell and Maksymilian del Mar (eds), *Authority in Transnational Legal Theory: Theorising Across Disciplines* (Edward Elgar Publishing 2016)

Krisch N, 'Pouvoir Constituant and Pouvoir Irritant in the Postnational Order' (2016) 14 International Journal of Constitutional Law 657

Krislov S, 'The Amicus Curiae Brief: From Friendship to Advocacy' (1963) 72 Yale Law Journal 694

Krivenko EY, *Rethinking Human Rights and Global Constitutionalism* (CUP 2017)

Krunke H, 'Courts as Protectors of the People: Constitutional Identity, Popular Legitimacy and Human Rights' in Martin Scheinin, Helle Krunke and Marina Aksenova (eds), *Judges as Guardians of Constitutionalism and Human Rights* (Edward Elgar Publishing 2016)

Kuehn RR, 'A Taxonomy of Environmental Justice' (2000) 30 Environmental Law Reporter 10681

Kumar P, 'Review Essay: M. Kotzur (Ed.), Peter Häberle on Constitutional Theory: Constitution as Culture and the Open Society of Constitutional Interpreters. Baden- Baden, Germany: Nomos, 2018, 323 Pp., €84' (2019) 65 Indian Journal of Public Administration 769

Kumm M, 'The Cosmopolitan Turn in Constitutionalism: On the Relationship between Constitutionalism in and beyond the State' in Jeffrey L Dunoff and Joel P Trachtman (eds), *Ruling the World? Constitutionalism, International Law and Global Government* (CUP 2009)

Kumm M, 'The Cosmopolitan Turn in Constitutionalism: An Integrated Conception of Public Law' (2013) 20 Indiana Journal of Global Legal Studies 605

Kumm M, 'Constituent Power, Cosmopolitan Constitutionalism, and Post-Positivist Law' (2016) 14 International Journal of Constitutional Law 697

Kysar DA, 'Global Environmental Constitutionalism: Getting There from Here' (2012) 1 Transnational Environmental Law 83

Lachs M, 'The Threshold in Law-Making' in Rudolf Bernhardt and others (eds), *Völkerrecht als Rechtsordnung, Internationale Gerichtsbarkeit, Menschenrechte (FS f. Hermann Mosler)* (Springer 1983)

Lahav A, *In Praise of Litigation* (OUP 2017)

Lauterpacht H, 'De l'interprétation Des Traités' (1950) 43/1 Annuaire de l'Institut de Droit International 366

Lavrik M, Jimenez A and Vilela M, 'The Global Pact for the Environment As a Next Step on the Way Forward for the Earth Charter' 1

Lawrence P and Köhler L, 'Representation of Future Generations through International Climate Litigation: A Normative Framework' (2017) 60 German Yearbook of International Law 639

Lazarus RJ, 'Super Wicked Problems and Climate Change: Liberate the Future' (2009) 1234 Cornell Law Review 1153

Lehmann JA, 'The Right to Privacy in Germany' (1968) 1 N.Y.U. Journal of International Law and Politics
Leijten I, 'Human Rights v. Insufficient Climate Action: The Urgenda Case' (2019) 37 Netherlands Quarterly of Human Rights 112
Leite JRM and Ayala P de A, 'Global Environmental Constitutionalism as a Constitutionalism of the Earth' in Jordi Jaria-Manzano and Susana Borràs (eds), *Research Handbook on Global Climate Constitutionalism* (Edward Elgar Publishing 2019)
Leiter B, 'Positivism, Formalism, Realism. Review Essay on Anthony Sebok's "Legal Positivism in American Jurisprudence"' (1999) 99 Columbia Law Review 1138
Lemley MA, 'The Imperial Supreme Court' (2023) 136 Harvard Law Review 97
Levitt JK, 'A Bottom-up Approach to International Lawmaking: The Tale of Three Trade Finance Instruments' (2017) 30 The Globalization of International Law 125
Lewis B, 'Human Rights Duties towards Future Generations and the Potential for Achieving Climate Justice' (2016) 34 Netherlands Quarterly of Human Rights 206
Lhotta R, 'Die kinetische Verfassung: Verfassungstheorie und Verfassungsbegriff bei Peter Häberle und Rudolf Smend' in Martin Möllers and Robert van Ooyen (eds), *Verfassungs-Kultur. Staat, Europa und pluralistische Gesellschaft bei Peter Häberle* (Nomos 2016)
Lhotta R and Zucca-Soest S, 'Legitimation und Integration durch Verfassung in einem Mehrebenensystem' in Christoph Hönninge, Sascha Kneip and Astrid Lorenz (eds), *Verfassungswandel im Mehrebenensystem* (VS Verlag für Sozialwissenschaften 2011)
Lin J, 'Climate Change and the Courts' (2012) 32 Legal Studies 35
Lixinski L, 'Across the Public/Private International Legal Divide in the Governance of Global Public Goods' (2020) 47 Denver Journal of International Law and Policy 1
Lobel J, 'Courts as Forums for Protest' (2004) 52 UCLA Law Review 477
Lomborg B, *The Skeptical Environmentalist: Measuring the Real State of the World* (CUP 2001)
López T, 'Sociedad y Naturaleza. Contribuciones de la América profunda a la superación de la crisis' [2013] Herramienta Web 1
Loughlin M, 'What Is Constitutionalisation?' in Petra Dobner and Martin Loughlin (eds), *The Twilight of Constitutionalism?* (OUP 2010)
Loughlin M, 'Constitutional Pluralism: An Oxymoron?' (2014) 3 Global Constitutionalism 9
Lowman MK, 'The Litigating Amicus Curiae: When Does the Party Begin After the Friends Leave?' (1991) 41 American University Law Review 1243
Luhmann N, *Soziale Systeme* (Suhrkamp 1984)
Luhmann N, *Political Theory in the Welfare State* (de Gruyter 1990)
Luhmann N, *Das Recht der Gesellschaft* (Suhrkamp 1993)
Luhmann N, *Die Gesellschaft der Gesellschaft* (Suhrkamp 1997)
Luhmann N, *Law as a Social System (1993)* (Fatima Kastner and others eds, OUP 2004)
Luhmann N, *Ökologische Kommunikation (1986)* (4th edn, VS Verlag für Sozialwissenschaften 2004)
Luhmann N, 'Are There Still Indispensable Norms in Our Society?' (2008) 14 Soziale Systeme 18
Luhmann N, *Theory of Society (Vol. 2)* (Stanford University Press 2013)
Lutz DS, 'Thinking About Constitutionalism at the Start of the Twenty-First Century' (2000) 30 Publius: The Journal of Federalism 115

MacCormick N, *Questioning Sovereignty. Law, State, and Nation in the European Commonwealth* (OUP 1999)
Magallanes CI, 'Using Human Rights to Recognize Human Responsibilities toward Nature' in Erin Daly and others (eds), *New Frontiers in Environmental Constitutionalism* (UNEP 2017)
Maliska MA, 'Rezeption von Häberle in Brasilien. Die Brasilianische Verfassung im Kontext der internationalen Öffnung, Kooperation und Integration' in Martin Möllers and Robert van Ooyen (eds), *Verfassungs-Kultur. Staat, Europa und pluralistische Gesellschaft bei Peter Häberle* (Nomos 2016)
Maljean-Dubois S, 'Climate Change Litigation', *Max Planck Encyclopedia of International Procedural Law* (OUP 2018)
Malm A and Hornborg A, 'The Geology of Mankind? A Critique of the Anthropocene Narrative' (2014) 1 The Anthropocene Review 62
Maltz EM, 'Unenumerated Rights and Originalist Methodology: A Comment on the Ninth Amendment Symposium' (1988) 64 Chicago-Kent Law Review 981
Marauhn T, 'Changing Role of The State' in Daniel Bodansky, Jutta Brunnée and Ellen Hey (eds), *The Oxford Handbook of International Environmental Law* (OUP 2012)
Marjanac S and Patton L, 'Extreme Weather Event Attribution Science and Climate Change Litigation: An Essential Step in the Causal Chain?' (2018) 36 Journal of Energy and Natural Resources Law 265
Marjanac S, Patton L and Thornton J, 'Acts of God, Human Infuence and Litigation' (2017) 10 Nature Geoscience 616
Markell D and Ruhl JB, 'An Empirical Assessment of Climate Change in the Courts: A New Jurisprudence or Business as Usual' (2012) 64 Florida Law Review 15
Martens W, 'Democracy for Transnational Regimes' in Bas Leijssenaar, Judith Martens and Evert Van der Zweerde (eds), *Futures of Democracy* (Wilde Raven Publishing 2014)
Martens W, 'Demokratie für transnationale Regimes' in Kornelia Hahn and Andreas Langenohl (eds), *Kritische Öffentlichkeiten – Öffentlichkeiten in der Kritik* (Springer 2017)
Martinez JS, 'Horizontal Structuring' in Michel Rosenfeld and András Sajó (eds), *The Oxford Handbook of Comparative Constitutional Law* (OUP 2012)
Martinez JS, 'The Anti-Slavery Movement and the Rise of Non-Governmental Organizations' in Dinah Shelton (ed), *The Oxford Handbook of Human Rights Law* (OUP 2013)
Marx K, 'On the Jewish Question (1843)' in Robert Tucker (ed), *The Marx-Engels Reader* (Norton & Company 1978)
Maslow AH, 'A Theory of Human Motivation' (1943) 50 Psychological Review 370
Mattheis C, 'The System Theory of Niklas Luhmann and the Constitutionalization of the World Society' (2012) 4 Goettingen Journal of International Law 625
Mattheis C, *Die Konstitutionalisierung des Völkerrechts aus systemtheoretischer Sichtweise* (Springer 2018)
Maurer A, 'Transnationales Recht' in Lars Viellechner (ed), *Verfassung ohne Staat* (Nomos 2019)
Max-Planck-Institut für ausländisches öffentliches Recht und Völkerrecht, 'Tätigkeitsbericht für die Jahre 2012, 2013 und 2014' (2015)

May J and Daly E, 'Can the U.S. Constitution Encompass a Right to a Stable Climate? (Yes, It Can.)' (2021) 39 UCLA Journal of Environmental Law and Policy 39

May JR and Daly E, *Global Environmental Constitutionalism* (CUP 2014)

May JR and Daly E, 'The Nature of Environmental Constitutionalism', *Global Environmental Constitutionalism* (2014)

May JR and Daly E, *Judicial Handbook on Environmental Constitutionalism* (Law Division, UNEP Programme 2017)

May JR and Daly E, 'Global Climate Constitutionalism and Justice in the Courts' in Jordi Jaria-Manzano and Susana Borràs (eds), *Research Handbook on Global Climate Constitutionalism* (Edward Elgar Publishing 2019)

Mayer B, 'Interpreting States' General Obligations on Climate Change Mitigation: A Methodological Review' (2019) 28 Review of European, Comparative and International Environmental Law 107

Mayer B, 'The State of the Netherlands v. Urgenda Foundation: Ruling of the Court of Appeal of the Hague (9 October 2018)' (2019) 8 Transnational Environmental Law 167

Mayer B, 'The Contribution of Urgenda to the Mitigation of Climate Change' (2023) 35 Journal of Environmental Law 167

Mbengue MM, 'Non-State Actors in International Environmental Law. A Rousseauist Perspective' in Jean D'Aspremont (ed), *Participants in the International Legal System Multiple Perspectives on Non-State Actors in International Law* (Routledge 2011)

McCormick S and others, 'Strategies in and Outcomes of Climate Change Litigation in the United States' [2018] Nature Climate Change 1

McCrudden C, 'Human Dignity and Judicial Interpretation of Human Rights' (2008) 19 European Journal of International Law 655

McDonald J, 'A Risky Climate for Decision-Making: The Liability of Development Authorities for Climate Change Impacts' (2007) 24 Environmental and Planning Law Journal 405

McDougal MS, Reisman WM and Willard AR, 'World Community: A Planetary Social Process' (1987) 1 U.C. Davis Law Review 808

McNair AD, *The Law of Treaties* (Clarendon Press 1961)

McRae D, 'Evolutionary Interpretation: The Relevance of Context' in Georges Abi-Saab and others (eds), *Evolutionary Interpretation and International Law* (Bloomsbury Publishing 2019)

Mello C de, 'Discurso de saudação do Ministro Gilmar Ferreira Mendes na Posse na presidência do Supremo Tribunal Federal (Solemn Ministerial Address on the Occasion of the Official Inauguration of Gilmar Ferreira Mendes as President of the Supreme Federal Court)'

Mendes G, 'Homenagem à doutrina de Peter Häberle e sua influência no Brasil (Speech on the Occasion of the Award of an Honorary Doctorate to Prof. Häberle by the University of Brasilía)'

Mendes G, 'A influência de Peter Häberle no constitucionalismo brasileiro' (2016) 2 Journal of Institutional Studies 30

Mendes GF and do Vale AR, 'O pensamento de Peter Häberle na jurisprudência do Supremo Tribunal Federal' (2008) 2 Observatório da Jurisdição Constitucional

Merkl A, 'Das doppelte Rechtsantlitz' [1918] Juristische Blätter

Merkl A, *Die Lehre von der Rechtskraft entwickelt aus dem Rechtsbegriff* (Franz Deuticke 1923)
Merkouris P, '(Inter)Temporal Considerations in the Interpretative Process of the VCLT: Do Treaties Endure, Perdure or Exdure ?' (2014) 45 Netherlands Yearbook of International Law 121
Merkouris P, *Article 31(3)(c) VCLT and the Principle of Systemic Integration. Normative Shadows in Plato's Cave* (Brill/Martinus Nijhoff Publishers 2015)
Merry SE, 'Legal Pluralism' (1988) 22 Law and Society Reivew 869
Mertens H-J, 'Lex Mercatoria – A Self-Applying System Beyond National Law?' in Gunther Teubner (ed), *Global Law without a State* (Dartmouth Publishing 1997)
Michaels R, 'Global Legal Pluralism' (2009) 5 Annual Review of Law and Social Science 1
Michelman F, 'Law's Republic' (1988) 97 The Yale Law Journal 1493
Michelman FI, 'The Supreme Court, 1985 Term – Foreword: Traces of Self-Government' (1986) 100 Harvard Law Review 4
Michelman FI, 'Human Rights and the Limits of Constitutional Theory' (2000) 13 Ratio Juris 63
Michelman FI, 'The Constitution, Social Rights, and Liberal Political Justification' (2003) 1 International Journal of Constitutional Law 13
Mikosa Ž, 'Implementation of the Aarhus Convention through Actio Popularis' in Jerzy Jendrośka and Magdalena Bar (eds), *Procedural Environmental Rights: Principle X in Theory and Practice* (Intersentia 2017)
Mileva N and Fortuna M, 'Environmental Protection as an Object of and Tool for Evolutionary Interpretation' in Georges Abi-Saab and others (eds), *Evolutionary Interpretation and International Law* (Hart/Bloomsbury Publishing 2019)
Milewicz K, 'Emerging Patterns of Global Constitutionalization: Toward a Conceptual Framework' (2014) 16 Indiana Journal of Global Legal Studies 413
Miller D, *On Nationality* (Clarendon Press 1995)
Miller D, *Principles of Social Justice* (Harvard University Press 1999)
Miller D, 'Social Justice and Environmental Goods' in Andrew Dobson (ed), *Fairness and Futurity: Essays on Environmental Sustainability and Social Justice* (OUP 1999)
Moeckli D and White ND, 'Treaties as "Living Instruments"' in Michael J Bowman and Dino Kritsiotis (eds), *Conceptual and Contextual Perspectives on the Modern Law of Treaties* (CUP 2018)
Moellendorf D, 'Climate Change and Global Justice' (2012) 3 WIREs Climate Change Climate Change 131
Möllers C, *The Three Branches: A Comparative Model of Separation of Powers* (OUP 2013)
Montesquieu, *Complete Works, Vol. 1 (The Spirit of Laws) [1748]* (T Evans 1777)
Moore SF, 'Legal Systems of the World: An Introductory Guide to Classifications, Typological Interpretations, and Bibliographical Resources' in Leon Lipson and Stanton Wheeler (eds), *Law and the Social Sciences* (Russell Sage Foundation 1987)
Mortenson JD, 'The Travaux of Travaux: Is the Vienna Convention Hostile To Drafting History?' (2013) 107 American Journal of International Law 780
Mueller ML, *Ruling the Root: Internet Governance and the Taming of Cyberspace* (MIT Press 2002)
Münch F, 'Die Martenssche Klausel und die Grundlagen des Völkerrechts' (1976) 36 Zeitschrift für ausländisches öffentliches Recht und Völkerrecht 347

Muniz-Fraticelli VM, *The Structure of Pluralism* (OUP 2014)
Musgrave L, 'Turning a Ripple into a Torrent: Riding the Waves of Climate Litigation' [2021] Paper presented at Clayton Utz seminar, Sydney, 16 March 2021
Nagel T, 'The Problem of Global Justice' (2005) 33 Philosophy and Public Affairs 113
Nanz P and Steffek J, 'Global Governance, Participation and the Public Sphere' (2004) 39 Government and Opposition 314
Neuborne B, 'Of Sausage Factories and Syllogism Machines: Formalism, Realism, and Exclusionary Selection Techniques' (1992) 67 New York University Law Review 419
Neves M, 'From Constitutionalism to Transconstitutionalism' in Paul Blokker and Chris Thornhill (eds), *Sociological Constitutionalism* (CUP 2017)
Niehaus M and Davies K, 'Voices for the Voiceless – Climate Protection from the Streets to the Courts' (2021) 12 Journal for Human Rights and the Environment 228
Nisbet MC, 'Public Opinion and Participation' in John S Dryzek, Richard B Norgaard and David Schlosberg (eds), *The Oxford Handbook of Climate Change and Society* (OUP 2011)
Nollkaemper A, 'Internationally Wrongful Acts in Domestic Courts' (2007) 101 American Journal of International Law 760
Nollkaemper A, *National Courts and the International Rule of Law* (OUP 2011)
'Nomination of Robert H. Bork to Be Associate Justice of the Supreme Court of the United States: Hearings Before the Committee on the Judiciary US Senate (Testimony of Robert Bork)' (1989)
Notaro N and Pagano M, 'The Interplay of International and EU Environmental Law' in Inge Govaere and Sasha Garben (eds), *The Interface Between EU and International Law – Contemporary Reflections* (Hart Publishing 2019)
Nussbaum MC, *The Cosmopolitan Tradition: A Noble but Flawed Ideal* (Harvard University Press 2019)
Nye JS, 'Globalization's Democratic Deficit: How to Make International Institutions More Accountable' (2001) 80 Foreign Affairs 2
O'Donoghue A, *Constitutionalism in Global Constitutionalisation* (CUP 2014)
O'Gorman R, 'Environmental Constitutionalism: A Comparative Study' (2017) 6 Transnational Environmental Law 435
OECD, *Climate Finance Provided and Mobilised by Developed Countries in 2013–18* (OECD Publishing 2020)
Oeter S, 'Regime Collisions from a Perspective of Global Constitutionalism' in Kerstin Blome and others (eds), *Contested Regime Collisions. Norm Fragmentation in World Society* (CUP 2016)
OHCHR, 'General Comment No. 26 on Children's Rights and the Environment with a Special Focus on Climate Change' (2021)
Okereke C, 'Climate Justice and the International Regime' (2010) 1 WIREs Climate Change 462
Olechowski T, 'Legal Hierarchies in the Works of Hans Kelsen and Adolf Julius Merkl' in Ulrike Müßing (ed), *Reconsidering Constitutional Formation II Decisive Constitutional Normativity* (Springer International Publishing 2018)
Oppenheim L, *International Law, a Treatise, Vol. 1* (2nd edn, Robarts 1912)
Osofsky HM, 'The Geography of Climate Change Litigation: Implications for Transnational Regulatory Governance' (2005) 83 Washington University Law Review 1789

Osofsky HM, 'Climate Change Litigation as Pluralist Legal Dialogue?' (2007) 26A Stanford Environmental Law Journal 181

Osofsky HM, 'The Geography of Climate Change Litigation Part II: Narratives of Massachusetts v. EPA' (2008) 8 Chicago Journal of International Law 573

Osofsky HM, 'Polycentrism and Climate Change' in Daniel A Farber and Marjan Peeters (eds), *Elgar Encyclopedia of Environmental Law: Climate Change Law (Vol. I)* (Edward Elgar Publishing 2015)

Ostrom E, 'A Polycentric Approach for Coping with Climate Change' [2009] The World Bank – Policy Research Working Paper 5095

Paddock LC, 'Environmental Justice' in Lee Paddock, Robert L Glicksman and Nicholas S Bryner (eds), *Elgar Encyclopedia of Environmental Law: Decision Making in Environmental Law (Vol. II)* (Edward Elgar Publishing 2016)

Page EA, 'Distributing the Burdens of Climate Change' (2008) 17 Environmental Politics 556

Parenteau P, 'Some Observations on How Courts in the United States and European Union View Their Role in Adjudicating Climate Litigation' (2023) 26 Environmental Liability: Law, Policy, and Practice 138

Paskalev V, 'May Science Be with You: Can Scientific Expertise Confer Legitimacy to Transnational Authority?' (2017) 8 Transnational Legal Theory 202

Paulus AL, 'Commentary to Andreas Fischer-Lescano & Gunther Teubner. The Legitimacy of International Law and the Role of the State' (2004) 25 Michigan Journal of International Law 1047

Paulus AL, 'International Law and International Community' in David Armstrong and others (eds), *Routledge Handbook of International Law* (Routledge 2008)

Paulus AL, 'The International Legal System as a Constitution' in Jeffrey L Dunoff and Joel P Trachtman (eds), *Ruling the world? Constitutionalism, International Law, and Global Governance* (CUP 2009)

Pauwelyn J, 'Is It International Law or Not, and Does It Even Matter?' in Joost Pauwelyn, Ramses Wessel and Jan Wouters (eds), *Informal International Lawmaking* (OUP 2013)

Pavlova M, *Technology and Vocational Education for Sustainable Development* (Springer 2009)

Payandeh M, *Judikative Rechtserzeugung* (Mohr Siebeck 2017)

Payandeh M, 'The Role of Courts in Climate Protection and the Separation of Powers' in Wolfgang Kahl and Marc-Philippe Weller (eds), *Climate Change Litigation – A Handbook* (Beck/Hart/Nomos 2020)

Pearce D, Campbell E and Harding D, 'Australian Law Schools: A Discipline Assessment for the Commonwealth Tertiary Education Commission' (1987)

Peel J, 'Climate Change Law: The Emergence of a Legal Discipline' (2008) 32 Melbourne University Law Review 922

Peel J, 'Issues in Climate Change Litigation' (2011) 5 Carbon & Climate Law Review 15

Peel J, Godden L and Keenan RJ, 'Climate Change Law in an Era of Multi-Level Governance' (2012) 1 Transnational Environmental Law 245

Peel J and Lin J, 'Transnational Climate Litigation: The Contribution of the Global South' (2019) 113 American Journal of International Law 679

Peel J and Osofsky HM, *Climate Change Litigation: Regulatory Pathways to Cleaner Energy* (CUP 2015)

Peel J and Osofsky HM, 'Litigation as a Mitigation Tool', *Climate Change Litigation: Regulatory Pathways to Cleaner Energy* (CUP 2015)

Peel J and Osofsky HM, 'Litigation as a Climate Regulatory Tool' in Christina Voigt (ed), *International Judicial Practice on the Environment: Questions of Legitimacy* (CUP 2019)

Peel J and Osofsky HM, 'Climate Change Litigation' (2020) 16 Annual Review of Law and Social Science 21

Percival R V., 'The Greening of the Global Judiciary' (2017) 32 Journal of Land Use and Environmental Law 333

Perez O, 'Normative Creativity and Global Legal Pluralism: Reflections on the Democratic Critique of Transnational Law' (2003) 10 Indiana Journal of Global Legal Studies 25

Pernice I, 'Multilevel Constitutionalism and the Treaty of Amsterdam: European Constitution-Making Revisited?' (1999) 36 Common Market Law Review 703

Pernice I, 'The Treaty of Lisbon: Multilevel Constitutionalism in Action' (2009) 15 The Columbia Journal of European Law 47

Peters A, 'Global Constitutionalism Revisited' (2005) 11 Legal Theory 39

Peters A, 'Compensatory Constitutionalism: The Function and Potential of Fundamental International Norms and Structures' (2006) 19 Leiden Journal of International Law 579

Peters A, 'The Constitutionalist Reconstruction of International Law: Pro and Cons' (2006) 1 NCCR Trade working papers 1

Peters A, 'Dual Democracy' in Jan Klabbers, Anne Peters and Geir Ulfstein (eds), *The Constitutionalization of International Law* (OUP 2009)

Peters A, 'Humanity as the A and Ω of Sovereignty' (2009) 20 European Journal of International Law 513

Peters A, 'Membership in the Global Constitutional Community' in Jan Klabbers, Anne Peters and Geir Ulfstein (eds), *The Constitutionalization of International Law* (OUP 2009)

Peters A, 'The Merits of Global Constitutionalism' (2009) 16 Indiana Journal of Global Legal Studies 397

Peters A, 'Rechtsordnungen und Konstitutionalisierung: Zur Neubestimmung der Verhältnisse' (2010) 65 Zeitschrift für öffentliches Recht 3

Peters A, 'Are We Moving towards Constitutionalization of the World Community?' in Antonio Cassese (ed), *Realizing Utopia: The Future of International Law* (OUP 2012)

Peters A, 'Global Constitutionalism' in Michael Gibbons (ed), *The Encyclopedia of Political Thought* (John Wiley & Sons 2015)

Peters A, 'The Refinement of International Law: From Fragmentation to Regime Interaction and Politicization' (2017) 15 International Journal of Constitutional Law 671

Peters B, 'On Public Deliberation and Public Culture – Reflections on the Public Sphere' [1997] InIIS-Arbeitspapier Nr. 7/97

Petersmann EU, 'Human Rights, Constitutionalism and the World Trade Organization: Challenges for World Trade Organization Jurisprudence and Civil Society' (2006) 19 Leiden Journal of International Law 633

Petersmann EU, *Multilevel Constitutionalism for Multilevel Governance of Public Goods* (Hart Publishing 2017)

Pettit P, *Republicanism: A Theory of Freedom and Government* (OUP 1998)

Picciotto S, 'Constitutionalizing Multilevel Governance?' (2008) 6 International Journal of Constitutional Law 457

Pickering J, Bäckstrand K and Schlosberg D, 'Between Environmental and Ecological Democracy: Theory and Practice at the Democracy-Environment Nexus' (2020) 22 Journal of Environmental Policy & Planning 1

Plessis A Du, 'South Africa's Constitutional Environmental Right (Generously) Interpreted: What Is in It for Poverty?' (2011) 27 South African Journal on Human Rights 279

Pogge T, *World Poverty and Human Rights* (Polity Press 2002)

Popper K, *The Open Society and Its Enemies* (Routledge & Kegan 2002)

Pörtner H-O and others, 'Climate Change 2022: Impacts, Adaptation and Vulnerability Working Group II Contribution to the Sixth Assessment Report of the Intergovernmental Panel on Climate Change' (2022)

Preston BJ, 'The Influence of Climate Change Litigation on Governments and the Private Sector' (2011) 2 Climate Law 485

Preston BJ, 'Characteristics of Successful Environmental Courts and Tribunals' (2014) 26 Journal of Environmental Law 365

Preuss UK, 'Disconnecting Constitutions from Statehood: Is Global Constitutionalism a Viable Concept?' in Petra Dobner and Martin Loughlin (eds), *The Twilight of Constitutionalism?* (OUP 2010)

Pring G (Rock) and Pring C (Kitty), 'Greening Justice – Creating and Improving Environmental Courts and Tribunals' (The Access Initiative 2009)

Prost M, *The Concept of Unity in Public International Law* (Hart Publishing 2012)

Rajagopal B, *International Law from Below: Development, Social Movements and Third World Resistance* (CUP 2003)

Rausch J, 'The Necessity Defense and Climate Change: A Climate Change Litigant's Guide' (2019) 44 Columbia Journal of Environmental Law 553

Raustiala K, 'States, NGOs, and International Environmental Institutions' (1997) 41 International Studies Quarterly 719

Raustiala K, 'The "Participatory Revolution" in International Environmental Law' (1997) 21 Harvard Environmental Law Review 537

Rawls J, *A Theory of Justice (1971)* (Revised Ed, OUP 1999)

Rawls J, *The Law of Peoples* (Harvard University Press 1999)

Rawls J, *Justice as Fairness – A Restatement* (Erin Kelly ed, Belknap Press 2001)

Raz J, 'On the Authority and Interpretation of Constitutions: Some Preliminaries' in Larry Alexander (ed), *Constitutionalism: Philosophical Foundations* (CUP 1998)

Rehg W,'Translator's Introduction', *Between Facts and Norms. Contributions to a Discourse Theory of Law and Democracy* (Polity Press 1996)

Reimann M, 'Introduction: The Yahoo! Case and Conflict of Laws in the Cyberage' (2003) 24 Michigan Journal of International Law 663

Rengarajan S and others, 'National Green Tribunal of India—an Observation from Environmental Judgements' (2018) 25 Environmental Science and Pollution Research 11313

Resnik J, 'Law's Migration: American Exceptionalism, Silent Dialogues, and Federalism's Multiple Ports of Entry' (2006) 115 Yale Law Journal 1564

Rich R, 'Bringing Democracy into International Law' (2001) 12 Journal of Democracy 20

Rippe KP, 'Diminishing Solidarity' (1998) 1 Ethical Theory and Moral Practice 355

Rittberger B and Schimmelfennig F, 'Explaining the Constitutionalization of the European Union' (2006) 13 Journal of European Public Policy 1148

Roberts A, 'Comparative International Law? The Role of National Courts in Creating and Enforcing International Law' (2011) 60 International and Comparative Law Quarterly 57
Roberts JT and Parks BC, 'Ecologically Unequal Exchange, Ecological Debt, and Climate Justice: The History and Implications of Three Related Ideas for a New Social Movement' (2009) 50 International Journal of Comparative Sociology 385
Robinson D, 'Defining "Crimes Against Humanity" at the Rome Conference' (1999) 93 American Journal of International Law 43
Rockström J and others, 'Planetary Boundaries: Exploring the Safe Operating Space for Humanity' (2009) 461 Nature 472
Rödl F, 'Fundamental Rights, Private Law, and Societal Constitution: On the Logic of the so-Called Horizontal Effect' (2013) 20 Indiana Journal of Global Legal Studies 1015
Rosenberg GN, *The Hollow Hope: Can Courts Bring About Social Change?* (2nd edn, University of Chicago 2008)
Rosenfeld M, 'Modern Constitutionalism as Interplay Between Identity and Diversity' in Michel Rosenfeld (ed), *Constitutionalism, Identity, Difference, and Legitimacy: Theoretical Perspectives* (Duke University Press 1994)
Rouvroy A and Poullet Y, 'The Right to Informational Self-Determination and the Value of Self-Development: Reassessing the Importance of Privacy for Democracy' in Serge Gutwirth and others (eds), *Reinventing Data Protection?* (Springer Sciene+Business Media 2009)
Rudolf W, '§ 90 Recht auf informationelle Selbstbestimmung' in Detlef Merten and Hans-Jürgen Papier (eds), *Handbuch der Grundrechte in Deutschland und Europa*, vol IV (CF Müller 2011)
Rushe A, 'Same-Sex Marriage under the Grundgesetz and the European Convention on Human Rights' (2017) 60 German Yearbook of International Law 711
Sands P and Peel J, *Principles of International Environmental Law* (4th edn, CUP 2018)
Santivasa S, 'The NGOs' Participation in the Proceedings of the International Court of Justice' (2012) 5 Journal of East Asia and International Law 377
Satterthwaite D, 'The Implications of Population Growth and Urbanization for Climate Change' (2009) 21 Environment and Urbanization 545
Scalia A, *A Matter of Interpretation* (Princeton University Press 1997)
Scalia A and Garner BA, *Reading Law. The Interpretation of Legal Texts* (Thomson/West 2012)
Scanlon J, Cassar A and Nemes N, *Water as a Human Right?* (IUCN, Gland, Switzerland and Cambridge, UK 2004)
Scelles G, 'Le phénomène juridique du dédoublement fonctionnel' in Walter Schätzel and Hans-Jürgen Schlochauer (eds), *Rechtsfragen der internationalen Organisation (FS f. Hans Wehberg)* (Vittorio Klostermann 1956)
Schaffer JK, 'The Co-Originality of Human Rights and Democracy in an International Order' (2015) 7 International Theory 96
Schaffer RP, 'Current Trends in Treaty Interpretation and the South African Approach' (1976) 7 Australian Year Book of International Law 129
Scheyli M, 'Der Schutz des Klimas als Prüfstein völkerrechtlicher Konstitutionalisierung?' (2002) 40 Archiv des Völkerrechts 273
Schill SW, 'Lex Mercatoria', *Max Planck Encyclopedia of Public International Law [MPEPIL]* (OUP 2014)

Schlink B, 'Das Recht der Informationellen Selbstbestimmung' (1986) 25 Der Staat 233
Schlosberg D, 'Reconceiving Environmental Justice: Global Movements and Political Theories' (2004) 13 Environmental Politics 517
Schlosberg D, 'Disruption, Community, and Resilient Governance – Environmental Justice in the Anthropocene' in Tobias Haller and others (eds), *The Commons in a Glocal World: Global Connections and Local Responses* (Routledge 2019)
Schmitz HP, 'Domestic and Transnational Perspectives on Democratization' (2004) 6 International Studies Review 403
Scholte JA, 'Civil Society and Democratically Accountable Global Governance' (2004) 39 Government and Opposition
Schwartz A, 'Patriotism or Integrity? Constitutional Community in Divided Societies' (2011) 31 Oxford Journal of Legal Studies 503
Schwartz P, 'The Computer in German and American Constitutional Law: Towards an American Right of Informational Self-Determination' (1989) 37 The American Journal of Comparative Law 675
Schwartz SH, 'Universalism Values and the Inclusiveness of Our Moral Universe' (2007) 38 Journal of Cross-Cultural Psychology 711
Schwartz SH, 'An Overview of the Schwartz Theory of Basic Values' (2012) 2 Online Readings in Psychology and Culture 1
Schwartz SH, 'Refining the Theory of Basic Individual Values' (2012) 103 Journal of Personality and Social Psychology 663
Schwartzmann S, 'Foro de foco: Diversidade e identidades étnicas no Brasil' (1999) 55 Novos Estudos CEBRAP 83
Schwöbel CEJ, 'Organic Global Constitutionalism' (2010) 23 Leiden Journal of International Law 529
Schwöbel CEJ, *Global Constitutionalism in International Legal Perspective* (Martinus Nijhoff Publishers 2011)
Scott J, 'The Multi-Level Governance of Climate Change' (2011) 5 Carbon & Climate Law Review 25
Segger M-CC, 'Sustainable Development in International Law' in David Armstrong and others (eds), *Routledge Handbook of International Law* (Routledge 2009)
Segger M-CC and Weeramantry JCG, *Sustainable Development Principles in the Decisions of International Courts and Tribunals: 1992–2012* (Routledge 2017)
Senn M, *Non-State Regulatory Regimes* (Springer 2011)
Setzer J and Benjamin L, 'Climate Litigation in the Global South: Constraints and Innovations' (2020) 9 Transnational Environmental Law 77
Setzer J and Byrnes R, 'Global Trends in Climate Change Litigation: 2019 Snapshot' (2019)
Shelton D, 'Normative Hierarchy in International Law' (2006) 100 American Journal of International Law 291
Shelton D, 'Common Concern of Humanity' (2009) 39 Environmental Policy and Law 83
Shelton D, 'Developing Substantive Environmental Rights' (2010) 1 Journal of Human Rights and the Environment 89
Shue H, *Basic Rights: Subsistence, Affluence, and U.S. Foreign Policy* (Princeton University Press 1980)
Shue H, 'Subsistence Emissions and Luxury Emissions' (1993) 15 Law & Policy 39
Shue H, *Climate Justice: Vulnerability and Protection* (2014)

Sidhu BK and Desai BH, 'Plastics Pollution: A New Common Concern of Humankind?' (2018) 48 Environmental Policy and Law 252

Siekmann RCR and Soek J (eds), *Lex Sportiva: What Is Sports Law?* (TMC Asser Press/Springer 2012)

Simits S, 'Das Volkszählungsurteil oder der lange Weg zur Informationsaskese – (BVerfGE 65, 1)' (2000) 83 Kritische Vierteljahresschrift für Gesetzgebung und Rechtswissenschaft 359

Simma B, 'Self-Contained Regimes' (1985) 16 Netherlands Yearbook of International Law 111

Singer P, *One World: The Ethics of Globalisation* (2nd edn, Yale University Press 2004)

Singer P, 'One Atmosphere' in Stephen M Gardiner and others (eds), *Climate Ethics: Essential Readings* (OUP 2010)

Slaughter A-M, *A New World Order* (Princeton University Press 2004)

Slaughter AM and Burke-White W, 'The Future of International Law Is Domestic (or, The European Way of Law)' (2006) 47 Harvard International Law Journal 327

Smend R, 'Verfassung und Verfassungsrecht (1928)' in Rudolf Smend (ed), *Staatsrechtliche Abhandlungen und andere Aufsätze* (4th edn, Duncker & Humblot 2010)

Soltau F, 'Common Concern of Humankind' in Kevin Gray, Richard Tarasofsky and Cinnamon Carlarne (eds), *The Oxford Handbook of International Climate Change Law* (OUP 2016)

Solum LB, 'Originalism versus Living Constitutionalism: The Coceptual Structure of the Great Debate' (2019) 113 Northwestern University Law Review 1432

Sommermann K-P, 'Transformative Effects of the Aarhus Convention in Europe' (2017) 77 Zeitschrift für ausländisches öffentliches Recht und Völkerrecht 321

Sørensen E and Torfing J, 'The Democratic Anchorage of Governance Networks' (2005) 28 Scandinavian Political Studies 195

Souza Galdino M, 'Jurisdição constitucional e teoria da decisão: As contribuições de Ronald Dworkin, Peter Häberle e Jürgen Habermas na Democratização do debate constitucional' (2016) 21 Revista Jus Navigandi 27

Special Rapporteur on Extreme Poverty and Human Rights Philipp Alston, 'Climate Change and Poverty (A/HRC/41/39)' (2019)

Spier J, '"The 'Strongest' Climate Ruling Yet": The Dutch Supreme Court's Urgenda Judgment' (2020) 67 Netherlands International Law Review 319

Spiro P, 'Non-Governmental Organizations and Civil Society' in Daniel Bodansky, Jutta Brunnée and Ellen Hey (eds), *The Oxford Handbook of International Environmental Law* (OUP 2008)

Squires J, 'Liberal Constitutionalism, Identity and Difference' in Richard Bellamy and Dario Castiglione (eds), *Constitutionalism in Transformation: European and Theoretical Perspectives* (Blackwell Publishers 1996)

Srinivasan UT, 'Economics of Climate Change: Risk and Responsibility by World Region' (2010) 10 Climate Policy 298

Stark A, *Interdisziplinarität der Rechtsdogmatik* (Mohr Siebeck 2020)

Steffen W and others, 'The Anthropocene: Conceptual and Historical Perspectives' (2011) 369 Philosophical Transactions of the Royal Society 842

Stephens T, *International Courts and Environmental Protection* (CUP 2009)

Stern N, 'The Stern Review on Economics of Climate Change' (2006)

Stevenson H, *Global Environmental Politics. Problems, Policy, and Practice* (CUP 2017)
Stevenson H and Dryzek JS, 'The Discursive Democratisation of Global Climate Governance' (2012) 21 Environmental Politics 189
Stevenson H and Dryzek JS, *Democratizing Global Climate Change* (CUP 2014)
Stone CD, 'Should Trees Have Standing? Towards Legal Rights for Natural Objects' (1972) 45 Southern California Law Review 450
Stone CD, *Should Trees Have Standing?* (3rd edn, OUP 2010)
Streck C, 'Innovativeness and Paralysis in International Climate Policy' (2012) 1 Transnational Environmental Law 137
Sunstein CR, 'What's Standing after Lujan? Of Citizen Suits, "Injuries," and Article III' (1992) 91 Michigan Law Review 163
Tamanaha B, *A General Jurisprudence of Law and Society* (OUP 2001)
Tamanaha BZ, 'A Non-Essentialist Version of Legal Pluralism' (2000) 27 Journal of Law and Society 296
Tanaka Y, 'Reflections on Time Elements in the International Law of the Environment' (2013) 73 Zeitschrift für ausländisches öffentliches Recht und Völkerrecht 139
Taylor P, 'Common Heritage of Mankind and Common Concern of Humankind', *Elgar Encyclopedia of Environmental Law: Principles of Environmental Law (Vol. VI)* (Edward Elgar Publishing 2018) 303
Teraya K, 'Emerging Hierarchy in International Human Rights and Beyond: From the Perspective of Non-Derogable Rights' (2001) 12 European Journal of International Law 917
Teubner G, '"Global Bukowina": Legal Pluralism in the World Society' in Gunther Teubner (ed), *Global Law without a State* (Dartmouth Publishing 1997)
Teubner G, *Global Law without a State* (Gunther Teubner ed, Dartmouth Publishing 1997)
Teubner G, 'The Two Faces of Janus: Rethinking Legal Pluralism' in Kaarlo Tuori, Zenon Bankowski and Jyrki Uusitalo (eds), *Law and Power: Critical and Socio-Legal Essays* (Deborah Charles Publications 1997)
Teubner G, 'Globale Zivilverfassungen: Alternativen zur staatszentrierten Verfassungstheorie' (2003) 63 Zeitschrift für ausländisches öffentliches Recht und Völkerrecht 1
Teubner G, 'A Constitutional Moment? The Logics of "Hitting the Bottom"' in Poul F Kjaer, Gunther Teubner and Alberto Febbrajo (eds), *The Financial Crisis in Constitutional Perspective: The Dark Side of Functional Differentiation* (Hart Publishing 2011)
Teubner G, 'Constitutionalizing Polycontexturality' (2011) 20 Social and Legal Studies 209
Teubner G, *Constitutional Fragments: Societal Constitutionalism and Globalization* (OUP 2012)
Teubner G, *Verfassungsfragmente* (Suhrkamp 2012)
Teubner G, 'Societal Constitutionalism: Nine Variations on a Theme by David Sciulli' in Paul Blokker and Chris Thornhill (eds), *Sociological Constitutionalism* (CUP 2017)
Teubner G, 'Quod Omnes Tangit: Transnational Constitutions without Democracy?' (2018) 45 Journal of Law and Society S5
'The Hague Principles for a Universal Declaration on Responsibilities for Human Rights and Earth Trusteeship'
Thériault S, 'Environmental Justice and the Inter-American Court of Human Rights' in Anna Grear and Louis J Kotzé (eds), *Research Handbook on Human Rights and the Environment* (Edward Elgar Publishing 2015)

Thornhill C, 'Constitutional Law from the Perspective of Power: A Response to Gunther Teubner' (2011) 20 Social and Legal Studies 244

Thornton F, 'The Absurdity of Relying on Human Rights Law to Go After Emitters' in Benoit Mayer and Alexander Zahar (eds), *Debating Climate Law* (CUP 2021)

Thorp T, 'Climate Justice: A Constitutional Approach to Unify the Lex Specialis Principles of International Climate Law' (2012) 8 Utrecht Law Review 7

Tladi D, 'Interpretation of Treaties in an International Law-Friendly Framework – The Case of South Africa' in Helmut Aust and Georg Nolte (eds), *The Interpretation of International Law by Domestic Courts – Unity, Diversity, Convergence* (OUP 2016)

Tobin J, 'Seeking to Persuade: A Constructive Approach to Human Rights Treaty Interpretation' (2010) 23 Harvard Human Rights Journal 1

Tomuschat C, 'Obligations Arising for States Without or Against Their Will' in Académie de Droit International (The Hague Academy of International Law) (ed), *Recueil des Cours*, vol 241 (Martinus Nijhoff Publishers 1993)

Tomuschat C, 'International Law: Ensuring the Survival of Mankind on the Eve of a New Century' in Académie de Droit International (The Hague Academy of International Law) (ed), *Recueil des Cours*, vol 281 (Martinus Nijhoff Publishers 2001)

Trachtman JP, 'The Constitutions of the WTO' (2006) 17 European Journal of International Law 623

Trachtman JP, 'Constitutional Economics of the World Trade Organization' in Jeffrey L Dunoff and Joel P Trachtman (eds), *Ruling the World? Constitutionalism, International Law and Global Government* (CUP 2009)

Tremmel JC, 'Introduction' in Joerg Chet Tremmel (ed), *Handbook of Intergenerational Justice* (Edward Elgar Publishing 2006)

Tully J, *Strange Multiplicity. Constitutionalism in an Age of Diversity* (CUP 1995)

Tully J, 'The Agonic Freedom of Citizens' (1999) 28 Economy and Society 161

Tushnet M, *Taking the Constitution Away from the Courts* (Princeton University Press 1999)

Uerpmann R, 'Internationales Verfassungsrecht' (2001) 56 Juristenzeitung 565

Ulfstein G, 'Evolutive Interpretation in the Light of Other International Instruments: Law and Legitimacy' in Anne van Aaken and Iulia Motoc (eds), *The European Convention on Human Rights and General International Law* (OUP 2018)

UN General Assembly, 'Report of the Secretary-General: Intergenerational Solidarity and the Needs of Future Generations (A/68/322)' (2013)

UN Special Rapporteur John H. Knox, 'Framework Principles on Human Rights and the Environment – Report of the Special Rapporteur on the Issue of Human Rights Obligations Relating to the Enjoyment of a Safe, Clean, Healthy and Sustainable Environment (A/HRC/37/5)' (2018)

UN Special Rapporteur on Human Rights and the Environment David Boyd, 'Special Report on Human Rights Obligations Relating to the Enjoyment of a Safe, Clean, Healthy and Sustainable Environment (A/74/161)' (2019)

UN Special Rapporteur on Human Rights and the Environment John H. Knox, 'Special Report on Climate Change and Human Rights' (2015)

UN Special Rapporteur on Human Rights and the Environment John H. Knox, 'Human Rights Obligations Relating to the Enjoyment of a Safe, Clean, Healthy and Sustainable Environment (A/HRC/31/52)' (2016)

UN World Commission on Environment and Development, *Our Common Future (Brundtland Report)* (OUP 1987)

UNEP, '21 Issues for the 21st Century – Results of the UNEP Foresight Process on Emerging Environmental Issues' (2012)

UNEP, 'The Status of Climate Change Litigation – A Global Review' (2017)

UNEP, *Environmental Rule of Law (First Global Report)* (2019)

UNEP, 'Emissions Gap Emissions Gap Report 2022' (2022)

United States Environmental Protection Agency, 'Toolkit for Assessing Potential Allegations of Environmental Injustice' (2004)

van Aaken A, 'Defragmentation of Public International Law Through Interpretation: A Methodological Proposal' (2009) 16 Indiana Journal of Global Legal Studies 483

van den Berge L, 'Montesquieu and Judicial Review of Proportionality in Administrative Law: Rethinking the Separation of Powers in the Neoliberal Era' (2017) 10 European Journal of Legal Studies 203

van Wyk D, 'Values, Values, Values or Mere Words, Words, Words? Values in the 1996 Constitution', *Constitution and Law IV: Developments in the Contemporary Constitutional State* (2000)

Vanderheiden S, 'Environmental and Climate Justice' in Teena Gabrielson and others (eds), *The Oxford Handbook of Environmental Political Theory* (OUP 2016)

Vattel E de, *The Law of Nations: Or, Principles of the Law of Nature, Applied to the Conduct and Affairs of Nations and Sovereigns* (T & JW Johnson 1854)

Venzke I, 'The Role of International Courts as Interpreters and Developers of the Law: Working Out the Jurisgenerative Practice of Interpretation' (2011) 34 Loyola of Los Angeles International and Comparative Law Review 99

Venzke I, *How Interpretation Makes International Law: On Semantic Change and Normative Twists* (OUP 2012)

Venzke I, 'Semantic Authority' [2016] ACIL Research Paper 2016–03

Verschuuren J, 'The State of the Netherlands v Urgenda Foundation: The Hague Court of Appeal Upholds Judgment Requiring the Netherlands to Further Reduce Its Greenhouse Gas Emissions' (2019) 28 Review of European, Comparative and International Environmental Law 94

Viellechner L, 'Constitutionalism as a Cipher: On the Convergence of Constitutionalist and Pluralist Approaches to the Globalization of Law' (2012) 4 Goettingen Journal of International Law 599

Viellechner L, 'Responsive Legal Pluralism: The Emergence of Transnational Conflicts Law' (2015) 6 Transnational Legal Theory 312

Viellechner L, 'Verfassung ohne Staat. Eine Einführung' in Lars Viellechner (ed), *Verfassung ohne Staat* (Nomos 2019)

Volkmann U, 'Der Aufstieg der Verfassung: Beobachtungen zum grundlegenden Wandel des Verfassungsbegriffs' in Thomas Vesting and Stefan Korioth (eds), *Der Eigenwert des Verfassungsrechts* (Mohr Siebeck 2011)

Volkmann U, *Grundzüge einer Verfassungslehre für die Bundesrepublik Deutschland* (Mohr Siebeck 2013)

von Bernstorff J, 'Procedures of Decision-Making and the Role of Law in International Organizations' (2008) 9 German Law Journal 1939

von Bogdandy A and Venzke I, *International Judicial Lawmaking* (Springer 2012)

von Bogdandy A and Venzke I, 'On the Democratic Legitimation of International Judicial Lawmaking' in Armin von Bogdandy and Ingo Venzke (eds), *International Judicial Lawmaking* (Springer 2012)
von Gerber CF, *Grundzüge des Deutschen Staatsrechts* (B Tauchnitz 1880)
von Giercke O, *Deutsches Privatrecht Band 1: Allgemeiner Teil und Personenrecht* (Duncker & Humblot 1895)
Vorländer H, 'Constitutions as Symbolic Orders' in Paul Blokker and Chris Thornhill (eds), *Sociological Constitutionalism* (CUP 2017)
Voßkuhle A, 'Verfassungsstil und Verfassungsfunktion: Ein Beitrag zum Verfassungshandwerk' (1994) 119 Archiv des öffentlichen Rechts 35
Waibel M, 'Interpretive Communites in International Law' in Andrea Bianchi, Daniel Peat and Matthew Windsor (eds), *Interpretation in International Law* (OUP 2015)
Waldron J, *Law and Disagreement* (OUP 1999)
Walker G, *Environmental Justice: Concepts, Evidence and Politics* (Routledge 2012)
Walker N, 'The Idea of Constitutional Pluralism' (2002) 65 Modern Law Review 317
Walker N, 'The Idea of Constitutional Pluralism' [2002] EUI Working Paper LAW No. 2002/1
Walker N, 'Big "C" or Small "c"?' (2006) 12 European Law Journal 12
Walker N, 'Beyond Boundary Disputes and Basic Grids: Mapping the Global Disorder of Normative Orders' (2008) 6 International Journal of Constitutional Law 373
Walker N, 'Taking Constitutionalism beyond the State' (2008) 56 Political Studies 519
Walker N, 'Beyond the Holistic Constitution?' in Petra Dobner and Martin Loughlin (eds), *The Twilight of Constitutionalism?* (OUP 2010)
Walker N, 'Constitutional Pluralism Revisited' (2016) 22 European Law Journal 333
Wallerstein I, *European Universalism – The Rhetoric of Power* (The New Press 2006)
Walter C, 'Constitutionalizing (Inter)National Governance – Possibilities for and Limits to the Development of an International Constitutional Law' (2001) 44 German Yearbook of International Law 170
Watt HM, 'Private International Law Beyond the Schism' (2011) 2 Transnational Legal Theory 347
WBGU (German Advisory Council on Global Change), 'World in Transition: A Social Contract for Sustainability' (2011)
Weber M, *Wirtschaft und Gesellschaft* (JCB Mohr (Paul Siebeck) 1922)
Weiler J, 'Prolegomena to a Meso-Theory of Treaty Interpretation at the Turn of the Century', *International Legal Theory Colloquium: Interpretation in International Law,IILJ, NYU School of Law, 14 February 2008*
Weiler JHH and Paulus AL, 'The Structure of Change in International Law or Is There a Hierarchy of Norms in International Law?' (1997) 8 European Journal of International Law 545
Weiss EB, *International Law for a Water-Scarce World* (Brill/Martinus Nijhoff Publishers 2013)
Wessel RA, 'Informal International Law-Making as a New Form of World Legislation?' (2011) 8 International Organizations Law Review 253
Weston BH, 'Climate Change and Intergenerational Justice: Foundational Reflections' (2008) 9 Vermont Journal of Environmental Law 375

Wiener A, 'Editorial: Evolving Norms of Constitutionalism' (2003) 9 European Law Journal 1

Wiener A, *The Invisible Constitution of Politics: Contested Norms and International Encounters* (CUP 2008)

Wiener A, *A Theory of Contestation* (Springer 2014)

Wiener A, 'Global Constitutionalism: Human Rights, Democracy and the Rule of Law' (2012) 1 Global Constitutionalism 1

Willetts P, 'The Cardoso Report on the UN and Civil Society: Functionalism, Global Corporatism, or Global Democracy?' (2006) 12 Global Governance 305

Wirth DA, 'Reexamining Decision-Making Processes in International Environmental Law' (1994) 79 Iowa Law Review 769

Wittgenstein L, *Philosophical Investigations* (1953)

Wolff HA, *Ungeschriebenes Verfassungsrecht unter dem Grundgesetz* (Mohr Siebeck 2000)

Wood MC, 'Atmospheric Trust Litigation: Securing a Constitutional Right to a Stable Climate System' (2018) 29 Colorado Natural Resources, Energy, and Environmental Law Review 321

Woodward BB, 'International Lawmaking and Civil Society' in Catherine Brölmann and Yannick Radi (eds), *Research Handbook on the Theory and Practice of International Lawmaking* (Edward Elgar Publishing 2016)

World Bank, 'World Development Report: Development and Climate Change' (2010)

Yasuaki O, 'In Quest of Intercivilizational Human Rights: Universal vs. Relative Human Rights Viewed from an Asian Perspective' (2000) 1 Asia-Pacific Journal on Human Rights and the Law 53

Young EA, 'The Constitution Outside the Constitution' (2007) 117 Yale Law Journal 408

Young IM, *Justice and the Politics of Difference (1990)* (Princeton University Press 2011)

Young MA, 'Climate Change Law and Regime Interaction' (2017) 5 Carbon & Climate Law Review 147

Yuval S, 'Should the Implementation of International Rules by Domestic Courts Be Bolstered?' in Antonio Cassese (ed), *Realizing Utopia: The Future of International Law* (2012)

Zajadło J and Widłak T, 'Constitutionalisation: A New Philosophy of International Law?' in Andrzej Jakubowski and Karolina Wierczyńska (eds), *Fragmentation vs the Constitutionalisation of International Law* (Routledge 2016)

Zangl B and Zürn M, 'Make Law, Not War: Internationale und transnationale Verrechtlichung als Baustein für Global Governance' in Michael Zürn and Bernhard Zangl (eds), *Verrechtlichung – Baustein für Global Governance?* (Stiftung Entwicklung und Frieden 2004)

Zarbiyev F, 'A Genealogy of Treaty Interpretation' in Andrea Bianchi, Daniel Peat and Matthew Windsor (eds), *Interpretation in International Law* (OUP 2015)

Zengerling C, *Greening International Jurisprudence* (Martinus Nijhoff Publishers 2013)

Zhao Y, Lyu S and Wang Z, 'Prospects for Climate Change Litigation in China' (2019) 8 Transnational Environmental Law 349

Ziegler KS, 'Domaine Réservé', *MPEPIL* (2013)

Zurn CF, 'Deliberative Democracy and Constitutional Review' (2002) 4/5 Law and Philosophy 467

Zürn M, 'Global Governance and Legitimacy Problems' (2004) 39 Government and Opposition 260

Links

',,Böse Zungen Nennen Das Verfassungslyrik" – Interview with Georg Oswald' (*Deutschlandfunk*, 29 July 2019) <https://www.deutschlandfunkkultur.de/jurist-oswald-ueber-klimaschutz-im-grundgesetz-boese-zungen.1008.de.html?dram:article_id=455043> accessed 31 August 2023

Bundesverfassungsgericht (GFCC), '25 Jahre "Volkszählungsurteil" des Bundesverfassungsgerichts' (*Press Release No. 106/2008 of 11 December 2008*) <https://www.bundesverfassungsgericht.de/SharedDocs/Pressemitteilungen/DE/2008/bvg08-106.html> accessed 31 August 2023

Bundesverfassungsgericht (GFCC), 'Constitutional Complaints against the Federal Climate Change Act Partially Successful (Press Release No. 31/2021 of 29 April 2021)'

Baazil D, 'After Climate Court Victories Comes the Problem of Enforcement' *Bloomberg* (18 August 2023) <https://www.bloomberg.com/news/articles/2021-08-18/climate-litigation-victories-face-enforcement-problems> accessed 31 August 2023

'Bid for Environmental Rights Pact to Kick off in Paris' (23 June 2017) <https://www.france24.com/en/20170623-bid-environmental-rights-pact-kick-off-paris> accessed 31 August 2023

'Brief of the United States as Amicus Curiae in Support of Appellees (Case City of New York v BP P.L.C., et Al., No. 1:18-Cv-00182)' (2019) <https://climatecasechart.com/case/city-new-york-v-bp-plc/> accessed 31 August 2023

Buchner BK and others, 'Global Landscape of Climate Finance' (2019) <https://www.climatepolicyinitiative.org/wp-content/uploads/2019/11/2019-Global-Landscape-of-Climate-Finance.pdf> accessed 31 August 2023

C40 Cities, 'The Future We Don't Want: Cities and Sea Level Rise' <https://www.c40.org/other/the-future-we-don-t-want-staying-afloat-the-urban-response-to-sea-level-rise> accessed 31 August 2023

'Climate Change Poses "Defining Challenge" of Our Time, Ban Says' *UN News* (7 October 2008) <https://news.un.org/en/story/2008/10/276912-climate-change-poses-defining-challenge-our-time-ban-says> accessed 31 August 2023

Cornwall W, 'In a San Francisco Courtroom, Climate Science Gets Its Day on the Docket' *Science* (22 March 2018) <https://www.sciencemag.org/news/2018/03/san-francisco-court-room-climate-science-gets-its-day-docket> accessed 31 August 2023

Dejusticia, 'About Us' <https://www.dejusticia.org/en/about/> accessed 31 August 2023

Dejusticia, '¿Qué le hace falta al gobierno para implementar la sentencia contra el cambio climático y la deforestación?' (2 December 2020) <https://www.dejusticia.org/que-le-hace-falta-al-gobierno-para-implementar-la-sentencia-contra-el-cambio-climatico-y-la-deforestacion/> accessed 31 August 2023

European Commission, ‘Press Remarks by President von Der Leyen on the Occasion of the Adoption of the European Climate Law’ (4 March 2020) <https://ec.europa.eu/commission/presscorner/detail/en/statement_20_381> accessed 31 August 2023

Equity Generation Lawyers, ‘O’Donnell v Commonwealth and Ors’ <https://equitygenerationlawyers.com/cases/odonnell-v-commonwealth> accessed 31 August 2023

‘Fridays for Future’ <https://fridaysforfuture.org> accessed 31 August 2023

Hasemyer D, ‘Fossil Fuels on Trial: Where the Major Climate Change Lawsuits Stand Today’ *Inside Climate News* (17 January 2020) <https://insideclimatenews.org/news/04042018/climate-change-fossil-fuel-company-lawsuits-timeline-exxon-children-california-cities-attorney-general> accessed 31 August 2023

Helgesen JE, ‘What Are the Limits to the Evolutive Interpretation of the Convention?’, *Dialogue between Judges at the European Court of Human Rights Strasbourg, 28 January 2011* <http://www.echr.coe.int/Documents/Dialogue_2011_ENG.pdf> accessed 31 August 2023

Human Rights Committee, ‘Call for Comments on Article 6 of the International Covenant on Civil and Political Rights’ <https://www.ohchr.org/en/calls-for-input/general-comment-no-36-article-6-right-life> accessed 31 August 2023

IUCN World Commission on Environmental Law, ‘Global Judicial Institute on the Environment’ <https://www.iucn.org/our-union/commissions/group/iucn-wcel-global-judicial-institute-environment-task-force> accessed 31 August 2023

Jansen Reventlow N, ‘The Climate Movement’s Racial Blind Spots’ *Project Syndicate* (2 November 2022) <https://www.project-syndicate.org/commentary/european-climate-movement-racial-blind-spots-by-nani-jansen-reventlow-2022-11> accessed 31 August 2023

Kahn D, ‘Oil Giant Accepts Climate Consensus, Denies Responsibility for Warming’ *Scientific American* (22 March 2018) <https://www.scientificamerican.com/article/oil-giant-accepts-climate-consensus-denies-responsibility-for-warming/> accessed 31 August 2023

Mitchell RB, ‘International Environmental Agreements (IEA) Database Project’ <https://iea.uoregon.edu> accessed 31 August 2023

Nicolson A, ‘A Sense of Place: New Frontiers for the Law (Inaugural Lecture of Prof Loretta Feris at University of Cape Town on 8 October 2014)’ (16 October 2014) <https://www.news.uct.ac.za/article/-2014-10-16-a-sense-of-place-new-frontiers-for-the-law> accessed 31 August 2023

‘Notícias STF – Ministros destacam interação do STF com a sociedade na abertura de audiência pública’ (2012) <https://stf.jusbrasil.com.br/noticias/3109764/ministros-destacam-interacao-do-stf-com-a-sociedade-na-abertura-de-audiencia-publica> accessed 31 August 2023

OHCHR, ‘Statement by United Nations High Commissioner for Human Rights, Michelle Bachelet’, *Human Rights for the Planet – High-Level International Conference on Human Rights and Environmental Protection, 5 October 2020* <https://www.ohchr.org/EN/NewsEvents/Pages/DisplayNews.aspx?NewsID=26343&LangID=E> accessed 31 August 2021

‘Oslo Principles on Global Climate Change Obligations’ (*Global Justice Program (Yale University)*) <https://globaljustice.yale.edu/oslo-principles-global-climate-change-obligations> accessed 31 August 2023

Our Children's Trust, 'Juliana v United States – Youth Climate Lawsuit' <https://www.ourchildrenstrust.org/juliana-v-us> accessed 31 August 2023

Our Children's Trust, 'Juliana v United States (Major Court Orders and Filings)' <https://www.ourchildrenstrust.org/court-orders-and-pleadings> accessed 31 August 2023

Oxfam, 'Confronting Carbon Inequality: Putting Climate Justice at the Heart of the COVID-19 Recovery' (2020) <https://policy-practice.oxfam.org/resources/confronting-carbon-inequality-putting-climate-justice-at-the-heart-of-the-covid-621052/> accessed 31 August 2023

Oxfam, 'Confronting Carbon Inequality in the European Union' (2020) <https://www.oxfam.org/en/research/confronting-carbon-inequality-european-union> accessed 31 August 2023

Peters A, 'Research Concept: Global Constitutionalism and Global Governance' (*Max Planck Institut für ausländisches Öffentliches Recht und Völkerrecht*) <https://www.mpil.de/de/pub/forschung/nach-rechtsgebieten/voelkerrecht/global-constitutionalism.cfm> accessed 31 August 2023

Peters A, 'Der Mensch im Mittelpunkt des Völkerrechts', *Lecture given on 27 November 2013 in the context of the farewell of Prof. Dr. Dr. h.c. Rüdiger Wolfrum as Director of the Max Planck Institute for Comparative Public Law and International Law and introduction of Prof. Dr. Anne Peters as new Director* (2013) <http://www.mpil.de/files/pdf3/Peters_Der_Mensch_im_Mittelpunkt_des_Voelkerrechts._Vortrag_zur_Amtseinfuehrung_als_neue_Direktorin_am_Max_Planck_Institut_fuer_Voelkerrecht_27.11.20131.pdf> accessed 31 August 2023

Planet Prosperity Foundation, 'Bringing Government to Court. Claiming a Green Energy Revolution' <http://www.planetprosperity.org/news/3-revolution-justified> accessed 31 August 2023

Planet Prosperity Foundation, 'Revolution Justified – About the Book' <https://www.revolutionjustified.org> accessed 31 August 2023

Planet Prosperity Foundation, 'The Climate Case' <https://www.planetprosperity.org/news/15-the-climate-case> accessed 31 August 2023

Rai J and others, 'Universalism and Ethical Values for the Environment', vol Draft 3/27 (UNESCO 2010) <https://unesdoc.unesco.org/ark:/48223/pf0000188607> accessed 31 August 2023

Rodrigo CM, 'New York City Officials Declare Climate Emergency' *The Hill* (26 June 2019) <https://thehill.com/policy/energy-environment/450506-new-york-city-officials-declare-climate-emergency> accessed 31 August 2023

Sabin Center for Climate Change Law, 'Juliana v United States'

Sachs J, 'A Proposal for Climate Justice' (*Lecture delivered at London School of Economics and Political Science (3 October 2017)*) <http://www.lse.ac.uk/Events/2017/10/20171003t1830vOT/a-proposal-for-climate-justice> accessed 31 August 2023 <http://climatecasechart.com/case/juliana-v-united-states/> accessed 31 August 2021

'Scalia Vigorously Defends a "Dead" Constitution' *NPR* (28 April 2008) <https://www.npr.org/templates/story/story.php?storyId=90011526> accessed 31 August 2023

Scientists for Future, 'Statement of Scientists and Scholars Concerning the Protests for More Climate Protection' (12 March 2019) <https://www.scientists4future.org/stellungnahme/statement-text/> accessed 31 August 2023

Systemic Justice, 'Our Vision for Community-Driven Litigation' (2023) <https://systemicjustice.ngo/2023/02/our-vision-for-community-driven-litigation/?trk=feed_main-feed-card_feed-article-content> accessed 31 August 2023

The Climate Reality Project, 'Climate Adaptation vs. Mitigation: What's the Difference, and Why Does It Matter?' (7 November 2019) <https://www.climaterealityproject.org/blog/climate-adaptation-vs-mitigation-why-does-it-matter> accessed 31 August 2023

'The People's Climate Case' <https://peoplesclimatecase.caneurope.org> accessed 31 August 2023

UN Harmony with Nature, 'Rights of Nature Law, Policy and Education' <http://www.harmonywithnatureun.org/rightsOfNature/> accessed 31 August 2023

UNEP, 'The Tricky Business of Reaching a Global Consensus on the Environment' (2019) <https://www.unenvironment.org/news-and-stories/story/tricky-business-reaching-global-consensus-environment> accessed 31 August 2023

United States Environmental Protection Agency, Overview of Greenhouse Gases' (2016) <https://www.epa.gov/ghgemissions/overview-greenhouse-gases> accessed 31 August 2023

Urgenda, 'Climate Case Explained' <https://www.urgenda.nl/en/themas/climate-case/climate-case-explained/> accessed 31 August 2023

'Urgenda Opnieuw Naar Rechter in Klimaatzaak, Nu Om Dwangsom Te Eisen van Staat' *NOS News* (27 June 2021) <https://nos.nl/artikel/2386855-urgenda-opnieuw-naar-rechter-in-klimaatzaak-nu-om-dwangsom-te-eisen-van-staat> accessed 31 August 2023

vzw Klimaatzaak asbl (Association without lucrative purpose), 'Klimaatzaak (Belgium)' <https://www.klimaatzaak.eu/en> accessed 31 August 2023

WTO, 'Statement of Director-General Ngozi Okonjo-Iweala on USTR Tai's Statement on the TRIPS Waiver' <https://www.wto.org/english/news_e/news21_e/dgno_06may21_e.htm> accessed 31 August 2023

Newspaper and magazine articles

Balch O, 'Meet the World's First "Minister for Future Generations"' *The Guardian* (2 March 2019) <https://www.theguardian.com/world/2019/mar/02/meet-the-worlds-first-future-generations-commissioner> accessed 31 August 2023

Bergkamp L, 'The Urgenda Judgment: A "Victory" for the Climate That Is Likely to Backfire' *Energypost.eu* (9 September 2015) <https://energypost.eu/urgenda-judgment-victory-climate-likely-backfire/> accessed 31 August 2023

Boyd A, 'Climate Change Litigation in Philippines a Game-Changer?' *Asia Times* (13 April 2018) <https://asiatimes.com/2018/04/climate-change-litigation-philippines-game-changer/> accessed 31 August 2023

Chazan G, 'Germany Sets Ambitious New Carbon Emissions Target' *Financial Times* (5 May 2021) <https://www.ft.com/content/75956e41-57b1-4c55-981e-aec7a21560a0> accessed 31 August 2023

Connolly K, '"Historic" German Ruling Says Climate Goals Not Tough Enough' *The Guardian* (29 April 2021) <https://www.theguardian.com/world/2021/apr/29/historic-german-ruling-says-climate-goals-not-tough-enough> accessed 31 August 2023

Ellison K, 'An Inconvenient Lawsuit: Teenagers Take Global Warming to the Courts' *The Atlantic* (9 May 2012) <https://www.theatlantic.com/national/archive/2012/05/an-inconvenient-lawsuit-teenagers-take-global-warming-to-the-courts/256903/> accessed 31 August 2023

Goldenberg S, 'Just 90 Companies Caused Two-Thirds of Man-Made Global Warming Emissions' *The Guardian* (20 November 2013) <https://www.theguardian.com/environment/2013/nov/20/90-companies-man-made-global-warming-emissions-climate-change> accessed 31 August 2023

Irfan U, 'Pay Attention to the Growing Wave of Climate Change Lawsuits' *Vox* (4 June 2019) <https://www.vox.com/energy-and-environment/2019/2/22/17140166/climate-change-lawsuit-exxon-juliana-liability-kids> accessed 31 August 2023

Jarvis B, 'Climate Change Could Destroy His Home in Peru. So He Sued an Energy Company in Germany.' [2019] *The New York Times Magazine* <https://www.nytimes.com/interactive/2019/04/09/magazine/climate-change-peru-law.html> accessed 31 August 2023

Khan RS, 'Pakistan Passes Climate Change Act, Reviving Hopes – and Skepticism' *Reuters* (24 March 2017) <https://www.reuters.com/article/us-pakistan-climatechange-lawmaking/pakistan-passes-climate-change-act-reviving-hopes-and-skepticism-idUSKBN16V19N> accessed 31 August 2023

Kormann C, 'The Right to a Stable Climate Is the Constitutional Question of the Twenty-First Century' [2019] *The New Yorker* <https://www.newyorker.com/news/daily-comment/the-right-to-a-stable-climate-is-the-constitutional-question-of-the-twenty-first-century> accessed 31 August 2023

Murphy K, 'Torres Strait Islanders Take Climate Change Complaint to the United Nations' *The Guardian* (12 May 2019) <https://www.theguardian.com/australia-news/2019/may/13/torres-strait-islanders-take-climate-change-complaint-to-the-united-nations> accessed 31 August 2023

Newburger E, 'Visionary of the Visayan Sea' *Harvard Law Today* (28 July 2008) <https://today.law.harvard.edu/feature/visionary-of-the-visayan-sea/> accessed 31 August 2023

Selig K, 'Judge Rules in Favor of Montana Youths in Landmark Climate Decision' *The Washington Post* (14 August 2023) <https://www.washingtonpost.com/climate-environment/2023/08/14/youths-win-montana-climate-trial/> accessed 31 August 2023

Tizon TA, 'Mayor Is on a Mission to Warm U.S. Cities to the Kyoto Protocol' *Los Angeles Times* (22 February 2005) <https://www.latimes.com/archives/la-xpm-2005-feb-22-na-greenteam22-story.html> accessed 31 August 2023

Todd M, 'Extinction Rebellion's Tactics Are Working. It Has Pierced the Bubble of Denial' *The Guardian* (10 June 2019) <https://www.theguardian.com/commentisfree/2019/jun/10/extinction-rebellion-bubble-denial-climate-crisis> accessed 31 August 2023

Watts J, 'We Have 12 Years to Limit Climate Change Catastrophe, Warns UN' *The Guardian* (8 October 2018) <https://www.theguardian.com/environment/2018/oct/08/global-warming-must-not-exceed-15c-warns-landmark-un-report> accessed 31 August 2023

Watts J, 'Dutch Officials Reveal Measures to Cut Emissions after Court Ruling' *The Guardian* (24 April 2020) <https://www.theguardian.com/world/2020/apr/24/dutch-officials-reveal-measures-to-cut-emissions-after-court-ruling> accessed 31 August 2023

Watts J, 'European States Ordered to Respond to Youth Activists' Climate Lawsuit' *The Guardian* (30 November 2020) <https://www.theguardian.com/environment/2020/nov/30/european-states-ordered-respond-youth-activists-climate-lawsuit> accessed 31 August 2023

'Youth Climate Lawsuit Against Federal Government Headed for Trial' *YaleEnvironment360* (2 June 2023) <https://e360.yale.edu/digest/juliana-youth-climate-lawsuit-trial> accessed 31 August 2023

Blogs

Auz J, 'Global South Climate Litigation versus Climate Justice: Duty of International Cooperation as a Remedy?' *Völkerrechtsblog* (28 April 2020) <https://voelkerrechtsblog.org/de/global-south-climate-litigation-versus-climate-justice-duty-of-international-cooperation-as-a-remedy/> accessed 31 August 2023

Banda ML, 'Inter-American Court of Human Rights' Advisory Opinion on the Environment and Human Rights' *American Society of International Law* (2018) <https://www.asil.org/insights/volume/22/issue/6/inter-american-court-human-rights-advisory-opinion-environment-and-human> accessed 31 August 2023

Bookman S, 'Indigenous Climate Litigation in Anglophone Settler-Colonial States' *Verfassungsblog/Völkerrechtsblog* (25 March 2022) <https://verfassungsblog.de/indigenous-climate-litigation-in-anglophone-settler-colonial-states/> accessed 31 August 2023

Brunswick S, 'Not a Kid Anymore: What's Next for Juliana v. United States' *Arizona State Law Journal* (6 April 2021) <https://arizonastatelawjournal.org/2021/04/06/not-a-kid-anymore-whats-next-for-juliana-v-united-states/> accessed 31 August 2023

Dolidze A, 'The Arctic Sunrise and NGOs in International Judicial Proceedings' (2014) 18 ASIL Insights <https://www.asil.org/insights/volume/18/issue/1/arctic-sunrise-and-ngos-international-judicial-proceedings> accessed 31 August 2023

Fuchs M-C, 'Rights of Nature Reach Europe The Mar Menor Case in Spain in the Light of Latin American Precedents' *Verfassungsblog* (24 February 2023) <https://verfassungsblog.de/rights-of-nature-reach-europe/> accessed 31 August 2023

Grünstein MA, 'Participación de la sociedad civil en el Proceso a través del amicus curiae' (*Instituto Chileno de Derecho Procesal*, 29 June 2016) <https://www.ichdp.cl/participacion-de-la-sociedad-civil-en-el-proceso-a-traves-del-amicus-curiae/> accessed 31 August 2023

Kimble J, 'The Ideology of Textualism' *American Constitution Society Expert Forum* (17 July 2017) <https://www.acslaw.org/expertforum/the-ideology-of-textualism/> accessed 31 August 2023

Laville S and Watts J, 'Across the Globe, Millions Join Biggest Climate Protest Ever' *The Guardian* (21 September 2019) <https://www.theguardian.com/environment/2019/sep/21/across-the-globe-millions-join-biggest-climate-protest-ever> accessed 31 August 2023

Lyle R, 'A Reckless Decision' [2022] *Verfassungsblog* <https://verfassungsblog.de/a-reckless-decision/> accessed 31 August 2023

Mührel J, 'All That Glitters Is Not Gold: The German Constitutional Court's Climate Ruling and the Protection of Persons Beyond German Territory Against Climate Change Impacts' *Völkerrechtsblog* (3 May 2021) <https://voelkerrechtsblog.org/all-that-glitters-is-not-gold/> accessed 31 August 2023

Nollkaemper A and Burgers L, 'A New Classic in Climate Change Litigation: The Dutch Supreme Court Decision in the Urgenda Case' *Blog of the European Journal of International Law* (2020) <https://bit.ly/38h3WEa> accessed 23 August 2023

Nugent C, 'Does Climate Change Violate Children's Human Rights? A European Court May Soon Decide' *Time* (30 November 2020) <https://time.com/5916362/climate-change-human-rights-portugal/> accessed 31 August 2023

Patarroyo P, 'Justiciability of "Implicit" Rights : Developments on the Right to a Healthy Environment at the Inter-American Court of Human Rights' *EJIL Talk* (2020) <https://www.ejiltalk.org/justiciability-of-implicit-rights-developments-on-the-right-to-a-healthy-environment-at-the-inter-american-court-of-human-rights/> accessed 31 August 2023

Posner RA, 'The Incoherence of Antonin Scalia' [2012] *The New Republic* <https://newrepublic.com/article/106441/scalia-garner-reading-the-law-textual-originalism> accessed 31 August 2023

Sönmezocak EB, 'The Case for Global Constitutionalism in Pandemic Times' (*Völkerrechtsblog*, 6 June 2020) <https://voelkerrechtsblog.org/the-case-for-global-constitutionalism-in-pandemic-times/> accessed 31 August 2023

Spijkers O, 'Pursuing Climate Justice through Public Interest Litigation: The Urgenda Case' *Völkerrechtsblog* (29 April 2020) <https://voelkerrechtsblog.org/articles/pursuing-climate-justice-through-public-interest-litigation-the-urgenda-case/> accessed 31 August 2023

Stucki S, 'In Defence of Green Civil Disobedience' *Verfassungsblog* (30 October 2020) <https://verfassungsblog.de/in-defence-of-green-civil-disobedience/> accessed 31 August 2023

Cases

Domestic courts

The Americas

Constitutional Court of Colombia, *Tierra Digna v Presidencia de La República,* T-622 (2016)

Corte Suprema de Justicia de Colombia, *Future Generations v Colombia,* STC 4360–2018 (2018)

District Court of Oregon, Judge Ann Aiken, *Kelsey Cascadia Rose Juliana v United States of America,* Case No. 6:15-Cv-01517-TC (11 October 2016)

Federal District Cout for the District of Oregon, Opinion and Order *Kelsey Cascadia Rose Juliana v United States of America,* Case No. 6:15-Cv-01517-AA (15 October 2018)

Supreme Court of Canada, *Reference re Same-Sex Marriage*, 3 S.C. R. 698, 2004 SCC 79 (2004)
Superior Court of Washington for King County, *Aji P v State of Washington*, Case No. 18–2–04448–1 SEA (14 August 2018) 1
U.S. Ninth Circuit Court of Appeals, *Juliana v United States,* No. 18–36082 (17 January 2020)
U.S. Supreme Court, *Marbury v. Madison*, 5 U.S. (1803) 137
U.S. Supreme Court, *Simon v. Eastern Kentucky Welf. Rights. Org*., 426 U.S. 26 (1976)
U.S. Supreme Court, *Allen v. Wright*, 468 U.S. 737 (1984)
U.S. Supreme Court, *Lujan v. Defenders of Wildlife*, 504 U.S. 555 (1992)

Europe

District Court of The Hague, *Urgenda v The Netherlands*, ECLI:NL:RBHDHA:2015:7196 (2015)
The Hague Court of Appeal, *Urgenda v The Netherlands*, ECLI:NL:GHDHA:2018:2610 (2018)
Supreme Court of the Netherlands, *Urgenda v The Netherlands*, ECLI:NL:HR:2019:2007 (2019)
German Federal Constitutional Court, Order of the First Senate of 24 March 2021, 1 BvR 2656/18
Norwegian Supreme Court, *Greenpeace Nordic Ass'n v. Ministry of Petroleum and Energy*, HR-2020–846-J (2020)
Swiss Supreme Court, *Union of Swiss Senior Women for Climate Protection v. Swiss Federal Council and Others* (No. A-2992/2017) (2020)
United Kingdom House of Lords Decision, UKHL 1, *Liversidge v Anderson,* AC 206 (1942)

Asia

Lahore High Court, *Asghar Leghari v Federation of Pakistan*,W.P. No. 25501/2015 (Frist Order Sheet, 4 September 2015)
Lahore High Court, *Asghar Leghari v Federation of Pakistan*,W.P. No. 25501/2015 (Second Order Sheet, 14 September 2015)
Lahore High Court, *Asghar Leghari v Federation of Pakistan*,W.P. No. 25501/2015 (Judgement of 25 January 2018)
Supreme Court of India, *Bandhua Mukti Morcha vs Union of India and Others*, 1984 AIR 802, 1984 SCR (267) (1983)
Supreme Court of Pakistan, *Shehla Zia and others v. WAPDA*, PLD 1994 SC 693 (1994)
Supreme Court of the Philippines, *Minors Oposa v Factoran*, 224 SCRA 792 (1993)

Australasia

High Court of New Zealand, *Thomson v The Minister for Climate Change Issues*, NZHC 733 (2017)
NSW Land and Environment Court, *Ironstone Community Action Group Inc. v. NSW Minister for Planning and Duralie Coal Pty. Ltd.*, [2011] NSWLEC 195 (Australia), 2011
NSW Land and Environment Court, *Walker v. Minister for Planning*, NSWLEC 741/157 LGERA 124 (2008)
NSW Land and Environment Court, *Bulga Milbrodale Progress Association Inc v Minister for Planning and Infra-structure and Warkworth Mining Limited*, NSWLEC 48 (2013)
NSW Land and Environment Court, *Gloucester Resources Limited v Minister for Planning*, NSWLEC 7 (2019)

Africa

High Court of South Africa, EarthLife Africa Johannesburg v. Minister of Environmental Affairs and Others, Case no. 65662/16 (2017)
Constitutional Court of South Africa, S v Makwanyane and Another, Case No. CCT/3/94 (6 June 1995)
Constitutional Court of South Africa, Fuel Retailers Association of Southern Africa v Director-General Environmental Management, Department of Agriculture, Conservation and Environment, Mpumalanga Province and Others, Case CCT 67/06 [2007] ZACC 13 (2007)

International Courts

International Court of Justice

ICJ, *Aegean Sea Continental Shelf (Greece v Turkey)*, Judgment, ICJ Rep 3, 32 (1978)
ICJ, *Legality of the Threat of Use of Nuclear Weapons*, Advisory Opinion (ICJ Rep 1996)
ICJ, *Gabčikovo-Nagymaros Project (Hungary v Slovakia)*, ICJ GL No 92, (1997) ICJ Rep 7, (1997) ICJ Rep 88, (1998) 37 ILM 162, ICGJ 66 (Judgement 1997)
ICJ, *Pulp Mills on the River Uruguay (Argentina v. Uruguay)*, ICJ GL No 135 (Judgment 2010)

UN Bodies

UN Committee on the Rights of the Child, *Sacchi et al v Argentina et al* (8 October 2021), Communication No. 104/2019 (Argentina), Communication No. 105/2019 (Brazil), Communication No. 106/2019 (France), Communication No. 107/2019 (Germany), Communication No. 108/2019 (Turkey)

UN Human Rights Committee, *Ioane Teitiota v. New Zealand* (7 January 2020), Communication No. 2728/2016

UN Human Rights Committee, *Daniel Billy et al v Australia* (21 July 2022), Communication No. 3624/2019

Inter-American Court/Commission of Human Rights

IACtHR, *Claude Reyes et al v Chile,* Case No. 12.108 (Judgement of 19 September 2006)

IACtHR, *Yakye Axa Indigenous Community v Paraguay*, Case No. 12.313 (Judgment of 17 June 2005)

IACtHR, *Case of the Kichwa Indigenous People of Sarayaku v Ecuador,* Case No. 12.456 (Judgement of 27 June 2012)

IACtHR, *Comunidades indígenas miembros de la asociación Lhaka Honhat (Nuestra Tierra) vs Argentina* (Judgement of 6 February 2020)

IACtHR, Advisory Opinion OC-23/17 – The Environment and Human Rights (2017)

European Court of Human Rights

ECtHR, *Golder v. United Kingdom*, Judgement of 21 February 1975, App. No. 4451/70

ECtHR, *Ireland v. the United Kingdom*, Judgment of 18 January 1978, App. No. 5310/71

ECtHR, *López Ostra v. Spain*, Judgement of 9 December 1994, App. No. 16798/90

ECtHR, *Guerra and Others v. Italy*, Judgement of 19 February 1998, App. No. 14967/89

ECtHR, *Goodwin v. United Kingdom*, Judgement of 11 July 2002, App. No. 28957/95

ECtHR, *Kyrtatos v. Greece*, Judgement of 22 May 2003, App. No. 41666/98

ECtHR, *Fadeyeva v. Russia*, Judgement of 9 June 2005, App. No. 55723/00

ECtHR, *Budayeva and Others v. Russia*, Judgement of 20 March 2008, App. Nos. 15339/02, 21166/02, 20058/02, 11673/02 and 15343/02

ECtHR, *Demir and Baykara v. Turkey*, Judgement of 12 November 2008, App. No. 34503/97

ECtHR, *Tătar v. Romania*, Judgement of 27 January 2009, App. No. 67021/01

ECtHR, *Öneryildiz v. Turkey*, Judgement of 30 November 2014, App. No. 48939/99

ECtHR, *Cordella and Others v. Italy*, Judgement of 24 January 2019, App. Nos. 54414/13 and 54264/15

General Court / European Court of Justice

EU GC, Danielsson and Others v Commission, T-219/95, ECLI:EU:T:1995:219 (1995)
EU GC, Carvalho and Others v Parliament and Council, T-330/18, ECLI:EU:T:2019:324 (2019)
CJEU, Plaumann & Co. v Commission of the European Economic Community, Case 25/62, ECLI:EU:C:1963:17 (1963)
CJEU, Trianel (Bund für Umwelt und Naturschutz Deutschland, Landesverband Nordrhein-Westfalen eV v Bezirksregierung Arnsberg), C-115/09, ECLI:EU:C:2011:289 (2011)
CJEU, Gemeinde Altrip and Others v Land Rheinland-Pfalz, C-72/12, ECLI:EU:C:2013:712 (2013)
CJEU, Lesoochranárske zoskupenie VLK, C-243/15, ECLI:EU:C:2016:838 (2016)

African Commission and Court on Human and Peoples' Rights

African Commission, SERAC and CESR v. Nigeria, Communication 155/96 (2001)

Others

Permanent Court of International Justice, S.S. Wimbledon (U.K. v. Japan), 1923 P.C.I.J. (ser. A) No. 1 (17 August 1923)

MIX
Papier aus verantwortungsvollen Quellen
Paper from responsible sources
FSC® C105338

If you have any concerns about our products,
you can contact us on
ProductSafety@springernature.com

In case Publisher is established outside the EU,
the EU authorized representative is:
Springer Nature Customer Service Center GmbH
Europaplatz 3, 69115 Heidelberg, Germany

Printed by Libri Plureos GmbH
in Hamburg, Germany